006.788
SNÉ

Mike Snell
Lars Powers

Microsoft® Visual Studio® 2010

UNLEASHED

D1331816

SAMS | 800 East 96th Street, Indianapolis, Indiana 46240 USA

Microsoft® Visual Studio® 2010 Unleashed

Copyright © 2011 by Pearson Education, Inc.

ISBN-13: 978-0-672-33081-0

ISBN-10: 0-672-33081-4

Library of Congress Cataloging-in-Publication data:

Snell, Mike.

  Microsoft Visual Studio 2010 unleashed / Mike Snell, Lars Powers.

     p. cm.

  ISBN 978-0-672-33081-0

 1. Microsoft Visual studio. 2. Web site development. 3. Application software[md]Development. I. Powers, Lars. II. Title.

  TK5105.8885.M57S654 2010

  006.7[md]dc22

                        2010029011

Printed in the United States of America

First Printing: July 2010

Trademarks

Warning and Disclaimer

Bulk Sales

Pearson offers excellent discounts on this book when ordered in quantity for bulk purchases or special sales. For more information, please contact:

U.S. Corporate and Government Sales
1-800-382-3419
corpsales@pearsontechgroup.com

For sales outside of the U.S., please contact:

International Sales
+1-317-581-3793
international@pearsontechgroup.com

Editor-in-Chief
Karen Gettman

Executive Editor
Neil Rowe

Acquisitions Editor
Brook Farling

Development Editor
Mark Renfrow

Managing Editor
Sandra Schroeder

Senior Project Editor
Tonya Simpson

Copy Editor
The Wordsmithery, LLC

Indexer
Lisa Stumpf

Proofreaders
Debbie Williams
Leslie Joseph

Technical Editor
Todd Meister

Team Coordinator
Cindy Teeters

Book Designer
Gary Adair

Composition
Mark Shirar

Contents at a Glance

Table of Contents

About the Authors

Mike Snell spends his work life helping teams build great software that exceeds the expectations of end users. Mike runs the Solutions division at CEI (www.ceiamerica.com). Mike and his team deliver architecture, consulting, and mentoring to clients looking to build great enterprise and commercial software. Mike is also a Microsoft Regional director (www.TheRegion.com).

Lars Powers is a Principal ISV Developer Evangelist with Microsoft in the Developer and Platform Evangelism group. He works with Microsoft's largest global ISV partners to help them craft solutions on top of Microsoft's next-generation technologies. Prior to joining Microsoft, Lars was an independent consultant providing training and mentoring on the .NET platform.

Dedications

To Mom, who was never prouder than that day when my first book hit the shelves. I miss you.
—Lars Powers

For Gail and Gordy Weeks, who bought me my first Windows PC (a Pentium 166 where I learned to write VB 3/4 code) and allowed me to marry their daughter. Thanks!
—Mike Snell

Acknowledgments

Lars Powers: I would like to thank all of the great application developers that I have the chance to interact with every month. Your enthusiasm for the nearly endless possibilities of software, and your unflinching efforts to push Microsoft to go farther and deeper with every Visual Studio release have rekindled my own love for this product. One day, I hope to rejoin your ranks!

Mike Snell: I would like to thank all the fine people involved with the making of this book. This includes Brook Farling, who every day went the extra mile to make sure we were able to just keep writing; Todd Meister, who continues to shine as our technical editor; Charlotte Kughen our copy editor, who fixed all our mistakes; and Tonya Simpson our project editor, who kept everyone focused on the many steps involved with a work like this. I would also like to acknowledge a few people on my team at CEI for hearing me out on all things Visual Studio, this includes Stephen Johnston, Geoff Tewksbury, Jason Agostoni, and Ryan Baker. Finally, I would like to thank my co-author, Lars Powers, for collaborating with me on another work we can both be proud to put our names on.

We Want to Hear from You!

As the reader of this book, you are our most important critic and commentator. We value your opinion and want to know what we're doing right, what we could do better, what areas you'd like to see us publish in, and any other words of wisdom you're willing to pass our way.

As an editor for Sams Publishing, I welcome your comments. You can email or write me directly to let me know what you did or didn't like about this book—as well as what we can do to make our books better.

Please note that I cannot help you with technical problems related to the topic of this book. We do have a User Services group, however, where I will forward specific technical questions related to the book.

When you write, please be sure to include this book's title and author as well as your name, email address, and phone number. I will carefully review your comments and share them with the author and editors who worked on the book.

Email: neil.rowe@samspublishing.com

Mail: Neil Rowe
         Executive Editor
         Sams Publishing
         800 East 96th Street
         Indianapolis, IN 46240 USA

Reader Services

Visit our website and register this book at informit.com/register for convenient access to any updates, downloads, or errata that might be available for this book.

Introduction

Visual Studio 2010 builds on the .NET development experience that has evolved through prior editions of the product. Those editions brought us code snippets, custom project templates, refactoring, data binding wizards, smart tags, modeling tools, automated testing tools, and project and task management. The related Framework releases included Windows Presentation Foundation (WPF) for building richer client solutions, Windows Communication Foundation (WCF) to help build more dynamic service-oriented solutions, and Windows Workflow Foundation (WF) to enable structured programming around business processes.

Visual Studio 2010 adds to the innovations. It includes a new, WPF-based code editor, support for cloud development on Azure, IDE extensions with the Managed Execution Framework (MEF), additional SharePoint development support, Silverlight programming, and much more. The .NET languages have also been extended to include dynamic language support, the new F# for functional programming, and other features for helping you write better code, faster.

The tools and languages combine to increase your productivity and success rate. This book is meant to help you unlock the many tools built into Visual Studio so that you can realize these gains.

Who Should Read This Book?

Developers who rely on Visual Studio to get work done will want to read this book. It provides great detail on the many features inside the latest version of the IDE. The book covers all of the following key topics:

▶ Understanding the basics of solutions, projects, editors, and designers

▶ Writing macros, add-ins, and wizards

▶ Using the new Managed Extensions Framework (MEF) to write compelling extensions to the Visual Studio editor

▶ Debugging with the IDE

▶ Refactoring code

▶ Sharing code with team members and the larger community

▶ Writing ASP.NET applications (including those based on ASP.NET MVC)

▶ Writing Silverlight web applications

▶ Implementing Service Oriented Architecture (SOA)-based applications, and consuming services, using the Windows Communication Foundation (WCF)

▶ Coding with Windows forms and with Windows Presentation Foundation (WPF)

▶ Working with data and databases and leveraging LINQ and Entity Framework to build data-centric applications

▶ Creating and hosting workflow-based applications using Windows Workflow Foundation (WF)

▶ Writing applications for the Azure cloud

This book is primarily a tools book. We have one primary focus: detailing and explaining the intricacies of the Visual Studio 2010 IDE to enable developers to be more productive. We do, however, cover the basics of object-oriented programming with VB and C# (see Chapter 3, "The .NET Languages"). The rest of the book is about building applications using the Visual Studio toolbox. These chapters assume you can write C# or VB code and help you optimize your productivity with Visual Studio.

Focusing on Visual Studio Professional

This book represents a departure for us from our previous versions. It is focused on Visual Studio Professional. The advanced Visual Studio SKUs that include Premium, Ultimate, Team Foundation Server, and Test Professional have grown so large they need their own book. The Professional edition has also gotten bigger with more options for building more types of applications than ever before. This was a difficult decision to make, but ultimately one that frees us to go even deeper into the core Visual Studio 2010 Professional product used by the vast majority of .NET developers all over the world. Be sure to look for additional coverage of these other Visual Studio products at the SAMS site and our blog (both listed below):

- ▶ Sams: www.samspublishing.com

- ▶ Our blog: www.visualstudiounleashed.com

Downloadable Content

Many of the chapters in the book include sample content you can download. In addition, look for content that extends the samples and discussion in the book. You can find both the downloadable content and additional content at the sites listed previously (SAMS and out blog).

How Is This Book Organized?

You can read this book cover to cover, or you can pick the chapters that apply most to your current need. We sometimes reference content across chapters, but for the most part, each chapter can stand by itself. This organization allows you to jump around and read as time (and interest) permits. There are four parts to the book; each part is described next.

Part I: An Introduction to Visual Studio 2010

The chapters in this part provide an overview of what to expect from Visual Studio 2008. Readers who are familiar only with prior versions of Visual Studio will want to review these chapters. In addition, we cover the new language enhancement for the 2010, .NET 4 versions of VB and C#.

Part II: An In-Depth Look at the IDE

This part covers the core development experience relative to Visual Studio. It provides developers with a base understanding of the rich features of their primary tool. The chapters walk through the many menus and windows that define each tool. We cover the base concepts of projects and solutions, and we explore in detail the explorers, editors, and designers.

Part III: Writing and Working with Code

Part III builds on the topics discussed in Part II by digging into the powerful productivity features of Visual Studio 2008. These chapters investigate the developer productivity aids that are present in the IDE, and discuss how to best use Visual Studio for refactoring and debugging your code.

Part IV: Extending Visual Studio

For those developers interested in customizing, automating, or extending the Visual Studio IDE, these chapters are for you. We explain the automation model and then document how to use that API to automate the IDE through macros. We also cover how you can extend the IDE's capabilities by writing your own add-ins.

Part V: Creating Enterprise Applications

Part V focuses on how to work with the IDE tools to write your applications. Each chapter provides an in-depth overview of how to use Visual Studio to help you design and develop an application. We cover writing applications using ASP.NET, web services and WCF, Windows forms, WPF, WF, and working with data and databases.

Conventions Used in This Book

The following typographic conventions are used in this book:

Code lines, commands, statements, variables, and text you see onscreen appears in a monospace typeface.

Placeholders in syntax descriptions appear in an *italic monospace* typeface. You replace the placeholder with the actual filename, parameter, or whatever element it represents.

Italics highlight technical terms when they're being defined.

A code-continuation icon is used before a line of code that is really a continuation of the preceding line. Sometimes a line of code is too long to fit as a single line on the page. If you see Â before a line of code, remember that it's part of the line immediately above it.

The book also contains Notes, Tips, and Cautions to help you spot important or useful information more quickly.

CHAPTER 1

A Quick Tour of Visual Studio 2010

Visual Studio 2010 and the .NET Framework 4.0 introduce many new features to an already full-featured toolset. This latest version is about increasing developer productivity while providing developers with choices and flexibility when building their solutions. If you've been developing for a long time, you've come to expect that a new release of the IDE comes with advanced programming models, more acronyms, a few fresh project types, and improved ways to view and organize code. The 2010 product is no exception. Some highlights for this release include

▶ An improved code editor built on WPF

▶ Windows 7 development support

▶ Improved support for Microsoft Office programming including SharePoint development

▶ A better experience on multiple monitors

▶ Support for simplified, parallel programming against multi-core devices

▶ Support for ASP.NET MVC

▶ Support for building Web applications using the latest versions of Silverlight

▶ One-click Web deployments

▶ Building for the cloud with Windows Azure

▶ Major additions and improvements to Windows Workflow and Windows Communication Foundation

▶ Increased support for database development on SQL Server and other database technologies such as Oracle and DB2

▶ Expanded team development with the new architecture explorer, support for UML, and automated testing improvements built in to the Premium and Ultimate editions

This chapter covers the core make-up and capabilities of Visual Studio 2010. We first help you sort through the product choices available to .NET developers. We then provide a comparison of the .NET programming languages. The remaining sections of the chapter cover the many possibilities open to .NET programmers including building Web, Windows, cloud, data, and service applications. Our hope is to give you enough information in this chapter to get the full picture of what is available to you when you build solutions using Visual Studio.

> **NOTE**
>
> Part I, "An Introduction to Visual Studio 2010," is broken into three chapters. This chapter provides a snapshot of all things Visual Studio. Chapter 2, "The Visual Studio IDE," is an introduction to getting the tool installed, running it, and creating that first project. It also serves to familiarize you with the basics of the IDE. Chapter 3, "The .NET Languages," is a quick primer on coding constructs in VB and C#. It also covers general programming against the .NET Framework.

The Visual Studio Product Line

With Visual Studio 2010, Microsoft has simplified the product line. There are now only three primary editions of the tool: professional, premium, and ultimate. This should make it easier to understand which tool you need for your development and price point. At a high level, these tools are differentiated as follows (each addition assumes an MSDN subscription, too):

▶ **Professional**—Includes the basic features of the IDE to build applications of all types on all .NET languages. Includes support for writing, debugging, and testing code.

▶ **Premium**—Builds on top of the Professional edition to include many features targeted toward the enterprise developer for testing and verifying code. Also includes database development tools.

▶ **Ultimate**—Includes every tool in the Visual Studio product line as well as surrounding products. It builds on Premium to add additional debugging and testing support, architecture tools, lab management, and more.

> **NOTE**
>
> You can see a detailed product comparison at http://www.microsoft.com/visualstudio/en-us/products.

Of course, there are some peripheral versions and products that surround Visual Studio. These include the Express editions, Test Professional, and Microsoft Expression. We take a deeper look at all these products in the coming sections.

Express Editions

Microsoft offers the Visual Studio Express Editions on a per-language basis (VB, C#, C++, Web, Windows Phone, and SQL Server 2008 R2). These editions are free, downloadable, low-barrier to entry versions targeted directly at the novice, hobbyist, student, or anyone else looking to write some code without breaking the bank. In conjunction with the Express Editions, Microsoft has made a few development kits available for things such as Facebook and Windows Live. There are also tutorials, videos, support sites, and fun projects to review. To get started, check out the URL www.microsoft.com/express/Resources/.

The Express Edition can be seen as Microsoft's answer to all the "freeware" tools available to today's developers. After all, if you are a college student looking to put up a buddy's website, you are more likely to look for a low-cost solution. Of course, five years down the road when you're making decisions for your company, Microsoft wants to be sure you've had a chance to work with its products. The Expression Edition fits this niche nicely. Figure 1.1 shows an example of the Web Platform Installer that is part of the Visual Web Developer 2010 Express installation. This installer enables you to download and install the IDE for creating web applications. In addition, as the figure shows, it enables you to install many base web applications that you can use in your solution, including applications for blogging, eCommerce, content management, and more.

FIGURE 1.1   The Web Platform Installer for Visual Web Developer 2010 Express enables you to install many application templates to kick-start your projects.

The Express Editions purposely do not have all the power of their professional patriarch (a Class Designer, test-driven development with unit testing, enterprise templates, XSLT support, source code control, and so on). However, they do have full language support (such as LINQ) and access to the .NET Framework items such as WPF.

The Express Editions also have a more streamlined user experience that does not expose the full complexity (or power) of the professional editions. However, developers are to create client/server form-based applications, websites, data-driven solutions, and even web services using these tools.

> **NOTE**
>
> For more information regarding the Visual Studio Express Editions or to download one of these editions, you can visit Microsoft's site at www.microsoft.com/express.

Professional Edition

Visual Studio Professional is the base entry for most developers who make a living writing code. Visual Studio Professional gives you all the language support (including VB, C#, F#, C++); the capability to write all types of applications, including Console, Windows, Windows Services, Class Libraries, Web, Cloud, WPF, Silverlight, Database, Office, SharePoint; and more.

Visual Studio Professional also gives you access to many additional tools that are key to building professional applications. The following features ship only with Visual Studio Professional (and above):

- ▶ Unit Testing and Test-Driven Development
- ▶ Access to Team Foundation Server (TFS) for source control, continuous integration, and work item tracking
- ▶ Office development including SharePoint
- ▶ Multi-core, parallel development
- ▶ Class Designer
- ▶ Server Explorer
- ▶ Refactoring
- ▶ And much more

> **NOTE**
>
> This book targets Visual Studio Professional only. A quick perusal of the book will allow you to see the depth and breadth of what you can do with this powerful tool.

Premium

Visual Studio 2010 Premium is targeted toward professional developers who build both corporate and commercial applications. It provides additional tools that help developers verify, test, and check their code against common issues. It also includes all the features inside Professional plus the following:

- ▶ Static code analysis
- ▶ Code metrics
- ▶ Code profiling
- ▶ Unit test code coverage and test impact analysis
- ▶ Performance profiling
- ▶ Coded UI tests
- ▶ Database change management, unit testing, data generation, schema and data comparison

> **NOTE**
>
> Visual Studio 2010 Premium combines the features of the Developer and Database role–based products from the prior edition (2008).

Ultimate

Visual Studio 2010 Ultimate is for developers who really need it all. It includes additional testing tools targeted toward both the technical and manual tester. It also provides architecture tools for creating UML models and exploring code visually. This version of the product is the everything-but-the-kitchen-sink option in a single package. The following highlights the Ultimate features:

- ▶ Historical debugging with IntelliTrace
- ▶ UML modeling support for use case, class, sequence, component, and activity diagrams (including generating sequence diagrams from code)
- ▶ Architecture Explorer, for coming up to speed on a code base
- ▶ Layer diagrams
- ▶ Web, load, and stress testing
- ▶ Test Professional, including test case management, manual testing, and test record and playback
- ▶ Test lab management

> **NOTE**
>
> Visual Studio 2010 Ultimate is similar to the prior edition, 2008 Team Suite. However, it adds even more features centered around architecture and testing.

MSDN

All editions of Visual Studio (above Express) now come with some form of an MSDN subscription. Depending on your edition, you get a little more of MSDN with each version up the product line. The following provides an overview of your MSDN benefit by product:

▶ **2010 Professional**—Includes a license for TFS, a client access license for TFS; 50 hours per month of Azure hosting; development editions of Windows 7, Windows Server 2008 R2, and SWL Server 2008; access to prior versions of Windows and SQL; two technical support incidents; priority forums; e-learning access; and MSDN magazine.

▶ **2010 Premium**—Includes everything in Professional with MSDN plus the following: 100 hours per month of Azure hosting; Expression Studio; Office 2010 Plus, Visio, and Project; development editions of Office, Dynamics, SharePoint, Windows embedded, and other Microsoft platform and server products; and four technical support incidents.

▶ **2010 Ultimate**—Includes all the preceding in Premium with the following extras: 250 hours per month of Azure hosting and access to Team Explorer Everywhere.

> **NOTE**
>
> Microsoft also sells a version of 2010 Professional with MSDN essentials. This is a limited MSDN version and does not include things like TFS access, SQL Server, Office, technical support, and MSDN magazine.

Related Tools

A number of additional tools outside Visual Studio surround the Windows development experience. This includes tools targeted toward the development team (Team Foundation Server and Team Explorer), those targeted toward designers (Microsoft Expression), and those targeted toward the tester (Test Professional). It's important to be aware of how these tools can help you build your next solution. This section provides a brief overview of each of these products.

Team Foundation Server (TFS)

TFS is the central hub that provides an integrated, application lifecycle management (ALM) experience around the many development tools from Microsoft. The first version of TFS was built with the release of 2005. This included source control, a centralized project management system, build automation, and reporting. By all accounts, these tools have been a great success. Microsoft has built upon this with the release of TFS 2010. Figure 1.2 shows TFS in relation to the many products that surround the ALM practices.

FIGURE 1.2   Team Foundation Server acts as the hub that provides ALM services to the many development products available from Microsoft.

As you can see from the figure, TFS is at the center of development and ALM coordination. The following highlights the many services provided by TFS:

▶ **Process Guidance/Template**—TFS includes two process templates out of the box: Microsoft Solutions Framework (MSF) for CMMI 5.0 and MSF for Agile 5.0. Both provide a set of work items, workflow, and reporting based on their specific methodology. Both also provide guidance to the team for executing key activities on the project (such as requirements management or build automation). The CMMI template is targeted toward those teams that have a strong need for auditing and traceability and might be looking to achieve a CMMI-level assessment. The MSF for Agile template provides tools for teams implementing a SCRUM approach to development.

▶ **Project Management**—TFS enables project managers to define their projects in terms of iterations and functional areas. It provides work items that are used to define, assign, and track work on the project. A work item can be a task on the project, a requirement, a bug, a test scenario, and so on. In general, a work item represents a generic unit of work on the project. Of course, work items are customizable and can have states, new fields, and business rules associated with them. Work items play a central part in ensuring project team communication and reporting. Project managers can use the Excel and Project add-ins to Office to manage the work items on a project.

▶ **Requirements Management**—TFS provides specific work items for managing requirements. In fact, 2010 introduces the concept of hierarchical work items. This means you can create work item children. For example, you might create a requirement work item and then define the tasks required to build that requirement. You might also define the test cases that will be used to verify the requirement. In this way, TFS enables rich reporting through the aggregation of the child work item data (such as tests passing for a requirement or work remaining at the requirement level).

▶ **Test Case Management**—TFS and Test Professional enable work items specific to test planning and test case management. You can define a set of test cases for a given requirement. Each test case can define the steps required to execute the test case along with the expected results.

▶ **Version Control**—The source control features in Team Foundation Server include enterprise-class features such as change sets, shelving, automatic build rules, the capability to associate work items to changed source, parallel development, a source control policy engine, branching, checkpoints, and more. The 2010 edition includes branch and changeset visualization.

▶ **Build Automation**—The TFS build tools allow for automatic, scheduled, and on-demand builds. Builds are reported against, documented, automatically tested, and analyzed for code coverage and churn (as an example). The build engine in 2010 has been rewritten to leverage Windows Workflow (WF) 4.0.

▶ **Reporting**—TFS provides a rich set of reports for tracking statistics and the overall health of your project. Reports include those built on SQL Reporting Services (that are accessible from the IDE, the Web, and SharePoint) as well as a new set of Excel reports for working directly with the data.

▶ **Collaboration and Dashboards**—TFS includes a SharePoint site for each project. This site provides full access to manage and create work items outside Visual Studio and Office. In addition, it provides a set of dashboard reports for quick analysis of what is happening on the project as well as items specific to the logged-in user. Of course, the SharePoint sites also provide rich collaboration around documents and through a team wiki.

▶ **Web Access**—TFS provides a web access version for working with work items over the web (outside SharePoint). This version also includes source control access through a web browser. The web access version, however, does not include the richer, dashboard features of the SharePoint TFS sites.

▶ **Integration with other IDEs**—TFS is accessible from Visual Studio, Office, SharePoint, and the Web. In addition, there is Team Explorer Everywhere for accessing the TFS features using other IDEs running on operating systems outside Windows. This includes the eclipse IDE and the MacOS.

Team Explorer

There are those team members who will not have a development tool such as Visual Studio, Test Professional, or Expression that provides access to TFS. In this case, they can get full access through Team Explorer. Team Explorer is targeted at project managers, business analysts, directors, and others on the team who need to access TFS but do not do direct development. This tool is purchased as a client access license (CAL). It includes a basic explorer, the Excel and Project add-ins, and full access to the SharePoint site, Web access, and reporting.

Test Professional

Visual Studio Test Professional 2010 provides test planning, test case management, and manual testing for those people dedicated to the testing role. This is a separate tool that should seem comfortable and familiar to testers. Test plans are created based on application requirements (to provide traceability). Test cases are created and tracked as work items.

When a tester runs a test plan, they work through each test case and each step in the test case. They indicate the success or failure of the given test. For failures, they can log bugs (also work items). The bugs can automatically include things such as diagnostic trace information, event log data, network information, and even video recording of the steps the tester was executing when the bug was found.

Test Professional also enables testers to create action recordings of their steps. These recordings can be played back to execute the same steps again. This helps automate many portions of manual tests.

Finally, Test Professional includes lab management, which is a suite of tools for provisioning test environments from a template. These environments are virtual machines that are meant to be set up and torn down as needed for testing. You also can create checkpoint environments for various builds.

Visual Studio Agents 2010 and Load Test Virtual User Packs

Visual Studio Ultimate is used to create web, load, and stress tests; however, when executing these tests, it is limited to simulating up to 250 simultaneous users. Sometimes you need to generate much more load for your tests. In this case, you need to purchase Visual Studio Load Test Virtual User Pack 2010.

This tool is a separate product that works with Visual Studio Agents 2010 (included with Ultimate) to generate massive loads for various load-testing scenarios. You use the VS Agents software to set up a central test controller. You can then put agents on different machines. You add virtual user packs to each agent (depending on how many users you want to simulate per machine). Each user pack you purchase enables you to simulate an additional 1,000 users. The controller then kicks off the agents. The agents report their data back to the controller, where things are centralized and aggregated for reporting.

The Expression Tools

A sister product line to Visual Studio is Microsoft Expression tools. These tools are targeted toward designers who build applications on the Microsoft platform. Microsoft Expression tools offer rich design experiences for building Web, Windows, and Silverlight applications.

The Expression tools are also built to enable workflow between designers and developers; that is, a designer can open a solution and work on the design without affecting the code a developer might be working on (and vice versa). In the latest version, the tools can also integrate into TFS for source control and work item tracking.

It is important that you are aware of these tools so that you know where you might use them, and also because they work with Visual Studio projects and project files by offering some similar capabilities (but in different ways). The following is a high-level overview of these tools:

- ▶ **Expression Web**—A design tool for creating ASP.NET Web Forms and websites that comply with CSS standards.

- ▶ **Expression Blend**—A tool for designing user interfaces based on XAML and Silverlight.

- ▶ **Expression Design**—A tool that enables a designer to create vector-based illustrations that include drawing, text, and more.

- ▶ **SketchFlow**—A tool for creating fast prototypes before moving forward with a solution.

- ▶ **Expression Encoder**—A tool for encoding video and audio and publishing it to Silverlight applications.

- ▶ **Expression Media**—A tool for organizing and managing design assets (files) into visual catalogs.

- ▶ **Expression Studio**—The full set of Expression tools for designers who need it all.

> **NOTE**
>
> For more information on the Expression products (which are not covered further in this book), see www.microsoft.com/expression/default.aspx.

Languages, Frameworks, and Application Templates

Programming in Visual Studio and the .NET Framework means you have a variety of languages from which to choose. .NET was built to be somewhat language agnostic. The common type system (CTS), the common language specification (CLS), the common language runtime (CLR), and the Framework all work to abstract language from .NET and provide developers with choice. Once deployed and compiled, applications written on .NET are very similar in runtime execution.

Programming Language Choices

What should be important to developers is selecting a language that allows you to be productive and has a high degree of support inside the IDE. Productivity is about developing with syntax that is familiar and logical to you. IDE support means the tools can generate code, help you write code, and provide features and artifacts that accelerate your coding. This is where many third-party (non-Microsoft-supported) languages often fall short. It takes a lot to provide IDE support to build the many application types Visual Studio enables.

The following provides an overview of the Microsoft-supported languages for .NET development with Visual Studio:

▶ **Visual Basic**—The VB implementation in Visual Studio is about productivity. Developers can rapidly build type-safe, object-oriented applications. Although VB developers have full access to all code constructs in .NET, they tend to use VB because of the productivity features inside the IDE and they are already familiar with it from past experience with VB (or a similar language built on basic).

▶ **Visual C#**—Visual C# is a programming language designed for those who are familiar and comfortable programming in C-style languages (such as C, C++, and Java). C# is type-safe, object-oriented, and targeted for rapid application development. C# developers tend to spend more of their time inside the Visual Studio code editor and less time with the designers.

▶ **Visual C++**—With C++, developers can build .NET managed applications. However, they can also create Windows-based applications that do not rely on .NET. Most C++ developers have a C++ background and are therefore more comfortable inside the C++ world than they are with other languages. A C++ developer also has access to build against Active Template Library (ATL), the Microsoft Foundation Class (MFC) libraries, and the C Runtime Library (CRT).

▶ **Visual F#**—The F# language is said to be multiparadigm because it allows for functional, object-oriented, and imperative programming. F# is now a core language inside of Visual Studio 2010. It brings .NET developers a solution to many difficult programming problems. There are many features of F# including lightweight function types, functions as values, function composition and pipelining, recursive functions, and lambda expressions, to name a few. F# makes for simpler programming of math, scientific, engineering, and symbolic analysis (such as machine learning) problems.

▶ **JScript 8.0**—A scripting language for .NET. This language is Microsoft's implementation of the ECMA standard for compliance. You can use this language to write a variety of applications including Windows and Web applications. On the Web, you can target both server-side as well as client-side processing. JScript 8.0 adds compilation and full object-oriented supports (typed variables, early and late binding, inheritance, overloading, and more) to JScript. It also now allows access to the .NET Framework.

NOTE

The basics of programming the languages of .NET are covered in Chapter 3.

> **NOTE**
>
> If you are familiar with one language but need to program in another (or translate), search for "Keywords Compared in Various Languages" on MSDN (http://msdn. microsoft.com).

The .NET Framework(s)

The .NET Framework represents the base classes, libraries, and useful functions that make programming in .NET so productive. The classes and functions found in the .NET Framework provide the majority of common features you need as a developer. Thanks to the CTS, each language can take advantage of this single Framework of functionality. Framework features include file I/O, web, workflow, collections, Windows, communication, and much, much more.

Of course, as the .NET languages evolve so does the Framework. However, to maintain backward compatibility, each version of the Framework remains as a separate entity. There are now at least six versions of the .NET Framework: 4.0, 3.5, 3.0, 2.0, 1.1, 1.0. There are also various versions of the .NET Compact Framework (used for mobile devices). There is even a Micro Framework for very small, resource-constrained devices (www.microsoft. com/netmf).

Versions 3.0/3.5 of the .NET Framework brought WPF, WCF, and WF support along with modifications for Windows Vista. The latest version (4.0) ships with Visual Studio 2010 and brings support for dynamic languages (dynamic language runtime or DLR) such as Ruby, profiling running applications, new types such as Tuple and BigInteger, a revised Windows Workflow (WF) engine, isolated storage improvements, and a whole lot more. Chapter 3 discusses many of these Framework elements in greater detail.

> **NOTE**
>
> See Chapter 2 for details on how you can target a specific version of the .NET Framework inside of Visual Studio 2010.

The Many Faces of a .NET Application

.NET has become the standard when building applications targeting the Microsoft Windows client or server products. It took only a few years, but it is now fair to say that .NET is everywhere; Windows programming and .NET programming are now synonymous. Many of the user applications we interact with have some if not all of their code base in .NET. This includes rich clients built on Windows, solutions built on Office (including parts of Office itself), smart clients that work across the Web, Web applications that run in a browser and execute on a Windows server, and mobile applications that run on devices such as phones. The good news is that the .NET developer is in high demand, and you can leverage your skills to target a wide audience across an array of user experiences.

Figure 1.3 shows the New Project dialog in Visual Studio 2010; it serves as an example of the myriad user solutions that are possible with .NET. This graphic cannot fit all of the possibilities available to you, but it does illustrate that Windows, Web, Silverlight, Office, SharePoint, and many other project types are within the reach of .NET developers working with Visual Studio.

FIGURE 1.3   The many application faces made possible by Visual Studio 2010.

As discussed, you have many project templates available for your next solution. What is needed, however, is some sort of road map with respect to user experience. Choosing the right project template is an important part of making the delivery of your solution successful. The following list is meant to provide an overview of the core presentation technologies available to the .NET developer:

► **Windows Forms Application (WinForm)**—Windows form applications are used to deliver business applications and tools built on the Windows platform. You typically select a WinForm application template when you need to build a solution that leverages the resources on the user's machine. This means the application is installed and users expect it to run more responsively than the typical Web application. WinForm applications can be stand-alone or data-driven (often client-server). WinForm applications might connect to web services and work in both connected an unconnected scenarios. Note that WinForm applications are being de-emphasized in the current versions of Visual Studio. If you're building a new application, you should consider WPF instead of WinForm.

▶ **WPF Application**—Windows Presentation Foundation (WPF) combines features of WinForms with XAML and 3D capabilities to allow you to create the richest, most full-featured client solutions that run on Windows. WPF applications are delivered similar to a WinForm application. You choose WPF when you need to deliver a unique visual experience for your Windows application by taking advantage of vector-based scaling and 3D. In addition, WPF solutions can be browser-hosted in a security sandbox on Windows machines.

▶ **ASP.NET Web Application (WebForm)**—ASP.NET applications allow you to build solutions that run inside a user's browser but communicate with a web server for application processing. These solutions use HTML, CSS, and AJAX on the client but communicate across HTTP to a server for centralized processing of code and data storage and retrieval. Choose ASP.NET if you need to target a wide client base with low (or no) installation and wish to centralize updates to the application (as you need only update the server).

▶ **Silverlight Application**—A Silverlight application is similar to WPF; you can develop highly interactive user experiences that combine video, animation, 3D, and vector-based scaling. However, Silverlight applications are delivered across the Web and run using a browser plug-in. Therefore, unlike WPF, they are not constrained to just Windows machines. They also work on a Mac.

▶ **Office**—Visual Studio enables you to build solutions based on the Office productivity tools, including Excel, Word, Project, Visio, Outlook, PowerPoint, and InfoPath. This includes support for both 2010 and 2007 versions of Office. Choose an Office project when you want to write a business-productivity application centered on the product of one of these tools (such as an Excel template or spreadsheet).

▶ **SharePoint**—SharePoint applications are for delivering functionality through the collaboration portal. You might write a Web Part to deliver information, work with a document type, or allow users to enter data. You might also define business process workflow centered on a document. Note that 2010 provides expanded capabilities for developers building SharePoint applications (including F5 debugging support).

▶ **NetCF**—The .NET Compact Framework 3.5 runs on small devices (phone and PDAs, which enables you to build applications that target mobile devices and mobile users. The .NET CF and mobile SDK is available as a separate download to Visual Studio.

▶ **XNA**—XNA Game Studio 4.0 allows you to build games for Windows, Xbox, and Zune. This, too, is a separate download to Visual Studio.

Each of these UI delivery technologies is supported by Visual Studio 2010. With them, you have many options for creating great user experiences on .NET. The sections that follow highlight a number of these technologies for building both Windows and Web solutions.

Developing Rich(er) Clients

Today's users demand a rich, interactive experience when they work with software. The line between what a web-based client can do versus one that runs on Windows has blurred thanks to many UI advancements, technologies, and tools, which can make it difficult to choose the right UI delivery for your next application. It also means that if you do decide to write a Windows-based client, you need to be sure you take full advantage of having the desktop resources at your disposal. Your application should perform well, look great, provide a high degree of interactivity, be able to work with larger datasets at any given time, and more. Here we look at the Windows-based client options for Visual Studio 2010 and creating smart, rich applications using WinForms, Windows Presentation Foundation (WPF), and Microsoft Office.

Windows (WinForms)

Visual Studio provides a mature, feature-rich set of tools for the rapid development of Windows applications that includes a drag-and-drop form designer and many controls inside the form toolbox. With these tools, developers can quickly lay out a Windows application that includes menus, toolbars, data access, tabs, re-sizing support, common controls for working with and printing files, and much more.

You create a Windows application by selecting the Windows Form Application project template in the New Project dialog. This type of application is also called a WinForm application as it is based on the WinForm technology in Visual Studio and the .NET Framework.

The first step in a WinForm application is determining the layout of your form. You might decide to create a document-centric application (such as Word or Excel), of a single utility application (such as Calculator or Disk Defragmenter), or some other type of application. Whatever your choice, layout is typically controlled through the docking of controls to the form (through the Properties dialog) and the use of Panel controls.

For example, Figure 1.4 shows a MenuStrip control docked to the top of a WinForm and a StatusStrip docked to the bottom of the form. The menu allows a user to set a folder from which to view pictures. The status indicator provides updates as the application processes.

FIGURE 1.4   Building a WinForm application inside Visual Studio 2010.

Docked to the center of the form is a SplitContainer control, which allows two panels to size relative to one another using a splitter bar. Together, these controls define the layout of the main, interactive section of the form. In this case, a user can open a folder of pictures and view them individually by selecting a thumbnail from the left side of the form. The form then displays the selection as a larger image to the right. These features are accomplished through ImageList, ListView, and PictureBox controls. Each control is added to the appropriate area of the form and then configured via the Properties window.

You can start to see that the initial layout and definition of a WinForm application is a rapid experience. You first need to decide your form layout. The tools make it easy from that point forward.

As with all .NET programming, you first create the visual design and layout of your user interface, and then write code to respond to events. The WinForm application has a standard model that includes such events as Load, Closing, and Closed. You also respond to the events triggered by the controls on the form. For more detailed information on building WinForm applications please refer to Chapter 18.

Windows Presentation Foundation (WPF)

WPF is a set of classes, tools, and controls with which developers can create even richer, more dynamic client solutions for Windows. This includes developing user experiences that combine traditional data view and entry with video, 3D graphics, shading, and vector-based scaling. The results are truly unique, visually appealing, rich applications.

WPF uses markup code to define the UI. This should be very familiar to web developers. The markup is based on XAML (Extensible Application Markup Language). The XAML is created for you using the Visual Studio WPF designer (or a similar tool from Microsoft called Expression Blend). The XAML is then processed by the .NET CLR. The CLR process this XAML on the client, outside the browser. Therefore, it is not bound by the limits of HTML and the browser. Instead, it can create vector-based, hardware-accelerated user experiences.

Visual Studio provides a familiar experience for creating WPF solutions. You first define a WPF project and add WPF forms to the project. When creating your solution, you select a project type based on whether the application runs as a browser add-in or as an installed desktop client. Figure 1.5 shows the WPF project templates. Selecting WPF Application creates a basic WPF application that is pushed to or installed on a client. It might have access to local resources on the client.

FIGURE 1.5   Creating a new WPF project with Visual Studio 2010.

The WPF Browser Application, on the other hand, is meant to be deployed through a URL and run as a browser extension. The application, called an XBAP (XAML browser application), runs inside a sandbox. It does not have rights to the client machine and is cleaned up as part of the browser's cache. The application does not require a download provided that the user has the right version of the .NET Framework on her machine. It can work with the browser's cookies and is supported by both IE and Firefox.

Making the wrong choice here is not too problematic. You can move the WPF forms between application types. Note that the other two application types highlighted in Figure 1.5 are

WPF User Controls and WPF Custom Control Library. Both are for creating reusable controls for WPF applications.

The next step in building your WPF form is to simply open it and drag and drop UI controls onto a design surface. One big difference for developers used to building WinForm applications, however, is that you now have control over the form layout code (or XAML), which is more akin to designing a web form with Visual Studio. Figure 1.6 shows the XAML designer in action.

FIGURE 1.6   Designing a WPF form.

Notice that the XAML controls are listed in the toolbox on the left. Although they are similar to Windows and web controls, they are their own set of controls just for WPF. Also, notice how the designer has a split view between the design surface and the XAML. These views stay in sync as you develop your code. Finally, the properties window shown on the right provides a familiar experience for WinForm developers when editing the many properties of a selected control. We cover the WPF designer in greater detail in Chapter 19.

Office-Based Solutions

Developers have been able to customize Office for a long time now; some of us still remember writing Excel macros on Windows 3.1 or automating Word with Word Basic. Thankfully, these days the tools used to write Office solutions are built into Visual Studio. With them, you can create Office-based projects and solutions that leverage Word, Excel,

Project, Visio, PowerPoint, Outlook, and InfoPath. Figure 1.7 shows the New Project dialog for Office solutions. The templates shown in the figure are for C#, but the same exist for Visual Basic.

FIGURE 1.7   The many Office project templates inside Visual Studio.

There are a few scenarios that might lead developers to create an application based on Office. The most common is when you need to extend a line-of-business (LOB) application to provide functionality inside the common, information-worker productivity tools of Office. This type of solution typically combines structured, corporate data with a business process workflow that's centered on a document (such as an invoice or a purchase request).

As an example, suppose you work with a financial, manufacturing, or payroll application. Each of these fills a specific need. However, users might need to work with the data that is housed inside the application and make key decisions that feed back into these systems. This work is often done through cut-and-paste and is not captured by the systems. Users lose productivity switching back and forth between the Office tools and the LOB application. This is precisely where you should consider creating an Office Business Application (OBA) to help bridge this gap.

Develop Documents, Templates, and Add-Ins

Notice the many templates in Figure 1.7. There are three separate templates for Excel 2010 (and for 2007), for example. Each of these templates provides a specific purpose. Office application templates allow you to create solutions built on a single document, a document template, or as an add-in to the given Office application. The following list provides a brief overview of these three project subtypes:

▶ **Document (Workbook in Excel)**—Document projects allow you to build a solution based on a specific document. There are typically not multiple instances of the document. As an example, suppose you have an Excel workbook that needs to read and write project resource billing information from and to an enterprise resource planning (ERP) system. This document might be updated weekly as part of a resource meeting. The data should be up-to-date and changes should feed the billing system. In this instance, you would create a solution based on this single document.

▶ **Template**—An Office Template project is one that is based on an Office template file (an Excel .xltx, for example). Creating a solution based on an Office template file gives you the flexibility to provide users with assistance when creating a new instance of a given template. You might push common document templates out to your users. When a user creates a new instance, the template might reach into data housed in other systems to help the user fill out the details of the document. You might then, in turn, capture the results in a database after routing the template through a basic SharePoint workflow.

▶ **Add-in**—An Add-in project allows you to extend the features and functionality of a given Office application. You create Add-ins to offer additional productivity and solutions inside a given application. You might, for example, write an Outlook Add-in that allows users to more easily file and categorize their email.

Whichever template you choose, Visual Studio 2010 provides a rich, design-time experience for building your Office solution. As an example, Figure 1.8 shows the Visual Studio 2010 design experience building a solution for a Word 2010 Template. In this example, a user is creating a quote for training. The fields in the document pull from a LOB database that includes customer information, resource data, and common pricing.

The Office templates in Visual Studio also provide design support for working with the Office Ribbon. In this way, your application can behave like the rest of Office. You can embed productivity features and aids on your own tab of the Office Ribbon. Figure 1.9 shows a simple example. The features shown apply to the document template for a sales quote discussed previously. In this example, a developer provides specific features based on the document template that are then accessed by the user from Word's Ribbon.

Create SharePoint Solutions

While not a true Windows client, SharePoint and Office have become nearly synonymous. Therefore, we thought it appropriate to discuss the SharePoint-specific capabilities of Visual Studio in this section. Companies leverage SharePoint for knowledge management, collaboration, and business process automation. Of course, this inevitably means customization and extension by developers. If you customized SharePoint using the existing tools for Visual Studio prior to 2010, you know that this presented a big challenge. The design-time support was not there, configuration was difficult, and debugging was very challenging.

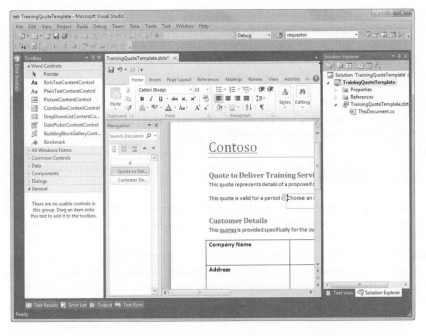

FIGURE 1.8   Designing a Word 2007 Template project in Visual Studio 2010.

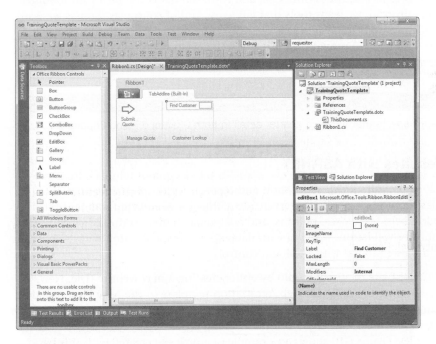

FIGURE 1.9   Creating a custom Ribbon for a Microsoft Office solution.

Visual Studio 2010 presents a much richer toolset for SharePoint developers. With it, you can create SharePoint workflows and build Web Parts based on ASP.NET. In addition, the debug experience has streamlined. SharePoint development is now a first-class consideration inside the IDE. This should help developers more easily extend SharePoint to meet the business demand this collaboration product has generated.

There are many more advancements, however, including access to open XML formats, the capability to add features to existing Outlook forms, custom task panes in Word and Excel, data binding, and improved deployment and security.

Creating Web Clients

The vast majority of applications built these days involve some semblance of a web component—be it a full-blown browser-based, web application; a smart client that works across the Web; or a web service. In fact, the line between a traditional rich client and a web application is blurring, and Technologies such as AJAX (Asynchronous JavaScript and XML), jQuery, Web Services, Smart Clients, XAML (Extensible Application Markup Language), and Silverlight have helped blur the line. You can now build rich user experiences as your needs dictate. Of course, Microsoft has remained suitably focused on expanding Visual Studio's capabilities with respect to web development.

Web developers want tools that help them through the common functions of building their application. Let's face it, the HTML, CSS, and XML standards can be a pain to follow by memory alone. Instead, we want tools that guide us. And of course, as soon as we want to work with code, we want to be able to access the entire related source and massage it as necessary. Visual Studio 2010 provides an array of web development templates from which to choose. This section presents many of these possibilities.

> **NOTE**
>
> We cover many aspects that follow in greater detail in both Chapter 17 and Chapter 20.

Building Websites with ASP.NET

Visual Studio 2010 provides a rich set of tools and controls for the web developer. It supports standard controls for building server-side ASP.NET and emitting standard HTML. Controls include labels, text boxes, buttons, and related data-entry controls. In addition, there are controls for validation, working with data, doing personalization with Web Parts, and managing the user process with the login controls.

You create an ASP.NET site in Visual Studio by either creating a new website (File, New, Web Site) or by selecting the ASP.NET Web Application template in the New Project dialog. The website template should be used to create projects that mimic basic, file-centric websites. This typically means all files (your markup and code) deployed to the website and managed as files. Figure 1.10 shows an example of a new site created with this basic project template. This template should feel comfortable to most developers who are used to working on file-driven websites.

FIGURE 1.10   The ASP.NET website project template.

A Web Application, on the other hand, provides a project model similar to other .NET applications. You can generate .DLLs, set references, sign assemblies, manage build properties, and do similar tasks in a familiar manner as writing other .NET applications. Figure 1.11 shows an example. Notice the References folder for setting .NET references and the multiple versions of the Web.config file. Your template choice ultimately depends on the manner in which you plan to build and manage your site.

FIGURE 1.11   The ASP.NET Web Application Project Template.

Develop and Design at the Same Time

You develop ASP.NET pages by editing the design and connecting code to that design. The design is referred to as markup. This is XHTML that defines the controls, their layout, and their look on your page. Visual Studio includes both a markup editor and a visual, WYSIWYG designer for laying out your page. Most web form developers switch between the Source (XHTML) and the Design (WYSIWYG) view of a web form many times during development. The Source view allows you full access to editing the XHTML of the page. Design view lets you see the page develop and gives access to the many shortcuts attached to controls in the designer. Visual Studio makes switching between these views simple. It provides a Split view. With it, you can see both the XHTML and the visual Designer. Figure 1.12 shows an example.

FIGURE 1.12   The Web Form Designer Split view.

Split view tries to keep both the source and the design in sync. This works when you drag items from the toolbox to either the Source or the Design view panes. However, the Design view can get out of sync when you are doing a lot of edits to your source. In these cases, the Design view indicates that it is out of sync (see the middle of Figure 1.12). Click on the Designer and everything is back in sync.

Centrally Manage Navigation and Design

Visual Studio 2005 introduced the capability to create master pages. These pages centralize the management of a site's design and navigation elements. In addition, master pages are supported by the designer, which allows for a richer design experience. A developer is able to see the page in the context of the site's central design while in design mode.

You create a master page by selecting the Master Page template from the Add New Item dialog. You then define your site navigation, header and footer information, styles, and anything else that should apply to each page in the site (or sub-area of a site). After you define the navigation, you can create new web forms that provide specific content that should be enclosed inside a master page. Figure 1.13 shows an example of working with a web form whose outer content is based on a master page.

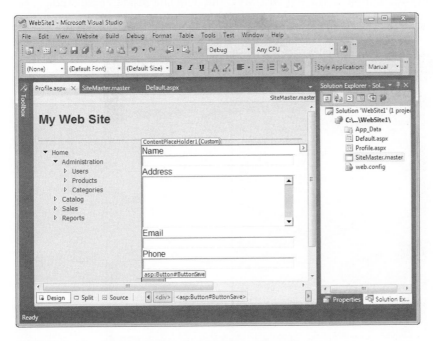

FIGURE 1.13   Creating pages that use a master page.

Building Loosely Coupled Web Applications with ASP.NET Model-View-Controller (MVC)

Visual Studio supports an alternative to building your application using standard Web Forms. This alternative is based on the Model-View-Controller design pattern. The purpose of this pattern is to separate the application's logic and data (model), its user interface display (view), and the code that helps the user interact with the UI and the data (controller).

Sites built using MVC are typically easier to maintain as there is decreased dependency between the application layers. They also support test-driven development as you can write tests for each layer. In addition, you can use the MVC construct to separate the duties by developer where you might have designers creating views while other developers are working on models or controllers. Another advantage of MVC is that developers have more fine control over the processing as a web page.

The ASP.NET implementation of the MVC is both a set of namespaces (System.Web.Mvc) and project templates. You create a site in which you intend to use MVC by selecting the ASP.NET MVC Web Application project template in the New Project dialog. Note that you can mix sites that use both MVC and standard Web Forms. In addition, ASP.NET MVC supports most ASP.NET constructs such as master pages, sessions, caching, profiles and membership, configuration, and the like. However, it does not support ASP.NET view state. Figure 1.14 shows an example of the ASP.NET MVC site template inside Visual Studio. See Chapter 17 for a detailed discussion of ASP.NET MVC 2.

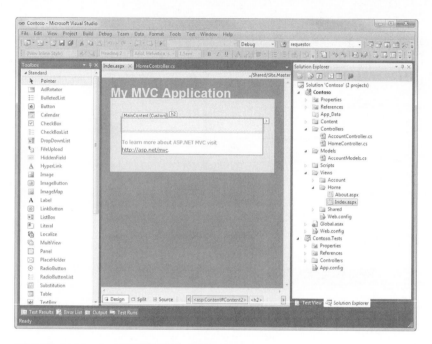

FIGURE 1.14   An ASP.NET MVC project.

Adding Richer Features with AJAX

AJAX represents the capability to leverage the ubiquitous support for JavaScript in web browsers to create a more interactive user experience. Client applications built to leverage AJAX still have a client-server paradigm. However, with AJAX the client can update portions of a given page without appearing to have posted back to the server (of course, it typically does). In addition, most AJAX-enabled applications put more processing on the client for things such as toggling sections of a page, working with tabs, auto-completing data entry, popping up dialogs, and more. The result is a step forward in interactivity for a user.

AJAX is not a Microsoft-specific technology. Instead, it is a programming model. However, Microsoft created a set of controls called the AJAX Extensions for Visual Studio. These controls allow developers to more easily create AJAX experiences. Figure 1.15 shows the controls inside the Visual Studio Toolbox.

FIGURE 1.15   The AJAX Extensions Controls in Visual Studio 2010.

The AJAX Extension Controls enable you to create a page that can receive partial, asynchronous updates (using UpdatePanel) and show update progress (using UpdateProgress). They also allow you to create your own controls and features that implement AJAX without having to write the client-side JavaScript.

In addition to these controls, Visual Studio 2010 supports IntelliSense, code comment documentation, and client-side debugging for JavaScript. It also contains the Microsoft AJAX Library, which is a JavaScript common library that supports object-oriented development for JavaScript. Finally, many of the ASP.NET controls have AJAX features built-in to give you control over partial postbacks versus full page refresh.

Developing for Silverlight

Microsoft's Silverlight is another exciting client technology for the Web. Silverlight allows for an even richer user experience than AJAX. You use it to create media-rich (images, video, graphic scaling), highly interactive experiences. Silverlight requires a browser add-on (or plug-in). It works with Windows, Mac, and Linux in a variety of browsers. Silverlight is based on WPF; it allows you to leverage XAML skills inside a browser and across platforms.

You create a Silverlight application in Visual Studio 2010 by selecting the Silverlight Application project template in the New Project dialog. When doing so, you need to select a host for your application. This can be an ASP.NET Web project or you can let Visual Studio generate a test page upon build. You can also set the target version of Silverlight on which you intend your application to be deployed. This is based on the versions of Silverlight you have installed. Figure 1.16 shows an example of configuring these two settings upon project creation.

FIGURE 1.16   Targeting a specific Silverlight version.

You create a Silverlight application like you might a WPF application. You have a designer for laying out a page. You can also edit the XAML directly. In addition, the Silverlight controls are available to you from the Toolbox. The real difference is the application host. This is typically an ASP.NET web project. You can see in Figure 1.17 that there is both a host project (generated by the Visual Studio template) and the Silverlight project.

FIGURE 1.17   A Silverlight Page Inside Visual Studio.

Designers and Developers

When discussing Silverlight (or even WPF), it's important to note the work that went into the technology and tools to support a strong designer-developer workflow. It's understood that traditionally developers have been left to try to "design" the UI. It goes without saying that many developers have not exactly shined as UI designers.

However, even in scenarios where designers are employed on projects, the design often falls short or the implementation is an arduous process. Designers have their own tools that often do not talk with those of the developers. Instead, a design is often provided to the development team as a picture or some basic HTML. Developers are left to try to realize the intricacies of the design while having to concern themselves with coding the solution. This can cause the design to never be exactly what was envisioned and developers to spend too much time trying to get the look right.

Silverlight and WPF try to right this wrong by keeping the UI markup (XAML) totally separate from the implementation code (C# or VB). In addition, Microsoft has provided design tools that let designers create real user interfaces that can be leveraged by the development team. There are no more "lost in translation" issues. Instead, a designer can create or open a XAML-based UI element, edit it using the power of Expression Blend (they do not have to learn Visual Studio), and save it back to the solution or send it to a developer. The developer can then open the same item inside of Visual Studio and begin responding to key UI events with their code. This back-and-forth can continue as the UI builds up over time. Nobody's code gets stepped on; everyone focuses on their strength.

Figure 1.18 shows a sample of the Expression Blend 3.0 tool. Notice that the same .xaml file that was in the Silverlight example is also open here. Designers can use a tool with which they are more familiar to lay out the UI and apply visual techniques such as 3D and animation. Also notice that the C# project file is being used to maintain continuity between the solutions. After the designers are finished, their save goes right back to the development team. They can even test their UI in the context of the application by building and running the project.

Making the Client Choice

The many options for developing rich user experiences on Windows invariably leads to this question: "What is the right UI technology for my next application?" Of course, the answer depends on your specific scenario. When making your decision, you should keep the intent of each technology in mind. The following should help you make the right decision:

> ▶ Windows forms still has a place in creating installed, business applications that connect with the operating system, leverage resources on the client, connect to databases, and more. They offer standard, workman-like user experiences for data entry, file manipulation, configuration, and related task-oriented solutions. Windows forms are easy to develop and do not typically involve much work from a design perspective. We suggest you continue with WinForms if you already have a significant investment in them. If you are building from scratch, however, you should take a good look at WPF as that is where Microsoft has focused its innovation.

FIGURE 1.18   Designing a WPF form inside of Expression Blend.

▶ WPF is a Windows technology that requires the .NET Framework on the client. It can run in a browser sandbox or as a fully featured Windows application. You should leverage WPF when you need to create a rich user experience with high design aesthetics (3D, animations, vector-scaled graphics), want a low cost of installation and update, and require distributed connectivity.

▶ Silverlight runs inside a browser. Silverlight is a very lightweight, cross-platform version of WPF. It provides many of the rich features of WPF, but it allows you to run on different platforms (Windows, Mac, Linux) and different browsers. Of course, Silverlight does require a browser plug-in. The browser plug-in runs a mini version of the CLR on the client. In this way, you still can write your code in C# or VB and have access to bits of the .NET Framework. However, clients must have the plug-in to run your application. Think of Silverlight as an alternative to Adobe's Flash product.

▶ ASP.NET Web applications are a great solution for creating functionality that runs ubiquitously. The only requirement is a web browser. Therefore, Web Form applications are still a great solution when you need to reach the widest possible audience and you do not wish to deal with client installations. In addition, most modern browsers support JavaScript. Therefore, you can still get some interactive features using AJAX in your ASP.NET application.

▶ Microsoft Office solutions are applicable when users tend to work directly with productivity documents. In these cases, you can combine the power of Word, Excel, or another Office product with your line-of-business data to create a rich solution. For instance, you might define an Excel document for creating an invoice or a timesheet. You could connect that document to a SharePoint library for managing approvals and workflow. All the while, the document can be built to get data from backend systems and write out results to the same.

Coding for the Cloud

Most of the distributed applications we write are deployed onto one or more servers for hosting and delivery out to the user base. This hosted environment might contain multiple web servers, a database server, and other servers as necessary. The environment then needs to be monitored and managed either internally or through a hosting provider. The management of this environment can be costly. Servers require repair and updates; as the demand for your application increases, you often have to add new hardware to scale with the demand.

Cloud computing is meant to help address these issues. In its basic form, cloud computing represents a hosting environment for your entire application (user interface, logic, database, and so on). The environment is meant to automatically scale with your demand and free you from hardware management and monitoring tasks. This is accomplished through massive amounts of distributed, automatically managed computing power.

Visual Studio developers that want to take advantage of cloud computing can do so via Windows Azure. You can think of this technology as the server operating system for hosting your application. The difference is that Azure is not a single server OS you install; rather, it is an OS that sits atop massive amounts of shared, computing power. You can develop, deploy, manage, and scale your application using the Windows Azure cloud as the single host for your application. Adding scale to that host is then simply a configuration change.

Creating a Cloud Application

You create an application destined for the cloud by selecting the Cloud Service template from Visual Studio's New Project dialog. Doing so brings up the New Cloud Service Project dialog as shown in Figure 1.19. Here, you select a role (or type) for your application. The ASP.NET Web Role, for example, tells Visual Studio to create a standard ASP.NET website for deploying in the cloud. This is also the role you would use to move your existing ASP.NET sites to the cloud.

Developing for the cloud is very similar to developing standard .NET applications. In the case of the Web Role, you simply develop your website as you might otherwise do it. This means adding pages, using standard controls, and coding to the ASP.NET event model. The Visual Studio solution template keeps the cloud service application and your ASP.NET site as separate projects in the solution. Figure 1.20 shows an example. Notice that the website looks like (and is) a standard ASP.NET site. The cloud service application serves as the configuration point for defining how the site should be deployed into the cloud.

FIGURE 1.19   Selecting the role for your cloud service project.

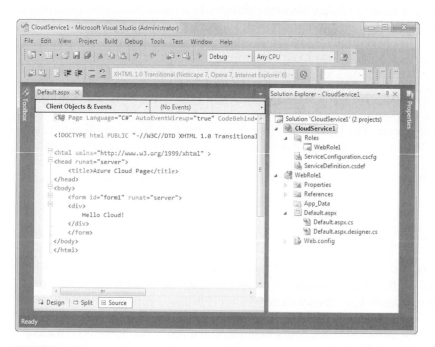

FIGURE 1.20   An ASP.NET website and its cloud configuration project.

Running a Cloud Application

You can run and debug your cloud-bound application from your client machine. That is, you are not required to deploy it into the cloud in order to run it at development time. This experience is very similar to debugging any local project. The primary difference is that the cloud is simulated locally. An application called the development fabric runs on your machine to host your application. The development fabric executes your application as if it were running on the Azure cloud. You can actually view and control this fabric by clicking on its icon in the task bar. Figure 1.21 shows a website running in the development fabric.

FIGURE 1.21   An application running locally inside the cloud development fabric.

Publishing to the Cloud

When you are ready to push your application into the actual cloud, you can do so directly within Visual Studio. You first must publish your solution by right-clicking the cloud service and selecting Publish. This creates a package file (.cspkg) and a configuration file inside your applications bin\Publish directory.

To deploy, you must have an Azure services account (windows.azure.com). In Azure you define and manage your projects and their services. In this case, you would create a hosted service under a specific project you name. The hosted service must map to a URL that provides access to your service. After your service is defined, you can then deploy. You can deploy a staged or production version. Clicking on the Deploy button for either Production or Stage takes you to a screen where you can upload your application package and configuration file. Figure 1.22 shows an example.

After deployment, you can start, suspend, configure, or upgrade the application from the Windows Azure management site. Of course, you can also now access it from its URL.

Working with Data

Data is the domain of the business developer. It makes sense then that the number one tool and framework for business development continues to provide new and better ways of accessing and exposing that data. Data access is everywhere inside Visual Studio and

FIGURE 1.22   Deploying a hosted service (website) to the Azure cloud.

the .NET Framework. Here we highlight some of the things you encounter when working with data inside Visual Studio 2010.

Design Your Data

A typed dataset allows you to create a .NET class that is based on your database table semantics but works as a dataset behind the scenes. This can simplify your programming as you are working with a class. Visual Studio can generate all the code for you. Typed datasets have been part of Visual Studio for a while now. You can auto-generate them based on your actual table schemas and edit the code that is generated to query, update, insert, and delete data.

Visual Studio 2010 provides design-time support for typed datasets. You create a typed dataset file (.xsd) by adding it to your project. You can then use the Toolbox and Server Explorer to build the dataset. Figure 1.23 shows an example. Tables from the Server Explorer were added to the design surface to build the dataset (and generate the underlying class code).

After you create the dataset, you can program against the actual class that represents your data. The class manages the task of working with your database. In addition, typed datasets support hierarchical updates. This feature allows you to save data in multiple, related tables through the typed dataset class. In Figure 1.23, this would mean you could edit both the employee details and the related territories and update both as a single process.

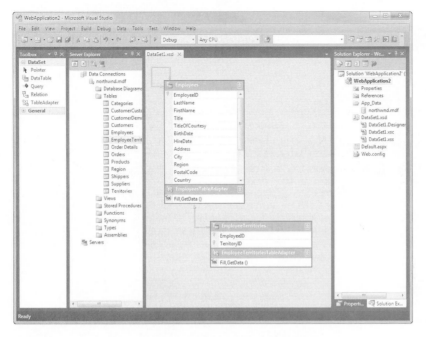

FIGURE 1.23   Building a typed dataset with the dataset designer.

Separate Data Design from Storage Schema

Most business applications rely on data that is stored in relational databases. Databases have a well-known structure of tables, columns, and relationships. This structure makes for a nice storage and reporting mechanism. However, the needs of an object-oriented, .NET developer and the database technology are often mismatched. The object developer thinks in terms of objects, properties, methods, relationships, encapsulation, and the like. A lot of time is spent (and a lot of code is written) to convert data from a database into an object-oriented structure and back again.

Visual Studio provides the Entity Data Model (EDM) as a means for mapping objects to database schemas. The EDM and Entity Framework allow you to design the data classes that are used by your application independent of the actual storage mechanism used to persist those classes to a database. You can program against these data classes (the design schema) in your application. You can then define a separate schema for doing the actual persistence (called the storage schema). You create a mapping specification to indicate how the design and storage schema are connected. In this way, the EDM allows your application data to evolve independent of your database schema. They are not coupled. If either schema changes, you change the map to keep them connected.

You create an EDM by selecting the ADO.NET Entity Data Model item from the Add New Item dialog (see Figure 1.24). Selecting this template launches the Entity Data Model Wizard.

FIGURE 1.24   ADO.NET Entity Data Model.

The EDM Wizard enables you to start with an Empty Model (as shown in Figure 1.25), which is great if you intend to model first and then build data storage. You can also generate an EDM from an existing database. This creates a set of class files that mimic your current database structure. However, your class files can then evolve independent of the underlying storage.

The EDM is a file (.edmx) in your solution. You can open it inside a designer for editing. Figure 1.26 shows an example. Notice the storage schema is being mapped to the design schema using the Mapping Details pane (at the bottom of the figure). There are also options for handling relationships (Toolbox) and browsing the model (Model Browser on the left). Once your EDM is complete, you can code directly against it inside your application as you would any class object.

Build Occasionally Connected Applications

Many applications written these days require access to data both on- and offline. For example, you might need report data or customer service records when traveling or at a customer site. You cannot always rely on being connected. Developers have been dealing with this issue in various ways. Visual Studio provides data synchronization services to provide a common, easy solution to this difficult problem.

Data synchronization allows you to sync and cache data between a central database and a user's client system. The cache is a version of SQL Server Compact Edition (CE). Microsoft

FIGURE 1.25 The Entity Data Model Wizard enables you to generate a model from an existing database or start with an empty model.

FIGURE 1.26 Mapping design schema to storage schema in the EDM designer.

takes advantage of these services in Windows 7, Vista, Office, and even its Zune software. You, too, can take advantage of these services in your applications.

You can add a local database cache to a WinForms or WPF application. You do so through the Local Database Cache item template. With it, you create a .sync file to configure how synchronization should happen between a local data store and a server. Opening the local database cache file in Visual Studio opens the Configure Data Synchronization dialog. Here you can set up tables that should be cached on a client, set up the server database, and configure the client database information. Figure 1.27 shows an example of configuring this dialog to sync certain tables between a server and a client database cache.

FIGURE 1.27   Configuring data synchronization.

Write Connected, Service-Oriented Solutions

Many business applications involve specific processes, or workflows, around documents, records, and related data. These business processes typically involve staged review and approval by business personnel; they might also require communication between various systems. A business process is also typically long-running—meaning the process is not a simple, single execution but rather a multistep process that has to "wait" before moving to the next step.

Building these processes into business application typically required a lot of custom development work with little guidance, or it meant tying your application to third-party tools.

Web services helped, but developers lacked an easy way to build them with support for multiple protocols, different transports, strong security, and transactional support.

Visual Studio 2010 provides in-the-box support for building business processes as workflows and reliably integrating them with other applications, systems, and partners. This section takes a look at Windows Workflow (WF) for defining reusable business process and Windows Communication Foundation (WCF) for unlocking that business process across system boundaries.

Develop an Application/Business Process

A workflow represents a set of actions (called activities) that typically model a business process and often involve user interaction. WF provides the framework, tools, and an execution engine for enabling workflows in your application. With it, you can create a workflow and know that it runs wherever the .NET Framework is installed.

You create a workflow model to describe the order and logic of how activities are to be executed based on the data in the workflow, your business rules and conditions, and system and user actions. A workflow is executed and managed by a workflow instance object. This object is run in process with your application and controls the execution and current state of the workflow. You interact with your workflows from within your application. This could be any type of application (Windows, ASP.NET, console, service, and so on). You typically submit data to the workflow and you might get a response, or you might use the workflow to kick off certain tasks or activities in your business process. The workflow can also persist itself during long-running transactions and then rehydrate on demand.

> **NOTE**
>
> If you've used WF in a prior version of .NET, you should know that WF in .NET 4.0 is almost a completely new version. For example, the SequentialWorkflow and StateMachineWorkflow classes from the prior version are now gone. Instead, you have a single, hierarchical model.

Building a workflow is a visual process. The thought behind this is that workflows themselves are traditionally illustrated as a set of steps (boxes) and connections (arrows). For this reason, workflows are represented as a FlowChart item template. You can add activities (or a sequence of activities) to a flowchart and connect them accordingly. Activities are added from the Toolbox items. There are many standard activities for handling things such as branching, looping, error handling, and compensation. You will most likely also code your own, custom activities and add them to the workflow. Figure 1.28 shows an example workflow in the designer. There are activities listed in the toolbox on the left. Notice that once added to the diagram, you can code the activity (including IntelliSense) from within the designer.

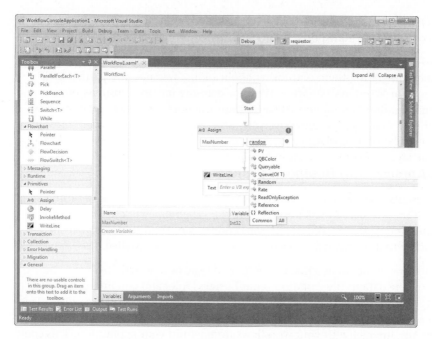

FIGURE 1.28   The Workflow designer inside Visual Studio.

A workflow can also have both variables and arguments. These concepts are similar to programming .NET C# or VB. A variable is used to store state (or data) inside the workflow (or activity). An argument is used to pass data into and out of a workflow. Notice the variable and arguments editor at the bottom of Figure 1.28. Here, you define the name, type, direction, and default value for variable or argument used by your given workflow.

Finally, notice the messaging activities listed on the Toolbox inside Figure 1.28. These activities allow you to define a receive and/or send port for the workflow. This enables your workflow to be listening for messages and then kick-off a hosted instance after a message is received. You can also use the send shape to communicate with other hosted services.

> **NOTE**
>
> See Chapter 23, "Embedding Workflow in Your Applications," for a more detailed discussion of Windows Workflow.

Create and Consume Services

Most organizations have multiple systems, each designed for a specific purpose. They might have systems for finance, HR, order management, inventory, customer service, and more. Each application houses specific business processes. However, most organizations need to unlock these business processes from their applications and reuse them as part of an integrated solution. This is where service-oriented solutions have helped. By exposing an application's business process as a service, multiple clients can take advantage of that process.

The promise of code reuse has been with us a long time. However, service-oriented code reuse became very popular with the advent of web services. The ubiquitous nature of HTTP and port 80 coupled with XML-based interfaces allowed for a new level of communication between application boundaries. Developers began wrapping key business functions as services and calling them from multiple clients.

Visual Studio 2010 and the .NET Framework 4.0 represent another step forward in this service-oriented paradigm. With these tools, you can create services based on Microsoft's Windows Communication Foundation. WCF is a framework that recognizes that developers need multiple layers of communication (not just the SOAP protocol carried over an HTTP transport), require strong security, often need to support transactions, and do not want to write all the plumbing code to do so.

You create WCF services as a code library, as a workflow, or as a web service application. Figure 1.29 shows the new project templates listed under the WCF project types. From here you can indicate that your web service contains a workflow or simply create a service library that calls custom code you write.

FIGURE 1.29   The WCF Project Templates.

You can also still create XML web services (.asmx) through the web project templates. This same template area also provides access to the WCF Service Application template. With it, you can create a WCF service that is configured similarly to a standard web service (and hosted in ASP.NET).

WCF is all about configuration. It frees you from having to write all the service plumbing code. Instead, you can focus on the functionality of your service. For example, you can add service endpoints to your service depending on which communication stack you intend to support (HTTP, TCP/IP, MSMQ, Named Pipes, and so on). Figure 1.30 shows the WCF configuration editor. Notice how the binding support for an endpoint is a configuration (and not coding) task.

FIGURE 1.30   Configuration of a WCF service.

After you've built your service, you need to host it so consumers (clients) can find it and call it. You have a lot of hosting options available to you including self-hosted, Windows service, IIS, and WAS (Windows Process Activation Service). Actually consuming the WCF service requires you to define a service reference and configure how you are going to talk with the service and pass messages. We discuss creating, hosting, and consuming services in detail later in this book (Chapter 22, "Service Oriented Applications").

> **NOTE**
>
> See Chapter 22, "Service-Oriented Applications," for a more detailed discussion of the tools for WCF and web services.

Summary

A new release of Visual Studio means a lot to all the various development camps out there. Visual Studio touches developers who write code in C++, C#, Visual Basic, and many other languages. Literally millions of developers boot up and launch their favorite tool every day. They spend the vast majority of their working hours, days, weeks, and months architecting and building solutions with the tool. Hopefully, this chapter oriented you to the many possibilities available for building your next application.

CHAPTER 2

The Visual Studio IDE

When you're traveling over new ground, it's often wise to consult a guide. At a minimum, a quick check of the map is in order before you set out for new adventures. The same holds true for approaching a new development tool the size and breadth of Visual Studio 2010. It is wise to familiarize yourself a bit with the tool before starting that first project off on the wrong foot.

This chapter is your quick, to-the-point guide. It serves to orient you before you set out. We cover the basics of installation; configuration; booting up the IDE; and getting to know the layout of the tool in terms of projects, menus, tools, editors, and designers. Let's get started.

Installing Visual Studio

The installation of Visual Studio 2010 remains similar to that of previous versions. The application plays host to many tools. Depending on your purchase, a subset of these items are available during install (see Chapter 1, "A Quick Tour of Visual Studio 2010," for a comparison of Visual Studio editions). If you are fortunate enough to own the Team Suite Edition, you are presented with the full set of options for installation. For those with Visual Studio Professional, however, you choose one or more development languages, determine if you want to install unit testing, decide if you need the features of Microsoft Office Development, and perhaps install SQL 2008 Express. Figure 2.1 shows the setup options selection dialog box for Visual Studio Professional.

FIGURE 2.1   Visual Studio 2010 Setup Options page.

Choosing a Language

Setting up your development machine should be relatively straightforward. We suggest that most developers keep language installs to a primary language and perhaps one backup. You might use a secondary language for viewing sample code from MSDN or similar sites. Typically, this means if your primary language is Visual Basic, you install C# as a secondary language (and vice versa). Choosing to install many languages, most of which you do not intend to use, not only takes up hard drive space, but also can clutter your environment with too many choices. Having a backup language, however, helps solve the problem of finding a great bit of code you want to learn more about only to discover you can't give it a test run because it is not available in your chosen language.

Whether or not to install the additional tools is entirely up to you (and the projects you will be working on). For example, if you intend to work with a lot of local database code, you want SQL Server 2008 Express. If your project requires you to unit test your code then you should be sure to install the Unit Testing Tools.

> **TIP**
>
> You might change your mind about your installation selections at a later date. In this case, you can always go back and rerun setup. Rerunning setup gives you the Add or Remove Features, Repair/Reinstall, or Uninstall options.

Configuring Your Development Environment Settings

Booting the new IDE for the first time results in a dialog box asking you to choose your environment settings. As Visual Studio becomes the central tool for so many developers, testers, architects, and even project managers, it's harder and harder to satisfy them all with a single tool. To aid in this dilemma, Microsoft has created an entire set of environment settings that are configured for the usual developer type. For instance, if you set your environment to C#, the New Project dialog box automatically highlights C# projects above other languages. Figure 2.2 shows the available environment settings options.

FIGURE 2.2   The Environment Settings options dialog box.

Managing Your Settings

Only your first use of Visual Studio launches the default settings dialog box. On subsequent visits, you go straight to the tool. However, you might consider switching your environment settings if you do a lot of switching from one language to another or if you switch roles. For example, C# developers might use the C# development settings most of the time. They might then toggle to another collection of settings when switching to VB or developing a Web-only application.

You manage your environment settings from the Tools menu's Import and Export Settings option. Figure 2.3 shows the first screen in this wizard. This screen enables you to choose to execute a settings export, import, or total reset.

TIP

If you are like most developers, you are probably particular about your environment setup. There is nothing worse than having to work on a machine that has a different IDE configuration. You can be thankful that you can use the Import and Export Settings Wizard to take your IDE settings with you.

FIGURE 2.3   The Import and Export Settings Wizard.

You can choose from several setting collections when importing. There are a few default collections, including those based on language and role (such as web developer or tester in the case of Team Systems). In addition, you can select a custom settings file. Figure 2.4 shows the import settings collection options.

FIGURE 2.4   Choosing a collection of settings for import.

Another key screen to the Import and Export Settings Wizard is the settings selection screen. On this screen, you decide which options are important for export or import. This enables you to pick and choose settings you plan to either export or import. For example, you might love the way a friend has configured her code editor in terms of font and contrasting colors, but you do not want all her other settings, such as her keyboard configurations. You can accomplish this by selecting to import only her code editor settings. Figure 2.5 provides a glimpse at the granular level to which you can manage your environment settings during import and export.

FIGURE 2.5   Choosing settings to export.

TIP

A great feature of the import and export settings tool is the capability to export/import any of your IDE customizations, including fonts and colors, start page customizations, menu and keyboard customizations, and more. These items can travel with you from machine to machine, so you do not have to spend valuable development time resetting them each time you rebuild or switch machines.

By default, settings are exported to your documents folder. In Windows 7, you typically find this folder at C:\Users\[user]\Documents\Visual Studio 10\Settings. Here you can find a .vssettings XML file representing the many settings for your instance of Visual Studio. This includes CurrentSettings.vssettings and any exported settings files. The

.vssettings files can be shared among users. They can also be used to migrate settings from one PC and one IDE version to another. You do so through the Import and Export Settings Wizard.

Getting Started

When you first launch Visual Studio 2010, you are presented with the Start Page for the IDE. This page has been revamped for the 2010 version to be more useful and shows off some of the new capabilities of an IDE built on top of Windows Presentation Foundation (WPF). Figure 2.6 shows an example of the Start Page.

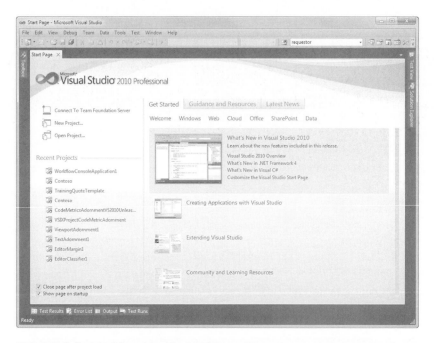

FIGURE 2.6   The Visual Studio 2010 Start Page.

The Start Page contains a number of useful links to get you moving quickly. Starting from the upper left, you have three primary options: connect to TFS, new project, and open project. You also can launch a recent project from the left side of the screen. Across the top are tabs for getting started, guidance and resource, and latest news. These all provide access to online content. See Chapter 7, "The .NET Community: Interacting Online," for more information on working with the Start Page.

> **TIP**
>
> The new Start Page gives you more control over the projects that show up in the recent projects list. You can highlight a project in the list and pin it to ensure it stays in the list. You can also easily delete projects from this list.

Startup Options

If you just don't like the Start Page or prefer to launch directly into the project you'll be spending the next few months of your life working on, you can customize what happens when the IDE boots. From the Options dialog box (Tools, Options or the Settings link on the Start Page), choose the Environment node and then the Startup leaf. Figure 2.7 shows some of the options available to you at startup.

FIGURE 2.7   Startup options.

From here, you can configure where to get your start page news(Start Page news channel). You set this to a valid RSS feed URL. You can also use the At Startup option to tell the environment to load the last solution, show the new or open project dialog boxes, open your browser's home page, or do nothing (show an empty environment). You can also configure how often your content is automatically refreshed from the server. Finally, you have the option here to use a custom start page. For more information on custom start pages click the Customize the Start Page link on the Welcome screen of the Start Page.

Creating Your First Project

The next, natural step is to create your first project. You might have an existing project you want to open or you might be starting fresh. In either case, creating or opening a project quickly exposes you to some of the basic project and file management features within the IDE.

To get started, you can click the File menu or the Projects link on the start page. Assuming you are using the File menu, you see the options to create a new project or website under the New submenu. Projects are simply templates that group files for Windows, Office, Web, and similar applications A website creates a set of web files that get promoted and managed as files (and not complied code).

You might have multiple projects grouped together to form a single application. In this case, each project might be grouped under a single solution. Figure 2.8 shows an example of the New Project dialog box. Notice that a Visual C#, ASP.NET Web Application is being created along with a new solution to house the project. For more information on this, see Chapter 4, "Solutions and Projects."

FIGURE 2.8   Creating a New Project.

Targeting Your Environment

Many of us work in environments that include applications built on various versions of the .NET Framework. You might be building your new applications on .NET 4.0, but still need to support one or more .NET 2.0 applications. Of course, this becomes even more prevalent as more versions are released. You do not, however, want to have to keep multiple versions of Visual Studio on your machine. Instead, you should be able to target the version of the Framework for which the application is written. This way you can work in a single IDE and take advantage of the latest productivity enhancements.

Visual Studio 2010 supports the ability to target a specific version of the .NET Framework for an application. This means you can use a single tool to develop against many applications built on various .NET Framework flavors. Setting the .NET Framework version of an application appropriately sets the toolbox, project types, available references, and even IntelliSense inside the IDE to be in sync with the chosen .NET Framework version. Figure 2.9 shows the New Project dialog box again; this time, the .NET Framework version selection (top-center) has been highlighted.

FIGURE 2.9   Creating an application to target a specific version of the .NET Framework.

After you select a Framework version, the IDE automatically adjusts the available project types, IntelliSense, reference-able libraries, and similar features. For instance, if you choose to add a reference to your project, only those libraries from the target version of the Framework are available to you in the Add Reference dialog box.

You can also decide to move your application to a different (hopefully newer) version of the .NET Framework at a later date. You can do so inside the project properties dialog box (right-click your project file inside of Solution Explorer and select Properties). Figure 2.10 shows an example. Notice the Target Framework drop-down. You can change this and the IDE then resets IntelliSense, references, your toolbox, and more to the newly selected target framework.

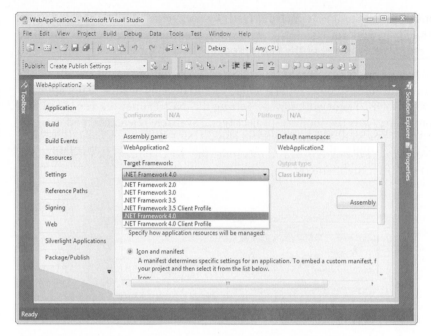

FIGURE 2.10   Resetting the target Framework of a Web application.

> **NOTE**
>
> The Framework setting is per project. Therefore, you can create a single solution that contains multiple projects and each can target a different version of the .NET Framework.

Of course, you can use Visual Studio 2010 to open an existing application built on a prior version of the .NET Framework. When doing so, you have the option of upgrading or keeping it tied to its current.NET Framework version. Figure 2.11 shows an example of the dialog box you see opening an older application with Visual Studio 2010. Note that you can choose to upgrade the target Framework version or continue to target an older version.

FIGURE 2.11   Opening an older application using Visual Studio 2010.

Many environments include developers using different versions of Visual Studio. You do have to be careful about opening these older applications inside of a newer version of

Visual Studio. While the code is not affected, the actual solution file is converted to 2010 (and thus rendered useless to prior versions). If this is your environment, we recommend creating multiple versions of the solution file: one for each version of Visual Studio in use by the team.

Navigating the IDE

After you've created your first project you should get started adding features to your application. This, of course, requires that you have some base understanding of the many components of the IDE. Figure 2.12 shows a sample website inside the IDE. Notice that the IDE layout is relatively generic: Toolbox on the left, Solution Explorer on the right, and code in the middle. You should expect a similar experience for your applications (at least until you've customized things).

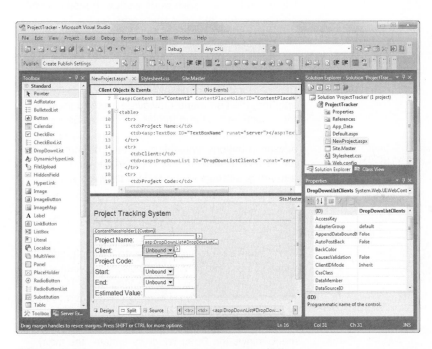

FIGURE 2.12   A simple Web application in the IDE.

Getting around inside the IDE is the first step to being productive. In the following sections, we break down the many items shown in Figure 2.12; it might be useful to refer to this graphic to provide overall context as we discuss a given item.

The Menus

If you've been working with previous versions of Visual Studio, you should find the Visual Studio 2010 menu bar to be standard fare. It is very intuitive; options are where you'd expect them; and new menus appear depending on your place within the IDE, the tools you've chosen to install, and your default programming language. For example, a Refactor menu appears when you are in the C# code editor; the Project menu shows up when you have a project open; and the File menu configures itself differently depending on the programming language you are using.

Table 2.1 lists (from left to right across the IDE) some of the more common menus, along with a description of each.

TABLE 2.1   Visual Studio 2010 Menus

Menu	Figure	Description
File	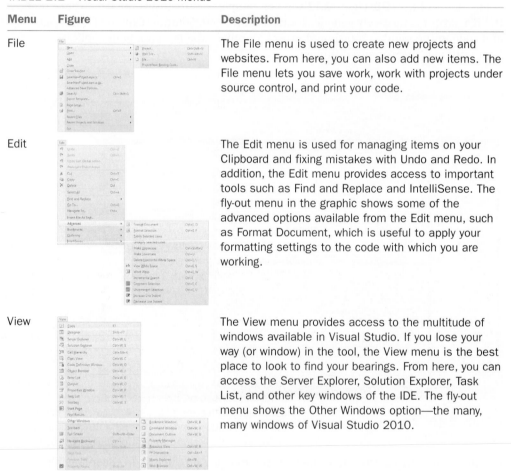	The File menu is used to create new projects and websites. From here, you can also add new items. The File menu lets you save work, work with projects under source control, and print your code.
Edit		The Edit menu is used for managing items on your Clipboard and fixing mistakes with Undo and Redo. In addition, the Edit menu provides access to important tools such as Find and Replace and IntelliSense. The fly-out menu in the graphic shows some of the advanced options available from the Edit menu, such as Format Document, which is useful to apply your formatting settings to the code with which you are working.
View		The View menu provides access to the multitude of windows available in Visual Studio. If you lose your way (or window) in the tool, the View menu is the best place to look to find your bearings. From here, you can access the Server Explorer, Solution Explorer, Task List, and other key windows of the IDE. The fly-out menu shows the Other Windows option—the many, many windows of Visual Studio 2010.

TABLE 2.1   Continued

Menu	Figure	Description
Refactor		The Refactor menu (C# only) provides access to options such as renaming code elements, extracting code from a method to a new method, and promoting local variables to parameters. See Chapter 10, "Refactoring Code," for more information on refactoring.
Website		The Website menu is available only when you're working with websites (and not web applications or other project types). It provides access to add new items, add references, copy your website to a deployment location, and work with project dependencies. You can also set the start page for the application and access ASP.NET configuration options for the given website.
Project		The Project menu is similar to the Website menu but is available to both web and non–web-based projects. From here, you can add new items and references to your projects, set the startup project, and change the build order for projects in your solution. In addition, you can access the Properties for a given project. This enables you to set things such as the version of the .NET Framework you are targeting, the default namespace, and many more items.
Build		The Build menu enables you to invoke the given compiler(s) for your solution. From here, you can force a build or rebuild on the entire solution or an individual project within the solution. You can also access the Configuration Manager from the Build menu. This dialog box enables you to control your target build in terms of debug versus release, CPU, and so on.

TABLE 2.1   Continued

Menu	Figure	Description
Debug		The Debug menu provides developers access to the debug commands for Visual Studio. These commands include options for starting your project inside a debugging session and attaching a new debug session to an existing, executing process. In addition, you can manage debug breakpoints from this menu. The fly-out menu shows some of the other debug windows available from this menu. For more information, see Chapter 11, "Debugging Code."
Data		The Data menu enables you to manage your data sources for a given application. You can add new items to your database from this menu. For additional information on working with data, see Chapter 21, "Working with Databases."
Format		The Format menu enables you to manipulate the layout of controls on a window or web form with respect to one another. For example, you can select a number of controls on your form and manage the vertical and horizontal spacing between them.
Tools		The Tools menu provides access to many of the tools that ship with Visual Studio. This includes managing Visual Studio Add-Ins and Macros that extend your environment (see fly-out menu). You can also access tools for connecting to other servers and applications, and managing your IDE settings. The items in this tool menu are covered in depth throughout the book.

TABLE 2.1   Continued

Menu	Figure	Description
Table	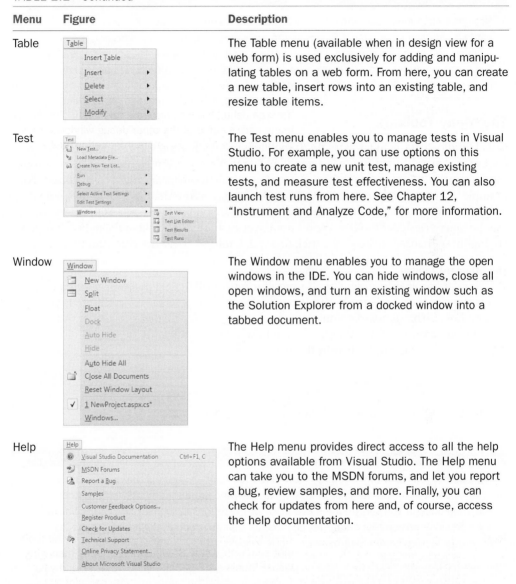	The Table menu (available when in design view for a web form) is used exclusively for adding and manipulating tables on a web form. From here, you can create a new table, insert rows into an existing table, and resize table items.
Test		The Test menu enables you to manage tests in Visual Studio. For example, you can use options on this menu to create a new unit test, manage existing tests, and measure test effectiveness. You can also launch test runs from here. See Chapter 12, "Instrument and Analyze Code," for more information.
Window		The Window menu enables you to manage the open windows in the IDE. You can hide windows, close all open windows, and turn an existing window such as the Solution Explorer from a docked window into a tabbed document.
Help		The Help menu provides direct access to all the help options available from Visual Studio. The Help menu can take you to the MSDN forums, and let you report a bug, review samples, and more. Finally, you can check for updates from here and, of course, access the help documentation.

NOTE

Note that each menu screenshot in Table 2.1 was taken using the C# menu default settings. In each case, Visual Basic has an equivalent, albeit slightly different, menu. In addition, the keyboard shortcut callouts in the menu items are also those of C#. Visual Basic developers should recognize a lot of them as the same. All menus can be customized to an individual developer's preference.

The Many Toolbars

Visual Studio 2010 includes close to 30 toolbars in just the professional edition. If you use a set of commands often, there is a good chance that there is a matching toolbar to group those commands. As a result, a large percentage of the toolbars are highly specialized. For example, if you are working with the Class Designer, you use the Class Designer toolbar to manage classes or change screen magnification. Or if you are building a SQL Query, you use the Query Designer toolbar. We do not cover each of these toolbars here because they are highly specialized. Instead, we stick to a quick tour to cover the common ground.

The Standard Toolbar

The Standard toolbar is present at all times during your IDE sessions (unless, of course, you customize things or turn it off). It provides quick access to all the commands you use over and over. The standard commands are on the top left: Create New Project, Add New Item, Open, Save, and Save All. These are followed by Cut, Copy, Paste, and Undo. Figure 2.13 shows the Standard toolbar in the IDE.

FIGURE 2.13   The Standard toolbar in Visual Studio 2010.

TIP

We suggest you learn the keyboard equivalents for such standard commands as Cut, Copy, Paste, Undo, and the like. In fact, most standard toolbar items have a shortcut you should learn. You can then remove many of these toolbar icons from the toolbar to save precious screen real estate for commands that have you reaching for the mouse anyway (and have harder-to-remember shortcut keys).

Additional items worth mentioning include the two navigation commands on the toolbar. These are the icons that look like a document (or code file) with an arrow on them. One icon's arrow points left and the other's points right. These navigation buttons enable you to move backward and forward through your code and your solution. They keep track of special lines in your code or windows you have visited and provide one-click access up and down this line. This can really help your productivity.

The button to the right of the navigation commands (the one that is a green arrow) is often called the Run or Play button. This initiates a build of your project and launches you into debug mode. Moving to the right, you see options for initiating a search within your code. This capability can be handy for quickly finding the place where you left off or the place you are looking for. To the right of this are icons for quick access to displaying one of the many windows of Visual Studio. Just as with the View menu, these icons give you quick access to the Solution Explorer, Properties window, Object Browser, Toolbox, and so on. You even have an icon for Other Windows (the icon on the far right), which gives access to even more windows.

Customizing Toolbars

In the event that the standard toolbars that ship with Visual Studio don't meet your needs, you can create custom toolbars that do. Select the Tool menu's Customize item or right-click a toolbar in the IDE and select Customize to launch the Customize dialog box as shown in Figure 2.14. From here, select which toolbars to show, indicate icon size for toolbar items, turn on and off tips and shortcut keys, and more.

FIGURE 2.14   The Customize dialog box in Visual Studio 2010.

You make customizations to the toolbar by selecting an item and choosing one of the option buttons on the right (move up, move down, delete, and so on). If things get messed up, you can use the Reset All button for a selected Toolbar to revert to the default state.

The Toolbars tab on the Customize dialog box enables you to select which toolbars are visible. This dialog box also includes the New button, which enables you to create new toolbars to group existing commands. This gives you a great deal of customization options. After you've click the New button, you name your new toolbar and use the Commands tab (see Figure 2.15) to add items to your custom toolbar.

FIGURE 2.15   The Customize dialog box's Commands tab.

You can also configure your keyboard shortcut combinations from the Customize dialog box. Use the Keyboard button (the bottom of Figure 2.14) to bring up the Options dialog box to the environment's keyboard options screen. Figure 2.16 shows an example. First, you find a command in the list; next, you press a shortcut key to map (or remap) a combination. Notice that if the option is already assigned a shortcut key, Visual Studio warns you before you make the reassignment.

FIGURE 2.16   Options dialog box keyboard assignments.

We recommend that you do some of your own exploration into the many toolbars (and toolbar customization options) within Visual Studio. Often their usefulness presents itself only at the right moment. For instance, if you are editing a Windows form, having the Layout toolbar available to tweak the position of controls relative to one another can be a valuable timesaver. Knowing that these toolbars are available increases the likelihood that you can benefit from their value.

The Solution Explorer

The Solution Explorer enables you to group and manage the many files that make up your application. A solution simply contains multiple projects (applications). A project groups files related to its type. For instance, you can create a website, Windows Form application, class library, console application, and more. The files inside the project containers represent your code in terms of web pages, forms, class files, XML, and other related items.

Figure 2.17 shows the Solution Explorer undocked from the IDE. Note that a single solution is open (you might only have one solution open at a time), and the solution contains a few applications (called projects). One is a Windows Presentation Foundation (WPF) application (TimeTrackingInterface); another is a website (ProjectTracker); the project at the top is a class library (AppFramework).

FIGURE 2.17   The Visual Studio 2010 Solution Explorer.

You use the Solution Explorer to navigate the many items in your project. You can access an item by first selecting it and then double-clicking it. Solution Explorer opens the given designer or editor associated with the type of file you request. For example, opening a file with the extension .cs opens the C# code editor. You can also add a new item (class, image, form) to your application from here by right-clicking a project or folder and selecting the Add menu. Finally, you also use the Solution Explorer during source control scenarios to check items in and out of the source database. For more information, the Solution Explorer is covered in depth in Chapter 4.

The Text Editors

Visual Studio 2010 has several text editors or word (code) processors. Each text editor is based on a common core that provides the basic set of functionality for each editor such as the selection margin, the capability to collapse nested items, and colorization. Each editor derives from this core and is customized to give you the editors for code (C#, VB, and so on), the XML editor, the HTML (or aspx) editor, the style sheet editor, and more.

The Code Editors

The code editor, for our money, is where the magic happens. It is here that you get down to business leveraging your favorite language to define objects and their functionality. Of course, you can write code outside the Visual Studio editor, but why would you? You can also write a novel using Notepad or do your taxes by hand. A good code editor means higher productivity, plain and simple. And Visual Studio has some of the best code editors around.

The code editor is front and center when you're writing the guts of your application. It handles indentation and whitespace to make your code clean and readable. It provides IntelliSense and statement completion to free you from having to look up (or memorize) every object library and keyword. It provides shortcut snippets to help you quickly generate common code such as property definitions. It groups code into blocks; it provides color codes for keywords and comments; it highlights errors; it shows new code relative to previously compiled code. All in all, the Visual Studio code editor does quite a bit to keep you focused, organized, and productive.

The C# Code Editor

Figure 2.18 shows the C# code editor. Some items to note include the following:

- ▶ The code is grouped into logical sections along the left side. You can use the minus signs to close a whole class, method, property, or similar group. This capability enables you to hide code you are not working on at the moment. You can also create your own custom, named regions to do the same thing.

- ▶ Code lines are numbered along the left edge of the editor. This feature can be turned on or off for different code editors in the tool.

- ▶ New code is signaled inside the section groups with a colored line. Yellow is used for new code that has yet to be saved. The highlighted line turns green after a save and disappears after you close and reopen the file. This feature enables you to track where you have made changes to code during your current session.

- ▶ The name of the open code file is listed as the code window's tab across the top. The asterisk indicates that the code has changed since the last time it was saved.

FIGURE 2.18   The C# code editor.

▶ IntelliSense is invoked as you type. You can use the arrow keys to quickly find the item in the list. Hovering over the item shows details for the given item (tip text to the right). You can press the Tab key to complete the item from IntelliSense.

▶ The code is highlighted in various colors. By default, keywords are navy blue, comments are green, text is black, types you create are light blue, string values are red, and so on.

▶ The two drop-downs at the top of the code editor enable you to navigate between the classes in the file (left-side drop-down) and methods, fields, and properties within a given class (right-side drop-down).

The Visual Basic Code Editor

The Visual Basic code editor works much the same way as the C# editor. Figure 2.19 shows similar code as in Figure 2.18, this time written using the Visual Basic code editor. Some of the differences between the editors are as listed here:

▶ Horizontal lines are used to separate methods and properties within the editor.

▶ The IntelliSense drop-down list is filtered into a common subset and all the possible values.

▶ The code navigation drop-downs at the top of the code editor enable you to navigate the entire, active object hierarchy (including events). The left-side drop-down shows namespaces, objects, and events. The right-side drop-down shows all methods for the given type, including those you have not yet overridden. The items you have implemented are highlighted as bold within the list.

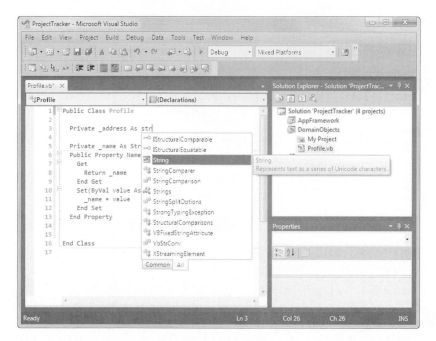

FIGURE 2.19   The Visual Basic code editor.

Of course there are many more text editors inside of Visual Studio. There are other language editors (C++ and F#), XML editors, XHTML editors, and more. Each of these have similar features to the two code editors shown here. We cover many of the specifics of these additional editors throughout the rest of the book.

Editor Customizations

Nearly every aspect of the many code editors can be customized to your every whim. From our experience, it seems no two developers see their code the same way. You can use the Options dialog box (Tools, Options) to change the editor's background color or the color and font of various text elements within the editor. You can also turn on line numbering, and manage indenting (tabs) and whitespace. You can set options based on language and editor. The full list of customizations for the editors is large.

Figure 2.20 shows the Options dialog box set for Fonts and Colors. From here, you can tweak the many display items in the editor in terms of their color, font, and font size.

If you dig a little deeper in the Options dialog box, you come across the Text Editor node in the option tree. From here, you can manipulate even more settings for the text editor in general for language-specific editors. For example, you can remove the horizontal procedure separators in the Visual Basic editor or turn off the automatic reformatting of code by the editor.

FIGURE 2.20   The Options dialog box set to Fonts and Colors.

One common change we see developers make is controlling how the editor automatically formats code inside the C# editor. It seems granular control of curly braces is a big deal to those who look at code all day. For instance, you might like to see all your curly braces on separate lines or you might prefer them to start on the line that starts the given code block. Alternatively, you may want a might depending on the type of code block. Fortunately, you can control all of that from the Options dialog box. Figure 2.21 shows some of these options available for formatting C# inside the editor. Notice how the option also shows an example of how the code is formatted by the editor.

FIGURE 2.21   Controlling code formatting from the Options dialog box.

The Visual Designers

Visual Designers are the canvases that you work on using the mouse to create items such as forms via drag, drop, move, resize, and the like. Visual Studio 2010 ships with many such visual designers. Together, they enable you to build the items that make up your application. Items include Windows forms, web forms, class diagrams, XML schemas, and more.

The visual designers all work in a similar way. First, they take center stage within the IDE as tabbed windows surrounded by various menus, toolbars, and panes. Second, you use the Toolbox (we discuss this in a moment) as a palette from which you place items (such as controls) onto the given designer. You then configure each item's many properties using the Properties window.

Figure 2.22 shows the WPF Form Designer in action (the middle, highlighted tab). Note that the Toolbox is on the left and the Properties window is on the bottom right. Additionally, note that this figure shows the Layout toolbar. This toolbar enables you to easily position controls relative to one another. We cover the majority of the visual designers in depth in the coming chapters. You can also get a better overview from Chapter 6, "Introducing the Editors and Designers."

FIGURE 2.22 The WPF/XAML Designer.

The Toolbox

The Visual Studio 2010 Toolbox provides access to the many controls when you're building web and windows forms. It also provides access to nearly anything that can be dragged onto one of the many designers used for creating forms, XML schemas, class diagrams, and more. As an example, if you are building a web form, the Toolbox provides the many controls, grouped for easier access, which can be added to the form. Furthermore, if you are working with a text editor, the Toolbox enables you to save clips of text for quick access.

Figure 2.23 shows the Toolbox in a standard configuration (undocked from the IDE) for building a web form. Note that the Standard group of controls is closed to highlight some additional control groups. The many controls inside this Toolbox are covered throughout the rest of the book. The bulk of the Toolbox controls are covered in Part V, "Creating Enterprise Applications."

FIGURE 2.23　The Visual Studio Toolbox configured for a web form.

> **TIP**
>
> You can customize the Toolbox to your liking. For example, you can add your own groups (called tabs). You can also configure the Toolbox to show more icons on the screen at a time. As you familiarize yourself with the various standard controls, you can turn off their text descriptions and simply show them as icons. To do so, right-click the control group (tab) and uncheck List View. Figure 2.24 illustrates the additional screen real estate you gain by turning off the text descriptions.

FIGURE 2.24   The Visual Studio Toolbox configured for more screen real estate.

The Properties Window

It seems that with every new release and every new tool, programming becomes less and less about writing code and more and more about dragging, dropping, and configuring. The many tools, controls, and rich designers that free us from the repetitive code also now require our attention in the form of maintenance. This work is typically done through the manipulation of the literally hundreds of properties that work in concert to define our application. This is where the Properties window comes into play. It enables us to control the size, appearance, and behavior of our controls. Furthermore, the Properties window groups common properties into sets for easier access. Finally, the Properties window also gives us access to connecting the events for a given control to the code inside our application.

Figure 2.25 shows the Properties window (undocked from the IDE) for a web button control. Note that the window can group similar properties into sections via banded categories, such as Appearance. You can also list properties in alphabetic order by clicking the AZ icon on the Properties window toolbar. Another item worth noting is the lightning bolt icon also on the toolbar (C# only). This gives you access to the events for the given control. From the list of events you can select an event and wire it to code in your project (or double-click it to generate an event handler).

FIGURE 2.25   The Properties window in Visual Studio 2010.

Managing the Many Windows of the IDE

To round out our whirlwind tour, we thought it important to provide you guidance on customizing and managing the plethora of windows available within the IDE (lest they leave you with a postage-stamp-size window in which to write your code). To manage these windows, you really need to know only two skills: pinning and docking.

Pinning

Pinning refers to the process of making a window stick in the open position. It is called pinning in reference to the visual cue you use to perform the act: a pushpin (refer to the highlighted area of the Solution Explorer title bar in Figure 2.26). Pinning is imperative because you sometimes want full-screen real estate for writing code or designing a form. In this case, you should unpin (hide) the various extraneous windows in your IDE. Note that when a window is unpinned, a vertical tab represents the window (see the highlighted Toolbox tab in Figure 2.26). Moving the mouse near this tab results in the window unfolding for your use. After you use it, however, it goes back to its hiding spot. Alternatively, you might be working to drop controls on a form. In doing so, you might want to pin (stick open) the Toolbox window (refer to Figure 2.22).

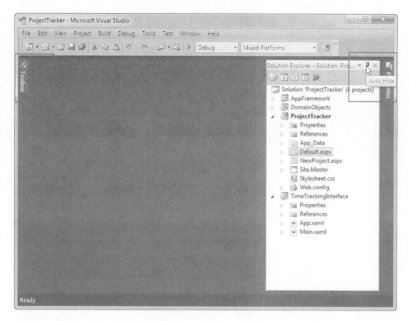

FIGURE 2.26   Pinning windows inside the IDE.

Docking

Docking is the process of connecting windows to various sticky spots within the IDE. Typically, this means docking to the left, top, right, or bottom of the IDE. For example, the Toolbox is, by default, docked to the left side of the IDE. You might prefer to put it at the bottom of the screen, docked below the active designer. You might also want to dock the Solution Explorer to the top of the screen and then un-pin it for quick access. You can see an example of these docking options in Figure 2.27.

You can also dock windows to one another. For example, you might want to dock the Properties window below the Solution Explorer. Or you might want the Properties window to be a tab within the same window to which the Solution Explorer is docked (refer to Figure 2.22).

To help with docking, Visual Studio 2010 has provided visual cues and helpers. First, click and hold the title bar with the mouse, and then drag the window to where you want to dock it. Visual Studio displays some docking icons.

Four icons are at the edge of the IDE, one each at the left, top, right, and bottom. These icons are used for docking the window at the given edge of the IDE. Using these icons results in the window being docked across the full length (or width) of the IDE. Figure 2.28 shows each of these icons as the Properties window is being docked.

There is also an icon that shows over the top of a window to which you might want to dock. This icon is used for docking the selected window relative to another window in the IDE. For example, you might want to dock the Properties window under the Solution Explore window (as shown in Figure 2.28). You do so with the bottom icon inside this icon group.

FIGURE 2.27   Some docking options in the IDE.

FIGURE 2.28   A window being docked.

Of course, you can also undock items. This is simply the process of floating windows off by themselves (outside, or on top of, the IDE). To do so, you simply grab (click with the mouse) a window by the title bar and move it off to the side of the IDE or just don't choose a docking icon.

Finally, when working with a window, you can right-click the title bar and tell Visual Studio how the window should behave. Figure 2.29 shows the available options. The down-arrow icon on the window provides access to the same features. The Float option indicates that the window floats wherever you put it, on top of the IDE. This can be useful if you find yourself moving windows about or need to use multiple monitors. You turn off this option by choosing Dock. You can also use the Dock as tabbed Document option to add a window to the center of your IDE to behave just like a designer or code editor.

FIGURE 2.29   The IDE window options.

Navigating IDE Windows

You can navigate open windows in the IDE without touching a mouse. This keeps your fingers on the keyboard and can lead to greater productivity. Visual Studio 2010 provides a couple of options here. The first is a simple window-switching hotkey. Suppose you have a number of code windows open in the IDE. To navigate forward (left to right) through them, you can use the key combination Ctrl+- (minus sign). This is for the standard development settings in the IDE; your settings might differ. To go backward (right to left), you use Ctrl+Shift+- (minus sign). This provides faster window-switching without requiring that you scroll with the mouse or search through your solution.

You can get similar results using a visual aid called the IDE Navigator. This tool is similar to the Alt+Tab feature of Windows that allows for fast application switching. To access it, you use Ctrl+Tab (and Ctrl+Shift+Tab). You use this key combination to open the dialog box and navigate open code windows and active tool windows. Figure 2.30 shows the result. Notice that active files are cycled through on the right. You can jump between the active tools and active file lists using the right- and left-arrow keys.

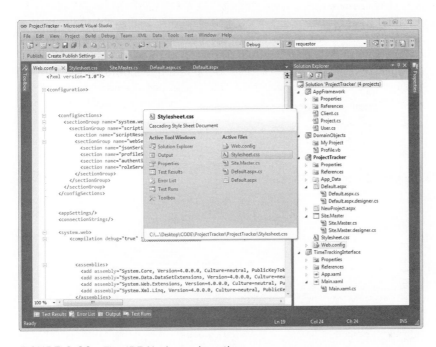

FIGURE 2.30 The IDE Navigator in action.

TIP

To change the keyboard combinations assigned to the IDE navigator, select the menu option Tools, Options. Under the Environment node, select Keyboard. Here you can set keyboard shortcut keys. You should change the settings assigned to Window.NextDocumentWindowNav and Window.PreviousDocumentWindowNav.

Customize Your Font

There is a setting called Environment Font inside the Options dialog box (Tools menu) under the Environment node, Fonts and Colors. This option enables you to set the font for the entire IDE to the selection of your choice. Figure 2.31 shows selecting this option from the list.

Changing this font changes your IDE. For example, suppose you set the Environment Font to Courier New. Dialogs, menus, the Toolbox, Solution Explorer, and more change. Figure 2.32 shows the results of such a change.

FIGURE 2.31   Setting the Environment Font.

FIGURE 2.32   The IDE with a new font setting.

Summary

The whirlwind tour is over. We've covered the basics of installation, creating your first project, and the standard items you encounter when journeying out on your own. You should now be oriented to the basic set of menus, toolbars, settings, and window management inside Visual Studio. Now that you have your bearings, you can begin pushing onward.

CHAPTER 3

The .NET Languages

Unlocking the productivity promises of the Visual Studio IDE is at the heart of this book. The IDE, of course, also ships from Microsoft in concert with new versions of the .NET languages and Framework. You need to have a solid grasp of programming the Visual Basic or C# language using the .NET Framework to take advantage of everything Visual Studio has to offer.

In this chapter we set aside the IDE (for the most part) and focus on the foundations of .NET programming. We start with a language primer on the basics; we then cover some more in-depth programming features and language-related IDE enhancements. The chapter concludes with an overview and map of the .NET Framework class library.

Language Primer

You have a few language choices available to you as a .NET programmer: Visual Basic, C#, C++, or F#. Which you choose is typically a result of your history, style, and intent. Developers who have worked with past incarnations of VB or another basic language will find they are at home inside Visual Basic. The language (including templates, tools, wizards, and so on) is all about developer productivity. Developers whose roots are in a C-based language (C++, Java, and so on) and want similar productivity in a straightforward way gravitate toward C#. Of course some developers will just want to stay in C++ even for their .NET applications.

New in Visual Studio 2010 is the F# language. This language has been available in various states previously; however, it is now part of the full Visual Studio product line. Similar to other .NET languages, F# supports object-oriented programming. What makes it different is that it is also a functional programming language. Functional programming elevates functions to first-class values (the "F" in F# is for functional). For example, a functional language allows you to easily pass functions as parameters, return functions as the result of a function, chain functions together to create new functions, create recursive functions, and more. These powerful features in F# allow you to more easily tackle complex algorithms with less code (and often less pain) than it would take with the standard OO-only languages of Visual Basic and C#. Having F# inside of Visual Studio also means you can leverage the .NET Framework, get the benefits of the CLR (including calling to and from other .NET code), have debugging, and other related tools support.

NOTE

F# is both a new language and new way of programming. You need to spend time to be able to "think" in F#. There is not room in this book to present the language. In addition, most .NET developers still write most of their code in Visual Basic or C#. Therefore, we focus on those two languages throughout this book.

Programming Objects

Programming in .NET is an object-oriented experience. You write your own classes and leverage those created by Microsoft (forms, controls, and libraries). In fact, every .NET application has at least one class, and more often it has hundreds. You can extend classes with new functionality (inheritance), define classes based on a contract (interface), and override the behavior of existing classes (polymorphism). This section looks at defining objects with .NET code.

Classes

Think of classes as the container for your code. Classes define how you hold data (properties) and perform actions (methods); they communicate how your class works after it's created (instantiated). When you create an instance of the class, it is an object and can then actually maintain data and execute code.

You define a class using the Class keyword. The following shows an example:

C#

```
public class Employee
{
}
```

VB

```
Public Class Employee

End Class
```

Fields and Properties

You add code to a class to define its data and behavior. Data for your class can be stored in fields or properties. Fields and properties are similar; both define data that is contained in the class. The difference is that properties can provide a means to protect the access (setting and getting) to field data. Fields are typically private variables defined at the class level and are thus defined as follows:

C#

```
public class Employee
{
  private string _name;
}
```

VB

```
Public Class Employee
  Private _name As String
End Class
```

You can define public fields on your class. In this case, they are accessible members from the class. However, it is a best practice to encapsulate public data inside a property. This way you can control whether or not to expose the ability to read or write a property. You then also control the reading and writing of the data. Properties are typically backed by an internal, private field. This is called data hiding and is implemented with the Private keyword. For example, the previously defined field can be encapsulated into a property as follows:

C#

```
public class Employee
{
  private string _name;

  public string Name
  {
    get { return _name; }
    set { _name = value; }
  }
}
```

VB

```
Public Class Employee
    Private _name As String

    Public Property Name() As String
        Get
```

```
            Return _name
        End Get
        Set(ByVal value As String)
            _name = value
        End Set
    End Property
End Class
```

You can also create read-only properties. This is useful when you want to reserve the writing of the property's value to code running inside the class. You create a read-only property by not implementing the set statement in the property definition. In VB, you also have to add the ReadOnly keyword. As an example, suppose you want to add an Id property to the Employee class defined previously. This Id can be read but only set by internal class code. You could implement a read-only property as follows:

C#

```
private int _id;


public int Id
{
  get { return _id; }
}
```

VB

```
Private _id As Integer
Public ReadOnly Property Id() As Integer
  Get
    Return _id
  End Get
End Property
```

Methods

Methods represent the blocks of code in your class that, when called, perform some specific action. This action could be reading or writing from a database, calling other methods, calculating a value, processing some business rules and returning a result, or whatever you need your code to do.

Methods are defined by their names and access levels (see the next section for more details on access levels). In VB, you also need to add the Sub keyword to define a method that does not return a value. In C#, this is done by indicating the return type of void before the method name. For example, if you were to add a Save method to the Employee class previously defined, the code would look as follows:

C#

```
public void Save()
```

```
{
  //implementation code goes here
}
```

VB

```
Public Sub Save()
  'implementation code goes here
End Sub
```

Methods often return values to the code that called the method. To define a method that returns a value you must indicate the method's return type (the class type of the returned data). In VB, you also use the keyword Function (instead of Sub). You use the Return keyword to indicate the value to return from your code. For example, if you were to add a method to calculate an employee's remaining sick day, you would do so as follows:

C#

```
public int GetRemainingSickDays()
{
  int _sickDays = 0;

  //calculate remaining sick days

  return _sickDays;
}
```

VB

```
Function GetRemainingSickDays() As Integer

  Dim _sickDays As Integer = 0

  'code to calculate remaining sick days

  Return _sickDays

End Function
```

In the prior example, note the return type defined in the method signature (first line of the method). Also note the use of the keyword Return to return a value from the method. In this case, that value is stored inside a variable defined as internal to the method.

Member Accessibility

The properties, fields, and methods in your application are referred to as class members. Each member in your class is defined to have a specific access level. As you've seen, if you want others to be able to access a member you must declare that member as public. If you want to reserve the member for accessibility only within the class, you declare it as private. These are two of the member accessibility levels available to you. The full complement of accessibility levels are defined in Table 3.1.

TABLE 3.1   Member Accessibility Level in .NET

Level	Description
Public	Indicates that a member is publicly available to any code that has access to the class.
Private	Indicates that the member is hidden and private to the class that contains the member. No code outside the class can directly access members defined as private.
Protected	Protected is similar to private. It indicates that the member is not exposed publicly. Rather, it is private to the class. However, protected members are also made available to any class that derives from the class that contains the protected method (see inheritance below for more details).
Internal	Indicates that a member is available to all code within the assembly that contains it. This means other classes within a compiled .dll or .exe can access the member. However, other assemblies that reference a given .dll cannot access internal members.
Protected Internal	Indicates that the member is accessible by all code within an assembly and any code that derives from a class that contains the given member.

In addition to class-member accessibility, classes themselves also use the same accessibility levels. You can declare a class as public, private, protected, and so on in order to define your intended usage. You want to make many classes private or protected to the class and deriving types. The classes you make public define the functionality you want to expose to other code.

Constructors

A constructor is code that is called when a new instance of your class is created. This code is used to define how you want your class created, typically by setting default values or some related initialization code. You create a constructor as you would a method. The difference is that you give the constructor the same name as the class. The following code shows an example for the Employee class:

C#

```
public Employee()
{
  //init default values of an empty employee object
}
```

VB

```vb
Public Sub Employee()
  'init default values of an empty employee object
End Sub
```

A class can have multiple constructors to change the way in which the object is created. In these instances, each constructor is defined with a different set of parameters. The version of the constructor that does not take parameters is referred to as the default constructor. The following shows a couple additional constructors added to the Employee class. One initializes an Employee object based on the calling code passing in an id parameter; the other uses the employee's email address to initialize the object.

C#

```csharp
public Employee(int id)
{
  //init default values for the employee defined by the given id
}

public Employee(string emailAddress)
{
  //init default values for the employee defined by the given email
}
```

VB

```vb
Public Sub Employee(ByVal id As Integer)
  'init default values for the employee defined by the given id
End Sub

Public Sub Employee(ByVal emailAddress As String)
  'init default values for the employee defined by the given email
End Sub
```

Static (Shared in VB) Members and Objects

Sometimes you do not want the full behavior of a class for all of your methods. Instead, you might want to define certain methods that are not part of an object. These methods often retrieve information or calculate values but are not part of a specific object. In these cases, you can create entire classes or just specific methods of a class as static (or shared in VB).

The Shared and Static keywords, when applied to a method, indicate that the method can be called without creating an instance of the class that contains it. Shared and Static can also be defined at the class level. In this case, you are indicating that the class only contains shared and static methods and it cannot be created as an instance. For example, you might add a static, helper method to the Employee class to check to see if an employee is active in the system before you create an instance. This declaration would look as follows:

C#

```csharp
public static bool IsActive(string emailAddress)
{
  //check to see if an employee has been added to the system
}
```

VB

```vb
Public Shared Function IsActive(ByVal emailAddress As String) As Boolean
  'check to see if an employee has been added to the system
End Function
```

Enumerations

Enumerations enable you to create a group of named values that help improve your code readability. Each item in an enumeration is a unique integer value. You can pass the enumeration value around as a name rather than an actual value. In this way, your code doesn't rely on arbitrary, "magic" numbers. Instead, the code is sensible and readable.

You create an enumeration using the enum keyword. For example, you might add an enumeration to the Employee class in order store the employment status of an employee. This would enable you to make decisions in your code based on the specific status of an employee. To define this enumeration, you add code as follows to the Employee class:

C#

```csharp
enum EmploymentStatus
{
  Salaried,
  Hourly,
  Contract,
  Other
}
```

VB

```vb
Enum EmploymentStatus
  Salaried
  Hourly
  Contract
  Other
End Enum
```

Inheritance

You can define a new class based on an existing class, which is called inheritance. You use inheritance to extend (or add to) the functionality of a base class. Classes that that extend a base class are said to derive their functionality from another class. That is, they contain all the functionality of the base class plus any additional functionality added to the new class.

You indicate inheritance in VB by using the Inherits keyword; in C# you add a colon and the base class name following the name of the new class. For example, suppose you implement a Manager class that derives from Employee. The Manager class contains all the members of an Employee but might add special properties and methods specific to a Manger. You define this new class as follows:

C#

```
class Manager: Employee
{
}
```

VB

```
Public Class Manager
  Inherits Employee

End Class
```

Note that you can actually define a base class that cannot be created. Instead, it only exists to form the basis for a new class. Other classes can derive from it, but you cannot create a direct instance of just the base class. This is done by adding the MustInherit (VB) or Abstract (C#) keyword in front of the class definition. The keyword NotInheritable (VB) or Sealed (C#) indicates that the class cannot be used as the basis for a new class.

NOTE

.NET programmers can only derive from a single class. They cannot inherit from multiple base classes. However, they can implement multiple interfaces (as discussed next).

Overriding Behavior

When you design your classes you might want to consider how other developers might extend them. That is, your classes might serve as the base class for future derived classes. If this is the case, you might also consider which (if any) features of your base class you want to allow a derived class to override. The derived class may then implement a new version of one of your base methods, for example. This process is often referred to as polymorphism in object-oriented programming.

To change the data or behavior of a base class you can either add to the base class or you can override an existing member of the base class. Doing the later gives you alternate behavior for the same function in your new class. You decide which members of your base class are available for override. You do so by marking them as virtual members; this indicates a derived class may fully replace your base class functionality.

As an example, suppose you want to enable the CalculateYearlyCost method of the Employee class to be overridden when the Employee is used as the base for the Manager class. In this case, the calculation for a Manager is different for that of an Employee. You would therefore mark the method inside the Employee class as virtual (C#) or Overridable (VB) as follows:

C#

```
public class Employee
{
  public virtual float CalculateYearlyCost()
  {
  }
}
```

VB

```
Public Class Employee
  Public Overridable Function CalculateYearlyCost() As Single

  End Function
End Class
```

You can then override this method in the derived class. You do so using the override (C#) or Overrides (VB) keyword. You can still call the method on the base class if you need to by using the base (C#) or MyBase (VB) keyword. The following shows an example:

C#

```
class Manager : Employee
{
  public override float CalculateYearlyCost()
  {
    //add new functionality, access underlying method using base keyword
  }
}
```

VB

```
Public Class Manager
```

```
Inherits Employee

Public Overrides Function CalculateYearlyCost() As Single
   'add new functionality, access underlying method using MyBase
End Function

End Class
```

Hiding Members

There is a second way you can override the functionality of a base class. This involves using the keyword, new (C#) or Shadows (VB) to redefine the base method. Overriding in this manner hides the base class members. However, the base class member is still called if an instance of the derived class gets down-cast to an instance of the base class. This type of overriding is referred to as hiding by name. As an example, you could replace the C# keyword override with "new" or the VB Overrides with "Shadows" to implement this type of behavior.

You need to be careful about hiding members versus overriding because down-casting can occur often. For example, you might be working with a collection of Employee objects (some of type Manager and some of type Employee). If you iterate over the list using the base class (for each employee), you get a different method called on the Manager class depending on if you hid the member (in which case the base class method is called) or override the member (in which case the derived class method is called).

Overloading Members

You can also create multiple versions of the same procedure. All versions of a procedure can be defined inside the same class or you can have a few versions in a base class and yet other versions in a derived class. This is useful when you need to preserve the name of the procedure but need to create different versions that each take different parameters. Creating multiple versions of a procedure is called overloading or hiding by signature (as in the method's calling signature).

Overloading a method must follow rules designed to make each overload somehow different from all the others. Of course each overload has the same name. However, you must change either the number of parameters the method accepts, the data type of one or more of those parameters, or the order of the parameters. You create a valid overload by changing one or more of these items to make the overload signature unique. Note that changing the return type, if the method returns a value, or a parameter modifier is not sufficient to create an overload.

As an example, suppose you were creating a method to return the number of vacation days left for an employee. You might allow the users of this method to get the vacation days left for the current year, a supplied month, or a supplied month and year. In this case, the users of your method see a single method with multiple overloads. You would implement this overloading similar to the following code:

C#

```csharp
public short GetVacationUsed()
{
  //returns all vacation used in the current year
}

public short GetVacationUsed(short monthNumber)
{
  //returns all vacation used in the given month of the current year
}

public short GetVacationUsed(short monthNumber, short year)
{
  //returns all vacation used in the given month and year
}
```

VB

```vb
Public Function GetVacationUsed() As Short
  'returns all vacation used in the current year
End Function

Public Function GetVacationUsed(ByVal monthNumber As Short) As Short
  'returns all vacation used in the given month of the current year
End Function

Public Function GetVacationUsed(ByVal monthNumber As Short, ByVal year As Short) _
  As Short
  'returns all vacation used in the given month and year
End Function
```

Defining Interface Contracts

An interface is used to define a class contract. An interface does not contain any actual functioning code. Rather, it indicates a common structure for code that can be implemented by another class. This enables you to create common contracts and use those contracts across multiple objects. You can then trust that each class that implements the interface does so completely and in the same manner.

An interface can define different types of class members including fields, properties, methods, events, and the like. To create an interface, you use the Interface keyword. For example, suppose you want to define a basic interface for a person. The Employee class might then be required to implement this interface. Other objects (such as User and

Customer) might also implement the same interface. The following shows an example of how you might define this interface:

C#

```
interface IPerson
{
    string Name();
    DateTime DateOfBirth();
    string EyeColor();
    short HeightInInches();
}
```

VB

```
Public Interface IPerson


  Property Name As String
  Property DateOfBirth As DateTime
  Property EyeColor As String
  Property HeightInInches As Short
End Interface
```

You implement the interface by adding the interface to the class definition on the class where you intend to implement the interface. In VB this is done by adding the Implements keyword under the class definition (similar to inheritance). In C# you add the interface to the class definition the same way you would indicate a base class (using a colon). You can separate multiple implemented interfaces by a comma.

> **NOTE**
>
> You implement an interface when you want to define the structure of a base class but do not intend to implement any base functionality. If you have common, base functionality for which you provide for extension, you should consider using inheritance.

Creating Structures

So far we have talked about programming classes. There is another type of class available to .NET programmers called a structure. Structures are similar to classes; they can contain properties, fields, enumerations, and methods; they can implement interfaces; they can have one or more constructors. The differences lie in how structures are managed by .NET.

Structures are considered value types. This means that when structures are used, the entire class is passed around as a value and not a reference. A class is a reference type. When you use a class and pass it around your application you are actually passing a reference to a class. Not so with a structure. This also changes how .NET manages the memory used for structures and classes. Structures use stack allocation and classes are managed on the heap. To put this in perspective for .NET developers imagine you have an instance of an Employee class. This instance might be created inside one object and passed to another object's method. If the second object makes a change to the Employee instance, this change is reflected inside all objects that maintain a reference to the instance. If, however, this were a structure, there would be copies of that object passed around and changes would be isolated to each copy.

There are other differences between classes and structures. For one, structures cannot be inherited from. They also have an implicit, public constructor that cannot be redefined. For these reasons, structures are best used when you need a light-weight container for data values and do not need the features of a reference type. Structures are often used to define custom data types.

You define a structure much like you define a class. In place of the class keyword, however, you use struct (C#) or structure (VB). For example, imagine you want to define a data type that represents a paycheck. You could create a structure to hold this information. The following shows an example:

C#

```csharp
public struct PayCheck
{
  private double _amount;

  public double Amount
  {
    get { return _amount; }
  }

  //add additional structure elements ...
}
```

VB

```vb
Public Structure Paycheck

  Private _amount As Double
  Public ReadOnly Property Amount() As Double
    Get
      Return _amount
    End Get
  End Property
```

```
'additional structure elements ...


End Structure
```

Organizing Your Code with Namespaces

A namespaces is used to group code that is specific to a company, an application, or a given library. Namespaces help .NET programmers overcome naming conflicts for classes and methods. For instance, you cannot have two classes with the same name in the same namespace because it would confuse the .NET runtime and developers. Instead, your class names are unique inside your namespace.

You declare a namespace at the top of your code using the keyword namespace. Alternatively, you can set the default namespace inside your project properties. In this way, you do not have to see the outer namespace definition inside each code file. A common practice for defining namespaces includes using your company name followed by the application being written and then perhaps the library to which the code belongs. As an example, you might define the namespace grouping for the Employee class as follows:

C#

```
namespace MyCompany.MyApplication.UserLibrary
{
  public class Employee
  {
  }
}
```

VB

```
Namespace MyCompany.MyApplication.UserLibrary


  Public Class Employee


  End Class


End Namespace
```

You do not have to add this namespace information at the top of every code file in your project. This can become redundant and is error prone as a developer might forget to include the namespace definition. As an alternative, you can set the root namespace for your entire project using the project properties window (right-click the project file and choose Properties). Figure 3.1 shows an example. This is a similar experience in both C# and VB. Note that you can define a root namespace here and still add additional namespace groupings in your code as necessary. Of course those additional namespace definitions fall inside the root namespace.

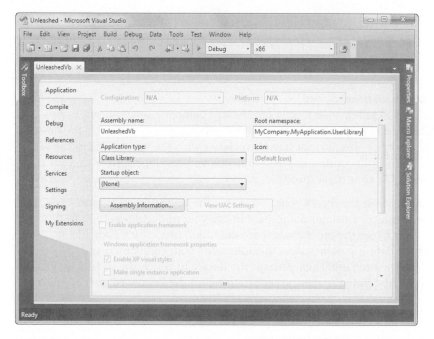

FIGURE 3.1   Setting the root namespace at the project level.

You access code inside a namespace by using the fully qualified definition of the namespace. For example, the .NET root namespace is System. If you were to access the String class you would do so by calling System.String. This is true for your code, too. To access the GetVacationUsed method you might call out as follows:

```
MyCompany.MyApplication.User.Employee.GetVacationUsed()
```

As you can see, accessing code using the fully-qualified namespace can be cumbersome in terms of typing and reading your code. Thankfully, you can import (with the using statement in C#) a namespace inside your code. This frees you from having to fully qualify each type call. Instead, the compiler resolves class names based on your imported namespaces. Of course the namespaces themselves are still required to prevent ambiguity in the compiler. Importing namespaces also help trim IntelliSense to those imported libraries.

In most cases, you do not get conflicts with imported namespaces. Type names are typically different enough in a given library that they do not overlap. If names do overlap, you can add qualification to eliminate the conflict.

You import namespaces using the using statement (C#) or imports (VB) keyword. As an example, the following shows namespaces imported into a class file for a Windows form application. The code includes the import statements for referencing the Employee class library:

C#

```csharp
using System;
using System.Collections.Generic;
using System.ComponentModel;
using System.Data;
using System.Drawing;
using System.Linq;
using System.Text;
using System.Windows.Forms;
using MyCompany.MyApplication.UserLibrary;

namespace TestHarnessCSharp
{
  public partial class Form1 : Form
  {
    public Form1()
    {
      InitializeComponent();
    }

    private void Form1_Load(object sender, EventArgs e)
    {
      Employee emp = new Employee();
      //do work
    }
  }
}
```

VB

```vb
Imports MyCompany.MyApplication.UserLibrary


Public Class Form1

  Private Sub Form1_Load(ByVal sender As System.Object, _
    ByVal e As System.EventArgs) Handles MyBase.Load

    Dim emp As New Employee()
    'do work ...


  End Sub


End Class
```

Notice in the preceding example that the C# code has a number of additional using (or imports) statements at the top of the file. This is because VB files automatically import many of the default namespaces in .NET.

Types, Variables, and Constants

All classes and interfaces you create in .NET are considered types. That is, they define a specific type of data. The underlying classes in the .NET Framework are also all strong types. In fact, the .NET languages of both C# and VB are based on strongly typed objects. This means when you define a variable you create an instance of a strongly typed class. The .NET runtime can then rely on this type information for handling casting, comparisons, and other rules.

Data Types

There are a number of built-in types (classes) that are used for common programming needs. These built-in types are referred to as data types and represent things such as a string of characters or a numeric value. You work with these data types like you would any structure or class. You can declare a variable of a certain type, create a new instance, or execute a method off of the type.

Most of the simple data types you use are value types (structures). There are a couple reference data types (classes). These are string (System.String) and object (System.Object). Recall that value types store data (and copies of data) and reference types are used to provide a reference to underlying data. Table 3.2 lists many of the common value types used in .NET programming (there are more than what is in this list). The list shows the underlying .NET Framework class, the range allowed in the data type, and the C# and VB data type names.

TABLE 3.2   Value Data Types by Language

.NET Framework	C# Data Type	VB Data Type	Range
System.Byte	byte	Byte	0 to 255
System.Int16	short	Short	-32,768 to 32,767
System.Int32	int	Integer	-2,147,483,648 to 2,147,483,647
System.Int64	long	Long	-9,223,372,036,854,775,808 to 9,223,372,036,854,775,807
System.Single	float	Single	$\pm 1.5 \times 10^{-45}$ to $\pm 3.4 \times 10^{38}$
System.Double	double	Double	$\pm 5.0 \times 10^{-324}$ to $\pm 1.7 \times 10^{308}$
System.Decimal	decimal	Decimal	$\pm 1.0 \times 10^{-28}$ to $\pm 7.9 \times 10^{28}$
System.Boolean	bool	Boolean	true or false

Many of the data types listed in Table 3.2 include unsigned versions. These are preceded with a u. The System.Byte data type is the exception. It is unsigned. The signed version is called sbyte. Signed values include both the negative and positive numbers in their range. Unsigned value types start and zero and include only positive numeric values.

Declaring Variables

When you declare a variable using a simple type you typically want to declare the variable using the type that represents the lowest possible range for your situation. For example, if you were to define a variable to hold the month value you might use System.Byte. If you were to define the year, you might use System.Int16. In this way, the lowest possible overhead is used for these types.

You declare a variable in C# by preceding the name of the variable with its type. In VB, you use the Dim statement. The type then comes after the variable's name. The following code shows an example of declaring variables in each language:

C#

```
byte month;
short year;
float paycheckAmount;
```

VB

```
Dim month As Byte
Dim year As Short
Dim paycheckAmount As Single
```

Of course, you can also define variables of other (more complex) types in the .NET Framework or types defined in your own class libraries. When you declare a variable you can also assign it a default value and/or instantiate a new instance. The following shows an example:

C#

```
byte month = 1;
short year = 2010;
float paycheckAmount = 0;
string name = "test";
Employee emp = new Employee();
```

VB

```
Dim month As Byte = 1
Dim year As Short = 2010
Dim paycheckAmount As Single = 0
Dim name As String = "test"
Dim emp As Employee = New Employee()
```

Type Conversion

Again, both VB and C# are strongly typed languages. Therefore, the variables you declare cannot be reused by assigning different type values. Rather, they must always represent the underlying type to which they were declared. This can be problematic. Sometimes, for instance, you have an integer that you need to pass to a method that only accepts a double. Or you need to parse a string value into an integer for a calculation. You might also have to convert a class to an interface type in order to use it with a specific method. These are all instances where you need to convert one type to another.

There are two conversions that you can make: implicit and explicit. An implicit conversion happens when you pass a smaller value type into a larger type that can contain the smaller value. In this case, if no data is lost the conversion is allowed. For example, you can pass a short into a long without issue. However, passing a float (or double) into an integer might result in data loss and is thus not allowed as an implicit conversion (you need to explicitly convert). As an example, the following code converts an integer value to a double. This code does not throw a type conversion error. Rather, it converts using implicit conversion.

C#

```
int intVal = 100;
double doubleVal = intVal;
```

VB

```
Dim intVal As Integer = 100
Dim doubleVal As Double = intVal
```

If there is a chance that the conversion results in data loss then you must explicitly indicate your intention to convert types. This is called casting. You can also cast values that might otherwise be implicitly converted. In fact, this often makes your code more readable.

In C#, you cast a variable to another type by putting the type to which you are casting in parenthesis in front of the type (or value) being cast as in the following:

C#

```
double doubleVal = 12.345;
int intVal = (int)doubleVal;
```

In VB, you cast a variable to another type using conversion keywords. These keywords have a 'C' (for cast) in front of them followed by the type to which you are casting. For example, you can cast to an integer using CInt, or a double using CDbl, or a string using CStr. The following shows an example:

VB

```
Dim doubleVal As Double = 12.345
Dim intVal As Integer = CInt(doubleVal)
```

There are times when you have a string value and need to convert it into a numeric. This cast is not allowed. However, most of the numeric types include the method Parse that enables you to parse a string into a numeric value. There is also TryParse that returns a boolean indicating if the parse will work. The following code shows an example:

C#

```csharp
string stringVal = "1234";
int intVal;
intVal = int.Parse(stringVal);
```

VB

```vb
Dim stringVal As String = "1234"
Dim intVal As Integer
intVal = Integer.Parse(stringVal)
```

The framework also includes the Convert class that enables you to convert one type to almost any other (including strings). This class is available to both VB and C# programmers.

Defining Constants

You might need to define values in your application that will not (and cannot) change during the execution of the application. In this case you need to declare a constant. A constant in .NET is said to be an immutable value. That is, they cannot change values. You declare a constant in your code (typically at the class level) using the keyword, const. Like fields, they can be private or public. The following shows an example:

C#

```csharp
private const int CompanyTaxNumber = 123456;
```

VB

```vb
Private Const CompanyTaxNumber As Integer = 123456
```

Operators

Operators are indicators in your code that express an operation to perform. An operator might be an assignment from one variable to another, a comparison between two values, or a mathematical calculation among values. There are many operators available to .NET programmers. We do not cover them all here, but many of the more common operators are discussed in the following sections.

Assignment

Assignment operators are used to assign one variable or value to another. The most simple example is the equal (=) operator. This simply assigns the value on the right of the operator to the variable on the left side of the assignment (as in x = y). Other operators enable you to do assignment with addition (+=), assignment with subtraction (-=), assignment with multiplication (*=), and assignment of a string value with concatenation (&=). There are also assignment operators for division, arithmetic shifting, and more. The following shows a few assignment code examples:

C#

```
public double CalculatePaycheck(double gross, double commission,
  double deductions)
{
  double paycheck = gross;    //define paycheck as gross pay
  paycheck += commission;     //add commission
  paycheck -= deductions;     //subtract deductions

  return paycheck;
}
```

VB

```
Public Function CalculatePaycheck(ByVal gross As Double, _
  ByVal commission As Double, ByVal deductions As Double)

  Dim paycheck As Double = gross  'define paycheck as gross pay
  paycheck += commission          'add commission
  paycheck -= deductions          'subtract deductions

  Return paycheck
End Function
```

Arithmetic

The arithmetic operations enable you to perform calculations on variables and using values. For example, you can use the multiplication operator (*) to multiply two numbers (x * y). The operators you expect are all available, such as addition (+), subtraction (-), division to return an integer (\), division to return a floating point (/), multiplication (*), and dividing for remainder (mod in VB, % in C#). There are other, less common operators, too.

You typically use assignment with arithmetic operators as in x = y * z. However, you can use the value of the calculation when making decisions in your code (without first assigning it to a variable)—there's more on this in the coming sections. As an example of basic arithmetic in code with assignment, the following code shows how you might calculate an employee's accrued vacations days at the given point in the year (the AccrualRate is either a constant or set based on the number of days of vacation an employee has).

C#

```
double accruedVacation = DateTime.Today.DayOfYear * AccrualRate;
```

VB

```
Dim accruedVacation as Double = DateTime.Today.DayOfYear * AccrualRate
```

Comparison

The comparison operators enable you to determine whether values are equal to one another, greater than, or less than. You typically use these operators comparing two variables, values, or expressions. The results of the comparison indicate whether or not (true or false) the comparison is valid (as in is x > y). The comparison operators include less than (<), less than or equal to (<=), greater than (>), greater than or equal to (>=), equal (= in VB and == in C#), and does not equal (<> in VB and != in C#). The following shows an example of assigning a variable of type boolean to a comparison result.

C#

```
bool check = accruedVacation > vacationTakenToDate;
```

VB

```
Dim check As Boolean = accruedVacation > vacationTakenToDate
```

You can also do type comparison to check to see if two objects point to the same reference (or not). In C#, this type of comparison is still done with the equal (=) and not equal (!=) operators. In VB, you use the keywords Is and IsNot, as in check = Employee1 Is Employee2.

Concatenation

The concatenation operations enable you to combine string values. In VB, the concatenation operator is an ampersand (&) sign used with two string variables or values. In C#, the plus (+) sign is used. The following shows an example:

C#

```
string fullName = firstName + " " + lastName;
```

VB

```
Dim fullName as String = firstName & " " & lastName
```

Logical and Conditional

The logical and conditional operators enable you to combine comparisons in different ways to help make decisions in your code (see the next section for even more details). For example, you might combine two comparisons to make sure they are both true. Alternatively, you might need to determine if at least one of the two comparisons is true.

You can do this and more with the logical operators. Table 3.3 lists many of the logical operators (for code examples see the next section).

TABLE 3.3   Logical and Conditional Comparison Operators

Purpose	C#	VB	Pseudo Code Example
Join two boolean expressions and get the result as in, result is true if both this and that are true	&	And	VB: check = (x>Y) And (x>0) C#: check = (x>Y) && (x>0)
Negate a boolean value or expression as in results equal the opposite of an evaluation	!	Not	VB:check = Not someVal C#: check = !someVal
Choose between one or another values as in result is true if that or that is true	|	Or	VB: check = (x>y) Or (x>0) C#: check = (x>y) ¦ (x>0)
Two values must evaluate to opposite values as in, result is true if this is true and that is false	^	Xor	VB: check = True Xor False C#: check = true ^ false
A short-circuited version of And where if the first condition does not pass evaluation the second condition does not get executed	&&	AndAlso	VB: check = (x>Y) AndAlso (x>0) C#: check = (x>Y) && (x>0)
A short-circuited version of Or where if the first condition does not pass evaluation then the second condition does not get executed	||	OrElse	VB: check = (x>y) OrElse (x>0) C#: check = (x>y) ¦ (x>0)

Making Decisions and Branching Code

You can use the operators discussed previously to test for specific conditions in your code. These tests are then evaluated in order to make a decision on what code to execute or where to branch off in your application. There are three primary decision structures in .NET programming: If...Then...Else, Select...Case, and Try...Catch...Finally (covered in the "Handling Errors" section later in the chapter).

If...Then...Else

You can use the If syntax in your code to test one or more conditions. Based on the results of your test, you might decide to execute one set of code if the condition proves true and another set of code if the condition proves false. You can also get into more complex scenarios by nesting If statements and using the logical operators discussed in the prior section.

In VB, you use the explicit If...Then statements nested with End If. In C#, you put your If conditions inside parenthesis and the statements nested inside brackets. For example, the following shows code to determine if an Employee can get her vacation request approved.

In this code, there is a nested if statement and an example of combining two conditions with 'and'.

C#

```csharp
public bool CanApproveVacationRequest(int daysRequested, int daysTaken,
  int daysAllowed, int daysAccruedToDate)
{
  //rule: employee can take vacation if it is accrued and not used
  if ((daysRequested < daysAllowed) & (daysTaken < daysAllowed))
  {
    if ((daysTaken + daysRequested) < daysAccruedToDate)
    {
      return true;
    } else {
      return false;
    }
  } else {
    return false;
  }
}
```

VB

```vb
Public Function CanApproveVacationRequest(ByVal daysRequested As Integer,
  ByVal daysTaken As Integer, ByVal daysAllowed As Integer,
  ByVal daysAccruedToDate As Integer) As Boolean

  'rule: employee can take vacation if it is accrued and not used
  If daysRequested < daysAllowed And daysTaken < daysAllowed Then
    If (daysTaken + daysRequested) < daysAccruedToDate Then
      Return True
    Else
      Return False
    End If
  Else
    Return False
  End If
End Function
```

Note that in VB, if you have a single line that executes based on an if condition then you can write that as a single line of code as in If x > 500 Then doSomething. In C#, if you have a single line that executes, you can eliminate the need for the braces and the statement following the If condition is executed based on the condition's evaluation.

Select...Case (Switch)

The Select...Case (switch in C#) code construct enables you to evaluate a single statement for a value. Based on this condition, you then can execute blocks of code depending on the value.

In C#, you define the condition inside parentheses following the keyword switch. You then define each case block with the keyword case, the value you are checking on, and a colon. You must then add a break statement at the end of the case to indicate the end of the case. You can use the default keyword to execute code if no case was realized. The following code shows an example:

C#

```csharp
private void CalculateAdditionalCompensation()
{
  switch (this.Status)
  {
    case EmploymentStatus.Contract:
      //code for contract employees
      break;
    case EmploymentStatus.Hourly:
      //code for hourly employees
      break;
    case EmploymentStatus.Salaried:
      //code for salaried employees
      break;
    case EmploymentStatus.SalariedCommissioned:
      //code for commissioned employees
      break;
    case EmploymentStatus.Other:
      //code for other employees
      break;
    default:
      //code that runs if bad status was set
      break;
  }
}
```

In VB, you write case Select...Case statements using the keyword Select followed by Case followed by the condition. Each condition is then preceded with Case. You can use Case Else to run code when no other condition value evaluates. The following shows a code example:

VB

```vb
Private Sub CalculateAdditionalCompensation()

  Select Case Me.Status
```

```
    Case EmploymentStatus.Contract
        'code for contract employees

    Case EmploymentStatus.Hourly
        'code for hourly employees

    Case EmploymentStatus.Salaried
        'code for salaried employees

    Case EmploymentStatus.SalariedCommissioned
        'code for commissioned employees

    Case EmploymentStatus.Other
        'code for other employees

    Case Else
        'code that runs if bad status was set

    End Select

End Sub
```

Looping

There are many times in your code when you need to execute a set of statements more than once. In these cases, you need to create a loop. The most common scenarios are looping through code a set number of times, looping until a condition becomes true or false, or looping through code once per element in a collection of objects (see working with groups of items later in this chapter).

For...Next

The For...Next construct enables you to execute a block of code statements a set number of times. This is accomplished through a counter that increments a set number of steps each time the loop executes. After the counter has reached a max value the looping completes.

In C#, you write a for statement inside parentheses. The for statement has three parts: counter declaration, condition for the counter, and counting step. Each part is separated by a semicolon. The following code shows an example of executing a code block once for each employee's direct report:

C#

```
for (int i = 0; i < numDirectReports; i++)
{
    //update employee based on num of direct report
}
```

In VB, your For statement is a little more readable. You indicate the counter, the initial value and the To value. Optionally, you can add the Step keyword to indicate how many times you want to increment the counter each time through the loop. The following shows a code example:

VB

```
For i As Integer = 1 To numDirectReports
  'update employee based on num of direct reports
Next
```

For...Each (Iterators)

Like For...Next, the For...Each construct enables you to execute a group of statements. However, For...Each executes once for each element in a group of elements (or a collection). For instance, if you add a block of code to the Employee class that needs to execute once for each DirectReport you could do so using the For...Next (as shown previously) and the execute based on the count of DirectReports. However, using For...Each allows you to iterate over each object in a collection. As you do, you get a reference to the given object that you can use in your code. This makes coding a little easier to write and to understand.

You implement For...Each similar as For...Next in both C# and VB. The following shows code that executes once for each Employee instance inside the collection DirectReports:

C#

```
foreach (Employee emp in DirectReports)
{
  //execute code based on each direct report
  //  using the item as in emp.Name
}
```

VB

```
For Each emp As Employee In DirectReports
  'execute code based on each direct report
  '  using the item as in emp.Name
Next
```

Do...While/Until

Sometimes you need to repeat a block of code as many times as required until a condition evaluates to true or false. You might be looking for a specific value or might be using a counter that increments based on logic (instead of standard steps). In these cases, you can use a Do...While or a While loop. A Do...While loop executes once before the condition is evaluated to determine if it should execute a second time. A While loop evaluates the condition first and then only executes if the condition evaluates to true.

In C#, you can create Do...While loops using the do keyword followed by your block of code in braces. The while statement is written at the end of the code block indicating that the statements are executed once before looping (use a while loop to evaluate a condition before looping). The following shows an example:

C#

```
do
{
  //get next project and calculate commission
  projectCommission = GetNextProjectCommision(empId);
  calculatedCommission += projectCommission;
  if (projectCommission == 0)
  break;
} while (calculatedCommission < MaxMonthlyCommission);
```

Notice in the prior code that use of the break keyword. This indicates that the code should break out of the Do...While loop. You can also use the continue keyword to skip remaining code in your code block and jump right to the while statement to force a condition evaluation (and possible another loop).

In VB, you can define the while (or until) statement at the top or bottom of the loop. If defined at the top, your statement is evaluated before the loop executes once. If at the bottom, the loop executes at least once before the statement is evaluated. The While keyword indicates that you wish to loop while a condition is true (until it becomes false). The Until keyword allows you to loop until a condition evaluates to true (while it is false). The following shows an example:

VB

```
Do
   'get next project and calculate commission
  projectCommission = GetNextProjectCommision(empId)
  calculatedCommission += projectCommission
  If projectCommission = 0 Then Exit Do
Loop While calculatedCommission < MaxMonthlyCommission
```

As mentioned before, there is also the basic While loop (without do). This simply loops a block of code while a condition evaluates to true. Also, like all looping constructs, you can nest Do...While loops to handle more complex situations.

Working with Groups of Items

A common scenario in computer programming is managing a group of similar items. For example, you might need to work with a set of values, such as ZIP codes to which a sales representative is assigned. Alternatively, you might need to work with a group of objects such as the paychecks an employee has received in a given year. In cases where you need to work with a group of elements you can do so using an array or a collection class. The former is great for working with a set, sequential list of items of the same type. The latter is more applicable for managing a variable sized group of objects.

Arrays

An array is a group of items of the same type (either value or reference types). For instance, you might create an array that contains all integer values or all string values. You also have to define the number of elements contained in your array when you first initialize it. There are ways to expand or contract this size but these typically involve copying the array into another array. If you need the flexibility of adding and removing items in a group you want to use a collection class and not an array.

When you define an array's size you need to know that they are zero-based arrays. That is, the first element in the array is item zero. Therefore, if you dimension an array as myArray(6), it contains seven items (0 through 6). Each item is contiguous and sequential. This enables you to set and access items quickly using the items index.

The typical array you create is one-dimensional, meaning that it contains a single group of indexed items. You declare this type of an array by indicating the number of elements in the array either on the declaration of the variable or before the array's first use. There are a few valid syntaxes for defining an array. The standard way in C# is to use the new keyword to set the size of the array. In VB, you can set the size of the array without using the keyword new. The following shows an example:

C#

```
short[] salesRegionCodes = new short[numRegions];
```

VB

```
Dim salesRegionCodes(numRegions) As Short
```

You access an array through its index value. Array objects inherit for the System.Array class. This gives you a number of properties and methods you can use including getting the type of values in the array (GetType), getting the total number of elements in all dimensions of an array (Length), and getting the upper bound value for a single dimension (GetUpperBound). The following code shows an example of using this last method and accessing an array through its index:

C#

```
for (int i = 0; i < salesRegionCodes.GetUpperBound(0); i++)
{
  short code = salesRegionCodes[i];
  //additional processing ...
}
```

VB

```
For i = 0 To salesRegionCodes.GetUpperBound(0)

  Dim code As Short = salesRegionCodes(i)
  'additional processing ...
Next
```

You can also initialize the values in an array inside the declaration statement. In this case, the number of elements you define sets the size of the array. The following is an example:

C#

```
double[] salesFigures = new double[] {12345.98, 236789.86, 67854.12};
```

VB

```
Dim salesFigures() As Double = {12345.98, 236789.86, 67854.12}
```

You can define arrays that have more than a single dimension (up to 32). A common scenario is a two-dimensional array where one dimension is considered rows and the other columns. You can use the Rank property to determine the number of dimensions in an array.

As an example of a multidimensional array consider one that contains sales figures for each sales representative (rows) in each region (columns). You might define this array as follows:

C#

```
double[,] salesByRegion = new double[6, 5];
```

VB

```
Dim salesByRegion(6, 5) As Double
```

Note that an array can also contain other arrays. These type of arrays are called jagged arrays (or arrays of arrays). They are considered jagged because each element in the array might contain an array of different size and dimension; therefore, there might be no real uniformity to the array.

Collection Classes and Generics

A collection class can give you more flexibility when working with objects. For example you can have objects of different types in a single collection; collections can be of varying lengths; you can easily add and remove items in a collection.

The standard collection classes are defined inside the System.Collections namespace. The classes in this namespace include a base class for creating your own, custom collections (CollectionBase), and more specific collections such as ArrayList, Stack, SortedList, Queue, and HashTable.

For example, you might create a simple, dynamic ArrayList to contain a set of sales figures. The following code shows how you can create a new ArrayList, add items to it, and loop through those items.

C#

```
ArrayList salesFigures = new ArrayList();
```

```
salesFigures.Add(12345.67);
salesFigures.Add(3424.97);
salesFigures.Add("None");

for (int i = 0; i < salesFigures.Count; i++)
{
  object figure = salesFigures[i];
  //process figures ...
}
```

VB

```
Dim salesFigures As New ArrayList()


salesFigures.Add(12345.67)
salesFigures.Add(3424.97)
salesFigures.Add("None")

For i As Integer = 0 To salesFigures.Count - 1
 Dim figure As Object = salesFigures(i)
 'process sales figure data ...
Next
```

Of course, there are many additional properties and methods available to you through the ArrayList and related collection classes. You should explore these for your specific scenarios.

Notice in the prior code that the collection class has two types of objects inside it: double and string. This can be problematic if you need to rely on a collection of objects all being of the same type. For example, you might want all your sales figures to be of type double; or you might want a collection of only Employee objects. In these cases, you need a strongly typed collection class. You can create these by coding your own, custom collection classes (inheriting from CollectionBase and implementing the interfaces specific to your needs). However, .NET also provides a set of classes called generics that allow for strongly typed groups of objects.

Generic collections can be found inside the System.Collections.Generic namespace. A generic collection class enables you to define the type that the class contains when you initialize it. This then restricts what types the class can contain. You can rely on this information within your code.

You define a generic list in C# using angle brackets (<>) with the type defined inside those brackets. In VB, you define the generic type inside parenthesis using the Of keyword. For example, the following defines a simple, generic list of items that can only include values of type double:

C#

```
List<double> salesFigures = new List<double>();
```

VB

```
Dim salesFigures As New List(Of Double)
```

There are many generic collection classes available to you including Dictionary, HashSet, LinkedList, List, Queue, SortedList, Stack, and more. You can also write your own generic collection classes.

Tuples (New)

The System.Tuple class enables you to create a set, ordered list of items and work with that list. After you've created the list, the list cannot be changed. This makes for easy storage (and access) of sequential items.

For example, if you wanted to create a Tuple to store the month names in the first quarter you could do so using the static member, Tuple.Create. Each item you want to add to the list you add inside parenthesis (and separated by commas). You can then access the items in your Tuple using the Item1, Item2, Item3 syntax. Note that the Tuple only exposes item properties for the number of items that exist inside the group. The following code shows an example:

C#

```
var q1Months = Tuple.Create("Jan", "Feb", "Mar");
string month1 = q1Months.Item1;
```

VB

```
Dim q1Months = Tuple.Create("Jan", "Feb", "Mar")
Dim month1 As String = q1Months.Item1
```

The Tuple class is based on generics. You define the type of object you enable for each member in the list. The Create method shown infers this type for you. However, you might want to be explicit. In this case, you can declare your types using the constructor as in the following:

C#

```
Tuple<int, string, int, string, int, string> q1MonthNumAndName =
        Tuple.Create(1, "Jan", 2, "Feb", 3, "Mar");
```

VB

```
Dim q1MonthNumAndName As Tuple(Of Integer, String, Integer, String,
                              Integer, String) =
  Tuple.Create(1, "Jan", 2, "Feb", 3, "Mar")
```

Programming with Attributes

Sometimes you need to provide metadata about the capabilities of your code. This metadata is meant to tell other code that is inspecting your code (through reflection) specific things about what the code might do. This includes information for the .NET runtime such as how you want your code compiled. There are many attributes available in the .NET Framework. You can also create your own, custom attributes to be applied to your code. In this case, you can write code to examine the metadata about your own application.

Declarative attributes can be applied to classes, properties, methods, parameters, and other elements inside your code. You can apply a single attribute or multiple attributes to an application. Some attributes also might take parameters to indicate additional information to the attribute code.

Note that by convention, all attributes end with the word Attribute in their names, such as SerializableAttribute. You typically leave the word attribute off your declaration, however, as it is not required.

In C#, attributes are placed on code using square brackets ([]). For example, you can use the ConditionalAttribute to indicate to the compiler which code should be compiled based on environment variables or command line options. You would apply this attribute to your code as shown:

C#

```
[System.Diagnostics.Conditional("DEBUG")]
public void EmployeeCalculationsTestMethod()
{
  //code that compiles in the debug version of the assembly
}
```

In VB, you decorate your code elements with an attribute by putting the attribute in angle brackets (<>) in front of the code element as in the following:

VB

```
<Conditional("DEBUG")> Public Sub EmployeeCalculationsTestMethod()
  'code that compiles in the debug version of the assembly
End Sub
```

Exception Handling

A lot of programming time is spent eliminating exceptions from our code. However, you can't always eliminate all scenarios that might cause an exception. In these cases, you need a way to anticipate the exception and then, if possible, handle the exception in your code. There is where the Try...Catch...Finally construct comes into play.

You put a Try statement around a block of code you expect might cause an exception. You typically do so if you intend to handle the error. If you are not intending to handle the error, you can let the error bubble up to the calling code. Of course, you need to have an outer-error handler (or manager) inside your outer code to prevent errors from bubbling up to users in nasty ways.

When an exception actually occurs inside your Try block, execution is immediately passed to a Catch block. This might be a general catch of all errors or a catch meant for a specific exception type. The code inside the catch block is then meant to handle the error. Handling an error might include logging the error, sending it to a message system, or actually trying something different (or trying again using a jump statement) as the result of the error.

The following shows a basic example. Inside the Try block is a calculation that does division. This try block has the possibility of raising an exception in the case where the division is done by zero. This condition raises the specific exception, DivideByZeroException. There is a catch block that consumes this (and only this) type of exception. You can add code to the catch block to either eat the exception (do nothing) or process it somehow. Also, if you want to re-throw the exception after handling it, you can that, too.

C#

```
try
{
  averageSales = salesToDate / avgRate;
}
catch (System.DivideByZeroException e)
{
  //handle the exception ...
  // if re-throwing use: throw e;
}
```

VB

```
Try
  averageSales = salesToDate / avgRate

Catch ex As System.DivideByZeroException
  'handle the exception ...
  ' if re-throwing use: Throw ex
End Try
```

You can have multiple catch blocks be both specific and generic. Note that if no exception type is found in a catch block the exception is actually not handled but gets bubbled up to the calling code (or to the runtime).

Note that you can also re-throw the error from your catch block using the Throw keyword. If you do not re-throw the exception, the runtime assumes you have handled the error and moves on. You can also use throw anywhere in your application where you want to raise an exception.

There is also a Finally block that you can write. This bit of code goes after your Catch blocks. It runs regardless of whether an exception is raised or not. It is useful for cleaning up any resources that might have been allocated inside the Try block.

Creating and Raising Events

There is not much functionality you can build using the .NET languages without events. Events enable one piece of code to notify another bit of code that something has just happened. Code that raises events are said to publish an event and those that receive the event notice are said to subscribe to events. A simple example is when you write a user interface for the Web or Windows. In these cases, you are consistently adding code that subscribes to events published by the UI such as a user clicking on a button control. Of course an event may have more than a single subscriber and subscribers may be subscribed to multiple events.

Create an Event

When you create an event you need to determine if you need to pass custom data to the subscribers. This custom data is referred to as event arguments (or args). If you do not need to pass custom data, then you simply declare the event using the keyword event and the existing delegate, EventHandler. For example, if you were to define a simple event that you would raise when an employee class is updated you might define that event as follows:

C#

```csharp
public event EventHandler RaiseEmployeeUpdatedEvent;
```

VB

```vb
Public Event RaiseEmployeeUpdatedEvent As EventHandler
```

By declaring the event you have effectively published it. Subscribers that have a reference to your class can then set up a subscription to your event. You then need to raise the event in the same class where you published it. This notifies the subscribers that the event has fired.

It is slightly more complicated to define events where you need to pass custom data. In this case, you must first create a custom class to maintain your event data. This class must inherit from the EventArgs base class. For example, you might create a custom event arguments class to contain the employee id for the employee updated event. In this case, your custom class contains a property to hold the Id value and a constructor for passing in this value as in the following code:

C#

```csharp
public class EmployeeUpdatedEventArgs : EventArgs
{
  public EmployeeUpdatedEventArgs(string id)
  {
    _id = id;
```

```
    }

    private string _id;
    public string EmployeeId
    {
      get { return _id; }
    }
}
```

VB

```
Public Class EmployeeUpdatedEventArgs
  Inherits EventArgs

  Public Sub New(ByVal id As String)
    _id = id
  End Sub

  Private _id As String
  Public ReadOnly Property EmployeeId() As String
    Get
      Return _id
    End Get
  End Property

End Class
```

When you use a custom event argument you need to declare your event to use the custom event argument class. You can do so using the version of the EventHandler class that is defined as a generic. In this case, you indicate the class that contains the argument as part of the generic definition of EventHandler. This class also automatically contains the sender argument (typically a copy of the object publishing the event). The following shows an example of defining this custom event handler:

C#

```
public event EventHandler<EmployeeUpdatedEventArgs> RaiseEmployeeUpdatedCustomEvent;
```

VB

```
Public Event RaiseEmployeeUpdatedCustomEvent As _
  EventHandler(Of EmployeeUpdatedEventArgs)
```

Raise an Event

You raise the event in the same class where the event is defined. An event is raised as the result of some action. In the case of the example, the action is the employee class has been updated. To raise the event you simply call it in the right spot and pass the appropriate parameters. In the case of the employee updated custom event, you pass an instance of the employee class as the sender and then the employee Id as part of an instance of the EmployeeUpdatedEventArgs as shown below:

C#

```csharp
public void UpdateEmployee()
{
  //do work to update employee ...

  //raise event to notify subscribers of the update
  RaiseEmployeeUpdatedCustomEvent(this, new EmployeeUpdatedEventArgs(this.Id));
}
```

VB

```vb
Public Sub UpdateEmployee()
  'do work to update employee ...

  'raise event to notify subscribers of update
  RaiseEvent RaiseEmployeeUpdatedCustomEvent(Me, _
    New EmployeeUpdatedEventArgs(Me.Id))
End Sub
```

Subscribe to and Handle an Event

The final step is to actually listen for (or subscribe to) the event. Here, you need to do two things. First, you must write a method that mimics the signature of the event. The content of this method is yours to write. It is called when the event fires. The following shows an example of a method (inside a class that subscribes to the employee class) that gets called when the event fires. Notice how this method uses the custom event type and must therefore match that signature.

C#

```csharp
private void OnEmployeeUpdate(object sender, EmployeeUpdatedEventArgs e)
{
  //do something in response to employee update
  string empId = e.EmployeeId;
}
```

VB

```vb
Private Sub OnEmployeeUpdate(ByVal sender As Object, _
  ByVal e As EmployeeUpdatedEventArgs)

  Dim empId As String = e.EmployeeId
```

```
    Console.WriteLine("Event Fired: id=" & empId)
End Sub
```

Second, you must register your event handler with the actual event. This is done by adding a pointer to the event using the += (C#) or AddHandler (VB) syntax. You typically add your handlers inside the subscribing class's constructor or initialization code. The following shows code to connect the OnEmployeeUpdate handler to the RaiseEmployeeUpdatedCustomEvent event:

C#

```
Employee _emp = new Employee();
_emp.RaiseEmployeeUpdatedCustomEvent += this.OnEmployeeUpdate;
```

VB

```
AddHandler _emp.RaiseEmployeeUpdatedCustomEvent, AddressOf OnEmployeeUpdate
```

When the code is run you undoubtedly access features of the class that fire the event (in this case Employee.UpdateEmployee). When you hit a method that triggers the event your subscribing code is called accordingly.

Language Features

Thus far you've looked at the basics of programming with the .NET languages including building objects and solving common coding issues with respect to looping, handling logic, and creating and consuming events. In this section we try to point out some additional elements that make the .NET languages special. Many of these items are not necessarily things you might use every day; however, they can provide you with additional skills when writing code and better understanding when reading it. The .NET language features covered here include the following:

- ▶ Local Type Inference (also called Implicit Typing)
- ▶ Object Initializers
- ▶ Collection Initializers (new)
- ▶ Extension Methods
- ▶ Anonymous Types
- ▶ Lambda Expressions
- ▶ Partial Methods
- ▶ Language Integrated Query (LINQ)
- ▶ Friend Assemblies
- ▶ XML Language Support (VB only)
- ▶ Unused Event Arguments (VB only)

▶ Automatically Implemented Properties (new for VB)

▶ Implicit Line Continuation in VB (new)

▶ Work with Dynamic Language / Objects (new)

▶ Covariance and Contravariance (new)

▶ Type Equivalence Support (new)

Infer a Variable's Data Type Based on Assignment

In the later versions of Visual Basic and C# (2008 and beyond), you can define variables without explicitly setting their data type. And, when doing so, you can still get the benefits of strongly typed variables (compiler checking, memory allocation, and more). The compilers actually infer the data type you intend to use based on your code. This process is called local type inference, or implicit typing.

As an example, consider the following lines of code. Here you create a variable of type String and assign a value.

C#

```
string companyName = "Contoso";
```

VB

```
Dim companyName As String = "Contoso"
```

Now, let's look at the same line of code using type inference. You can see that you do not need the string portion of the declaration. Instead, the compiler is able to determine that you want a string and strongly type the variable for you. In C#, this is triggered by the keyword, var. This should not be confused with the var statement in languages such as JavaScript. Variables defined as var are strongly typed. In VB, you still simply use the Dim statement but omit the data type.

C#

```
var companyName = "Contoso";
```

VB

```
Dim companyName = "Contoso"
```

These two lines of code are equivalent in all ways. Although in the second example no data type was declared, one is being declared by the compiler. This is not a return to a generalized data type such as Variant or Object. Nor does this represent late-binding of the variable. Rather, it is simply a smarter compiler that strongly types the variable by choosing a data type based on the code. You get all the benefits of early-bound variables while saving some keystrokes.

For example, take a look at Figure 3.2. This is the C# compiler in action (the VB compiler does the same thing). You can see that even at development time, the compiler has determined that this variable is of type System.String.

FIGURE 3.2   Type inference in action.

There are a few things for you to be aware of when using type inference. The first is that it requires your local variable to be assigned a value in order to do the compiler typing. This should not be a big deal because if your variable is not assigned it is not used.

The second item you should consider is that type inference works only with local types. It does not work with class-level variables (also called fields) or static variables. In these cases, using local type inference results in an error being thrown by the compiler in C#. In VB, you would get the same error provided that Option Strict is set to On. If you are not using Option Strict in your VB code, the variable is not strongly typed. Instead, the variable is assigned the generic Object data type.

Local type inference can be useful in other declaration scenarios as well. This includes defining arrays, creating variables during looping, defining a variable inside a Using statement, and defining a variable that contains the result of a function call. In each of these cases, the compiler can infer your data type based on the context of the code.

As another example, the following code creates a Using statement and infers the type of the variable cnn (as a SqlConnection object). Note that a Using block defines a block of code for which a given resource is being used. The use of a Using block guarantees that the runtime disposes of the used object (in this case, the database connection) when done.

C#

```
using (var cnn = new System.Data.SqlClient.SqlConnection()) {
  //code to work with the connection
}
```

VB

```
Using cnn = New System.Data.SqlClient.SqlConnection
  'code to work with the connection
End Using
```

In Visual Basic, you can turn local type inference off and on for a given file. By default, a new VB code file is set to allow type inference. However, if you want to turn it off at the file level, you can do so by setting Option Infer Off at the top of the code file.

Create an Object and Set Its Properties with a Single Line of Code

There is a shortcut for both declaring an instance of a class and setting the initial value of all or some of its members. With a single line of code, you can instantiate an object and set a number of properties on that object. During runtime, the object is first created and then the properties are set in the order in which they appear in the initialization list. This feature is called object initializers.

Let's look at an example. Suppose you have a class called Employee that has a number of properties such as FirstName, LastName, FullName, Title, and the like. Using object initialization, you can both create an instance of this class and set the initial values of some (or all) of the Employee instance's properties. To do so, you first construct the object. In Visual Basic, you follow this construction with the With keyword (C# does not require an equivalent indicator). You then place each property initialization inside a set of curly braces. Examples are as shown here:

C#

```
Employee emp = new Employee { FirstName = "Joe",
  LastName = "Smith", Title = "Sr. Developer" };
```

VB

```
Dim emp As New Employee With {.FirstName = "Joe", _
  .LastName = "Smith", .Title = "Sr. Developer"}
```

This single line of code is the equivalent of first creating an Employee class and then writing a line of code for each of the listed properties. Notice that in VB, you need to precede the initialization using the With keyword; you also access each property using a dot. In C#, you do not need the dot or a keyword indicator.

Of course, you can also use object initialization with parameterized constructors. You simply pass the parameters into the constructor as you normally would. You then follow the constructor with the initialization. For example, suppose that the Employee class had a constructor that took the first and last name respectively. You could then create the object with the parameters and use object initialization for the Title as shown here:

C#

```
Employee emp = new Employee("Joe", "Smith")
  { Title = "Sr. Developer" };
```

VB

```
Dim emp As New Employee("Joe", "Smith") With _
  {.Title = "Sr. Developer"}
```

Object initialization also enables you to write some code in the initialization. In addition, with VB you can use properties of the object you are initializing to help initialize other properties. This is not valid in C#. The C# compiler does not allow you to access the variable until the assignment is complete. To see an example of this, the following code initializes an Employee object and sets the Employee.FullName property by concatenating the first and last names. Notice that the VB code uses the object itself.

C#

```
Employee emp = new Employee { FirstName = "Joe",
  LastName = "Smith", FullName = "Joe" + " Smith"};
```

VB

```
Dim emp As New Employee() With {.FirstName = "Joe", _
  .LastName = "Smith", _
  .FullName = .FirstName & " "" & .LastName}
```

You can also nest object initialization. That is, if a given property represents another object, you can create the other object as part of the initialization. You can also nest an initialization of the other object within the initialization of the first object. A simple example makes this clear. Suppose that the Employee class has a property called Location. The Location property might point to a Location object that includes the properties for City and State. You could then create the Employee object (along with the nested Location object) as shown here:

C#

```
Employee emp = new Employee { FirstName = "Joe",
  LastName = "Smith", Location = new Location
  { City = "Redmond", State = "WA" } };
```

VB

```
Dim emp As New Employee() With {.FirstName = "Joe", _
  .LastName = "Smith", _
  .Location = New Location With _
  {.City = "Redmond", .State = "Washington"}}
```

Define a Collection and Initialize Its Values (New)

You can now define a collection class or an array and, at the same time, set the initial values in your object. This turns multiple lines of code calling simple add methods into a single line. This is especially useful if you have a list of items that your application works with and you need to both declare the list and initialize these values.

As an example, you might need to define an array to contain the geographic locations for your sales office. You could define this array and initialize it as follows:

C#

```
string[] salesGeos = {"South", "Mid Atlantic", "Mid West"};
```

VB

```
Dim salesGeos() As String = {"South", "Mid Atlantic", "Mid West"}
```

You can use similar syntax to define and initialize a collection class including those based on a generic. For example, the following defines a List of Employee objects and adds two new Employee classes to that list. Note that the VB code requires the From keyword.

C#

```
List<Employee> empList = new List<Employee>
  {new Employee("1234"), new Employee("3456")};
```

VB

```
Dim empList As New List(Of Employee) From _
  {New Employee("1234"), New Employee("3456")}
```

Create an Instance of a Nonexistent Class

The .NET languages enable you to create an object that does not have a class representation at design time. Instead, an unnamed (anonymous) class is created for you by the compiler. This feature is called anonymous types. Anonymous types provide crucial support for LINQ queries. With them, columns of data returned from a query can be represented as objects (more on this later). Anonymous types are compiled into class objects with read-only properties.

Let's look at an example of how you would create an anonymous type. Suppose you want to create an object that had both a Name and a PhoneNumber property. However, you do not have such a class definition in your code. You could create an anonymous type declaration to do so as shown here:

VB

```
Dim emp = New With {.Name = "Joe Smith", _
  .PhoneNumber = "123-123-1234"}
```

C#

```
var emp = new { Name = "Joe Smith",
  PhoneNumber = "123-123-1234"};
```

Notice that the anonymous type declaration uses object initializers (see the previous discussion) to define the object. The big difference is that there is no strong typing after the variable declaration or after the New keyword. Instead, the compiler creates an anonymous type for you with the properties Name and PhoneNumber.

There is also the Key keyword in Visual Basic. It is used to signal that a given property of an anonymous type should be used by the compiler to further define how the object is treated. Properties defined as Key are used to determine whether two instances of an anonymous type are equal to one another. C# does not have this concept. Instead, in C# all properties are treated like a VB Key property. In VB, you indicate a Key property in this way:

```
Dim emp = New With {Key .Name = "Joe Smith", _
  .PhoneNumber = "123-123-1234"}
```

You can also create anonymous types using variables (instead of the property name equals syntax). In these cases, the compiler uses the name of the variable as the property name and its value as the value for the anonymous type's property. For example, in the following code, the Name variable is used as a property for the anonymous type:

VB

```
Dim name As String = "Joe Smith"
Dim emp = New With {name, .PhoneNumber = "123-123-1234"}
```

C#

```
string name = "Joe Smith";
var emp = new {name, PhoneNumber = "123-123-1234" };
```

Add Methods to Existing Classes

You can add custom features to an existing type as if the type always had the custom features. In this way, you do not have to recompile a given object, nor do you have to create a second, derived object to add these features. Rather, you can add a method to an existing object by using a new compiler feature called extension methods.

Adding methods varies between VB and C#. In VB, you first import the System.Runtime.CompilerServices namespace into your code file. Next, you mark a given Sub or Function with the ExtensionAttribute directive. Lastly, you write a new Sub or Function with the first parameter of the new method being the type you want to extend. The following shows an example. In this example, we extend the Integer type with a new method called DoubleInSize:

VB

```
Imports System.Runtime.CompilerServices


Public Module IntegerExtensions
  <Extension()> _
  Public Function DoubleInSize(ByVal i As Integer) As Integer
    Return i + i
  End Function
End Module
```

The C# compiler does not require the same import or method attribute. Instead, you first create a static class. Next, you create a static method that you intend to use as your extension. The first parameter of your extension method should be the type you want to extend. Additionally, you apply this modifier to the type. Notice the following example. In it, we extend the int data type with a new method called DoubleInSize.

C#

```
namespace IntegerExtensions
{
  public static class IntegerExtensions
  {
    public static int DoubleInSize(this int i)
    {
      return i+i;
    }
  }
}
```

To use an extension method, you must first import (using in C#) the new extension methods into a project. You can then call any new method as if it had always existed on the type. The following is an example in both VB and C#. In this case, a function called

DoubleInSize that was added in the preceding example is being called from the Integer (int) class.

VB

```
Imports IntegerExtensions


Module Module1
  Sub Main()
    Dim i As Integer = 10
    Console.WriteLine(i.DoubleInSize.ToString())
  End Sub
End Module
```

C#

```
using IntegerExtensions;


namespace CsEnhancements
{
  class Program
  {
    static void Main(string[] args)
    {
      int i = 10;
      Console.WriteLine(i.DoubleInSize().ToString());
    }
  }
}
```

Add Business Logic to Generated Code

A partial method (like a partial class) represents code you write to be added as a specific method to a given class upon compilation. This enables the author of a partial class to define a method stub and then call that method from other places within the class. If you provide implementation code for the partial method stub, your code is called when the stub would be called (actually the compiler merges your code with the partial class into a single class). If you do not provide a partial method definition, the compiler goes a step further and removes the method from the class along with all calls to it.

The partial method (and partial class) was created to aid in code generation and should generally be avoided unless you are writing code generators or working with them because they can cause confusion in your code.

Of course, Visual Studio has more and more code generation built in. Therefore, it is likely you will run into partial methods sooner or later. In most cases, a code generator or designer (such as LINQ to SQL) generates a partial class and perhaps one or more partial methods. The Partial keyword modifier defines both partial classes and partial methods. If you are working with generated code, you are often given a partial class that allows you to create your own portion of the class (to be merged with the code-generated version at compile time). In this way, you can add your own custom business logic to any partial method defined and called by generated code.

Let's look at an example. The following represents an instance of a partial class, Employee. Here there is a single property called Salary. In addition, there is a method marked Partial called SalaryChanged. This method is called when the value of the Salary property is modified.

VB

```vb
Partial Class Employee

  Private _salary As Double

  Property Salary() As Double
    Get
      Return _salary
    End Get
    Set(ByVal value As Double)
      _salary = value
      SalaryChanged()
    End Set
  End Property

  Partial Private Sub SalaryChanged()
  End Sub

End Class
```

C#

```csharp
partial class Employee {

  double _salary;

  public double Salary {
    get {
      return _salary;
    }
    set {
```

```
      _salary = value;
      SalaryChanged();
    }
  }


  partial void SalaryChanged();
}
```

The former code might represent code that was created by a code generator. The next task in implementing a partial method then is to create another partial Employee class and provide behavior for the SalaryChanged method. The following code does just that:

VB

```
Partial Class Employee
  Private Sub SalaryChanged()
    Dim newSalary As Double = Me.Salary
    'do something with the salary information ...
  End Sub
End Class
```

C#

```
partial class Employee
{
  partial void SalaryChanged()
  {
    double newSalary = this.Salary;
    //do something with the salary information ...
  }
}
```

When the compiler executes, it replaces the SalaryChanged method with the new partial method. In this way, the initial partial class (potentially code-generated) made plans for a method that might be written without knowing anything about that method. If you decide to write it, then it gets called at the appropriate time. However, it is optional. If you do not provide an implementation of the partial method SalaryChanged, the compiler strips out the method and the calls to the method—as if had never existed.

Access and Query Data Using the .NET Languages

Visual Studio 2008 introduced the language feature set called LINQ (for Language-Integrated Query). LINQ is a programming model that takes advantage of many of the features discussed in this section. It provides language extensions that change the way you access and work with data. With it, you can work with your data using object syntax and query collections of objects using VB and C#.

You can use LINQ to map between data table and objects (see Chapter 21, "Working with Databases"). In this way, you get an easier, more productive way to work with your data.

This includes full IntelliSense support based on table and column names. It also includes support for managing inserts, updates, deletes, and reads.

The last of these, reading data, is a big part of LINQ in that it has built-in support for easily querying collections of data. Using LINQ features, you can query not only your data but any collection in .NET. There are, of course, new keywords and syntax for doing so. Query operators that ship with Visual Basic, for example, include Select, From, Where, Join, Order By, Group By, Skip, Take, Aggregate, Let, and Distinct. The C# language has a similar set of keywords. And, if these are not enough, you can extend the built-in query operators, replace them, or write your own.

You use these query operators to query against any .NET data that implements the IEnumerable or IQueryable interface. This may include a DataTable, mapped SQL Server objects, .NET collections including Generics, DataSets, and XML data.

Let's look at an example. Suppose you had a collection of employee objects called employees and you wanted to access all the employees at a specific location. To do so, you might write the following function:

C#

```
public static List<Employee> FilterEmployeesByLocation
  (List<Employee> employees, string location)
{
  //LINQ query to return collection of employees filtered by location
  var emps = from Employee in employees
             where Employee.Location.City == location
             select Employee;

  return emps.ToList();
}
```

VB

```
Public Function FilterEmployeesByLocation( _
  ByVal employees As List(Of Employee), _
  ByVal location As String) As List(Of Employee)

  'LINQ query to return collection of employees filtered by location
  Dim emps = From Employee In employees _
             Where Employee.Location.City = location

  Return emps.ToList()
End Function
```

Take a look at what is going on in the previous listing. The function takes a list of employee objects, filters it by a region passed to it, and then returns the resulting list. Notice that to filter the list, we create a LINQ, in-memory query called emps. This query can be read like this: Looking at all the employee objects inside the employees collection, find those whose city matches the city passed into the function. Finally, the emps.ToList() method call in the return statement converts the in-memory query results into a new collection.

This is just a brief overview of LINQ. There are many things going on here, such as compile-time checking and schema validation—not to mention the LINQ language syntax. You will undoubtedly want to spend more time with LINQ.

Write Simple, Unnamed Functions Within Your Code

The latest versions of the .NET languages (2008 and later) enable you to write simple functions that might or might not be named, execute in-line, and return a single value. These functions exist inside your methods and not as separate, stand-alone functions. These functions are called *lambda expressions*. It's useful to understand lambda expressions because they are used behind the scenes in LINQ queries. However, they are also valid outside of LINQ.

Let's take a look at an example. Suppose you want to create a simple function that converts a temperature from Fahrenheit to Celsius. You could do so within your Visual Basic code by first using the keyword Function. Next, you can indicate parameters to that function (in this case, the Fahrenheit value). Lastly, you write an expression that evaluates to a value that can be returned from the lambda expression. The syntax is as follows:

VB

```
Dim fahToCel = Function(fahValue As Integer) ((fahValue - 32) / 1.8)
```

The C# syntax is a bit different. In C#, you must explicitly declare a delegate for use by the compiler when converting your lambda expression. Of course, you declare the delegate at the class-level scope. After you have the delegate, you can write the expression inside your code. To do so, you use the => operator. This operator is read as "goes to." To the left side of the operator, you indicate the delegate type, a name for the expression, and then an = sign followed by any parameters the expression might take. To the right of the => operator, you put the actual expression. The following shows an example of both the delegate and the expression:

C#

```
//class-level delegate declaration
delegate float del(float f);

//lambda expression inside a method body
del fahToCel = (float fahValue) => (float)((fahValue - 32) / 1.8);
```

Notice that in both examples, we assigned the expression to a variable, fahToCel. By doing so, we have created a delegate (explicitly converting to one in C#). We can then call the variable as a delegate and get the results as shown here:

VB

```
Dim celcius As Single = fahToCel(70)
```

C#

```
float celcius = fahToCel(-10);
```

Alternatively, in Visual Basic, we could have written the function in-line (without assigning it to a variable). As an example, we could have written this:

VB

```
Console.WriteLine((Function(fahValue As Integer) ((fahValue - 32) / 1.8))(70))
```

Notice in this last example that the function is declared and then immediately called by passing in the value of 70 at the end of the function.

The C# language has its own quirk, too. Here you can write multiple statements inside your lambda expression by putting the statements inside curly braces and setting off each statement with a semicolon. The following example has two statements inside the lambda expression. The first creates the new value; the second writes it to a console window. Notice, too, that the delegate must be of type void in this instance and that you still must call the lambda expression for it to execute.

C#

```
//class level delegate declaration
delegate void del(float f);

del fahToCel = (float fahValue) => { float f =
  (float)((fahValue - 32) / 1.8); Console.WriteLine(f.ToString()); };
fahToCel(70);
```

Lambda expressions are used in LINQ queries for things such as the Where, Select, and Order by clauses. For example, using LINQ, you can write the following statement:

VB

```
Dim emps = From emp In db.employees
  Where(emp.Location = "Redmond")
  Select emp
```

C#

```
var emps = from emp in db.employees
  where emp.Location == "Redmond"
  select emp;
```

This LINQ code gets converted to lambda expressions similar to this:

VB

```
Dim emps = From emp In db.employees.Where(Function(emp) emp.Location = _
    "Redmond").Select(Function(emp) emp)
```

C#

```
var emps = from emp in db.employees
   where (emp => emp.Location == "Redmond")
   select (emp => emp);
```

Split an Assembly Across Multiple Files

The 2005 version of C# introduced the concept of Friend assemblies; the feature was added to VB in 2008. It enables you to combine assemblies in terms of what constitutes internal access. That is, you can define internal members but have them be accessible by external assemblies. This capability is useful if you intend to split an assembly across physical files but still want those assemblies to be accessible to one another as if they were internal.

> **NOTE**
>
> Friend assembles *do not* allow for access to private members.

You use the attribute class InternalsVisibleToAttribute to mark an assembly as exposing its internal members as friends to another assembly. This attribute is applied at the assembly level. You pass the name and the public key token of the external assembly to the attribute. The compiler then links these two assemblies as friends. The assembly containing InternalsVisibleToAttribute exposes its internals to the other assembly (and not vice versa). You can also accomplish the same thing by using the command-line compiler switches.

Friend assemblies, like most things, come at a cost. If you define an assembly as a friend of another assembly, the two assemblies become coupled and need to coexist to be useful. That is, they are no longer a single unit of functionality. This can cause confusion and increase management of your assemblies. It is often easier to stay away from this feature unless you have a specific need.

Work with XML Directly Within Your Code (VB Only)

You can embed XML directly within your Visual Basic code. This can make creating XML messages and executing queries against XML a simple task in VB. To support this feature, VB enables you to write straight XML when using the data types called System.Xml.Linq.XElement and System.Xml.Linq.XDocument. The former enables you to create a variable and assign it an XML element. The latter, XDocument, is used to assign a variable to a full XML document.

> **NOTE**
>
> What we cover here is how VB enables you to write XML code. The two objects (XElement and XDocument) are still important to C# developers. However, C# developers work with the properties and methods of these objects directly and not write and parse XML directly within a code editor.

Writing XML within your code is a structured process and not just simple strings assigned to a parsing engine. In fact, the compiler uses LINQ to XML behind the scenes to make all of this work. Let's look at a simple example. The following code creates a variable, emp, of type XElement. It then assigns the XML fragment to this variable.

```
Dim emp As XElement = <employee>
                        <firstName>Joe Smith</firstName>
                        <title>Sr. Developer</title>
                        <company>Contoso</company>
                        <location state="WA">Redmond</location>
                      </employee>
```

You can create a similar fragment as an XDocument. You simply add the XML document definition (`<?xml version="1.0"?>`) to the header of the XML. In either scenario, you end up with XML that can be manipulated, passed as a message, queried, and more.

In most scenarios, however, you do not want to hard-code your XML messages in your code. You might define the XML structure there, but the data comes from other sources (variables, databases, and so on). Thankfully, Visual Basic also supports building the XML using expressions. To do so, you use an ASP-style syntax, as in `<%= expression %>`. In this case, you indicate to the compiler that you want to evaluate an expression and assign it to the XML. For XML messages with repeating data, you can even define a loop in your expressions. As an example, let's look at building the previous XML using this syntax. Suppose you have an object e that represents an employee. In this case, you might write your XElement assignment as shown here:

```
Dim e As Employee = New Employee()
Dim emp As XElement = <employee>
                        <firstName><%= e.FirstName %></firstName>
                        <lastName><%= e.LastName %></lastName>
                        <title><%= e.Title %></title>
                        <company><%= e.Company %></company>
                        <location state=<%= e.Location.State %>>
                            <%= e.Location.City %>
                        </location>
                      </employee>
```

Remove Unused Arguments from Event Handlers (VB Only)

Visual Basic now enables you to omit unused and unwanted arguments from your event handlers. The thought is that this makes for code that reads more cleanly. In addition, it enables you to assign methods directly to event handlers without trying to determine the proper event signature.

As an example, suppose you had the following code to respond to a button click event:

```
Private Sub Button1_Click(ByVal sender As System.Object, _
  ByVal e As System.EventArgs) Handles Button1.Click

  'your code here

End Sub
```

You could remove the arguments from this code (or never put them in). Your new code functions the same and looks as follows:

```
Private Sub Button1_Click() Handles Button1.Click
  'your code here
End Sub
```

Create an Automatically Implemented Property (New for VB)

Beginning with the 2008 version, C# allows for a simplified property declaration called auto-implemented properties. With this feature, you can declare a property without having to declare a local, private field to back the property. Instead, the compiler does this for you. This can be useful when you do not need logic inside the property's assessors. This feature has been added to VB for the 2010 version.

As an example, suppose you want to define the property Name on the Employee class. You can declare this property without setting a private field variable as shown here:

C#

```
public string Name { get; set; }
```

VB

```
Public Property Name As String
```

Notice that there is no logic in the get or set statements. Instead, the compiler creates an anonymous field to back the property for you.

Drop the Underscore in VB for Line Continuation (New)

The latest version of VB now has a feature for implicit line continuation. This enables you to drop the need for the underscore (_) commonly used to indicate line continuation. For example, the following code shows a valid method signature without the need for the underscore required for line continuation:

```
Private Sub OnEmployeeUpdate(ByVal sender As Object,
  ByVal e As EmployeeUpdatedEventArgs)
```

There are many places in VB where you can eliminate the underscore and instead allow the compiler to use implicit continuation. These include after commas, after an open parenthesis, after an open curly brace, after concatenation, and more. For a full list see "Statements in Visual Basic" inside MSDN.

Work with Dynamic Languages/Objects (New)

To date, everything in .NET has been about strongly typed languages where the compiler knows in advance the properties and methods that a given class exposes. However, there are objects (and languages) out there that do not have a static structure against which you can program. Instead, they are designed to get their information at runtime based on data inside an HTML form, a text file, XML, a database, or similar. These objects and languages are said to be dynamic in that they get their structure only at runtime. These items have been mostly off limits to .NET developers until now. Dynamic support has been added to .NET for the purpose of simplifying the access to dynamic APIs provided by languages such as IronPython and IronRuby, or even those found in Office Automation.

The Dynamic Data Type

The C# language has a new data type called dynamic. This type is similar to object in that it might contain any actual type (in fact, in VB you simply use object to get dynamic-like behavior). The difference in C#, however, is that any value defined as dynamic only has its actual type inferred at runtime (and not at compile time). This means you do not have type checking against valid methods and properties (that is, the compiler does not stop you from writing code against methods it cannot see at design time). Instead, type checking is only done when the code executes. Of course this means that your dynamic type should be an actual type at the right time or you get errors.

You can define dynamic fields, properties, variable, or return types of methods. For example, the following shows a property defined as a dynamic.

```
public dynamic DyProperty { get; set; }
```

At first glance, it would seem the dynamic keyword simply makes the type behave like types declared as object. In fact, the differences are so slight that VB combines the concept of object and dynamic. However in C#, the keyword dynamic indicates that the property can contain any value and that no type checking is done at compile time regardless of what the code looks like that uses the property. That is in contrast to types declared as object where the compiler evaluates expressions that use the type and prevents certain code (such as doing arithmetic with objects). Whereas dynamic types do not get this scrutiny by the compiler and thus either execute properly or throw an error if a problem exists.

Dynamics are useful for dealing with types and code outside of .NET such as IronPython (discussed below). However, you have to be careful when using them for your own needs. Because no resolution is done until runtime, you do not get strong type checking by the compiler or with IntelliSense. Figure 3.3 shows an example of the experience inside Visual Studio. In this case, the new Employee type is being declared as a dynamic. This can be problematic as you have to know the method you want to call and the parameters you want to pass. You could get the method right and not provide the right number of parameters in your call. The compiler allows it but an exception is thrown at runtime.

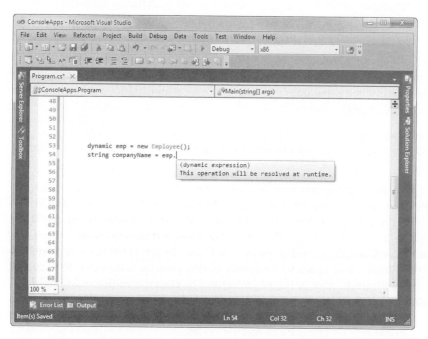

FIGURE 3.3   Using dynamics means no type checking even in IntelliSense.

Creating a Custom Dynamic Object

A dynamic object is one that gets its type information for things such as properties and methods at runtime. This is typically due to the fact that the object is meant to represent dynamic information such as that contained in an HTML or XML script file. In both cases, the underlying HTML and XML files you create are unique to your needs. Therefore you cannot code directly against these models. Instead, you often have to code against static objects and write syntax such as `MyXml.GetElement("EmployeeId")`. In this example, the Get Element method then searches for the given XML element and returns the same. With a dynamic object, the object can be written to interrogate your XML (or similar data) and enables developers to code against the dynamic object as if it contained the EmployeeId property. For example, they could use your dynamic object to write their code as: MyXml.EmployeeId. The dynamic object still has to interrogate the underlying structure for an EmployeeId but this does simplify the coding for those working with your object and a dynamic structure such as XML or HTML.

You can create dynamic objects using either VB or C#. To do so, you inherit from the DynamicObject class inside the System.Dynamic namespace. You then override the members inside this class. These members serve as the basis for your dynamic items. For example, you can override the TrySetMember and TryGetMember to indicate the code that should be run when a user attempts to set or get a dynamic property on your object (such as calling MyXml.EmployeeId). In this case, if a user is trying to return a dynamic property the TryGetMember method is called. Your code then determines how to return information for the dynamic property (you might interrogate a file for instance).

There are many members on DynamicObject for which you can provide functionality. In addition to the two aforementioned members, the other notables include TryInvokeMember for invoking dynamic methods and TryCreateInstance for creating new instances of a dynamic object.

You might also add your own methods and properties to a dynamic object. In this case, the dynamic object first looks for your property or method before calling out to the appropriate Try member.

Let's look at an example. Suppose you were to write a dynamic object to represent an Employee. In this case, perhaps you get data scraped from a web page or inside an XML file. You therefore want to convert this data to an object for easier programming. In this case you can create a new class called Employee and make sure it inherits from DynamicObject. In our example, we use a simple HashTable of key value pairs to simulate the employee data. When a user creates an instance of this class he is expected to pass the employee data to the dynamic class in the constructor. The skeleton of this class might then look as follows:

C#

```
class Employee : System.Dynamic.DynamicObject
{
  Hashtable _memberData;

  public Employee(Hashtable employeeData)
  {
    _memberData = employeeData;
  }
}
```

VB

```vb
Public Class Employee
  Inherits System.Dynamic.DynamicObject

  Dim _memberData As Hashtable

  Public Sub New(ByVal employeeData As Hashtable)
    _memberData = employeeData
  End Sub

End Class
```

The next step is to override one or more of the Try members of DynamicObject in order to add our own functionality. In this simple example, we override the TryGetMember method to provide functionality for reading a property. This method takes two parameters: binder and result. The binder parameter is an object that represents the dynamic call made to your object (such as its name). The result parameter is an outbound parameter of type object. You use it to pass back any value you intend to pass as the property read. Finally, the method returns a bool. This indicates true if the member was determined to exist; otherwise you return false.

In the example, we simply look inside the HashTable for a given key (based on the binder.Name property). If it exists, we set the result to its value and return true. Otherwise, we set the result to null and return false. The following shows the code for this additional member of our Employee class (assumes you're using (imports in VB) System.Dynamic):

C#

```csharp
public override bool TryGetMember(
  GetMemberBinder binder, out object result)
{
  if (_memberData.ContainsKey(binder.Name))
  {
    //set the out parameter, results to the value in the
    //  hash table for the given key
    result = _memberData[binder.Name];

    //indicate that member existed
    return true;
  }
  else
  {
    //property does not exist in hash table
    result = null;
    return false;
  }
}
```

VB

```
Public Overrides Function TryGetMember(ByVal binder As GetMemberBinder,
  ByRef result As Object) As Boolean

  If _memberData.ContainsKey(binder.Name) Then
    'set the out parameter, results to the value in the
    ' hash table for the given key
    result = _memberData(binder.Name)

    'indicate that member existed
    Return True
  Else
    'property does not exist in hash table
    result = Nothing
    Return False
  End If

End Function
```

> **NOTE**
>
> Note that classes that inherit from DynamicObject can be passed as instances to other languages that support the dynamic interoperability model. This includes IronPython and IronRuby.

Using the Dynamic Object

You use a dynamic object like you would any other. You can create an instance, call methods and properties, and so on. However, you do not get type checking by the compiler. Again, this is because the object is late bound at runtime. In C# you indicate a late bound, dynamic object using the keyword dynamic. In VB, you simply declare your type as object. VB figures out if you are using late binding.

As an example, suppose you want to use the dynamic version of the Employee class created in the previous section. Recall this class simulates converting data into an object. In this case, this simulation is handled through a HashTable. Therefore, you need to declare an instance of the Employee class as dynamic (or object in VB) and then create an instance passing in a valid HashTable. You can then call late bound properties against your object. Recall these properties are evaluated inside the TryGetMember method you overrode in the previous example. The following shows a Console application that calls the dynamic Employee object:

C#

```
class Program
{
  static void Main(string[] args)
  {
```

```
    Hashtable empData = new Hashtable();
    empData.Add("Name", "Dave Elper");
    empData.Add("Salary", 75000);
    empData.Add("Title", "Developer");

    dynamic dyEmp = new Employee(empData);

    Console.WriteLine(dyEmp.Name);
    Console.WriteLine(dyEmp.Salary);
    Console.WriteLine(dyEmp.Title);
    Console.WriteLine(dyEmp.Status);

    Console.ReadLine();
  }
}
```

VB

```
Module Module1

  Sub Main()

    Dim empData As New Hashtable()
    empData.Add("Name", "Dave Elper")
    empData.Add("Salary", 75000)
    empData.Add("Title", "Developer")

    Dim dyEmp As Object = New Employee(empData)

    Console.WriteLine(dyEmp.Name)
    Console.WriteLine(dyEmp.Salary)
    Console.WriteLine(dyEmp.Title)
    Console.WriteLine(dyEmp.Status)

    Console.ReadLine()

  End Sub

End Module
```

This code all passes the compiler's test and executes accordingly. However, the last call to dyEmp.Status is not valid. In this case, the dynamic object returns false and thus throws an error. Figure 3.4 shows the results including the console output and the error message trying to access a bad member.

FIGURE 3.4   The dynamic object executing in the Console and throwing an error in Visual Studio.

TIP

You can use the features discussed here to load a dynamic language library such as IronPython. In this case, you load the dynamic language library and can then use this library inside your code. For more on this see, "Creating and Using Dynamic Objects (C# and Visual Basic)" inside MSDN.

Covariance and Contravariance (New)

The latest versions of the .NET languages support the concepts of covariance and contravariance. These concepts enable you to reduce restrictions on strong typing when working with delegates, generics, or generic collections of objects. In certain situations, decreasing the type restrictions might increase your ability to re-use code and objects and decrease the need to do a lot of casting or converting in order to provide the right type to a method.

Covariance is the ability to use a more derived type than that which was originally specified by an interface or function signature. For example, you could assign a list of strings to a generic list that only takes objects if that list supports covariance (as strings inherit from objects and are thus more derived). Contravariance is similar; it is the ability to use a less derived type for a given parameter or return value. That is, you might assign an object type as the return type for a method that returns a string (provided that method supports contravariance).

It is important to note that the target object has to support covariance or contravariance. This is not a change to the entire language. Instead, it introduces a couple new keywords to allow support for these concepts when appropriate.

Variance in Generic Collections

Many of the generic interfaces in the latest version of the .NET Framework now support variance. This includes the interfaces IEnumerable<T> and IEnumerator<T> (among others) that support covariance. This means you can have support for variance inside your collections.

For example, you might have a list of Manager objects. Recall that Manager derives from Employee. Therefore, if you need to work with the Manager list as an Employee collection you can do so using List and the IEnumerable interface. The following code shows an example:

C#

```
IEnumerable<Manager> managers = new List<Manager>();
IEnumerable<Employee> employees = managers;
```

VB

```
Dim managers As IEnumerable(Of Manager) = New List(Of Manager)()
Dim employees As IEnumerable(Of Employee) = managers
```

The preceding code compiles and executes because Manager inherits from Employee and is thus more derived. Using covariance, you can use a list of Manager objects with a list of Employee objects. For example, you might have a method that takes a list of Employee objects as a parameter. Using covariance support, you can pass the manager list instead.

Additional Considerations

Support for variance has additional ramifications for your coding. These include the following:

▶ **Custom Generic Classes**—If you create your own custom generic classes you can declare support for variance. You do so at the interface level using the out (covariant) and in (contravarient) keywords on generic type parameter.

▶ **Delegate Variance**—Using variance, you can assign methods to delegates that return more derived types (covariance). You can also assign those methods that accept parameters that have a less derived type (contravariance).

▶ **Func and Action**—The generic delegates, Func and Action now support variance. This enables you to more easily use these delegates with other types (and thus increase the flexibility of your code).

The .NET Framework

The .NET Framework continues to evolve. This latest version layers on top of the many previous versions that brought us support for generics, AJAX Web Extensions, LINQ, Windows Presentation Foundation (WPF), Windows Communication Foundation (WCF), Windows Workflow Foundation (WF), SQL Synch Services, and more. Version 4.0 adds to this list to include support for parallel computing, improved security, better performance, the dynamic language runtime (DLR), and improvements in Web, WPF, and WCF applications.

A Map to the .NET Framework

We cannot begin to cover all of the features of the .NET Framework in this limited space. Therefore, we simply highlight some of the key areas that fuel the current version of the .NET Framework. Think of this section as a high-level map to help guide you when exploring the Framework. Many of these items are also covered in more depth throughout the book.

▶ **System.AddIn (Add-In Framework)**—Provides classes and methods for developers looking to build applications that can be extended based on a common add-in framework. For example, the AddInStore class allows for the discovery and management of add-ins. The framework also provides versioning, isolation, activation, and sandboxing. If you are building a new application and hope to allow for add-ins, you should dig deeper on this namespace.

▶ **System.CodeDom**—Includes the classes used to represent the structure of a code file. The classes in this namespace can be used to generate and compile code.

▶ **System.Collections**—Provides the collection classes inside the Framework including ArrayList, HashTable, SortedList, and others. Use the System.Collections.Generic namespace to get generic, type-safe equivalent collections.

▶ **System.ComponentModel**—Provides classes used to help with the runtime and design time execution of .NET controls including data-binding and progress monitoring.

▶ **System.Configuration**—Provides classes for reading, writing, and managing application configuration information.

▶ **System.Data (ADO.NET)**—Provides the classes required to work with data and databases. This includes the DataTable and DataSet. There is also the namespace, System.Data.SqlClient for working with SQL databases. For more information on working with ADO.NET see Chapter 21, "Working with Databases."

▶ **System.Diagnostics**—Contains classes for working with diagnostic information about your application. This includes and EventLog and Process class. There is also the EventSchemaTraceListener class to allow for cross-domain, cross-thread, cross-computer, end-to-end, lock-free logging and tracing.

▶ **System.Diagnostics.Contracts**—Provides support for code contracts including preconditions and other data that is not typically defined inside a method signature.

▶ **System.Drawing**—Provides classes (like Pen, Brush, and Graphics) related to drawing with GDI+.

▶ **System.Dynamic**—Provides support for dynamic objects that get their members are runtime (see content earlier in this chapter for more details).

▶ **System.EnterpriseServices**—Provides the services architecture for creating serviced components that run under COM+.

▶ **System.Globalization**—Used to define language and culture information for writing multi-lingual, multi-cultural applications.

▶ **System.IO**—Provides classes for reading and writing file and data streams. This includes classes such as File, Directory, and Stream. Note there is also the System.IO.Pipes namespace that provides support for writing code that communicates at the pipe level across processes and across computers.

▶ **System.Linq (LINQ)**—Defines standard LINQ query operators and types. The System.Data.Linq namespace holds the connection between databases and the LINQ subsystem. There are more LINQ-related namespaces, too. These include System.Data.Linq.Mapping for handling the O/R mapping between SQL and LINQ and System.Xml.Linq for working between XML and the LINQ subsystem.

▶ **System.Media**—Used for accessing and playing sounds and music.

▶ **System.Messaging**—Provides support for working with message queues.

▶ **System.Net**—Provides support for programming with network protocols including the HTTP, FTP, and TCP/IP. It also includes peer-to-peer networking support found in the System.Net.PeerToPeer namespace.

▶ **System.Security**—Provides the classes used to implement security inside the .NET runtime.

▶ **System.ServiceModel (WCF)**—Encapsulates what is known as WCF. With it you can easily create service-based applications that work across multiple protocols, transports, and message types. WCF is covered more in Chapter 22, "Service-Oriented Applications."

▶ **System.Threading**—Provides support for writing multi-threaded applications. This includes System.Threading.Tasks which provides support for parallel computing on multiple threads and multiple cores. This namespace simplifies the task of writing for these environments. Note there is also the PLINQ (or parallel LINQ uses this support in LINQ for objects programming).

▶ **System.Web (ASP.NET)**—Includes many classes and controls. For example, the framework directly supports AJAX programming with the ScriptManager and UpdatePanel controls. There are also controls, such as ListView, for displaying data. For more on the ASP.NET framework, see Chapter 17, "Creating ASP.NET Applications."

▶ **System.Windows (WPF)**—Provides the WPF presentation technology for Windows applications. This technology is spread throughout the namespace and includes support for creating Windows applications based on XAML, XBAP, vector graphics, and both 2D and 3D scenarios. For more information, see Chapter 19, "Creating Richer, Smarter User Interfaces."

▶ **System.Workflow.Activities and System.Activities (WF)**—Provides classes for writing workflow applications and the custom activities found inside a workflow application. For more on WF, see Chapter 23, "Embedding Workflow in Your Applications."

▶ **System.Xml**—Provides support for working with XML and XSL.

Summary

This chapter provided a primer on the .NET languages. It should serve to get you running on the many features and programming constructs made possible by these languages. Our intent is to help you write more and better code during your development day. This chapter also presented a high-level roadmap of the .NET Framework. This Framework is becoming so large that developers (and books) are often forced to specialize in a particular area. We suggest that you look at our list and then jump off to your own specialty area for further exploration.

CHAPTER 4

Solutions and Projects

Solutions and projects are the containers Visual Studio uses to house and organize the code you write within the IDE. Solutions are virtual containers; they group and apply properties across one or more projects. Projects are both virtual and physical in purpose. Besides functioning as organizational units for your code, they also map one to one with compiler targets. Put another way, Visual Studio turns projects into compiled code. Each project results in the creation of a .NET component (such as a DLL or an EXE file).

In this chapter, we cover the roles of solutions and projects in the development process. We see how to create solutions and projects, examine their physical attributes, and discuss ways to best leverage their features.

Understanding Solutions

From a programming perspective, everything that you do within Visual Studio takes place within the context of a solution. As we mentioned in this chapter's introduction, solutions in and of themselves don't do anything other than serve as higher-level containers for other items. Projects are the most obvious items that can be placed inside solutions, but solutions can also contain miscellaneous files that may be germane to the solution itself, such as "read me" documents and design diagrams. Really, any file type can be added to a solution. Solutions can't, however, contain other solutions. In addition, Visual Studio loads only one solution at a time. If you need to work on more than one solution concurrently, you need to launch another instance of Visual Studio.

So what do solutions contribute to the development experience? Solutions are useful because they allow you to treat different projects as one cohesive unit of work. By grouping multiple projects under a solution, you can work against those projects from within one instance of Visual Studio. In addition, a solution simplifies certain configuration tasks by allowing you to apply settings across all the solution's child projects.

You can also "build" a solution. As mentioned previously, solutions themselves aren't compiled, per se, but their constituent projects can be built using a single build command issued against the solution. Solutions are also a vehicle for physical file management: Because many items that show up in a solution are physical files located on disk, Visual Studio can manage those files in various ways (delete them, rename them, move them). So it turns out that solutions are very useful constructs within Visual Studio.

The easiest way to explore solution capabilities and attributes is to create a solution in the IDE.

Creating a Solution

To create a solution, you first create a project. Because projects can't be loaded independent of a solution within Visual Studio, creating a project causes a solution to be created at the same time.

> **NOTE**
>
> There actually is a way to create a blank, or empty, solution without also creating a project. If you expand the Other Project Types node that appears in the Installed Templates list, you will see an option for Visual Studio Solutions. This contains a Blank Solution template. Blank solutions are useful when you are creating a new solution to house a series of already-existing projects; the blank solution obviates the need to worry about extra, unneeded projects being created on disk.

Launch the New Project dialog box by using the File menu and selecting the New, Project option (shown in Figure 4.1) or by using the Ctrl+Shift+N keyboard shortcut.

The New Project dialog box is displayed with defaults for the project name, location, and solution name (see Figure 4.2). We take a detailed look at the various project types offered there when we discuss projects later in this chapter. Notice that a Solution Name field is displayed at the bottom of the dialog box. This field allows you to customize the name of your solution before you create the solution. Clicking OK at this point does two things: A project of the indicated type and name is created on disk (at the location specified), and a solution, with links to the project, also is created on disk using the provided name.

Assuming that you have selected something other than the Blank Solution project type, Visual Studio now displays the newly created solution and project in the Solution Explorer window (we cover the Solution Explorer in depth in Chapter 5, "Browsers and Explorers"). In effect, Visual Studio has created the solution hierarchy shown in Figure 4.3.

Assuming that you have accepted the default locations and left the Create Directory for Solution box checked, the physical directory/file structure is created as shown in Figure 4.4.

FIGURE 4.1   The File, New, Project menu.

FIGURE 4.2   The New Project dialog box.

In this example, the first WindowsFormsApplication1 folder holds the solution file and has a subfolder for each project. The second WindowsFormsApplication1 folder contains the new Windows forms project. The source files are placed in the root of this folder, and any compiled output files sit underneath the bin directory and then under the specific build configuration (for example, Debug or Release).

FIGURE 4.3   A simple solution hierarchy.

FIGURE 4.4   The solution file hierarchy.

CAUTION

By default, the solution is named after the project. There is potential for confusion here because you now have two folders/entities named WindowsFormsApplication1. One refers to the solution; the other, the project. This is not an ideal way to physically organize your code on disk. It is recommended that you give the solution itself a unique name during the project creation process by simply overriding the default name given in the Solution Name field (see Figure 4.2).

The Solution Definition File

Visual Studio stores solution information inside two separate files: a solution definition file and a solution user options file. For the preceding example, Visual Studio created the solution definition file WindowsFormsApplication1.sln and the solution user options file WindowsFormsApplication1.suo in the indicated folder.

The solution definition file is responsible for actually describing any project relationships in the solution and for storing the various solution-level attributes that can be set. The solution user options file persists any customizations or changes that you, as a Visual Studio user, might have made to the way the solution is displayed within the IDE (such as whether the solution is expanded or which documents from the solution are open in the IDE). In addition, certain source control settings and other IDE configuration data are stored here.

The solution user options file is, by default, marked as a hidden file, and its content is actually binary. Because its internal structure is not publicly documented, we won't attempt to dissect it here. The solution definition file, however, is simply a text file. Listing 4.1 shows the file content for a fairly complex sample solution.

LISTING 4.1   Sample Solution File

```
Microsoft Visual Studio Solution File, Format Version 11.00
# Visual Studio 2010
Project("{FAE04EC0-301F-11D3-BF4B-00C04F79EFBC}") = "Contoso.Fx.Integration",
➥"ClassLibrary1\Contoso.Fx.Integration.csproj", "{DA0BA585-76C1-4F5E-B7EF-
➥57254E185BE4}"
EndProject
Project("{FAE04EC0-301F-11D3-BF4B-00C04F79EFBC}") = "Contoso.Fx.Common",
➥"Contoso.Fx.Common\Contoso.Fx.Common.csproj", "{A706BCAC-8FD7-4D8A-AC81-
➥249ED61FDE72}"
EndProject
Project("{FAE04EC0-301F-11D3-BF4B-00C04F79EFBC}") = "Contoso.Fx.Analysis",
➥"Contoso.Fx.Analysis\Contoso.Fx.Analysis.csproj", "{EB7D75D7-76FC-4EC0-
➥A11E-2B54849CF6EB}"
EndProject
Project("{FAE04EC0-301F-11D3-BF4B-00C04F79EFBC}") = "Contoso.Fx.UI",
➥"Contoso.Fx.UI\Contoso.Fx.UI.csproj", "{98317C19-F6E7-42AE-AC07-72425E851185}"
EndProject
Project("{2150E333-8FDC-42A3-9474-1A3956D46DE8}") = "Architecture Models",
➥"Architecture Models", "{60777432-3B66-4E03-A337-0366F7E0C864}"
    ProjectSection(SolutionItems) = postProject
        ContosoSystemDiagram.sd = ContosoSystemDiagram.sd
    EndProjectSection
EndProject
Project("{FAE04EC0-301F-11D3-BF4B-00C04F79EFBC}") = "Contoso.UI.WindowsForms.
OrderEntry", "Contoso.UI.WindowsForms.OrderEntry\Contoso.UI.WindowsForms.
OrderEntry.csproj", "{49C79375-6238-40F1-94C8-4183B466FD79}"
EndProject
Project("{2150E333-8FDC-42A3-9474-1A3956D46DE8}") = "Class Libraries", "Class
➥Libraries", "{E547969C-1B23-42DE-B2BB-A13B7E844A2B}"
EndProject
Project("{2150E333-8FDC-42A3-9474-1A3956D46DE8}") = "Controls", "Controls",
➥"{ED2D843C-A708-41BE-BB52-35BFE4493035}"
EndProject
Global
    GlobalSection(SolutionConfigurationPlatforms) = preSolution
```

```
        Debug|Any CPU = Debug|Any CPU
        Release|Any CPU = Release|Any CPU
    EndGlobalSection
    GlobalSection(ProjectConfigurationPlatforms) = postSolution
        {DA0BA585-76C1-4F5E-B7EF-57254E185BE4}.Debug|Any CPU.ActiveCfg = Debug|
        ➥Any CPU
        {DA0BA585-76C1-4F5E-B7EF-57254E185BE4}.Debug|Any CPU.Build.0 = Debug|
        ➥Any CPU
        {DA0BA585-76C1-4F5E-B7EF-57254E185BE4}.Release|Any CPU.ActiveCfg = Release
        ➥|Any CPU
        {DA0BA585-76C1-4F5E-B7EF-57254E185BE4}.Release|Any CPU.Build.0 = Release|
        ➥Any CPU
        {A706BCAC-8FD7-4D8A-AC81-249ED61FDE72}.Debug|Any CPU.ActiveCfg = Debug|
        ➥Any CPU
        {A706BCAC-8FD7-4D8A-AC81-249ED61FDE72}.Debug|Any CPU.Build.0 = Debug|
        ➥Any CPU
        {A706BCAC-8FD7-4D8A-AC81-249ED61FDE72}.Release|Any CPU.ActiveCfg = Release
        ➥|Any CPU
        {A706BCAC-8FD7-4D8A-AC81-249ED61FDE72}.Release|Any CPU.Build.0 = Release
        ➥|Any CPU
        {EB7D75D7-76FC-4EC0-A11E-2B54849CF6EB}.Debug|Any CPU.ActiveCfg = Debug| Any
        ➥CPU
        {EB7D75D7-76FC-4EC0-A11E-2B54849CF6EB}.Debug|Any CPU.Build.0 = Debug|
        ➥Any CPU
        {EB7D75D7-76FC-4EC0-A11E-2B54849CF6EB}.Release|Any CPU.ActiveCfg =
        ➥Release |Any CPU
        {EB7D75D7-76FC-4EC0-A11E-2B54849CF6EB}.Release|Any CPU.Build.0 = Release
        ➥|Any CPU
        {98317C19-F6E7-42AE-AC07-72425E851185}.Debug|Any CPU.ActiveCfg = Debug|
        ➥Any CPU
        {98317C19-F6E7-42AE-AC07-72425E851185}.Debug|Any CPU.Build.0 = Debug|
        ➥Any CPU
        {98317C19-F6E7-42AE-AC07-72425E851185}.Release|Any CPU.ActiveCfg =
        ➥Release |Any CPU
        {98317C19-F6E7-42AE-AC07-72425E851185}.Release|Any CPU.Build.0 = Release
        ➥|Any CPU
        {49C79375-6238-40F1-94C8-4183B466FD79}.Debug|Any CPU.ActiveCfg = Debug|
        ➥Any CPU
        {49C79375-6238-40F1-94C8-4183B466FD79}.Debug|Any CPU.Build.0 = Debug|
        ➥Any CPU
        {49C79375-6238-40F1-94C8-4183B466FD79}.Release|Any CPU.ActiveCfg =
        ➥Release |Any CPU
        {49C79375-6238-40F1-94C8-4183B466FD79}.Release|Any CPU.Build.0 =
        ➥Release |Any CPU
    EndGlobalSection
    GlobalSection(SolutionProperties) = preSolution
```

```
        HideSolutionNode = FALSE
    EndGlobalSection
    GlobalSection(NestedProjects) = preSolution
        {ED2D843C-A708-41BE-BB52-35BFE4493035} = {E547969C-1B23-42DE-B2BB-
        ➡A13B7E844A2B}
        {EB7D75D7-76FC-4EC0-A11E-2B54849CF6EB} = {E547969C-1B23-42DE-B2BB-
        ➡A13B7E844A2B}
        {A706BCAC-8FD7-4D8A-AC81-249ED61FDE72} = {E547969C-1B23-42DE-B2BB-
        ➡A13B7E844A2B}
        {DA0BA585-76C1-4F5E-B7EF-57254E185BE4} = {E547969C-1B23-42DE-B2BB-
        ➡A13B7E844A2B}
        {98317C19-F6E7-42AE-AC07-72425E851185} = {ED2D843C-A708-41BE-BB52-
        ➡35BFE4493035}
    EndGlobalSection
EndGlobal
```

At the beginning of the file are references to the projects that belong to the solution. The references contain the project's name, its GUID, and a relative path to the project file itself (more on project files in a bit).

You can also see some of the various configuration attributes applied to the solution; the Debug and Release settings, for instance, show up here. Note that this project contains several solution folders: Architecture Models, Class Libraries, and Controls. They are represented in the solution file in much the same way as projects. In fact, the only difference is that they do not have a relative file path associated with them.

Working with Solutions

After you have created a solution, the primary vehicle is in place for interacting with your code base. In essence, this boils down to controlling the way its constituent projects and files are built and deployed. Solutions also provide functionality outside the scope of projects. The primary tool for manipulating solutions and projects is the Solution Explorer. This tool is discussed in depth in Chapter 5. Here, we look at the general procedures used to manage solutions by using the menu system in Visual Studio; keep in mind that most of the commands and actions discussed here can be initiated from the Solution Explorer.

Solution Items

In practice, the content you add most often to a solution is project related. But items can be added directly to a solution as well. Collectively, the term *solution items* refers to any nonproject file that is attached to a solution. Because we know that solutions can't be compiled, it stands to reason that files added at the solution level serve no practical purpose from a compilation perspective. There are various reasons, however, that you might want to add solution items to your solution. For instance, adding solution items to your solution is a convenient way to store documentation that applies to the solution as a whole. Because you can add any type of file to a solution, this could take the form of documents, notes to other developers, design specifications, or even source code files from other solutions that could have some effect or bearing on the work at hand.

By default, Visual Studio supports a few types of solution items that can be created directly from within the IDE. They are grouped within four categories. Within each category are various file types that can be generated by Visual Studio. Table 4.1 shows the supported types.

TABLE 4.1   File Types Supported Within a Solution by Add New Item

Category	Item Type	File Extension
General	Text file	.txt
	Style sheet	.css
	XML schema	.xsd
	Bitmap file	.bmp
	Cursor file	.cur
	Visual C# class	.cs
	Visual Basic class	.vb
	HTML page	.html
	XML file	.xml
	XSLT file	.xsl
	Icon file	.ico
	Native resource template	.rct

NOTE

Keep in mind that you are in no way limited as to the type of file you can add to a solution. Even though Visual Studio supports only a limited number of file types that can be created within the IDE, you always have the option of creating a file *outside* the IDE and then adding it to a solution by using the Add Existing Item command.

Figure 4.5 shows the Add New Item – Solution Items dialog box that appears when you try to add a new item to a solution.

Solution Folders

To assist in organizing the various files in your solution, you can use solution folders. Solution folders are virtual folders implemented entirely within Visual Studio. Creating a solution folder does not cause a physical file folder to be created on disk; these folders exist solely to provide another grouping level within the solution. Solution folders can be nested and are especially useful in large solutions that contain many different projects and miscellaneous files. For example, you might want to group all of your web service projects under a single solution folder called Services and group the Windows forms elements of your solution under a UI folder. On disk, files added to a virtual folder are physically stored within the root of the solution directory structure.

FIGURE 4.5   Adding a new solution item.

Visual Studio creates solution folders automatically if you add a non-project item to an existing solution. For instance, if we want to add a text file to the current solution, Visual Studio automatically adds a solution folder titled "Solution Items" to contain the text file. Similarly, you might see a "Misc Files" folder in some solutions. This is simply a solution folder as well.

Beyond providing a way to visually group items, solution folders also allow you to apply certain commands against all the projects contained within an individual folder. For example, you can "unload" all the projects within a virtual folder by issuing the unload command against the virtual folder (this makes the projects temporarily unavailable within the solution, and can be useful when trying to isolate build problems or solution problems). After unloading the projects in a folder, another right-click on the solution folder allows you to reload the projects.

Solution Properties

You can set several solution-level properties from within the IDE. The Solution Property Pages dialog box gives you direct access to these properties and allows you to do the following:

▶ Set the startup project of the solution (this project runs when you start the debugger)

▶ Manage interproject dependencies

▶ Specify the location of source files to use when debugging

▶ Modify the solution build configurations

You launch this dialog box from the View, Property Pages menu or with the Shift+F4 keyboard shortcut. On this dialog box, the property page categories are represented in a tree view to the left; expanding a tree node reveals the individual property pages available.

Specifying the Startup Project   Figure 4.6 shows the Startup Project property page. The Startup Project property page indicates whether the startup project should be the currently selected project, a single project, or multiple projects.

FIGURE 4.6   The Startup Project property page.

The default, and most typically used option, is to specify a single startup project. The project to run is specified in the drop-down box. If Current Selection is selected, the project that currently has focus in the Solution Explorer is considered the startup project.

You can also launch multiple projects when the debugger is started. Each project currently loaded in the solution appears in the list box with a default action of None. Projects set to None are not executed by the debugger. You can also choose from the actions Start and Start Without Debugging. As their names suggest, the Start action causes the indicated project to run within the debugger; Start Without Debugging causes the project to run, but it is not debugged.

Setting Project Dependencies   If a solution has projects that depend on one another—that is, one project relies on and uses the types exposed by another project—Visual Studio needs to have a build order of precedence established among the projects. As an example, consider a Windows application project that consumes types that are exposed by a class library project. The build process fails if the class library is not built first within the build sequence.

Most of the time, Visual Studio is able to determine the correct sequence. Sometimes, you might need to manually indicate that a project is dependent on other, specific projects. For instance, a UI project might depend on another class library project. To supply this information, you use the Project Dependencies property page (see Figure 4.7). By selecting a project in the drop-down, you can indicate which other solutions it depends on by placing a check mark on any of the projects shown in the Depends On list.

FIGURE 4.7   Project dependencies.

Source File Location for Debugging   In certain situations, you might need to explicitly point the Visual Studio debugger at source files to use when the debugger executes. One such scenario occurs when you are trying to debug a solution that references an object on a remote machine. If the source is not available locally for that remote object, you can explicitly point Visual Studio at the source files.

The Debug Source Files property page (see Figure 4.8) has two different list boxes. The top box contains a list of folders that hold source code specific to your debugging scenario. The bottom list box allows you to indicate specific files that the debugger should ignore (that is, should not load) when debugging.

FIGURE 4.8   Source file locations.

To add an entry to either box, first place your cursor within the box and then click on the New Line button (upper right of the dialog box). This allows you to enter a fully qualified path to the desired folder. You remove an entry by selecting the item and then clicking on the Cut Line button. The Check Entries button allows you to double-check that all entries point to valid, reachable folder paths.

If the loaded solution has any Visual C++ projects, you probably see several items already added into the Directories Containing Source Code list box.

Build Configuration Properties   Build configurations are covered in depth in Chapter 11, "Debugging Code." On the Build Configuration property page (see Figure 4.9), you indicate how Visual Studio builds the projects contained within the solution. For each project, you can set a configuration and platform value. In addition, a check box allows you to indicate whether to build a particular project.

See Chapter 11 for information on how to effectively use build configurations in your development.

Now that we have covered the concept of a solution in depth, let's examine the role of projects within Visual Studio.

Getting Comfortable with Projects

Projects are where all the real work is performed in Visual Studio. A project maps directly to a compiled component. Visual Studio supports various project types. Let's reexamine the project creation process.

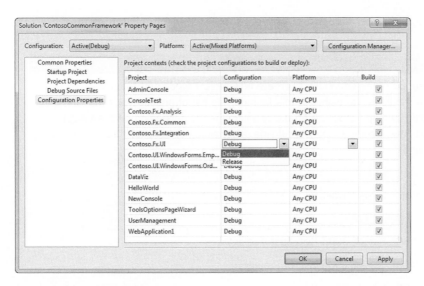

FIGURE 4.9   Build configuration properties.

Creating a Project

As we saw earlier when discussing solution creation, you create projects by selecting the New, Project option from the File menu. This launches the New Project dialog box (see Figure 4.10).

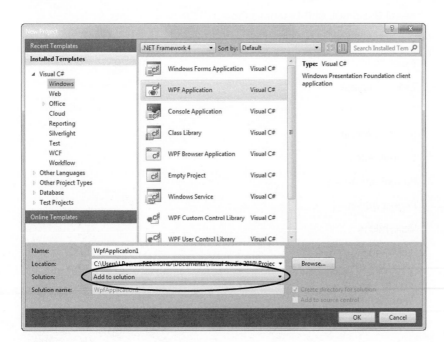

FIGURE 4.10   Adding a project to the current solution.

Table 4.2 shows some of the various project types supported in Visual Studio out of the box.

NOTE

Visual Studio supports the capability to create new project types and templates. Because Visual Studio is extensible in this fashion, the list of project types that you see in your particular copy of Visual Studio can vary greatly depending on the Visual Studio SKU you have installed, and any add-ins, extensions, or "Starter Kits" you have installed on your PC.

TABLE 4.2   Supported Project Types

Category	Project Type
Database	SQL Server 2005 Database Project
	SQL Server 2005 Server Project
	SQL Server 2005 Wizard
	SQL Server 2008 Database Project
	SQL Server 2008 Server Project
	SQL Server 2008 Wizard
	SQL Server Data-Tier Application
	Visual Basic SQL CLR Database Project
	Visual C# SQL CLR Database Project
Office	Excel Add-in
	Excel Template
	Excel Workbook
	InfoPath Add-in
	Outlook Add-in
	PowerPoint Add-in
	Project Add-in
	Visio Add-in
	Word Add-in
	Word Document
	Word Template
Test	Test Project

TABLE 4.2   Continued

Category	Project Type
Web	ASP.NET AJAX Server Control
	ASP.NET AJAX Server Control Extender
	ASP.NET Dynamic Data Entities Web Application
	ASP.NET Dynamic Data Linq to SQL Web Application
	ASP.NET Empty Web Application
	ASP.NET MVC 2 Empty Web Application
	ASP.NET MVC 2 Web Application
	ASP.NET Server Control
	ASP.NET Web Application
	ASP.NET Web Service Application
	Dynamic Data Entities Web Application
	Dynamic Data Linq to SQL Web Application
	WCF Service Application
Windows	Class Library
	Console Application
	Empty Project
	Windows Forms Application
	Windows Forms Control Library
	Windows Service
	WPF Application
	WPF Browser Application
	WPF Custom Control Library
	WPF User Control Library

NOTE

Visual Studio 2010 does not ship with any project templates for mobile or smart device development. Development options for phones and Windows CE devices will be made available as a separate download for Visual Studio 2010.

As outlined previously, creating a new project also creates a new containing solution. However, if you are creating a project and you already have a solution loaded in the IDE, the New Project dialog box offers you the opportunity to add the new project to the existing solution. Compare Figure 4.10 with Figure 4.2; notice that there is a new option in the form of a drop-down box that allows you to indicate whether Visual Studio should create a new solution or add the project to the current solution.

Website Projects

Developers have two different ways to create web projects within Visual Studio 2010: web application projects are created using the New Project dialog that we just discussed. Website projects are created in a slightly different fashion. Instead of selecting File, New, Project, you select File, New, Web Site. This launches the New Web Site dialog box (see Figure 4.11).

FIGURE 4.11   Creating a new website project.

As with other project types, you initiate website projects by selecting one of the predefined templates. In addition to the template, you also select a target source language and the location for the website. The location can be the file system, an HTTP site, or an FTP site. Unlike other project types, websites are not typically created within the physical folder tree that houses your solution. By default, even selecting the file system object places the resulting source files in a Web Sites folder under the Visual Studio 2010 projects folder.

> **NOTE**
>
> The *target source language* for a website project simply represents the default language used for any code files. It does not constrain the languages you can use within the project. For instance, a website project created with C# as the target language can still contain Visual Basic code files.

After you have created the website, you manage and maintain it just like the other project types within the IDE.

You might be wondering about the difference between a web application project and a website project. One key difference is the way that these two different project types are built. Web application projects use the same build model as the other .NET project types; that is, all the code in the project is compiled into a single assembly. Website projects, on the other hand, support a dynamic build model in which the code for a particular page is generated at runtime the first time a user hits the page. In this model, each page has its own assembly. There are many other differences between the two project types that we discuss in depth in Chapter 17 "Creating ASP.NET Applications."

Working with Project Definition Files

As with solutions, projects maintain their structure information inside a file. These files have different extensions depending on their underlying language. For instance, Visual Basic project files have a .vbproj extension, and Visual C# project files have a .csproj extension.

Each project definition file contains all the information necessary to describe the source files and the various project properties and options. This includes the following:

▶ Build configurations

▶ Project references and dependencies

▶ Source code file locations/types

Visual Basic and Visual C# project definition files are based on the same schema. Listing 4.2 contains a snippet from a Visual C# project definition file.

LISTING 4.2   Contents of a Visual C# Project Definition File

```
<Project DefaultTargets="Build" xmlns="http://schemas.microsoft.com/
➥developer/msbuild/2003" ToolsVersion="4.0">
  <PropertyGroup>
    <Configuration Condition=" '$(Configuration)' == '' ">Debug</Configuration>
    <Platform Condition=" '$(Platform)' == '' ">AnyCPU</Platform>
    <ProductVersion>10.0.20506</ProductVersion>
    <SchemaVersion>2.0</SchemaVersion>
```

```
    <ProjectGuid>{E22301F1-5AD6-4514-A05D-266158AB1CAB}</ProjectGuid>
    <OutputType>WinExe</OutputType>
    <AppDesignerFolder>Properties</AppDesignerFolder>
    <RootNamespace>WindowsApplication2</RootNamespace>
    <AssemblyName>WindowsApplication2</AssemblyName>
    <TargetFrameworkVersion>v2.0</TargetFrameworkVersion>
  </PropertyGroup>
  <PropertyGroup Condition=" '$(Configuration)¦$(Platform)' == 'Debug¦AnyCPU' ">
    <DebugSymbols>true</DebugSymbols>
    <DebugType>full</DebugType>
    <Optimize>false</Optimize>
    <OutputPath>bin\Debug\</OutputPath>
    <DefineConstants>DEBUG;TRACE</DefineConstants>
    <ErrorReport>prompt</ErrorReport>
    <WarningLevel>4</WarningLevel>
  </PropertyGroup>
  <PropertyGroup Condition=" '$(Configuration)¦$(Platform)' == 'Release¦AnyCPU' ">
    <DebugType>pdbonly</DebugType>
    <Optimize>true</Optimize>
    <OutputPath>bin\Release\</OutputPath>
    <DefineConstants>TRACE</DefineConstants>
    <ErrorReport>prompt</ErrorReport>
    <WarningLevel>4</WarningLevel>
  </PropertyGroup>
  <ItemGroup>
    <Reference Include="System" />
    <Reference Include="System.Data" />
    <Reference Include="System.Deployment" />
    <Reference Include="System.Drawing" />
    <Reference Include="System.Windows.Forms" />
    <Reference Include="System.Xml" />
  </ItemGroup>
  <ItemGroup>
    <Compile Include="Form1.cs">
      <SubType>Form</SubType>
    </Compile>
    <Compile Include="Form1.Designer.cs">
      <DependentUpon>Form1.cs</DependentUpon>
    </Compile>
    <Compile Include="Program.cs" />
    <Compile Include="Properties\AssemblyInfo.cs" />
    <EmbeddedResource Include="Properties\Resources.resx">
      <Generator>ResXFileCodeGenerator</Generator>
      <LastGenOutput>Resources.Designer.cs</LastGenOutput>
```

```
      <SubType>Designer</SubType>
    </EmbeddedResource>
    <Compile Include="Properties\Resources.Designer.cs">
      <AutoGen>True</AutoGen>
      <DependentUpon>Resources.resx</DependentUpon>
    </Compile>
    <None Include="Properties\Settings.settings">
      <Generator>SettingsSingleFileGenerator</Generator>
      <LastGenOutput>Settings.Designer.cs</LastGenOutput>
    </None>
    <Compile Include="Properties\Settings.Designer.cs">
      <AutoGen>True</AutoGen>
      <DependentUpon>Settings.settings</DependentUpon>
      <DesignTimeSharedInput>True</DesignTimeSharedInput>
    </Compile>
  </ItemGroup>
  <Import Project="$(MSBuildBinPath)\Microsoft.CSharp.targets" />
</Project>
```

This project definition file would look relatively the same as a Visual Basic project. Although we don't cover Visual C++ development in this book, you might be surprised to know that project definition files in Visual C++ use an entirely different schema. For completeness, and to contrast with the Visual Basic/Visual C# content, Listing 4.3 shows a sample Visual C++ project definition file in its entirety.

LISTING 4.3   Visual C++ Project Definition File

```
<?xml version="1.0" encoding="Windows-1252"?>
<VisualStudioProject
    ProjectType="Visual C++"
    Version="10.00"
    Name="Contoso.Fx.UI.BrowserShim"
    ProjectGUID="{BE574BF5-7FDA-46F2-A42E-4A35E5E338A0}"
    RootNamespace="ContosoFxUIBrowserShim"
    Keyword="MFCActiveXProj"
    SignManifests="true">
    <Platforms>
        <Platform Name="Win32" />
    </Platforms>
    <ToolFiles>
    </ToolFiles>
    <Configurations>
        <Configuration Name="Debug¦Win32" OutputDirectory="Debug"
            IntermediateDirectory="Debug" ConfigurationType="2"
```

```
    UseOfMFC="2" CharacterSet="1">
<Tool Name="VCPreBuildEventTool" />
<Tool Name="VCCustomBuildTool" />
<Tool Name="VCXMLDataGeneratorTool" />
<Tool Name="VCWebServiceProxyGeneratorTool" />
<Tool
    Name="VCMIDLTool"
    PreprocessorDefinitions="_DEBUG"
    MkTypLibCompatible="false"
    TypeLibraryName="$(IntDir)/$(ProjectName).tlb"
    HeaderFileName="$(ProjectName)idl.h"
    ValidateParameters="false"
/>
<Tool
    Name="VCCLCompilerTool"
    Optimization="0"
    PreprocessorDefinitions="WIN32;_WINDOWS;_DEBUG;_USRDLL"
    MinimalRebuild="true"
    BasicRuntimeChecks="3"
    RuntimeLibrary="3"
    TreatWChar_tAsBuiltInType="true"
    UsePrecompiledHeader="2"
    WarningLevel="3"
    Detect64BitPortabilityProblems="true"
    DebugInformationFormat="4"
/>
<Tool Name="VCManagedResourceCompilerTool" />
<Tool
    Name="VCResourceCompilerTool"
    PreprocessorDefinitions="_DEBUG"
    Culture="1033"
    AdditionalIncludeDirectories="$(IntDir)"
/>
<Tool Name="VCPreLinkEventTool" />
<Tool
    Name="VCLinkerTool"
    RegisterOutput="true"
    OutputFile="$(OutDir)\$(ProjectName).ocx"
    LinkIncremental="2"
    ModuleDefinitionFile=".\Contoso.Fx.UI.BrowserShim.def"
    GenerateDebugInformation="true"
    SubSystem="2"
    TargetMachine="1"
/>
<Tool Name="VCALinkTool" />
<Tool Name="VCManifestTool" />
```

```
    <Tool Name="VCXDCMakeTool" />
    <Tool Name="VCBscMakeTool" />
    <Tool Name="VCFxCopTool" />
    <Tool Name="VCAppVerifierTool" />
    <Tool Name="VCWebDeploymentTool" />
    <Tool Name="VCPostBuildEventTool" />
</Configuration>
<Configuration
    Name="Release¦Win32"
    OutputDirectory="Release"
    IntermediateDirectory="Release"
    ConfigurationType="2"
    UseOfMFC="2"
    CharacterSet="1"
    >
    <Tool Name="VCPreBuildEventTool" />
    <Tool Name="VCCustomBuildTool" />
    <Tool Name="VCXMLDataGeneratorTool" />
    <Tool Name="VCWebServiceProxyGeneratorTool" />
    <Tool
        Name="VCMIDLTool"
        PreprocessorDefinitions="NDEBUG"
        MkTypLibCompatible="false"
        TypeLibraryName="$(IntDir)/$(ProjectName).tlb"
        HeaderFileName="$(ProjectName)idl.h"
        ValidateParameters="false"
    />
    <Tool
        Name="VCCLCompilerTool"
        Optimization="2"
        PreprocessorDefinitions="WIN32;_WINDOWS;NDEBUG;_USRDLL"
        MinimalRebuild="false"
        RuntimeLibrary="2"
        TreatWChar_tAsBuiltInType="true"
        UsePrecompiledHeader="2"
        WarningLevel="3"
        Detect64BitPortabilityProblems="true"
        DebugInformationFormat="3"
    />
    <Tool Name="VCManagedResourceCompilerTool" />
    <Tool
        Name="VCResourceCompilerTool"
        PreprocessorDefinitions="NDEBUG"
        Culture="1033"
        AdditionalIncludeDirectories="$(IntDir)"
    />
```

4

```xml
            <Tool Name="VCPreLinkEventTool" />
            <Tool
                Name="VCLinkerTool"
                RegisterOutput="true"
                OutputFile="$(OutDir)\$(ProjectName).ocx"
                LinkIncremental="1"
                ModuleDefinitionFile=".\Contoso.Fx.UI.BrowserShim.def"
                GenerateDebugInformation="true"
                SubSystem="2"
                OptimizeReferences="2"
                EnableCOMDATFolding="2"
                TargetMachine="1"
            />
            <Tool Name="VCALinkTool" />
            <Tool Name="VCManifestTool" />
            <Tool Name="VCXDCMakeTool" />
            <Tool Name="VCBscMakeTool" />
            <Tool Name="VCFxCopTool" />
            <Tool Name="VCAppVerifierTool" />
            <Tool Name="VCWebDeploymentTool" />
            <Tool Name="VCPostBuildEventTool" />
        </Configuration>
    </Configurations>
    <References></References>
    <Files>
        <Filter Name="Source Files"
            Filter="cpp;c;cc;cxx;def;odl;idl;hpj;bat;asm;asmx"
            UniqueIdentifier="{4FC737F1-C7A5-4376-A066-2A32D752A2FF}">
            <File RelativePath=".\Contoso.Fx.UI.BrowserShim.cpp"></File>
            <File RelativePath=".\Contoso.Fx.UI.BrowserShim.def"></File>
            <File RelativePath=".\Contoso.Fx.UI.BrowserShim.idl"></File>
            <File RelativePath=".\Contoso.Fx.UI.BrowserShimCtrl.cpp">
            </File>
            <File RelativePath=".\Contoso.Fx.UI.BrowserShimPropPage.cpp">
            </File>
            <File RelativePath=".\stdafx.cpp">
                <FileConfiguration Name="Debug|Win32"      >
                    <Tool Name="VCCLCompilerTool"
                        UsePrecompiledHeader="1" />
                </FileConfiguration>
                <FileConfiguration Name="Release|Win32">
                    <Tool Name="VCCLCompilerTool"
                        UsePrecompiledHeader="1" />
                </FileConfiguration>
            </File>
        </Filter>
```

```
<Filter
    Name="Header Files"
    Filter="h;hpp;hxx;hm;inl;inc;xsd"
    UniqueIdentifier="{93995380-89BD-4b04-88EB-625FBE52EBFB}">
    <File RelativePath=".\Contoso.Fx.UI.BrowserShim.h"></File>
    <File RelativePath=".\Contoso.Fx.UI.BrowserShimCtrl.h"></File>
    <File RelativePath=".\Contoso.Fx.UI.BrowserShimPropPage.h">
    </File>
    <File RelativePath=".\Resource.h"></File>
    <File RelativePath=".\stdafx.h"></File>
</Filter>
<Filter Name="Resource Files"
Filter="rc;ico;cur;bmp;dlg;rc2;rct;bin;rgs;gif;jpg;jpeg;jpe;resx;tiff;tif;
➥png;wav"
    UniqueIdentifier="{67DA6AB6-F800-4c08-8B7A-83BB121AAD01}">
    <File RelativePath=".\Contoso.Fx.UI.BrowserShim.ico"></File>
    <File RelativePath=".\Contoso.Fx.UI.BrowserShim.rc"></File>
    <File RelativePath=".\Contoso.Fx.UI.BrowserShimCtrl.bmp"></File>
</Filter>
<File RelativePath=".\ReadMe.txt"></File>
</Files>
<Globals></Globals>
</VisualStudioProject>
```

Working with Projects

As source code containers, projects principally act as a settings applicator. They are used to control and organize your source code files and the various properties associated with the whole build and compile process (we cover the build process in depth in Chapter 11). As with solutions, projects can contain various different items that are germane to their development. Projects are language specific. You cannot mix different languages within a specific project. There is no similar limitation with solutions: A solution can contain many projects, each one in a different language.

Project Items

After a project is created, by default it contains one or more project items. These default items vary depending on the project template you selected and on the language of the project. For instance, creating a project using the C# Windows application template results in the formation of a Form1.cs file, a Form1.Designer.cs file, and a Program.cs file. Projects are also preconfigured with references and properties that make sense for the given project type: The Windows application template contains a reference to the System.Windows.Forms assembly, whereas the class library template does not.

NOTE

You might be wondering if you can create your own project templates for you and others to use. The answer is most definitely yes! We cover creating and distributing custom project templates in Chapter 7, "The .NET Community: Interacting Online."

Projects, like solutions, can also have subfolders within them that you can employ to better manage and group project items. Unlike solutions, the folders you create within a project are physical; they are created on disk within your project directory structure. These are examples of physical project items. Source code files are also physical in nature.

Projects can also contain virtual items—items that are merely pointers or links to items that don't actually manifest themselves physically within your project structure. They are, for example, references to other assemblies, database connections, and virtual folders (virtual folders are described in Chapter 5). Figure 4.12 illustrates a fully described solution and project.

FIGURE 4.12   Project structure.

Project Properties

Like solution properties, project properties are viewed and set using a series of property pages accessed through the Project, Properties menu. These property pages are hosted within a dialog box referred to as the Project Designer. Figure 4.13 shows the Project Designer that is displayed for a sample Visual Basic class library project. Different languages and different project types actually surface different property pages within the Project Designer. For instance, the Application property page for a Visual Basic project looks different and contains slightly different information than an identical Visual C# project (although the basic intent of the page remains unchanged).

In general, you use project properties to control the following:

▶ General project attributes such as the assembly name and project type

▶ The way that the project is built/compiled

▶ Debugger configuration for the project

▶ Resources used by the project

▶ Signing and security settings

FIGURE 4.13   Setting properties using the Project Designer.

4

> **NOTE**
>
> The project designer is also easily accessed from the Solution Explorer window. For C#
> projects, you can double-click on the Properties folder under the project. Visual Basic
> projects have a My Projects item that does the same thing. And, of course, you can
> always right-click on the project name and then select Properties from the pop-up menu.

Let's examine some of the more common project property pages and discuss briefly the
options that can be set on each.

Application   The Application property page allows you to set the assembly name,
root/default namespace, application/output type, and startup object. For Windows forms
applications, authentication modes and visual styles are also controlled via this property
page. Note that the options available in this dialog depend on the project type and the
chosen language.

- ▶ **Assembly Name**—This is the filename of the assembly that the project is compiled
  into. Typically, it defaults to the project name. The extension used is determined by
  the output type of the project.

- ▶ **Root/Default Namespace**—This specifies a namespace to be used by any types
  declared within the project. This can also be declared manually in code.

- ▶ **Output Type (C#)/Application Type (VB)**—This value determines the fundamental project type (for example, class library, Windows application, console
  application).

▶ **Startup Object**—This object is used to set the entry point for the project. For Windows applications, this is the default form (or in the case of C#, the program entry point for the form) that should be launched when the application is executed. For console applications, the startup object is the main subroutine procedure that implements the console. Class library projects do not have an entry point and will be set to (Not set) for C# projects, and (None) for VB projects.

▶ **Icon**—This is the icon to associate with the assembly. It is not pertinent to class library or web projects.

▶ **Resource File**—This text box can be used to specify a path and filename for a resource file. Resource files contain nonexecutable content, such as strings, images, or even persisted objects, that need to be deployed along with an application.

▶ **Visual Styles (VB)**—The Enable XP Visual Styles check box allows you to indicate whether the application supports XP themes when the user interface is rendered. This option is not applicable for non-Windows application projects.

▶ **Windows Application Framework Properties**—Visual Basic provides a series of properties that apply specifically to Windows application projects. These properties allow you to set the splash screen associated with the project, the authentication mode supported by the project (Windows or application-defined), and the shutdown mode of the project. The shutdown mode specifies whether the application should shut down when the initial form is closed or when the last loaded form in the application is closed.

Build (C# Only)   The Build property page is used with Visual C# projects to tweak settings associated with build configurations. Using this dialog box, you can select whether the DEBUG and TRACE constants are turned on, and you can specify conditional compilation symbols. Settings that affect the warning and error levels and the build output are also housed here. For more exploration of the options available here, see Chapter 10.

Build Events   Visual Studio triggers a pre- and post-build event for each project. On the Build Events page, you can specify commands that should be run during either of these events. This page also allows you to indicate when the post-build event runs: always, after a successful build, or when the build updates the project output. Build events are particularly useful for launching system tests and unit tests against a project that has just been recompiled. If you launch a suite of, say, unit tests from within the post-build event, the test cycle can be embedded within the build cycle.

NOTE

If you specify commands in the pre- or post-build events, Visual Studio creates a batch file for each event and places it into the bin/debug directory. These files, titled PreBuildEvent.bat and PostBuildEvent.bat, house the commands you enter on the Build Events property page. In the event of an error running the build event commands, you can manually inspect and run these files to try to chase down the bug.

Compile (VB Only)   The Compile property page is used by Visual Basic projects to control which optimizations are performed during compile and also to control general compilation options for the output path and warnings versus errors raised during the compilation process. It is analogous to the C# Build property page.

- ▶ **Compile Options**—You use the Option Strict, Option Explicit, and Option Infer drop-downs to turn on or off these settings. You can also control whether the project performs binary or text comparisons with the Option Compare drop-down.

- ▶ **Compiler Conditions**—Visual Basic allows you to customize the level of notification provided upon detecting any of a handful of conditions during the compilation process. For instance, one condition defined is Unused Local Variable. If this condition is detected in the source code during the compile, you can elect to have it treated as a warning or an error, or to have it ignored altogether.

- ▶ **Build Events**—Visual Basic allows you to access the Build Events property page (see the preceding section for an explanation) via a Build Events button located on this screen.

- ▶ **Advanced Compile Options**—You can choose to disable all compiler warnings, treat all warnings as errors, and generate an XML documentation file during the compile process. This results in an XML file with the same name as the project; it contains all the code comments parsed out of your source code in a predefined format.

Debug   The Debug property page allows you to affect the behavior of the Visual Studio debugger.

- ▶ **Start Action**—You use this option to specify whether a custom program, a URL, or the current project itself should be started when the debugger is launched.

- ▶ **Start Options**—You use this option to specify command-line arguments to pass to the running project, set the working directory for the project, and debug a process on a remote machine.

- ▶ **Enable Debuggers**—You use the check boxes in this section to enable or disable such things as support for debugging unmanaged code, support for SQL stored procedure debugging, and use of Visual Studio as a host for the debugger process.

Publish   The Publish property page enables you to configure many ClickOnce-specific properties. You can specify the publish location for the application, the install location (if different from the publish location), and the various installation settings, including prerequisites and update options. You can also control the versioning scheme for the published assemblies.

References (VB Only)   The References property page is used within Visual Basic projects to select the assemblies referenced by the project and to import namespaces into the project.

This screen also allows you to query the project in an attempt to determine whether some existing references are unused. You do this by using the Unused References button.

Reference Paths (Visual C#)   The Reference Paths property page allows you to provide path information meant to help Visual Studio find assemblies referenced by the project. Visual Studio first attempts to resolve assembly references by looking in the current project directory. If the assembly is not found there, the paths provided on this property page are used to search for the assemblies. Visual Studio also probes the project's `obj` directory, but only after attempting to resolve first using the reference paths you have specified on this screen.

Resources   Resources are items such as strings, images, icons, audio, and files that are embedded in a project and used during design and runtime. The Resources property page allows you to add, edit, and delete resources associated with the project.

Security   For ClickOnce applications, the Security property page allows you to enforce code access security permissions for running the ClickOnce application. Various full-trust and partial-trust scenarios are supported.

Settings   Application settings are dynamically specified name/value pairs that can be used to store information specific to your project/application. The Settings property page allows you to add, edit, and delete these name/value pairs.

Each setting can be automatically scoped to the application or to the user, and can have a default value specified. Applications can then consume these settings at runtime.

Signing   The Signing property page allows you to have Visual Studio code sign the project assembly—and its ClickOnce manifests—by specifying a key file. You can also enable Delay signing from this screen.

Summary

Solutions and projects are the primary vehicles within Visual Studio for organizing and managing your code. They allow you to divide and conquer large solutions, and they provide a single point of access for various settings (at both the solution and project levels). Solutions are the top-level container, and the first work item that Visual Studio creates when creating a new code project.

To summarize what we have learned about solutions:

▶ Solutions can be built (triggering a build of each of its projects) but cannot be compiled.

▶ Visual Studio can load only one solution at a time; to work on multiple solutions concurrently, you must have multiple copies of Visual Studio running.

▶ You can create folders within a solution to help group its content; these folders are virtual and do not represent physical file folders.

▶ Solutions are primarily used to group one or more projects together. Projects within a solution can be a mix of the various supported languages and project types.

▶ Solutions cannot contain other solutions.

▶ Besides projects, solutions can also contain miscellaneous files (called solution items) that typically represent information pertinent to the solution (readme files, system diagrams, and the like).

Although solutions are an important and necessary implement, it is the Visual Studio project that actually results in a compiled .NET component. Projects are created and based on templates available within the IDE that cover the various development scenarios, ranging from web application development to Windows application development to smart device development.

To summarize what we have learned about projects:

▶ Projects exist to compile code into assemblies.

▶ Projects are based on a project template; project templates define the various artifacts, references, and so on that make sense for the project's context.

▶ Like solutions, projects also support subfolders to help you better organize your code. These folders are actual, physical folders that are created on disk.

▶ Projects contain project items. They can be source code files, references, and other items such as virtual folders and database connections.

We have seen how solutions and projects are physically manifested; in the next chapter, we cover the primary Visual Studio tools used to interact with solutions and projects.

Browsers and Explorers

Visual Studio provides a cohesive and all-encompassing view of your solutions, projects, and types within your projects through windows called browsers and explorers. These windows (which are confusingly also referred to as view windows) attempt to provide a visually structured representation of a large variety of elements—some code-based, others not.

In general, you access and display these windows through the View menu. Some of these windows, such as the Solution Explorer and Class View, are staples of a developer's daily routine. Others touch on elements that are used during specific points within the development cycle or by more advanced Visual Studio IDE users.

In this chapter, we examine each of the basic browser and explorer windows in detail.

Solution Explorer

The Solution Explorer is the primary tool for viewing and manipulating solutions and projects. It provides a simple but powerful hierarchical view of all solution and project items, and it enables you to interact with each item directly via context menus and its toolbar.

Using Solution Explorer, you can launch an editor for any given file, add new items to a project or solution, and reorganize the structure of a project or solution. In addition, the Solution Explorer provides instant, at-a-glance information as to the currently selected project; the startup project for the solution; and the physical hierarchy of the solution, its projects, and their child items.

The Solution Explorer is simply a window hosted by Visual Studio. It can be docked, pinned, and floated anywhere within the Visual Studio environment. It is composed of a title bar, a toolbar, and a scrollable tree-view region (see Figure 5.1).

The tree view provides a graphics- and text-organizational view of the currently loaded solution. Figure 5.1 shows all the various items and projects represented for a fourteen-project solution loaded in the IDE.

FIGURE 5.1   The Solution Explorer.

Visual Cues and Icons

Each item in the Solution Explorer is represented by a name and by an icon. Table 5.1 summarizes which icon is used to represent the supported item types.

TABLE 5.1   Solution Explorer Item Types and Icons

Icon	Item	Notes
	About Box	Visual Basic only.
	Application Diagram	
	ASP.NET Web Site	This represents the root node for an ASP.NET website project.
	Bitmap File	
	Class Diagram	

TABLE 5.1   Continued

Icon	Item	Notes
	Component Class	
	Custom Control	
	DataSet	
	Dialog	Visual Basic only.
	Folder	Solution folders or project folders.
	Global Application Class	
	HTML Page	
	Icon File	
	Interface (Visual Basic)	
	Interface (Visual C#)	
	Logical Datacenter Diagram	
	Master Page	Web projects only.
	Module	Visual Basic only.
	My Project File	Visual Basic equivalent to the C# Properties folder.
	Partial Class	
	Project Reference	Visual C# only.
	Properties Folder	Visual C# equivalent to the Visual Basic My Project File folder.
	References Folder	Visual C# only.
	Resources Folder	
	Settings Folder	

TABLE 5.1   Continued

Icon	Item	Notes
	Site Map	Web projects only.
	Skin File	Web projects only.
	Solution	This is the topmost, root node visible within Solution Explorer.
	Style Sheet	
	System Diagram	
	Text File	
	User Control	Any class that inherits directly from the UserControl class.
	User Control (Web)	Class that inherits from TODO.
	VBScript/JScript File	
	Visual Basic Class File	
	Visual Basic Project	This is the root node for a Visual Basic project.
	Visual C# Project	This is the root node for a Visual C# project.
	Visual C# Class File	
	Web Configuration File	
	Web Form (.aspx)	
	Web Project	
	Web Service	
	Windows Form	Refers to a file containing a class that implements the Form class.
	Windows Form (Inherited)	
	Windows Form (MDI Parent)	Visual Basic only.

TABLE 5.1   Continued

Icon	Item	Notes
	XML File	
	XML Schema File	
	XSLT File	

NOTE

The icons shown in Table 5.1 are a representative list of icons that correspond to specific project and solution items within the IDE. Other files added to a project or solution are represented by the icon associated with their file types. For example, a Word document is represented by the standard Word document icon in the Solution Explorer.

Signal Icons

To provide a visual cue about the status of a particular item, the Solution Explorer overlays an additional graphical element on the item icon. These overlays are called signal icons. For example, when source code control is enabled, the Solution Explorer visually indicates whether an item is checked out via a graphical overlay. Table 5.2 describes the version control signal icons used by the Solution Explorer to indicate the current version control status of the item. Note that the version control state of an item is dependent on the actual version control system you are using (for instance, Visual Source Safe or Team Foundation Source Control).

TABLE 5.2   Version Control Signal Icons

Icon	Description
	Item not found. The item was specified as part of the solution/project, but can't be located.
	Checked in. The item is under source code control and is currently checked in.
	Checked out (exclusive). The item is under source code control and is currently checked out exclusively.
	Checked out (shared). The item is under source code control and is currently checked out in a shared mode.
	Disabled. The item is located within a project that is under source control, but this item could not be added to source control.
	Editable. The item is available for editing.
	Excluded. The item has been specifically excluded from version control.

TABLE 5.2   Continued

Icon	Description
	Orphaned. The item has been orphaned within the version control system because one or more dependency links have been broken.
	Pending Add. The item is scheduled to be added to the source control system during the next check-in.
	Read Only. The item is not available for editing (this is the opposite of Editable).

The Solution Explorer supports different management actions depending on whether you are currently interacting with a solution or a project. In fact, supported commands might vary by project type as well. As an example, the Copy Web Project command button is available for web projects but not class library projects, whereas the Properties command button is available for all item types.

Table 5.3 shows the various toolbar command buttons supported by the Solution Explorer, along with their specific context.

TABLE 5.3   Solution Explorer Toolbar Buttons

Icon	Context	Description
	All	Properties button. Launches the solution properties dialog.
	Solution, solution item, solution folder	Add New Solution Folder button. Creates a new solution folder in the currently loaded solution.
	Project, project item	Refresh. Refreshes the solution explorer's tree view of the project.
	Web project, web project item	Nest Related Files. Visual Studio has the capability to group certain project item constructs together. This is most commonly done with items such as code behind files. This is a toggle button: Clicking it "on" causes related files to be nested underneath the "parent" file. Clicking it "off" causes all files to show up at the same level under the project.
	Project, project item	View Class Diagram. Creates a class diagram project item and launches the viewer for that item. All the types contained within the project will be automatically added to the diagram.
	Web project, web project item	Copy Web Site. Copies the website to a specified location (available only for web projects).

TABLE 5.3   Continued

Icon	Context	Description
	Web project, web project item	ASP.NET Configuration. Launches a browser to the ASP.NET Web Site Administration tool. This is useful for setting up global security parameters and application-specific options.
	Solution, solution item, project, project item (only if items in the solution are currently hidden)	Unhide All. Unhides any hidden items in the solution.
	Project code files	View Code. Opens the current item in the code editor.
	Project code files with a UI (Windows Form or Web Form)	View Designer. Opens the designer for the currently selected item.

Managing Solutions

Clicking on the solution in Solution Explorer immediately exposes all the valid management commands for that solution. You access these commands through either the Solution Explorer toolbar or the context menu for the solution (which you access by right-clicking on the solution). Through the toolbar and the solution's context menu, the Solution Explorer allows you to do the following:

▶ View and set the properties for a solution

▶ Build/rebuild a solution

▶ Directly launch the configuration manager for a solution

▶ Set project dependencies and build order

▶ Add any of the various Visual Studio–supported solution and project items

▶ Add the solution to the source control

You can initiate some of these actions by using the Solution Explorer toolbar; you can access the balance in the context menu for a solution, as shown in Figure 5.2.

FIGURE 5.2   The solution context menu.

Managing Projects

Just as with solutions, Solution Explorer provides various ways to manage projects within a solution. They include these:

- ▶ Opening a project item
- ▶ Building or rebuilding a project
- ▶ Adding items to a project
- ▶ Adding a reference to a project
- ▶ Cutting, pasting, renaming, or deleting a project within the solution tree
- ▶ Unloading a project

> **NOTE**
>
> The current startup project for a solution is indicated with a bold font (as is the OrderEntry project in Figure 5.1). If multiple projects are selected as startup projects, the solution name is instead bolded.

The default action when you double-click an item is to open it within its default editor or designer. Multiple select and drag-and-drop operations are also supported. For instance, multiselecting several code files allows you to open them simultaneously in their editor windows.

You can move and copy items within a solution, within a project, or between projects through the standard drag and drop using the left mouse button. You can also drag certain items from within a project and drop them onto a suitable designer surface. This is an easy way, for instance, to add classes to a class diagram: Simply highlight the code files that contain the types you want to add and drag them onto the class diagram designer window.

Class View

The Class View window is similar in design and function to the Solution Explorer window. It, too, provides a hierarchical view of project elements. However, the view here is not based on the physical files that constitute a solution or project; rather, this window provides a view of the various namespaces, types, interfaces, and enums within a project.

The Class View window is composed of four major visual components: a toolbar, a search bar, a tree view of types (called the Objects pane), and a members pane, as shown in Figure 5.3.

Toolbar

The Class View window's toolbar provides easy access to command buttons for adding virtual folders, moving forward and back through the Objects pane items, and controlling which objects are displayed.

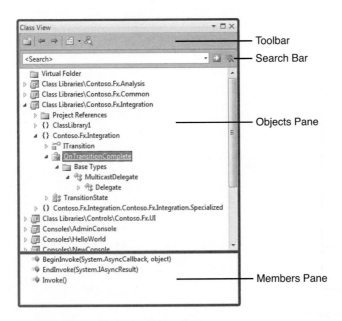

FIGURE 5.3   The Class View window.

Table 5.4 describes the various Class View toolbar buttons.

TABLE 5.4   Class View Toolbar Buttons

Icon	Description
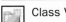	Class View New Folder. Creates a virtual folder used to organize objects within the Objects pane.
	Back. Causes the previously selected item to become the currently selected item.
	Forward. Causes the most recently selected item to become the currently selected item. This button is available only after you've used the Back button.
	Class View Settings. Displays a drop-down that allows selection of object types to display within the Objects pane and the members pane. The available options include these: Show Base Types, Show Derived Types, Show Project References, Show Hidden Types and References, Show Public Members, Show Protected Members, Show Private Members, Show Other Members, Show Inherited Members.
	View Class Diagram. Creates a class diagram project item and launches the viewer for that item. All the types contained within the project are automatically added to the diagram.

Search Bar

The search bar is a drop-down text box that provides a quick and easy way to filter the objects shown in the Objects pane. When a search term (such as type name or namespace name) is entered, the Class View window clears the Objects pane and then repopulates it with only those objects that match the search term. Figure 5.4 shows the results of a search for ITransition.

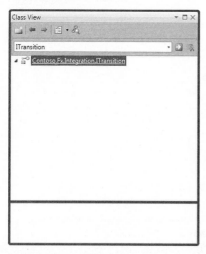

FIGURE 5.4   Filtering the Objects pane.

To restore the Objects pane and remove the filter, click on the Clear Search button to the right of the Search button.

Recent search terms are saved for reuse in the drop-down list.

Objects Pane

The Objects pane encloses a tree of objects grouped, at the highest level, by project. Each object is identified by an icon and by its name. Expanding a project node within the tree reveals the various types contained within that project. Further parent-child relationships are also visible, such as the namespace-to-class relationship and the type-to-parent-type relationship.

Table 5.5 shows the icons used in the Objects pane.

TABLE 5.5   Objects Pane Icons

Icon	Description
	Class/Struct
	Delegate
	Enum
	Namespace
	Module
	Interface

Certain signal images are also overlaid on top of these icons to visually represent scope and access information for each object. These access type signal icons are shown in Table 5.6.

TABLE 5.6   Scope/Access Signal Icons

Icon	Description
🔒	Private
🔲	Internal/Friend
(n/a)	Public
🔑	Protected

The depth of the various levels shown for each object is dictated by the view settings in place at the time. For example, turning on the Show Base Types option appends an additional base type level to the tree for each type. The Objects pane's principal duty is to allow quick and easy navigation back and forth through the object tree for each project. It exposes, in other words, an object-oriented view of each project.

Right-clicking within the Objects pane displays the shortcut menu. The menu is essentially identical to the shortcut menu exposed by the Solution Explorer, with the exception of various Sort and Group By selections. These are the Sort options available:

- ▶ **Sort Alphabetically**—The projects, namespaces, and types in the Objects pane are sorted in ascending, alphabetic order.

- ▶ **Sort by Object Type**—The types in the Objects pane are alphabetically sorted by their general classification (for example, in the following order: classes, enums, interfaces, structs).

- ▶ **Sort by Object Access**—The types are sorted by their access modifiers (public, private, protected, and so on).

- ▶ **Group by Object Type**—Another folder level is added to the tree for each distinct object type present. For example, if a project contains both class and interface types, a class folder and an interface folder are displayed in the Objects pane tree, with their correlated types contained within.

Members Pane

The Members pane reacts to the selection(s) made in the Objects pane by displaying all the members—properties, events, constants, variables, enums—defined on the selected type. Each member has a distinctive icon to immediately convey information such as scope and type; even member signatures show up here (note that the same signal icons used by the Objects pane, and documented in Table 5.7, are used here as well).

TABLE 5.7   Members Pane Icons

Icon	Description
	Constant
	Method/Function
	Property
	Field

The Members pane is ideal for quickly visualizing type behavior and attributes: Just select the class/type in the Objects pane and browse its members in the Members pane.

> **NOTE**
>
> Many developers find that the bulk of their development tasks are more easily envisioned and acted on within the Class View window rather than in the Solution Explorer window. The available actions among the two are virtually identical, but the Class View window provides a much more code-focused perspective of your projects. Developers can spelunk through inheritance trees and see, at a glance, other various members implemented on each defined type within their projects. The downside to using the Class View is that source code control information is not visually surfaced here.

The Members pane also exposes a context menu that has invaluable tools for browsing and editing code. For one, you can directly apply the Rename refactoring to a selected member. Other capabilities exposed here include the capability to immediately view the definition code for a member, to find every code location where the selected member is referenced, and to launch the Object Browser with the primary node for the member already selected for you.

The capability to alter the filter and display settings is also presented here. Figure 5.5 illustrates all the available commands on this menu.

Server Explorer

The Server Explorer window serves two purposes: It exposes various system services and resources that reside on your local machine and on remote machines, and it provides access to data connection objects. As with the other Visual Studio explorer windows, the systems, services, resources, and data connections are viewed in a graphical tree format. Systems appear under a top-level Servers node (your local machine shows up by default), and data connections appear under a top-level Data Connections node.

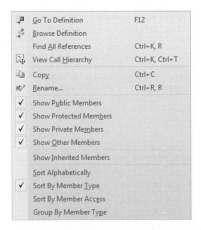

Go To Definition	F12	
Browse Definition		
Find All References	Ctrl+K, R	
View Call Hierarchy	Ctrl+K, Ctrl+T	
Copy	Ctrl+C	
Rename...	Ctrl+R, R	
✓ Show Public Members		
✓ Show Protected Members		
✓ Show Private Members		
✓ Show Other Members		
Show Inherited Members		
Sort Alphabetically		
✓ Sort By Member Type		
Sort By Member Access		
Group By Member Type		

FIGURE 5.5   The Members pane context menu.

NOTE

The Server Explorer window content and configuration are not specific to a solution or project. Server Explorer settings are preserved as part of the IDE environment settings and are thus not subject to change on a per-solution (or project) basis.

A toolbar appears at the top of the Server Explorer window, providing one-click access to the Add Data Connection and Add Server functions (see Figure 5.6). You can also force a refresh of the window contents (a button is also provided to cancel the refresh because querying remote machines might be a lengthy process).

NOTE

The Express and Standard editions of Visual Studio do not have support for servers within the Server Explorer window; they are limited to data connections only. In fact, these versions of Visual Studio actually refer to this window as the Data Explorer window.

Data Connections

Data Connections represent a physical connection to a local or remote database. Through an established connection, you can gain access to and manipulate the various objects within a database. Each category of object shows up as a folder node under the Data Connections node. The tree items under each node allow you to directly interact with their physical database counterparts through a suite of designers and editors collectively referred to as Visual Database Tools. These tools are covered in depth in Chapter 21, "Working with Databases."

FIGURE 5.6   The Server Explorer window.

The following objects are exposed in the Server Explorer:

▶ Data Diagrams

▶ Tables

▶ Views

▶ Stored procedures

▶ Functions

▶ Synonyms

▶ Types

▶ Assemblies

In general, you can create new database objects, edit or delete existing ones, and, where appropriate, query data from a database object (such as a table or view).

NOTE

The level of functionality and the number of object types you can access through the Server Explorer depend on both the version of Visual Studio you are using and the version of the database you are connecting to. In other words, not all functions are supported across all databases. The Visual Database Tools interact most effectively with Microsoft SQL Server, although most basic functions are supported against a variety of other relational databases.

Server Components

The Servers node in Server Explorer exposes various remote or local services and resources for direct management or use within a Visual Studio project. In essence, it is a management console for server-based components. By default, your local machine is visible here as a server; to add other servers, right-click on the Servers node and select Add Server or click on the Connect to Server button in the Server Explorer toolbar. A dialog box prompts you for a computer name or IP address for the server; this dialog box also supports the capability to connect via a different set of credentials.

Under the Servers node, the following component categories appear as child nodes:

- Event Logs
- Management Classes
- Management Events
- Message Queues
- Performance Counters
- Services

Other component categories might also choose to register for display under the Servers node; the preceding list, however, represents the default, out-of-the-box functionality provided by Visual Studio 2010.

Event Logs

Under the Event Logs node, you can administer the separate application, security, and system event logs for the connected server. This includes clearing event log entries or drilling into and inspecting individual event log entries. Highlighting an event log or event log entry causes its properties to display in the Visual Studio property window, enabling you to view and edit their values. If you drag and drop one of the event logs into a project, a System.Diagnostics.EventLog or System.Diagnostic.EventLogEntry component instance is automatically created.

Management Classes

The items under the Management Classes node represent various Windows Management Instrumentation (WMI) classes. Each of these classes maps to a logical or physical entity associated with a server. The available classes here are shown in Table 5.8.

TABLE 5.8   WMI Management Class Nodes

Title	WMI Class
Desktop Settings	Win32_Desktop
Disk Volumes	Win32_LogicalDisk
My Computer	Win32_ComputerSystem

TABLE 5.8   Continued

Title	WMI Class
Network Adapters	Win32_NetworkAdapter
Network Connections	Win32_NetworkConnection
NT Event Log Files	Win32_NTEventLogFile
Operating Systems	Win32_OperatingSystem
Printers	Win32_Printer
Processes	Win32_Process
Processors	Win32_Processor
Services	Win32_Service
Shares	Win32_Share
Software Products	Win32_Product
System Accounts	Win32_SystemAccount
Threads	Win32_Thread

A thorough discussion of WMI is beyond the scope of this chapter and this book; in summary, however, each of these nodes exposes various WMI class property groups (such as precedents, antecedents, settings, dependents), and, in turn, each of these property groups exposes a span of commands, enabling you to directly affect a resource on the server. One simple example of how you might use this capability is to set access information for a share exposed on a remote server. When you expand nodes in the Server Explorer down to the share (via the Disk Volumes node), access to the share information is gained via the shortcut menu on the share. In this example, you would select the SetShareInfo action, which initiates a WMI dialog box allowing you to change various share attributes such as the description and maximum allowed users.

Management Events
The Management Events node contains a list of event queries; essentially, these are "listeners" that you establish to periodically poll the WMI eventing system on the server. These event queries are established through a dialog box (see Figure 5.7; you launch the dialog box by selecting Add Event Query on the shortcut menu). When an event is created, a child node to the Management Events node is created, and under this node, actual event instances appear.

Message Queues
If message queuing is installed on the target server, the Message Queues node displays all the available message queues, along with any messages currently residing in each queue.

Performance Counters
Every performance counter installed on the target computer can be viewed in the Performance Counters node. Each performance counter is displayed within its category. Performance counter instances, if available, are also displayed.

FIGURE 5.7   Creating a Management Event query.

Services

Each installed service is enumerated under the Services node.

Programming with Server Explorer

Beyond allowing you to examine and manipulate data connections and server resources, the Server Explorer serves another task: By dragging and dropping items from the Server Explorer onto a Visual Studio design surface, you can quickly create components in code that directly reference the item in question. As an example, dragging the Application Log node (from Servers, Event Logs) onto an existing Windows form creates a System.Diagnostics.EventLog component instance that is preconfigured to point to the application log. You can then immediately write code to interact with the event log component. You could use the same process to quickly embed message queue access into your application or read from/write to a performance counter. Table 5.9 lists the various possible drag-and-drop operations, along with their results.

TABLE 5.9   Server Explorer Drag and Drop

Under This Node...	Dragging This...	Does This
Event Logs	Event Log Category (e.g., Application or System)	Creates a System.Diagnostics.EventLog component instance, configured for the appropriate event log

TABLE 5.9   Continued

Under This Node...	Dragging This...	Does This
Management Classes	Management Class instance	Creates the appropriate WMI/CIMv2 component instance
Management Events	Management Event Query	Creates a System.Management.ManagementEventWatcher component instance
Message Queues	Message Queue instance	Creates a System.Messaging.MessageQueue component instance for the selected queue
Performance Counters	Performance Counter or counter instance	Creates a System.Diagnostics.PerformanceCounter component instance, configured for he appropriate counter
Services	Service	Creates a System.ServiceProcess.ServiceController, provisioned for the indicated service

NOTE

Data connection items in the Server Explorer cannot be dragged onto a design surface. For more information regarding drag-and-drop development of database solutions, see Chapter 21.

Object Browser

The Object Browser is similar in functionality and look and feel to the Class View window. It provides a hierarchical view of projects, assemblies, namespaces, types, enums, and interfaces. Unlike the Class View window, however, the Object Browser is capable of a much wider scope of objects. In addition to the currently loaded projects, the Object Browser is capable of displaying items from the entire .NET Framework, up to and including COM components and externally accessible objects. This is a great tool for finding and inspecting types, regardless of where they are physically located.

Changing the Scope

You can use the toolbar's Browse drop-down to filter or change the scope of the objects displayed within the Object Browser. The scoping options offered are shown in Table 5.10.

TABLE 5.10   Object Browser Scoping Options

Scope	Effect
All Components	This is a superset of the other scopes offered. Selecting this shows all types and members within the .NET Framework, the current solution, any libraries referenced by the current solution, and any individually selected components.

TABLE 5.10   Continued

Scope	Effect
.NET Framework	Shows all objects within a specific version of the .NET Framework (for example, .NET Framework 2.0, .NET Framework 3.0).
My Solution	Shows all objects with the currently loaded solution, including any referenced components.
Custom Component Set	Shows any objects specifically added to the custom component set.

Editing the Custom Component Set

A custom component set is a list of components that you manually specify. Using a custom list might be useful in situations in which you want to browse a list of components from a variety of different "buckets." Instead of wading through each of the other scopes, you could include only those types that you care about in the component list.

You add to the custom component list by selecting the Edit Custom Component Set option in the Browse drop-down or by clicking on the ellipsis to the right of the drop-down. This launches an editor dialog box in which you can add or remove entries in this list (see Figure 5.8).

FIGURE 5.8   Editing the custom component set.

Adding a component to the set is as easy as selecting from one of the pre-populated object lists (available via the .NET, COM, or Projects tabs) or by browsing directly to the container assembly via the Browse tab. You can select an object or objects and then click the Add button. The current set members show up at the bottom of the dialog box. You can also select a current member and remove it from the list by clicking the Remove button.

Browsing Objects

The Object Browser consists of a toolbar and three different panes: an Objects pane, a members pane, and a description pane. Again, the similarity here to the Class View window is obvious. The toolbar, Objects pane, and members pane function identically to the Class View Objects pane and members pane. You click down through the tree view to view each individual object's members; the toolbar aids in navigating deep trees by providing a Forward and Back button. Figure 5.9 shows the Object Browser in action.

FIGURE 5.9   The Object Browser.

The hierarchical relationships, icons, and actions possible within the panes are the same (and therefore we won't rehash them here). The description pane, however, is a new concept.

Description Pane

When an item is selected in either the Object Browser's Objects pane or members pane, the description pane provides detailed information about the selected item. The data provided is quite extensive, and includes the following:

- ▶ The name of the selected object

- ▶ The name of the parent of the selected object

- ▶ Code comments and in-line help associated with the selected object

Where possible, the description pane will embed hyperlinks within the data that it displays to allow you to easily navigate to related items. As an example, a declared property of type string might show the following description:

```
public string SystemContextId { set; get; }
    Member of Contoso.Fx.Integration.ContextToken
```

Note the use of hyperlinking: Clicking on the string identifier navigates to the string data type within the Object Browser window. Similarly, clicking on the Contoso.Fx.Integration.ContextToken hyperlink navigates the browser to the class definition for the ContextToken class.

> **TIP**
>
> You can click on an assembly in the Objects pane and quickly add it as a reference to the current project by clicking on the Add to References button, located on the Object Browser's toolbar.

Document Outline

The Document Outline window (opened from the View, Other Windows menu) exposes a hierarchical view of elements residing on a Windows form, a web form, or a WPF window. This is a fantastic tool for "re-parenting" form items or changing the z-order of a control within its parent. In addition, it assists with understanding the exact logical structure of a form that might have a lot happening on it from a visual perspective.

Figures 5.10 and 5.11 show the Document Outline windows for a simple web form and a slightly more complicated WPF window.

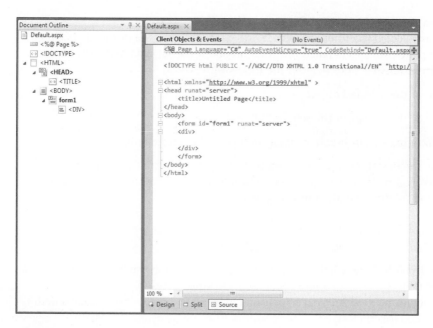

FIGURE 5.10   A web form.

FIGURE 5.11   A WPF form.

The Document Outline toolbar allows you to control the display of the types within the tree view and also facilitates reordering and repositioning elements within the outline.

Editing Elements

The Document Outline makes it easy to instantly jump from the hierarchical element view directly to the underlying code for an item. If an item is currently being edited in the designer/code window, it is highlighted within the outline tree. Conversely, selecting an item within the outline view causes the item to be selected/highlighted within the designer/code window. Each project type has slightly different behavior within the Document Outline tool. In general, you can use drag-and-drop actions within the tree view to move elements around in the outline. Windows Forms applications actually have a toolbar you can use within the Document Outline window (see Table 5.11 for a description of the toolbar buttons).

TABLE 5.11   Windows Forms Document Outline Toolbar Commands

Icon	Description
	Type Name Display Style. This drop-down button allows you to control how type names are displayed in the tree view: None—No type names are displayed. Short—The local, unqualified type name is displayed. Long—The fully qualified type name is displayed.
	Expand All. Causes all the parent nodes to expand.
	Collapse All. Causes all the parent nodes to collapse.
	Move Down in Container. Moves the currently selected item down one place within its order in the current container.
	Move Up in Container. Moves the currently selected item up one place within its order in the current container.
	Move Out of Current Container. Moves the currently selected item out of its current container and places it in the next, higher container (or within the root level if no container exists).
	Move into Next Container. Moves the currently selected item out of its current container (or root level) and into the next container.

5

Summary

In this chapter, we have seen that browsers and explorers are Visual Studio windows that typically provide a hierarchical view of their content. They tend to share common interface elements (tree views, toolbars, and elements), and they are, in effect, the primary means for visualizing and interacting with project elements within the IDE.

Browsers and explorers provide simple point-and-click interfaces for

- ▶ Visualizing and organizing your solutions and projects on a file-by-file basis.

- ▶ Visualizing and organizing your projects on a type-by-type, class-by-class basis.

- ▶ Querying and interacting with server resources such as databases, performance counters, and message queues.

- ▶ Browsing through type libraries.

Although certain browsers/explorers touch underlying concepts that are fairly deep and complicated (WMI, for instance), they are all geared toward a common goal: extending the reach of the IDE as a rapid application development tool for tasks beyond simple code file editing.

CHAPTER 6

Introducing the Editors and Designers

Although Visual Studio provides an impressive array of functionality for nearly all areas of the development process, its editors and designers are the real heart of the IDE. They are the bread-and-butter tools of the programmer: They enable you to write code, edit resources, design forms, and construct schemas. And, of course, each of these tools has key features designed to boost your productivity and the quality of your output.

This chapter is squarely focused on using these editors and designers to create solutions within the IDE.

The Basics

Broadly speaking, a Visual Studio editor is a text editor (think word processor) that enables you to write specific output efficiently (Visual Basic code, HTML, XAML, and so on). A designer, on the other hand, is a visual editor, enabling you to work with visual concepts directly instead of text. Many document types are supported by both designers and editors: You can build a form, for instance, by using the drag-and-drop convenience of the Windows Forms designer or by handcrafting the code within a text editor; or you can build an XML file using the same mechanisms.

The Visual Studio text editor provides the core text-editing functionality for all the editors. This functionality is then inherited and added upon to create editors specific for a given document type. Thus, you have a code editor for source code files, an XML editor for markup, a CSS editor for style sheets, and so on.

Likewise, designers manifest themselves in ways specific to their roles. The HTML designer is part text editor and part graphical tool, and the Windows and web forms designers are superb WYSIWYG form builders.

The Text Editor

There are a few text-editing features that we all take for granted: selecting parts of an existing body of text, inserting text into a document, copying and pasting text, and so on. As you would expect, the text editor window supports all of these features in a way that is familiar to anyone who has used a Windows-based word processor.

You select text, for instance, by using the following familiar actions:

1. Place the cursor at the start of the text you want to select.
2. While holding down the left mouse button, sweep the mouse to the end of the text you want to select.
3. Release the left mouse button.

In addition to this "standard" selection method, the Visual Studio text editor supports "column mode" selection. In column mode, instead of selecting text in a linear fashion from left to right, line-by-line, you drag a selection rectangle across a text field. Any text character caught within the selection rectangle is part of the selected text. This is called column mode because it allows you to create a selection area that captures columns of text characters instead of just lines. The procedure is largely the same:

1. Place the cursor at the start of the text you want to select.
2. While holding down the Alt key *and* the left mouse button, expand the bounds of the selection rectangle until it includes the desired text.
3. Release the left mouse button and the Alt key.

After you've selected text, you can copy, cut, or drag it to a new location within the text editor. As with text selection, the commands for cutting, copying, and pasting text remain unchanged from their basic, standard implementations in other Windows applications: You first select text and then cut or copy it using the Edit menu, the toolbar, or the text editor's shortcut menu.

By dragging a text selection, you can reposition it within the current text editor; place it in another, previously opened text editor window; or even drag the selection into the command or watch windows.

Line Wrapping and Virtual Space

The default behavior of the text editor is not to automatically wrap any text for you. In other words, as you type, your text or code simply keeps trailing on to the right of the editor. If you exceed the bounds of the currently viewable area, the editor window scrolls to the right to allow you to continue typing. However, the text editor window can behave more like a word processor, in which the document content is typically constrained horizontally to its virtual sheet of paper.

> **TIP**
>
> With word wrapping turned on, Visual Studio automatically wraps your text onto the next line. You can also have the IDE place a visual glyph to indicate that a wrap has taken place. Both of these options are controlled on the Options dialog box, under the Text Editor, All Languages, General page (shown in Figure 6.1).

FIGURE 6.1   Editor Options dialog box.

If you override the default behavior, turn wrapping on, and then type a line of code that exceeds the editor's width, you can see that the editor window (see Figure 6.2) automatically wraps the source to fit within the boundaries of the window and provides an icon to the far right of the editor to indicate that a wrap has taken place. Word wrapping is useful for keeping all of your code in plain sight (without the need for scrolling horizontally).

The other option on the Text Editor Options dialog box, Enable Virtual Space, is a mutually exclusive feature to word wrapping. That is, you can enable virtual space *or* word wrapping, but not both. Virtual Space refers to the capability to type text anywhere within the editor window without entering a bunch of spaces or tabs in the text area. This feature is useful in situations in which you want to place, for example, a code comment to the right of a few lines of code. Instead of tabbing each code comment over (or inserting padding spaces before them) to get them to indent and line up nicely, you can simply place the cursor at the exact column within the text editor where you want your comments to appear. See Figure 6.3 for an example; the code comments in the screenshot were not preceded by any spaces or tabs. They were simply typed directly into their current positions.

FIGURE 6.2   Word wrapping in the editor.

FIGURE 6.3   Virtual spacing in the editor window.

Visual Studio Designers

Designers are much more visual in nature than the text editors within Visual Studio; they provide a graphical perspective of a particular solution artifact. Thus, a form appears within a designer just as it would to the end user, as visual constructs made up of buttons, borders, menus, and frames. The code to implement the items shown in a designer is actually written by Visual Studio itself.

Like the various editors, the designers are all similar in form and function. They occupy space within the tabbed documents area of the IDE (just as the editors do). They might take on different behaviors depending on their target use. The Windows Forms designer and the component designer appear nearly the same, but there are subtle differences in their uses.

Coding with the Code Editor

Writing code and creating other syntax-based files are really all about typing text. The text editor window is the Visual Studio tool directly mapped to the task of creating source code text files. It is the keystone of development inside the IDE. It supports text entry and basic text operations such as selecting text regions, dragging and dropping text fragments, and setting tab stops. With basic text features alone, the editor would be sufficient to code with. However, the features layered on top for debugging, code formatting, code guidance, and customization really make this tool shine.

As we mentioned previously, the text editor actually has a few different personalities within the IDE. The code editor is designed to support creating and editing of source code files; the XML editor is targeted at XML files; and the CSS editor is targeted at CSS files. Although there are subtle differences in the way that code or markup is displayed in these windows, they all share the user interface and the same set of editing functionality.

TIP

Each editor type is fully customizable. Just fire up the Options dialog box (by choosing Tools, Options) and locate the Text Editor node. Under this node are separate pages that allow customization of each editor type.

Opening an Editor

There are two ways to launch a text editor (or any other editor in the IDE, for that matter). The first way involves using the Solution Explorer: Select an existing code file, text file, or other type file and double-click on the file. If it is a code file, you can also right-click on it and select View Code. The file content is loaded into a new editor window.

The second way to launch an editor window is to choose File, New, File. This launches the New File dialog box. Selecting a code template from this dialog box launches a code editor prefilled with the initial code stubs relevant to the template selected.

TIP

The text editor windows live as tabbed windows front-and-center within the IDE. If multiple code editors are open, they are each accessible by their tabs. If a lot of editors are open at one time, finding the window you are looking for by cycling through the tabs can be cumbersome. There are four ways to quickly locate and select a code editor window. First, you can use Solution Explorer. Double-clicking on the code file again within the Solution Explorer selects and displays the associated code editor window. Second, you can use the Window menu. Each open code editor window is shown by name in the windows list under the Window menu. Third, to the far right of the editor tabs, right next to the Close icon, is a small drop-down button in the image of an arrow. Clicking on the arrow drops down a list of all open editor windows, allowing you to select one at will. And finally, Visual Studio has its own version of the Windows switcher: Hold down the Ctrl key and tap the Tab key to cycle through a list of all windows open in IDE.

Writing Code in the Code Editor

Because the code editor's primary purpose is "word processing" for source code, let's first look at writing the simplest of routines—a "Hello, World" function—from the ground up using the code editor.

Figure 6.4 shows a code editor with an initial stubbed-out console file. This was produced by creating a new Visual C# Console project using the Solution Explorer. Double-clicking on the Program.cs file within that new project displays the source code for this console application.

FIGURE 6.4   Code template for a console code file.

As you can see, Visual Studio, as a result of the template used for creating the project, has already filled in some code:

```
using System;
using System.Collections.Generic;
using System.Linq;
using System.Text;

namespace HelloWorld
{
    class Program
    {
        static void Main(string[] args)
        {
        }
    }
}
```

To demonstrate the code editor in action, you create a console application that outputs the "Hello, World!" string to the console window.

Within the Main routine, add the following:

```
Console.WriteLine("Hello, World!");
```

To begin writing the code, simply place your cursor in the window by clicking within the Main routine's braces, press Enter to get some space for the new line of code, and type the Console.WriteLine syntax.

These and other productivity enhancers are discussed at great length in the next chapter. Here, we focus on the basics of editing and writing code in the editor window.

Now that you have seen the code editor in action (albeit for a very simple example), you're ready to dig more into the constituent components of the editor window.

TIP

Visual Studio 2010 now supports "zooming" within any open code editor/text editor. Hold down the Ctrl key and then use the mouse scroll wheel to zoom the editor view in or out.

Anatomy of the Code Editor Window

Editor windows, as you have seen, show up as tabbed windows within the IDE and are typically front-and-center visually in terms of windows layout. As you can see with the code editor window in Figure 6.5, each text editor window consists of three primary regions: a code pane, a selection margin, and an indicator margin. There are also both horizontal and vertical scrollbars for navigating around the displayed file.

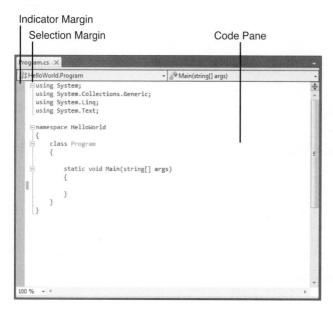

FIGURE 6.5   The components of the code editor window.

These regions, and their functionality, remain the same for all editor types within the IDE.

The code editor adds an additional set of UI elements that are not present with the other editors: Two drop-down boxes at the top of the code editor window enable you to quickly navigate through source code by selecting a type in the left drop-down and then selecting a specific type member (property, field, function, and so on) in the right drop-down (these drop-downs are called class and method name, respectively, in Visual Basic). This jogs the current cursor location directly to the indicated type.

> **NOTE**
>
> The type drop-down displays only those types that are declared in the file currently displayed in the editor; it won't display a list that is global to the entire solution, project, or even namespace. Likewise, the type member drop-down displays only members for the selected type.

The Code Pane

The code pane is the place where the document (source code, XML, and so on) is displayed and edited. This region provides basic text-editing functionality, in addition to the more advanced productivity features of the editor, such as IntelliSense.

Right-clicking within the code pane provides a shortcut menu (see Figure 6.6) that includes standard cut, copy, and paste tools, along with an assortment of other handy editing actions.

	Refactor	▸
	Organize Usings	▸
	Create Unit Tests...	
	Insert Snippet...	Ctrl+K, X
	Surround With...	Ctrl+K, S
	Go To Definition	F12
	Find All References	Ctrl+K, R
	View Call Hierarchy	Ctrl+K, Ctrl+T
	Breakpoint	▸
	Run To Cursor	Ctrl+F10
	Cut	Ctrl+X
	Copy	Ctrl+C
	Paste	Ctrl+V
	Outlining	▸

FIGURE 6.6   Code editor shortcut menu for a WinForms file.

The Indicator Margin

The indicator margin is the slim, gray-colored margin to the far left of the editor. This margin area is used to mark a line of code that contains a breakpoint or bookmark.

Figure 6.7 shows the "Hello, World" example with a bookmark placed on the Main routine and a breakpoint placed on the Console.WriteLine command.

```
Program.cs  X
HelloWorld.Program                    Main(string[] args)
using System;
using System.Collections.Generic;
using System.Linq;
using System.Text;

namespace HelloWorld
{
    class Program
    {
        static void Main(string[] args)
        {
            Console.WriteLine("Anyone listening?");
        }
    }
}
100 %
```

FIGURE 6.7   A bookmark and a breakpoint.

Clicking within the indicator margin toggles a breakpoint on or off for the line of code you have selected (we cover more on the topic of breakpoints later in this chapter and in Chapter 11, "Debugging Code").

The Selection Margin

The selection margin is a narrow region between the indicator margin and the editing area of the code pane. It provides the following:

▶ The capability to select an entire line of text by clicking within the selection margin.

▶ A visual indication—via colored indicator bars—of those lines of code that have changed during the current editing session.

▶ Line numbers (if this option has been turned on). See the following section in which we discuss customizing the text editor's behavior.

You can clearly see the "changed text" indicator and line numbers in action in Figure 6.8.

FIGURE 6.8   Changed text indicators and line numbers.

TIP

Visual Studio provides a dedicated toolbar for the text editor. You can view this toolbar by selecting View, Toolbars, Text Editor. It exposes buttons for the Member List, Quick Info, Parameter List, and Word Completion IntelliSense features, in addition to indenting buttons, commenting buttons, and bookmark navigation buttons. The navigation buttons are arguably the most useful because they provide easily accessible forward and back navigation through your code.

Code Navigation Tools

As the lines of code in any given project increase, effectively navigating through the code base—that is, quickly and easily finding lines of interest among the potentially thousands or even millions of lines of code—becomes an issue.

The text editor comes equipped with several tools to help you mark lines of code, search and replace text across source files, and, in general, maintain your situational awareness from within a long code listing.

Line Numbering

As we mentioned in the discussion of the text editor's selection margin, line numbering can be enabled for any given document loaded into an editor. This option is controlled in the Options dialog box within the Text Editor, All Languages, General page, or selectively under the individual languages and their General page.

By themselves, line numbers would be fairly useless. The capability to immediately jump to a line of code completes the equation and provides some real benefit from a navigation perspective. While within a text editor, press the Ctrl+G to jump to a line of code. This triggers the Go To Line dialog box (see Figure 6.9), which provides a text box for specifying the line number to jump to and even indicates the valid "scope" for the jump by providing a line number range for the current document. Entering a valid line number here moves the cursor position to the start of that line.

FIGURE 6.9   Jumping to a line.

Bookmarks

Bookmarks tackle the problem of navigating through large code files. By placing a bookmark on a line of code, you can instantly navigate back to that line of code at any time. When dealing with a series of bookmarks, you can jump back and forth through the bookmarked lines of code, which turns out to be a surprisingly useful feature. If you are a developer who is dealing with a large base of source code, there are inevitably points of interest within the source code that you want to view in the editor. Recall that the text editor window provides a means of navigating via type and member drop-downs; these are not, however, the best tools for the job when your "line of interest" is an arbitrary statement buried deep within a million lines of code.

Bookmarks are visually rendered in the indicator margin of the text editor (refer to Figure 6.8; a bookmark appears on line 11).

To add a bookmark or navigate through your bookmarks, you use either the text editor toolbar or the Bookmarks window.

You can view the Bookmarks window, shown in Figure 6.10, by choosing View, Other Windows, Bookmark Window. Notice that this window provides a toolbar for bookmark actions and provides a list of all available bookmarks, along with their actual physical location (filename and line number within that file).

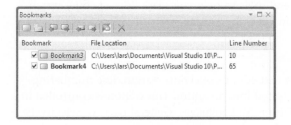

FIGURE 6.10   The Bookmarks window.

To toggle a bookmark for a given line of code, you first place your cursor on the desired line within the text editor and then click on the Toggle Bookmark button. The same process is used to toggle the bookmark off. Using the Forward and Back buttons within the bookmarks window jumps the text editor's cursor location back and forth through all available bookmarks.

TIP

Use the Bookmarks window to navigate through code across projects. You are not limited to bookmarks placed within a single code file; they can, in fact, be in *any* loaded code file. The list of bookmarks in this window is also a useful mechanism for quickly toggling a bookmark on or off (via the check box next to the bookmark) and for assigning a meaningful name to a bookmark. Right-clicking on a bookmark allows you to rename it something more meaningful than "Bookmark7."

Bookmark Folders   One interesting feature with the Bookmarks window is the capability to create a bookmark folder. This is an organizational bucket for related bookmarks. For instance, you might want to place bookmarks for a specific math algorithm under a folder called MathFuncs. To do this, you first create a folder by using the New Folder button on the toolbar. You can rename the folder to whatever makes sense for your particular scenario. Then you can create a bookmark and drag and drop it into the folder.

See Figure 6.11 for a look at a populated Bookmarks window. Note that two folders are in use, in addition to bookmarks being shown for various source code files.

Call Hierarchy

The Call Hierarchy window is yet another way to navigate through your projects. This window lets you easily follow the calls to and from every method, property, or constructor. With the code editor open, just right-click on the member name and select View Call Hierarchy. This launches the Call Hierarchy window. The member name appears in a tree view in the left pane of this window; this tree view itemizes the various calls made to and from the member. If you click on one of the calling sites, you can then view the calls to and from that method, and so on.

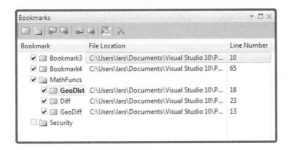

FIGURE 6.11   The Bookmarks window with folders.

Figure 6.12 shows an example of this iterative information displayed for successive callers. Clicking on any of the caller or callee nodes shows you the specific location of that code in the right pane, and double-clicking on that information in the right pane immediately jumps the code editor to that line of code.

FIGURE 6.12   Using the Call Hierarchy window to explore code relationships.

NOTE

Unfortunately, the Call Hierarchy window is only available for use with C# code.

The usefulness of this tool doesn't stop at caller/callee information. If you right-click on any node in the tree, you are able to jump directly to the code that implements the method/property, find all references to the selected method/property within your code, or even directly copy the code content represented by the node. All of these commands and more are available right from a node's right-click, pop-up menu.

Searching Documents

The text editor window provides an extensive search-and-replace capability. Three primary methods of searching are supported: Quick Find (ideal for finding text fragments within the current document or set of open documents), Search In Files (ideal for finding text in a file residing anywhere within a folder structure), and Find Symbol (ideal for searching on objects or members by name). All of these search mechanisms are triggered through the Find and Replace window, which you can launch under the Edit menu or with the Ctrl+F shortcut; a drop-down button on the Find and Replace window controls the mode of the window, which directly maps to the three search methods just itemized.

This same window is used to perform text substitution. This Replace functionality has two different modes that equate to the first two search modes. Thus, you have Quick Replace, which functions in a similar fashion to Quick Find, and Replace In Files, which functions in a similar fashion to Search In Files.

That makes a total of five different function modes for the Find and Replace tool:

▶ Quick Find

▶ Find In Files

▶ Find Symbol

▶ Quick Replace

▶ Replace In Files

Let's take a closer look at each of these search-and-replace modes individually.

Quick Find/Quick Replace

Figure 6.13 illustrates the Find and Replace window in Quick Find mode. You have three pieces of information to fill in here: what you are searching for, what you want to search in, and the options to use to fine-tune your search parameters.

FIGURE 6.13   Quick Find mode.

The Find What drop-down, obviously, specifies the string to search for. This drop-down holds the last 20 strings used in a Find operation, making it easy to reuse a previous search. Just select the string from the list.

The Look In drop-down sets the scope of the search. For Quick Find searches, you have a few options to choose from:

- ▶ **Current Document**—This option indicates the currently active document within the text editor.

- ▶ **Selection**—If a portion of a document is selected within a text editor, this option limits the search to only the selected text.

- ▶ **All Open Documents**—With this option, the search is performed across any open documents.

- ▶ **Current Project**—Searches only the files within the current project.

- ▶ **Entire Solution**—This option expands the search to include all files within the solution.

- ▶ **Current Block**—If the cursor is currently positioned within an object or namespace code block, the "current type" option allows you to search within that code block. Note that this option includes the name of the code block itself. Consider this example: A code editor window is open, and the cursor is placed within the definition for a class called MessageBus, within the Contoso.Fx.Integration namespace. The Look In drop-down displays an option called Current Block (Contoso.Fx.Integration.MessageBus) to limit the scope of the search to just this class. If the cursor is not positioned within a code block, this option simply does not display.

Fine-Tuning Your Search   Below the Look In control is a series of check boxes for fine-tuning the search. The effects these options have on your search are self-explanatory:

- ▶ Match Case causes the search to be executed against the exact case you used in the Find What drop-down.

- ▶ Match Whole Word forces the search to match only on the entire string as entered in the Find What drop-down.

- ▶ Search Up causes the search to move from bottom to top in a document (as opposed to the default top-to-bottom search).

- ▶ Use Wildcards/Use Regular Expressions changes how the search engine performs matching on the Find What string. A standard search does a character match for the target string. You can also, however, use wildcard conventions (such as Message* to find any string starting with the text Message) or a full-blown regular expression to perform even more intricate searches. You would enter a regular expression as the Find What string.

TIP

If you elect to use wildcards or regular expressions for your search, there is a tool that can help you to write the correct syntax for the search phrase. If the Use check box is selected, a small button located directly to the right of the Find What drop-down becomes enabled. This button displays the Expression Builder: a fly-out menu of expression syntax choices and their descriptions. The context of this menu changes depending on whether you have indicated Wildcard or Regular Expressions.

Finding Search Results   After you have specified all the criteria for your search, the Find Next button at the bottom of the search window launches the search. Any matches within the scope specified are highlighted for you within the document. Clicking on the Find Next button moves to the next match until no more matches are found.

You also have the option of placing a bookmark against any matches. Just click the Bookmark All button.

Replacing Text   You set the Quick Replace mode (see Figure 6.14) by clicking on the right-most of the two mode buttons (in the same fashion that you set Quick Find mode). The Quick Replace process is virtually identical to Quick Find; a single additional field, used to specify the replacement text, is added to the dialog box. The Find What, Look In, and Find Options fields all remain the same in form and function.

FIGURE 6.14   Quick Replace mode.

Two buttons are added to the dialog box to initiate the string replacement: Replace, which replaces the first instance found with the Replace With text, and Replace All, which replaces all instances found with the Replace With text. Note that any replacements you make can always be undone via the Undo command under the Edit menu.

These two buttons take the place of the Bookmark All button, which is not available in this mode.

NOTE

Although a complete discussion of regular expressions is outside the scope of this book, you should note that the Replace With box is capable of supporting tagged expressions. For more information on how you might use this to your advantage during replace operations, consult a regular expression reference manual and look at the MSDN Regular Expressions help topic for Visual Studio.

Find In Files/Replace In Files

Figure 6.15 depicts the Find and Replace dialog box in Find In Files mode. The operation of this mode is similar to Quick Find, with a few minor differences. You still have to specify the "what" and the "where" components of the search. And you still can fine-tune your search, although you lose the Search Up and Search Hidden options because they don't make sense for a file-based search. The major differences with this mode are

1. The available search scopes you can specify in the Look In drop-down

2. The way search results are displayed.

FIGURE 6.15   Find In Files mode.

Let's look at these two differences in turn.

The search scope is notable in that, in addition to the standard solution, document, and project scopes, it allows you to specify a folder location to search. There is a Choose Search Folders button located just to the right of the Look In drop-down that allows you to add folder locations to the drop-down.

Building Search Folder Sets   Clicking the Choose Search Folders button launches a dialog box; this dialog box allows you to build up a set of directories as the scope of the search. You can name this folder set and even set the search order for the directories. Figure 6.16 captures this dialog box as a search set called ClassLibCode is built. You can see that three directories have been added to the set and that you can add more by simply browsing to the folder with the Available Folders control and adding them to the Selected Folders list.

FIGURE 6.16   Building a Search Folder set.

The Find Results Window   With Quick Find, the search results are highlighted (or book-marked) right within the text editor window. The Find In Files mode displays its search results in a separate, dedicated Find Results window (see Figure 6.17). You can redirect the output to one of two results windows by selecting either the Find Results 1 Window or Find Results 2 Window option at the bottom of the Find and Replace dialog box. The two windows are identical; two options provided here allow you to keep different search results separate and avoid the confusion that the commingling of matches would cause if you were constrained to just one output window.

In Figure 6.17, you see the results of a simple search conducted across all the files in a solution. The contents of the Find Results window provides the following information:

- ▶ A description of the search performed (for example, Find all "MessageBus", Subfolders, Find Results 1, "Entire Solution").

- ▶ The matches returned from the search. Match information includes the file path and name, the line number within the file, and a verbatim repeat of the line of code containing the match.

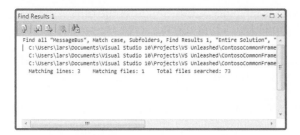

FIGURE 6.17   The Find Results window.

▸ A summary of the find results, including the number of matching lines of code, the number of files containing matches, and the total number of files searched.

Double-clicking on one of the results lines in the window jogs the cursor location directly to the matching line within the editor. Note that this window has a toolbar. From left to right, the buttons on this toolbar allow you to do the following:

▸ Jump to the matched line of code within the text editor. (First place your cursor on the match inside the Find Results window and then click on the Go to the Location of the Current Line button.)

▸ Move back and forth through the list of matches. Each matched item is highlighted in the Find Results window and in the Text Editor window.

▸ Clear the Find Results window.

▸ Cancel any ongoing searches.

Replacing In Files   The Replace In Files mode builds from the Find In Files mode by providing all the same functionality and adding the ability to cycle through matching results in the Text Editor window. The Replace, Replace All, and Skip File buttons also make an appearance in this mode (see Figure 6.18).

We've already covered the Replace and Replace All functions. Each file that matches the search phrase is opened in a separate text editor window, and the replacements are made directly in that window. If you're performing a Replace All, the replacements are made and then saved directly into the containing file. You also have the option, via the Keep Modified Files Open After Replace All check box, to have Visual Studio keep any files touched open inside their respective text editors. This allows you to selectively save or discard the replacements as you see fit.

You can elect to skip files during the search-and-replace process by using the Skip File button. This button is available only if more than one file has been selected as part of the search scope. Clicking this button tells the search engine to skip the current file being processed and continue with the next in-scope file.

Find Symbol

The last search mode supported by the Find and Replace dialog box is called Find Symbol. It is used to search out lines of code in which a symbol is defined, referenced, or used. This tighter search scope makes Find Symbol the preferred mechanism for, say, finding all places where a class called CustomAnalyzer is referenced. You could use the other Find modes to locate this text, but the Find Symbol algorithm's tighter scope is much more relevant to this kind of search because it doesn't rove over any nonsymbol text in the document. In addition, the Find Symbol function uses reflection and the compiler to find symbol references; this is not a simple text search with a different scope.

FIGURE 6.18   Replace in Files mode.

The Find Symbol search also has two other distinguishing characteristics from the normal Find/Replace. It is able to search external components even in the absence of source code. As an example, you can opt to select .NET Framework in the Look In drop-down. Figure 6.19 shows the results of searching for the String symbol in the Framework itself.

FIGURE 6.19   The Find Symbol Results window.

The second difference with Find Symbol is the capability to immediately jump to a referenced object's definition or browse its definition using the object browser. You can access both of these functions, Go To Definition and Browse Definition, by right-clicking on any of the matches displayed in the results window.

NOTE

If you are searching for a symbol within a library where you do not have access to the source code, the option to view the symbol's definition in source (for example, Go To Definition) is obviously not available. However, you can still leverage the Browse Definition function to instantly pull the definition open in the object browser. It turns out that this is a great way to understand and explore libraries not of your own creation.

Incremental Search

Incremental Search functions without the aid of a dialog box. With a text editor open, select Edit, Advanced, Incremental Search (or press Ctrl+I). While Incremental Search is active, you see a visual pointer cue composed of binoculars and a down arrow. If you start typing a search string, character-by-character, the first match found will is highlighted within the text editor window itself. With each successive character, the search string is altered and the search itself is reexecuted. The current search string is displayed on the Visual Studio status bar. Figure 6.20 illustrates an Incremental Search in progress; the characters *MESS* have been entered, and you can see the first match flagged within the text editor.

FIGURE 6.20   Incremental Search.

By default, the search function works from the top of the document to the bottom, and from left to right. You can reverse the direction of the search by using the Ctrl+Shift+I key combination.

To jump to the next match within the document, use the Ctrl+I key combination.

Clicking anywhere within the document or pressing the Esc key cancels the Incremental Search.

NOTE

Incremental Searches are always performed in a manner that is not case-sensitive and will always match on substrings.

Debugging in the Text Editor

The text editor—more specifically, the code editor—has several interactive features that facilitate the code debugging process. Debugging activities within the text editor primarily center on breakpoints and runtime code control. We cover general Visual Studio debugging in greater detail in Chapter 11.

A breakpoint is simply a location (for example, a line of code) that is flagged for the debugger; when the debugger encounters a breakpoint, the currently executing program is paused immediately before executing that line of code. While the program is in this paused state, you can inspect the state of variables or even affect variable state by assigning new values. You can also interactively control the code flow at this point by skipping over the next line of code or skipping directly to another line of code and continuing from there—all without actually leaving the IDE.

Setting a Breakpoint

To set a breakpoint using the code editor, first locate the line of code you want to pause on and then click that line of code within the indicator margin. This will set the breakpoint, which can now be visually identified by a red ball in the indicator margin. Hovering over the breakpoint indicator margin displays a ToolTip indicating some basic information about that breakpoint: the code filename, the line number within that code file, the type you are in (if any), and the line number within that type.

In Figure 6.21, a breakpoint has been set within a class called MessageMapper. The ToolTip information shows that you are on line 3 in the MessageMapper type, but within the overall code file (Integration.cs), you are on line number 12.

Clicking on the breakpoint again removes it.

The breakpoint we have set is a simple one in that it suspends the program on that line of code without regard for any other variable or factor. Simple breakpoints are, however, only the tip of the iceberg. Breakpoints support an extensive set of conditions used to fine-tune and control what will actually trigger the breakpoints. For instance, you can set a breakpoint to activate the state of a variable or the number of times program execution will "hit" the breakpoint. You also can configure conditional breakpoints by simply pointing and clicking within the code editor window.

FIGURE 6.21   Setting a breakpoint.

Configuring a Breakpoint

Right-clicking on the breakpoint indicator reveals the context menu (see Figure 6.22) for configuring the breakpoint.

🔵	Delete Breakpoint	
🟤	Disable Breakpoint	Ctrl+F9
	Location...	
	Condition...	
	Hit Count...	
	Filter...	
	When Hit...	
	Edit labels...	Alt+F9, L
🔵	Export...	

FIGURE 6.22   Configuring a breakpoint.

It is from here that you can indicate special conditions for triggering the breakpoint and even disable or enable the breakpoint. Disabling the breakpoint, rather than deleting it, keeps its location intact if you ever need to re-enable it.

TIP

Visual Basic actually provides a command word that allows you to programmatically trigger a breakpoint within your code. The Stop statement, like a breakpoint, suspends execution of the executing code. This capability is useful when you're running the application outside the IDE. Any time a Stop statement is encountered during runtime, the Visual Studio debugger launches and attaches to the program.

Although C# doesn't have an equivalent statement to Visual Basic's Stop command, you can use the Debugger class to achieve the same thing: simply call Debugger.Break to force a breakpoint programmatically. The Debugger class lives in the System.Diagnostic namespace.

Controlling the Flow of Running Code

When a program is run within the IDE, it continues along its path of execution through the code base until it hits a breakpoint or Stop statement, is paused manually, or terminates either by reaching the end of its code path or by a manual stop.

TIP

The DVR-like controls and their shortcut keys (available under the Debug menu or on the Debug toolbar) are, by far, the easiest way to start, pause, or stop code within the IDE.

When a breakpoint is hit, the code editor visually indicates the line of code where execution has paused. Figure 6.23 shows a slightly modified version of the "Hello, World" program, suspended at a breakpoint. A yellow arrow in the indicator margin flags the next statement that will execute when you resume running the program. In this case, because the breakpoint is also here, the next statement indicator appears in the margin embedded within the breakpoint glyph.

FIGURE 6.23   Stopping at a breakpoint.

When execution is paused, you can change the next line of code to be executed. By default, of course, this is the line of code where operations were paused (recall that execution stops just before running the line of code matched with the breakpoint). But you can manually specify the next line of code to run by right-clicking on the target line and then selecting Set Next Statement.

In Figure 6.24, this feature has been used to jump out of the WriteLine loop. Normal flow through the code has been circumvented, and instead of continuing to spin through the for loop, the program immediately executes the line of code just after the loop. You can see the arrow and highlighting that show the next line of code and the breakpoint are no longer at the same location within the code file.

FIGURE 6.24   Setting the next run statement.

You can also create a sort of virtual breakpoint by selecting Run To Cursor from the editor's context menu. This causes the program to run until it hits the line of code that you have selected, at which point it pauses much as if you had set a breakpoint there.

Printing Code

To print the current text editor's contents, select Print from the File menu. The Print dialog box is fairly standard, allowing you to select your printer and set basic print properties. Two Visual Studio–specific options bear mentioning here. The Print What section in this dialog box controls whether line numbers are produced in the printout and whether collapsed regions are included in the printed content.

Colors and Fonts

By default, the font colors and markup that you see in the text editor window are sent to the printer as is (assuming that you are printing to a color printer). If you so desire, you can tweak all these settings from the Fonts and Colors page in the Options dialog box (see Figure 6.25).

FIGURE 6.25   The Fonts and Colors Options dialog box.

This is the same dialog box used to control font and color settings for many of the IDE's constituent parts. You access the printer settings by selecting Printer in the Show Settings For drop-down at the top of the dialog box.

Figure 6.26 provides a snapshot of output produced by printing a code file.

```
C:\Users\lars\Documents\Visual Studio 10\...\ContosoCommonFramework\NewConsole\Program.cs        1

 1 using System;
 2 using System.Collections.Generic;
 3 using System.Linq;
 4 using System.Text;
 5
 6 namespace HelloWorld
 7 {
 8     class Program
 9     {
10         static void Main(string[] args)
11         {
12             for (int i = 0; i <= 5; i++)
13             {
14                 Console.WriteLine("Hello, World! try#{0}", i);
15             }
16
17             Console.WriteLine("Anyone listening?");
18
19
20         }
21     }
22 }
23
```

FIGURE 6.26   Code printout.

Using the Code Definition Window

The code definition window is a "helper" window that works in close conjunction with the code editor window by displaying definitions for symbols selected within the code editor. It is actually a near clone of the code editor window, with one big exception: It is read-only and does not permit edits to its content.

The code definition window content is refreshed anytime the cursor position is moved within the code editor window. If the cursor or caret is placed in a symbol/type, the code definition window shows you how that symbol is defined.

Figure 6.27 shows an open code editor and a code definition window; the cursor in the editor is positioned on an internal field, _state, defined within the class InternalToken.

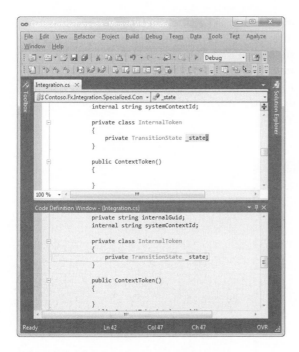

FIGURE 6.27   The Code Definition window.

The code definition window has reacted to the cursor position by showing the source code that actually defines the type of the _state field. You can see from the figure that the code definition window is a fairly featured adaptation of a text editor window: It supports bookmarks, breakpoints, and various navigation aids. Although you cannot edit code using this window, you are not prevented from copying code out of the window.

You can open a code definition window by using the View menu.

TIP

The Code Definition window also works well with the Class View window. If you single-click a class within the Class View window, the Code Definition window refreshes to show you the code implementation for that class.

Creating and Editing XML Documents and Schema

The text editor is equally adept, and just as productive, at editing documents with XML content—including XML schemas. The XML editor is launched whenever you open a file with the .xml extension inside of Visual Studio. It is also launched for .xsl files and .config files, and is always available when you use the Open With command in the Solution Explorer against any item in a project.

Because XML documents contain structured content involving the concepts of nodes and tags, attributes, and node containership, the XML editor supports document outlining in a similar fashion to the code editor: You can expand or collapse nodes within the editor to expose or hide a node's content (see Figure 6.28). And just as with the code editor, syntax checking and IntelliSense are fully supported by the XML editor. The XML editor is aware of the syntactical requirements for the current document and provides appropriate IntelliSense and formatting help where possible.

FIGURE 6.28   Editing an XML document.

Using the XML Editor, you can also carry out these actions:

- Edit XSD schema documents
- Generate a schema document from an XML document
- Edit XSLT style sheets
- Edit Document Type Definition (DTD) documents and XML-Data Reduced (XDR) documents
- Insert XML snippets

For a proper treatment of the various editing, validation, and productivity aids available in this editor, see Chapter 8, "Working with Visual Studio's Productivity Aids." Here, let's explore two of the core XML functions: schema generation and XSLT style sheet editing.

Inferring Schema

The XML Editor can automatically generate an XML schema document (XSD) based on a valid XML document. While the XML document is open, select Create Schema from the XML main menu. This creates an XSD document and opens it in the XML Schema Designer (more on this in the next section). From there, you can make any necessary changes to the XSD document and save it to disk. You can also include it in your project at this point.

> **NOTE**
>
> If you run the Create Schema command against an XML document that already contains a DTD or XDR schema, the XML inference algorithm uses these schemas as the basis for the conversion as opposed to the actual data within the XML document.

Designing XML Schemas

Visual Studio 2010 has radically enhanced its support for XML schema design. This is evident right off the bat when you open an XML schema file (.xsd). A visual design window and an XML Schema Explorer window, working in tandem, quickly allow you to inspect, edit, and build out your schema. Figure 6.29 shows the same schema we just inferred from our simple "product catalog" XML file opened in the Visual Studio IDE. Note the schema explorer to the right, and the schema design surface to the left. Let's examine the various views in detail.

FIGURE 6.29   Editing a simple XML schema.

Schema Views

Visual Studio provides five different ways to visualize and/or edit the information in an XML schema, delivered by three different tools. We have already covered the XML Editor. Because XML schemas are verbalized using XML itself, the editors' functions apply just as well to schema editing as they do to document editing.

That leaves us with two remaining tools: the XML Schema Explorer and the XML Schema Designer. Just as you have come to expect with most explorer/designer pairs in the IDE, these two tools work hand-in-hand.

The XML Schema Explorer

The schema explorer is a tree view representation of schema content (Figure 6.30). Using this explorer, you can expand any of the schema container elements to view their child elements. The toolbar on this explorer window lets you search for schema elements and change the sort order as well.

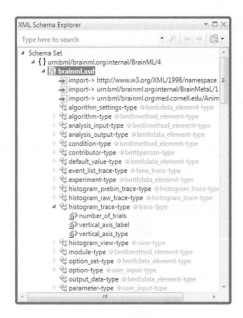

FIGURE 6.30   The XML Schema Explorer.

While this hierarchical view of the schema is useful in its own right, the real purpose of the explorer window is to select items to view and/or edit in the design window. In fact, the explorer and designer windows are inseparable pairs: closing the designer automatically closes the explorer.

The XML Schema Designer

The schema design window is where all of the schema editing takes place. You can edit or view a schema (or set of schemas) by dragging items from the XML Schema Explorer window onto the XML Schema Designer surface.

After you have added the schema to the design surface, the schema design window provides you with three different views into the schema's structure and content:

▶ The Start View is the default view. As its name implies, this is a launching page into the other views. The Start View also provides summary statistics for the XML schema (such as a count of the global elements, attributes, and types), and provides a quick and easy way to add these items to the design surface.

▶ The Graph View is a 2D view of the nodes and node relationships within a schema. The Graph View is primarily useful in visualizing the complexity and types of relationships within a schema. You can't use this to directly edit the nodes or node relationships. Use the toolbar buttons at the top of the designer to change the way that the graph is displayed: left to right, right to left, top to bottom, or bottom to top. Double-clicking on a node opens the schema's XML in the XML editor, with the XML for that node highlighted. See Figure 6.31 for a picture of the Graph View with a complex schema file loaded.

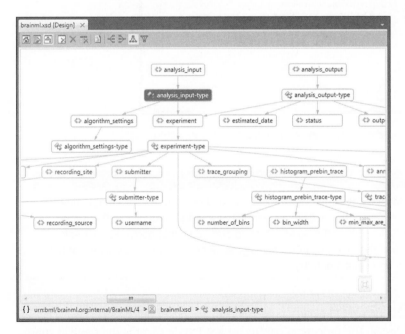

FIGURE 6.31   Using the Schema Designer's Graph View.

▶ The Content Model View is a graphical, hierarchical view of the nodes and node elements, attributes, types, and groups. This view is particularly useful if you are trying to understand the details of a particular portion of the schema. For instance, by double-clicking on a type, you can quickly gain a fairly complete understanding of that type's schema including elements, attributes, types, and groups—in addition to any constraints or relationships that are defined in the schema. This view also provides a simple way to select nodes: An A-Z list of all nodes within the schema appears in the listbox to the left of the design surface. Clicking on the node in this list displays the node details on the design surface (see Figure 6.32).

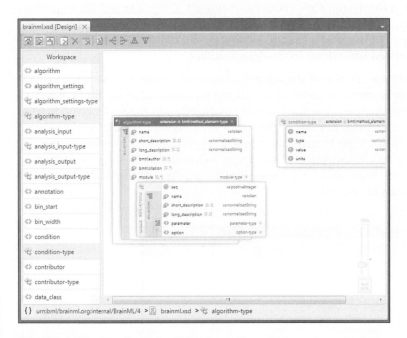

FIGURE 6.32   The Content Model View with multiple nodes selected.

TIP

Using the Content Model View, it is easy to compare and contrast two or more nodes within a schema. Just select the nodes you want to view in the node list to the left of the design surface (using Ctrl+left mouse button to add additional nodes to your selection). You can then use the design surface's image scaler to get a high-level view of the nodes or to zoom in on specific details.

Editing XSLT Style Sheets

XSLT files are XML files, so the process of editing an XSLT style sheet is the same as that described for editing an XML document. There are, however, a few additional features specific to XSLT documents. For one, keywords are recognized and shaded appropriately in the editor just as with a code document. Second, the XML editor automatically processes the current state of the document against the standard schema for XSLT style sheets and shows any validation errors to you directly. And finally, Visual Studio is fully aware of any script embedded in an XSLT document. You can set breakpoints within a script block, and there is full debug support for script enabling you to step through code, see the current state of variables, and so forth. Figure 6.33 shows an XSLT style sheet with a breakpoint set within a section of embedded script.

FIGURE 6.33   Debugging script embedded into an XSLT document.

Running XSLT Against XML

After a style sheet has been created and attached to an XML document, you can execute that XSLT style sheet and view the output within a new editor window. To attach the XSLT sheet to the XML document, use the Properties window for the XML document and set the Stylesheet property. Entering the full path and filename of the XSLT in this property attaches the style sheet. Alternatively, you can manually code the style sheet into the XML document's prolog section by typing an `xml-stylesheet` Processing Instruction prolog into the document, like this:

```
<?xml-stylesheet type='text/xsl' href='myxsl.xsl'?>
```

When a style sheet is associated, selecting the Show XSLT Output option from the XML menu runs the transforms against the XML document and shows you the results in a separate editor window.

Working with Cascading Style Sheets

The CSS Editor allows you to build and edit cascading style sheet documents. Because CSS documents are, at their core, text documents, the editor doesn't need to provide much more than standard text-editing features to be effective. There are, however, a few built-in tools available from the editor that enable you to add style rules and build styles using dialog boxes as opposed to free-form text entry.

Adding Style Rules

Right-click within the CSS editor to access the shortcut menu. From there, select the Add Style Rule option. The Add Style Rule dialog box allows you to input an element, class name, or class ID and even define a hierarchy between the rules. Committing the change from this dialog box injects the necessary content into the CSS editor to create the rule.

Defining Style Sheet Attributes

After you've added a style to the CSS document by either writing the style syntax manually or using the aforementioned Add Style Rule dialog box, you can edit the attributes of that style using the Style Builder dialog box. You launch this dialog box by right-clicking anywhere within the previously entered style section and then selecting the Build Style option. When you use this dialog box, it is possible to fully describe the style across several different categories from font to layout to list formatting.

Developing Windows Client Applications

There are two principal .NET technologies used to develop Windows client applications: Windows Forms (WinForms) and Windows Presentation Foundation (WPF). Both of these technologies are essentially a set of classes and user interface controls exposed by the .NET Framework that enable developers to quickly build out applications that are installed, and run, under the Microsoft Windows operating system.

Both the WinForms framework and the WPF framework are mature technologies, however WPF represents Microsoft's long-term technical strategy for user interface development. It provides a huge leap beyond WinForms for crafting applications that must blend multimedia, document, and high-impact user interface elements together.

WPF uses a markup language called XAML (Extensible Application Markup Language) to describe application objects, property values, and behavior. In this respect, it is similar to a web application that uses HTML to describe the various elements of a web page. WPF as a technology heavily leverages vector graphics and graphics hardware acceleration to display an application's user interface.

Regardless of the type of client application you need to build, the process is much the same: Both the WinForms designer and the WPF designer enable drag-and-drop development, and both have project templates available in Visual Studio.

Creating a Windows Forms Project

The process of building a Windows Forms application starts the same as all other project types within Visual Studio: You select the Windows Application project template from the New Project dialog box and set up the location for the application's source. From there, Visual Studio stubs out an initial project, and the Windows Forms designer loads, as shown in Figure 6.34.

FIGURE 6.34   Initial form in the Windows Forms designer.

As you can see from the figure, a design-time "mock-up" of the actual form is visible within the designer. This is the canvas for your user interface. Using this canvas, you can add controls and visual elements to the form, tweak the look and feel of the form itself, and launch directly to the code that is wired to the form. To investigate how the designer works, start with a simple design premise: Say you want to take the blank form that Visual Studio generated for you and create a login dialog box that allows users to input a name and password and confirm their entries by clicking an OK button. A Cancel button should also be available to allow users to dismiss the form.

> **NOTE**
>
> Don't get confused about the various representations that a form can have, such as message box or dialog box. From a development perspective, they are all windows and are therefore all forms.

The designer in this exercise allows you, the developer, to craft the form and its actions while writing as little code as possible. Using drag-and-drop operations and Property dialog boxes, you should be able to customize the look and feel of the application without ever dealing with the code editor.

Customizing the Form's Appearance

There are a few obvious visual elements in the designer. For one, the form itself is shown complete with its borders, title bar, client area, and Min/Max/Close buttons. In addition, you can see grab handles at the bottom, right, and bottom-right corner of the form. The grab handles are used to resize the form. To change other attributes of the form, you use the property grid for the form. The property grid enables you to set the background color, border appearance and behavior, title text, and so on.

In Figure 6.35, the title of the form has been changed to Login, and the border behavior has been changed to match a dialog box as opposed to a normal, resizable window.

FIGURE 6.35   Editing the form's size, border and title.

Adding Controls to a Form

Controls are adornments to a form that have their own user interface. (There is such a thing as UI-less controls; we cover such controls later in this chapter in the section "Authoring Components and Controls.") They provide the principal interaction mechanism method with a form. Put another way, a form is really just a container for the various controls that implement the desired functionality for the form.

You can add controls to a form quite easily by dragging and dropping them from the toolbox. Continuing the metaphor of the designer as a canvas, the toolbox is the palette.

The Toolbox   The toolbox is a dockable window within the IDE; it is viewable only when you are editing a project element that supports toolbox functionality. To make sure that the toolbox is visible, select it from the View menu (or use the Ctrl+W, X shortcut).

The toolbox groups the controls in a tabbed tree. Expand the tab grouping (such as Common Controls or Menus & Toolbars), and you see a list of the available controls. In this case, you want two text box controls to hold the login ID and password text, a few label controls to describe the text box controls, and the OK and Cancel buttons to commit or cancel the entries. You can find all of these controls under the Common Controls tab (see Figure 6.36).

FIGURE 6.36   The WinForms toolbox.

To place a control on the form, drag its representation from the toolbox onto the form. Some controls, referred to as components, don't actually have a visual user interface. The timer is one example of a component. When you drag a component to a form, it is placed in a separate area of the designer called the component tray. The component tray allows you to select one of the added components and access its properties via the Properties window.

> **TIP**
>
> The toolbox is customizable in terms of its content and arrangement. You can add or remove tabs from the toolbox, move controls from one tab to another through simple drag and drop, and even rename individual items within the toolbox. To perform many of these actions, bring up the toolbox context menu by right-clicking on a tab or an item.

Arranging Controls   When you are designing a form, control layout becomes an important issue. You are typically concerned about ensuring that controls are aligned either horizontally or vertically, that controls and control groups are positioned with equal and common margins between their edges, that margins are enforced along the form borders, and so on.

The designer provides three distinct sets of tools and aids that assist with form layout. First, you have the options available to you under the Format menu. With a form loaded in the designer, you can select different groups of controls and use the commands under the Format menu to align these controls vertically or horizontally with one another, standardize and increase or decrease the spacing between controls, center the controls within the form, and even alter the controls' appearance attributes so that they are of equal size in either dimension.

The other layout tools within the designer are interactive in nature and are surfaced through two different modes: snap line and grid positioning. You can toggle between these two modes via the Windows Forms Designer Options dialog box (choose Tools, Options and then the Windows Forms Designer tab). The property called LayoutMode can be set to either SnapToGrid or SnapLines.

Using the Layout Grid   The layout grid is, as its name implies, a grid that is laid on top of the form. The grid itself is visually represented within the designer by dots representing the intersection of the grid squares. As you drag and move controls over the surface of the grid, the designer automatically snaps the control's leading edges to one of the grid's square edges.

> **TIP**
>
> Even with the grid layout turned on, you can circumvent the snapping behavior by selecting a control, holding down the Ctrl key, and using the arrow keys to move the control up, down, right, or left one pixel at a time.

The size of the grid squares (and thus the spacing of these guide dots) is controlled by the GridSize property (also located in the Options dialog box). A smaller grid size equates to a tighter spacing of guide dots, which in turns equates to more finely grained control over control placement.

Figure 6.37 shows the login form with the layout grid in evidence. Note that the grid was used to make sure that

FIGURE 6.37   The layout grid.

▶ The text boxes are aligned with one another (and are the same length).

▶ The labels are aligned vertically with the text boxes and horizontally with each other.

▶ The buttons are aligned vertically and have an appropriate buffer area between their control edges and the form's border.

Using Snap Lines   Snap lines are a slightly more intelligent mechanism for positioning controls. With snap lines, there is no grid visible on the form's surface. Instead, the designer draws visual hints while a control is in motion on the form.

Figure 6.38 illustrates snap lines in action; this figure shows the process of positioning the OK button.

FIGURE 6.38   Using snap lines.

Note that the control—in this case, an OK button—has "snapped" into a position that is located a set distance away from the form border (indicated by the thin blue line extending down from the button to the form edge). The button snap position also sufficiently spaces the control from its neighboring Cancel button, as indicated by the thin blue line extending from the right edge of the button to the left edge of the Cancel button. The snap line algorithm has also determined that you are trying to create a row of buttons and thus need to vertically align the current control to its neighbor. This is actually done using the interior text of the buttons; the thin pink line running under the text of both buttons clearly shows that they are perfectly aligned.

The snap line algorithms automatically take into account the recommended margins and spacing distances as discussed in the Windows User Interface Guidelines written and adopted by Microsoft. This feature takes the guesswork out of many layout decisions and helps to ensure some commonality and standards adherence within the Windows Forms applications.

> **NOTE**
>
> Changes made to the layout modes of the designer typically do not take effect immediately. You might need to close the designer and reopen it after making a change (such as switching between SnapLine mode and SnapToGrid mode).

Resizing Controls and Editing Attributes   When a control is in place on its parent form, you can interact with the control in various ways. You can set control properties using the Properties window. You also can alter the sizing and shape of the control by dragging the grab handles on the sides of the control.

Writing Code

Although the designer excels at enabling developers to visually construct a user interface, its capability to actually implement behavior is limited. You can use the designer to place a button, but responding to a click on the button and reacting in some way are still the domain of code.

At the code level, a form is simply a class that encapsulates all the form's behavior. For simplicity and ease of development, Visual Studio pushes all the code that it writes via the designer into clearly marked regions and, in the case of Windows forms, a separate code file. The file is named after the primary form code file like this: *FormName.Designer.language extension.* As an example, the login form is accompanied by a Login.Designer.cs file that implements the designer-written code.

Listing 6.1 shows what Visual Studio has generated in the way of code to implement the changes made through the designer.

LISTING 6.1   Windows Forms Designer–Generated Code

```
namespace Contoso.UI.WindowsForms.OrderEntry
{
    partial class Login
    {
        /// <summary>
        /// Required designer variable.
        /// </summary>
        private System.ComponentModel.IContainer components = null;

        /// <summary>
        /// Clean up any resources being used.
        /// </summary>
```

```csharp
/// <param name="disposing">true if managed resources should be disposed;
/// otherwise, false.</param>
protected override void Dispose(bool disposing)
{
    if (disposing && (components != null))
    {
        components.Dispose();
    }
    base.Dispose(disposing);
}

#region Windows Form Designer generated code

/// <summary>
/// Required method for Designer support - do not modify
/// the contents of this method with the code editor.
/// </summary>
private void InitializeComponent()
{
    this.label1 = new System.Windows.Forms.Label();
    this.label2 = new System.Windows.Forms.Label();
    this.textBoxID = new System.Windows.Forms.TextBox();
    this.textBoxPassword = new System.Windows.Forms.TextBox();
    this.buttonCancel = new System.Windows.Forms.Button();
    this.buttonOk = new System.Windows.Forms.Button();
    this.SuspendLayout();
    //
    // label1
    //
    this.label1.AutoSize = true;
    this.label1.Location = new System.Drawing.Point(61, 23);
    this.label1.Name = "label1";
    this.label1.Size = new System.Drawing.Size(17, 13);
    this.label1.TabIndex = 0;
    this.label1.Text = "ID:";
    //
    // label2
    //
    this.label2.AutoSize = true;
    this.label2.Location = new System.Drawing.Point(26, 46);
    this.label2.Name = "label2";
    this.label2.Size = new System.Drawing.Size(52, 13);
    this.label2.TabIndex = 1;
    this.label2.Text = "Password:";
```

```
            //
            // textBoxID
            //
            this.textBoxID.Location = new System.Drawing.Point(85, 20);
            this.textBoxID.Name = "textBoxID";
            this.textBoxID.Size = new System.Drawing.Size(195, 20);
            this.textBoxID.TabIndex = 2;
            //
            // textBoxPassword
            //
            this.textBoxPassword.Location = new System.Drawing.Point(85, 46);
            this.textBoxPassword.Name = "textBoxPassword";
            this.textBoxPassword.Size = new System.Drawing.Size(195, 20);
            this.textBoxPassword.TabIndex = 3;
            //
            // buttonCancel
            //
            this.buttonCancel.DialogResult =
               System.Windows.Forms.DialogResult.Cancel;
            this.buttonCancel.Location = new System.Drawing.Point(205, 72);
            this.buttonCancel.Name = "buttonCancel";
            this.buttonCancel.Size = new System.Drawing.Size(75, 23);
            this.buttonCancel.TabIndex = 4;
            this.buttonCancel.Text = "Cancel";
            //
            // buttonOk
            //
            this.buttonOk.Location = new System.Drawing.Point(124, 72);
            this.buttonOk.Name = "buttonOk";
            this.buttonOk.Size = new System.Drawing.Size(75, 23);
            this.buttonOk.TabIndex = 5;
            this.buttonOk.Text = "OK";
            //
            // Login
            //
            this.AcceptButton = this.buttonOk;
            this.AutoScaleDimensions = new System.Drawing.SizeF(6F, 13F);
            this.AutoScaleMode = System.Windows.Forms.AutoScaleMode.Font;
            this.CancelButton = this.buttonCancel;
            this.ClientSize = new System.Drawing.Size(292, 109);
            this.Controls.Add(this.buttonOk);
            this.Controls.Add(this.buttonCancel);
            this.Controls.Add(this.textBoxPassword);
            this.Controls.Add(this.textBoxID);
```

```
            this.Controls.Add(this.label2);
            this.Controls.Add(this.label1);
            this.FormBorderStyle =
                System.Windows.Forms.FormBorderStyle.FixedDialog;
            this.MaximizeBox = false;
            this.MinimizeBox = false;
            this.Name = "Login";
            this.ShowInTaskbar = false;
            this.SizeGripStyle = System.Windows.Forms.SizeGripStyle.Hide;
            this.Text = "Login";
            this.ResumeLayout(false);
            this.PerformLayout();


        }

        #endregion

        private System.Windows.Forms.Label label1;
        private System.Windows.Forms.Label label2;
        private System.Windows.Forms.TextBox textBoxID;
        private System.Windows.Forms.TextBox textBoxPassword;
        private System.Windows.Forms.Button buttonCancel;
        private System.Windows.Forms.Button buttonOk;
    }
}
```

Creating a Windows Presentation Foundation Project

Windows Presentation Foundation projects behave much like WinForms projects do. In fact, one of the design goals for the WPF designer and editor was to act in ways that would be familiar to developers who are used to Windows Forms development. Just as we previously did with our WinForms project, we start the development and design process by selecting a template—WPF Application—from the File, New Project dialog.

Two XAML files are automatically created within the project: Windowl.xaml, which represents the main window for the app, and App.xaml, which represents the application itself. These are analogous to the Form1.cs/Form1.vb and Program.cs/Module1.vb files created in a new Windows Forms project.

The first difference you notice with WPF projects is that, by default, you are presented with two different panes: In one pane, you see the design surface for the window, and in another you see an editor that contains the XAML declarations for the form. This design view is actually the same that is used for web applications (which we investigate as part of the next topic). See Figure 6.39 for a look at the Window1 file loaded in the IDE.

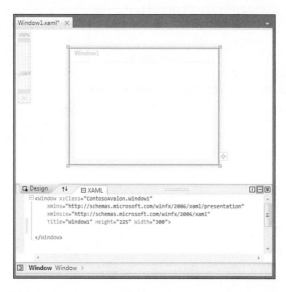

FIGURE 6.39   The initial window in the WPF designer.

Each of these panes is simply a different view of the same window: a visual view and a text/XML view. I can add a button to the window, for example, by dragging it from the toolbox onto the design surface, or by typing the XAML declaration directly into the XAML pane like this:

```
<Button Height="23.07" Name="button1" Width="75.362">Button</Button>
```

Both the design and the XAML view are kept in sync with one another automatically.

Because WPF is based on vector graphics, you can zoom in and out in the designer using the slider control in the upper left of the designer. Figure 6.40 shows the Window1 form, with a button, zoomed in at 10x.

Using the Split Panes

You have control over how the design and XAML panes are displayed and positioned within the IDE. There is a small button flagged with two-way arrows that, when pressed, swaps the position of the two panes. You can also change the panes from a horizontal to a vertical orientation (or vice versa) by clicking on the Horizontal Split or Vertical Split button. And, finally, you can collapse either pane by clicking on the Collapse/Expand Pane button.

There is one other feature of interest that is unique to the WPF designer: You can navigate back and forward through objects that you have selected by using the back and forward selectors shown in the bottom area of the designer. The controls for pane management, object navigation, and view zoom are highlighted for you in Figure 6.41.

FIGURE 6.40   10x magnification in the WPF designer.

FIGURE 6.41   WPF editor controls.

Adding Controls

WPF windows are populated with controls by using the same drag-and-drop action from the toolbox that is used with Windows Forms and Web Forms development. Control positioning and sizing is aided through snap lines and sizing boxes that look a bit different than their WinForms counterparts but perform the same tasks (see Figure 6.42).

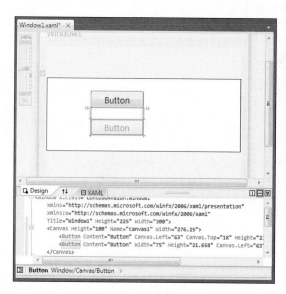

FIGURE 6.42   Positioning controls in the WPF designer.

We cover WPF development in more depth in Chapter 19, "Creating Richer, Smarter User Interfaces."

Developing Web Forms

Web forms represent the user interface element to a web application. Traditionally with .NET, the term web form is used to refer specifically to pages processed dynamically on the server (using ASP.NET). We use a broader definition here and use the term to refer to any web page, static or dynamic, that can be developed and designed within the Visual Studio IDE.

The HTML designer (also referred to as the Web designer) is the sister application to the Windows Forms and WPF designers; it allows you to visually design and edit the markup for a web page. As with the two client application designers, it works in conjunction with the HTML designer and source view to cover all the bases needed for web page design. We cover the entire web application development process in depth in Chapter 17, "Creating ASP.NET Applications"; in the following sections, we cover the basics of the web designers and editors.

Designing a Web Form Application

Web page design starts first with a web project. As previously discussed, there are two different ways for you to construct a web page or website with Visual Studio. Both of these approaches are represented by their own unique project templates. Specifically, we are talking about "web application" versus "website" projects. In Chapter 4, we broached some of the core differences between these two project types; even more detail is waiting for you in Chapter 17. However, because the actual construction of a web page with the Web designer remains exactly the same between the two project types, we concentrate here on illustrating our points by walking through a "website" project.

Select File, New Web Site, and from the dialog box select the ASP.NET Web Site option. After you set the source code directory and source language, click OK to have Visual Studio create the project and its initial web page.

The Web designer looks similar to the WPF designer; it has a design surface that acts as a canvas, allowing objects from the toolbox to be placed and positioned on its surface. Although they look slightly different from the pane controls we saw in the WPF designer, they have the same basic functions. You can work in a "split" mode in which the designer and markup editor are visible in separate panes, or you can elect to work strictly with either the designer or the editor open.

Now examine what happens when you try to mimic the login form that was previously built using Windows forms. (There is actually a prebuilt login form component that you could use here; for the sake of demonstrating the development process, however, we will go ahead and cobble together our own simplistic one for comparison's sake.)

Adding and Arranging Controls

The process of adding and arranging controls doesn't change from the Windows Forms or WPF designer process. Simply drag the controls from the toolbox onto the designer's surface. In this case, you want two labels, two text boxes, and an OK button (because this isn't a dialog box, you can dispense with the Cancel button). Changing control properties is also handled the same way via the Properties window. You can select the labels and command buttons and set their text this way.

NOTE

As you add controls to a web page, you should note that the default layout mode is relative. That is, controls are not placed at absolute coordinates on the screen but instead are placed relative to one another. Absolute positioning is accommodated via style sheets. For instance, you can select a label control, edit its style properties, and select Absolutely Position as the position mode. This will now allow you to range freely over the form with the control.

A formatting toolbar is provided by default; it supplies buttons for common text formatting actions such as changing font styles, colors, paragraph indenting, and bulleting.

To line up control edges the way you want, you can press Shift+Enter to insert spacing between the controls as necessary (this generates a break tag, <br>, in the HTML). In this case, a break was added between the first text box and the second label, and between the second text box and the first button. Figure 6.43 shows the design in progress. The text boxes don't line up and you probably want to apply a style for the label fonts and buttons; but the general layout and intent are evident. Note that the designer provides a box above the currently selected control that indicates both the control's type and the instance name of the control on the page.

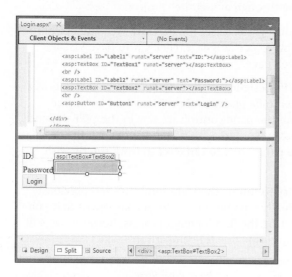

FIGURE 6.43   Creating a web form.

As a further aid for control alignment, be sure to turn on the ruler, the positioning grid, or both; they are accessed from the View menu, under Ruler and Grid.

Editing Markup

As controls and other elements are added and manipulated on the designer's surface, HTML is created to implement the design and layout. As a designer or developer, you are free to work at either the visual level with the designer or the text/source level with the HTML Source Editor. Like the other editors within Visual Studio 2010, the HTML Source Editor supports IntelliSense and other interactive features for navigating and validating markup.

Looking back at Figure 6.42, you can see the markup generated by the designer when the controls were added to the login page.

As with the other designer/editor pairs, you can write your own HTML and see it implemented immediately in the design view. The HTML editor has a toolbar as well: The HTML source editing toolbar provides quick access to code "forward and back" navigation, commenting, and schema validation options (we discuss schema validation in the section "Browser Output and Validation").

One key feature realized with the HTML editor is source format preservation: The HTML source editor works hard to respect the way that you, the developer, want your markup formatted. This includes the placement of carriage returns and whitespace, the use of indentation, and even how you want to handle word and line wrapping. In short, Visual Studio never reformats HTML code that you have written!

Working with Tables   HTML tables provide a quick and easy way to align controls on a web page. With Visual Studio 2010, there is a dedicated Insert Table dialog box that provides extensive control over table layout and appearance. To place a table onto the design surface, select Insert Table from the Table menu. The Insert Table dialog box supports custom table layouts in which you specify the row and column attributes and the general style attributes such as borders and padding. Through this dialog box, you can also select from a list of preformatted table templates.

After you've added a table to the designer, it is fully interactive for drag-and-drop resizing of its columns and rows.

Formatting Options   In addition to preserving the format of HTML that you write, Visual Studio 2010 provides fine-grained control over how the designer generates and formats the HTML that it produces. You use the HTML page and its subpages in the Options dialog box (Tools, Options, Text Editor, HTML) to configure indentation style, quotation use, word wrapping, and tag casing (see Figure 6.44).

FIGURE 6.44   HTML formatting options.

Settings can be applied globally for all markup, or you can set options on a per-tag basis by clicking the Tag Specific Options button (Text Editor, HTML, Format). As an example, this level of control is useful if your particular coding style uses line breaks within your table column tags (<td>), but not with your table row tags (<tr>). In Figure 6.45, the tr tag is being set to support line breaks before and after the tag, but not within the tag.

FIGURE 6.45   Setting HTML formatting options at the tag level.

Managing Styles and Style Sheets

Visual Studio has a complete set of tools for managing styles and cascading style sheets. The Manage Styles and Apply Styles windows are both used to perform common style editing tasks, including applying a style to the current HTML document, or attaching/detaching a cascading style sheet file to/from the current HTML document. The third tool, the CSS Properties window, enumerates all the CSS properties for the currently selected page element, allowing for quick changes for any of the property values.

A typical workflow for editing styles might look like this:

1. Open a web page
2. Define a new style
3. Apply the style
4. Tweak the style

Figure 6.46 shows the Manage Styles window, and its capability to itemize and preview any of the formatting elements within a style sheet. The Options button at the upper-right of the window is used to control the way that the list of elements within a style sheet is shown (by order, by type, and so on), or to filter the elements that are shown (all, only those used in the current page, and so on).

FIGURE 6.46 The Manage Styles window.

Both the Manage Styles window and the Apply Styles window are accessed from the View menu.

Browser Output and Validation

The result of all the design effort put into an HTML document is its final rendering within a browser. With various flavors of browsers in use supporting various levels of HTML specifications (including XHTML), it is difficult to ensure that the page's design intent actually matches reality. Visual Studio's browser target settings help with this problem by enabling you to easily target a specific HTML standard or browser. As you type HTML into the source editor, Visual Studio validates the syntax on the fly against your selected browser target. If a piece of markup violates the rules of your particular validation target, it is flagged by the familiar red squiggly line (complete with a ToolTip explaining the exact violation), and the error is listed within the Task List window.

The target can be selected on the HTML designer or source editor toolbar; just pick the target from the drop-down.

> **NOTE**
>
> The validation rules for a given browser or standard can actually be customized to support targets that do not ship out of the box with Visual Studio.

Standards Compliance   The HTML code generated by the HTML designer is, by default, XHTML compliant; tags, for instance, are well formed with regard to XHTML requirements. Using the various XHTML validation targets helps you to ensure that the code you write is compliant as well.

Visual Studio also focuses on providing compliance with accessibility standards—those standards that govern the display of web pages for persons with disabilities. You launch the Accessibility Checker by using the Check Page for Accessibility button on the HTML Source Editing or Formatting toolbars.

Figure 6.47 shows the Accessibility Validation dialog box. You can select the specific standards you want to have your HTML validated against. You can also select the level of feedback that you receive (errors, warnings, or a text checklist). Each item flagged by the checker appears in the Task List window for resolution. For more details on the two standards supported here (WCAG and Access Board Section 508), see their respective websites: http://www.w3.org/TR/WCAG10/ and http://www.access-board.gov/508.htm.

FIGURE 6.47   Setting accessibility validation options.

Authoring WinForms Components and Controls

Referring to our earlier discussion of Windows forms, components are non-visual controls or classes. This is a good generic definition, but a more specific one is this: A component is any class that inherits from System.ComponentModel.IComponent. This particular interface provides support for designability and resource handling. If you need a designable control that does not have a user interface of its own, you work with a component. Controls are similar in function but not form; a control is a reusable chunk of code that does have a visual element to it.

Because Visual Studio provides a dedicated design surface for creating Windows Forms components, we cover this separately in this section. WPF projects also allow for custom controls and components, but in a fashion that is much more streamlined and integrated with the overall development of forms in the WPF world. We cover some of that content in our WPF chapter later in the book (Chapter 19).

Creating a New Component or Control

Starting from an existing WinForms project, you kick off the process of authoring a component by using the Add New Item dialog box (from the Project menu). Selecting Component Class in this dialog box adds the stub code file to your current project and launches the component designer. To start control development, you use the Add New User Control dialog box.

> **NOTE**
>
> Essentially two different "types" of WinForms controls can be authored within Visual Studio: custom controls and user controls. Custom controls inherit directly from the System.Windows.Forms.Control class; they are typically code intensive because you, the developer, are responsible for writing all the code necessary to render the control's visual portion. User controls (sometimes called *composite controls*) inherit from the System.Windows.Forms.UserControl class. User controls are advantageous because you can build them quickly by compositing other controls together that are already available in the toolbox. These controls already have their user interface portion coded for you.

Both the control and the component designers work on the same principles as the Windows Forms designer: The designers allow you to drag an object from the toolbox onto the design surface.

Assume that you need a component that sends a signal across a serial port every x minutes. Because Visual Studio already provides a timer and a serial port component, which are accessible from the toolbox, you can use the component designer to add these objects to your own custom component and then leverage and access their intrinsic properties and methods (essentially, using them as building blocks to get your desired functionality).

Figure 6.48 shows the component designer for this fictional custom component. Two objects have been added: a timer and a process component.

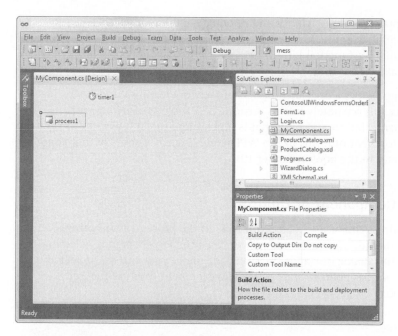

FIGURE 6.48   The component designer.

A similar scenario can be envisioned with a user control. You can take the example of a login "form," consisting of two text boxes, two labels, and two buttons, and actually make that a control—one that can be easily included in the toolbox and dropped onto a Windows form or web form.

Further Notes on Writing Component Code

Because the component has no visual aspect to it, you don't have the layout and formatting features that you see with the Windows Forms designer. However, the concept of drag-and-drop programming is alive and well. Visual Studio, behind the scenes, injects the code to programmatically add the given class to the component's container. From there, you can edit the various objects' properties, double-click an object to get to its code, and so on.

When you drag the timer and process objects over from the toolbox, Visual Studio aggregates these objects into the component by automatically writing the code shown in Listing 6.2.

LISTING 6.2   Component Designer–Generated Code

```
namespace Contoso.UI.WindowsForms.OrderEntry
{
```

```csharp
partial class Component1
{
    /// <summary>
    /// Required designer variable.
    /// </summary>
    private System.ComponentModel.IContainer components = null;

    /// <summary>
    /// Clean up any resources being used.
    /// </summary>
    /// <param name="disposing">true if managed resources should be
    /// disposed; otherwise, false.</param>
    protected override void Dispose(bool disposing)
    {
        if (disposing && (components != null))
        {
            components.Dispose();
        }
        base.Dispose(disposing);
    }

    #region Component Designer generated code

    /// <summary>
    /// Required method for Designer support - do not modify
    /// the contents of this method with the code editor.
    /// </summary>
    private void InitializeComponent()
    {
        this.components = new System.ComponentModel.Container();
        this.timer1 = new System.Windows.Forms.Timer(this.components);
        this.serialPort1 = new System.IO.Ports.SerialPort(this.components);

    }

    #endregion

    private System.Windows.Forms.Timer timer1;
    private System.IO.Ports.SerialPort serialPort1;


}
```

Writing code "behind" one of the objects placed on the component designer canvas is easy: Double-click the object's icon, and the code editor is launched. For instance, double-clicking on the timer icon on the designer surface causes the timer1_Tick routine to be created and then launched in the code editor.

Creating Classes with the Class Designer

The final designer we cover in this chapter is the Class Designer. The Class Designer, via its class diagram, allows you to get a view of your code as it exists statically (or at rest). You also get real-time synchronization between the model and the actual code. You should think of the class designer more as a visual code editor and less like a diagram. If you make a change to code, that change is reflected in the diagram. When you change the diagram, your code changes too.

Creating a Class Diagram

There are a couple of ways to create a class diagram. The first is to add a class diagram to your project from the Add New Item dialog box. Here, you select a class diagram template (.cd) and add it to the project. You can then add items to this diagram from the Toolbox or from existing classes in the Solution Explorer.

The second way to add a class diagram to a project is to choose View Class Diagram from the context menu for a given project. In this way, Visual Studio generates a class diagram from an existing project. This option is shown in Figure 6.49.

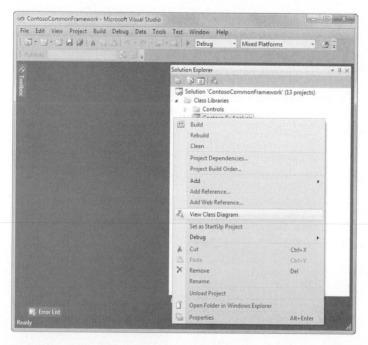

FIGURE 6.49   Launching the Class Designer.

In either case, you end up with a .cd file in your project that represents the visual model of your classes. Clearly the View Class Diagram option saves you the time of dragging everything onto the diagram. Figure 6.50 shows an example of the Class Designer file. We cover each window shown in this designer.

FIGURE 6.50   The Class Designer.

Displaying Members

You use the arrow icon (points up or down) in the upper-right corner of each object in the designer to toggle whether to show or hide its members. This is useful if you need to conserve screen real-estate, or if you are interested only in members of a particular class.

You can also use the Class Designer toolbar to indicate how members are grouped for display and what additional information is shown. For example, you can sort members alphabetically, group them by their kind (property, method, and so on), or group by access (public, private, and so on). You can then indicate whether you want to display just member names, their names and types, or the full signatures.

Adding Items to the Diagram

You add items to the Class Designer by using either the Toolbox or the Solution Explorer. The Toolbox is for adding new items. You use the Solution Explorer to add existing classes to the diagram. In both scenarios, you simply drag and drop the item onto the Class Designer window. If the item already exists, Visual Studio builds out the class details for you. In fact, if the class file contains more than one class, each class is placed as an object on the diagram.

Figure 6.51 shows an example of the Class Designer Toolbox tools. Notice that you can define all object-oriented concepts here, including classes, interfaces, inheritance, and so on.

FIGURE 6.51   The Class Designer Toolbox.

When you add a new item such as a class or struct to the designer, the designer prompts you for the item's name and location. You can choose to generate a new file to house the item or place it in an existing file. Figure 6.52 shows the New Class dialog box. Here, you can give the class a name, set its access modifier, and indicate a filename.

FIGURE 6.52   Adding a new class to the Class Designer.

Defining Relationships Between Classes

One of the biggest benefits of the class diagram is that it visually represents the relationships between classes. These relationships are much easier to see in a diagram than through code. The following relationships can be represented:

▶ **Inheritance**—Indicates whether a class inherits from another class

▶ **Interface**—Indicates whether a class implements one or more interfaces

▶ **Association**—Indicates an association between classes

Let's look at implementing each of these relationships through an example.

Inheritance

First, let's look at inheritance with the class designer. Suppose that you have a base class called EmployeeBase. This class represents a generic employee in your system. You then want to create a concrete Employee class that inherits from Product. To do this with the Class Designer, you make sure that both classes are on the screen. You then select the Inheritance tool from the Class Designer Toolbox. This tool has its own special icon that shows an arrow pointing upward. This visual cue indicates that you want to draw the inheritance from the implementation class to the base class.

When the drawing is complete, the inheritance arrow should point toward the base class. Figure 6.53 shows an example. Also, notice that the Employee class now contains an icon indicating that it inherits Product.

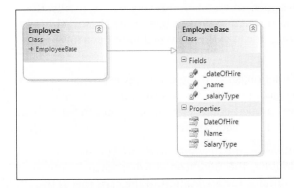

FIGURE 6.53   Class inheritance.

Interface

The next visual relationship we look at is an interface. For this example, suppose that all the business entities in your system implement a similar contract. This contract might define properties for ID and name. It might also define methods such as Get, Delete, and Save.

To implement this interface, you again use the Inheritance tool from the Class Designer Toolbox. You drag it from the class doing the implementation toward the interface. Figure 6.54 shows the result of an implemented interface. Notice the lollipop icon above the Customer class; it denotes the interface implementation.

FIGURE 6.54   Implementing an Interface.

Association

The final relationship to look at is association. This relationship is typically a loose one in the UML world. However, in the Class Designer, an association is very real. Typically, this means that two classes have an association through the use of one of the classes. This relationship is also optional in terms of viewing. It can exist, but you do not have to show it in the diagram.

For example, suppose that you have an Order object. This object might expose an OrderStatus property. Suppose that it also has a property for accessing the Customer record associated with the order. These two properties are associations. You can leave them as properties, or you can choose to show them as associations.

You can also draw these property associations on the diagram. To do so, you select the Association tool from the Toolbox. This tool has the same icon as Inheritance. You then draw the association from the class that contains the association to the class that is the object of the association. You can also right-click the actual property that represents the association and choose Show as Association from the context menu (or Show as Collection Association for associations that are part of a collection).

The result is that the association property is displayed on the association arrow. This indicates that the class from where the association originates contains this property (it is shown only on this line, however). Figure 6.55 illustrates this.

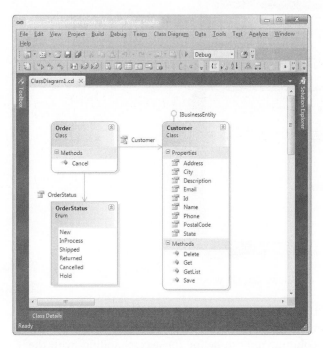

FIGURE 6.55   Creating an association.

Defining Methods, Properties, Fields, and Events

The most exciting part of the Class Designer is that it allows you to do more than define classes and relationships. You can actually stub out code and do refactoring (see Chapter 10, "Refactoring Code," for details).

There are two ways to add code to your classes, structs, interfaces, and the like. The first is to type directly into the designer. For example, if you are in the Properties section of a class, you can right-click and choose to add a new property. This places the property in your class and allows you to edit it in the diagram. This method works for other class members as well. It does have a couple of drawbacks, however. You can't, for instance, define a full method signature or indicate access levels. For that, you need the Class Details window.

The Class Details window allows you to fully define methods, fields, properties, and events for a class. It also works with other constructs such as interfaces, delegates, and enums. To use this window, right-click a class and choose Class Details from the context menu. Selecting this menu item brings up the Class Details editor for the selected class. Figure 6.56 shows the Class Details window in action.

FIGURE 6.56   Creating a method in the Class Details window.

Notice that when working in the Class Details window, you still get IntelliSense. In this example, the Cancel method is being added to the Order class. You can indicate a return type for the method with the Type column. You can define the access modifier with the Modifier column. You can also set the parameters of the method. In this case, the method takes the parameter reasonCode.

Finally, there are the Summary and Hide columns. The Hide column indicates whether you want to show an item on the diagram. This capability allows you to hide various members when printing or exporting as an image. The Summary column allows you to add your XML documentation to the class. Clicking the ellipsis button (not shown) in this field brings up the Description dialog box. Here, you can enter your XML summary information for the given member. Figure 6.57 shows an example for the Cancel method.

FIGURE 6.57   Creating code comments for a method.

Summary

Visual Studio provides a full array of editors and designers. They cover the gamut of solution development activities from WYSIWYG positioning of graphical controls to finely tuned text editing for a certain language, syntax, or markup.

This chapter described how to leverage the basics within these editors and designers. It also described how the editor and designer relationship provides two complementary views of the same solution artifact, in effect working together to provide you, the developer, with the right tool for the right task at hand.

In subsequent chapters, we look at the more advanced options and productivity features available within these tools and even look at end-to-end development efforts involved in building a web application with ASP.NET or Silverlight, and building a Windows application using Windows Forms or Windows Presentation Foundation.

The .NET Community: Interacting Online

The image of a developer coding away, disconnected from others and from vast amounts of information on the Internet is an anachronism. Instead, development is now a very connected experience. It is common when programming to expect to take advantage of the large and diverse .NET community. Take a quick look across the Internet and you can find countless bits of content and help for building applications. Microsoft continues to add community features to Visual Studio. These features connect developers with the content in the cloud. They help you quickly gain access to information, sample code, and productivity aids provided by other developers and communities. Visual Studio helps to package this content, manage it, and streamline access to it.

This chapter covers how developers can take advantage of the community capabilities of Visual Studio 2010. You see how to gain access to community content that is right for you, how to get community-driven support, and how to find and consume code from the developer community. Finally, you also learn how you can bundle your own code samples and productivity aids for sharing with the .NET community.

The Community Features of Visual Studio

Software development has become a more connected experience. Web services, RSS feeds, websites, and the like provide access to rich content well beyond what was once stored on a local hard drive or network. This content is no longer simply supplied by and managed by Microsoft.

Microsoft provides a huge amount of developer help, samples, and information, but it also recognizes the contributions of the greater .NET community. Visual Studio 2010 provides links to all of this content. The intent is to provide developers with important (and targeted) product, development, and learning information where developers will find it: in their IDE. Taking advantage of this content helps you increase your productivity and use of best practices.

The Visual Studio team has refined the community connections and features in the IDE over the years so it is intuitive and unobtrusive (yet readily available). You do not have to go searching to find and connect to your community. Rather, these communities are delivered to you through your development tool. If you are looking to find specific information, explore what is available, or publish your own community content, you can do so directly from within Visual Studio 2010. The following sections illustrate what is available from the IDE in terms of the Visual Studio Start Page and the Help menu.

The Visual Studio Start Page

Developers new to Visual Studio 2010 first encounter the IDE through the Start Page. The Start Page acts as a simple portal to your development experience and includes links to community content.

The Start Page is divided into two primary sections. On the left is the projects area, which includes links for creating a new project, opening an existing one, or clicking on a recent project. The right side contains a lot of information inside three tabs:

- ▶ **Getting Started**—This tab provides links to content for starting with Visual Studio, Windows, Web, Cloud, Office, SharePoint, and Data-driven applications. This is also one place where you can link to community inside the Community and Learning Resources link.

- ▶ **Guidance and Resources**—Provides helpful content on things related to Development Process, MSDN Resources, and Additional Tools.

- ▶ **Latest News**—This tab is an RSS reader and can be connected to the latest news on all things .NET-related.

Figure 7.1 shows a sample of the Start Page in the IDE. Notice that the sample Start Page (or portal) shown in Figure 7.1 is for a developer who has set default settings in the IDE to Visual C# Development Settings (Tools, Import and Export Settings). The Start Page (and other items in the IDE such as toolbars and layout) change to reflect the setup of your default profile in the IDE (see Chapter 2, "The Visual Studio IDE," for more information). For example, if you select Visual Basic Development Settings, your Get Started / Welcome tab includes links targeted to a Visual Basic developer.

Projects Area

The projects section of the Start Page provides quick links to connecting to a Team Foundation Server (TFS) to open a project from source control, create a new project, or open an existing one. Using these links, you can quickly start a new project, create a new website, or browse to another project not listed here. Having quick access to these features makes the Start Page more useful as a launch point for your daily development work.

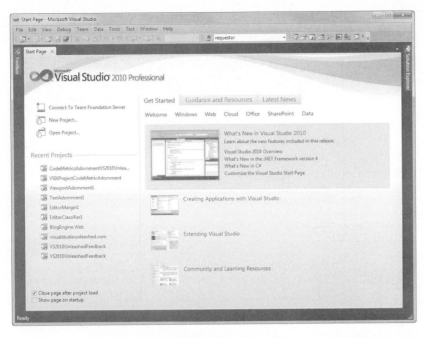

FIGURE 7.1   The Visual Studio Start Page.

This area also includes a list of projects you have been working on. This allows you to easily access one or more projects in which you are currently engaged. Clicking on a project in this list opens that project for editing. Figure 7.2 shows an example of a projects area on the Start Page.

Get Started

The Get Started tab on the Start Page provides developers who are new to Visual Studio 2010 (or those looking to learn something new) a common place to start. The links in this list typically revolve around creating a new project, using a template or starter kit, answering a question, or learning something new. This feature can be a great launch point for doing your own exploration. Figure 7.3 shows an example of the Get Started tab from a C# developer's Start Page. Of course, this section changes based on your developer profile (VB, C#, C++, Web, and so on).

In Figure 7.3, you can see that the Get Started area provides links directly to MSDN help in terms of what's new. You can also connect directly to community-related websites (Community and Learning Resources) or download add-ins and starter kits (Extending Visual Studio). Clicking one of these links brings up additional options as shown in Figure 7.4.

FIGURE 7.2   The Projects area on the Visual Studio Start Page.

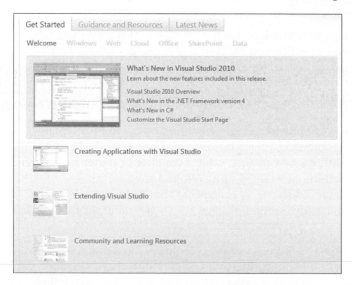

FIGURE 7.3   The Get Started tab on the Visual Studio Start Page.

Guidance and Resources

The Visual Studio Guidance and Resources tab on the Start Page shows announcements and headlines relative to Visual Studio. Figure 7.5 shows an example. You can see that the feature contains information from the Patterns and Practices group at Microsoft. Visiting the Microsoft Patterns and Practices area is a great way to find information about best practices and development process regardless of your chosen language.

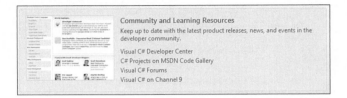

FIGURE 7.4   Clicking on a link inside the tab window displays multiple options.

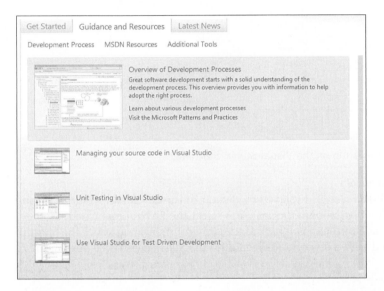

FIGURE 7.5   The Guidance and Resources tab on the Visual Studio Start Page.

Latest News

The Latest News tab (the top right on Figure 7.5) on the Start Page provides links to all the current news and important information about Visual Studio. This information includes announcements on training, new betas, new tools, webcasts, and more. It helps keep you informed even if you do not have time for browsing the MSDN website. Figure 7.6 shows an example of some of the news captured when beta 2 of 2010 was first released.

Content for the news channel comes to the IDE via an RSS feed. For those of you unfamiliar with the term *RSS*, it stands for *Really Simple Syndication*. RSS is provides an XML-structured list that contains summaries and links to key information found within a particular website. You can see from Figure 7.6 that you can reset the URL to the Start Page's Latest News. Note that when you first use this tab, you will have to use the Enable RSS Feed button to turn on this feature; it is off by default.

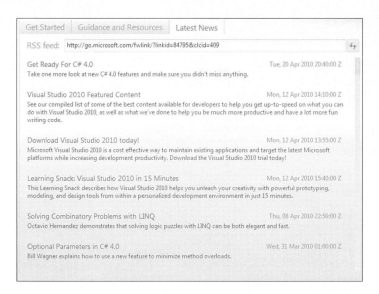

FIGURE 7.6   The Latest News tab on the Visual Studio Start Page.

Setting a Custom News Channel

You can customize which RSS feed is displayed by default in the Latest News tab. To do so, you use the Options dialog box (Tools, Options). You select the Environment node from the tree view on the left side of the dialog box. Under Environment, you select the Startup leaf and you are presented with a few options regarding the Start Page. These options are shown in Figure 7.7.

FIGURE 7.7   You can use the Startup node to set Start Page settings.

The second option inside the Startup options dialog box is Start Page news channel. Here you can set a URL to a default RSS feed. This option allows for easy customization and connection to any RSS channel. Changing this setting changes the default RSS data that is displayed in the Latest News tab of the Start Page.

TIP

Some common MSDN RSS feeds and their URLs can be found inside the MSDN developer centers from Microsoft. You can access the list of developer centers at http:/ /msdn.microsoft.com/en-us/aa937802.aspx. From this page, select a developer center. You can then look for a list of information that has an RSS logo associated to it (as shown in Figure 7.8). Click the RSS logo. Copy the resulting URL from the Address bar to the Start Page news channel inside the Options dialog box (shown in Figure 7.7).

FIGURE 7.8   An RSS link inside one of the MSDN developer centers.

Selecting What to Do at Startup

You can choose what Visual Studio does at the time of application startup. Refer to Figure 7.7. Notice the first option, At Startup. This drop-down list enables you to choose to either show the Start Page, load your last solution, show the open or new project dialog box, show an empty environment, or open a home page. Most of these options are self-explanatory. The last one (open home page), however, requires a little explanation. By setting this value, Visual Studio opens to the home page for the development center based on your IDE settings. For example, if you configured your IDE as primarily a VB developer the VB developer center opens for you when Visual Studio starts (provided you select the home page option). Figure 7.9 shows an example for a C# developer.

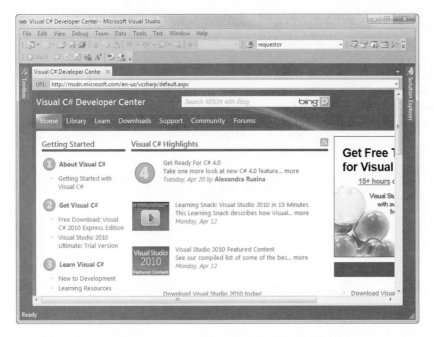

FIGURE 7.9   You can load a language-based, startup home page inside the IDE.

TIP

If you choose not to see the Start Page when your IDE starts (show empty environment), or you close the Start Page and need to get back to it, you can still navigate to the Start Page. You do so by using the Start Page toolbar icon as shown in Figure 7.10. Alternatively, you can choose View, Start Page from the IDE menu bar.

FIGURE 7.10   Accessing the Start Page using the toolbar icon.

Creating a Custom Start Page

You can have full control over what is displayed when you (or your team) open the IDE. The Start Page is a .xaml WPF form that you can customize. You can either start with a blank WPF form and turn it into a start page or use the start page project template. The project template makes thing easier because it already contains a fully functioning start page. To get the project template, you download it from the Visual Studio Code Gallery (http://visualstudiogallery.msdn.microsoft.com). Search for "Custom Start Page Project Template" to find this free download from Microsoft. Note that you also need the Visual Studio 2010 SDK (again found through a quick search).

Once installed, you can create a new start page project from File, New Project. Then select Visual C#, Extensibility. There you should find the Custom Start Page template.

The Solution contains two projects: the start page and a start page control. The start page project contains the actual start page (StartPage.xaml) and creates the VSIX required for deployment (more on VSIX later in this chapter). The start page control is a WPF user control you use to add custom content to your start page. Figure 7.11 shows the default view of the two projects.

FIGURE 7.11   You can edit the Start Page displayed inside your IDE.

Remember, the Start Page is a WPF form. Therefore, you can create a totally custom Start Page or customize the existing Start Page.

As an example, suppose you want to add a tab to the Start Page to show the current state of the project. You could edit the XAML file to add the tab group and a related control that reads a report from a website URL. For more on XAML coding, see Chapter 19, "Creating Richer, Smarter User Interfaces."

After the project is complete, you build it and use the VSIX file for deployment. When run, it will install the new start page. You then can then use the Options dialog box

(Figure 7.7) to select the new start page. Figure 7.12 shows an example of a daily project status indicator pulled from the project website. Having this on the developer's IDE at startup keeps all eyes on the current state of the project.

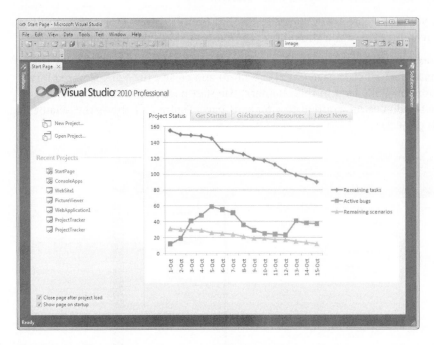

FIGURE 7.12   You can customize the IDE Start Page to show your own information.

Accessing Help

The Visual Studio Help menu is there for you when you get stuck and need to reach out for some assistance. The Help menu provides access to the Visual Studio Documentation (either local or online). It lets you quickly search for an answer to a question, access code samples, or even report a bug with Visual Studio or the Framework. Figure 7.13 shows the Help menu.

Manage Your Help Settings

The Visual Studio help system has been re-vamped for 2010. The Microsoft Document Explorer application is no longer a part of the help system. Instead, Microsoft is moving to a system that creates a stronger link between the online help and your local help. You can choose to access all your help locally, online, or through a combination of the two. You can also get updates to your local help on a regular basis.

How you receive help is controlled through the Help menu link, Manage Help Settings. Clicking this link brings up the Help Library Manager as shown in Figure 7.14. From here, you can determine if you want to use online or local help (or a combination); you can also get updates to your help system, add and remove local content, and find content online or browse to local downloads.

FIGURE 7.13   The Visual Studio Help menu connects you to help and your community.

FIGURE 7.14   The help settings allow you to control how you get help inside the IDE.

Choose Between Online and Local Help

The new Help system has been simplified somewhat to use compressed XML files, which makes authoring, downloading, and accessing the help content easier. You can use the Help Library Manager to indicate what help you want available locally and what you want to only access via the Internet.

To get started managing your help settings, you can click on Choose Online or Local Help link from the dialog box shown in Figure 7.14. The Settings dialog box shown in Figure 7.15 opens. This is where you set your preference as to whether or not to use any local version of help. We suggest that if you travel or work unconnected from the Internet, you might want some portion of the help system available locally. The Library Location option simply indicates where your help is stored on the machine.

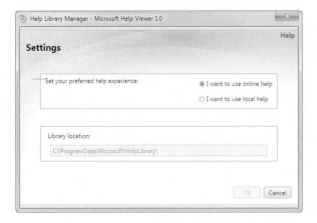

FIGURE 7.15   You can switch between online and offline help.

Adding Help Content to Your Local Collection

You can choose which content areas you download and sync locally by selecting the Find Content Online link (refer to Figure 7.14). This brings up all the Visual Studio help content areas as shown in Figure 7.16. Notice that you can see which items are already local (Status column). For those that are not local, you can click the Add link from the Actions column to add them to your local sync.

FIGURE 7.16   Adding help content to your local machine.

Update Your Local Help

You can periodically update your local help files. New help is released often by Microsoft, so it is a good idea to check for updates on a regular basis. You do so by clicking the

Check for Updates Online link (refer to Figure 7.14), which brings up the Checking for Updates dialog box as shown in Figure 7.17. If updates are found (as shown in the figure) then clicking the Update button downloads those updates locally.

FIGURE 7.17   You can update your local help system.

Using the Visual Studio Documentation

The online version of the Visual Studio documentation is similar to other versions. Clicking help takes you to msdn.microsoft.com. From there you can navigate the MSDN library.

The local help version is a copy of the content found online inside the MSDN library. You still access this content with a web browser. However, the local version includes a new Search box and a related navigation control. The search box allows just that, search across your local help. The navigation control is a fast way to see where you are in the help system; it allows you to navigate up or down in your current branch of the help tree and access related content to your selected topic. Figure 7.18 shows an example. Notice that the browser is set to a local URL. The left-side navigation is not the full help system tree. Rather, it shows you where you are at the present time and gives access both up and down to additional content. You can, of course, use the browser's Back button, too. The related links area gives you access to other information related to your selected topic.

MSDN Forums

The MSDN Forums item on the Help menu allows you to search the community forums for answers to questions you have about Visual Studio or the .NET Framework and related languages. When you click this button, Visual Studio navigates to a general page for the MSDN Community Forums. This page allows you to search, browse, and login to the forums. Figure 7.19 shows an example.

The MSDN Community Forums allow developers to find information relevant to a common problem or to post specific issues and receive feedback from the community. The intent of these moderated forums is to provide a community of developers to aid other developers.

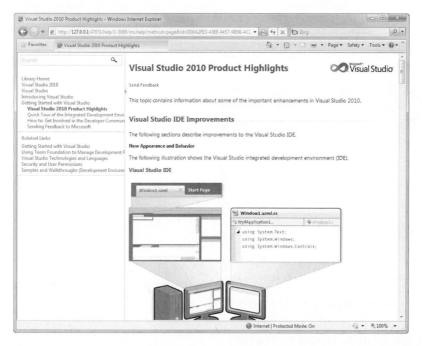

FIGURE 7.18 The Visual Studio local help system includes a quick navigation pane (on the left).

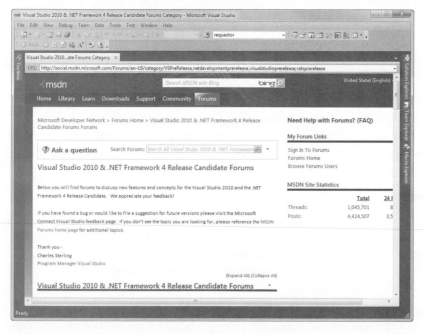

FIGURE 7.19 Search for an answer to your question.

When you reach out to the MSDN forums, you start the process of getting an answer to your question by first searching to find out whether your question was already asked (and possibly already answered). You have the option to search only the new stuff (VS 2010 and .NET Framework 4.0) or all MSDN forums. Figure 7.20 shows an example of setting this option.

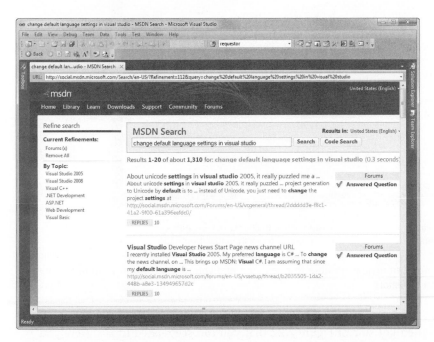

FIGURE 7.20   You can set your search options to the new stuff or all of MSDN forums.

For example, suppose you want to search the forums for answers to a question pertaining to changing the default language for Visual Studio. In this case, the new forums do not have much to offer (at present). However, this question was asked and answered inside prior editions. Therefore, you can set your search settings accordingly and click the Search button. MSDN searches the community forum for relevant matches. Figure 7.21 shows the matches returned by the sample question.

FIGURE 7.21   The sample search results from the MSDN forums.

In this example, the results show that someone has already asked a similar question in the MSDN forums. Results are displayed based on Bing's (Microsoft's search engine for the Web) relevance rating to your search text. If you are specific enough, you can typically find your question in the first few search results.

When you select a search result from the forums you are taken to a page showing the question and the various replies and answers. Figure 7.22 shows an example of a topic page. From here, you can quickly see any replies to the given question. Those replies that have been flagged as answers to the question are highlighted in green, which makes it much easier to find real answers to your questions and not have to filter through a large number of replies that did not really answer the question. You can also vote on the best answers (you must have an account and be logged in). Those replies that have the largest number of votes float to the top of the list.

FIGURE 7.22   You can review answers to questions and vote on those that provide the best answer to a given question.

Notice, too, on the right side of Figure 7.22 that you can see related topics. Here you can pick a topic that includes an answer (check mark) or one that still needs to be answered (question mark). Select the latter if you think you can add to the discussion of a specific question.

Finally, if you are signed in, you have access to a few more options. You can use the Alert Me button (at the top of the posted question) to receive alerts when a new post is added to the discussion thread (more on this a bit later). You can also quickly access the forums, threads, and other users in which you might have a specific interest.

Starting a New Thread

Of course, often your search does not come up with a suitable answer. In these cases, you can post the question to the appropriate community forum. You can browse forums directly and post your thread or question right there. You can also quickly post a question using the Ask a Question button from the home page (see the upper left of the page shown in Figure 7.19).

To post a question (or do much else on the forums) you must have a Windows Live account and be logged in. When you start, you decide if you want to ask a question or start a discussion. Figure 7.23 shows an example. In either case, before your new item is listed, the page shows a list of possible topics that already match your question or discussion topic (as shown in the middle of Figure 7.23).

FIGURE 7.23   You can ask a question or start a discussion on the MSDN Forums.

If you end up posting a new topic or question, you need to select the correct forum and tag the content accordingly. Figure 7.24 shows tagging your content and selecting a forum. Finally, you can select the Alert Me link to make sure you are notified in the event people reply to your post.

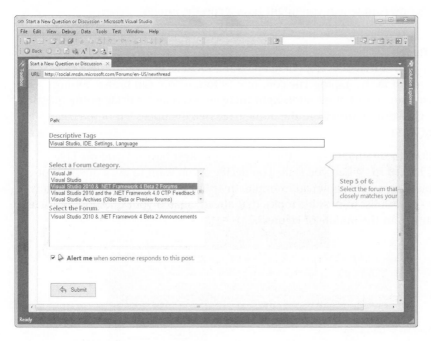

FIGURE 7.24   Completing a MSDN Forum post.

After you've completed the form, your new question or discussion topic is added to the appropriate forum and marked unanswered. Typically, each forum has a group of people who peruse these unanswered questions and provide assistance.

NOTE

Microsoft is providing preferential support in the MSDN Forums to people with MSDN subscriptions. This support is being rolled out in the 2010 timeframe.

Navigating Forums and Topics

The MSDN Community Forums are organized into a wide variety of high-level forum categories. These categories include web development, .NET, Visual Studio, Visual Basic,

C#, and many more. Each forum category is further refined by the actual forums in the given category.

You click on a forum category to navigate to the forums list for the given category. You can find forums that might be of particular interest to you in the Visual Studio category (or any of the other forums on the forum home page). Figure 7.25 shows the main page for the Visual Studio 2010 Beta 2 category. From here, you can find forums related to developing different types of applications with Visual Studio 2010.

FIGURE 7.25   The Visual Studio 2010 category home page.

Selecting a given forum from a category takes you to the main page for that forum. From here, you can find announcements related to the forum and the actual discussion threads. You can browse the discussion threads, or you can filter them by most popular, posts with code, posts flagged as helpful, and posts that have no reply. You can also sort the topics by recent replies, most views, and most replies. The forums keep track of which items you have and have not read. You can mark all items as read or mark as unread. Of course you can also search the forum.

As an example, Figure 7.26 shows some of the topics found on the Visual Studio 2010 Install and Setup forum. Notice you can see which items are unanswered (designated by the question mark icon). You can also see the number of replies and views for each item.

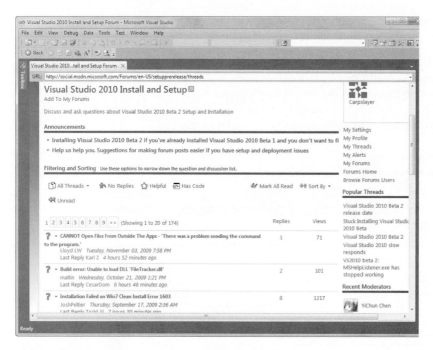

FIGURE 7.26   You can filter how you view the discussion topics in a given forum.

The forums are decorated with many icons. Some are shown in Figure 7.26. The icons help you to navigate through topics. As you look through the topics, you quickly learn that not all topics are questions and not all questions are answered. The icons also help guide you to the content within a given topic. For instance, a check mark over a document icon indicates that the topic is an answer to a question. Helpful items have a star icon. There are many icons with which you should become familiar. Figure 7.27 shows the icons and what they mean.

What do the Thread icons mean?
The following table lists the Thread icons and their meanings.

Icon	Legend	Icon	Legend
	Thread Has Code		All Threads
	Helpful Post	?	Unanswered Thread
	No Replies		Answered Thread
	Sort By		General Discussion Thread
	Start New Thread		Proposed Answer
	User		Sticky Thread
	Alerts		Locked Thread
	Reply		Abusive Thread
	Quote	X	Deleted Thread
	Edit	!	Escalated Thread

FIGURE 7.27   The icons used to help you understand the forums.

Managing Your Thread Alerts

Typically, when you start a new thread or post a new question, you ask to receive alerts when someone replies to your post or answers your question. In addition, if you find a topic that is of particular interest, you can request to be alerted when new posts are made to the thread. The MSDN Community Forums enable you to receive these alerts via email, instant messenger, or a mobile device. This capability allows the community to stay in touch with its participating members without forcing them to constantly log in and check for activity.

Your forum alerts are managed against your Windows Live ID. This allows all alerting functionality to be managed in a central location. For example, you might get alerts from eBay, MSN, the forums, or other calendar-type applications. You can control all these alerts from your Windows Live ID. Figure 7.28 shows some of the options you have for managing forum alerts. You can get to these options by clicking on My Alerts inside the forums and then selecting the Configure Alerts link.

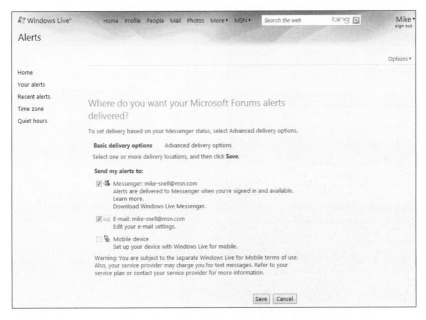

FIGURE 7.28   You can manage your Windows Forum alerts in the same place you manage all your Windows Live alerts.

Notice in Figure 7.28 that there are basic options and advanced delivery options. The latter allows for alerts to be sent based on your MSN Messenger status. If you are logged in, you can get an IM; if not, the alert can be forwarded to your email or phone.

Reporting a Bug and Other Customer Feedback Options

Most developers we've met love to work with cool software and are always looking for ways it might be improved. This holds especially true for their tools, the biggest of which is Visual Studio. There are a couple options to help Microsoft make this tool better. One option is to allow Microsoft to collect data about your customer experience with the product. The other includes making suggestions and reporting any issues, anomalies, or actual bugs you find in your day-to-day programming.

Help Improve Visual Studio

You can choose to participate in the Visual Studio Customer Improvement Program. This option is first presented at the time you install the product. If you ever want to change your original selection you can do so by selecting the Customer Feedback Options menu item from the Help menu. This brings up the dialog box shown in Figure 7.29. Here you can choose to participate or not. If you choose to participate, Visual Studio collects usage data from you and sends it anonymously back to Microsoft. Microsoft then uses that data to identify usage trends with Visual Studio and to help improve the overall product.

FIGURE 7.29   You can choose to help improve Visual Studio.

Report a Bug or Make a Suggestion

Often you think of something that would make for a great addition or perhaps you find a flaw (or bug) in the software. Using the Report a Bug item on the Help menu, you can post your suggestions and log any bugs you find.

The process for reporting bugs and making suggestions is similar to that of starting a new thread in the MSDN forums. After you log in, you see the Microsoft Connect website. Figure 7.30 shows the main page of this site.

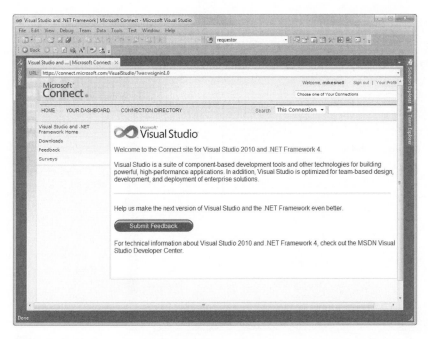

FIGURE 7.30   You can report a bug or make a suggestion for Visual Studio.

The process starts by first searching for a similar suggestion or bug, which helps to reduce the creation of duplicate submissions. If you find an item similar to the one you had planned to post, you can rate the item in terms of relative importance. Adding an importance vote helps Microsoft to focus on items of highest relevance to the community. You can also add a workaround to the item (if you know one), add the item to your watch list for additional monitoring, or indicate that you can reproduce the issue. You can also add comments to a suggestion or bug. Adding your comments to an item allows you to provide similar evidence or clarification to a reported bug or suggestion. Figure 7.31 shows the screen for an active bug.

Microsoft actively monitors these lists. In fact, most items are marked with Microsoft comments and are closed or resolved in new builds and service packs. In addition, if you find a bug for which you know a workaround, you can attach your workaround to the item. This is another way the .NET community can help itself.

Samples

Selecting the Samples link from the Help menu takes you to a ReadMe.htm page for Visual Studio 2010 samples. Here you learn how to access up-to-date samples on MSDN and how to find samples that have been downloaded to your hard drive.

You click a link from the samples read me page to access the sample downloads from MSDN. This takes you to a development center on MSDN. Which developer center you go to is based on your IDE preferences. Figure 7.32 shows the developer center for C#.

Add a Workaround; Indicate You Can Reproduce; Add to Watch List

Vote on a Bug's Importance

Add a Comment

FIGURE 7.31   You can report, monitor, and comment on bugs.

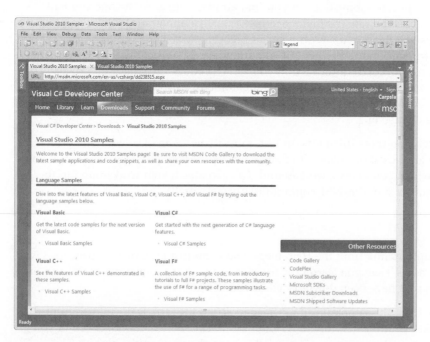

FIGURE 7.32   You access samples from the developer centers on MSDN.

Notice in Figure 7.32 that you can click one of the sample links, which takes you to the MSDN Code Gallery where the sample is stored. From here, you can get release details about the sample, download the actual sample code, participate in discussions about the sample, and more. Of course you can also just browse the MSDN Code Gallery. Figure 7.33 shows an example of the C# samples for Beta 2.

Selecting a sample enables you to download it locally. Most samples are stored as .zip files. You can extract these files to your local machine and begin using them. Most samples include a Visual Studio project file that makes it easy to open the sample.

Samples are also stored locally. You can access local samples from the Visual Studio samples read me page. Alternatively, you can navigate to the local file path C:\Program Files (x86)\Microsoft Visual Studio 10.0\Samples\1033. This folder contains similar sample files that are available online. The difference is that these sample files were installed when you installed the product. The online versions maintain the latest updates. The files in this folder are also .zip files and need to be extracted before you begin using them.

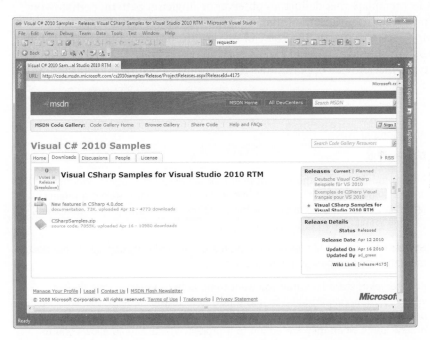

FIGURE 7.33   The MSDN Code Gallery maintains the latest samples for Visual Studio.

Discovering and Consuming Shared Content

We have all been given programming tasks in which we just know someone must have already tackled the problem, and we've all faced tight deadlines. In these cases, it is often wise to hit the Internet to find out whether there is community content you can use to your advantage. At a minimum, you might find a partial solution that can speed your development effort and increase your understanding of how you might solve your particular problem.

Visual Studio provides a formal mechanism for publishing, finding, and consuming shared content. In the following sections, we look at discovering and leveraging this content. We also demonstrate how you can be an active participant in this community.

Examining Shared Content Types

Visual Studio provides a number of code-sharing opportunities. For example, you might download a project template that defines an observer or singleton pattern, perhaps you find a code snippet that inserts a common method for accessing a database, or maybe you write a timesaving add-in or macro that you can share with the community. Visual Studio allows developers to write these types of extensions and more. Table 7.1 describes the many content types that provide opportunities for community sharing and consumption in Visual Studio 2010.

TABLE 7.1   Shared Content Types

Content	Description
Project Template	Project templates are the sets of files that define a new project. When you create a new project using Visual Studio, you are asked to select a project template. Visual Studio allows for the creation of your own project templates and the consumption of the same.
Starter Kit	Starter kits are just like project templates but typically include additional documentation and step-by-step instructions.
Item Template	Item templates are files that you want to be able to reuse across projects. When you use Visual Studio to add a new item to your project, you are selecting and adding an item template. Item templates define the contents and structure of new items when they are added to a project. Visual Studio allows you to create and consume custom item templates
Code Snippet	Code snippets are bits of code that you can add to the Visual Studio IntelliSense feature. You can create your own code snippets and share them with your community. A number of useful snippets are also available for download. We cover creating a custom code snippet in Chapter 8, "Working with Visual Studio's Productivity Aids."

TABLE 7.1   Continued

Content	Description
Sample	A number of MSDN sample applications are available for download and installation. These files are typically .zip files and come in multiple languages (C# and VB being the most common). In addition, a number of samples are available when installing Visual Studio (see samples discussion previously in this chapter).
Control	Controls can be both user and custom controls written for .NET. They might be free to the community and include source code, or they might be made for commercial purposes. You can write and share your own controls using Visual Studio.
Add-Ins & Macros	Add-ins and macros are typically extensions and enhancements to the development environment. Visual Studio supports the creation and sharing of these items. We cover macros in great depth inside Chapter 14, "Writing Macros"; add-ins are covered in Chapter 15, "Writing Add-Ins and Wizards."

Finding the Right Content

The first trick to leveraging the knowledge that exists out there is finding it. You can, of course, always search the internet for content. You can also find content right from the IDE. To do so, you can create a new project (File, New, Project). From the New Project dialog box you can select Online Templates (far left, which displays a list of templates maintained by Microsoft on the Visual Studio Gallery site. Figure 7.34 shows an example.

The Online Templates option in the New Project dialog box enables you to find templates by technology (see the left side of Figure 7.34), sort those templates by relevance and framework version (the top middle of Figure 7.34), and do a text-based search for templates (the upper right of Figure 7.34).

> **NOTE**
>
> We are using the word *template* here because that is what they are called in the dialog box. However, by using the New Project dialog box you are really installing *starter kits*. Starter kits are sample applications and learning tools that allow you to examine a full solution. If you need just a Visual Studio item template, you can find these, too, inside the Add New Item dialog box under the Online templates link.

Templates are stored at http://visualstudiogallery.msdn.microsoft.com. You can browse this site directly. It contains templates for many versions of Visual Studio. You can also find tools and controls (in addition to templates). The items listed on this site include ratings, reviews, and discussions. Most of the items are free. There are other items that have a free trial and still others that require purchase. The latter are mostly controls (not samples). Figure 7.35 shows a sample from the gallery.

Filter Templates by Technology   Choose a Sort Order   Search for Templates

View Template
Details

FIGURE 7.34   You can find templates online.

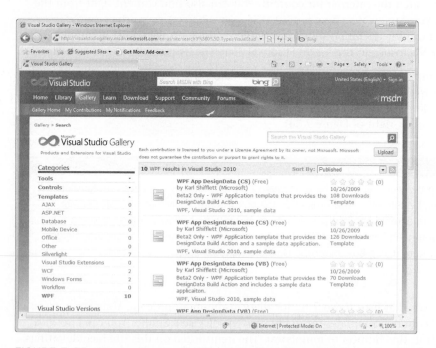

FIGURE 7.35   You can browse the Visual Studio Gallery directly.

Installing and Storing Shared Content

In Visual Studio 2010 you can install an online template (starter kit) directly from the New Project dialog box. Notice the options at the bottom of Figure 7.34. When you install the template, Visual Studio downloads the content and stores it accordingly, which in most cases means installing it in a local folder of your choosing. You have to respond to one dialog box that allows you to accept any license terms (Figure 7.36).

FIGURE 7.36   You can accept license terms of the downloaded content.

Real Visual Studio project and item templates (not starter kits, macros, add-ins, or snippets) are installed in one of the appropriate Visual Studio locations. There are paths for projects, project templates, and item templates. Figure 7.37 shows the Options dialog box that can be used to manage these paths. Note that if you have a lot of varied project and item templates, you may choose to set these paths to a network share. This enables you to share templates among a development team.

Participating in the Community

No matter how good Visual Studio gets, most developers often think of great additions or extensions to the existing functionality. These extensions might be project-specific, or they might apply to all Visual Studio users. Of course, developers also like to write code. Therefore, it is not surprising that some go so far as to write their own custom extensions (add-ins, snippets, macros, and the like). This feat is often successful for single, personal use. The trouble comes when you want to share your timesaving creation with the rest of the team. Often, you end up writing a page of installation instructions and doing one-on-one troubleshooting with each developer as he or she installs your "timesaver."

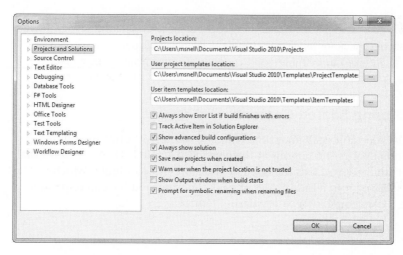

FIGURE 7.37   Setting project and item template storage locations.

Visual Studio 2010 offers a solution in the form of a packaging mechanism that allows developers to publish, exchange, and install Visual Studio content. Previously, we looked at consuming community content. Now we demonstrate how you can package your own creations and exchange them with team members, with friends, or through community websites.

Starter Kits Versus Templates

In other chapters, we demonstrate how to create snippets, macros, and add-ins (see Table 7.1 for chapter references). What we have not covered is creating starter kits and templates (both project and item templates). These items are very useful for large teams that want to disseminate standards and provide guidance. They are also useful for providing content to the community.

A project template and a starter kit are fundamentally the same thing. They are only discussed differently to set expectations of those consuming these items. People who use a starter kit expect to use it as a learning tool and therefore you are expected to provide a high-degree of documentation and step-by-step instruction when creating something called a starter kit. Project and item templates are similar to the templates that you use inside Visual Studio to create new projects and items. In most cases, these templates provide a starting point for something that you create often. The documentation of these items is typically stored elsewhere (if at all).

Again, Visual Studio does not distinguish between starter kits and templates. Therefore we discuss creating templates. You can use what is discussed here to package your starter kits, too.

Creating a Project Template

Project templates are what appear in Visual Studio's New Project dialog box. Projects are grouped by project type (C#, VB, Windows, Office, and so on). These project types are defined by a tree control. Figure 7.38 shows the New Project dialog box in action. You choose a project type or group and then the actual templates themselves.

FIGURE 7.38   The New Project dialog box.

You can create a project template manually or use the Visual Studio Export Template Wizard. The wizard simply makes the task of putting together the right XML files and zipping your project slightly easier. To create a project template, you follow these basic steps:

1. Create a project in Visual Studio (or start with an existing project).
2. Determine where (if any) parameters should exist in your template.
3. Choose the Export Template option from the File menu.
4. (Optional) Edit the .vstemplate XML.

Next, let's look at each of these steps.

Step 1: Create Your Project

Most templates you create start with an existing Visual Studio template (or an empty project). Typically, developers look to templates to enforce standards and practices and provide guidance to teams. Therefore, the hardest part of creating a project template is defining the template itself in terms of what content should go into it. As an example, perhaps your team uses a common set of libraries, resources, or controls. You can define a project template that has these items either built in or referenced.

Step 2: Determine Project Parameters

Project parameters define the items that are set by default when Visual Studio sets up a new project based on the given template. For example, when you create a new project, the namespace of the code files is set to the namespace of the project. This is a project parameter. Visual Studio uses a number of reserved template parameters for this purpose. Table 7.2 provides an overview of these parameters.

TABLE 7.2   Reserved Template Parameters

Content	Description
clrversion	The version of the Common Language Runtime (CLR).
GUID[1-10]	A unique project ID. You can set up to 10 project IDs using GUID1, GUID2, and so on.
itemname	The name of the given item that the user types into the Add New Item dialog box—for example, MyNewClass.cs.
machinename	The user's computer name.
projectname	The name of the given project that the user types into the Add New Project dialog box—for example, MySmartClient.
registeredorganization	The Registry key value for the organization set during Windows installation.
rootnamespace	The namespace that is set as the root for the current project.
safeitemname	Similar to the itemname but with all unsafe characters and spaces removed.
safeprojectname	Similar to the projectname but with all unsafe characters and spaces removed.
time	The current time on the user's computer.
userdomain	The domain the user has logged in to.
username	The name of the active user.
webnamespace	The name of the website is used as the default namespace for web applications.
year	The current year as represented by the user's computer.

The Export Template Wizard helps you with these parameters. After you define them manually in your code, the Export Template Wizard picks up the settings.

As an example, suppose you have a project template titled SmartClient. When a user chooses to create a project based on this template, you want the template to behave as another template in the dialog box. For instance, you want the project's namespace to be defined as the project name the user has chosen.

To implement parameters in the template, you define the parameter's position within the code. In the namespace example, you must use the reserved template parameter safeprojectname in place of the actual namespace defined throughout the code files in the project. This indicates to Visual Studio that when a new project is created, the namespace should be set to the safe project name as defined by the user. The following code example shows how to define the code:

```
namespace $safeprojectname$ {
    class Framework {
```

> **NOTE**
>
> Your code will not build with these parameters in place. Therefore, it is best to debug your code before setting up parameters.

After you've defined your parameters, the Export Template Wizard picks them up and places them in the .vstemplate XML file. We look at this in the "Step 3: Export Your Template" section.

Defining Custom Parameters In addition to the aforementioned Visual Studio parameters, you can define your own custom parameters to be passed to your templates. The process is similar to using the reserved template parameters. You first define the parameters using the $parameter$ syntax in your code as shown here:

```
string myCustomValue = "$CustomParameter1$";
```

You then edit the .vstemplate XML (generated in the next step) to include a <CustomParameters> node in which you define your replacements. We look at this XML in more detail in the next major section; however, the following defines a custom parameter in the .vstemplate file:

```
<TemplateContent>

    ...

    <CustomParameters>
        <CustomParameter Name="$CustomParameter1$" Value="Some Custom Value"/>
    </CustomParameters>
</TemplateContent>
```

Visual Studio replaces the content of the custom parameter when a user creates a new instance of the project template. In the preceding example, the value of the variable myCustomValue is set to Some Custom Value.

> **NOTE**
>
> The Export Template Wizard does not recognize custom parameters. You have to edit the .vstemplate XML manually to include the CustomParameters node.

Step 3: Export Your Template

Now that you have defined your template and decided on template parameters, the next step is to run the Export Template Wizard. This wizard is used for both project and item templates. You access it from the File menu.

Figure 7.39 shows the first step in the wizard. Here, you are asked to choose the template type (project or item). You then must select a project from within the current, open Visual Studio solution. This project serves as the basis for your template.

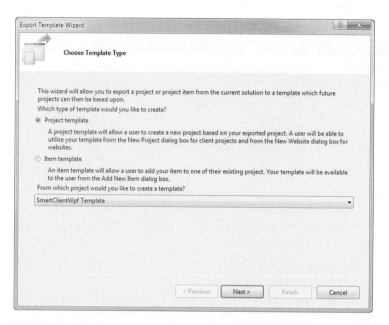

FIGURE 7.39   You use the Export Template Wizard to create a project or item template.

The next step in the Export Template Wizard allows you to define a few additional parameters for your template. You can set an icon and a preview picture for the template, indicate a name and description that show up in the New Project dialog box, and also choose the location where your template is placed. Figure 7.40 shows an example of this dialog box.

Notice that in the dialog box shown in Figure 7.40 we have not checked the Automatically Import the Template into Visual Studio option. This is for two reasons. First, before importing we want to edit the .vstemplate file the wizard generates. Second, you might want to package the template for installation and test out that installation (we look at this topic in the next major section). By default, the template is output to the directory Documents\Visual Studio 10\My Exported Templates\. The exported template is a single, .zip file. All templates in Visual Studio are zip files. To edit the template before deploying, you can unzip the file and gain access to the many files defined by the template (including .vstemplate).

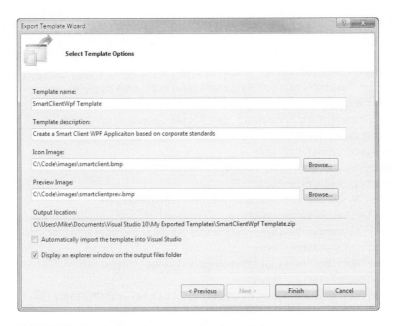

FIGURE 7.40   Define the export template options.

Step 4 (Optional): Edit the .vstemplate XML

A fourth, optional step in the process is to edit the .vstemplate XML. The Export Template Wizard generates a default .vstemplate for you. You can open the .zip file, edit the XML, rezip (compress) the file, and place it directly into the template folder or package for installation. Listing 7.1 shows a sample .vstemplate file.

LISTING 7.1   A Sample .vstemplate File

```
<VSTemplate Version="3.0.0"
  xmlns="http://schemas.microsoft.com/developer/vstemplate/2005" Type="Project">
  <TemplateData>
    <Name>SmartClientWpf Template</Name>
    <Description>A Smart Client WPF App based on corporate standards</Description>
    <ProjectType>CSharp</ProjectType>
    <ProjectSubType>
    </ProjectSubType>
    <SortOrder>1000</SortOrder>
    <CreateNewFolder>true</CreateNewFolder>
    <DefaultName>SmartClientWpf Template</DefaultName>
    <ProvideDefaultName>true</ProvideDefaultName>
    <LocationField>Enabled</LocationField>
    <EnableLocationBrowseButton>true</EnableLocationBrowseButton>
    <Icon>__TemplateIcon.bmp</Icon>
```

```
      <PreviewImage>__PreviewImage.bmp</PreviewImage>
    </TemplateData>
    <TemplateContent>
      <Project TargetFileName="SmartClientWpf Template.csproj"
        File="SmartClientWpf Template.csproj" ReplaceParameters="true">
        <ProjectItem ReplaceParameters="true"
          TargetFileName="Framework.cs">Framework.cs</ProjectItem>
        <Folder Name="Properties" TargetFolderName="Properties">
          <ProjectItem ReplaceParameters="true"
            TargetFileName="AssemblyInfo.cs">AssemblyInfo.cs</ProjectItem>
          <ProjectItem ReplaceParameters="true"
            TargetFileName="Resources.resx">Resources.resx</ProjectItem>
          <ProjectItem ReplaceParameters="true"
            TargetFileName="Resources.Designer.cs">Resources.Designer.cs</ProjectItem>
          <ProjectItem ReplaceParameters="true"
            TargetFileName="Settings.settings">Settings.settings</ProjectItem>
          <ProjectItem ReplaceParameters="true"
            TargetFileName="Settings.Designer.cs">Settings.Designer.cs</ProjectItem>
        </Folder>
      </Project>
    </TemplateContent>
  </VSTemplate>
```

Notice that the wizard added the ReplaceParameters attribute to the Project and ProjectItem nodes and set its value to true. This setting indicates to Visual Studio that it should swap any parameters in the target file during project creation. In the example, Framework.cs is the target file that contains the parameter, $safeprojectname$.

TIP

You can actually create templates that contain multiple projects. To do so, you still create a .vstemplate file for each project in the solution. You then create a .vstemplate root file that describes the multi-project template. The data inside this XML is used by the New Project dialog box. The file also contains pointers to each individual project's .vstemplate file.

Installing the Template

The simple way to install your template on a local machine is to copy it to the templates directory (Documents\Visual Studio 10\Templates\). You can put the template inside one of the folders found in this location. It is then available for use. Figure 7.41 shows an example of the SmartClientWpf Template project ready for use.

FIGURE 7.41   The installed template in the New Project dialog box.

When the project is generated, Visual Studio inserts the safe filename for the project namespace. Recall that this was the reserved parameter you had set. The following code is inserted into Framework.cs:

```
namespace SmartClientWpf_Template1 {
    class Framework {
```

TIP

You can package templates for installation. This allows you to distribute them to other developers and post them on the Visual Studio Gallery. We look at creating a packaged solution and installing it the "Packaging Your Creation for Wider Distribution" section.

Creating Item Templates

Item templates represent the various items or files you can add to Visual Studio projects. Selecting Add New Item opens a dialog box that enables you to select from the various Visual Studio items (class files, for example). You can also create your own, custom items. Examples of custom items are timesaving devices that stub out the shell of a class or a fully implemented, specific type of class. Figure 7.42 shows the Add New Item dialog box with the custom item, DataFramework.

FIGURE 7.42   A custom item template in the Add New Item dialog box.

The good news is that you create item templates the same way you create project templates. You start with an existing item, edit it, and then use the Export Template Wizard to create an item template from the item. In Step 1 of the wizard, you choose Item Template (refer to Figure 7.39).

There are a couple of additional steps to creating an item template. You must select the files in your project that you want to use to generate item templates. Each item template is based on a single file. You then select any references you want to add to a project when someone uses your new item template. The list of available references from which to choose is built based on the project from which you are exporting.

Note that you can also define the same set of parameters for item templates that you can for project templates. Also, item templates are copied to the same location as project templates (but inside a different folder).

Packaging Your Creation for Wider Distribution

There are three primary ways you can package your content for distribution: VSIX, MSI, and VSI. Each of these has their place depending on your needs. The following describes each option:

▶ **VSIX**—The Visual Studio Extension file format (.vsix) is used for creating content that you intend to publish to the Visual Studio Gallery. The VSIX items are then installed and managed via the Visual Studio Extension Manager (Tool, Extension Manager). The VSIX projects are also available in the Online Templates in the New Project Dialog.

VSIX can package project and item templates, toolbox controls, and more. You cannot, however, use VSIX to deploy macros, add-ins, and code snippets (you would use VSI for that). In addition, you cannot write to the GAC or registry with VSIX (it is a file-based deployment).

▶ **MSI**—The Windows Installer (MSI) is used to create custom setup packages. These are great for deploying your applications. They can write to the GAC and the registry (among other things). MSIs, however, cannot be used to deploy project and item templates to Visual Studio.

▶ **VSI**—The Visual Studio Content Installer (VSI) is great for deploying macros, add-ins, and code snippets. However, it cannot write to the GAC or registry. In addition, VSI packaged content cannot be deployed to the Visual Studio Gallery. You can still create item and project templates with VSI (you just cannot deploy them into the gallery).

The VSIX and VSI deployment methods are the primary means for distributing your community content. Of course, VSIX is the preferred option if you intend to use the Visual Studio Gallery. We look at both of these options in greater detail.

Packaging Content with VSI

The Visual Studio Installer (VSI) helps developers install content that is targeted at the Visual Studio IDE. This includes macros, add-ins, and code snippets. A VSI file has the .vsi extension and bundles the other files that make up the package. After it has been created, a VSI can be easily installed into the right directories on a developer's computer to make that macro, add-in, or snippet available at run time.

The good news is that creating these files is a relatively straightforward process. Of course, the first step is to define and debug your creation (see Chapter 13, "Introducing the Automation Object Model," Chapter 14, "Writing Macros," and Chapter 15, "Writing Add-ins and Wizards," for more information on extending Visual Studio). When you are ready to share your creation, you need to follow these steps (we elaborate on them later):

1. Create a .VSContent file that contains XML describing your content.
2. Gather the file or files that define your creation.
3. Compress your files into a .zip file.
4. Rename the .zip file using the .vsi extension.
5. Optional: Add an end-user license agreement (EULA) to your VSI.
6. Optional: Sign your .vsi file.

This process is the same no matter the content type (macros, add-ins, and snippets). The install tool gets its information regarding your contents through the settings of your .VSContent XML file.

The Elements of a VSContent XML File

The VSContent file is an XML structure that contains elements for all pertinent items needed by the Visual Studio Content Installer. Your content is defined by a Content node (or element). This element is meant to define a single item of content you want to share (such as a macro file or control defined in a .dll file). Listing 7.2 presents the high-level structure of the VSContent file. This is neither a real example nor the official XSD. Rather, it serves to present the elements and their relations to one another.

LISTING 7.2   The Structure of a .VSContent File

```
<VSContent xmlns="http://schemas.microsoft.com/developer/vscontent/2010">
  <Content>
    <FileName></FileName>
    <DisplayName></DisplayName>
    <Description></Description>
    <FileContentType></FileContentType>
    <ContentVersion></ContentVersion>
    <Attributes>
      <Attribute name="" value=""/>
    </Attributes>
  </Content>
</VSContent>
```

TIP

The actual XSD that defines the structure of a VSContent file is a bit lengthy to reprint here. However, if you would like to examine the XSD file that defines the structure for valid VSContent XML, you can do so. The file is stored at C:\Program Files (x86)\Microsoft Visual Studio 10.0\Xml\Schemas\1033\ and is named vscontent.xsd.

You can point to multiple content types and their associated files using a single .vsi file. You do so by creating multiple instances of the Content element, one for each item you want to share. For example, a single .vsi file could contain a Content node that installs a code snippet and another Content node that points to a .vsmacro file containing macros.

Each element inside Listing 7.2 is covered in depth in Table 7.4. We walk through an actual example of creating and using a VSContent file in a coming section.

TABLE 7.4   Elements of a VSContent File

Element	Description
FileName	This element represents the name of the file that contains the item to be installed as the content.
	A single Content element can contain multiple FileName elements, depending on the situation. For example, you may define a VSContent file to install an add-in. The add-in might contain both an .Addin file and a .dll file.
DisplayName	This is the name of your content. The Visual Studio Content Installer displays this name when users install your creation.
Description	This element is used as the ToolTip text for your content inside the Visual Studio Content Installer.

TABLE 7.4   Continued

Element	Description
FileContentType	This represents the type of content defined by the given Content node. This value is enumerated and therefore must be one of the following settings: Addin, Macro Project, Code Snippet, VSTemplate, Toolbox Control.
ContentVersion	This element represents a version number for your content. The only valid setting at this time is 1.0. All other settings result in an error.
Attributes	This element is used to group Attribute elements.
Attribute	You can use attributes to further define code snippet and VSTemplate content. These settings are discussed further in the next section.

Using Attributes to Define VSTemplates and Code Snippets   The Attribute element inside the VSContent file provides the Visual Studio Content Installer additional information for your given content type that include project templates, item templates, and code snippets. The Attributes node is not used for the content types Addin, Macro Project, and Toolbox Control.

The Attribute element consists of a name/value pair. You set the name and value of the element using XML attributes in the following format:

```
<Attribute name="" value=""/>
```

Both the name and the value attributes are defined with enumerated values. These enumerated values define the possible setting combinations you can define for code snippets and templates.

For code snippets, only the value lang is applicable for the name attribute. Setting the lang attribute on code snippets allows you to indicate the development language to which the snippet applies. Possible entries for the value attribute when defined with lang include csharp, jsharp, vb, and xml. For example, if your code snippet is meant to work with Visual Basic, you would define your attribute as shown here:

```
<Attribute name="lang" value="vb"/>
```

When defining content of type VSTemplate, you can use the following enumerated items for the name attribute:

- ▶ **TemplateType**—Defines the type of template your content represents. Values are either Project for project templates or Item for item templates.

- ▶ **ProjectType**—Defines the type of project contained in your template. Possible enumerated items for the value attribute are Visual Basic, Visual C#, Visual J#, and Visual Web Developer.

- ▶ **ProjectSubType**—Defines the subcategory in which your template is placed in the New Project dialog box. Possible entries include Windows, Office, Smart Device, Database, Starter Kits, and Test.

Recall the Smart Client project template you created earlier. Listing 7.3 represents the VSContent file used to define the installation for the Smart Client. Notice the three attribute definitions used to define template, project and project sub type.

LISTING 7.3   The VSContent File for the Smart Client Example

```
<VSContent xmlns="http://schemas.microsoft.com/developer/vscontent/2010">
  <Content>
    <FileName>Smart Client.zip</FileName>
    <DisplayName>Smart Client</DisplayName>
    <Description>Install a smart client project template</Description>
    <FileContentType>VSTemplate</FileContentType>
    <ContentVersion>1.0</ContentVersion>
    <Attributes>
      <Attribute name="TemplateType" value="Project"/>
      <Attribute name="ProjectType" value="Visual C#"/>
      <Attribute name="ProjectSubType" value="Windows"/>
    </Attributes>
  </Content>
</VSContent>
```

An Example: Packaging a Macro   As with most things, the best way to understand the Visual Studio content packaging process is to work through a real example. In this case, we take a few of the macros defined in Chapter 14, "Writing Macros," and bundle them for sharing with other developers.

After you've debugged and tested your creation, the first step in packaging it is to define the VSContent file. For this example, we've created a macro file that contains a few macros from previous chapters, including the flowerbox macro (Chapter 11, "Debugging Code") that places common comment structure above the Visual Basic Subs and Functions and a couple of IDE resize macros. We use the macro file as content for our package. The name of the macro file is VisualStuioUnleashed2010.vsmacros.

An easy way to define the VSContent file is to create an XML file inside Visual Studio (File, New, File), which opens the New File dialog box. From here, select XML File. Remember, the VSContent file is simply an XML file with a special extension in the filename (.VSContent). In this way, you can create and edit your VSContent file directly in Visual Studio. You have to edit the filename from .xml to VSContent. However, using Visual Studio enables you to take advantage of the built-in XML editor that includes IntelliSense.

The first step in defining the content of this file is to set the XML namespace (xmlns) to the proper schema. You do this by adding the following root node to the file:

```
<VSContent xmlns="http://schemas.microsoft.com/developer/vscontent/2005">
```

After you've done this, Visual Studio recognizes the intended structure for the XML and guides you through defining additional elements. Figure 7.43 shows an example of creating the VSContent file inside the IDE. Note that for the example, you define the FileName element to point to the macro file. You also must set the FileContentType to the enumerated value Macro Project. This ensures that the example is installed in the proper location for macros.

FIGURE 7.43   Defining the VSContent file inside the Visual Studio IDE.

The next step is to place all your files into a single directory where they can easily find each other. You need to include in your bundle any files that are called out in the VSContent file (.vsmacros, .dll, .addin) and the VSContent file itself. For some files and projects, you might have to dig a little. For this macro project, the .vsmacros file created as a new macro project is stored in the VSMacros80 folder. This folder exists inside the path Documents\Visual Studio 2010\Projects\.

In this example, you create a folder named VS2010 Unleashed Macros. In it, you place the macro file named VisualStuioUnleashed2010.vsmacros and the VSContent file named VS2010_Unleashed.vscontent.

The third step is to compress (.zip) your files. The process of compressing the files should be familiar to all developers. You can use Windows's built-in capability to compress files, or you can use a compression tool. In this example, use the Windows compression tool. You select the .vsmacros and VSContent files, right-click, and then choose Send To, Compressed (Zipped) Folder.

The result of Step 3 is the creation of a file named VisualStudioUnleashed2010.zip. Now you're ready for the easiest step. Right-click the `.zip` file and choose Rename from the context menu. Remove the `.zip` extension and replace it with `.vsi`. Of course, you need to be showing file extensions for this to work. You can do so in Windows 7 using Windows Explorer, Organize, Folder and Search Options. That's it. If you are on a machine with Visual Studio installed, the new file takes on the `.vsi` icon (used for both .vsi and VSContent files).

All that remains is to distribute the .vsi file to the intended audience. Of course, it would be prudent to do a couple of test installations first. Let's look at the Visual Studio Content Installer tool in action.

Both the .vsi and the .vscontent files are Visual Studio Content Installer (VSContentInstaller.exe) files. They have the same icon. The reason is that both can be used to install the content.

There are some differences between the two, however. The .vsi file is fully self-contained. It does not require additional files for installation, whereas the .vscontent file must exist in a directory that also contains the related content files. In addition, when you run the VSContent file, you are not warned about the lack of a signature (if one is lacking). Therefore, you might think that there is a bug or that these files are more appropriate for internal installations. The .vsi file, on the other hand, prompts you with a security warning dialog box if the content is not signed by a publisher. This, along with the single file and compression factor, seems to make the .vsi file ideal in larger, distributed scenarios.

Let's examine the installation process for the .vsi file. First, you double-click the file to invoke the Visual Studio Content Installer. Figure 7.44 shows the example loaded in the tool.

From this screen, you can select View Files in Windows Explorer to examine the files that will be installed by the .vsi. Also, notice that the Publisher Information section is blank. The reason is that the bundle is not signed. When you click the Next button, the tool prompts you with a warning regarding the lack of signature. Again, this warning is not shown if you are installing from the VSContent file directly. For now, click Yes and move on. In the sidebar, we discuss signing your work.

Next, the installer prepares you to finish the installation. When you click the Finish button, the installer writes the files to the appropriate folders based on content type. If the given file already exists, the installer prompts you to find out whether you want it left as is or overwritten. Finally, the installer finishes its job and reports back. Figure 7.45 shows a successful installation.

FIGURE 7.44   The first step in the Visual Studio Content Installer.

FIGURE 7.45   A successful installation.

SIGNING YOUR WORK

To sign your .vsi files with Authenticode, you must get a valid software publisher certificate (.spc) from a certificate authority (CA). Of course, this requires that you have a company set up and that you fill out an application as such. Visual Studio does have a few test tools to help developers understand the process before working with a CA. These tools include the following:

▶ Zip to Exe Conversion Tool (MakeZipExe.exe)

▶ Certificate Creation Tool (MakeCert.exe)

▶ Software Publisher Certificate Test Tool (Cert2spc.exe)

▶ Sign Tool (SignTool.exe)

The vision for these tools is as follows: You use the MakeZipExe.exe tool to convert your .zip file to an .exe file (because code signing requires an .exe or a .dll). You then use the SignTool.exe to sign the resulting .exe. You then convert this file into a .vsi file for publication.

If you do not have a valid certificate from a CA, you can create a test certificate (not to be used for publishing) with the MakeCert.exe tool. You then must convert this certificate into a software publisher certificate (.spc) using the Cert2spc.exe.

Packaging Content with VSIX

You can use Visual Studio to create Visual Studio Extension projects that can then be distributed within VSIX files. These projects are used to distribute project and item templates as well as sample applications you might distribute for learning purposes. You can also package Visual Studio controls you want to share (or sell).

Recall that the first step toward creating community content is to code it, build it, debug it, and export it. This process puts your shared content in a .zip file that will add to the VSIX project. Refer to the prior section if you need to refresh.

Step 1: Install the SDK   To get started packaging your community-bound code, you must have the VSIX project template installed. You get this project template by installing the Visual Studio 2010 SDK. This is available as a separate download from Microsoft's website (you can find it with a quick search). Figure 7.46 shows an example of the install dialog box. Notice the destination folder for the install (in case you need to navigate there in the future).

Step 2: Create a VSIX Project   After the SDK is installed, you have a few new tools and templates that help you extend Visual Studio. This includes the VSIX Project template. You can find this template inside the Extensibility node on the New Project dialog box in both VB and C#. Figure 7.47 shows an example of the VSIX project template inside this dialog box.

FIGURE 7.46   You must install the Visual Studio SDK to create VSIX projects.

FIGURE 7.47   The Visual Studio SDK installs the VSIX extensibility project.

This project contains a reference to the namespace, Microsoft.VisualStudio.CoreUtility that contains the libraries used to build and deploy VSIX projects. The project template also includes the following items:

▶ **source.extension.vsixmanifest**—A file that contains the XML defining your VSIX project.

▶ **VSIXProject.cs**—A class file you can use to write any custom code related to your VSIX installation.

▶ **VSIXProject_large.png**—A graphic file used to create a preview graphic for your project. You can edit this file inside Visual Studio or replace it. The key is that your graphic size should be 318 high by 351 wide.

Note that this file (and the one below) are different than the actual project and item template graphics you create in the export process. Those graphics are used after the item is deployed. These graphics are shown in the gallery before installation.

▶ **VSIXProject_small.png**—A graphic file used for a small icon of your project when shown in a list. This image should be square, 50 by 50.

Figure 7.48 shows these files inside a VSIX project template.

FIGURE 7.48   The files of a VSIX project template.

Step 3: Add Your Content   The next step is to add to the project the content you want to share. Again, this is a .zip file of a project you created and exported (see the preceding section for more details). You can add this content to your project by right-clicking your project and selecting Add, Existing Item. Recall that your exported template should be in your documents directory (Documents\Visual Studio 10\My Exported Templates). You have to show all files to find the .zip file.

After your exported template is added to the project, use the Properties dialog box to set its Copy to Output Directory property to Copy Always. This ensures that an install of your shared template is always deployed to the output directory. Figure 7.49 shows an example of this property.

FIGURE 7.49   Set the Copy to Output Directory property to Copy Always.

Step 4: Edit the VSIX Manifest   Before you deploy you should add information about your project for those looking to browse before they download. You can do this by editing the source.extension.vsixmanifest file. You can open this file in an XML editor (right-click and choose Open With). Alternatively, you can open the file inside the Visual Studio VSIX manifest editor. This editor is shown in Figure 7.50.

The editor allows you to set nearly all of the values of the manifest. This includes the project's unique ID, the author, version, product name, description, and much more. Notice in Figure 7.50 you can also select your project's icon and preview image. You can also provide a link to a website for more information and a link to any documentation.

The manifest editor also contains a number of additional options. The References section allows you to indicate a payload, installed extension, or other reference on which your project depends. This is an advanced option for those creating toolbox controls and other Visual Studio extensions (beyond project templates).

The Content section of the manifest editor is where you indicate content you want to deploy as part of your VSIX project. The Add Content dialog box is shown in Figure 7.51. You first select a content type (project or item template, toolbox control, and so on). You then select the actual file that contains this content.

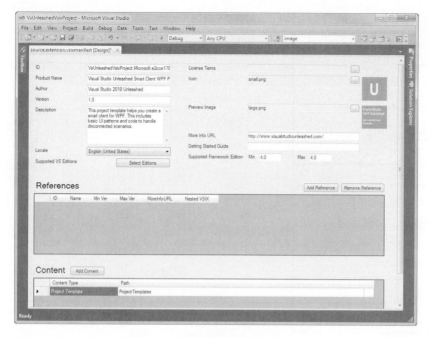

FIGURE 7.50 You can edit the VSIX manifest inside a designer.

FIGURE 7.51 You must add your content to the VSIX manifest.

You can also indicate the editions of Visual Studio to which your extension applies, which you can do by selecting the Select Editions button. This brings up the dialog box shown in Figure 7.52. Here you can select those editions of Visual Studio 2010 to which your extension is valid.

Step 5: Build the Project The next step is to compile your code. Visual Studio validates your manifest and raises any errors that invalidate the XML schema.

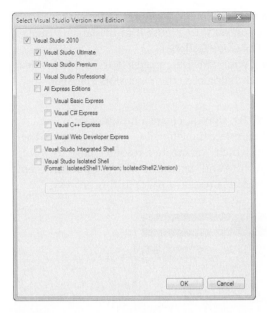

FIGURE 7.52   You can select the editions of Visual Studio for which your extension should apply.

Step 6: Test Your Install   You can find your compiled project inside the Bin folder of your project. The file has a .vsix extension. Double-click this file to test the installation. This launches the Visual Studio Extension Installer. Figure 7.53 shows an example of this dialog box. The Visual Studio Extension Installer gives the same experience someone would get if the project has been downloaded from the Visual Studio Gallery. Click the Install button to install the extension. After the installation is complete, your new project template (or related extension) should be available for use inside Visual Studio.

FIGURE 7.53   Test your VSIX installation before deploying.

Step 7: Share Your Content on the MSDN Code Gallery (optional)   You can distribute your VSIX file to other developers in many ways. If you want to expose it to the larger Visual Studio community you can post it on the MSDN Code Gallery (code.msdn.microsoft.com). Recall that putting your code here makes it accessible inside the Online Templates section of the New Project dialog box, the Extension Manager, and elsewhere in Visual Studio.

To use this site, you must have a Windows Live ID, sign in, create a unique user name, and agree to the terms and conditions. You then select the Upload Content link from the home page. This takes you through a wizard in which you create a resource page for your extension. This page allows you to upload your files and determine when to publish them to the world. Figure 7.54 shows the first step (create a resource page) in this process.

FIGURE 7.54   You define a resource page to publish your content to the gallery.

The second screen in this wizard allows you to accept terms and conditions.

The final screen provides instructions on managing your resource page, publishing your content, and protecting your work. It also provides help and guidance on the process. Finally, it contains a link to your actual resource page. This page is where you add the content and finally publish it to the world.

Figure 7.55 shows an example of your resource page. Notice that you must still add your files to the site. You then save the added files and edit the home page for your resource. This is a Wiki page that contains information specific to your project. You must edit this content before you are allowed to publish. The last step is to actually publish the resource by clicking the Publish This Resource button at the top of the page. The content is then available on the MSDN Code Gallery.

FIGURE 7.55   You upload your files to your resource page.

Summary

This chapter presented the many community options inside Visual Studio 2010. Developers can expect to feel part of a larger community that surrounds .NET. Microsoft has built in a community to .NET. You see it with the Start Page inside Visual Studio, in the options on the Help menu, and within the capability to search for, use, and create community content.

Don't forget that being part of the developer community means giving back to it once in a while. Visual Studio provides the tools to make that happen. You can create and share project and item templates, code snippets, macros, add-ins, and controls. After you've created these items, Visual Studio provides the Visual Studio Content Installer framework and the VSIX project template (in the SDK) to package your shared content for distribution. Now, the next time you write a great timesaving macro, snippet, or project template you have the know-how to package it up and share it with others.

CHAPTER 8

Working with Visual Studio's Productivity Aids

In Chapter 6, "Introducing the Editors and Designers," we discussed the basic capabilities of the designers and editors in Visual Studio 2010. In this chapter, we delve a bit deeper into their capabilities and those of other Visual Studio tools by examining the many productivity aids provided by the IDE. Many of these productivity enhancers are embedded within the text editors. Others are more generic in nature. But they all have one common goal: helping you, the developer, write code quickly and correctly.

If you recall from Chapter 6, in our coverage of the editors we used a very basic code scenario: a console application that printed `"Hello, World!"` to the console. In Figure 8.1, you see what the final code looks like in the code editor window.

If you have followed along by re-creating this project and typing the "Hello, World!" code in Visual Studio, you notice that the productivity features of the code editor have already kicked into gear. For one, as you start to type code into the template file, the code editor has tabbed the cursor in for you, placing it at a new location for writing nicely indented code.

Second, as you type your first line of code, Visual Studio reacts to your every keystroke by interpreting what you are trying to write and extending help in various forms (see Figure 8.2). You are given hints in terms of completing your in-progress source, provided information on the members you are in the process of selecting, and given information on the parameters required to complete a particular method. These features are collectively referred to as IntelliSense, and we explore its forms and functions in depth in this chapter.

As you type, the IDE is also constantly checking what you have written with the compiler. If compile errors exist, they are dynamically displayed for you in the output window.

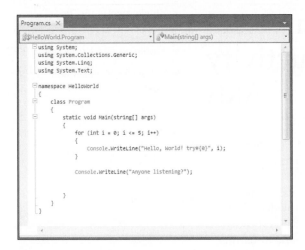

FIGURE 8.1   "Hello, World" in the code editor.

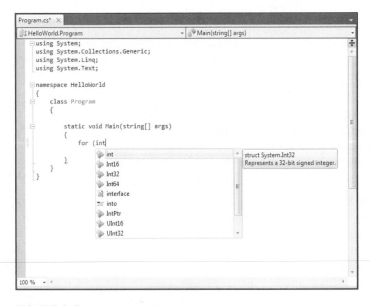

FIGURE 8.2   IntelliSense in action.

So, for this one simple line of code, Visual Studio has been hard at work improving your coding productivity by doing the following:

▶ Intelligently indenting the code

▶ Suggesting code syntax

▶ Displaying member descriptions to help you select the correct code syntax

▶ Visually matching delimiting parentheses

▶ Flagging code errors by constantly background compiling the current version of the source code

These features subtly help and coach you through the code-writing process by accelerating the act of coding.

Basic Aids in the Text Editor

The text editor user interface has several visual constructs that help you with common problem areas encountered during the code-writing process. These basic aids provide support for determining what has changed within a code document and what compile problems exist in a document. Additionally, the discrete syntax elements for each individual language are visually delineated for you using colored text.

Change Tracking

When you are in the midst of editing a source code file, it is tremendously useful to understand which lines of code have been committed (that is, saved to disk) and which have not. Change tracking provides this functionality; a yellow vertical bar in the text editor's selection margin spans any lines in the editor that have been changed but not saved. If content has been changed and subsequently saved, it is marked with a green vertical bar in the selection margin.

By looking at the yellow and green tracking bars, you can quickly differentiate between

▶ Code that hasn't been touched since the file was loaded (no bar)

▶ Code that has been touched and saved since the file was loaded (green bar)

▶ Code that has been touched but not saved since the file was loaded (yellow bar)

Change tracking is valid only for as long as the editor window is open. In other words, change tracking is significant only for the current document "session"; if you close and reopen the window, the track bars disappear because you have established a new working session with that specific document.

Figure 8.3 shows a section of a code file displaying the change tracking bars.

Coding Problem Indicators

The Visual Studio compiler works in conjunction with the code editor window to flag any problems found within a source code document. The compiler can even work in the background, enabling the editor window to flag problems as you type (as opposed to waiting for the project to be compiled).

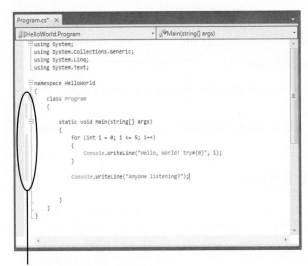

Change Tracking Indicators

FIGURE 8.3   Change tracking.

Coding problems are flagged using "squiggles": wavy, color-coded lines placed under the offending piece of code. These squiggles are the same mechanism Microsoft Word uses to flag spelling and grammar problems. The squiggle colors indicate a specific class of problem. Table 8.1 shows how these colors map to an underlying problem.

TABLE 8.1   Coding Problem Indicator Colors

Color	Problem
Red	Syntax error; the code will not compile because of the syntax requirements and rules of the language.
Blue	Semantic error; this is the result of the compiler not being able to resolve the type or code construct within the current context. For instance, a type name that doesn't exist within the compiled context of the current project is flagged with a blue squiggle. Typically, these are good indicators for typos (for example, misspelling a class name).
Purple	Warning; the purple squiggle denotes code that has triggered a compiler warning.

Hovering the mouse pointer over the problem indicator reveals the actual compiler error or warning message, as demonstrated in Figure 8.4.

Active Hyperlinking

Text editors support clickable hyperlinks within documents; clicking on a link launches a browser redirected at the URL. One great use of this feature is to embed URLs for supporting documentation or other helpful reference information within code comments.

FIGURE 8.4   Coding problem indicators.

Syntax Coloring

The text editor can parse and distinctly color different code constructs to make them that much easier to identify on sight. As an example, the code editor window, by default, colors any code comments green. Code identifiers are black; keywords are blue; strings are colored red, and so on.

In fact, the number of unique elements that the text editor is capable of parsing and coloring is immense: The text editor window recognizes more than 100 different elements. And you can customize and color each one of them to your heart's content through the Fonts and Colors section, under the Environments node in the Options dialog box. Do you like working with larger fonts? Would a higher contrast benefit your programming activities? How about squeezing more code into your viewable screen real estate? These are just a few reasons you might stray from the defaults with this dialog box.

Figure 8.5 shows the fonts and colors page in the Options dialog box that allows you to specify foreground and background colors for code, HTML, CSS, or other elements. Select the element in the Display Items list and change its syntax coloring via the Item Foreground and Item Background drop-downs.

FIGURE 8.5   Setting font and color options.

NOTE

The dialog box shown in Figure 8.5 actually enables you to control much more than the syntax coloring for the text editor; you can change the coloring schemes used in all the different windows within Visual Studio. The item you select in the Show Settings For drop-down determines the portion of the IDE you are customizing and alters the list of items in the Display Items list.

You can always use the Use Defaults button at the upper right of the dialog box to restore the default coloring schemes.

Outlining and Navigation

Certain documents, such as source code files and markup files, have a natural parent-child aspect to their organization and syntax. XML nodes, for instance, can contain other nodes. Likewise, functions and other programming language constructs such as loops and try/catch blocks act as a container for other lines of code. Outlining is the concept of visually representing this parent-child relationship.

Code Outlining

Code outlining is used within the code editor; it allows you to collapse or expand regions of code along these container boundaries. A series of grouping lines and expand/collapse boxes are drawn in the selection margin. These expand/collapse boxes are clickable, enabling you to hide or display lines of code based on the logical groupings.

TIP

Both Visual Basic and C# provide a way to manually create named regions of code via a special region keyword. Use #region/#endregion (#Region and #End Region for Visual Basic) to create your own artificial code container that is appropriately parsed by the code outliner. Because each region is named, this is a handy approach for organizing and segregating the logical sections of your code. In fact, to use one example, the code generated for you by the Windows Forms Designer is automatically tucked within a "Windows Forms Designer generated code" region.

One quick way to implement a region is with Surround With. In the editor, highlight the code that you want to sit in a new region, right-click on the highlighted text, select Surround With from the context menu, and then select #region (or #Region for VB).

Code outlining is best understood using a simple example. First, refer to Figure 8.1. This is the initial console application code. It contains a routine called Main, a class declaration, a namespace declaration, and several using statements. The code outline groupings that you see in the selection margin visually indicate code regions that can be collapsed or hidden from view.

Because the class declaration is a logical container, the selection margin for that line of code contains a collapse box (a box with a minus sign). A line is drawn from the collapse box to the end of the container (in this case, because you are dealing with C#, the class declaration is delimited by a curly brace). If you click on the collapse box for the class declaration, Visual Studio hides all the code contained within that declaration.

Figure 8.6 shows how the editor window looks with this code hidden from view. Note that the collapse box has changed to a plus sign, indicating that you can click on the box to reshow the now-hidden code and that the first line of code for the class declaration has been altered to include a trailing box with an ellipsis.

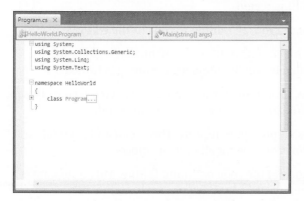

FIGURE 8.6 A collapsed outlined region.

The HTML Editor also supports outlining in this fashion. HTML elements can be expanded or collapsed to show or hide their containing elements.

Using the Outlining Menu

Several code outlining commands are available under the Edit, Outlining menu (see Figure 8.7).

FIGURE 8.7   The Edit, Outlining menu.

▶ **Toggle Outlining Expansion**—Based on the current cursor position in the editor window, hides or unhides the outline region.

▶ **Toggle All Outlining**—Hides or unhides all outline regions in the editor.

▶ **Stop Outlining**—Turns off automatic code outlining (any hidden regions are expanded). This command is available only if automatic outlining is turned on.

▶ **Stop Hiding Current**—Removes the outline for the currently selected region. This command is available only if automatic outlining has been turned off.

▶ **Collapse to Definitions**—Hides all procedure regions. This command is useful for distilling a type down to single lines of code for all of its members.

▶ **Start Automatic Outlining**—Enables the code outlining feature. This command is available only if outlining is currently turned off.

Code outlining is a convenience mechanism: By hiding currently irrelevant sections of code, you decrease the visible surface of the code file and increase code readability. You can pick and choose the specific regions to view based on the task at hand.

> **TIP**
>
> If you place the mouse pointer over the ellipsis box of a hidden code region, the contents of that hidden region are displayed to you in a ToolTip-style box; this is done without your having to actually expand and reshow the code region.

Tag Navigation

One problem with large or complex code files, be they web forms, WPF Windows, or XML documents, is navigation through the multiple levels and layers of nested tags. Envision a web page containing a button within a table within a table within a table. When you are editing the HTML (through either the designer or the editor), how can you tell exactly where you are? Put another way, how can you tell where the current focus is within the markup hierarchy?

Using the Tag Navigator

The tag navigator is Visual Studio's answer to this question. The navigator appears as a series of buttons at the bottom of the WPF, Web, and XML Schema designers. A breadcrumb trail of tags is shown that leads from the tag that currently has focus all the way to the outermost tag. If this path is too long to actually display within the confines of the editor window, it is truncated at the parent tag side; a button enables you to display more tags toward the parent.

Figure 8.8 shows the tag navigator as implemented by the web designer. While you're editing the OK button in the sample login page, the tag navigator shows the path all the way back to the parent enclosing <html> tag.

FIGURE 8.8   The Web designer's tag navigator in action.

Each tag button displayed by the navigator can be used to directly select the inclusive or exclusive contents of that tag. A drop-down triggered by the tag button contains options for selecting the tag or selecting the tag content. The former causes the tag itself, in addition to all of its enclosed content, to be selected. The latter excludes the tag begin and end, but still selects all of its enclosed content.

The navigator is a great mechanism for quickly moving up and down within a large tag tree.

Using the Document Outline Window

The Document Outline window displays a tree-view representation of the elements on a web page, WPF window, or Windows Form. This hierarchical display is a great navigation tool because it allows you to take in the entire structure of your document in one glance and immediately jump to any of the elements within the page.

To use the Document Outline window, choose Document Outline from the View, Other Windows menu. Figure 8.9 shows a sample outline for a WPF window.

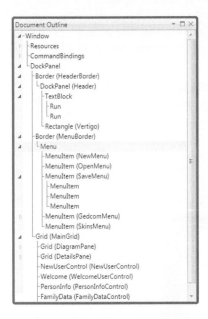

FIGURE 8.9   The Document Outline of a WPF window.

Clicking on an element navigates to that element (and selects it) within the designer window, and, of course, you can expand or collapse the tree nodes as needed.

> **NOTE**
>
> The features and look and feel of the document outline window change by document type. For instance, the WPF document outline shows a thumbnail image of the UI element when you hover over the node in the outline window. The Windows Forms outline window actually allows you to move and re-parent items within the form. Using just the outline window you could move a button from within one tab container and place it within another by just dragging the corresponding node and dragging it to the new parent in the outline.

Smart Tags and Smart Tasks

Smart tags and smart tasks (the terms can essentially be used interchangeably) are menu- or IntelliSense-driven features for automating common control configuration and coding tasks within the IDE. Designers and editors both implement smart tags in various scenarios. In the following sections, we examine a few of the ways that smart tags make your life easier, starting first with the HTML designer.

HTML Designer

As controls are placed onto the HTML designer, a pop-up list of common tasks appears. These tasks, collectively referred to as *smart tasks*, allow you to "set the dials" for a given control to quickly configure it for the task at hand.

You use the common tasks list to quickly configure a control's properties, as well as walk through common operations you might perform with it. For example, when you add a GridView control to a web page, a common task list appears that allows you to quickly enable sorting, paging, or editing for the GridView. When you add a TextBox control to a web page, a common task list appears that enables you to quickly associate a validation control with the control.

The Windows Forms designer also plays host to smart tags.

Windows Forms Designer

With the Windows Forms designer, the functionality of smart tags remains consistent; they do, however, take a slightly different form. A form control that supports this functionality shows a smart tag glyph somewhere within its bounds (typically to the top right of the control). This glyph, when clicked, opens a small drop-down of tasks. Figure 8.10 contains a snapshot of the smart tag in action for a tab control.

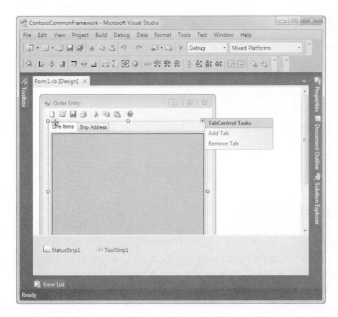

FIGURE 8.10   A Windows Forms TabControl smart tag.

Code Editor

Smart tags can also appear within code. You can find one example on interfaces. Normally, implementing an interface is a fairly code-intensive task. You have to individually create a member to map to each member defined on the interface. The smart tag in this case allows you to automatically create those members using two different naming modes:

▸ **Explicit naming**—Members have the name of the derived interface.

▸ **Implicit naming**—Member names do not reference the name of the derived interface.

See Figure 8.11 to view this smart tag in action.

In general, this type of smart tag is called a Generate From Usage smart tag. It's meant to solve a fairly common workflow issue: With certain development styles (especially, test-driven development or TDD), it is often the case that you are referencing members and types that have not yet been created. In the preceding example, this is an interface, but it could just as easily be another class, a property, or a method. As you type the name of the interface (in this example, 'IContosoConsole'), notice that the first letter of the interface will be decorated with an underline glyph. Hovering over this glyph reveals the smart tag drop-down, which displays the implementation options. The Generate From Usage smart tag enables you to automatically stub out the required type or member so that you can continue with your current coding task without having to switch context and develop, in full, the referenced item.

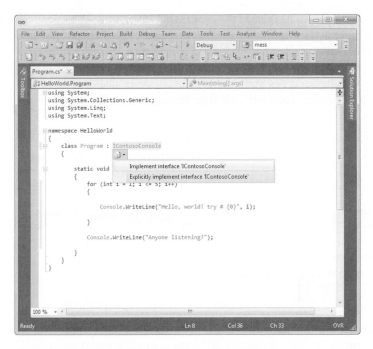

FIGURE 8.11   An implement interface smart tag.

Visual Studio supports the following Generate From Usage scenarios:

▶ Properties

▶ Methods

▶ Interfaces

▶ Classes

▶ Structs

▶ Enums

IntelliSense

IntelliSense is the name applied to a collection of different coding aids surfaced within the text editor window. Its sole purpose is to help you, the developer, write a syntactically correct line of code *quickly*. In addition, it tries to provide enough guidance to help you write lines of code that are correct *in context*—that is, code that makes sense given the surrounding lines of code.

As you type within the text editor, IntelliSense is the behind-the-scenes agent responsible for providing a list of code fragments that match the characters you have already entered, highlighting/preselecting the one that makes the most sense given the surrounding context, and, if so commanded, automatically inserting that code fragment in-line. This saves you the time of looking up types and members in the reference documentation and saves time again by inserting code without your having to actually type the characters for that code.

We spend a lot of time in this section discussing IntelliSense in the context of editing code, but you should know that IntelliSense also works with other document types such as XML documents, HTML documents, and XSLT files.

> **TIP**
>
> Attaching a schema to an XML document is beneficial from an IntelliSense perspective. The schema is used to further enhance the capabilities of the List Members function (see the "List Members" section later in this chapter).

There are many discrete pieces to IntelliSense that seamlessly work in conjunction with one another as you are writing code. You can trigger all of these IntelliSense features directly from the Edit, IntelliSense menu, or by pressing Ctrl+Space. Many of the features can be found as well on the text editor's context menu or by right-clicking anywhere in the editor window. Let's look at them one by one.

Complete Word

Complete Word is the basic timesaving kernel of IntelliSense. After you have typed enough characters for IntelliSense to recognize what you are trying to write, a guess is made as to the complete word you are in the process of typing. This guess is then presented to you within a list of possible alternatives (referred to as the *completion list*) and can be inserted into the code editor with one keystroke. This is in contrast to your completing the word manually by typing all of its characters.

Figure 8.12 illustrates the process: Based on the context of the code and based on the characters typed into the editor, a list of possible words is displayed. One of these words is selected as the most viable candidate; you may select any entry in the list (via the arrow keys or the mouse). Pressing the Tab key automatically injects the word into the editor for you.

FIGURE 8.12   IntelliSense: Complete Word.

NOTE

Complete Word takes the actual code context into account for various situations. For instance, if you are in the midst of keying in the exception type in a try/catch block, IntelliSense displays only exception types in the completion list. Likewise, typing an attribute triggers a completion list filtered only for attributes; when you're implementing an interface, only interface types are displayed; and so on. This IntelliSense feature is enabled for all sorts of content: Beyond C# and Visual Basic code, IntelliSense completion works for other files as well, such as HTML tags, XAML, CSS style attributes, .config files, and HTML script blocks, just to name a few. Visual Basic offers functionality with Complete Word that C# does not: It provides a tabbed completion list, in which one tab contains the most commonly used syntax snippets, and the other contains *all* the possible words.

You can manually invoke Complete Word at any time by using the Ctrl+Space or Alt+right-arrow key combinations.

TIP

Holding down the Ctrl key while the completion list is displayed makes the list partially transparent. This is useful if, during the process of selecting an item from the list, you need to see any of the lines of code that are hidden behind the list.

Standard Versus Consume First Mode

If you look carefully at Figure 8.12, you can notice that the top item of the completion list references a shortcut command: Ctrl+Alt+Space. When invoked, this command toggles the behavior of Complete Word (and its derivatives such as List Members) between standard and consume-first modes. Standard mode works as previously described: Visual Studio offers you the closest matches to what you are typing; the current closest match is highlighted in the completion list. You can easily insert the highlighted item by pressing Enter, or you can select to insert another item from the list.

Consume-first mode is subtly different: It also displays the closest matches to your typed text, but instead of highlighting an item in the completion list, it simply places a focus rectangle on the closest match. It preserves your current typing at the top of the list. The net result is that hitting enter won't automatically place one of the completion list items into your code; instead, it places whatever you are in the process of typing. This mode is meant to cater to scenarios where you are referencing a type or member that doesn't (yet) exist. In this scenario, you actually don't want Visual Studio to automatically assume that you are trying to reference a code construct that currently exists. In this mode, you have the explicit option to select an existing code element, or to continue typing and enter the name for a code element that has yet to be created. This gives you more flexibility while sacrificing a bit of the speed of standard mode (if you are referencing an existing item, consume-first mode requires an extra mouse-click to insert the item because it won't be highlighted in the completion list).

Quick Info

Quick Info displays the complete code declaration and help information for any code construct. You invoke it by hovering the mouse pointer over an identifier; a pop-up box displays the information available for that identifier.

Figure 8.13 shows Quick Info being displayed for the Console.ReadLine function. You are provided with the declaration syntax for the member, a brief description of the member, and a list of its exception classes. The description that shows up in the Quick Info balloon also works for code that you write: If you have a code comment associated with a member, IntelliSense parses the comment and uses it to display the description information.

FIGURE 8.13   IntelliSense: Quick Info.

List Members

The List Members feature functions in an identical fashion to Complete Word; for any given type or namespace, it displays a scrollable list of all valid member variables and functions specific to that type. To see the List Members function in action, perform the following steps in an open code editor window:

1. Type the name of a class (Ctrl+Space gives you the IntelliSense window with possible class names).

2. Type a period; this indicates to IntelliSense that you have finished with the type name and are now "scoped in" to that type's members.

3. The list of valid members is displayed. You can manually scroll through the list and select the desired member at this point, or, if you are well aware of the member you are trying to code, you can simply continue typing until IntelliSense has captured enough characters to select the member you are looking for.

4. Leverage Complete Word by pressing the Tab key to automatically insert the member into your line of code (thus saving you the typing effort).

This feature also operates in conjunction with Quick Info: As you select different members in the members list, a Quick Info pop-up is displayed for that member.

As noted earlier in our discussion of Complete Word, List Members can function in either standard or consume-first modes.

> **NOTE**
>
> IntelliSense maintains a record of the most frequently used (selected) members from the List Members and Complete Word functions. This record is used to help avoid displaying or selecting members that you have rarely, if ever, used for a given type.

Parameter Info

Parameter Info, as its name implies, is designed to provide interactive guidance for the parameters needed for any given function call. This feature is especially useful for making function calls that have a long list of parameters and/or a long overload list.

Parameter Info is initiated whenever you type an opening parenthesis after a function name. To see how this works, perform these steps:

1. Type the name of a function.
2. Type an open parenthesis.
3. A pop-up box shows the function signature. If there are multiple valid signatures (for example, multiple overloaded versions of this function), you can scroll through the different signatures by using the small up- and down-arrow cues. Select the desired signature.
4. Start typing the actual parameters you want to pass in to the function.

   As you type, the parameter info pop-up continues coaching you through the parameter list by bolding the current parameter you are working on. As each successive parameter is highlighted, the definition for that parameter appears.

In Figure 8.14, the first parameter for the Console object's SetWindowPosition function is currently being entered.

Organize Usings

Organize Usings is a C#-only IntelliSense item. It provides two separate functions: Remove Unused Usings and Sort Usings. It also provides a third command, Remove and Sort, that combines the two actions into one. All three commands live under the Organize Usings menu item on the editor shortcut menu, or under the main Edit, IntelliSense menu.

The Remove Unused Usings function is a great aid for uncluttering your code. It parses through the current body of code and determines which Using statements are necessary for the code to compile; it then removes all other Using statements. The Sort command is straightforward as well; it simply rearranges all of your Using statements so that they appear in A–Z alphabetical order by namespace.

Code Snippets and Template Code

Code snippets are pre-stocked lines of code available for selection and insertion into the text editor. Each code snippet is referenced by a name referred to as its alias. Code snippets are used to automate what would normally be non–value-added, repetitive typing. You can create your own code snippets or use the default library of common code elements provided by Visual Studio.

FIGURE 8.14   IntelliSense: Parameter Info.

Using the Code Snippet Inserter

You insert snippets by right-clicking at the intended insertion point within an open text editor window and then selecting Insert Snippet from the shortcut menu. This launches the Code Snippet Inserter, which is a drop-down (or series of drop-downs) that works much like the IntelliSense Complete Word feature. Each item in the inserter represents a snippet, represented by its alias. Selecting an alias expands the snippet into the active document.

Each snippet is categorized to make it easier to find the specific piece of code you are looking for. As an example, to insert a constructor snippet into a C# class, we would right-click within the class definition, select Insert Snippet, select Visual C# from the list of snippet categories, and then select ctor. Figure 8.15 shows this workflow in process; note that as you select a snippet category, a placeholder is displayed in the text editor window to help establish a breadcrumb trail.

After the constructor snippet is expanded into the text editor, you still, of course, have to write meaningful code inside of the constructor; but, in general, snippets eliminate the process of tedious coding that really doesn't require much intellectual horsepower to generate.

Figure 8.16 shows the same process being followed for a Visual Basic code window. The process is identical with the exception that Visual Basic makes more extensive use of categories.

FIGURE 8.15   The C# ctor code snippet.

FIGURE 8.16   Visual Basic code snippet.

Visual Basic also exhibits slightly different behavior than C# after a snippet has been expanded into the code window. Figure 8.17 shows the results of drilling down through multiple categories and, in this example, selecting the Create Transparent Windows Form snippet. Notice that the inserter has injected the template code into the Visual Basic code for you, but the inserter (at least in this case) wasn't intelligent enough to know the name of the form you are trying to make transparent.

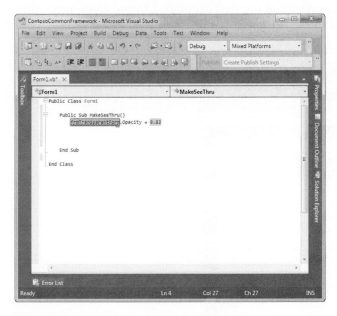

FIGURE 8.17   A form transparency snippet.

The snippet code has the form name filled in with a default, dummy name that is already highlighted. You merely start typing the form name you need, and it replaces the dummy name. The opacity value is also a dummy value that you can quickly correct at this time.

TIP

Snippets may have one or more placeholder values: fragments of code that you will want and probably need to change. You can cycle through each of the placeholder values by pressing the Tab key. When a placeholder is highlighted (in blue), you can start typing to replace the syntax with something that makes sense for your specific code context.

Surrounding Code with Snippets

C# and XML documents have one additional style of code snippets that bears mentioning: Surround With snippets. Surround With snippets are still snippets at their core (again, these are simply prestocked lines of code), but they differ in how they are able to insert themselves into your code.

Using a Surround With snippet, you can stack enclosing text around a selection with the text editor. As an example, perhaps you have a few different class declarations that you would like to nest within a namespace. Using the Surround With snippet is a simple two-step process: Highlight the class definitions and fire up the Code Snippet Inserter. This time, instead of selecting Insert Snippet from the shortcut menu, you select Surround With. The insert works the same way, but this time has applied the snippet (in this case, a namespace snippet) in a different fashion. Compare the before and after text shown in Figures 8.18 and 8.19. We have encapsulated the class definitions within a new namespace that sits within yet another namespace—all with just a few mouse clicks.

FIGURE 8.18   Before inserting a Surrounds With snippet.

Creating Your Own Code Snippets

Because code snippets are stored in XML files, you can create your own snippets quite easily. The key is understanding the XML schema that defines a snippet, and the best way to do that is to look at the XML source data for some of the snippets included with the IDE.

Snippets are stored on a per-language basis under the install directory for Visual Studio. For example, with a US English installation of Windows 7, the Visual Basic snippets can be found, by default, in the folders under the C:\Program Files\Microsoft Visual Studio 10.0\Vb\Snippets\1033 directory. Although snippet files are XML, they carry a .Snippet extension.

FIGURE 8.19   After inserting a Surrounds With snippet.

The XML Snippet Format   Listing 8.1 provides the XML for the C# constructor snippet.

LISTING 8.1   C# Constructor Snippet

```xml
<?xml version="1.0" encoding="utf-8" ?>
<CodeSnippets  xmlns="http://schemas.microsoft.com/VisualStudio/2005/CodeSnippet">
    <CodeSnippet Format="1.0.0">
        <Header>
            <Title>ctor</Title>
            <Shortcut>ctor</Shortcut>
            <Description>Code snippet for constructor</Description>
            <Author>Microsoft Corporation</Author>
            <SnippetTypes>
                <SnippetType>Expansion</SnippetType>
            </SnippetTypes>
        </Header>
        <Snippet>
            <Declarations>
                <Literal Editable="false">
                    <ID>classname</ID>
                    <ToolTip>Class name</ToolTip>
                    <Function>ClassName()</Function>
                    <Default>ClassNamePlaceholder</Default>
                </Literal>
            </Declarations>
```

```
        <Code Language="csharp"><![CDATA[public $classname$ ()
    {
        $end$
    }]]>
            </Code>
        </Snippet>
    </CodeSnippet>
</CodeSnippets>
```

The basic structure of this particular snippet declaration is described in Table 8.2. A more complete schema reference is available as a part of the Visual Studio MSDN help collection; it is located under Integrated Development Environment for Visual Studio, Reference, XML Schema References, Code Snippets Schema Reference.

TABLE 8.2   XML Snippet File Node Descriptions

XML Node	Description
<CodeSnippets>	The parent element for all code snippet information. It references the specific XML namespace used to define snippets within Visual Studio.
<CodeSnippet>	The root element for a single code snippet. This tag sets the format version information for the snippet. Although multiple CodeSnippet elements are possible within the parent <CodeSnippets> element, the convention is to place one snippet per file.
<Header>	A metadata container element for data that describes the snippet.
<Title>	The title of the code snippet.
<Shortcut>	Typically, the same as the title, this is the text that appears in the code snippet insertion drop-downs.
<Description>	A description of the snippet.
<Author>	The author of the snippet.
<SnippetTypes>	The parent element for holding elements describing the snippet's type.
<SnippetType>	The type of the snippet: Expansion, Refactoring, or Surrounds With. You cannot create custom refactoring snippets. This property is really used to tell Visual Studio where the snippet can be inserted within the editor window: Expansion snippets insert at the current cursor position, whereas Surrounds With snippets are inserted before and after the code body identified by the current cursor position or selection.
<Snippet>	The root element for the snippet code.
<Declarations>	The root element for the literals and objects used by the snippet.

TABLE 8.2 Continued

XML Node	Description
<Literal>	A string whose value can be interactively set as part of the snippet expansion process. The Editable attribute on this tag indicates whether the literal is static or editable. The ctor snippet is an example of one without an editable literal; contrast this with the form transparency snippet that you saw—an example of a snippet with an editable literal that allows you to set the form name as part of the snippet insertion.
<ID>	A unique ID for the literal.
<ToolTip>	A ToolTip to display when the cursor is placed over the literal.
<Function>	The name of a function (see Table 8.3) to call when the literal receives focus. Functions are available only in C# snippets.
<Default>	The default string literal to insert into the editor.
<Code>	An element that contains the actual code to insert.

The trick to writing a snippet is to understand how literals and variable replacement work. Say that you want to create a C# snippet that writes out a simple code comment indicating that a class has been reviewed and approved as part of a code review process. In other words, you want something like this:

```
// Code review of ContextToken.
//    Reviewer: Lars Powers
//    Date: 1/1/2010
//    Approval: Approved
```

In this snippet, you need to treat four literals as variable; they can change each time the snippet is used: the class name, the reviewer's name, the date, and the approval. You can set them up within the declarations section like this:

```
<Declarations>
    <Literal Editable="False">
        <ID>classname</ID>
        <ToolTip>Class name/type being reviewed</ToolTip>
        <Function>ClassName()</Function>
        <Default>ClassNameGoesHere</Default>
    </Literal>
    <Literal Editable="True">
        <ID>reviewer</ID>
        <ToolTip>Replace with the reviewer's name</ToolTip>
        <Default>ReviewerName</Default>
    </Literal>
```

```
    <Literal Editable="True">
        <ID>currdate</ID>
        <ToolTip>Replace with the review date</ToolTip>
        <Default>ReviewDate</Default>
    </Literal>
    <Literal Editable="True">
        <ID>approval</ID>
        <ToolTip>Replace with Approved or Rejected</ToolTip>
        <Default>Approved</Default>
    </Literal>
</Declarations>
```

Notice that you are actually calling a function to prepopulate the class name within the snippet. Functions are available only with C#; they are documented in Table 8.3. The rest of the literals rely on the developer to type over the placeholder value with the correct value.

TABLE 8.3   Code Snippet Functions

Function	Description
GenerateSwitchCases (enumliteral)	Creates the syntax for a switch statement that includes a case statement for each value defined by the enumeration represented by enumliteral (C#/J#).
ClassName()	Inserts the name of the class containing the code snippet (C#/J#).
SimpleTypeName(typename)	Takes the type name referenced by typename and returns the shortest name possible given the using statements in effect for the current code block. Example: SimpleTypeName(System.Exception) would return Exception if a using System statement is present (C#).
CallBase(parameter)	Is useful when stubbing out members that implement or return the base type: When you specify get, set, or method as the parameter, a call will be created against the base class for that specific property accessor or method (C#).

You should also provide some basic header information for the snippet:

```
<Header>
    <Title>review</Title>
    <Shortcut>review</Shortcut>
    <Description>Code review comment</Description>
    <Author>L. Powers</Author>
    <SnippetTypes>
        <SnippetType>Expansion</SnippetType>
    </SnippetTypes>
</Header>
<Snippet>
```

The last remaining task is to implement the <Code> element, which contains the actual text of the snippet and references the literals that we have previously defined.

```
<Code Language="csharp">
    <![CDATA[// Review of $classname$
    //    Reviewer: $reviewer$
    //    Date: $currdate$
    //    Approval: $approval$]]>
</Code>
```

When the code snippet is executed, our literals (bracketed by the $ symbols in the preceding code) are replaced by their specified default values and are highlighted to allow the snippet user to easily replace them after they are in the editor. Our $classname$ literal is a bit different in that it places a call to the ClassName() function to get the name of the current, enclosing class.

At this point, the snippet is syntactically complete. Although this snippet is writing comments into the editor, the same exact process and structure applies for emitting code into the editor. If you want to write a Surrounds With snippet, you change the <SnippetType> to Surrounds With.

Now, you need to make Visual Studio aware of the snippet.

Adding a Snippet to Visual Studio   You can use Visual Studio's own XML editor to create the XML document and save it to a directory (a big bonus for doing so is that you can leverage IntelliSense triggered by the XML snippet schema to help you with your element names and relationships). The Visual Studio installer creates a default directory to place your custom snippets located in your Documents folder: *user*\My Documents\Visual Studio 2010\Code Snippets\Visual C#\My Code Snippets. If you place your XML template here, Visual Studio automatically includes your snippet for use.

TIP

If you have placed your snippet file in the correct folder and it still doesn't show up within the Code Snippets Manager dialog box, you probably have a syntax error within the file. A good way to check this is to try to import the snippet file using the Import button. Visual Studio immediately tells you if the snippet file is valid or not.

The Code Snippets Manager, which is launched from the Tools menu, is the central control dialog box for browsing the available snippets, adding new ones, or removing a snippet (see Figure 8.20). As you can see, the review snippet shows up under the My Code Snippets folder.

FIGURE 8.20   The Code Snippets Manager.

You can also opt to include other folders besides the standard ones. To do so, click on the Add button to enter additional folders for Visual Studio to use when displaying the list of snippets.

Figure 8.21 shows the results of the custom snippet.

FIGURE 8.21   The results of a custom code snippet.

Snippets can also be browsed and shared online (see Chapter 7, "The .NET Community: Interacting Online," for a discussion of online communities). A great way to further your understanding of code snippet structure and functions is to browse your way through the snippet files included in Visual Studio, as well as those created by the developer community as a whole.

Snippets in the Toolbox

Although this capability is technically not part of the official code snippet technology within Visual Studio, you can also store snippets of code in the toolbox. First, select the text in the editor and then drag and drop it onto the toolbox. You can then reuse this snippet at any time by dragging it back from the toolbox into an open editor window.

Brace Matching

Programming languages make use of parentheses, braces, brackets, and other delimiters to delimit function arguments, mathematical functions/order of operation, and bodies of code. It can be difficult to visually determine whether you have missed a matching delimiter—that is, if you have more opening delimiters than you have closing delimiters—especially with highly nested lines of code.

Brace matching refers to visual cues that the code editor uses to make you aware of your matching delimiters. As you type code into the editor, any time you enter a closing delimiter, the matching opening delimiter and the closing delimiter are briefly highlighted. In Figure 8.22, brace matching helps to indicate the matching delimiters for the interior `for` loop.

You also can trigger brace matching simply by placing the cursor directly to the left of an opening delimiter or the right of a closing delimiter. If you are browsing through a routine congested with parentheses and braces, you can quickly sort out the matching pairs by moving your cursor around to the various delimiters.

Although this feature is referred to as brace matching, it actually functions with the following delimiters:

▶ Parentheses: ()

▶ Brackets: [ ], <>

▶ Quotation marks: " "

▶ Braces: {}

In the case of C#, brace matching also works with the following keyword pairs (which essentially function as delimiters using keywords):

▶ # region, #endregion

- #if, #else, #endif

- case, break

- default, break

- for, break, continue

- if, else

- while, break, continue

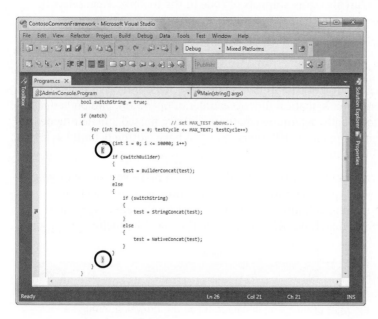

FIGURE 8.22   Brace matching.

Customizing IntelliSense

Certain IntelliSense features can be customized, on a per-language basis, within the Visual Studio Options dialog box. If you launch the Options dialog box (located under the Tools menu) and then navigate to the Text Editor node, you find IntelliSense options confusingly scattered under both the General and IntelliSense pages.

Figure 8.23 shows the IntelliSense editor Options dialog box for Visual C#.

Completion Lists in this dialog box refer to any of the IntelliSense features that facilitate autocompletion of code, such as List Members and Complete Word. Table 8.4 itemizes the options available in this dialog box.

FIGURE 8.23   IntelliSense options.

TABLE 8.4   IntelliSense Options

Option	Effect
Show Completion List After a Character Is Typed	This causes the Complete Word feature to automatically run after a single character is typed in the editor window.
Place Keywords in Completion Lists	If this box is checked, language keywords are displayed within the completion list. As an example, for C#, this would cause keywords such as class or string to be included in the completion list.
Place Code Snippets in Completion Lists	Checking this box places code-snippet alias names into any displayed completion lists.
Committed by Typing the Following Characters	This check box contains any of the characters that cause IntelliSense to execute a completion action. In other words, typing any of the characters in this text box while a completion list is displayed causes IntelliSense to insert the current selection into the editor window.
Committed by Pressing the Space Bar	Checking this adds the space character to the list of characters that fire a completion commit.
Add New Line on Enter at End of Fully Typed Word	Checking this box causes the cursor to advance down an entire line if you fully type a word in the IntelliSense list box. This is useful for those scenarios in which fully typed keywords are unlikely to be followed on the same line with other code.
Pre-select Most Recently Used Member	If this box is checked, IntelliSense maintains and use a historical list of the most frequently used members for a given type. This "MFU" list is then used to preselect members in a completion list.

The Task List

The Task List is essentially an integrated to-do list; it captures all the items that, for one reason or another, need attention and tracking. The Task List window then surfaces this list and allows you to interact with it. To show the window, select the View menu and choose the Task List entry. Figure 8.24 illustrates the Task List window displaying a series of user tasks. Tasks belong to one of three categories—comment tasks, shortcut tasks, and user tasks—and only one category can be displayed at a time.

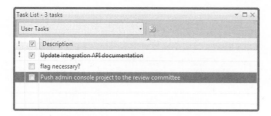

FIGURE 8.24   The Task List window.

The drop-down at the top of the Task List window enables you to select the current category. Each category has slightly different columns for each task category type, but each category has a Priority column and a Description column. For instance, user tasks and shortcut tasks provide a check box that is used to track task completion; shortcut and comment tasks display a filename and line number; and so on.

You can sort the tasks by any of the columns shown in the list. Right-clicking on the column headers provides a shortcut menu that allows you to control the sort behavior, as well as which columns (from a list of all supported columns) should be displayed.

Comment Tasks

Comment tasks are created within your code. Placing a code comment with a special string literal/token causes Visual Studio to add that comment to the comment task list. Three of these tokens are defined by Visual Studio: HACK, TODO, and UNDONE. To see these tasks in your task window, ensure that you have selected Comments from the drop-down at the top of the task list.

As an example, the following C# code results in four different comment tasks in the task list:

```
namespace Contoso.Fx.Integration.Specialized
{
    //TODO: Implement second constructor
    public class MessageMapper : IMessageSink
    {
        public MessageMapper()
        {
        }
```

```
    }

    //TODO: Check on IMap interface implementation
    public class MessageBus : MessageMapper
    {
        public MessageBus()
        {
            //UNDONE: MessageBus ctor
        }
    }

    //HACK: re-write of TokenStruct
    public class ContextToken
    {
        public ContextToken()
        {
        }
        public ContextToken(string guid)
        {
        }
    }
}
```

Double-clicking on the comment task takes you directly to the referenced comment line within the editor window.

Custom Comment Tokens

If needed, you can add your own set of tokens that are recognized as comment tasks. From the Tools, Options dialog box, select the Task List page under the Environment section; this dialog box provides options for adding, editing, or deleting the list of comment tokens recognized by the task list.

In Figure 8.25, a REVIEW token has been added to the standard list. Note that you can also set a priority against each of the tokens and fine-tune some of the display behavior by using the Task List Options check boxes, which control whether task deletions are confirmed, and by setting whether filenames or complete file paths are displayed within the task list.

Shortcut Tasks

Shortcut tasks are actually links to a line of code. You add them using the Bookmarks menu by placing the cursor on a line within the editor and then selecting Edit, Bookmarks, Add Task List Shortcut. The actual content of that line of code shows up as the task description.

Double-clicking on the task takes you directly to the bookmarked line within the editor window.

FIGURE 8.25   Adding a custom comment task token.

User Tasks

User tasks are entered directly into the task window. A Create User Task button appears next to the category drop-down on the Task List window (refer to Figure 8.24); this button adds a new entry within the list. You can type directly into the description column to add the task's title.

Unlike shortcut and comment tasks, user tasks aren't linked to a specific line of code.

> **NOTE**
>
> Visual Studio's automation model provides complete control over task lists. Using the exposed automation objects such as TaskList and TaskListEvents, you can, for example, programmatically add or remove tasks from the list; respond to a task being added, edited, or even selected; and control the linking between a task and an editor.

Summary

Visual Studio 2010 carries a staggering number of features designed to boost your productivity. This chapter described the many facets of the IntelliSense technology, ranging from statement completion to the new code snippet technology, and you learned how to work with the various IntelliSense features to both write code faster and improve the quality of your code.

We covered how to navigate and browse through sometimes complicated and congested code files.

We also introduced code snippets and discussed the different types of code snippets and their usefulness.

Finally, we covered how to use the Task List window to its fullest potential, to help organize and track the various to-do items inherent with any programming project.

From a productivity standpoint, Visual Studio 2010 truly is more than the sum of its parts: In synergy with one another, each of these features knocks down substantial hurdles and pain points for developers, regardless of their backgrounds, skill levels, or language preferences.

8

CHAPTER 9

Testing Code

Developers have always been responsible for testing their code before it is released to testers or users. In years past, this meant walking through every line of code in the debugger (including all conditions and errors). To do so, you often had to create test-harness applications that mimicked the functionality required to execute your code. Stepping through all your code in a debugger made for a fine goal but was not always realized (and very difficult to verify). In fact, the entire exercise was often skipped during code changes and updates. In addition, this process made it difficult to see if your code changes affected other parts of the system. The result was lower-quality builds sent to testers and users and thus higher defect rates and wasted time going back and forth between developers and testers.

This method of developer testing (and its results) highlighted a need to provide more robust, automated unit testing of code. As a result, unit test frameworks were developed. The first such framework for .NET was NUnit (nunit.org). This framework is available as open-source for most .NET languages. It allows you to write code that tests other code. A similar framework was built into Visual Studio 2005 and has been carried forward through the current edition.

The unit test framework in Visual Studio enables you to build tests as you build your application. Alternatively, if you subscribe to test-driven development, you can write your tests before you write your code. In either case, a disciplined approach to unit testing can lead toward building a full set of tests in unison with your application.

This full set of tests can often represent a regression test for most components or even the entire system. The result is increased confidence in activities that were previously high-risk, such as last-minute fixes, refactoring, and late additions. When these activities occur, you can leverage your full set of unit tests to find out what, if anything, was broken as a result of the change.

This chapter covers the many tools, technologies, and techniques for developer testing. With this information in hand, you are able to begin realizing the many benefits of automated, developer testing including fewer bugs, easier to understand code, and additional confidence in code changes.

Unit Testing Basics

Unit testing in Visual Studio is about creating tests that test the code inside the working layers of your application. This includes the many classes that make up your business and data domain. The user interface, on the other hand, is typically tested using alternate methods of automated testing. These methods are targeted more at testers. These features and products are included in the Premium edition of Visual Studio and thus not covered here. Our focus is the code you write to test the code you write. Of course this assumes you follow good, layered architecture techniques when writing your applications. In this section we cover the basics of writing unit tests. We drill in on these basics in coming sections.

Creating a Test Project

Your developer test must exist inside a test project. This is a project that has the right references to the unit testing framework and the configuration required to be run via the test tool built inside of Visual Studio. There are two primary ways you can initiate the creation of a unit test project. You can create a test project from within the IDE, or you can automatically generate unit tests into a new test project for existing code. We start with the first option.

The Test Project Template
You create a new test project in Visual Studio through the New Project dialog box (File, New, Project). Inside this dialog box you navigate to the Test Projects node in the Installed Templates tree. Figure 9.1 shows an example. Notice that you can select to put your test project inside a new solution or an existing solution. In most cases, you add test projects to existing solutions as they must reference the projects within your solution.

GOOD PRACTICE FOR CREATING TEST PROJECTS AND TEST CLASSES

You should define a policy on how many test projects you wish to create for your solution. Typically, you create a test project as a one-to-one ratio with a project you want to test. For example, if you have a project for your business objects and another project for your data services you might create two test projects (one for each). This is not required. It simply makes for an easily understood organization of your code.

A similar approach holds true for test classes. You should create a single test class for each class you have in your target project you wish to test. For example, if you are creating a test project for your business domain objects that includes a Customer and an Order object you should create a CustomerTest and OrderTest class. Again, this is not required; rather, it makes for a good, logical organization of your code.

FIGURE 9.1   You can create a new Test Project for your solution from the New Project dialog box.

The Test Project

Visual Studio sets a reference to the unit test framework (Microsoft.VisualStudio.QualityTools.UnitTestFramework) when you create a new test project. In addition, it adds two files to your solution (inside the Solution Items folder). These are both testing configuration (or settings) files. They are named Local.testsettings and TraceAndTestImpact.testsettings. Finally, the test project also creates a test class for you to use to write unit tests. Figure 9.2 illustrates each of these items inside the Solution Explorer. We explore each of these items in more detail in coming sections.

You can add additional test files to your test project by right-clicking the test project and choosing Add, New Test (you can also access this from the Project menu, which brings up the Add New Test dialog box as shown in Figure 9.3). From here you have the following options:

▶ **Basic Unit Test**—This template creates a simple test class with a blank test method. You typically use this template if you are creating your tests from scratch (and not using the auto-generation features).

FIGURE 9.2   The Test Project (and related items) inside the Solution Explorer.

FIGURE 9.3   You can add new tests to a test project through the Add New Test dialog box.

▶ **Database Unit Test**—This template is used to create a unit test that executes against a stored procedure in your database (you need the Premium edition of Visual Studio to use this feature).

▶ **Ordered Test**—This template enables you to create a sequential list of tests to be executed as a group (see "Creating Ordered Tests" later in this chapter).

▶ **Unit Test**—This template creates a blank unit test class that uses an object to track test context. This is the type of unit test class that is auto-generated (see "Generating Tests from Existing Code").

▶ **Unit Test Wizard**—This template launches the Unit Test Wizard used to auto-generate tests based on existing code in your solution (see "Generating Tests from Existing Code").

The Test Menu

The Test menu can be used to access all the features of developer testing inside Visual Studio. This includes the ability to add a unit test class to your test project (Test, New Test). You can use this menu to load information about a previous test run (Load Metadata File). You can also run tests from here (in run-only or debug mode). You can select which test settings in your solution to apply to the next test run you execute; you can also edit test settings from here. Finally, you can access the many windows used to view and organize the tests in your application. Figure 9.4 shows an example that illustrates the many features of this menu.

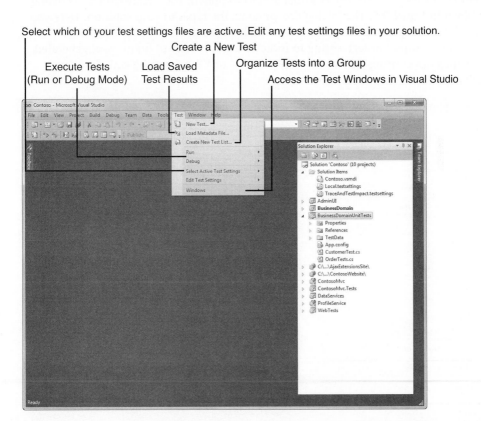

FIGURE 9.4   The Visual Studio Test menu can be used to access developer testing features in Visual Studio.

Generating Tests from Existing Code

Visual Studio also provides a means of automating the creation of unit tests. You can right-click an existing class and choose Create Unit Tests from the context menu. Alternatively, you can select the Unit Test Wizard item template to do the same. In either case, Visual Studio actually generates a set of unit tests based on the code in your class.

What is generated is a good start toward building your unit tests. Visual Studio actually examines the methods and properties in the class from which you want to generate tests and writes out real, possible tests. Of course, you have to finish each test by adding the appropriate variable values and the right assertions, but what is generated by the tools makes for a nice start.

Let's look at an example. Suppose that you have a Customer object that contains properties such as Name, Address, Phone, and Email. Imagine it also contains methods such as Save, GetList, and Delete. You can use Visual Studio to generate new unit tests for this class by either selecting Unit Test Wizard from the Add New Test dialog box or right-clicking in the actual class file and selecting Create Unit Tests.

Taking either of these steps instructs Visual Studio to present the Create Unit Tests dialog box as shown in Figure 9.5. This dialog box presents the types in your solution. Here you can select the members from those types for which you want to have tests generated. You can also use the Output project setting to indicate a test project to house your generated tests. This includes creating a new test project (in C# or VB) or putting code into any existing test project.

FIGURE 9.5   You can let Visual Studio generate unit tests for existing code.

The Add Assembly button at the bottom of the dialog box enables you to select an assembly (.dll file) outside of your project. You can generate tests for any .NET assembly.

Manage Test Generation Settings

The Settings button opens a dialog box that enables you to manage the various settings for generating your unit tests. Figure 9.6 shows an example of this dialog box. Notice you can use the macro text [File], [Class], and [Method] to indicate how Visual Studio should name the files, classes, and test methods it generates.

FIGURE 9.6   You can control how Visual Studio generates your unit tests.

Notice that there are additional settings inside the General group. These enable you to set each generated test as inconclusive, to enable comments in the generated code, and more.

> **NOTE**
>
> The Create Unit Tests Wizard enables you to generate unit tests to all the projects in your solution. Selecting a class and generating tests adds a reference from the test project to the project containing the code being tested.

The Generated Test Code

Visual Studio generates a test for every method and property you select in the Create Unit Tests dialog box. For example, Listing 9.1 shows what Visual Studio generated as a unit test for the Name property (the VB code would look similar). Notice that this test creates a new instance of the Customer object and names the related variable target. It then defines an expected result. In this case, the Name property is of type string so the test code creates a string variable called expected. It also defines a string variable called actual. It then sets the Customer.Name property to the expected value and reads back the actual value (after setting the property). Finally, the code confirms that this property set was successful via the Assert.AreEqual line. This is a valid property test. All that is left for a developer is to put a valid value into the variable expected (note the TODO) and remove the Assert.Inconclusive call.

LISTING 9.1   A Sample of an Auto-Generated Unit Test for a Property

```
[TestMethod()]
public void NameTest() {
  Customer target = new Customer(); // TODO: Initialize to an appropriate value
  string expected = string.Empty; // TODO: Initialize to an appropriate value
  string actual;
  target.Name = expected;
  actual = target.Name;
  Assert.AreEqual(expected, actual);
  Assert.Inconclusive("Verify the correctness of this test method.");
}
```

You have a little more work to do when testing methods. If the method returns a value you can check the method's return value to ensure you got back what was expected. If the method does not return a value, you have to write some additional code to verify the code executed property. Listing 9.2 shows an auto-generated test for a method that does not return a value. Of course, if the method call returns an error that is considered a failed test. However, you should still write more verification and assertions than that in your unit tests (see Creating Effective Unit Tests).

LISTING 9.2   A Sample of an Auto-Generated Unit Test for a Method

```
[TestMethod()]
public void SaveTest() {
  Customer target = new Customer(); // TODO: Initialize to an appropriate value
  target.Save();
  Assert.Inconclusive("A method that does not return a value cannot be verified.");
}
```

NOTE

When generating test code for constructors, Visual Studio appends the text ConstructorTest to the name of the class. If there is more than one constructor, Visual Studio starts appending numbers to each constructor as in CustomerConstructorTest1.

Writing an Actual Unit Test

You can start to see how you can leverage the unit tests that are generated for you. Let's take a look at writing an actual unit test to help better understand them. Recall that a unit test is simply test code you write to call your application code. This test code asserts that various conditions are either true or false as a result of the call to your application code. The test either passes or fails based on the results of these assertions. If, for example, you expect an outcome to be true and it turns out false, then a test fails.

After you have a test project and a test class, there are three steps to creating a typical unit test:

1. Apply the TestMethod attribute to the test code.
2. Execute the code in question passing in known values if there are parameters.
3. Use assertions to evaluate the test results.

Let's look more closely at a real example. Suppose that you have a data service that returns a customer's profile from the database. This method takes the customer's identification number as a parameter. The function signature for this method might look as follows:

```
public Customer GetCustomerProfile(int customerId)
```

You can then write a simple test to call this method and pass a known ID value from the database. A good tenant of unit testing with databases is to test a known state of the database. This test might then confirm that what is returned not only works but also is correct. Listing 9.3 shows an example of such a test.

LISTING 9.3   A Sample Unit Test

```
[TestMethod()]
public void GetCustomerProfileTest() {
  CustomerProfile custProfileService = new CustomerProfile();
  int customerId = 1234;
  Customer customer = custProfileService.GetCustomerProfile(customerId);
  Assert.AreEqual(customer.Id, 1234);
}
```

Notice that this code is similar to other C# code (the VB code is similar, too). You mark the method as a test by adding the TestMethod attribute. Inside the code, you create an instance of the object being tested and make a call to the method you want to test. If this call fails (or any exception is thrown), the test fails. You then do an assertion in the test to make sure that the object returned matches the expected results. If this assertion is false (the values are not equal), the test fails. If the assertion is true, the test succeeds. You might add a few more assertions to round out this test (validating other known items about this customer). In addition, you might create some additional tests for this method such as what happens when you attempt to retrieve a customer that does not exist.

This gives you an understanding of the basics of writing an actual unit test. We dig deeper in a moment.

Running Your Tests

There are a few places in Visual Studio that let you kick off an execution of your unit tests. Two such places are the Test Tools toolbar and the Test menu. Each of these gives you a similar set of options. Figure 9.7 shows these options. The top portion of the figure is the Test Tools toolbar. The bottom portion is actually a shot of the Add or Remove buttons option for the toolbar; this is useful as it illustrates the meaning of each toolbar icon and shows shortcut keys for running tests.

FIGURE 9.7   The Test Menu enables you to start your tests with or without debugging.

Notice that you can run your tests with the debugger activated or run without debugging. The former allows you to break into the debugger if a test fails. This capability can be useful if you are troubleshooting code through tests. The latter is a more likely scenario; with this option, you simply run your unit tests and view their results. Notice, too, that you have the option to run tests in the current context or the entire solution. The current context option runs any selected tests, or the test where your cursor currently resides, or all tests for a given class if you are viewing the class code (and not test code). It can sometimes be difficult to understand how Visual Studio sees the current context. In this case, either run all the tests in the solution or use execute tests from Test View (see "Organizing Your Tests").

> **NOTE**
>
> When you run a test project, any referenced projects are recompiled along with your test project.

Viewing Test Results

When you run your tests, the results are shown in the Test Results window (typically docked to the bottom of the IDE). The Test Results window provides an overview of which tests passed and which failed. Figure 9.8 shows this window in action and provide highlights on many of the features of this window. Notice that the given test run is considered failed as a whole if one or more tests fail. In this case, 16 of 18 tests passed. However, the overall test failed due to the two test failures.

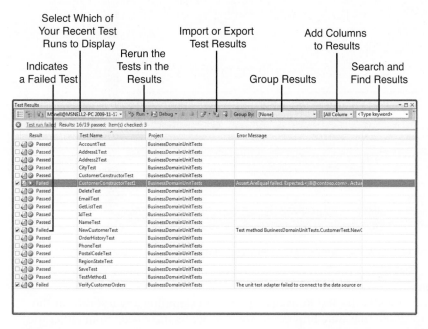

FIGURE 9.8   The Test Results window enables you to view test run results and re-run selected tests.

The Test Results window has a toolbar that gives you a lot of options and control. One option enables you to review the results of any test runs executed during a Visual Studio session. This includes the ability to show all test runs at once. Another option allows you to easily re-run the tests in a given test run. You can use yet another option to export your results to a file and share these results with someone else (who can import them using the same toolbar). You can also add more columns to your test results in order to view more data and better organize your results (there are more than 20 columns from which to choose).

If you double-click a passed test you see a details page about that test. This details page includes the test name, results, duration of the test, and the start and end time. If you double-click a failed test, you see the line of code in the class being tested that caused the test to fail. If, however, you want to see the details of a failed test, you can do so by right-clicking the test result and choosing View Test Results Details. Figure 9.9 shows an example of the details page for a failed test. Notice that the page includes the error message, a stack trace, and a link to the code that caused the failure.

FIGURE 9.9   You can view the details behind any test result (failed or passed).

Viewing Test Runs

Visual Studio also provides the Test Runs dialog box for examining any test runs in the current session (or those that were imported). You can access this dialog from either the Test Tools toolbar or from the menu, Test | Windows | Test Runs. Figure 9.10 shows an example of this dialog box. You can double-click a given run to load the details of the results into the Test Results window.

Configuring Testing Options and Settings

Visual Studio provides the ability to control and customize the testing environment through the Options dialog box. In addition, you can control test settings specific to your solution inside setting configuration files. This section explores how you can use both of these configuration scenarios to better manage your test environment.

Test Project Options

You can control how Visual Studio generates test projects. You do so inside the Options dialog box (Tools, Options) under the Test Tools, Test Project node. Figure 9.11 shows an example of this dialog box. From here, you can control the default language (VB or C#) for the test project type used by Visual Studio when you create or generate a new test project. Notice that you can also choose to override the default language setting in the IDE for test projects.

FIGURE 9.10   The Test Runs dialog enables you to see the results for all runs in a current Visual Studio session.

FIGURE 9.11   You can use the Options dialog box to customize the defaults for how Visual Studio creates test project templates.

The Test Project options also enable you to select which files should be included in the test project by default when it creates a new test project. Your options here are controlled by language. Options include files for basic unit test, database unit test, ordered test, or unit test (opens the create Unit Test Wizard).

Manage Test Results

By default, Visual Studio keeps a record of the last 25 test runs you've executed. If you exceed this limit, Visual Studio deletes the oldest test run from your hard drive before writing out the new test run results. You can increase (or decrease) this limit from the

Options dialog box (Tools, Options). From here, select the Test Tools node and the Test Execution sub-node to bring up the options shown in Figure 9.12. Notice the option, "Limit Number of Old Test Runs To."

FIGURE 9.12   You can indicate the number of test runs to keep from the Options dialog box.

Controlling Test Settings

Visual Studio provides a settings file that allows you to control how your tests execute. In most cases, you can leave this setting file in its default mode. However, there are many instances where you might need to edit the settings such as running deployment scripts that are part of tests, controlling test timeouts, and more.

The test settings files can be found at the solution level inside Solution Explorer (refer to Figure 9.2). Each of your test settings files has the extension .testsettings. You can configure which .testsettings file is active at any given time through the menu by using Test, Select Active Test Settings. Figure 9.13 shows an example of selecting an active settings file.

The .testsettings files in Visual Studio are simply XML configuration files. You can edit the XML directly. However, Visual Studio provides a dialog box to making changing settings easier. You can launch the Test Settings dialog box by double-clicking a .testsettings file. Figure 9.14 shows an example of the dialog box with the Test Timeouts node selected.

Selecting a node on the left of the Test Settings dialog box enables you to configure various settings associated with that node. The following provides an overview of the settings you can manage for each of the Test Settings nodes:

▶ **General**—Provides options for naming the settings file, providing a description, creating a naming scheme for each of your test runs (refer to Figure 9.10 for how test runs are named).

FIGURE 9.13   You can select the active test settings file from the Test menu.

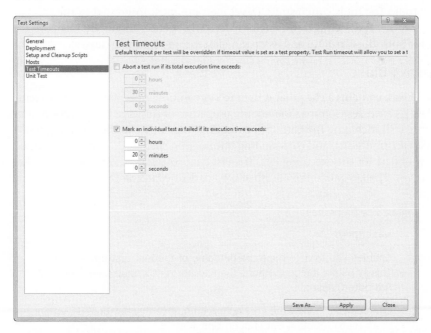

FIGURE 9.14   The Test Settings dialog box enables you to manage the settings around how your tests execute (including test timeouts).

► **Deployment**—Enables you to specify additional files and folders to deploy as part of running your tests. By default, the assemblies being tested automatically deploy to the test bin, which enables you to add any additional items you might want to deploy before running tests (such as a file-based database).

► **Setup and Cleanup Scripts**—Enables you to select a script to run either before or after your tests run (or both). This is different than running code before a test class runs. Here, you can define code to run before (or after) any test groups run.

► **Hosts**—Enables you to specify a host on which the tests can execute. Typically this is the default host (Visual Studio). You might also need to configure your tests to run inside an ASP.NET server host.

► **Test Timeouts**—Enables you to indicate how long Visual Studio (or your host) should wait before aborting a long-running test. You can also mark tests that run too long as failures. Figure 9.12 shows an example of this dialog box.

► **Unit Test**—Provides advanced options for loading additional assemblies that are required for your tests to execute.

The Unit Testing Framework

The unit testing framework is part of Visual Studio (and not the .NET Framework itself). Unit testing in Visual Studio includes a set of framework classes, the tools, and the execution host. You can find the namespace that contains the unit testing framework classes at Microsoft.VisualStudio.TestTools.UnitTesting. Developers are most interested in the attribute classes and the Assert class in this namespace. This section highlights the core usage scenarios for both the attribute and assertion classes (among other classes).

The TestContext Class

The unit test framework contains a class that is used to store information pertaining to executing tests. This class is called TestContext. You use the properties of this class to get information about your running tests including the path to the test directory, a URL to the executing test (in the case of ASP.NET unit tests), and data-binding information such as the data connection or the current row of data for the executing test. The test context information is stored inside properties of this class. The key properties and their use are defined inside Table 9.1.

TABLE 9.1   TestContext Key Properties

Property	Description
CurrentTestOutcome	Enables you to determine the outcome of the last test that executed. This is useful inside methods marked as TestCleanup (see "The Test Attribute Classes").
DataConnection	Enables you to view the connection string used by any data-driven unit tests (see "Creating Data-Bound Unit Tests").
DataRow	Enables you to access columns in a row of data when working with data-bound unit tests (see "Creating Data-Bound Unit Tests").

TABLE 9.1   Continued

Property	Description
RequestedPage	Provides access to the Page object for the requested page in an ASP.NET unit test (see "Writing ASP.NET Hosted Unit Tests").
TestDeploymentDir	Enables you to view the path to the directory where your unit tests are deployed and executing. This is useful if you need to read or write a file in that directory.
TestLogsDir	Enables you to view the path to the directory where your test results are written.
TestName	Enables access to the name of the currently executing test.

TestContext is not accessible to your code by default. You access TestContext by first defining a property of the same name and type inside your test class (this property is automatically generated for you when you generate unit tests from existing code). The unit test framework automatically creates an instance of a TestContext object when it runs your tests. It then looks for a TestContext property in your source code. If it finds it, the framework assigns an instance of TestContext to your property. You can then use your property to access information about the executing test context. The following code shows how you might define the TestContext property in a C# unit test:

```
public TestContext TestContext { get; set; }
```

Visual Studio actually generates a full property when creating the TestContext object. The following demonstrates the code Visual Studio generates for this property:

```
private TestContext testContextInstance;

public TestContext TestContext {
  get {
    return testContextInstance;
  }
  set {
    testContextInstance = value;
  }
}
```

NOTE

Some attribute classes require that you define a parameter of type TestContext to your decorated method. This is true for ClassInitialize (see below). In this case, the unit test framework automatically passes an instance of a TestContext object to your method when it executes.

The Test Attribute Classes

The unit tests you write are run by Visual Studio using the unit test execution host. This host has to examine your code and find the unit tests within in it and run them accordingly. To do so, it relies on attributes. Recall that an attribute is used to provide metadata about your code. Other code (such as the unit test host) can use reflection to determine various bits of information about your code.

As you've seen in the brief samples thus far, you signify unit tests by decorating your code with the attribute classes defined inside the unit namespace. For example, a test class has the TestClass attribute; a test method is indicated using the TestMethod attribute. Table 9.2 presents a list of the most common attribute classes found in the unit testing namespace.

TABLE 9.2　Visual Studio Test Attribute Classes

Test	Description
AssemblyCleanup	Used to define a method that should be run after all the tests in a given assembly have been executed by the framework. This is useful if you need to clean up resources after all tests have executed.
	Note that only one method in a given assembly can contain this attribute.
AssemblyInitialize	Used to define a method that should be run before any tests in a given assembly have been executed by the framework. This is useful if you need to initialize resources for all tests in an assembly.
	Note that only one method in a given assembly can contain this attribute.
ClassCleanup	Used to indicate a method that should be run once after all tests are executed in a given test class. This can be useful if you need to reset the system state (such as a database) after your tests have completed.
ClassInitialize	Used to indicate a method that should be run once by the test execution host before any other tests are run in the given test class. This can be useful if you need to reset a database or execute any code to prepare the test environment.
	Requires that your method take a parameter of type TestContext.
DataSource	Used to provide connection information for a data-driven unit test (see "Creating Data-Bound Unit Tests").
DeploymentItem	Used to indicate any additional files (.dll, .txt, or otherwise) that need to be deployed to the folder in which your tests run.
ExpectedException	Used to indicate that a given test method is expected to receive a certain exception for the code called within the test method. This type of test method is considered successful if the given exception type is received as part of the test execution (otherwise the test fails). This capability is useful for testing expected error conditions in your code (see "Testing Your Exceptions").

TABLE 9.2   Continued

Test	Description
HostType	Used if you want to override the default test host (Visual Studio). In most test scenarios, you do not need to use this attribute. If, however, you write tests to run in another host process (such as ASP.NET) you can use this attribute (along with UrlToTest and AspNetDevelopmentServerHost).
Ignore	Added to a TestMethod to indicate that method should be ignored when run by the test execution host.
TestClass	Used to indicate that a given class is a test class that contains one or more unit tests (test methods).
TestCleanup	Used to indicate a method that should be run once after each test method is executed. You can use this method to do any cleanup after each test method runs in a given test class. Cleanup at the class-level can be done via the ClassCleanup attribute.
TestInitialize	Used to indicate that a given method should be run once before each test method is executed. This capability is useful if you need to reset the system state before each test method within a given test class. If you only need to initialize for all the methods in a given test class, use ClassInitialize.
TestProperty	Used to define a property (name and value pair) attribute to a test method. This property information can be read inside the code of the test method.
TestMethod	Used to decorate a method as a unit test inside a test class. Test methods must have no return value (void). They succeed or fail based on error conditions and assertions. Test methods cannot take parameters as the host cannot pass parameters to the method. There are ways to simulate parameters, however. See "Creating Data-Bound Unit Tests" for more information.
Timeout	Used to indicate a timeout (in milliseconds) for a given test method. If the test exceeds this timeout period, it is stopped and considered failed.

You can see from Table 9.2 that there are a number of attribute classes that give you control over your unit tests. As an example, if you were writing a test class for the Customer object, you might define a test class, CustomerTest. Listing 9.4 shows how you might stub out a few tests for this class. This listing demonstrates the many attributes you might use in a typical test class. Notice the methods to initialize the test class and clean up following the test run.

The next step is to write code inside each of these test methods. The code should make calls to the Customer object and then make assertions with respect to the results. These assertions are made using the Assert class, which we cover next.

LISTING 9.4   An Example Test Class

```
using System;
using BusinessDomain;
```

```csharp
using Microsoft.VisualStudio.TestTools.UnitTesting;
using System.Data;
using System.Collections.Generic;

namespace BusinessDomainUnitTests {

  [TestClass()]
  public class CustomerTest {

    public TestContext TestContext { get; set; }

    [ClassInitialize()]
    public static void InitTests(TestContext testContext) {
      //call code to reset the test db (Utilities.ResetTestDb();)

    }

    [ClassCleanup()]
    public static void CleanupPostTests() {
      //call code to reset the test db (Utilities.ResetTestDb();)

    }

    [TestMethod()]
    public void CustomerConstructorTest() {
      //test the default constructor

    }

    [TestMethod()]
    public void CustomerConstructorTest1() {
      //test the constructor that takes a customer id

    }

    [TestMethod()]
    [DeploymentItem("BusinessDomain.dll")]
    public void DeleteTest() {

    }

    [TestMethod()]
    [DeploymentItem("BusinessDomain.dll")]
    public void GetListTest() {
```

```
    }

    [TestMethod()]
    [DeploymentItem("BusinessDomain.dll")]
    [Timeout(5000)]

    public void SaveTest() {

    }

  }

}
```

Unit Test Setup and Tear Down

A good practice for your unit tests is to write them for a known state of the system; this includes the database, files, and anything that makes up the entire system. This ensures that developers can rely on these items being there when they write their tests. Of course the tests themselves often disrupt this state. You might have a test that deletes data, changes it, adds new records, and the like. In this case, you need to be able to re-initialize the state of the system prior to executing your tests (and/or after executing your tests). to ensure both a steady state to test against and a one-click test run experience for developers (another good practice for unit testing).

You typically need to write code to keep your system in a steady state. This code might copy a known, good test database down to the test directory (you could also do this with a DeploymentItem attribute); reset your database using SQL; use a data generation plan to create your database; copy files; or verify other deployment items.

The code to reset your system is specific to your environment. However, to ensure this code is called when your tests run you have a few attribute classes with which to work: ClassInitialize and ClassCleanup, or TestInitialize and TestCleanup. The former set are run at the start (or end) of a test run in the entire unit test class. The latter are run before (or after) each test executes in a given test class.

In most cases, you run initialize and cleanup at the class level. As an example, if you had a Utilities class that included a method to reset your database you could ensure it is called by marking a method as ClassInitialize. Note that this method takes a TestContext object (which is passed to it by the unit test framework). A good practice is to reset the system again after the unit tests execute. The following code shows an example of two test methods doing both setup and cleanup.

```
[ClassInitialize()]
public static void InitTests(TestContext testContext) {
```

```
   Utilities.ResetTestDb();
}


[ClassCleanup()]
public static void CleanupPostTests() {
   Utilities.ResetTestDb();
}
```

Controlling Setup and Cleanup at the Test Execution Level

Sometimes your setup and cleanup needs to be executed at a higher level than just the running test class. Your scripts might need to run before any test classes execute. In this case, you can use your .testsettings file (see the earlier section "Controlling Test Settings") to define a script to execute when any tests are run (and after they have run).

Figure 9.15 shows an example of the Test Settings dialog box, Setup and Cleanup Scripts node. You can use this area to define setup and cleanup scripts to execute when any test in your solution executes.

FIGURE 9.15   You can define setup and cleanup scripts to execute when any test in your solution executes.

The Assert Classes

The UnitTesting namespace also includes the Assert static type. This object contains methods for evaluating whether the results of a test were as expected. You call these static methods and expect a true/false condition. If the boolean condition fails, the assertion fails. The assertions do not actually return results. Rather, they automatically notify the unit test framework at runtime if the assertion fails or succeeds.

As an example, you might write a unit test to load a known record from the database. You would then write assertions about this known record to prove that you can retrieve the data from the database and properly call the right sets and gets on a specific object. The following shows a simple assertion for testing that two variables contain the same value. If the values match (AreEqual) then the assertion passes without issue. If the values don't match, the assertion fails and the unit test framework marks the test as failed.

```
Assert.AreEqual(cust.Id, customerId);
```

The AreEqual method is just one example of the many assertion methods available to you from the Assert class. For the most part, these assertion methods are variations on a concept: compare two values and determine the results. A more complete list can be found inside Table 9.3.

TABLE 9.3   Test Assertions

Test	Description
AreEqual/AreNotEqual	Used to test whether two values are equal to one another (or not).
AreSame/AreNotSame	Used to test whether two objects are the same object (or not).
Fail	The Assert.Fail method is used to fail a condition without doing any evaluation. This might be useful if your evaluation is based on logic and you get to a point in your code where the logic represents a failed test.
Inconclusive	Used to indicate that a given test has not failed or succeeded (but has inconclusive results).
IsInstanceOfType/IsNotInstanceOfType	Used to determine whether an object is of a specified type (or not).
IsNull/IsNotNul	Used to test whether an object contains a null reference (or not).
IsTrue/IsFalse	Used to test whether a condition is true (or false).

Each assertion method has a number of overloads. These overloads enable you to compare various data types, such as strings, numeric values, objects, and generic collections of objects, to one another. In addition, there are overloads that enable you to simply do the assertion and those that both do the assertion and enable you to enter a message that is displayed when the assertion fails. For example, the following is the same assertion as was written previously but using the version that includes an error message for failed assertions.

```
Assert.AreEqual(cust.Id, customerId, "Customer Id numbers do not match.");
```

As an example, consider some of the methods stubbed out in the prior code listing (Listing 9.4). You would fill these methods out by writing some code to execute against the Customer class and then making assertions about the results. Listing 9.5 shows an example of the test for the constructor on the Customer class. Notice that we test a known data record by loading a Customer instance from that record id; we then use the results using the Assert class.

LISTING 9.5   An Example Unit Test Showing the Use of the Assert Class

```
[TestMethod()]
public void CustomerConstructorTest1() {

  //test the constructor that takes a customer id

  int customerId = 1; //test data for a customer
  Customer cust = new Customer(customerId);

  //verify the right data is being returned for the test customer
  //  verify the property sets and reads
  Assert.AreEqual(cust.Id, customerId,
    "Customer Id numbers do not match.");

  Assert.AreEqual(cust.Email, "jdevlop@contoso.com");
  Assert.AreEqual(cust.Name, "Joe Developer");
  Assert.AreEqual(cust.City, "Redmond");
  Assert.AreEqual(cust.PostalCode, "00000");
  Assert.AreEqual(cust.RegionState, "WA");
  Assert.AreEqual(cust.Address1, "100 Microsoft Way");
  Assert.IsTrue(cust.Address2 == "");
  Assert.IsTrue(cust.Phone == "");
}
```

The Assert class also contains a version of the AreEqual/AreNotEqual methods that uses a generic data type. These methods enable you to compare two generic types against one another for equality. In this case, you indicate the generic type using standard generic notation, <T> (or (of T) in VB) and pass the two generic types you want to compare. The following shows an example:

```
Assert.AreEqual<Customer>(cust1, cust2);
```

Verifying Collections of Objects

The UnitTesting namespace also contains the assertion classes, CollectionAssert. With it, you can verify the contents of collection classes. For instance, you can call the Contains method to assert whether a given collection contains a specific element (or DoesNotContain). You can use the AllItemsAreInstancesOfType to check that a collection only contains like instances. You can compare two collections to see if they are equal (AreEqual/AreNotEqual) or that they are simply equivalent; they have the same elements but might be in a different order (AreEquivalent/AreNotEquivalent).

Verifying Strings

The StringAssert class contains methods for verifying strings and portions of strings. For example, the Contains method enables you to check that a string contains a specific substring. You can use the StartsWith method to assert whether a string begins with a certain set of characters, or EndsWith to check the ending of a string. Finally, the Matches/DoesNotMatch methods enable you to check whether or not a string matches a regular expression you define.

Testing Your Exceptions

You should write unit tests to verify your code behaves as expected in both positive and negative conditions. The positive conditions can be verified using the Assert methods as discussed previously. However, many times you want to verify that your code returns the correct exception when you call or use it in a certain manner. In this case, you can use the ExpectedException attribute to test for specific error conditions.

You use the ExpectedException attribute by adding it to a test method. The attribute takes the type of expected exception as a parameter. If the test method results in an exception being thrown and the type of that exception is as you defined in the attribute then the test is considered a success. If an exception is not thrown or an exception of a different type is thrown, then the test is considered as failed.

As an example, suppose you want to test what happens when you try to create a new customer that has incomplete details. In this case, your code might be written to throw a custom exception of type InvalidCustomerException. You would then decorate your test method as follows:

```
[TestMethod()]
[ExpectedException(typeof(InvalidCustomerException),
  "The Invalid Customer Exception was not thrown.")]
public void NewCustomerTest() {

  //create a bad, new customer instance ...
}
```

Notice that in the prior code if the exception is not thrown, there is an error message provided as the result of the test ("The Invalid Customer Exception was not thrown."). This error message is an optional parameter of the ExpectedException attribute.

You can combine assertions with the ExpectedException attribute. In this case, both the assertions need to pass and the exception needs to be thrown for the test method to be considered passed.

> **NOTE**
>
> The resulting exception must be of the exact same type as the expected exception. The resulting exception cannot, for instance, inherit from the expected exception. In this case, the test is considered as failed.

Creating Data-Bound Unit Tests

It is often more practical to write a single unit test and run it multiple times with different parameter values than to create many, similar tests. In fact, a tenant of good unit tests is to ensure you have covered a variety of parameter conditions. Of course, unit tests do not actually take parameters; this makes it difficult to get data into them. In this case, you need to bind your unit tests to test data. You then tell the unit test framework to run your test for each row in the test data. Of course, you can use the bound test data inside your unit test to call your code in multiple ways.

Connecting to Data

You bind a unit test to test data using the DataSource attribute class inside the unit test framework. This attribute class enables you to specify either a direct connection string to test data or the name of the connection string stored inside your project's configuration file. In either case, you can connect to an actual database such as SQL Server or Access, a .csv file (typically created with Notepad or Excel), or an .xml file.

The DataSource attribute class has three overloads. The first simply takes a single parameter, dataSourceSettingName. In this case, you are expected to pass the name of the data source settings as defined inside a configuration file. The second overload takes both a connectionString and a tableName. In this case, you pass a valid connection string to the DataSource and indicate the name of the table you intend to bind to the unit test. The final overload takes providerInvariantName, connectionString, tableName, and dataAccessMethod. The provider name is used to indicate the type of provider such as a CSV provider, SQL Server, or similar. The connection string is based on your chosen provider and indicates how you access the data. The table name is the name of the table (or file) that contains your data. Finally, the data access method determines how your data is bound to the unit test: sequentially or randomly.

As an example, imagine you are writing a unit test to verify a customer's orders and account information. In this case, you might be loading a given customer, getting his orders to date, determining his credit limit, and checking his account balance. You might write a single unit test to do all of these things for a given customer. You can then bind that unit test to rows of customer test data to validate multiple scenarios. Imagine that your test data is stored inside a .csv file inside your test application. In this case you can apply the DataSource attribute to your test method as follows:

```
[TestMethod(),
DataSource("Microsoft.VisualStudio.TestTools.DataSource.CSV",
  "¦DataDirectory¦\\OrderTestData.csv", "OrderTestData#csv",
  DataAccessMethod.Sequential),
DeploymentItem("BusinessDomainUnitTests\\OrderTestData.csv")]
public void VerifyCustomerOrders() {

  //code to validate customer order and account info

}
```

Notice that in the preceding code example, the first parameter of the DataSource call defines the .CSV provider. The next parameter is a connection string to the actual data file. The third parameter (OrderTestData#csv) simply indicates that the table name does not exist (it is the file name). The last parameter, the enumeration DataAccessMethod.Sequential, indicates that each row should be bound to the unit test in sequential order. Finally, notice that the DeploymentItem attribute has been added to make sure the test data file is deployed along with the running unit test.

Connecting Using a Configuration File   In another example you might have your connection information stored inside a configuration file. This is useful if you do not want to hardcode this information in your unit tests. You might, for instance, have a test database that is used across many unit tests. It might change between development and test environments. In this case, having your connection information inside a configuration file makes it easier to manage.

The first step in this scenario is to define a configuration file. To do so, you simply add an app.config file to your unit test project (right-click the project file and select Add, New Item). Getting the format of the configuration file right is the only trick. You have to add a configuration section specific to the Visual Studio test tools. Note that this configuration section must indicate version 10 of the unit test framework. The following shows an example:

```
<configSections>
  <section name="microsoft.visualstudio.testtools"
    type="Microsoft.VisualStudio.TestTools.UnitTesting.TestConfigurationSection,
Microsoft.VisualStudio.QualityTools.UnitTestFramework, Version=10.0.0.0, Culture=
neutral, PublicKeyToken=b03f5f7f11d50a3a" />
</configSections>
```

You then add a connection string section. You give your connection string a name and provide information on both the connection and the data provider. The specifics of your

connection string, of course, depend on your provider and the type of data. Data stored in
.xlsx, .csv, .xml files, Access, Oracle, or SQL databases all have their own connection string
idiosyncrasies. As an example, the following uses the OleDb provider to define a connection string to a delimited text file (.csv):

```
<connectionStrings>
  <add name="OrderTestDataCnn"
    connectionString="Provider=Microsoft.Jet.OLEDB.4.0; Data Source=
¦DataDirectory¦TestData\; Extended Properties='text;HDR=Yes;FMT=Delimited'"
    providerName="System.Data.OleDb" />
</connectionStrings>
```

The last step is to create a data source section embedded inside a test tools section. The
data source defines a name for your test data source and points to your connection string.
You can also indicate the data access method here (sequential or random) and the table
name (if applicable). Your final configuration file should look similar to Listing 9.6.

LISTING 9.6   An Example Unit Test Configuration File

```
<?xml version="1.0" encoding="utf-8" ?>
<configuration>
  <configSections>
    <section name="microsoft.visualstudio.testtools"
      type="Microsoft.VisualStudio.TestTools.UnitTesting.TestConfigurationSection,
Microsoft.VisualStudio.QualityTools.UnitTestFramework, Version=10.0.0.0, Culture=
neutral, PublicKeyToken=b03f5f7f11d50a3a" />
  </configSections>
  <connectionStrings>
    <add name="OrderTestDataCnn"
      connectionString="Provider=Microsoft.Jet.OLEDB.4.0; Data Source=
¦DataDirectory¦TestData\; Extended Properties='text;HDR=Yes;FMT=Delimited'"
      providerName="System.Data.OleDb" />
  </connectionStrings>
  <microsoft.visualstudio.testtools>
    <dataSources>
      <add name="OrderTestDataSource"
        connectionString="OrderTestDataCnn" dataTableName="OrderTestData#csv"
        dataAccessMethod="Sequential"/>
    </dataSources>
  </microsoft.visualstudio.testtools>

</configuration>
```

Note that you can have multiple connection strings defined in a single configuration file (each named uniquely of course).

You can then use your configured test data source inside your test method. To do so, you simply indicate the data source name inside the DataSource attribute of the test method. This makes for cleaner code, reusable connection strings, and central management of the connection in case it changes from machine to machine. The following shows an example of the data source being used:

```
[TestMethod(),
DataSource("OrderTestDataSource")]
public void VerifyCustomerOrders() {

  //code to validate customer order and account info

}
```

Notice that in this example, the test data is stored in a .csv file called OrderTestData.csv. This file was added to a directory called TestData inside the test project. The directory and file then are deployed to the bin directory when the tests are run. This is the result of the connection string being set to "|DataDirectory|TestData\". You can also explicitly set this deployment by adding a DeploymentItem attribute to the test method.

You can use the Properties dialog box to configure unit test connection strings. For an example, see the upcoming section, "Managing Unit Test Attribute Properties."

Using Test Data in Your Assertions

You access the test data bound to your test method through the test context object. Recall that this object is provided to you by the framework as long as you set a property of type, TestContext (see "The TestContext Class"). You use the DataRow method of the TestContext object to retrieve the current row bound to the currently executing test. You can pass your field name or index number to this method to retrieve the right column. Typically you set variables to each of the fields in the test data. You can then use these variables throughout your assertions inside your unit test.

Listing 9.7 shows an example usage of test data (jump ahead to Figure 9.18 to see the layout of the test data). Notice that each column has to be cast or converted into the correct data type. You can then write assertions accordingly.

LISTING 9.7   An Example of a Unit Test Using Bound Data

```
[TestMethod(),
DataSource("OrderTestDataSource")]
public void VerifyCustomerOrders() {

  //get data row values
  string email = (string)TestContext.DataRow["email"];
  int numOrders = (int)TestContext.DataRow["num_orders_todate"];
  double creditLimit = Convert.ToDouble(TestContext.DataRow["credit_limit"]);
  double accountBalance = Convert.ToDouble(TestContext.DataRow["account_balance"]);

  //create a customer based on email address
  Customer cust = new Customer(email);

  //validate customer orders and account information
  Assert.IsTrue(cust.OrderHistory.Count == numOrders,
    "Order count does not match.");
  Assert.IsTrue(cust.Account.Balance == accountBalance,
    "Account balance does not match.");
  Assert.IsTrue(cust.Account.CreditLimit == creditLimit,
    "Credit limit does not match.");
  Assert.IsTrue(cust.Account.CreditLimit > cust.Account.Balance,
    "Credit limit must be less than balance.");

}
```

Running and Viewing Data-Driven Results
You run your data-driven unit tests as you would any other unit tests. The primary difference is that the entire unit test is considered as failed if only one of the given rows in the test data fail. You can then double-click your failed test result to get additional details. The data-driven results are shown in a separate pane under the common results for the unit test. Figure 9.16 shows an example.

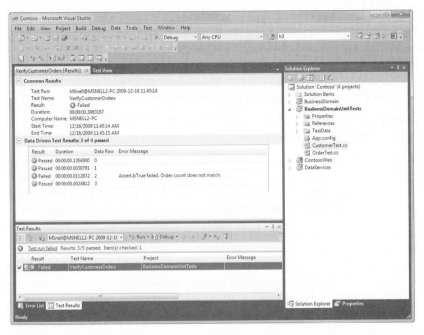

FIGURE 9.16   Your data-driven unit test results are displayed under the common results for the unit test as a whole.

Notice that three of the four data row unit tests actually passed. You can see the error message (from the assertion) of the row that failed. Double-clicking this failed data row brings up the specifics of that failure including the error stack trace and a link to the line of code that failed.

Writing ASP.NET Hosted Unit Tests

You can choose to have your unit tests hosted and run inside of ASP.NET instead of the default VSTest host process. This is useful if you're writing tests that work with ASP.NET objects such as Page and Session. You might want to test a Web service or some other application logic specific to your web interface. In either case, you have the option to host your ASP.NET unit tests in either IIS or the Visual Studio development server. Doing so ensures your test has full access to the ASP.NET environment variables.

Defining ASP.NET Attributes

You indicate a unit test should be run inside of ASP.NET by adding attributes to the test method. Many of these attributes are found in the UnitTesting.Web namespace. Therefore, you should first add a using statement (imports in VB) to the top of any test class file you intend to use with ASP.NET. This statement should read as follows:

```
using Microsoft.VisualStudio.TestTools.UnitTesting.Web;
```

You should also set a reference from your unit test application to your website. This ensures you can access the classes in the site. This includes the pages themselves and any other class files you might have in the App_Code directory or elsewhere.

There are three primary attributes you define when creating ASP.NET unit tests: UrlToTest, HostType, and AspNetDevelopmentServerHost. The UrlToTest attribute allows you to indicate a page that should be called for the execution of the given unit test. This page is called by the test framework and the context of that web request is available to your unit test (via the Page object). You can code against the ASP.NET environment inside your unit test as if you were writing code in a Web page's code-behind file.

The HostType attribute allows you to change the host type to ASP.NET. You do so by passing ASP.NET as a string value to the attribute.

If you are using IIS as your host, you need only set UrlToTest and HostType. If, however, you are using the ASP.NET Development Server (that works with Visual Studio) you must also add the attribute, AspNetDevelopmentServerHost. You pass the path to the web application as a parameter of the attribute. You also pass the name of the web application root.

Listing 9.8 shows an example of using all three attributes to define an ASP.NET unit test that runs against a local development server. Notice that you obtain a reference to the ASP.NET objects from the TestContext object's RequestedPage property. You can use this property to cast directly to the type of the requested page (in this case, ShoppingCartPage). Of course the RequestedPage property is of type System.Web.UI.Page and therefore gives you access to objects such as Server, Session, Request, and Response.

LISTING 9.8   An ASP.NET Unit Test

```
[TestMethod()]
[HostType("ASP.NET")]
[AspNetDevelopmentServerHost("C:\\CODE\\Unleashed\\Contoso\\ContosoWeb", "/")]
[UrlToTest("http://localhost:55136/ShoppingCart.aspx")]
public void AddShoppingCartItemTest() {

  //get the requested page
  Page reqPage = TestContext.RequestedPage;
  Assert.IsTrue(reqPage.Title == "Shopping Cart", "Page title does not match.");

  //cast to actual page type
  ShoppingCartPage actualPage = (ShoppingCartPage)reqPage;
  Assert.IsNotNull(actualPage.Cart, "There is no cart on the page.");

  //validate cart usage
  actualPage.Cart.AddItem("Product 1", 1, 12.75);
  actualPage.Cart.AddItem("Product 2", 2, 26.95);
  Assert.IsTrue(actualPage.Cart.Items.Count == 2, "Item count does not match.");
  Assert.AreEqual(actualPage.Cart.CalculateCartTotal(), 66.65);

}
```

Generating an ASP.NET Unit Test

You can generate ASP.NET unit tests automatically using Visual Studio. In many cases, this is the preferred method of creating your ASP.NET unit tests as it sets up your test project to work with ASP.NET and automatically configures your attributes.

You generate an ASP.NET unit test as you would any other unit test. You start by opening some code (either a code-behind file to a page or a another class file). You can then right-click inside the code and select Create Unit Tests. This launches the Create Unit Tests Wizard (refer to Figure 9.5). Here you can select the methods for which you want to generate tests. This includes page events, button click, and other control events. In fact, you can write unit tests that find controls on a page and verify their contents.

Configuring Your Test Project Host

A common scenario is to have a separate unit test project for working with your website. This project can focus on tests specifically related to the functions of your site. You can create additional test projects to work with other code libraries. This type of separation makes the writing and running of unit tests a more straightforward process.

You can also configure your test project settings to be specific to your host. In this way, you do not have to define the many ASP.NET attributes on each unit test. Instead, you can configure your .testsettings file to work with a specific host by double-clicking your .testsettings file (Solution Items, Local.testsettings). This opens the Test Settings dialog box as shown in Figure 9.17.

FIGURE 9.17   You can use a .testsettings file to configure your entire test project to work with an ASP.NET site.

> **TIP**
>
> If your solution contains multiple unit test projects, you might want multiple versions of the .testsettings file. You can then easily switch between configurations for ASP.NET and the standard, VSTest hosts.

From this dialog box, you select the Hosts node on the left. Next, in the Host type, select ASP.NET. This gives you some additional options including URL to Test, Path to Web Site, and Web Application Root. You can set each of these options to defaults for your entire unit test project.

Configuring Unit Test Attributes

As you have seen, there are many attributes you can apply to a unit test. Configuring each of these attributes in the code editor is certainly a viable option. However, Visual Studio provides some assistance inside the Properties dialog box. You can select a given unit test, view the Properties window and then configure which attributes you want to apply to the test method. Visual Studio then generates the attribute code for your test method. Let's look at an example.

Defining a Connection with the Properties Dialog Box

The first step to using the Properties window to configure unit tests is to select the unit test you want to configure. You can do this using the Test View window. You access this window from the Test menu (Test, Windows, Test View). You can then right-click a test in the given list and choose Properties to show the Properties pane for the selected test. Figure 9.18 shows an example.

FIGURE 9.18   You can select your test inside the TestView window and then configure attributes of your unit test using the Properties window.

Notice in that in the Properties window there are properties defined for the many attributes you can apply to a test method. Changing one of these property values results in Visual Studio generating the attribute and code inside your code file (there is a two-way sync between code and this window).

The Data Connection String property makes it easier to define the DataSource attribute, for example. Clicking the ellipsis button on this property launches a wizard that allows you to define a connection string to a SQL database, CSV file, or XML file (of course you can connect to other data sources but you have to write your own connection string for those). In our previous example, we were using a CSV file. Selecting this option allows you to navigate to a CSV file and even preview the data inside the file. Figure 9.19 shows an example of this wizard. After it's complete, the wizard updates the attribute in your code including DataSource and DeploymentItem. The following shows the resulting configuration code:

```
[TestMethod(),
  DeploymentItem("BusinessDomainUnitTests\\TestData\\OrderTestData.csv"),
  DataSource("Microsoft.VisualStudio.TestTools.DataSource.CSV",
    "|DataDirectory|\\OrderTestData.csv", "OrderTestData#csv",
  DataAccessMethod.Sequential)]
public void VerifyCustomerOrders() { ...
```

FIGURE 9.19   You can bind your unit tests to test data including a simple .csv file.

Creating Ordered Tests

Visual Studio enables you to group unit tests together, set their sequence of execution, and treat the results as if a single test was run. This can be useful if you need to write unit tests that are dependent on one another. For example, you might insert a record in one test and rely on that record being there in a later test. Of course, this goes against a good practice for unit testing; each test should be able to execute independently. Thankfully, you can create an ordered test that groups the individual unit tests into a new, self-contained test.

You add an ordered test to your test project by right-clicking the project and selecting Add, Ordered Test. You can also select the Ordered Test template from the Add New Test dialog box (refer to Figure 9.3).

An ordered test is simply an XML file based on the OrderedTest schema. You do not, however, need to hand-edit the XML. Instead, Visual Studio gives you the Ordered Test designer to help you. An example of this designer is shown in Figure 9.20.

FIGURE 9.20   You add existing unit tests to an ordered to test to create a new test that executes two or more tests in a specific order.

The left-side of the dialog box is where you find all your tests in your solution. Tests are shown by the selected list (see the next section, "Organizing Your Tests"). You select individual tests from the left side and use the arrow (>) to include the tests in your ordered test. You can use the up and down arrows on the right-side to change the order in which your tests execute.

When you run your ordered test, Visual Studio executes each unit test in the order you defined. If any fail, the entire ordered test fails. Of course you can view the details of the failed ordered test to see which tests passed and which failed.

Organizing Your Tests

Most unit test projects end up with many tests; often numbering in the hundreds. It is also common to have multiple unit test projects in a single solution. Managing all of these tests and running only those that are currently of interest can be a challenge. Visual Studio provides some help: Test View and Test List Editor.

The Test View Window

The Test View window enables you to see all the tests in your current solution, select the ones with which you want to work, and either run them or manage their attribute properties.

You access the Test View window from the Test menu (Test, Windows, Test View). Figure 9.21 shows an example. Notice that you can select one or more tests, right-click and execute the selected tests in a single test run. This saves you from having to run all your unit tests at once when you are focusing on a single test method (or a small group of test methods).

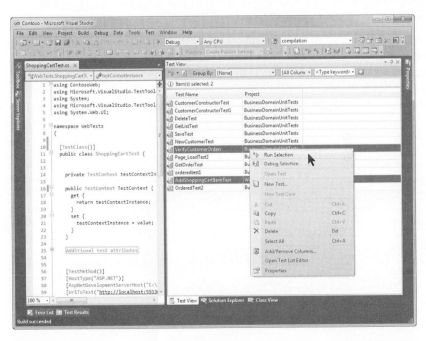

FIGURE 9.21   The Test View window enables you to easily select a set of tests you want to run.

There is a toolbar at the top of the Test View window. This toolbar enables you to search for a test by keyword and to change how tests are grouped or filtered. This makes finding your tests easier. For example, you can change the Group By option to Class Name to see all tests for a specific class. Figure 9.22 shows an example.

FIGURE 9.22   You can use the Group By option to help you find your unit tests.

The Test List Editor

Visual Studio also provides the Test List Editor. It has similar features of Test View; it allows you find tests, group them, and execute a set of tests. Unlike Test View, however, The Test List Editor also enables you to save lists of test you define. This way you can create and re-use these lists when you need to execute a set of tests.

You access the Test List Editor from the Test menu (Test, Windows, Test List Editor). This brings up a window similar to that shown in Figure 9.23. On the left side are lists of tests. By default, this includes Lists of Tests, Tests Not in a List, and All Loaded Tests. If you select a list that has tests (such as All Loaded Tests) you can either run the whole list or use the check boxes on the right of the window to select individual tests from the list to run.

FIGURE 9.23   You can select tests in the Test List Editor and run them as a group.

You can use the Test List Editor to create new test lists to store tests you want to run as a group on a regular basis. You can do so by right-clicking Lists of Tests in the Test List Editor explorer and then selecting New Test List. The Create New Test List dialog box opens. This dialog box enables you to name your test list and set its hierarchy in the lists of tests (see Figure 9.24).

FIGURE 9.24   You can define new lists of tests you want to re-use.

To add a unit test to a newly created list you can use drag and drop. First, select the All Loaded Tests list to show all tests that are currently loaded. Next, select any tests you want to add to your new list. Click and drag these tests to the custom test list name on the left side of the Test List Editor to associate these tests with your new test list. Figure 9.25 shows an example of a few custom tests lists and tests within a custom test list.

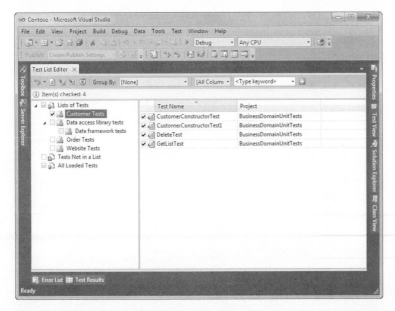

FIGURE 9.25   You can define custom lists of tests and add unit tests to them.

When you have the list of tests you want to run, you can do so from the toolbar on the Test List Editor. You choose the Run Checked Tests option (refer to Figure 9.23 for an example).

Summary

This chapter showed how you can use the unit test framework to define test projects and create test class files using the TestClass attribute. Each test method should include the TestMethod attribute. You can also data-bind unit tests using the DataSource attribute class.

Visual Studio allows you to generate unit tests from existing code. It also provides the Properties dialog box from Test View to help with generating your test attribute code.

You can write unit tests that are hosted by ASP.NET (either in IIS or the Visual Studio development server). An ASP.NET unit test uses the TestContext object to access information about the ASP.NET environment including the executing page, session, and server variables.

Writing unit tests can lead to fewer issues found in production. Having a suite of tests for your code makes that code easier to understand and more reliable. You will also gain confidence with code changes as you will be able to tell what code was broken as a result of a change.

CHAPTER 10

Refactoring Code

Whether or not you realize it, if you are like most developers, you are always refactoring code. Every time you change your code to reduce duplication or rename items for the sake of clarity, you are refactoring. Refactoring is simply putting a name to a common development task. The strict definition of the term is "a change made to the internal structure of software to make it easier to understand and cheaper to modify without changing its observable behavior." That is, refactoring does not add features to the application. Instead, it improves the general maintenance of the code base.

The term refactoring has received a large amount of attention. A number of good books have been written touting the many benefits of refactoring code as you are building your application. This is when you are closest to the code and thus able to quickly make these maintenance-type changes. Many of these books are on the subject of agile development. Refactoring has become one of the key tenets of the agile developer. In agile development, your code base builds feature by feature to satisfy a series of tests. This can result in code that works wonderfully but does not look as though it was designed as a cohesive unit. To combat this problem, you would be wise to go over the code base at frequent intervals and thus improve the general quality of the code (remove duplication, create common interfaces, rename items, put things into logical groups, and so on).

A new set of features has been developed inside code editors to aid with refactoring. These features have their basis in a real need. No developer wants to introduce errors into a relatively stable code base simply for the sake of improving maintenance—especially when running a tight schedule.

Imagine explaining to your manager or client that the large spike in bugs is a result of sweeping changes you made to the code to improve future maintenance and readability. We can be thankful that the C# editor inside Visual Studio 2010 provides a reliable set of refactoring tools.

These tools let you make changes to the code base without the concern of creating more problems than you are solving.

REFACTORING FOR THE DATABASE DEVELOPER

There are a couple of features built into Visual Studio for refactoring database elements. We cover these in Chapter 21, "Working with Databases."

Visual Studio Refactoring Basics

The Visual Studio refactoring tools work to ensure that you see the promises of refactoring: increased reuse of your code, fewer rewrites, reduced duplication, and better readability. These tools work to instill confidence in the edits they make to your code. They do so by using a common refactoring engine based on the C# compiler rather than string matching and search-and-replace. The engine and compiler work together to cover the entire code base (and its references) to find all possible changes that need to be made as part of a given refactor operation. The engine even searches out code comments and tries to update them to reflect new type names. In addition, you can preview changes to your code before they happen. This adds further to your comfort level with the modifications these tools are making to your code.

Table 10.1 presents a high-level overview of the many refactoring operations that are possible with the C# editor. We cover each of them in detail in the coming sections. First, however, we cover some of the common elements of the refactoring process. These elements include both invoking a refactoring tool inside Visual Studio and previewing the refactoring changes as they happen.

TABLE 10.1   Refactoring Tools Inside the Visual Studio 2010 C# Editor

Tool	Description
Rename	Renames fields, properties, namespaces, methods, types, and local variables.
Extract Method	Creates a new method using existing code within an existing method.
Reorder Parameters	Changes the order of parameters for a given method and updates all callers.
Remove Parameters	Removes a parameter from a method and updates callers.
Encapsulate Field	Quickly creates a property from an existing field.
Extract Interface	Creates an interface from an existing class or structure.

Invoking the Refactoring Tools

The refactoring tools are available from wherever you work on your C# code inside Visual Studio. You can invoke them in several ways. For example, if you are working inside the code editor, you can invoke the Rename tool using a smart tag. You can also select and right-click code to reveal the refactoring options; these same options are available on the menu bar through the Refactor menu. Finally, you can refactor directly from the Class Designer as you edit and change various items within a given class.

Using the Refactor Menu (and Right-Click)

The most common place to invoke the refactoring commands is from the actual refactoring menu. This menu item is added to the IDE when you have a C# code window open and active. Figure 10.1 shows the menu being invoked. Note that the portion of code you are trying to refactor is highlighted in the IDE. In this case, we want to rename the class Product because we have determined that all our products are books. Therefore, we rename the class Product to Book.

FIGURE 10.1   You can access a refactoring operation from the Refactor menu.

The same Refactor menu is available via a right-click within the code editor. In this case, you highlight a word or section of code (or simply position the cursor accordingly) and then right-click inside the editor, which brings up the context version of the Refactor menu as shown in Figure 10.2. Notice that the second item in this menu is Refactor. Selecting this option reveals the fold-out version of the refactor menu.

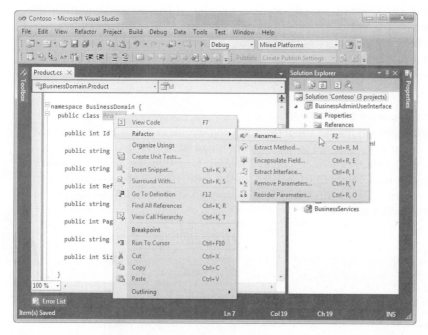

FIGURE 10.2   The Refactor menu invoked via a right-click with the mouse.

Refactoring in the Code Window via Smart Tags

The smart tag was originally introduced in Microsoft Office. As discussed in Chapter 8, "Working with Visual Studio's Productivity Aids," the goal of the smart tag is simple: Try to understand what the user is typing and offer additional, "smart" functionality. For example, as you type in the Word editor, it tries to understand what you've typed. The editor then provides you with additional functionality and the ability to control formatting options based on that information.

The C# code editor provides a similar smart tag feature. The editor detects your typing and understands when you have made a change to your code that is the equivalent of a refactor. In these cases, the editor creates a smart tag that can be used to invoke the refactoring tool. This allows you to stay in the code editor but still take advantage of the increased productivity and reduced error rate that the refactoring tool can provide.

As an example, suppose you have a property named Id. You want to rename this item to Identifier. You open the class file and position your cursor near the property name. You then type the new property name. The C# code editor detects your change and underlines the final character of the changed name. Figure 10.3 shows an example of this. Notice the small rectangle beneath the property name.

```
public int ISBN { get; set; }
```

FIGURE 10.3   Renaming a property invokes a smart tag for refactoring.

This small rectangle hovering under the change is your visual cue that the C# code editor thinks it can help you. You can position your mouse cursor next to the rectangle to reveal an in-line menu that indicates how the editor might help. Figure 10.4 shows the smart tag as it is invoked when renaming the ReferenceNumber property to ISBN (as these products are all books).

```
namespace BusinessDomain {
    public class Book {

        public int Id
                         at/  Rename 'Product' to 'Book'
        public string   at/  Rename with preview...

        public string Description { get; set; }
```

FIGURE 10.4   The rename smart tag menu in action.

TIP

You can also invoke smart tags without grabbing for the mouse by pressing the key combination Shift+Alt+F10.

Using the Class Designer to Refactor

Visual Studio 2010 provides a Visual Designer for working with classes. This Class Designer enables you to view the contents of your classes and their relationships. It can also be used as a productivity tool: You can create new classes and modify existing classes directly within the designer.

CLASS DESIGNER COVERAGE

Note that the class designer is covered in Chapter 6, "Introducing the Editors and Designers."

The Visual Studio Class Designer exposes the refactoring tool when you're working with C# classes. This ensures that code modifications made using this Visual Designer take full advantage of refactoring. For instance, suppose you want to rename a property from within the Class Designer but also want to make sure that the references to that property are automatically updated. You can do so by right-clicking the property within the Class Designer and choosing the Refactor menu's Rename option. Figure 10.5 shows refactoring (renaming the Creator property to Author) from directly within the Class Designer.

FIGURE 10.5   Invoking refactoring from within the Visual Studio Class Designer.

Previewing Changes

As you become comfortable with the refactoring tools, you might decide to simply let them do their thing without much oversight on your part. However, if you are like most developers, no one (or no tool) touches your code without your consent. Fortunately for us, the refactoring tools provide a preview option. This option lets you follow the tool through its changes and, in turn, accept or reject a given change.

The Preview Changes dialog box is invoked as an option (check box) on a given refactoring operation (or, in the case of a smart tag, from a second menu item on the smart tag menu). Figure 10.6 provides an example of selecting the Preview Reference Changes option from the Rename refactor operation.

After the refactoring operation is invoked with Preview Changes, Visual Studio presents you with the Preview Changes dialog box. The top portion of this dialog box lists all the changes the given refactor operation intends to make. This list is presented as a tree, with the outer branch representing where you intend to originate the change. The leaves under this branch are all files where changes happen. Nested beneath the filenames are the actual places within the code where a change is made. You use this list to select each item you would like to preview. Figure 10.7 shows an example of the changes required in our simple example of changing the Id property of the Product object.

FIGURE 10.6   Invoking a refactor operation with Preview reference changes checked.

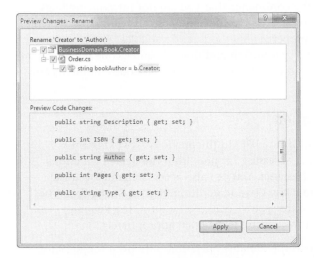

FIGURE 10.7   Previewing changes of a Rename operation.

As each item in the Preview Changes tree is clicked, the corresponding code is displayed below the tree in the Preview Code Changes section of the dialog box. This enables developers to quickly review where changes are being made. To prevent a given change, you can simply uncheck the item in the tree view. Of course, you can prevent entire file changes by unchecking farther up in the hierarchy at the file level. When you are finished with your preview and satisfied with the proposed changes, you simply click the Apply button to commit the changes to your code.

Renaming Code

Renaming code elements is the most common refactoring operation. In fact, while Rename is part of the refactoring support in the C# editor, a similar rename feature exists in the VB editor. Database projects also now include the ability to reliably rename elements in your database schema. Here we stick to our coverage of the C# refactoring tools. However, both the VB and database rename operations work in a similar fashion.

Most developers do not typically wait until the code base is operational and say to themselves, "Okay, now I will go back and rename items for clarity." Although this does happen on some teams as part of a set code refactoring step, the more likely scenario is that as you build your application, you consistently rename items to correct mistakes or make things clearer and more readable. Of course, as the code base builds, renaming classes, methods, fields, and the like becomes more and more difficult without introducing new bugs into your code.

The capability to rename items with the confidence that you are not introducing bugs into your code is paramount. With the C# editor, you can rename all relevant code items including namespaces, classes, fields, properties, methods, and variables. The compiler helps make sure that your code does not get broken and that all source code references are found. In fact, the Rename operation can even search through your code comments and update them accordingly.

Accessing the Rename Operation

You can rename from many places within the IDE. In the previous "Invoking the Refactoring Tools" section, we looked at accessing Rename from the Refactor menu, a right-click, a smart tag, and the Class Designer. You can also access Rename from the Object Browser, Solution Explorer, and Class View. In addition, if you use the Properties dialog box to change the name of a control you've placed on a form, the Rename operation is invoked behind the scenes and the control is renamed appropriately.

From the Object Browser, you can access the Rename operation only from the Refactor menu. Of course, you need to be browsing your own types in your solution. You select the item you want to rename and then click the Refactor menu. Figure 10.8 shows an example of the Object Browser and Rename operation (top of screen shot) working together.

FIGURE 10.8   Accessing the Rename operation from the Object Browser.

You can rename within the Solution Explorer for filenames that equate to class names. For instance, suppose you have a file named Customer and want to change the class and file-name to Shopper. You do so by right-clicking and choosing Rename. Visual Studio allows you to rename the file. When you do so, it prompts you to see if you also want to rename the class. If you choose yes, Visual Studio searches the code within the file for any class that has the same name as the file. So if you have a Customer class and a Customer.cs file, a Rename operation to Shopper renames the file as well as the class (and all references to the class).

> **NOTE**
>
> Although an undo on the Rename operation rolls back a change, in the case of a file-name change, Undo reverts the code but does not change the filename back to its original name.

Finally, you can also rename from within Class View (View, Class View). This can be helpful if you look at your code from a namespace and object perspective (rather than a file-based perspective). To do so, you right-click the item you want to rename and select the Rename option. Figure 10.9 shows an example of renaming the State property of the Order object (to Status) from within Class View. Note that renaming a class from within Class View has no effect on the filename for the file that contains the class.

FIGURE 10.9   Accessing Rename from the Class View.

TIP

You can access the Rename operation from a set of command keys. Past versions of Visual Studio introduced the concept of chords. They are like traditional keyboard commands, but you press (or play) them in sequence. For instance, to invoke the Rename operation without touching your mouse, position your cursor over what you want to rename. Then press the sequence Ctrl+R, R (where you continue to hold Ctrl when pressing the second R). Pressing this combination in sequence will bring up the Refactoring, Rename dialog box relative to the code element behind your cursor.

Working with the Rename Dialog Box

The Rename dialog box enables you to specify a few options when invoking a given Rename refactor operation. Refer to Figure 10.6 for an example of the dialog box. The text box on the form enables you to define the rename itself. In the New Name section, you indicate the new name of the element to be renamed. The Location text box indicates the namespace of the element to be renamed. Of course, all referenced locations are also searched. The Rename dialog box presents developers with a few options when doing a rename. The three check boxes below the Location text box enable you to set the options as described in Table 10.2.

TABLE 10.2 The Rename Dialog Box Options

Option	Description
Preview Reference Changes	This option enables you to indicate whether you want to preview the changes before they are applied to your code. This capability can be especially useful if you are renaming for the first time or you intend to rename items inside strings or comments.
	Renaming strings and comments does not use the compiler. Instead it uses string matching (see Figure 10.10 for an example). In this case, previewing a change before applying it can be especially helpful. For example, you may want to rename a type, but not similar text in a label.
Search in Comments	This option enables you to indicate whether the Rename operation should search your comments for possible textual references that should be renamed. Comments often refer to types and hence need to be synced with changes.
	Figure 10.10 shows the Preview Changes – Rename dialog box with both a `Strings` folder and a `Comments` folder expanded in the tree. Note that the string matching is case-sensitive. Therefore, you might want to be vigilant when writing comments that refer to types.
Search in Strings	This preference enables you to indicate whether the Rename operation should search inside your literal strings for references to a given item name. String literals include constants, control names, form names, and so on. This capability is most useful if there is a tight coupling between your code and the elements within your user interface. Again, this too is case-sensitive.

Extract Method

When developers go back and take a look at their code, perhaps during a periodic code review or after a particularly long session of heads-down development, they often find methods that are too long or coarse-grained, contain duplicate code, or are just poorly organized. A common thing to do is pass over the code and create fine-grained, discrete methods to reduce these issues and make for a more readable, reusable, and maintainable code base.

The problem, of course, is that doing this is time-consuming and often introduces bugs into the code. The C# code editor in Visual Studio 2010 provides an Extract Method refactoring tool to ensure a quick, bug-free experience when you're working to better organize your code. With this tool, you can create a new method using existing code.

10

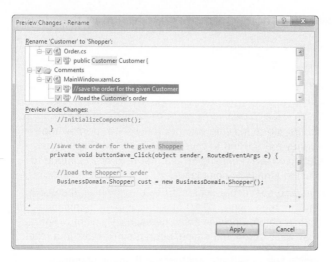

FIGURE 10.10   The Preview Changes – Rename dialog box.

Accessing the Extract Method Refactor

To access the Extract Method refactor operation, you first must select a portion of code to refactor. You then can use the Refactor menu and select the Extract Method menu item. You can also invoke the Extract Method from the context menu via a right-click.

> **TIP**
>
> To invoke the Extract Method operation from the keyboard, first select the section of code you want to extract. Next, play the chord Ctrl+R, Ctrl+M.

Extracting Methods

With the Extract Method operation, you can create (or extract) a new method from multiple lines of code, a single line, or an expression within a given line of code. In each case, the method is created immediately following the method from which the code was extracted. The extracted code is replaced by a call to the new method.

Listing 10.1 provides an example of a method that is unnecessarily long. We've added line numbers for reference purposes. When you're reviewing code, methods such as these are common and exactly what you should be looking for. The method is designed as a static call that returns a given customer's Order object based on the customer's ID number and the order ID number. However, the order, the order line items, and the customer details are all retrieved from discreet database calls and stored in domain-specific objects. These objects are then stored on the order as properties.

LISTING 10.1   A Long Static Method

```
01  public static Order GetCustomerOrder(int customerId, int orderId) {
```

```
02
03     DataAccess.DAL dal = new DataAccess.DAL();
04     Order order = new Order();
05
06     //get order details
07     System.Data.DataTable dtOrder = dal.GetData("customerOrder", orderId);
08
09     //validate order against customer
10     if (customerId != (int)dtOrder.Rows[0]["customer_id"]) {
11       throw new ApplicationException("Invalid order for the given customer.");
12     }
13     order.Id = (int)dtOrder.Rows[0]["id"];
14
15     //get order items
16     List<OrderItem> items = new List<OrderItem>();
17     System.Data.DataTable dtItems = dal.GetData("orderItems", orderId);
18     foreach (System.Data.DataRow r in dtItems.Rows) {
19       OrderItem item = new OrderItem((int)r["product_id"], orderId);
20       item.Name = (string)r["name"];
21       item.Description = (string)r["description"];
22       item.Quantity = (int)r["quantity"];
23       item.UnitPrice = (double)r["unit_price"];
24       items.Add(item);
25     }
26     order.Items = items;
27
28     //get customer details
29     System.Data.DataTable dtCustomer = dal.GetData("customer", customerId);
30     Shopper cust = new Shopper(customerId);
31     order.Customer = cust;
32
33     return order;

34  }
```

Opportunities for method extraction inside this one method are numerous. You might consider extracting the call to initialize the Order object, the call to get order items, and the call to get customer details, which results in better organized code (thus, more readable), more opportunities for reuse, and an easier-to-maintain code base. Let's look at doing these extractions.

First, you extract the call that sets up the order. Knowing what to select for extraction requires a bit of experience with the tool. In this case, extract lines 3–13, which is the code from the DataAccess setup through the order initialization. However, doing this confuses the Extract Method operation somewhat because you are setting up both a DataAccess object and an Order object in the first two operations. The Extract Method

10

understands you need these two objects later in your method. Therefore, it creates both objects as out parameters of the method. What you want is the method to return an instance of the Order object and set up its own DataAccess object. You can accomplish this with the following steps:

1. Select lines 4–13 (order creation through initialization).

2. Select the Extract Method refactor operation (menu, right-click, or keyboard chord).

3. Visual Studio presents the Extract Method dialog box, as shown in Figure 10.11. This dialog box presents the new method name (NewMethod by default) and the method signature. If the method signature does not look right, you can cancel the operation and refine your code selection. In this case, the method is private; static; returns an Order object; and takes customerId, orderId, and DataAccess objects. We do not want the latter in our function signature but deal with this momentarily.

FIGURE 10.11   Extracting code from an existing method to a new method.

4. Rename the method to something meaningful. In this case, rename it to InitCustomerOrder.

5. Click the OK button to allow the method to be extracted.

6. The new method is created, and the old method is replaced by the following call:

```
Order order = InitCustomerOrder(customerId, orderId, dal);
```

You still have one issue with the extracted method: It takes an instance of DataAccess when you would prefer that it created its own instance. Fortunately, you can use another refactoring operation to deal with this issue. In this case, use the Remove Parameters refactor. This refactoring operation is covered later in this chapter. It is important to point out that removing the parameter results in removing it from both the method signature and the call to the method. It does not, however, put the call to create that DataAccess object inside the new method (nor does it remove it from the old method). You must take these steps manually.

Next, let's extract the call to get order items. Begin by selecting lines 16–25 (see Listing 10.1). Note that we do not want to select the call to set the order's property (line 26); we simply want to return an object that represents all line items for a given order. Figure 10.12 shows the selection and method extraction. In this case, name the new method GetOrderItems. After the method is extracted, it is replaced by the following call to the new method:

```
List<OrderItem> items = GetOrderItems(orderId, dal);
```

Again you have the issue with the DataAccess object being passed into the new method. You solve this issue in the same manner as you did previously.

Finally, let's look at extracting the portion of the method that gets the customer details. By now, this procedure should be reasonably straightforward. You select the code (lines 29–30) and choose the Extract Method operation. You name the new method GetShopper and deal with the extracted DataAccess parameter.

FIGURE 10.12   Extracting code to a method to return order items.

10

The newly organized (and much shorter) method looks like Listing 10.2. In addition, you now have three new tight, discreet methods that you may be able to reuse in the future (and perhaps make public). These new methods are in Listing 10.3.

LISTING 10.2   The Static Method After the Extractions

```
public static Order GetCustomerOrder(int customerId, int orderId) {

  Order order = InitCustomerOrder(customerId, orderId);

  //get order items
  List<OrderItem> items = GetOrderItems(orderId);
  order.Items = items;

  //get customer details
  Shopper cust = GetShopper(customerId);
  order.Customer = cust;

  return order;

}
```

LISTING 10.3   The Extractions

```
private static Shopper GetShopper(int customerId) {

  DataAccess.DAL dal = new DataAccess.DAL();

  System.Data.DataTable dtCustomer = dal.GetData("customer", customerId);
  Shopper cust = new Shopper(customerId);
  return cust;
}

private static List<OrderItem> GetOrderItems(int orderId) {

  DataAccess.DAL dal = new DataAccess.DAL();

  List<OrderItem> items = new List<OrderItem>();
  System.Data.DataTable dtItems = dal.GetData("orderItems", orderId);
  foreach (System.Data.DataRow r in dtItems.Rows) {
    OrderItem item = new OrderItem((int)r["product_id"], orderId);
    item.Name = (string)r["name"];
    item.Description = (string)r["description"];
    item.Quantity = (int)r["quantity"];
    item.UnitPrice = (double)r["unit_price"];
```

```
      items.Add(item);
  }
  return items;

}

private static Order InitCustomerOrder(int customerId, int orderId) {

  DataAccess.DAL dal = new DataAccess.DAL();
  Order order = new Order();

  //get order details
  System.Data.DataTable dtOrder = dal.GetData("customerOrder", orderId);

  //validate order against customer
  if (customerId != (int)dtOrder.Rows[0]["customer_id"]) {
    throw new ApplicationException("Invalid order for the given customer.");
  }
  order.Id = (int)dtOrder.Rows[0]["id"];
  return order;

}
```

NOTE

Extract Method does not allow you to choose where to put the extracted method. Many times you might find a bit of code that really needs to be extracted into a method of another, different class. For this, you have to extract the method and then move things around manually.

Extracting a Single Line of Code

Sometimes, you might want to extract a single line of code or a portion of a line of code as its own method. For example, you might have a calculation that is done as part of a line of code but is common enough to warrant its own method. Alternatively, you might need to extract an object assignment to add additional logic to it. In either case, the C# code editor supports this type of extraction.

Let's look at an example. Suppose you have the following line of code that calculates an order's total inside a loop through the order items list:

```
total = total + item.Quantity * item.UnitPrice;
```

You might want to extract the portion of the assignment that calculates a line item's total (quantity * unit price). To do so, you select the portion of code and invoke the Extract Method refactor. Figure 10.13 shows this operation in action.

10

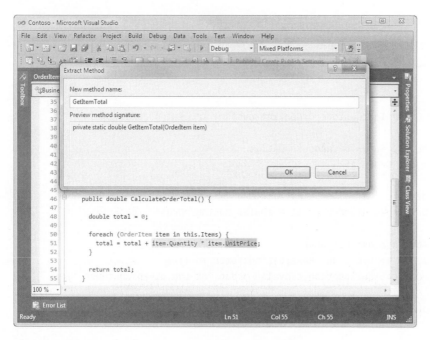

FIGURE 10.13   Extracting a portion of a line of code.

Notice that, by default, the new method would like an instance of `OrderItem`. You might prefer to pass both quantity and unit price instead. You would have to make this change manually. Alternatively, if quantity and unit price were assigned to variables before the extraction was done, you would get a new method that accepted these parameters (instead of an OrderItem instance). Figure 10.14 demonstrates this fact.

The resulting refactor replaces a portion of the line of code with the following:

```
total = total + GetItemTotal(qty, unitPrice);
```

It also adds the new method as follows:

```
private static double GetItemTotal(int qty, double unitPrice) {
  return qty * unitPrice;
}
```

Generate Method Stub

You can get Visual Studio to automatically generate a method stub for you. This is not strictly a refactoring operation but can provide some similar increases in productivity. The scenario where this is applicable is as follows. Suppose you are writing code that calls a method off one of your objects. However, that method does not exist. You can still write code to make the call to the nonexistent method. Visual Studio then recognizes that this method does not exist and provides you with a smart tag (see Figure 10.15) to create the method.

FIGURE 10.14   An alternative extraction of a portion of a line of code.

FIGURE 10.15   Generate a method stub for a nonexistent method.

Clicking on the smart tag results in Visual Studio extracting the method call to a newly generated method in the target assembly and class. Figure 10.16 shows the new method. Note that Visual Studio provides a readable name for the method's parameter provided you used a variable inside the calling method.

```csharp
1  using System;
2  using System.Collections.Generic;
3  using System.Linq;
4  using System.Text;
5
6  namespace DataAccess {
7      public class DAL {
8
9          public System.Data.DataTable GetData(string p, int orderId) {
10             throw new NotImplementedException();
11         }
12
13     }
```

FIGURE 10.16   The generated method stub.

Extract Interface

When classes contain the same subset of members, defining a common contract that each class shares can be useful. You do this, of course, via an interface. Some basic advantages to defining interfaces are that your code becomes more readable, is easier to maintain, and operates the same for like members. However, developers often don't realize the commonality between their classes until after those classes are coded. This sometimes makes creating interfaces a painful operation.

The C# editor in Visual Studio 2010 provides the Extract Interface refactoring operation to make this process easier. It enables you to take an existing class or struct and automatically generate a matching interface that the existing class then implements.

Accessing the Extract Interface Refactor

To access the Extract Interface refactor operation, you first must position your cursor in a class, a struct, or another interface that contains the members you want to extract. You then can use the Refactor menu and select the Extract Interface menu item. You can also invoke Extract Interface from the context menu via a right-click and from the Class Designer.

> **TIP**
>
> To invoke the Extract Interface operation from the keyboard, first position your cursor in the class, struct, or interface that contains the members you want to extract. Next, play the chord Ctrl+R, Ctrl+I.

Extracting Interfaces

To better understand the Extract Interface operation, let's look at an example. Suppose you review your code and notice that a number of your domain objects share similar properties and methods. Let's say the objects Customer, Vendor, Manufacturer, SalesAgent, and Product all contain properties for Id, Name, and Description and methods for Save and Delete. In this case, you should consider extracting this commonality into a standard interface that each of your domain objects would implement. Let's look at how the Extract Interface refactoring operation aids in this regard.

First, you position your cursor on the target class whose members you want to extract. In the example, choose the Vendor class. Invoking the Extract Interface operation presents a dialog box named the same. Figure 10.17 shows this dialog box relative to the example.

FIGURE 10.17   Extracting an interface.

Notice that you first define a name for the interface. By default, the tool names the interface with the name of the class preceded by the letter I for interface—in this case, IVendor. Of course, we are going to use our interface across our domain, so we change this to IDomainObject.

The Extract Interface dialog box also shows the generated name and the new filename for the interface. The generated name is simply the fully qualified name of the interface. This is used by the class for implementation of the interface. The New File Name text box shows the C# filename for the interface. All extracted interfaces result in the creation of a new file. The tool tries to keep the filename in sync with the interface name.

The last thing to do is select which members of the object you want to publish as an interface. Of course, only public members are displayed in this list. For this example, select the following public members: Id, Name, Description, Save, and Delete.

10

Clicking the OK button generates the interface. The only change that is made to the Vendor class is that it now implements the new interface, as in the following line of code:

```
public class Vendor : BusinessDomain.IDomainObject
```

The interface is then extracted to a new file. Listing 10.4 shows the newly extracted interface.

LISTING 10.4   The Extracted Interface

```
using System;
namespace BusinessDomain {
    interface IDomainObject {
        void Delete();
        string Description { get; set; }
        int Id { get; set; }
        string Name { get; set; }
        void Save();
    }

}
```

The next step in the example is to go out to each additional domain object and implement the new interface. This has to be done without the benefit of refactoring. However, Visual Studio provides a smart tag for implementing an interface. Figure 10.18 shows the smart tag that results from typing IDomainObject after the Vendor class declaration.

In this case, you have two options: implement the interface or explicitly implement the interface. The former checks the current class to see whether there are implementations that apply. The latter generates code that explicitly calls the interface items. It puts all this code inside a region for the given interface. This capability can be very useful if you're stubbing out a new class based on the interface. The following lines of code provide an example of an explicit interface member declaration:

```
void IDomainObject.Save() {
  throw new NotImplementedException();
}
```

Refactor Parameters

You sometimes need to change your method signatures by removing an item, by adding a local variable as a parameter, or by reordering the existing parameters. These changes require that all calls to the method also be changed. Doing this manually can introduce new bugs into the code. For example, suppose you want to swap the order of two parameters with the same type (int, for example). If you forget to change a call to the method, it might still work; it just won't work right. These bugs can be challenging to find. Therefore, Visual Studio provides refactoring operations for removing, promoting, and reordering parameters.

FIGURE 10.18   Implementing an interface.

Remove Parameters

The Remove Parameters refactor operation enables you to select one or more parameters from a given method, constructor, or delegate and have it or them removed from the method. It also works to update any callers to the method and remove the value passed to the parameter.

You invoke the Remove Parameters operation by positioning your cursor inside the method signature and then selecting the Remove Parameters menu item from the Refactor menu. You can also get to this operation through the context menu (right-click). In addition, this operation is available from the Class Designer from inside both the class designer and the Class Details window.

TIP

To invoke the Remove Parameters operation from the keyboard, first position your cursor in the method that contains the parameters you want to remove. Next, play the keyboard chord Ctrl+R, Ctrl+V.

Let's look at an example. Suppose you have a method with the following signature:

```
public static Order GetCustomerOrder(int customerId, int orderId)
```

This method returns an Order object based on both a customer and an order identification number. Suppose you determine that the order ID is sufficient for returning an order. In this case, you invoke the Remove Parameters refactor and are then presented with the Remove Parameters dialog box (see Figure 10.19). Method parameters are listed at the top. To remove one, you select it and click the Remove button. The item to be removed is then updated with strikethrough. If you change your mind, you can use the Restore button to cancel individual parameter removals.

FIGURE 10.19   The Remove Parameters dialog box.

When you are ready to make the removal, you can choose to preview the changes or simply apply them all at once. The preview option works the same as other previews. It shows you each change in a tree view and enables you to see the details behind the change. You can, of course, also uncheck specific changes. When finished, you apply the final set of removals to your code.

> **CAUTION**
>
> It is common to declare a local variable inside a method and pass that local variable in a call to another method. If you use the refactoring operation to remove the parameter on the method you are calling, the local variable still exists in your calling method. Be careful to make sure that this is what you intended; if not, you have to remove the local variable manually.

Reorder Parameters

You move parameters around in a method typically just for readability and maintenance. You might want the more important parameters to appear first on the method signature, or you might try to keep the order similar across like methods or overloads. The Reorder

Parameters refactor operation enables you to change the order in which parameters exist on a given method, constructor, or delegate. It also works to update any callers to the method and rearrange the parameters passed on the call.

You invoke the Reorder Parameters operation by positioning your cursor inside the method signature that contains the parameters you want to reorder and then selecting the Reorder Parameters menu item from the Refactor menu. You can also get to this operation through the context menu (right-click). In addition, this operation is available from the Class Designer.

TIP

To invoke the Reorder Parameters operation from the keyboard, first position your cursor in the method that contains the parameters you want to rearrange. Next, play the keyboard chord Ctrl+R, Ctrl+O.

Let's look at an example. Suppose you have the following method signature:

```
private static Order InitCustomerOrder(int orderId, int customerId)
```

This method is called InitCustomerOrder. Suppose that because the customer parameter comes first in the method name, you want to make that the first parameter of the method. To do so, you position the cursor on the method and invoke the Reorder Parameters refactor. This presents the Reorder Parameters dialog box (see Figure 10.20).

FIGURE 10.20   The Reorder Parameters dialog box.

This dialog box enables you to modify the order of the parameters on the given method. At the top, it lists all the parameters of the method. To the right of this list, there are two buttons. The up-arrow button moves the selected parameter in the list up. The down arrow does the opposite. You use these buttons to get the order of the parameters the way you want them. Figure 10.20 shows this example loaded into the Reorder Parameters dialog box.

Notice that as you change parameter order, the resulting method signature is displayed below the parameter list. You also have the option to preview any changes that are made to callers of the method. Clicking the OK button applies the changes to both the method and its callers.

Encapsulate Field

It's common to have a private field in your object from which you need to create a property. These fields might have been built as private because they were used only internally to the object. Alternatively, a developer might have simply defined a public field instead of encapsulating it as a property. In either case, if you need to make an actual property out of a field, you can do so with the Encapsulate Field refactor operation.

Accessing Encapsulate Field

The Encapsulate Field operation enables you to quickly generate properties from a given field. Properties, of course, enable you to protect the field from direct access and to know when the given field is being modified or accessed. To encapsulate a field, you position your cursor over the field and select the Encapsulate Field option from the Refactor menu. You can also do use the context menu (right-click) or the Class Designer.

TIP

To invoke the Encapsulate Field operation from the keyboard, first position your cursor on the field that you want to encapsulate. Next, play the keyboard chord Ctrl+R, Ctrl+F.

The Encapsulate Field Dialog Box

The Encapsulate Field dialog box, shown in Figure 10.21, enables you to set a few options for this refactor. First, it presents the field you are refactoring in a read-only text box. Next, it enables you to define a name for the new property. The good news is that the tool tries to name your property correctly. For example, if you have a private field named _rating, the tool chooses Rating for the property name by default.

An additional option on this dialog box is the choice of which references you would like to have updated. This refers to existing references to the field. Suppose you have a public field. This field might be called both from within the object that defines the field and by other, external objects. You might want to force external callers to use the new property.

FIGURE 10.21   The Encapsulate Field dialog box.

For this, you would use the External setting. In this case, the object that contains the field would still reference the local, private field (and not the property). Setting the Update Reference option to All results in both the external and internal callers using the property.

When you apply the encapsulation, the tool changes your internal field to private (if it was not already private) and then generates a property. The property includes both `get` and `set` accessors for the field. If the field was declared as read-only, the encapsulation generates only a `get` accessor.

Let's look at the code. Suppose you have the following field declaration:

```
private int _rating;
```

You want to encapsulate this private into a public property. The code that is generated is as follows:

```
private int _rating;
public int Rating {
    get { return _rating; }
    set { _rating = value; }
}
```

In addition, should you choose the All value for the update references option in the Encapsulate Field dialog box, your internal callers to the field (the field was private) would be updated to use the property internally.

10

Summary

This chapter showed how the refactoring tools built into the C# editor for Visual Studio 2010 can greatly increase productivity and decrease unwanted side effects (bugs) when you're making sweeping changes to your code to improve maintenance, reuse, and readability. The refactoring tools don't simply make changes using text searches and replacements; they use the Visual Studio compiler to make and validate the code changes and this improves confidence in, and reliability of, the tools.

These tools can be accessed using the keyboard, the Refactor menu, a context menu, the Class Designer, and elsewhere. The refactoring tools enable you to change your code in many ways. You can easily rename items in your code. You can take existing lines of code and extract them to new methods. Your objects can be used as the basis to define new interfaces. You can modify method signatures using the Remove and Reorder refactoring operations. Finally, you can take existing fields and quickly encapsulate them into properties.

CHAPTER 11

Debugging Code

Today's developers might spend as much time debugging their code as they do writing it. This is due in some part to the nature of today's highly dependent and distributed applications. These applications are built to leverage existing functionality, frameworks, building blocks, libraries, and so on. In addition, they often communicate with other applications, services, components, databases, and even data exchanges. Developers also demand more assistance from their debugger to help increase their productivity. The Visual Studio 2010 debugger addresses these needs by offering some great debugging scenarios. Some highlights include the following:

▶ Breakpoint and tracepoint management

▶ Visualizers and debugger DataTips

▶ Edit and Continue

▶ Just-my-code debugging

▶ The Exception Assistant

▶ Debugging support at design time

▶ Client-side script debugging

▶ Support for debugging WCF applications

▶ Debugging support for LINQ

▶ Debugging multi-threaded and parallel code

▶ Remote debugging

We cover all of these features and more in this chapter. Of course, if you are just getting started with .NET, more than just this list is new to you. The Visual Studio debugger has been evolving since the first release of .NET, which provided a unified debugger with the capability to debug across languages. In this chapter, we start by covering the basics of debugging an application. We then discuss the Visual Studio 2010 debugger in depth.

Debugging Basics

A typical scenario for a developer is to start building a web page or form and build up the code that surrounds it. In addition, the developer might rely on a framework or a few building blocks that provide added functionality. The application might also communicate with a services layer and most often a database. Even the most typical applications have a lot of moving parts. These moving parts make the task of finding and eliminating errors in the code all the more complex. The tools that help you track down and purge errors from your code not only have to keep up with this complexity, but also must ease the effort involved with the debugging process. In the following sections, we cover how a developer uses the tools built into Visual Studio 2010 to debug a typical development scenario.

The Scenario

We want to define an application scenario that we can use both to introduce the basics of debugging and to function as a base for us to build on throughout the chapter when demonstrating the many features of the debugging tools. In this scenario, imagine you are writing a web page that enables customers to view and edit their profiles. This page offers new functionality to a larger, existing application. The following are some of the conditions that surround this application scenario:

▶ The customers' profiles are stored in a SQL 2008 database.

▶ A data access library abstracts all access to the database.

▶ A web service exists to provide access to the customers' profile information.

Your task is to write a page using the web service to return profile information for customers. The page should display customer profile information and enable a user to edit this data. You also need to write changes to a customer profile back to the database using the data access library. The application you are debugging in this scenario is written in C#. However, the debugging tools in Visual Studio are equally applicable to both C# and Visual Basic. That is, everything we discuss here applies to both languages unless specified otherwise.

The Many Phases of Debugging

Nearly every time developers open the IDE, they are in some way debugging their code. The line between debugging and writing code, in fact, is becoming more and more blurred. For example, the code editor helps eliminate errors in your code as you write it. It highlights items where errors are present and enables you to fix them. You are then both writing and debugging simultaneously.

In addition, the compiler acts as another debugging tool. The first time you click the Run button, the compiler checks your code and reports a list of errors for you to fix before continuing. This is debugging. The steps or phases of the debugging process include the following:

▶ **Coding**—The editor helps you by pointing out issues and possible resolutions.

▶ **Compiling**—The compiler checks your code and reports errors before continuing.

▶ **Self-checking**—You run the application in debug mode and step through screens and code to verify functionality.

▶ **Unit testing**—You write and run unit tests to check your application (see Chapter 9, "Testing Code").

▶ **Code analysis**—You run the Static Code Analyzer to verify that your application meets project standards (requires Visual Studio Premium).

▶ **Code review**—Your code is reviewed by a peer or an architect and issues are logged accordingly.

▶ **Responding to bug**—When a bug has been logged against the code, you must re-create and debug a specific scenario.

In this chapter, we concentrate on two of these phases: self-checking and responding to bugs. These are the two phases in which developers get the most use of the debugging tools built into Visual Studio. For the purposes of this chapter, we assume that the code is written and compiles. Let's start by looking at how to self-check the code.

Debugging the Application (Self-Checking)

In this scenario, you have just started writing a web page to edit a customer's profile. Assume that you've laid out the page, connected to the profile web service, and written the code to save a user's profile to the database. You now need to start self-checking your work to make sure that everything operates as you expect.

The first step is to start your application in debug mode. This allows you to break into your code if an error occurs. In development, this is typically your default setting. You first invoke debug mode by clicking the Run button (the green arrow on either the Standard or the Debug toolbar). Figure 11.1 shows the sample application about to be run in debug mode for the first time. Notice the cursor hovering over the Run button.

Enabling Debugging on a Website

This example is a web application. As such, it requires you to set up debugging on server-side code whose errors and information are output to a remote client. Of course, in the vast majority of cases, developers code and debug on a single development machine. However, sometimes you might have to debug a process on a test server.

In either case, you have to enable debugging through a setting in the configuration file (web.config) for your application. Visual Studio prompts you to enable debugging when you first press the Run button. Figure 11.2 shows this prompt. Clicking the OK button adds the configuration information to the file and starts the debugging session.

FIGURE 11.1   Use the Run button to start the application in debug mode.

FIGURE 11.2   You can choose to allow Visual Studio to enable debugging of an ASP.NET site (and thus modify the Web.config for you).

NOTE

It is important that you turn off debugging in your config file before deploying your web application to production. Having debugging enabled in a production environment is a security risk. With debugging enabled, ASP.NET writes the details of your errors to a web page. These details provide valuable clues to would-be attackers about how your application is put together. In some instances, the error could include user credentials that are being used to access secured resources.

To turn off debug mode, you must edit the web configuration file. Specifically, you edit the Compilation element under the system.web node. You set debug equal to false (as in off). The following is an example of the XML with debug mode turned on:

```
<system.web>
  <compilation debug="true" targetFramework="4.0"/>
    ...
</system.web>
```

Starting in Debug Mode

The most typical scenario for starting a debug session is just clicking the Run button on the toolbar. This works with all application types including Windows and ASP.NET. This action instructs Visual Studio to compile the application and bring up the initial form or page.

Applications can also be started without debugging; this includes both Windows and ASP.NET applications. This capability is useful if you intend to attach to a running process or simply want to walk through an application as a user might see it (without breaking into the IDE). You use the Debug menu, Start Without Debugging option to start your application without attaching it to the Visual Studio Debugger. Figure 11.3 shows an example of invoking this action.

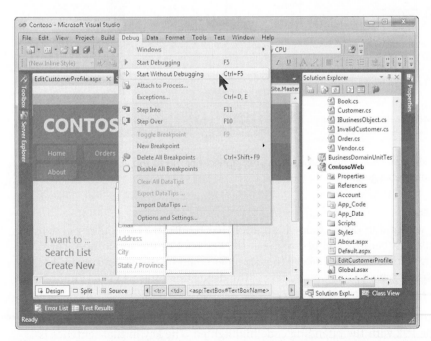

FIGURE 11.3   You can start an application without debugging turned on.

You can also start by stepping into code, line by line. This approach is useful if you want to see all of your code as it executes (rather than just errors). You might desire this if you are getting some unexpected behavior. Stepping line by line gives you an exact understanding of what is going on with your code (rather than just your assumed understanding).

Stepping into code on a web form is typically done by first opening the main source. You then right-click and select the Run to Cursor option from the shortcut menu. Figure 11.4 shows an example. This command tells Visual Studio to run the application until it gets to this point. At that time, the IDE opens into debug mode, where you can step through each line of code (or continue, and so on).

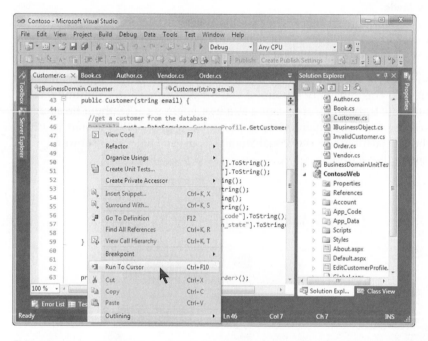

FIGURE 11.4   You can have Visual Studio run your application up to the current line of code and then break into debugging.

Breaking on an Error

Not everything you find in debug mode is an error that results in a break in the code. Often, issues arise just because you're looking at the behavior of the application. For example, a control could be out of place, the tab order could be wrong, and so on. For these items, you still have to rely on your eyes. The debugging tools in Visual Studio help you respond to hard errors in your code.

By default, when unhandled exceptions occur in your code, the debugger breaks execution and bring up the IDE with the offending code highlighted. The key in that sentence is "unhandled exceptions." They represent places in your code where you do not have try-catch blocks to manage an exception. This is typically a good default setting. However, you often need to see handled exceptions as well.

Fortunately, the errors that result in a break in the IDE are a configurable set. For example, you might handle a specific exception in your code and not want to be dumped to the IDE every time it occurs. Rather, you want to be notified only of those exceptional conditions. The Exceptions dialog box allows you to manage the set of exceptions you're concerned with. You access this dialog box by choosing Debug, Exceptions (or pressing Ctrl+D, E in C# or Ctrl+Alt+E in VB). Figure 11.5 shows the dialog box.

FIGURE 11.5   You can select the exceptions on which you wish Visual Studio to break.

In the Exceptions dialog box, the various exceptions are categorized by namespace for easy access (there is also a Find feature). The two columns of check boxes are of primary interest: one for Thrown and one for User-unhandled. Notice that, by default, the setting for nearly all exceptions in the .NET Framework is User-unhandled. This indicates that the debugger should break execution only when a given exception is thrown and it is not handled by your code.

Adding Thrown to the mix tells the debugger to break execution even if you have code to handle a given exception. The debugger reacts by breaking on the line of the exception, before your handler is called. If you intend to use this option, you should consider simply setting it at the category level. For example, you might toggle Thrown for the entire category Common Language Runtime Exceptions. Setting up more granularity is certainly possible. However, doing so often results in more confusion as the debugger breaks in different places depending on the given exception thrown.

Debugging an Error

The first step in debugging your application is to click the Run button. Your application is then running in debug mode. As it happens, the sample application we discussed in our scenario throws an exception upon its initial startup. The debugger responds by breaking into the code and showing the offending line. Figure 11.6 shows a typical view of the editor when it breaks on an error.

FIGURE 11.6   The Visual Studio debugger breaking on an exception.

There are a few items out of interest about the standard debug session shown in Figure 11.6. First, Visual Studio has highlighted the line on which the error was thrown. You can see this clearly by the arrow and the highlighted text.

Next, notice the window in the upper right of the image. This is the Exception Assistant. It provides details on the exception and offers tips for troubleshooting and fixing the given issue. From this window, you can access a few actions, including searching online help for more information on the exception.

At the bottom of the screen are a few additional helpful windows. The Locals window on the left automatically shows the value assigned to all local variables in the code where the exception was thrown. This gives you easy access to key information that might be contributing to the issue. Notice that to the right of this window is an inactive tab called Watch 1 (bottom of screen). This is a watch window; it keeps track of any custom watch scenarios you set up (more on this later).

The window on the bottom right of the screen is the Call Stack. It shows the order in which various components of an application were called. You can look at the Call Stack to find out how you got to where you are. You can also use it to navigate to any code referenced in the stack (see "Debugging Multithreaded Applications" later in this chapter for more on the call stack). Finally, the inactive tab next to this gives you access to the Immediate Window. The Immediate Window allows you to type in code commands and get the results in the editor (more on this to come).

Debugging Different Processes   After you examine the error in this example (Figure 11.6), you can see that it is being thrown inside the web service process. The code called by the web service is being run in a separate process from that of the startup application (the web user interface). When you debug an application, you debug (or shadow) a running process such as an executable (.exe). Visual Studio, by default, considers the startup application's process as the primary process being debugged.

To debug code that is running in a different process (such as the web service process), you must both have the source code and be attached to the executing process (running a debug build). If all the code for a given application is in a single solution, Visual Studio automatically attaches to each process. In the example, this includes both the web user interface process and the web service process. Therefore, in this case, you do not need to manually attach to another process.

The debugger does not, however, automatically break into the IDE on errors raised outside of the startup process. Instead, it respects breakpoints you set inside code executing in other processes. If an error is thrown in a separate process (and no related breakpoints exist in that process), the debugger breaks into the IDE inside the process that called into the process that threw the error.

As in the example, we have both a web UI application and a web service. The UI application calls the web service; the web service code contains the error. Each of these applications is running in a separate process. Therefore, even if both code projects are in the same solution, when the IDE encounters the error from the web service, it breaks on the web UI application (and not on the Web service) as the web UI application was the startup (and attached-to) process. To debug the error in the web service, then, you would need to set a breakpoint in the web service code (or step into that code from the web UI application).

> **NOTE**
>
> Recall that you need to enable debugging for web applications using the configuration file (web.config). This holds true for web service applications as well. Refer to Figure 11.2 for details.

Sometimes you need to manually attach to an already-running process. You might want to attach the IDE to a running web server, or you might have a web service application (as in the example) to which you want to bind debugging. Whatever the scenario, Visual Studio allows you to attach to the process and begin a debug session. To attach to a running process, like a web server, you choose the Attach to Process option from the Debug menu. This brings up the dialog box shown in Figure 11.7.

FIGURE 11.7   You can attach the debugger to a running process (such as a web server).

To connect the Visual Studio debugger to a process, you simply highlight it and click the Attach button (as shown in Figure 11.7). Note that any currently attached processes are grayed out. This is a visual indicator that you are already attached to a given process. In this example, the web UI process is grayed out. You can see that you can add the service process to the debug session. Clicking attach means that you are debugging both processes. Therefore, if you attach to the web service process prior to making a call to it, the IDE also breaks inside the web service code (provided it contains errors).

Setting a Breakpoint   To get the debugger to break into your code when it reaches a specific line, you set a breakpoint on that line. You do so by clicking on the indicator bar for the given line. Alternatively, you can right-click on the line and choose Insert Breakpoint from the Breakpoint context menu.

In the example, you might be unsure where the error originates in the web service code. It seems from the error that it has something to do with the data access class and therefore you could set a breakpoint there. Alternatively, you could set a breakpoint prior to the web service being called. You can then rerun the application, attach to the web service process when the breakpoint is hit, and then step into the web service code (or just hit run again and allow Visual Studio to break when it hits the error). However, this scenario requires you to stop your debug session and rerun the application. Let's assume that we do not want to do this. Rather, we have already attached to the web service process (in the prior step); we now need to set a breakpoint in the data access code (Figure 11.8 shows an example); we then can rerun the call to the web service without rerunning the entire application. Let's look at that next.

FIGURE 11.8   You can set a breakpoint on a specific line of code.

Continuing the Debugging   After you've navigated off the executing code during a debug session, it can often be hard to find your way back. The line that was executing could be buried in any one of the open code windows. Thankfully, you can use the Show Next Statement button (yellow arrow icon) on the Debug toolbar to take you back, which returns you to the line that was executing when the debugger broke.

In the example, you want to rerun the call to the web service without restarting the application. This allows you to hit your new breakpoint and step through the code. You must move the current execution point in the code by right-clicking the line where you want execution to start (or rerun) and selecting Set Next Statement from the context menu. Figure 11.9 shows this menu option.

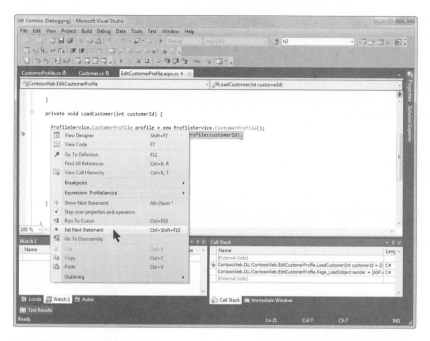

FIGURE 11.9   You can back up in your code using Set Next Statement.

Now that you have backed up the execution point, you are ready to continue the debugging by clicking the Run button again. This is essentially indicating that you are done with the break and want to continue execution (until an error is caught or a breakpoint is hit).

Stepping to Find the Error   In the example, the debugger now breaks execution as soon as it hits the breakpoint in the web service process. This allows you to step through the code. To step line by line through the code, you can click the Step Into button on the Debug toolbar (or press the F11 function key). This executes the code one line at a time, enabling you to view both execution flow and the state of the application as code executes. If you execute example, you see the error. It seems that the SqlDataAdapter object was not given a Command object prior to trying to use it to fill a DataSet.

In most scenarios, you can make this fix during the debug session and continue stepping through or running the code; this is referred to as Edit and Continue. Unfortunately, in this example you cannot make the change while debugging. You cannot invoke Edit and Continue when the debugger has been attached to an already running process. Figure 11.10 shows the message you get when you try.

Instead of using Edit and Continue, you can bookmark the line where you want to make the change using the Text Editor toolbar. You then click the Stop button on the Debug toolbar to stop the debug session. The code change can now be made.

FIGURE 11.10   Visual Studio throws an Edit and Continue error when trying to edit code in a process that it did not start (and you attached to).

To continue through self-checking, you restart the debugging process. However, before restarting, you might want to clear the breakpoint you set by selecting the Breakpoints toolbar item from the Debug toolbar. This brings up the Breakpoints window, as shown in Figure 11.11. From this window, you can view all breakpoints in the application. Here, you select and clear the breakpoint by clicking the Delete button from the toolbar on the Breakpoints pane. Finally, you click the Run button to continue the debug self-check session.

FIGURE 11.11   You can manage your breakpoints using the Breakpoints window.

Debugging Basics Summary

This scenario walked through the many phases of debugging a simple error. This example was meant to introduce the basics of doing debugging in Visual Studio 2010. If you are familiar with prior IDE versions, you probably noticed a lot of similarities.

Walking through the scenario demonstrated the many tools inside the debugging environment, including the Debug toolbar and menu, the Breakpoints window, the watch window, and so on. Now that you have a grasp of the basics, in the next section we intend to explore these debug elements in greater detail.

The Visual Studio Debugger

The debugger built into Visual Studio 2010 is one of the largest and most complex tools in the IDE. With such a large feature-set area, we cannot cover every scenario you might encounter. However, we hope to expose the most commonly applicable features in this section. We continue to work with the customer profile scenario from our previous example.

The Debug Menu and Toolbar

The Debug menu and its related toolbar provide your first-level access to starting debug sessions, stepping into code, managing breakpoints, and accessing the many features of debugging with Visual Studio. There are two states to the debug menu: at rest (or inactive) and in debug mode. Figure 11.12 shows the menu in the at-rest state.

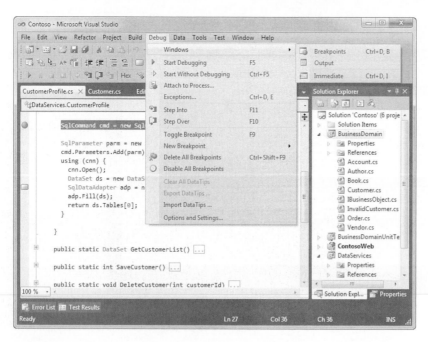

FIGURE 11.12   The Debug menu outside of a debug session.

In the at-rest state, the Debug menu provides features to start a debug session, attach code to a running process, or access some of the many debug windows. Table 11.1 lists all the features available from the Debug menu at rest.

TABLE 11.1   Debug Menu Items at Rest

Menu Item	Description
Windows, Breakpoints	Opens the Breakpoints window in the IDE. This window provides access to all the breakpoints in the option solution.
Windows, Output	Shows the Output window in the IDE. The Output window is a running log of the many messages that are emitted by the IDE, the compiler, and the debugger. Therefore, the information transcends just debug sessions.
Windows, Immediate	Opens the Immediate window in the IDE. This window allows you to execute commands. For example, during application design, you can call your methods directly from the Immediate window. This will start the application and enter directly into a debug session.
Start Debugging	Starts your application in debug mode.
Start Without Debugging	Starts your application without connecting the debugger to the executing process. In this mode, the developer sees what users would see (instead of breaking into the IDE for errors and breakpoints).
Attach to Process	Allows you to attach the debugger (and your code) to a running process (executable). If, for example, you started the application without debugging, you could then attach to that running process and begin debugging.
Exceptions	Opens the Exceptions Option dialog box. This dialog box enables you to choose how the debugger breaks on any given exception.
Step Into	Starts the application in debug mode. For most projects, clicking the Step Into command invokes the debugger on the first executing line of the application. In this way, you can step into the application from the first line.
Step Over	When not in a debug session, the Step Over command simply starts the application the same way as clicking the Run button would.
Toggle Breakpoint	Toggles the breakpoint on or off for the current, active line of code in a text editor. The option is inactive if you do not have a code window active in the IDE.
New Breakpoint, Break at Function	Brings up the New Breakpoint dialog box. This dialog box enables you to indicate a function name to define for which to create a breakpoint. This can be useful if you know a function's name but do not want to search your code files for it.
New Breakpoint, New Data Breakpoint	This option is available only for native, C++ applications. It allows you to define a breakpoint that breaks into the IDE when a value in a specific memory location changes.
Delete All Breakpoints	Removes all breakpoints from your solution.

TABLE 11.1   Continued

Menu Item	Description
Disable All Breakpoints	Disables (without removing) all the breakpoints in your solution.
Clear All DataTips	Enables you to clear any data tips you might have pinned to the IDE (including comments). See DataTips later in this chapter.
Export DataTips	Allows you to export your data tips as an XML file for sharing with other developers. See DataTips later in this chapter.
Import DataTips	Allows you to import an XML data tips file for use inside your debug sessions. See DataTips later in this chapter.
Options and Settings	Brings up the Options dialog box for debugging. See "Debug Options" later in this chapter.

When the debugger is engaged and you are working through a debug session, the state of the Debug menu changes. It now provides several additional options over those provided by the at-rest state. These options include those designed to move through the code, restart the session, and access even more debug-related windows. Figure 11.13 shows the Debug menu during a debug session.

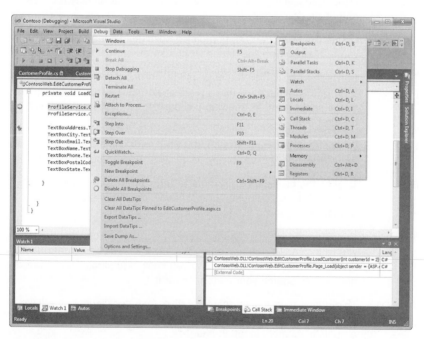

FIGURE 11.13   The Debug menu during a debug session.

Let's look at the many options provided by the Debug menu during a debug session. Table 11.2 presents the many items available from the debug menu in this state. When reading through the table, refer to the preceding figures to get context on any given item.

TABLE 11.2   Debug Menu Items for an Active Debug Session

Menu Item	Description
Windows, Breakpoints	Allows you to open the Breakpoints window during a debug session.
Windows, Output	Opens the Output window during an active debug session in order to read output messages emitted by the compiler and debugger.
Windows, Parallel Tasks	Enables you to view parallel tasks in a visual window. See "Debugging Parallel Applications" later in this chapter.
Windows, Parallel Stacks	Enables you to view executing threads and tasks in a visual window. See "Debugging Parallel Applications" later in this chapter.
Windows, Watch	Opens one of many possible watch windows in the IDE. Watch windows represent items and expressions you are keeping a close eye on through a debug session.
Windows, Autos	Opens the Autos window. This window shows variables (and their values) in the current line of code and the preceding line of code.
Windows, Locals	Opens the Locals window in the IDE. This window shows variables in the local scope (function).
Windows, Immediate	Opens the Immediate window where you can execute a command.
Windows, Call Stack	Shows the list of functions that are on the stack. Also indicates the current stack frame (function). This selected item is what defines the content from the Locals, watch, and Autos windows.
Windows, Threads	Shows the Threads window in the IDE. From here, you can view and control the threads in the application you are debugging.
Windows, Modules	Shows the Modules window in the IDE. This window lists the DLLs and EXEs used by your application.
Windows, Processes	Shows the Processes window in the IDE. This window lists the processes to which the debug session is attached.
Windows, Memory	Opens the Memory window for a view at the memory used by your application. This is valid only when address-level debugging is enabled from the Options dialog box.
Windows, Disassembly	Opens the Disassembly window. This window shows the assembly code corresponding to the compiler instructions. This is valid only when address-level debugging is enabled from the Options dialog box.

TABLE 11.2   Continued

Menu Item	Description
Windows, Registers	Opens the Registers window so that you can see register values change as you step through code. This is valid only when address-level debugging is enabled from the Options dialog box.
Continue	Continues executing the application after broken into the IDE. The application continues running on the active line of code (the breakpoint, a line that threw an error, or a line set using Set Next Statement).
Break All	Enables you to break the application into the debugger manually (without having to hit a breakpoint) during a debug session. The application breaks on the next line that executes. This capability is useful to gain access to the debug information such as watch windows. It can also be used to gain access to the debug session when your application appears to have hung.
Stop Debugging	Terminates the debugging session. It also terminates the process you are debugging, provided that the process was started by Visual Studio.
Detach All	Detaches the debugger from the executing process. This enables your application to continue running after the debugger is through with it.
Terminate All	Stops debugging and terminates all processes to which you are attached.
Restart	Stops the debugging session and restarts it. Similar to clicking both Stop Debugging and Start Debugging in sequence.
Attach to Process	Enables you to attach the active debug session to one or more additional processes such as an executing web server or a Windows service.
Exceptions	Brings up the Exceptions dialog box, which enables you to manage how the IDE breaks on specific exception types in the .NET Framework and other libraries.
Step Into	Advances the debugger a line. If you choose to "step into" a function, the debugger does so line by line.
Step Over	Functions the same as Step Into with one major difference: If you choose to "step over" a function, the line calling the function is executed (along with the function), and the debugger sets the next line after the function call as the next line to be debugged.
Step Out	Tells the debugger to execute the current function and then break back into debugging after the function has finished. This capability is useful if you step into a function but then want to have that function just execute and yet return you to debug mode when it is complete.
QuickWatch	Brings up the QuickWatch window when the debugger is in break mode. The QuickWatch window shows one variable or expression you are watching and its value.
Toggle Breakpoint	Turns an active breakpoint on or off.

TABLE 11.2   Continued

Menu Item	Description
New Breakpoint	Brings up the New Breakpoint dialog box (see Table 11.1 for more information).
Delete All Breakpoints	Deletes all breakpoints in your solution.
Disable All Breakpoints	Disables breakpoints in the solution without deleting them. You can also disable individual breakpoints. This capability is very useful if you want to keep the breakpoints around for later but simply don't want to hit that one at the moment.
Clear All DataTips	Allows you to clear any data tips you might have pinned to the IDE (including comments). See "DataTips" later in this chapter.
Clear All DataTips Pinned to	Clear only those DataTips pinned to the active file. See "DataTips" later in this chapter.
Export DataTips	Enables you to export your DataTips as an XML file for sharing with other developers. See "DataTips" later in this chapter.
Import DataTips	Enalbes you to import an XML DataTips file for use inside your debug sessions. See "DataTips" later in this chapter.
Save Dump As	Enables you to save a memory dump for the active debug session.
Options and Settings	Brings up the Options dialog box for debugging. See "Debug Options" later in this chapter.

The Debug Toolbar

The Debug toolbar provides quick access to some of the key items available on the Debug menu. From here, you can manage your debug session. For example, you can start or continue a debug session, stop an executing session, step through lines of code, and so on.

Figure 11.14 presents the Debug toolbar during an active debug session. In design mode, the Continue button reads Start Debugging, and a number of these items are disabled. We have added callouts for each item on the toolbar. You can cross-reference these callouts to Table 11.2 for further information.

FIGURE 11.14   The Debug toolbar during an active debug session (break mode).

> **NOTE**
>
> In Figure 11.14, the Breakpoints window icon on the right of the figure with the callout "Debug Windows" actually is a drop-down menu. This menu provides access to the many debug windows that are available to developers. See Figure 11.13 for a sample of the menus you can access from this toolbar item.

Debug Options

You can control the many debugging options in Visual Studio through the Options dialog box. You can access these options from the Tools menu (Tools, Options) and then select the Debugging node from the left-side of the dialog box. Alternatively, you can open the options right to Debugging from the Debug menu (Debug, Options and Settings).

There are six sets of options available under the Debugging node. The following provides an overview of each:

▸ **General**—Provides access to the many debugging switches (more than 20) to turn on and off Visual Studio debugging behavior. This includes enabling and disabling breakpoint filters, using just-my-code debugging, creating breakpoint filters, handling warnings, and many other options (see Figure 11.15).

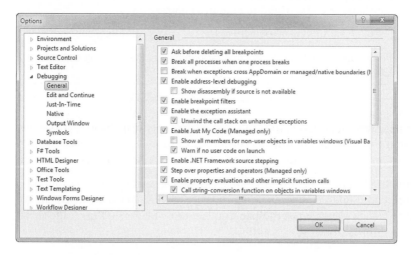

FIGURE 11.15   You can use the Options dialog box to control how Visual Studio behaves during a debugging session.

▸ **Edit and Continue**—Enables you to enable and disable edit-and-continue as a feature.

▸ **Just-In-Time**—Enables you to indicate the type of code (managed, native, and script) for which you want to enable or disable Visual Studio debugging (also called Just-In-Time debugging).

▸ **Native**—Enables you to control native (non-managed) code debugging.

▶ **Output Window**—Provides management features for the Output Window such as which messages are shown.

▶ **Symbols**—Enables you to choose which debug symbols are loaded for your debug session. You can also choose additional debug symbol files (.pdb and .dbg). These files can be helpful if you do not have the source code associated with a particular library you need to debug, such as the .NET Framework itself or a third-party component.

The majority of the settings you manage can be found on the General screen. Figure 11.15 shows the many options for this dialog box. We will cover the features behind these options throughout the remainder of this chapter.

These many options help you customize your debug experience. However, as we debug code in this chapter, we are assuming the default options for the debugger.

Stepping In, Out, and Over Code

Probably the most common debug operation for developers is stepping through their code line-by-line and examining the data emitted by the application and the debugger. Code stepping is just that, examining a line, executing the line, and examining the results (and then repeating the process over and over). Because this is such a dominant activity, becoming efficient with the step operations in Visual Studio is important for maximizing the use of your time during a debug session. Here, we cover each of the stepping options and provide examples.

Beginning a Debug Session (Stepping into Code)

The Step Into command is available from the Debug menu and toolbar (you can also press F11 as a shortcut). There are two behaviors commonly associated with this one command. The first is related to when you invoke the command for an application that is not currently running in debug mode. In this case, the application is compiled and started, and the first line is presented to you in the debug window for stepping purposes. This is, in essence, stepping into your application. Figure 11.16 shows a WPF application in debug mode as the result of a call to Step Into.

> **NOTE**
>
> For web applications, using Step Into or Step Over does not work the same as with other applications. Instead, your application simply runs in debug mode in the case of websites. The debugger does not break on the first line of your application. To do this, you must set a breakpoint or choose the Run to Cursor option (see the following section).

A call to the Step Over command (Debug menu, toolbar, or F10) while your application is at rest will result in the same behavior as Step Into. That is, your application (provided it is not a website) is compiled and started in a debug session on the first line of code.

Run to Cursor One of the more handy (and overlooked) features of the debug toolset is Run to Cursor. This feature works the way it sounds. You set your cursor position on some code and invoke the Run to Cursor command (right-click or Ctrl+F10). The application is compiled and run until it hits the line of code where your cursor is placed. At this point, the debugger breaks the application and presents the line of code for you to step through. This capability is especially handy because this is how many developers work. They are looking at a specific line (or lines) of code and want to debug this line. They do not need to start from the first line and might not want to be bothered with breakpoints. The Run to Cursor feature is therefore an efficient means to get the debugger on the same page as you. Figure 11.17 shows this feature being invoked from the context menu.

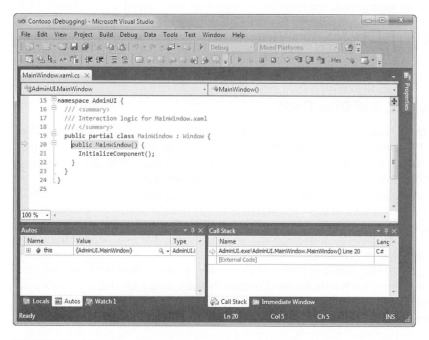

FIGURE 11.16   Using Step Into to start an application.

Run to Cursor works even if the user is required to activate some portion of the code prior to the code's reaching the cursor position. In this way, it acts like an invisible, temporary breakpoint. For instance, consider an example in which users are presented with a default web page. From here, they can select to edit their profiles. If you set the Run to Cursor command on a line inside the edit profile screen, the debugger still executes the application and waits until the user (tester or developer) invokes the given line of code.

Start Debugging   You can also start your debug session by selecting the Start Debugging option (green "play" arrow) from the Debug menu or toolbar (or F5). This starts a debug session but does not break into code unless an exception occurs or a breakpoint is encountered. This is a common operation for developers testing their code without wanting to walk through it or those who use a lot of breakpoints.

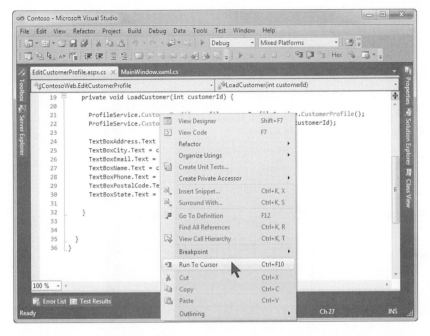

FIGURE 11.17   You can tell the debugger to stop when it hits a given line of code using the Run to Cursor command.

Break All   If your application is already running in a debug session and you want to enter break mode, you can do so at any time by invoking the Break All command from the Debug menu or toolbar (or Ctrl+Alt+Break). The Break All feature is represented by the pause icon on the toolbar. Clicking this button stops your application on the next executing line and enables you to interrogate the debugger for information. The Break All command is especially useful if you need to break into a long-running process or a loop that seems to have stalled your application.

Walking Through Your Code

During a debug session, you have basically three options for moving through your code. You can step into a line or function, step over a given function, or step out of a function. Let's look at each option.

Step Into   The Step Into command (F11 for C# and F8 for VB) enables you to progress through your code one line at a time. Invoking this command executes the current line of code and positions your cursor on the next line to be executed. The important distinction between stepping into and other similar commands is how Step Into handles lines of code that contain method calls. If you are positioned on such a line, calling Step Into takes you to the first line inside that method.

As an example, look at Figure 11.18. It shows an example of the Customer object making a call to a data access method named GetCustomer. In this case, both projects are loaded in the solution; thus, you have access to their debug symbols. Therefore, a call to Step Into results in your stepping into the first line of GetCustomer.

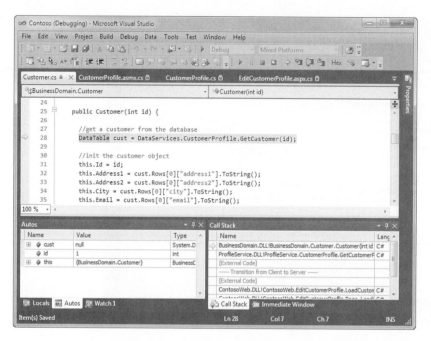

FIGURE 11.18   Stepping into a line of code can take you into another class.

Figure 11.19 shows stepping into this method. Notice that you are now positioned to step line by line through the method (line 15). Of course, when you reach the end of this method, the debugger returns you to the next line in the calling function (back to line 31 as depicted in Figure 11.18).

Step Over   The Step Over command (F10 for C# and Shift+F8 for VB) enables you to maintain focus on the current procedure without stepping into any methods called by it. That is, calling Step Over executes line-by-line but does not take you into any function calls, constructors, or property calls.

As an example, consider Figure 11.18. Here, the debugger is positioned on the call to GetCustomer. If you call the Step Over command, the GetCustomer function executes in its entirety without your stepping through it. Instead, the next line to execute in step mode is the line following the call to GetCustomer (line 31). Of course, any exception thrown by the function you step over results in the debugger breaking into your code (and the function) as normal.

Step Out   The Step Out command (Shift+F11 and Ctrl+Shift+F8 for VB) is another useful tool. It allows you to tell the debugger to finish executing the current method you are debugging but return to break mode as soon as it is finished. This is a great tool when you get stuck in a long method you wish you had stepped over. In addition, you might step into a given function only to debug a portion of it and then want to step out.

FIGURE 11.19   The results of stepping into a function.

As an example, refer again to Figure 11.19. Recall that you stepped into this method from the code in Figure 11.18. Suppose that you start stepping through a couple of lines of code. After you take a look and verify that a connection is made to the database, you simply want to have the function complete and return to debugging back in the calling function (line 31 of Figure 11.18). To do so, you simply invoke Step Out.

Continuing Execution

When you are in a debug session, the Start Debugging (or Run) command changes to Continue. The Continue command is available when you are paused on a given line of code in the debugger. It enables you to let the application continue to run on its own without stepping through each line. For example, suppose you walked through the lines of code you wanted to see, and now you want to continue checking your application from a user's perspective. Using Continue, you tell the application and debugger to keep running until either an exception occurs or a breakpoint is hit.

Ending a Debug Session

You can end your debug session in few ways. One common method is to kill the currently executing application. This might be done by closing the browser window for a web application or clicking the Close (or ∞) button of a Windows application. Calls in your code that terminate your application also end a debug session.

There are also a couple of options available to you from the Debug window. The Terminate All command kills all processes that the debugger is attached to and ends the debug session. There is also the Detach All option. Figure 11.20 shows both options from the Debug menu. Detach All simply detaches the debugger from all running processes without terminating them. This capability can be useful if you've temporarily attached to a running process, debugged it, and want to leave it running.

FIGURE 11.20   You can detach from a running process but leave the process running.

Indicating When to Break into Code

You control the debugger through breakpoints and tracepoints. With these, you can tell the debugger when you are interested in breaking into code or receiving information about your application. Breakpoints enable you to indicate when the debugger should stop on a specific line in your code. Tracepoints were first introduced in Visual Studio 2005. They are a type of breakpoint that enables you to perform an action when a given line of your code is reached. This typically involves emitting data about your application to the output window. Mastering the use of breakpoints reduces the time it takes to zero in on and fix issues with your code.

Setting a Breakpoint

The most common method of setting a breakpoint is to first find the line of code on which you want the debugger to stop. You then click in the code editor's indicator margin for the given line of code. Doing so places a red circle in the indicator margin and high-lights the line of code as red. Of course, these are the default colors; you can change the look of breakpoints in the Tools, Options dialog box under the Environment node, Fonts and Colors.

There are a few additional ways to set breakpoints. For instance, you can right-click a given line of code and choose Insert Breakpoint from the Breakpoint context menu. You can also choose New Breakpoint from the Debug menu (or press Ctrl+D, N in C# or Ctrl+B in VB) to open the New Breakpoint dialog box in which you can set a function breakpoint.

Setting a Function Breakpoint   A function breakpoint is just a breakpoint that is set through the New Breakpoint dialog box. It is called a function breakpoint because it is typically set at the beginning of the function (but does not need to be). From the New Breakpoint dialog box, you can manually set the function on which you want to break, the line of code in the function, and even the character on the line.

If your cursor is on a function or on a call to a function when you invoke this dialog box, the name of the function is automatically placed in the dialog box, or you can type a function name in the dialog box. Figure 11.21 shows the New Breakpoint dialog box in action. Notice that you can manually set the line and even the character on the line where the breakpoint should be placed (for lines of code that include multiple statements).

FIGURE 11.21   You can set a function breakpoint for a given function by name.

NOTE

If you specify an overloaded function in the New Breakpoint dialog box, you must specify the actual function on which you want to break. You do so by indicating the correct parameter types for the given overload. For example, the GetCustomer function in the example takes a customerId parameter (as an int). If you had an overload that also looked up a customer by name (as a string), you indicate this overload in the Function field as LoadCustomer(string).

Recognizing the Many Breakpoints of Visual Studio

Visual Studio 2010 has a number of breakpoint icons. These icons enable you to easily recognize the type of breakpoint associated with a given line of code. For instance, a round, filled circle is a common breakpoint, whereas a round, hollow circle represents a common breakpoint that has been disabled. We've provided Table 11.3 for reference purposes. It shows some of the more common icons associated with breakpoints and presents a description of each.

TABLE 11.3   The Breakpoint Icons

Icon	Description
	This icon indicates a standard, enabled breakpoint. When the debugger encounters this line of code, it stops the application and breaks into debug mode.
	This icon indicates a standard tracepoint. When the debugger hits this line of code, it performs the action associated with the tracepoint.
	The plus icon inside the breakpoint indicates an advanced breakpoint that contains a condition, hit count, or filter.
	The plus icon inside the tracepoint indicates an advanced tracepoint that contains a condition, hit count, or filter.
	An empty or hollow breakpoint indicates a disabled breakpoint. The breakpoint is still associated with the line of code. However, the debugger does not recognize the disabled breakpoint until it has been reenabled. Hollow icons are associated with types of breakpoint icons such as tracepoints, advanced items, and even breakpoint errors and warnings. In all conditions, the hollow icon indicates that the item is disabled.
	Represents a breakpoint warning indicating that a breakpoint cannot be set due to a temporary condition. This can be the result of debugging not being enabled for a website or debug symbols not being loaded. This type of icon is set by Visual Studio as a warning. Note: Conditional items also include the plus sign inside the icon.
	Represents a tracepoint warning (see preceding description).
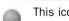	Indicates that the breakpoint is also the next line to be executed by Visual Studio (step into).

Working with the Breakpoints Window

The Breakpoints window in Visual Studio provides a convenient way to organize and manage the many conditions on which you intend to break into the debugger. You access this window from the Debug menu or toolbar (or by pressing Ctrl+D, B in C# or Ctrl+Alt+B in VB). Figure 11.22 shows the Breakpoints window inside Visual Studio.

The Breakpoints Window Toolbar   The Breakpoints window has its own toolbar that enables you to manage the breakpoints listed in the grid below the toolbar (refer to Figure 11.22). The commands available from the toolbar are described in detail in Table 11.4.

FIGURE 11.22   The Breakpoints window.

TABLE 11.4   The Breakpoints Window Toolbar

Item	Description
New ▾ Break at Function... Ctrl+D, N New Data Breakpoint...	Brings up the new Breakpoints window, enabling you to set a breakpoint at a function.
✕	Enables you to delete the selected breakpoint in the list.
⨯	Deletes all breakpoints in the window.
⨯	Toggles all breakpoints as either on or off. If even one breakpoint in the list is enabled, clicking this icon the first time disables it (and all others that are enabled). Clicking it a second time (or when all breakpoints are disabled) enables all breakpoints.
⬆	Enables you to export your breakpoints to an XML file. This can be useful if you have a lot of breakpoint information you want to share. You can share your breakpoints to allow others to debug your code.
⬇	Enables you to import breakpoints from an XML file.
⬚	Enables you to go to the source code associated with the selected breakpoint.
⬚	Enables you to go to the disassembly information associated with the selected breakpoint.

11

TABLE 11.4   Continued

Item	Description
	Enables you to choose which columns you want to view in the Breakpoints window. Each column provides information about a given breakpoint. For example, you can see information on the condition associated with each breakpoint, the filename, the function, the filter, the process, and so on.

Managing Each Individual Breakpoint   The Breakpoints window also gives you access to each individual breakpoint. It serves as a launching point for setting the many options associated with a breakpoint. For example, you can disable a single breakpoint by toggling the check box associated with the breakpoint in the list. In addition, you can set the many properties and conditions associated with a breakpoint. Figure 11.23 shows a disabled tracepoint and a disabled breakpoint; it also shows the context menu associated with an individual breakpoint.

FIGURE 11.23   You can manage individual breakpoints inside the Breakpoints window.

Notice that from this context menu, you can delete the breakpoint and navigate to its related source code (Go To Source Code). More important, however, is the access to setting the conditions and filters associated with the breakpoint. We cover using each of these options next.

Labeling Breakpoints   You can provide labels for your breakpoints, which enables you to define categories of breakpoints and quickly find them in the Breakpoints window. For example, you might want to set a number of breakpoints and tracepoints related to a specific scenario in your code such as managing a customer profile or creating a new order. These breakpoints are useful when you need to modify and review this code.

However, when you are working on unrelated code, you might want to turn a whole group of breakpoints off. Breakpoint labels support this scenario.

You label a breakpoint by selecting Edit Labels from the breakpoint context-menu (refer to Figure 11.23 to see an example). The Edit Breakpoint Labels dialog box opens as shown in Figure 11.24. Here you can add a new label and apply that label to the selected breakpoint. Alternatively, you can select one or more labels from the existing labels previously defined.

You can work with the breakpoint labels inside the Breakpoints window. You can sort the list by the Labels column as shown in Figure 11.25. In addition, you can use the Search feature to find breakpoints based on keywords contained in the labels.

Breaking Based on Conditions

Often, setting a simple breakpoint is not sufficient (or efficient). For instance, if you are looking for a particular condition to be true in your code—a condition that seems to be causing an exception—then you would prefer to break based on that condition. This saves the time of constantly breaking into a function only to examine a few data points and determine that you have not hit your condition.

FIGURE 11.24   You can use the Edit Breakpoint Labels dialog box to label breakpoints in order to make them easier to find and work with as a group.

FIGURE 11.25   You can sort or search breakpoints based on their labels.

There are five types of conditions you can add to a breakpoint: Location, Condition, Hit Count, Filter, and When Hit. You add a condition to a breakpoint from within the Breakpoints window. Select a given breakpoint and then right-click to open the context menu for the given breakpoint. Refer to Figure 11.23 for an example. You can see that each possible condition is listed for the breakpoint. The following sections highlight the conditional options available for breakpoints.

Setting a Breakpoint Condition   A breakpoint condition enables you to break into the debugger or perform an action (tracepoint) when a specific condition is either evaluated as true or has changed. Often, you know that the bug you are working on occurs only based on a very specific condition. Breakpoint conditions are the perfect answer for troubleshooting an intermittent bug.

To set a condition, you select the breakpoint on which you want to apply a condition. You then choose the Condition option from the context (right-click) menu to open the Breakpoint Condition dialog box, as shown in Figure 11.26. Notice that when setting the condition, you have access to IntelliSense.

FIGURE 11.26   You can use the Breakpoint Condition dialog box to set a boolean code condition that tells the debugger when to stop on your breakpoint.

When you set a condition, you have two options: Is True and Has Changed. The Is True option enables you to set a Boolean condition that, when evaluated to true, results in the debugger's breaking into the given line of code.

For example, suppose you are notified of an error that happens only for a specific customer. You might go to the Customer class and set a breakpoint inside the function that gets a customer from the database (in our example, this is the constructor). You might then add the Is True condition, id=1234, to the breakpoint (where id is the parameter to the method). This tells the debugger not to stop on this line of code unless this condition is met. Figure 11.27 shows this condition in the dialog box. It also shows the two options available for conditions at the bottom of the dialog box.

FIGURE 11.27   An example of a breakpoint condition.

The option, Has Changed, tells the debugger to break when the value of an expression changes. The first pass through your code sets the value for the first evaluation. If the value changes after that, the debugger breaks on a given line. This capability can be useful when you have fields or properties with initial values and you want to track when those values are being changed. In addition, Has Changed can be useful in looping and if...then scenarios in which you are interested in only whether the results of your code changed a particular value.

TIP

Your breakpoint information is persisted between debug sessions. That is, when you close Visual Studio for the day, your breakpoints are still there when you return. This validates the time you might spend setting some sophisticated debugging options because they can remain in your application and be turned on and off as required. The options can also be exported to a file and shared with other developers or other computers.

Breaking on Location   You can edit a breakpoint to break based on a specific location in a file. Most breakpoints already work this way. That is, they automatically know the file, line number, and character on which to break. However, there are times when you might want to edit this information. For example, suppose your code is slightly out of sync with the running build. You might need to edit your breakpoints to break on a different line of code.

Figure 11.28 shows an example of the File Breakpoint window as accessed from the Location option on the breakpoint context menu. You might also use this feature to quickly set a breakpoint on a specific line without searching your source code.

FIGURE 11.28   The File Breakpoint window enables you to set a breakpoint at a specific location in your code.

Setting a Breakpoint Filter   Breakpoint filters enable you to specify a specific machine, process, or thread on which you want to break. For instance, if your error condition seems to happen only on a certain machine or within a certain process, you can debug this condition specifically with a filter. Filters are most useful in complex debugging scenarios in which your application is highly distributed.

To use this feature, you can specify the machine by name, the process by name or ID, or the thread by name or ID. You can also specify combinations with & (and), || (or), and ! (not). This allows you to get to a specific thread on a specific process on a certain machine. Figure 11.29 shows the dialog box in which you set breakpoint filters. In this figure, the breakpoint is being configured to stop provided that the running process is the development web server (WebDev.WebServer.EXE).

FIGURE 11.29   You can set a breakpoint filter to stop the debugger inside a specific process or thread, or on a specific machine.

Using a Hit Count with a Breakpoint   Using the Hit Count command, you can tell the debugger that you want to break when a given line of code is reached a number of times. Typically, you can find a better condition than breaking based on Hit Count. However, this feature is useful in those cases in which you can't determine the actual condition but know that when you pass through a function a certain number of times, something bad happens. In addition, the Hit Count option might be more useful in tracepoint scenarios in which you are emitting data about what is happening in your code. You might want to write that data only periodically.

Figure 11.30 shows the Breakpoint Hit Count dialog box. Notice that this screenshot was taken during an active debug session. You can tell because the current hit count reads one (1).

FIGURE 11.30   You can set the debugger to break when it hits a line of code a set number of times.

You have the option of clicking the Reset button and turning the hit count back to zero and continuing debugging from that point. Note that you can add any condition to a breakpoint during an active debug session.

This dialog box also provides a few options for setting the actual hit count. In the drop-down list under When the Breakpoint Is Hit, the following options are available:

▶ Break Always (the default and does not invoke the hit count option)

▶ Break When the Hit Count Is Equal To

▶ Break When the Hit Count Is a Multiple Of

▶ Break When the Hit Count Is Greater Than or Equal To

TIP

You can combine all the breakpoint conditions we've discussed on a single breakpoint. For example, you may add a condition and a filter to a given breakpoint. Doing so allows you to create even more specific scenarios for debugging your application using breakpoints.

Working with Tracepoints (When Hit Option)

Tracepoints enable you to emit data to the Output window or run a Visual Studio macro when a specific breakpoint is hit. You then have the option to break into the debugger (like a regular breakpoint), process another condition, or just continue executing the application. This capability can be very useful if you want to keep a running log of what is happening as your application runs in debug mode. You can then review this log to get valuable information about specific conditions and order of execution when an exception is thrown.

You can set tracepoints explicitly by right-clicking a line of code and choosing Insert Tracepoint from the Breakpoint menu. In addition, selecting the When Hit command from the context menu (refer to Figure 11.25) for a breakpoint in the Breakpoints window opens a tracepoint dialog box, named When Breakpoint Is Hit, as shown in Figure 11.31.

FIGURE 11.31   You can set a tracepoint using the When Breakpoint Is Hit dialog box.

The options available for the When Breakpoint Is Hit dialog box include printing a message to the output window, running a macro, and continuing execution. You can choose any combination of these options. The first, printing a message, enables you to output data about your function. There are a number of keywords you can use to output data, such as $FUNCTION for the function name and $CALLER for the name of the calling function. A list of keywords is shown in the instructional text within the dialog box in Figure 11.29. You can also output your specific variable values. You do so by enclosing the variable names in curly braces.

The Continue execution option enables you to indicate whether this is a true tracepoint or a breakpoint that contains a tracing action. If you choose to continue, you get only the trace action (message and/or macro). If you indicate not to continue, you get the trace action, plus the debugger stops on this line of code, just as with a regular breakpoint. This is essentially applying a When Hit action to a standard breakpoint.

Finally, when you select the Run a Macro option, the dialog box gives you a list of all the macros loaded in your environment for selection.

You can also combine tracepoint actions with conditions. When you do so, the action fires only when the breakpoint condition is met.

As an example, suppose a tracepoint is set inside the web service GetCustomerProfile. Imagine this tracepoint prints a message to the output window when the line of code is hit and simply continues executing the application. The message we intend to print is as follows:

```
Function: $FUNCTION, Thread: $TID $TNAME, Id: {id}
```

This message prints the function name, the thread ID and name (if any), and the value of the variable, id. Figure 11.32 shows two passes through the tracepoint output in the Output window (Debug, Windows, Output).

FIGURE 11.32   You can view the results of tracepoints inside the Output window.

Viewing Data in the Debugger

After the debugger has thrown you into break mode, the next challenge is to filter all the data your application is emitting. Getting to the right data helps you find problems faster and fix them faster. Visual Studio tries to make the data available where you want it. For example, DataTips show you variable values right in the code editor. There are many similar examples in the way Visual Studio shows debugging data when and where you need it, which are covered throughout the following sections.

Watching Variables

A common activity in a debug session is to view the values associated with the many types in your application. There are various windows available to help you here. The two most obvious are the Locals and Autos windows.

Locals Window   The Locals window shows all the variables and their values for the current debug scope, which gives you a view of everything available in the current, executing method. The variables in this window are set automatically by the debugger. They are organized alphabetically in a list by name. In addition, hierarchy is also shown. For example, if a given variable relates to an object type, that object's members are listed inside the variable (as a tree-based structure).

Figure 11.33 shows an example of the Locals window. In it, you can see the sample application paused inside the Customer constructor. Notice that the customer instance (this) is expanded to show the various properties and fields associated with this object. As values are set, the results are shown in the Value column.

FIGURE 11.33   The Locals window shows you variable values for the currently executing method.

TIP

You can edit a value in the Locals or Autos window by right-clicking the variable and choosing Edit Value from the context menu. You can then change the value of the variable directly from within the window (similar to changing variable values using the Immediate window).

The Autos Window   Often, viewing all the locals provides too many options to sort through. This can be true when there is just too much in scope in the given process or function. To home in on the values associated with the line of code you are looking at, you can use the Autos window, which shows the value of all variables and expressions that are in the current executing line of code or in the preceding line of code. This allows you to really focus on just the values you are currently debugging.

Figure 11.34 shows the Autos window for the same method as was shown in Figure 11.33. Notice the difference in what is shown. Also, notice that Visual Studio has even added specific expressions that differ from the code to the watch list. For example, the call to cust.Rows[0]["name"] is automatically shown as an item in the Autos window. In addition, this.Name is also shown as an item. You can see the Autos window tries to anticipate the items you might need to review and shows their values.

FIGURE 11.34   You can use the Autos window to automatically get variable values for the last executed and the currently executing line of code.

The Watch Windows   The Visual Studio Watch windows enable you to set a custom list of variables and expressions that you want to keep an eye on. In this way, you decide the items in which you are interested. The Watch windows look and behave just like the Locals and Autos windows. In addition, the items you place in Watch windows persist from one debug session to another.

You access each Watch window from the Debug menu (Debug | Windows | Watch) or toolbar. The four Watch windows are named Watch 1, Watch 2, Watch 3, and Watch 4. Having four Watch windows enables you to set up four custom lists of items you want to monitor. This capability can be especially helpful if each custom list applies to a separate scope in your application.

You add a variable or an expression to the Watch window from either the code editor or the QuickWatch window. If you are in the code editor, select a variable or highlight an expression, right-click, and choose the Add Watch menu item. This takes the highlighted variable or expression and places it in the Watch window. You can also drag and drop the highlighted item into a Watch window.

QuickWatch   The QuickWatch window is similar to the other Watch windows. However, it enables you to focus on a single variable or expression. The QuickWatch window has been used less often since DataTips were introduced in 2005. From the QuickWatch window, you can write expressions and add them to the Watch window. When writing your expression, you have access to IntelliSense. Figure 11.35 shows the QuickWatch window.

FIGURE 11.35 The QuickWatch window enables you to define expressions and monitor their results during a debug session.

The item you add to QuickWatch is evaluated when you click the Reevaluate button. Clicking the Add Watch button sends the variable to the Watch 1 window.

DataTips

DataTips enable you to highlight a variable or an expression in your code editor and get watch information right in the editor. This feature is more in tune with how developers work. For example, if you are looking at a line of code, you might highlight something in that line to evaluate it. You can do this by creating a QuickWatch. However, you can also simply hover over the item and its data is unfold in a DataTip. In addition, Visual Studio 2010 now enables you to pin your data tips directly to your code window to they are always visible during a debug session, inside your code editor.

Figure 11.36 shows a DataTip active in a debug session. Here, the cursor is positioned over the variable that is of type Customer. Clicking on the plus sign to expand this variable unfolds the many properties and fields of the object. If the member list is long, you can scroll through it using an arrow at the bottom of the window. You can also right-click any member in the list and edit its value, copy it, or add it to the watch window (as shown). Also, notice the magnifying glass icon next to the items in the list; it allows you to select a specific visualizer for a given item (more on visualizers shortly).

FIGURE 11.36   You can use DataTips to quickly visualize your object data in the debugger.

You can also select an expression and have it evaluated as a DataTip. For example, if you select the portion of line 36 in Figure 11.36 that reads cust.Rows[0]["name"], a DataTip shows this variable and its value of true.

Pinning a Data Tip   In Figure 11.36, the highlighted member, City, has a pin icon on the far right of the window. This icon enables you to pin your DataTip to the code window, which ensures this DataTip is displayed each time you pass through the code in the debugger. This is a faster, more accessible version of a Watch window.

You can pin all sorts of code items as DataTips. You can pin an entire object, or, in the case of the example, a single member. You can also move pinned DataTips around in the editor to position them accordingly. After a DataTip is pinned, you can highlight the it to remove it, unpin it, or add your own comment to the DataTip. In Figure 11.37, we have pinned two DataTips to the code editor. The first (this) represents an entire object and contains a comment. The second (this.City) is simply selected in the editor.

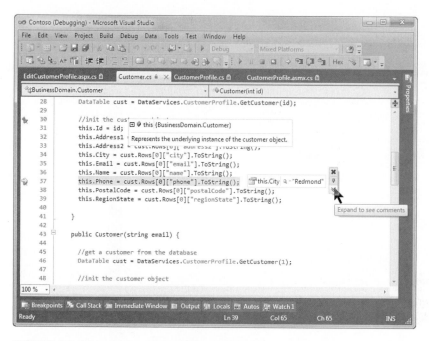

FIGURE 11.37 You can pin DataTips to the code editor to provide easier variable watching during a debug session.

Visualizing Data

When you are looking at variable values, what you really want to get to is the data behind the object. Sometimes this data is obscured by the object model itself. For example, suppose you are looking for the data that is contained in a DataSet object. To find it, you have to dig many layers deep in a watch window or a DataTip. You have to traverse the inner workings of the object model just to get at something as basic as the data contained by the object. If you've spent much time doing this, you know how frustrating it can be.

Visual Studio offers a quick, easy way to access the data contained in an object. It does so through a tool called a visualizer. Visualizers are meant to present the object's data in a meaningful way.

A few visualizers ship with Visual Studio by default, including the following:

▶ **HTML**—Shows a browser-like dialog box with the HTML interpreted as a user might see it.

▶ **XML**—Shows the XML in a structured format.

- ▶ **Text**—Shows a string value in an easy-to-read format.

- ▶ **WPF Tree Visualizer**—Enables you to view the WPF application events in a meaningful way. We cover WPF applications in Chapter 19, "Creating Richer, Smarter User Interfaces."

- ▶ **DataSet**—Shows the contents of the DataSet, DataView, and DataTable objects.

There is also a framework for writing and installing visualizers in Visual Studio so that you can write your own and plug them into the debugger. You can also download additional visualizers and install them. The possibilities of visualizers are many—as many ways as there are to structure and view data. A few ideas might be a tree-view visualizer that displays hierarchical data or an image visualizer that shows image data structures.

You invoke a visualizer from one of the many places you view data values, including Watch windows and DataTips. Visualizers are represented by a magnifying glass icon. Refer to Figures 11.36 or 11.37 to see an example of launching a visualizer using the icon. Rather than digging through the object hierarchy to get at the data, you can invoke the DataSet visualizer right from a DataTip. Figure 11.38 shows the visualizer in action for the customer DataSet object in the sample application.

Using the Edit and Continue Feature

Edit and Continue enables you to change code as you debug without killing your debug session. You can make a modification to a line of code or even fix a bug and keep working in break mode. Visual Basic developers who worked in versions prior to .NET should recall this powerful tool. Its absence in .NET made it one of the most requested features. The good news is that Edit and Continue was added in 2005 to both Visual Basic and C#. In 2008, this feature was also added to Visual C++.

There is no trick to invoking Edit and Continue. You simply make your code change during a debug session and then keep running through your code with a Step command or Continue.

The feature is turned on by default. If it is turned off, you can reenable it using the Options dialog box available from the Tools menu.

Not all code changes you make are eligible for Edit and Continue. In fact, it should be used only in minor fixes. As a best practice, any major additions to your code should not be done in debug mode. If your change is within the body of a method, it has a higher likelihood of passing the Edit and Continue test. Most code changes outside the method body require the debugger to restart. Some common changes that are not eligible for Edit and Continue include these:

- ▶ Changing code on the current, active statement

- ▶ Changing code on any calls on the stack that lead to the current, active statement

- ▶ Adding new types, methods, fields, events, or properties

- ▶ Changing a method signature

FIGURE 11.38   You can use the DataSet visualizer to quickly view the contents of a data table inside a grid.

For a more exhaustive list, search MSDN for "Edit and Continue." From there, you can link to the Edit and Continue documentation for your chosen language. You can then select the link, titled "Supported Code Changes." Here you can review the full list of supported and unsupported changes for your chosen language.

Advanced Debugging Scenarios

Debugging can sometimes be a complex process. We've looked at many of the straightforward scenarios presented by Windows and Web applications. However, debugging remote processes, multithreaded applications, and multi-core (parallel) applications, for example, present their own needs in terms of configuration and tools. This section presents a few of the more common, advanced debugging scenarios you will encounter.

Remote Debugging

Remote debugging allows you to connect to a running application on another machine or domain and debug that application in its environment. This is often the only way to experience errors that are occurring on specific hardware. We've all heard the developer's cry, "Works on my machine." Remote debugging helps those developers figure out why their application doesn't work in other environments.

Remote debugging makes a lot of sense in various scenarios, such as debugging SQL server–stored procedures, web services, web applications, remote services or processes, and so on.

The hardest part about remote debugging is getting it set up properly. The actual debugging is no different from the debugging we've discussed thus far. However, the setup requires you to jump through a lot of hoops in terms of installation and security. These hoops are necessary because you do not, by default, want developers to easily connect debug sessions to applications on your servers.

There is some good news. Visual Studio tries to minimize and simplify the setup and configuration of remote debugging. Microsoft has written the Remote Debugging Monitor (msvsmon.exe) for this purpose. However, developers still find the setup tasks somewhat arduous (but rewarding when finished). We do not cover the setup in great detail here because it is often environment-specific. We suggest querying MSDN for "Remote Debugging" to get the full walk-through and troubleshooting advice for your specific situation.

We do offer the following, however, as a set of high-level tasks that you need to complete to get remote debugging working:

1. Install the remote debugging monitor (msvsmon.exe) on the remote machine being debugged. You install it using the setup application, rdbsetup.exe. You can also run it from a file share.

2. Configure remote debugging permissions. Typically, this means one of two things. You can set up identical accounts (username and password) on both machines (debugging and server). The debugging account may be local or a domain account. However, the server account should be a local account. Alternatively, you can give your user account administrative access to the machine being debugged, but this is often a security risk that should not be taken lightly.

3. Run the remote debugging monitor on the remote machine. This is a Windows application (with a GUI). You can also set the monitor to run as a Windows service. This capability can be useful for specific server scenarios and ASP.NET remote debugging.

4. If your debug machine is running XP with SP2, you have to configure your security policy and firewall for remote debugging (see the MSDN documentation "How to: Set Up Remote Debugging"). If you are running Windows 7 or Vista, you might have to elevate privileges when running Visual Studio (run as Administrator).

5. Run Visual Studio on your debug machine as you would to debug any process. Open the project that contains the source for the process you want to debug.

6. Attach to the running process on the remote machine using Attach to Process. You have to browse to the machine you want to debug and find the process running on that machine.

As you can see, getting remote debugging set up can be a challenge. However, if you have a test environment that you typically debug, the setup should be a one-time operation. From there, you should be able to debug in a more realistic environment as well as walk through SQL stored procedures.

Debugging WCF Services

For the most part, you debug a web service (or Windows Communication Foundation service) using the same tools and techniques we've discussed to this point. The key to debugging services is properly attaching to them. There are basically two options for this. The first option is to step into a service directly from within code you are debugging (a client calling a service). The second option is to attach to a service that has already been called by a client. Let's look at these options.

Stepping into a WCF Service

You can step directly into a WCF service provided that your calling code (or client) has a two-way contract with the service. This is called a Duplex Contract and it enables the client and the service to communicate with one another. Each can initiate calls. This is useful when your server needs to call back to the client or raise events on the client. You use the ServiceContractAttribute to set this up (see Chapter 22, "Service-Oriented Applications," for more information).

Your client must also be synchronous for this to work. That is, the client cannot make a call to the WCF service asynchronously and then begin doing something else. Instead, it must call and wait.

Attaching to a WCF Service

You can use the Attach to Process option (covered earlier) to debug both WCF and Web Services (.asmx). In these cases, the service is already running typically in a process outside of your current debug environment. To attach and debug to this process, you must make sure you have the code for the service loaded inside of Visual Studio. Next, the service process must be hosted by IIS or the ASP.NET Development Server. Finally, the service must have been invoked by a WCF-based client to gain access to its execution.

Debugging Multithreaded Applications

A multithreaded application is one in which more than a single thread is running in a given process. By default, each process that runs your application has at least one thread of execution. You might create multiple threads to do parallel processing. This can significantly improve performance, especially when run on today's multicore processors and hyperthreading technology. However, multithreading comes at a cost. The code can be more complex to write and more difficult to debug. If you've ever written a multithreaded application, you already know this. For example, just stepping line-by-line in a multithreaded application to debug it might have you jumping from one thread to another. You would then have to keep track of this flow in your head in order to make sense of the diagnostic information you see.

Fortunately, Visual Studio provides a few tools that make the job a bit easier. We do not cover coding a multithreaded application here; rather, we cover the debug options available to you for debugging one such as

▶ The ability to view threads in your source during a debug session

▶ The Debug Location toolbar used to view processes, threads, and flagged threads

▶ The Thread window used to work with a list of threads in your application

▶ Breakpoint filters that enable you to set a breakpoint for an individual thread

Let's look at each of these features in more detail.

Discovering and Flagging Threads

Visual Studio enables you to visualize the threads in your application in debug mode. When you are stopped on a breakpoint, your application is paused and all threads in that application are halted. The threads are still there. They are put in a suspended state so you can examine their statuses. They do not continue until you continue the execution of your code. However, in a multithreaded scenario, threads outside the one on which your code broke might not be easily visible in the debugger. To see them in the Debug menu, you can use the Show Threads in Source option from the Debug menu, as shown in Figure 11.39.

FIGURE 11.39   Select the Show Threads in Source icon from the Debug toolbar to tell Visual Studio to visually display threads in the debug session.

Selecting Show Threads in Source highlights other threads that exist in your code in the indicator margin (or gutter) of the code window during a debug session. The icon used to highlight these items looks like two wavy lines (or cloth threads). Figure 11.40 shows an example of a multithreaded application in a debug session.

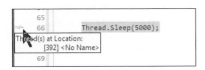

FIGURE 11.40   The thread icon indicates that a thread is stopped on a line of code in the debug session.

NOTE

Most debug scenarios are single-threaded. Therefore, you will not see another thread executing. You must write an application that uses more than one thread in order to see the thread icon in the debugger.

Notice the graphic on the left of line 66. This indicates that a thread exists at this location in your source code. Hovering over the indicator shows the thread (or threads) that are referenced by the indicator. Each thread is shown by its ID number (in brackets) and name (if any).

Now that you've found a thread, you might want to flag it for further monitoring. This simply helps group it with the threads you want to monitor versus those you do not care about. You can flag a thread right from the indicator margin. To do so, right-click the indicator and choose the Flag option on the context menu. Figure 11.41 shows an example.

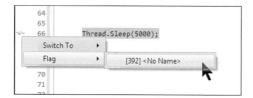

FIGURE 11.41   You can flag a thread to help you keep track of it in the Thread window.

Flagged threads show up highlighted in the Threads window (Debug, Windows, Threads). You can use this window to flag additional threads (or unflag them). Flagged threads provide special grouping in both the Thread window and the Debug Location toolbar. We cover these features next.

Managing Debug Processes and Threads

You can switch between the processes you are debugging and the threads within those processes by using the Debug Location toolbar (you might have to right-click the toolbar area and add this toolbar to the IDE). This toolbar is shown in Figure 11.42. On the left is the Process list. Here you can select a process to view details about that process, including executing threads. Many multithreaded applications are run within a single process, however.

FIGURE 11.42   The Debug Location toolbar.

The Thread list (Figure 11.43) on the toolbar shows a list of threads for the selected process. Notice that the threads are shown with their IDs, names, and flag indicators. You can select a thread in this list to jump to source code associated with the thread. If no source code is associated with a selected thread, the thread name is shown as red when you select it. You can filter the list to show only flagged threads by toggling the second button to the right of the Thread list (shown with two flags). The first button to the right flags (or unflags) the current, active thread. Finally, the list on the right shows the call stack. The active stack frame in the call stack is what is shown in the debug windows (Watch, Local, Autos, and so on).

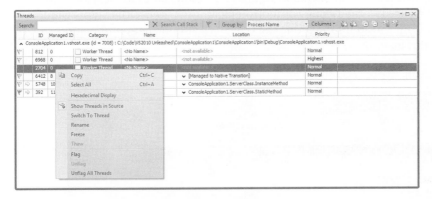

FIGURE 11.43   The Threads window provides total control over the threads in a debug session.

You can also manage threads from within the Threads window (Debug, Windows, Threads). Here you see all threads listed for a given process. Figure 11.43 shows an example. Notice that the left of the list shows flagged threads. We have flagged a thread in a sample application. Notice also that these threads can be named. This allows for easy recognition in the Name column.

There are several options available when you right-click a thread in the window. The options are shown in the context menu in Figure 11.43. Notice the Switch to Thread option, which allows you to switch the active thread being debugged. The active thread is shown with a yellow arrow in the thread list (to the right of the flag). Switching active threads changes the debug context and content in the debug windows. You can also Freeze (or pause) threads using this context menu. (Of course, you can then thaw (or resume) them, too.) Freezing a thread is equivalent to suspending it. The icons for freezing and thawing selected threads are on the far right side of the toolbar in the Threads window. The Threads window has a number of other features. You can use it to search the calls stack, group threads by process, id, category, priority, suspended state, and more.

TIP

When debugging multi-threaded applications, it's often easier to freeze all but one thread. This allows you to focus on what is happening with the given thread.

Inspecting Individual Threads   When your application hits a breakpoint, all executing threads are paused. This enables you to inspect them individually. As you've seen, you can use the Debug Locations toolbar (refer to Figure 11.42) to change the selected thread.

Doing so reconfigures the debug windows. This includes the call stack and watch windows (including Autos and Locals).

For example, imagine you are working on an application that has a main thread of execution. It might then create two additional threads on which it does work. When you break into the application, you can inspect the main thread and its current state or any of the other threads spawned by the application. Figure 11.44 shows an example. Notice the Main Thread is selected in the Debug Locations toolbar. Next, notice the Locals window pertains to this main thread information. The Call Stack also includes information about the lifetime of this main thread.

FIGURE 11.44   You can use Visual Studio to inspect individual threads during a debug session.

As further illustration, suppose that you selected another thread from the Debug Locations toolbar. Figure 11.45 shows the Worker1 thread selected (threads were named inside the code). Notice that the code window changes to the current line being executed by this thread. Because this is not the active thread, this icon is a different type of arrow and the selection is green (by default). In addition, the Locals window now shows values for this thread and the Call Stack shows the lifeline of this code.

FIGURE 11.45   Selecting another thread in a debug session allows you to view the call stack for that thread and inspect its variables.

Breaking Based on a Specific Thread   You can also break on a line of code when it hits a thread. To do so, set a breakpoint in your code and choose a breakpoint filter (covered earlier). Figure 11.46 shows an example. You can choose to break based on the thread ID or its name. In this case, the breakpoint is hit based on the thread ID.

FIGURE 11.46   You can add a breakpoint filter to stop Visual Studio on a specific thread.

Debugging Parallel Applications

A parallel application is one that executes code simultaneously. This includes multithreading applications. Therefore, the multithreading debugging discussed thus far is applicable to parallel applications. However, there are additional features of the .NET languages, the framework, and the Visual Studio Debugger to help support parallel coding scenarios. These features are an attempt to take advantage of the recent proliferation of manycore processors. Developers want to take advantage of this computer power, which means developers need to begin changing the way they write their applications to take advantage of the multiple cores, each capable of running one or more threads in parallel.

This section covers two of the new debugging features that help support parallel programming: Parallel Stack and Parallel Tasks. Some of these features also apply to multithreaded applications. However, the main focus of these features is parallel applications written for multi-core. Recall that parallel programming means task-based programming using the new features of .NET 4.0. You can refer to Chapter 3, "The .NET Languages" for a short discussion on parallel programming (System.Threading.Task, Parallel.For, and so on). You can also skip ahead to Chapter 21, "Working with Databases" for a discussion on PLINQ.

The Parallel Stacks Window

As more cores become available and more programming is done to support those cores, more threads will be executing. You therefore need additional support for debugging the processing complexities of your application. The Parallel Stacks window provides some help. It gives you a view of either all threads or all tasks executing at any given moment in time. The view is a diagram that shows the threads or tasks in your application, how they were created, and full call stack information for each thread or stack.

Parallel Stacks Thread View   You access the Parallel Stacks window in an active debug session from the Debug menu (Debug, Windows, Parallel Stacks). This window provides a visual diagram of the threads executing in your application. Figure 11.47 shows an example of the threads view in the Parallel Stacks window.

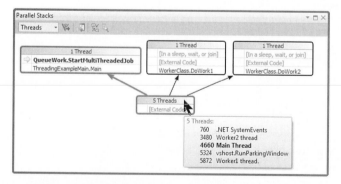

FIGURE 11.47   Use Threads view of the Parallel Stacks window to visualize your threads.

In this example, notice that there are five (5) threads in the application. However, only three are shown. As you can see, if you hover over one of the thread call stack boxes you can see the thread IDs and their names (if they have been named). Hovering over the initial grouping (5 Threads) shows three threads represented by the code in this application (Main, Worker1, Worker2). It also shows the external code threads that are hidden by default in the diagram (.NET SystemEvents and vshost.RunParkingWindow).

TIP

You can visualize external code (including that being executed by the framework) in the Parallel Stacks Window by right-clicking in the window and selecting Show External Code.

The arrows in the diagram indicate that the application creates three threads: Main, Worker1, Worker2. You can see how the threads were spawned, their ID, their name, and their call stack. You can use each thread's call stack information to switch to the code associated with a thread (and thus debug its context) by double-clicking.

Notice the toolbar in this window has the Threads option selected (as opposed to tasks). You can toggle between tasks (see the next section) and threads. The other options for this toolbar are shown in Figure 11.48.

FIGURE 11.48   The toolbar in the Parallel Stacks window.

Switching to method view using the toolbar (refer to Figure 11.48) changes the diagram to highlight (or pivot on) a specific method in your code. In this view, you can see all threads that enter the given method along with their call stacks up to that method. You can then see the exit points from the method and the call stacks following the method's exit.

Figure 11.49 shows an example of method view. In this simple example, there are two (2) threads that both call into the WorkerClass.DoMoreWork method. You can highlight this method by double-clicking on it in the standard, threads view. You then select the method view from the toolbar to show the diagram from the point-of-view of the method. Notice that you can see the two threads and their call stacks leading up to the entrance to the DoMoreWork method. You can also see that this method made an additional call out to the EvenMoreWork method for both threads.

FIGURE 11.49   Use the method view to show all threads that enter and exit a method along with the related call stack information.

Parallel Stacks Task View   You can toggle the Parallel Stacks window to show tasks instead of threads. You can use the drop-down in the toolbar to switch from threads to tasks. You can then use the same diagram tool and related features to visualize tasks as you would threads. Both tasks and threads are joined together in this same tool window as they are such similar concepts. Of course, this feature requires that your application is coded to use tasks.

Recall that tasks are bits of work that can be executed in parallel by two or more processor cores. You code tasks using the task scheduling service in the .NET Framework's parallel task library (System.Threading.Task namespace). The task scheduler provides a number of services such as managing thread pools on each core and providing synchronization services for your code. This is an additional layer of abstraction over simply managing your own threads or using the ThreadPool class. Instead, the framework handles cores and threads. Therefore, trying to debug task-based applications at the thread level is a challenge given the framework (and not your code) is typically managing the threads.

Visual Studio provides two principal windows for looking at the task-level abstraction of multi-core development: Parallel Stacks (in tasks view) and the Parallel Tasks windown. We discuss the latter in moment. First, let look at what can be done to view tasks using the Parallel Stacks window.

> **TIP**
>
> If you are debugging unfamiliar, but parallel code and are unsure if it uses tasks or threads you can enable external code in the Parallel Tasks window (right-click, select Show External Code). In thread view you can see if there are calls to the Task class. This indicates the code was written using multi-task (and not simply multi-threads).

You switch to task view by selecting Tasks in the drop-down of the Parallel Stacks toolbar. This shows the call stacks for each task being executed. It also shows you the status of the task (waiting, running, scheduled). Figure 11.50 shows you an example. The debugger is stopped inside a simple task-based application that tries to do multiple work steps simultaneously (queued up with calls to Task.Factory.StartNew). Visual Studio displays this as two tasks. The first (on the left) is in the waiting state (indicated by the question mark icon). The second is running (indicated by the arrow). Notice you can see full call stacks for each task.

FIGURE 11.50   You can switch the Parallel Stacks window to Tasks view in order to view the tasks running in your debug session.

This abstracted view helps you see the tasks in your application without worrying so much about on which processor and thread they are executing. Of course, you can switch to thread view to see this information, too. Figure 11.51 shows the same code at the same breakpoint in the same window but for threads view. Notice that in this simple example, the parallel framework has created threads that are very similar to the tasks (two main threads executing the work). If, however, you start to add a lot more work to this application you start to see inactive threads that are sitting in the pool waiting to do work. You also start to see a single thread executing larger call stacks (due to reuse) that do not align with your task view.

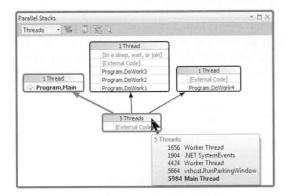

FIGURE 11.51   The Threads view of the same spot in a debug session depicted by the Tasks view shown in Figure 11.50.

The Parallel Tasks Window

Another way to look at the tasks running in your application is through the Parallel Tasks window (Debug, Windows, Parallel Tasks). This window is actually similar to the Threads window (refer to Figure 11.43) but it shows the abstraction layer of tasks for those developers doing multi-core, task-based development.

Figure 11.52 shows an example of this window running for a parallel application. Notice that for each task (in this case there are seven) you can view the task ID, status, location, the task (or entry point for the task), the thread assignment, and application domain. Note that this example groups the tasks by their status (running, waiting, scheduled, deadlocked). This is done by right-clicking the status column and selecting Group by Status from the context menu.

ID	Status	Location	Task	Thread Assignment	AppDomain
⌄ 🏷 Running (1)					
7	▶ Running		Action<object>()	8220 (Worker Thread)	1 (TaskDebugging.vshost.ex
⌄ 🏷 Scheduled (4)					
2	ⓘ Scheduled		DoWork5()		1 (TaskDebugging.vshost.ex
3	ⓘ Scheduled		DoWork1()		1 (TaskDebugging.vshost.ex
4	ⓘ Scheduled		DoWork7()		1 (TaskDebugging.vshost.ex
5	ⓘ Scheduled		DoWork8()		1 (TaskDebugging.vshost.ex
⌄ 🏷 Waiting (2)					
1	❓ Waiting	TaskDebu	DoWork1()	7876 (Worker Thread)	1 (TaskDebugging.vshost.ex
6	❓ Waiting	TaskDebu	DoWork2()	8292 (Worker Thread)	1 (TaskDebugging.vshost.ex

FIGURE 11.52   You can use the Parallel Tasks window in a similar manner as you would the Threads window.

You can also use the parallel tasks window to flag tasks for viewing. You do so using the arrows on the left-side of each task in the dialog box. You can also right-click a task to freeze or thaw its associated thread. Alternatively, you can use the right-click command, Freeze All Threads But This, to focus in on a specific thread and task.

The location column shows the current location of the task. If you hover over this location you see the call stack for the task. This is all code called thus far in the given task. This mouse-over is actually actionable. It is called a stack tip. The stack tip enables you to switch between stack frames and view the code inside a given call in the stack. Figure 11.53 shows an example of selecting an item from a stack tip. You can double-click this item to be taken to the code and change the debug context to focus on this call.

ID	Status	Location	Task	Thread Assignment	AppDomain
⌄ 🏷 Running (1)					
2	▶ Running	TaskDebugging.Program.DoWork4	DoWork4()	3936 (Worker Thread	1 (TaskDebug
⌄ 🏷 Waiting (3)					
1	❓ Waiting	TaskDebugging.Program.DoWork7	DoWork7()	1504 (Worker Thread	1 (TaskDebug
3	❓ Waiting	TaskDebugging.Program.DoWork8	DoWork8()	5688 (Worker Thread	1 (TaskDebug
4	❓ Waiting	TaskDebugging.P			

> [In a sleep, wait, or join]
> [External Code]
> TaskDebugging.exe!TaskDebugging.Program.DoWork3() Line 43 + 0xa bytes
> TaskDebugging.exe!TaskDebugging.Program.DoWork2() Line 39 + 0x5 bytes
> TaskDebugging.exe!TaskDebugging.Program.DoWork1() Line 35 + 0x5 bytes

FIGURE 11.53   The Location column includes an actionable stack tip window that represents the call stack for the given task.

Debugging a Client-Side Script

Visual Studio lets you debug your client-side script (Javascript and VBScript) by enabling script debugging in the browser. This can be done in Internet Explorer using the Internet Options dialog box (Tools, Internet Options). From this dialog box, select the Advanced tab and then navigate to the Browsing category (see Figure 11.54). Here you need to uncheck the Disable Script Debugging option (checked by default). This tells IE that if it encounters a script error, it should look for a debugger (such as Visual Studio).

FIGURE 11.54   You can enable client-side script debugging from IE's Options dialog box.

Next, set breakpoints inside your .aspx or .html files within your <script> blocks. You can then stop on these lines and debug them with Visual Studio. There are some limitations, however. If you are having trouble, review "Limitations on Script Debugging" in the MSDN documentation.

Debugging Crash Information (Dump Files)

It is often not possible to re-create all environment- or user-specific scenarios in a development environment. Of course many application bugs or crashes happen without the developer present, or a copy of Visual Studio running. In these cases, you can output a dump file of the application state at the time of the issue.

Dump files save information about the state of your application. Dump files are typically created in response to a major bug or an application failure (crash). The dump file can then be sent to a developer. A developer can open the file, connect it with the source code and debug symbols, and debug the state of the application at the time of the issue.

Dumping Debug Information

You can save running (but paused or on a breakpoint) .NET managed code as minidump files. You have a few options for creating these files. In a debugging setting, you can use Visual Studio to create these files and share them with other developers as necessary. Of course, other applications can also create minidump files which then can be opened by Visual Studio for debugging. Your options for creating dump files include

▶ Use the Save Dump As option from the Debug menu in an active debug session of Visual Studio.

▶ Attach to a running (or crashed) remote process from Visual Studio (see the information about attaching to a process earlier in this chapter). You can then break into that process and save the dump file using the Save Dump As option.

▶ Microsoft provides the utility UserDump as part of their OEM Support Tools. You can use this utility to create dump files that Visual Studio can read.

▶ Microsoft provides the Autodump+ utility as part of the Microsoft Debugging Tools for Windows. It, too, creates dump files for use by Visual Studio.

We focus on how Visual Studio creates dump files. A quick web search will lead you to the download for other dump-creating utilities.

Using Visual Studio to Create a Dump File   Creating a dump file with Visual Studio is straightforward. You stop (or break into) the application at the point you want to capture. This might be at a place in the testing where there is a known issue. You then select the Save Dump As option from the Debug menu. The Save Dump As dialog box is then displayed as shown in Figure 11.55.

FIGURE 11.55   You can save a minidump file with or without heap information.

Notice that when you save a dump file you can choose between creating the file with heap information and without. The heap information is often not required for many managed code debugging scenarios. Thus, you can save your file without it and conserve hard drive space.

Debugging with a Dump File

The first step to debugging with a dump file is to open the file from the File menu (File, Open, File) or by double-clicking the dump file. When you open a dump file, the new Dump File summary page appears. This page displays information about the dump file, such as when the dump file was created, the version of the OS and CLR that was running when the dump file was written, and the versions of the various other components (modules) that were running at the time. Figure 11.56 shows an example of this new summary page. Notice that you can use the modules search box to determine if a specific .dll or .exe was loaded at the time of the dump.

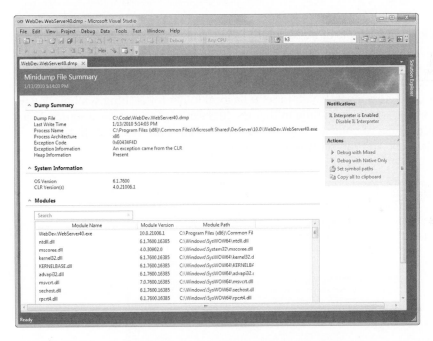

FIGURE 11.56   The minidump summary page shows you both detailed information and next steps (actions) when you open a dump file.

The summary page shown in Figure 11.56 represents a dump file from a break in the Contoso application discussed earlier in the chapter. Recall that this application includes a page that allows a customer to manage her profile that's stored in a database. In this case, an error has occurred. Imagine a scenario where the developer looking at the error could not debug it. Therefore, he might create a dump file and pass it to another developer to take a look. Alternatively, the dump could have come from a tester that encountered the error or from the web server.

The dump summary page provides a few actions. The two developers use the most are Set Symbol Paths and Debug with Mixed. The Set Symbol Paths option enables you to indicate the paths to the symbol files (.pdb) that match the build of the application from which the dump originated. By default, Visual Studio looks for symbol files in the location where your code executed. Therefore, if you dump and open that dump on the same machine, you have nothing more to set up. Visual Studio finds your symbol files. If, however, symbol files are created on a per-build basis and dumps can originate from anywhere, you have to use Set Symbol Paths to indicate where Visual Studio should find your latest symbols.

IMPORTANT

Symbol files (.pdb) are important if you intend to debug a built application. For this reason, we recommend you store your symbol files in a safe location along with the compiled versions of your deployed code to make debugging a production issue using a dump much easier.

Figure 11.57 shows an example of the Options, Debugging, Symbols dialog box. In the top part of the dialog box you can set up a symbol location, whichmight be a server where builds are dropped or a local folder on your machine. Notice, too, that you can load the Microsoft Public Symbols from their servers. The middle section of the dialog box, Cache Symbols in This Directory, enables you to set up a local folder for caching symbols downloaded from a server, which saves time in that the files can load from a local source. You indicate which modules of your symbol files should be loaded (or excluded) in the last part of the dialog box. You can set this option to All Modules.

FIGURE 11.57   You can use the Symbols options to indicate a location for symbol files and set up a local cache.

The other option, Debug with Mixed, enables you to start the debugger using the data found in the minidump file. It is helpful to know that a .NET symbol file (.pdb) essentially contains information about your source files, variable names, and code line numbers. When you debug a dump file, Visual Studio looks at the .pdb files it finds (searching your code or your symbol directory) and tries to use this information to find your code files on your machine. If it can locate your code it opens the code file and gives you a rich debugging experience. Figure 11.58 shows an example of a dump file after clicking the Debug with Mixed option. Notice that the line where the code broke is highlighted. You can also get full call stack and Watch window information. In this case, the error was the connection string to the database.

FIGURE 11.58   You can re-create a debugging experience using a minidump file.

Summary

This chapter presented the Visual Studio 2010 debugger. We covered setting breakpoints in code as well as setting conditions for when those breakpoints are hit. We discussed stepping through code after hitting that breakpoint. In addition, we presented tracepoints, which perform an action (such as printing a message to the output window) when a line of code is hit in the debugger. The chapter also examined the many ways you can see the data presented by the debugger, including the Watch windows, visualizers, and DataTips.

The advanced debugging scenarios covered included remote processes, web services, multithreaded applications, multi-core, and client-side script. Lastly, we showed how you can use the minidump features to take a snapshot of a running application and debug it at a later time on a different machine.

The Visual Studio 2010 debugger is sure to speed your overall development effort. This is a key skill to have. Honing your skills with the debugging tools is yet another way to unlock additional productivity.

Deploying Code

Visual Studio is primarily a coding and development tool. But after you have built an application, the next problem you face is how to get it into the hands of the users. This is not an insignificant problem space. Applications might have a variety of prerequisites that need to be verified: Is the right version of the .NET Framework installed? Does the target machine have SQL Server installed? Is a supported operating system detected?

In addition to prerequisites, the actual install process involves myriad variables. Some applications are simple enough to enjoy the ability to do "xcopy deployment." In other words, you simply copy the executable over to the target machine and away you go. But there are certainly more complicated scenarios as well. For instance, your application might store some data in the registry and might require registry values to be set upon install. Or there might be a particular folder structure required. Or maybe a database schema needs to be configured, and data populated, during the deployment process.

Visual Studio can help with all of these scenarios. In this chapter we examine how you can use Visual Studio to package and deploy .NET client applications. We also investigate how you can deploy server-based, ASP.NET web applications.

An Overview of Client Deployment Options

There are two primary installation and deployment technologies available within Visual Studio: ClickOnce and

Windows Installer. Both of these vehicles are similar in that they enable you to move binaries and components from one location and install them onto a target client machine. But there are definitely pros and cons to dealing with each.

Introducing ClickOnce Deployments

ClickOnce was created to try and match the low-deployment factor of web applications. With web applications, users can merely open a browser and click on a link to access functionality. In fact, with ClickOnce, you can publish a set of binaries to a web server or file share, and users can simply click on a link to the ClickOnce package to have the application installed onto their machine.

There are three ways to deploy an application using ClickOnce:

▶ **Web/Share Deployment**—In this model, your application executables or DLLs are first published to a web server or network share. You can then provide a link (either a web URL or network path) to binaries. Users can click on this link to have the applications automatically installed onto their current machine (thus the moniker "ClickOnce"). No further interaction is required from the user.

▶ **CD Deployment**—With this method, binaries are packaged and copied onto a CD or DVD. Users then browse the content of the media and launch the install process with one click. This method is primarily used for situations where users are isolated and do not have the required Internet access or network access to make the web/share deployment method useful.

▶ **Web/Share Execution**—This scenario is nearly identical to the first method we discussed. Binaries are published to a web location or network share, and a link to that location is then provided to users. When the user clicks that link the binaries are immediately copied over and the application starts without making a permanent home for the app on the user's PC. After a user closes the application, it is like it was never there in the first place; all of the application binaries are removed, there are no entries placed within the Start menu or within the Add or Remove Programs list in the Control Panel, and so on. To the user, it appears as if the application has been run directly from the Internet (or network share), although in fact the binaries have been cached on to the local machine.

ClickOnce applications are extremely easy to deploy for developers, and they are extremely easy for users to install because little interaction is required and there is little overall footprint on the client. However, this simplicity comes with a price. Generally speaking, ClickOnce deployments can't do any of the more complicated things we referenced in the introduction to this chapter, such as modifying registry settings, or installing third-party software. If your install scenario is too complicated for ClickOnce to handle, you have to turn to Windows Installer.

Introducing Windows Installer-Based Deployments

The Windows Installer is the traditional way to get a piece of software installed under Windows. The basic process looks like this:

1. You bundle your application and its resources within a "setup package." This package is actually a .msi file, and is a cohesive unit of deployment that is understood by the Windows Installer runtime.

2. The .msi file is delivered to the end users.

3. Running the .msi file launches a wizard that guides the user through the install process. This typically includes querying for information such as where the software should be installed on the hard drive, and specifying various options that the software might support in terms of feature set selection.

With very few limitations, you can craft a setup wizard to handle a variety of situations including different payloads based on the running OS version, adding a shortcut to the Windows startup group, adding registry entries, and installing device drivers.

> **NOTE**
>
> Certain applications have special deployment requirements. We re-examine the topic of deployment for the other major application types within each chapter that covers those types. For example, for Azure, cloud-based applications, you should read Chapter 25, "Developing Applications in the Cloud with Windows Azure."

Publishing a Project with ClickOnce

You create a ClickOnce install by first configuring the correct "publish" options for your project. These are all located on the project properties dialog box, under the Publish tab (see Figure 12.1).

You can see that this property page holds a variety of settings including where to host the ClickOnce installation, and how we want to handle the offline versus online aspects of ClickOnce. To make things easy for our first deployment, we let the Publish Wizard walk us through setting these options. Click on the Publish Wizard button at the bottom of the Publish property page to get started.

The first page of the wizard captures where we want to publish our application. This can be a path to a file share, or a URL pointing to a website or FTP site directory.

Page two of the wizard (Figure 12.2) identifies how users install the application. There are three choices here: via a website, via a network share, or from physical media (CD/DVD).

The first two selections require you to enter the exact location where users can download the software. At first glance, it's not clear what is different about the location specified here and the location specified on page one. Let's clarify what is happening with an example. Let's assume, for instance, that we want users of our application to be able to install the Windows Forms client by visiting a link on the Contoso website. In this scenario, we might end up with the following values:

- **Publishing folder location**—c:\inetpub\wwwroot\ContosoCSRInstall

- **Installation folder location**—http://www.contoso.com/CSR/Install.htm

FIGURE 12.1 Setting ClickOnce publication properties.

FIGURE 12.2 Setting the install type in the Publish Wizard.

The first path is the physical path that Visual Studio uses to copy the installation files to their home. The second path is the path (in this case, a URL) that the world uses to access those installation files.

The third and final page of the wizard varies slightly depending on the install option we selected on page two. For website and network share installs, we must indicate whether the application should be available online and offline, or just online. Offline capable applications have a shortcut added to the Start menu and can be uninstalled through the normal Add/Remove Programs control panel. Online-only applications are run directly from the Installation folder location. If we had selected the CD/DVD installation option, then we have the opportunity to specify whether or not the application updates itself when online.

After the wizard finishes, the project builds and immediately tries to publish using the information collected. Visual Studio then launches a browser and navigates to the install location. For a look at what a default ClickOnce install web page looks like, see Figure 12.3. The look and feel of a ClickOnce page can be easily customized by editing the HTML.

FIGURE 12.3   A ClickOnce install point (web page).

NOTE

You don't need to go through the entire Publish Wizard every time you want to deploy or re-deploy your application. After you have the options set the way you want them on the Publish property page, you can republish using those settings by selecting Publish from the Visual Studio Build menu.

Now let's move on, and see how we can accomplish the same end result using Visual Studio and the Windows Installer technology.

Publishing a Project with the Windows Installer

For deploying complicated installations, the Windows Installer is a great approach. For those situations where you want to get an application up and running in a short time with minimal user interaction, the Windows Installer can be overkill. This is where ClickOnce can be a better option.

Just as with ClickOnce, Visual Studio directly supports deployment of applications using the Windows Installer technology. The approach is different (as are the underlying technologies); Windows Installer deployments are created with the use of a separate project template/project type. So our first step is to add a deployment project to our existing ContosoCSR solution.

Right-click the solution, select Add, New Project, and then find the Visual Studio Installer template group by first expanding Other Project Types and then Setup and Deployment. You should see a set of project templates that include the Setup Wizard project type (see Figure 12.4). For our purposes, we start with the wizard. Give your setup project a name, and click OK to add it to the solution. This immediately launches the Setup Wizard.

FIGURE 12.4   Windows Installer project types.

The first screen in the Setup Wizard is the welcome screen. Next, you are asked to indicate the type of setup project that should be created. There are four options here. The first two are self-explanatory: You can create a Windows application setup project or a web application setup project. For the purposes of this chapter, select the Create a Setup for a Windows Application option (Figure 12.5).

FIGURE 12.5   Creating a Windows application setup project.

NOTE

The other two options for creating a redistributable package (refer to Figure 12.5) enable you to create a Windows Installer merge module, or a standalone CAB file. We won't cover either in this chapter because they stray from our primary goal of quickly getting a Windows form deployed. In terms of gaining a rudimentary understanding of these options, a merge module is a shared install component that is meant to be re-used across multiple setup projects, and a CAB file is used to bundle files together in one compressed container file.

The next page of the wizard provides a way to indicate the exact files to include in the setup project. Of course, we want to include the compiled binaries that constitute our application; these are listed as Primary Output. But you also have the option to include things such as documentation files, source files, or satellite assemblies that you might have for localizing the application. Select Primary Output and then click Next (Figure 12.6).

FIGURE 12.6   Including files in the installation package.

The next page of the wizard prompts for any other files (contained within the project or not) that should be added to the installation set. This is the ideal place to specify documentation/read-me files, graphics files, or any other supporting file that might not be directly included or referenced in your Windows Forms project. Finally, the last page of the wizard summarizes the selections we have made; click Finish to create the setup project.

When a setup project is first created, Visual Studio initially displays the File System editor. There are actually six different setup editors supported by Visual Studio: the File System editor, the Registry editor, the File Types editor, the User Interface editor, the Custom Actions editor, and the Launch Conditions editor. Each of these different views of a setup project are accessed by first selecting the setup project in the Solution Explorer, and then selecting the View, Editor menus in the IDE. Deployment editors are used in conjunction with one another to build the correct end-state for every target system that installs your application. Let's examine each in turn.

The File System Editor

Every client install involves copying files off the install media and placing those files in specific locations on the end user's system. This is the File System editor's domain. In essence, it maps which files go where. The interface for this editor (see Figure 12.7) is meant to mimic the folder structure on the target system, so we have a left pane that shows the various default folders we can copy files to, and the right pane identifies the files to copy into each folder. By default, you see that the primary output files that we selected earlier in the wizard are already placed within the Application Folder destination.

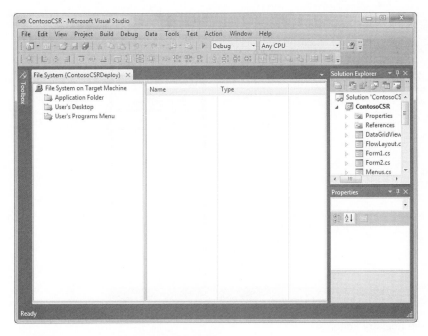

FIGURE 12.7   The File System Editor.

The folders that are listed in the File System editor are actually alias names for physical directories. You can examine, and set, the physical mapping between the folder alias and the actual directory through the properties window for the folder. Click on the folder and look for the DefaultLocation property in the property window. The value for the Application Folder, for example, is set to [ProgramFilesFolder][Manufacturer]\ [ProductName]. For the user's desktop, it is set to DesktopFolder. These location names are referred to as Special Folders. They represent another level of abstraction for predefined directories that exist in a Windows install. The DesktopFolder, for example, physically represents c:\Users\<username>\Desktop on Windows 7, and the System Folder represents c:\windows\system32.

To add a folder that doesn't appear in the current folder list, right-click anywhere in the left pane, and select any of the stock special folders or create a custom folder. (Custom folders are used in scenarios where you want to create your own directory that doesn't appear in a normal Windows installation.) To add a file to a folder, right-click in the right pane of the editor and then select Add. From there, you can browse to any of the files or project outputs.

The Registry Editor

The Registry Editor is used to create or modify registry entries on the target computer. The left pane of the editor shows the four HKEY "hives," and the User/Machine hive. You can walk down through the registry folder structure, find the location for your registry key, and then right click in the right pane to specify the key name and default value (see Figure 12.8).

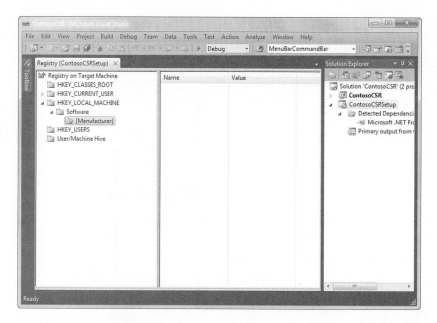

FIGURE 12.8   The Registry Editor.

The File Types Editor

The File Types Editor (Figure 12.9) is used to make file associations for your application. For example, if our Contoso CSR application was able to read and write to a certain file format, we would probably have a custom file extension (perhaps .tik for customer service ticket). The setup process could make that file name extension to application executable association for us so that users opening a .tik file would automatically have the Contoso CSR app loaded.

To make a file type association, right-click File Types on Target Machine within the editor, and select Add File Type from the pop-up menu. This adds a new entry. Using the properties window, you enter the filename extensions with the Extensions property. The executable to be associated with that filename extension is then entered into the Command property field (see Figure 12.10).

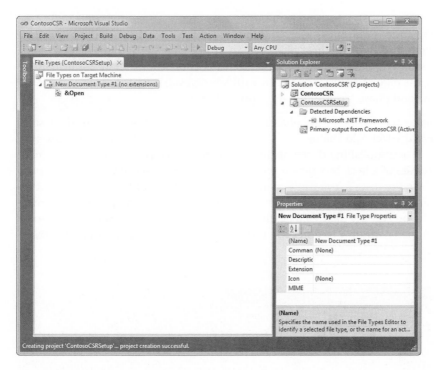

FIGURE 12.9   The File Types Editor.

FIGURE 12.10   Mapping a command to a filename extension.

The User Interface Editor

The User Interface Editor enables you to customize the appearance of the Install Wizard that is used by the Windows Installer. You can think of the Installer Wizard as a series of dialog boxes that are meant to either collect information from the user (such as an install path or installation options) or relay information to the user (such as a progress indicator for keeping track of the install process). The Windows installer provides a basic set of these screens that are grouped into the three phases of an install. The Start phase consists of an initial welcome screen, a dialog box to capture the installation folder, and a confirmation screen. The Progress phase has just one screen with a progress bar that measures current progress. And the End phase has a summary "Finished" screen.

To add a new dialog box to one of the phases, right-click on the phase name in the User Interface Editor and select Add Dialog. You can select from a stable of canned windows that are capable of accomplishing different things (Figure 12.11). For example, there are a few different varieties of Check box dialog boxes used to put up a set of yes/no configuration options during the install. You can't change the look and feel of these screens, but you can customize the text and certain other properties by using the properties window. As an example, if you add the dialog box called Check boxes (B) to your Start phase, you would use the property window to enter the text for the four check boxes supported by that dialog box.

FIGURE 12.11   Selecting a dialog box to add to add to the installer.

To change the order of dialog boxes within a particular phase, click on one of the dialog box entries and then move that screen up or down in the list using the Action menu and the Move Up and Move Down commands.

The Custom Actions Editor

If you have unique installation requirements not covered by the provided set of setup activities, you can implement them using the Custom Actions Editor. For instance, your software might need to register itself over the Internet. The Custom Actions Editor isn't used to actually build the custom action per se; it merely lets you identify an executable or script file that needs to be run and when that file should be run during the install process. There are four phases from which we can pick: Install, Commit, Rollback, and Uninstall. In our example, if we want to run a .exe file to register the CSR application over the Internet, we might want to make that happen in the Install phase, with a corresponding action in the Uninstall phase to de-register the application.

To indicate which file to run during which phase, right-click on the target phase in the Custom Actions Editor and select Add Custom Action. In the resulting box, select the executable or script file to run (Figure 12.12).

FIGURE 12.12   Adding a custom action.

The Launch Conditions Editor

The last editor to cover is the Launch Conditions Editor. Most application installers need to check for a set of pre-existing conditions for beginning the setup process. You might only support certain operating systems, or you might require certain other components to be already installed on the target machine. Figure 12.13 shows the Launch Conditions Editor open in the IDE.

FIGURE 12.13   The Launch Conditions Editor.

If our ContosoCSR application required SQL Server to be pre-installed, we would check for that condition using the Launch Conditions Editor. First, we have to decide what we look for to determine the launch condition. We could look for the presence of certain files on the target machine, we could look for certain key values in the registry, or we could look for an application in the installer database which is kept on every Windows PC. In this case, we check the registry. Specifically, we look for the presence of SQL Server Express version 10 by checking the value of CurrentVersion under HKEY_LOCAL_MACHINE\SOFTWARE\Microsoft\Microsoft SQL Server\SQLEXPRESS\MSSQLSERVER\CurrentVersion. This is a two step process using the editor. First, we need to add the search for that registry key, and then we need to set up a condition check that compares the results of that search against our setup requirements and returns a boolean YES or NO.

To add the registry key search, right-click on the Search Target Machine node in the left pane of the editor. Then select Add Registry Search (note that we could have also selected one of the other two search types from this same menu). With the search entry added, we give it a descriptive name (SQLExpress-v10), and with the search selected we use the property window to indicate where we need to perform the search within the registry. In Figure 12.14 you can see the values we have entered for the search. Take note of the value for Property: REGISTRYVALUE1. This is how we refer to this search. We could change Property value, but the default value works just fine for now.

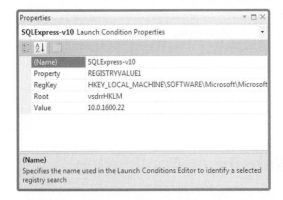

FIGURE 12.14   Setting properties for a registry search.

With the search added into the editor, we can now add the condition check. Right-click the Launch Conditions node and then select Add Launch Condition. Just as with our search entry, we want to give this condition a name and then use the properties window to configure the condition. There are three fields to fill in: The Condition property contains the name of the search that we want to evaluate; the InstallURL contains an optional URL that directs users to a download location if they don't have SQL Express installed; and the Message property contains the message we want to present to users if they don't have our prerequisite database installed.

Figure 12.15 shows the properties fully populated for our launch condition.

FIGURE 12.15   Setting the launch condition properties.

NOTE

We have been interacting with these editors by right-clicking in their panes to access the action menu. The action menu is also available as a top-level menu in the IDE whenever one of the setup editors is loaded. Its contents are dynamic and change to correspond to the valid commands for the currently open editor.

So we have now covered the two principal ways to deploy client applications. You can also deploy ASP.NET applications from the IDE.

Publishing an ASP.NET Website or Application

Visual Studio provides two sets of tools for ASP.NET deployment. The first, accessed via the Build menu, is called the Web Deployment Tool.

Using the Web Deployment Tool, you can take an existing web application project, compile it, bundle all of the folders, files, settings, and databases that are used by that application into a Web package, and then deploy that package to a web server. One advantage to compiling your website before deploying is that the compiler finds compile-time errors for you before deploying onto the target server. Another advantage you gain by compiling your application is increased page performance. Because all of the pages within the site are precompiled, the need to compile dynamically during the first page hit is removed.

The second tool is the Copy Web Site Tool. This tool is designed to deploy websites, as opposed to web applications (for a thorough treatment on the difference, please consult Chapter 4, "Solutions and Projects," and Chapter 17, "Creating ASP.NET Applications"). As its name implies, the Copy Web Site Tool takes all of the files contained within your website and copies them over to a destination folder structure on the target server. This tool is useful because of its synchronization capabilities. Instead of just copying files in one direction (from source to target), it actually performs a full synchronization between the target and source, which means that a file on the server that has a newer data stamp will be copied down to your project. This is great for scenarios where multiple developers or even multiple teams of developers are publishing to the same site and there is no central source control repository available.

In contrast to the Web Deployment Tool, the Copy Web Site Tool is capable of copying to remote machines.

Let's continue with a brief walkthrough on both deployment mechanisms.

Using the Web Deployment Tool

The Web Deployment Tool is accessed via the Build menu; specifically, via the Publish command (Figure 12.16).

FIGURE 12.16   Launching the Web Deployment Tool from within the IDE.

Before we jump into the tool, we need to configure our publication settings. Access the project properties page and navigate to the Package/Publish and Deploy SQL tabs to get to the publication settings.

Package/Publish Options

The Package/Publish tab houses all of the default information that is used by the Web Deployment Tool (Figure 12.17).

The first-drop down on this window provides a way to indicate which files should be included during the deployment process. There are three options: only the files needed to run the application (for example., all web pages, config files, binaries, and so on), all of the files within the project (including non-essential files such as readme.txt files, Word documents, and so on), or all of the files within the project folder (which also grabs files that appear in the project folder but aren't, for whatever reason, included in the project in Visual Studio).

The bottom half of the screen contains the fields you populate to indicate where your bundled and packaged app will be saved (note that the default is to package everything inside of a zip file), and the IIS website to deploy to.

Note the check box toward the middle of this window. If you check Include All Databases Configured in Deploy SQL Tab, the deployment tool uses the information provided on the Deploy SQL tab and publishes the referenced databases to the target database servers in addition to moving the ASP.NET application.

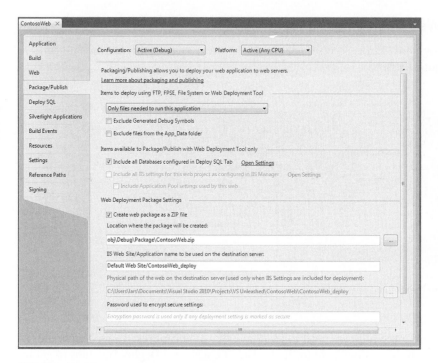

FIGURE 12.17   Web deployment options.

Deploy SQL Options

When used in conjunction with the Deploy SQL options on the prior tab, this window enables you to specify a list of SQL Server databases that should be published along with the web application (Figure 12.18).

There are three major groups of properties that need to be filled in here. You first add an entry to the top table by clicking the Add button and then giving a name to the database connection. You specify a connection string for both the source database and for the target database. Finally, you indicate what elements of the database should be published via the Database scripting options drop-down: schema only, data only, or data and schema.

> **NOTE**
>
> If you need to run a SQL script as part of the deployment, you can supply the location of that script on the Deploy SQL window as well. Click on the Add Script button, and then navigate to the script file. Notice that there is already a script entry in the list; this is the script that the deployment tool generates based on the settings you have provided. Custom scripts that are added are executed in the order they are listed. For instance, if you need a script to execute *before* the general schema and data script that the tool generates, you add the script to the list and then use the arrow keys to the right of the list to move it above the default script.

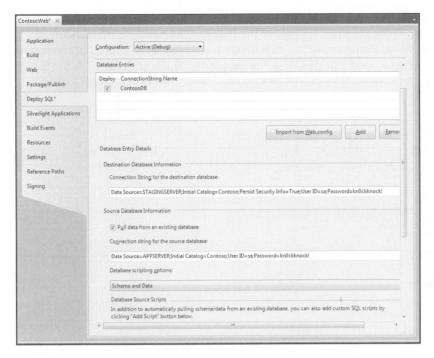

FIGURE 12.18   Specifying databases to be included in our deployment.

All of the options on this property page are tied to a particular configuration. This is set using the drop-down box at the very top of the page. For instance, if you refer to Figure 12.18, you can see that we have the Active (Debug) configuration selected in the drop-down at the top. If we changed that to Release, we would have a blank slate to provide an entirely different set of SQL deployment properties applicable only to the Release build configuration.

> **TIP**
>
> If you are wondering why you can provide multiple database entries on this page, consider the scenario where you will be publishing to a staging server and a production server. In that scenario, you would want two entries here (with two different sets of connection strings, SQL scripts, etc.). Because you can change the name of these entries, it is easy to keep their respective property sets separate and prevent mistakes. You might name one, for instance, "LocalToStage," and another "LocalToProd" to keep everything straight.

Now that we have our deployment options set the way we need them to be, let's try to publish our web application. Go to the Build menu and select Publish (alternatively, you can right-click on the project in the Solution Explorer window and select Publish from there).

Launching the Publish Process

The dialog box that launches when you select the Publish command on the Build menu captures the final set of details needed to start deployment (Figure 12.19). All of the details on this screen can be saved as part of a deployment profile. The large buttons at the top of the dialog box are used to rename, delete, or save the current profile.

FIGURE 12.19   The Publish Web dialog box.

The method of deployment is selected by using the Publish Method drop-down. Prior to Visual Studio 2010, we could select one of three different deployment methods: FTP, FrontPage Server Extensions (FPSE), or a file system path could be used. Visual Studio 2010 adds a fourth option: One-Click Publishing. One-Click Publishing is a slightly more robust addition to the list. This method uses IIS remote management services to copy the relevant application files locally to a remote or local server. In fact, there are web hosting providers that support One-Click Publishing, which makes this method particularly attractive for targeting off-site web servers that are being maintained by a third party.

The rest of the options in this dialog box are dynamic and depend on the method we choose. For FTP deployments, as an example, we would need to provide the appropriate FTP login information. For One-Click Publishing profiles, we are required to provide a Service URL and an application URL.

After all the required properties have been filled, click on the Publish button to start the process.

> **NOTE**
>
> One-Click Publishing will perform dynamic or incremental website updates. In other words, it can detect which files have changed and only deploy those files. This is a great feature to leverage when publishing over the Internet: for large sites, it can significantly speed up the publishing process.

Using the Copy Web Site Tool

The Copy Web Site Tool is accessed from the Website menu. It has a left pane that shows all of the source files (those files that are to be deployed), and a right pane that lists all of the files that currently exist on the source (see Figure 12.20). As we mentioned initially, this tool actually performs a two-way synchronization. If you look closely at Figure 12.20, you see arrows next to each of the files. Arrows pointing to the right indicate that the file will be pushed up to the target location, and arrows pointing to the left indicate files that will be copied down to the local project.

FIGURE 12.20   The Copy Web Site Tool.

The first thing you need to do after launching the copy tool is to establish a connection to a remote website. Click on the Connect button and you are presented with a connection dialog box (Figure 12.21).

FIGURE 12.21   Connecting to a website prior to copying.

You can clearly see your connection options to the left: file system, local IIS installation, FTP site or Remote Site. To copy files, select the ones that need to be moved as part of the deployment, and then click on one of the action buttons in the center of the screen. Reading from top to bottom, these buttons copy selected files to the remote website, copy files from the remote website to the local project, do a two way sync (that is, copy selected files in both directions), or stop a copy that is in progress.

> **NOTE**
>
> The Remote Site option uses FrontPage Server Extensions behind the scenes to communicate with the web server. FPSE is actually not enabled by default on Windows Server 2008 (or Windows Vista/Windows 7), nor does it show up as an available feature for installation. If you need to administer websites using FPSE on Windows Server 2008 or Windows Vista/Windows 7, you will need to download a separate file containing the server extensions, run that setup file on the target server, and then follow the instructions for enabling the extensions on a particular website sitting within IIS. At the time of this writing, you can find the FPSE install files here: http://go.microsoft.com/fwlink/?LinkId=86544

Summary

This chapter provided an introduction to the various tools available within Visual Studio for deploying both client applications and server-side, ASP.NET applications. For client applications, we covered an overview of the two principal deployment technologies, ClickOnce and Windows Installer, and discussed the specific reasons why you might choose one over the other. We explored these two technologies in-depth by examining how to use Visual Studio to publish a sample WinForms application using both methods.

We also discussed the tools available for deploying ASP.NET websites and web applications from a local machine off to a web server, and demonstrated the tools within the IDE for accomplishing the same.

12

Introducing the Automation Object Model

Visual Studio is built to be "extensible." It ships with its own API to enable you, the developer, to control many of the pieces of the IDE.

The API is called the Visual Studio automation object model, and understanding its capabilities is the key to unlocking your ability to program and control the IDE itself by writing code in the form of macros and add-ins (discussed in Chapter 14, "Writing Macros," and Chapter 15, "Writing Add-ins and Wizards").

In this chapter, we discuss the layout and structure of the automation object model. We map the various objects in the object model to their IDE counterparts, delve into the various ways to interact with these objects through managed code, and, we hope, start to see a glimpse of the possibilities in terms of Visual Studio customization.

To drive home the object model concepts and place them in context, we have provided various code snippets and listings, nearly 100% of which are written in Visual Basic. The reason is that Visual Basic is the language of macros (other languages are not supported), and macros are by far the easiest and quickest way to reach out and touch elements of the IDE. As such, macros are a perfect vehicle for exploring and understanding the object model. In Chapters 14 and 15, we move beyond the object model and work to understand how to use, write, and run macros and add-ins (add-ins don't suffer from the Visual Basic limitation, so we switch gears and provide most of our add-in code using C#).

Don't worry too much about the mechanics of writing an add-in or macro at this point; concentrate instead on understanding the automation objects and how they are referenced and used. For the ambitious, know that the code listings here can be pasted directly into the Macros IDE Editor and run as is.

An Overview of the Automation Object Model

The automation object model is a structured class library with a top-level root object called DTE (or DTE2; more on this in a bit), which stands for Development Tools Environment. By referencing the assembly that implements the DTE/DTE2 object, you can instance this root object and use its members and child classes to access the IDE components.

Object Model Versions

The automation object model is actually implemented across four different, complementary primary interop assemblies (PIAs): EnvDTE, EnvDTE80, EnvDTE90, and EnvDTE100. EnvDTE is the original automation assembly distributed with Visual Studio .NET 2003. EnvDTE80 was the library distributed with Visual Studio 2005. EnvDTE90 is distributed with Visual Studio 2008 (yet another assembly, EnvDTE90a is installed with Visual Studio 2008 Service Pack 1). And finally, EnvDTE100 is the automation assembly required by Visual Studio 2010. The reason for multiple assemblies is simple: They help balance the need for new features against the need to preserve backward compatibility. For instance, with Visual Studio 2008, Microsoft was faced with a common design decision: replace or upgrade the previous assembly shipped with Visual Studio 2005 (EnvDTE80) and risk introducing incompatibilities with current macros and add-ins, or ship a new assembly that could be leveraged in cases in which the new functionality was desired (existing code would still target the previous, unchanged library).

The latter path was chosen, and thus EnvDTE100 (100 represents version 10.0) contains automation types and members that are new to Visual Studio 2010, while EnvDTE90 (for Visual Studio 2008) and EnvDTE80 (for Visual Studio 2005) provide the base level of functionality and backward compatibility.

Within the EnvDTE100 assembly, you find types that supersede their predecessors from the EnvDTE90 assembly, and the same is true for types within EnvDTE90 that supersede types implemented in EnvDTE80, all the way back to the original EnvDTE assembly. In these cases, the type name has been appended with a number to indicate the revised version. Thus, we have DTE and DTE2; Solution, Solution2, and Solution3; and so on.

Table 13.1 provides a side-by-side listing of some of the most important types implemented in the EnvDTE libraries. This type list is incomplete; it should be considered for reference only. This table is useful, however, for identifying some of the newly minted types in the new automation assembly; in the next section, we see how these types can be organized into broad Visual Studio automation categories and how they map onto physical IDE constructs.

TABLE 13.1   Partial List of Automation Types

Type	Description
AddIn	Represents a VS add-in.
Breakpoint, Breakpoint2	Represents a debugger breakpoint.
BuildDependencies	For the selected project, represents a collection of BuildDependency objects.
BuildDependency	For the selected project, the projects that it depends on for a successful build.
BuildEvents	Exposes a list of events relevant to a solution build.
Command	Represents a command action in the IDE.
Commands, Commands2	A collection of all commands supported in the IDE.
CommandWindow	Represents the command window.
Configuration	Represents a project's configuration properties.
Debugger, Debugger2, Debugger3, Debugger4, Debugger5	Represents the Visual Studio debugger.
DebuggerEvents	Exposes events from the debugger.
Document	Represents an open document in the IDE.
Documents	A collection of all open documents in the IDE.
DTE	Represents the IDE; this is the top-level, root object for the automation object model.
EditPoint	Represents a text operation point within a document.
Events	Exposes all automation events.
ExceptionGroups	Represents the exception grouping categories supported by Visual Studio.
Find	Represents the Find capability for text searches in the IDE.
HTMLWindow, HTMLWindow3	Represents an HTML document window.
OutputWindow	Represents the Output window.
Program, (Process2)	Represents a program running within the IDE; useful for examining processes and threads within the program. EnvDTE80 functionality is provided by the Process2 object.
Project	Represents a project loaded in the IDE.
ProjectItem	Represents an item contained within a given project.
ProjectItems	A collection of all items contained within a project.

13

TABLE 13.1   Continued

Type	Description
Property	Represents a generic property for an object (this can be used across various objects in the automation library).
SelectedItem	Represents projects or project items that are currently selected in the IDE.
Solution, Solution2, Solution3, Solution4	Represents the solution currently loaded in Visual Studio.
SourceControl, SourceControl2	Represents the source control system of record within Visual Studio.
TaskItem	Represents an item in the Task List window.
TaskItems, TaskItems2	A collection of all items in the Task List window.
TaskList	Represents the Task List window.
Template	Represents a Visual Studio template.
TextDocument	Represents a text file open in the IDE.
TextPane, TextPane2	Represents a pane within an open text editor window.
TextWindow	Represents a text window.
ToolBox	Represents the Toolbox window.
ToolBoxItem, ToolBoxItem2	Represents an item within the Toolbox window.
ToolBoxTab, ToolboxTab2, ToolboxTab3	Represents a tab of items on the Toolbox window.
Window, Window2	Represents, generically, any window within the IDE.
Windows, Windows2	A collection of all windows within the IDE.

Automation Categories

Because any automation effort with Visual Studio starts with the object model, you should first understand how it maps onto the IDE constructs and determine the exact capabilities it exposes.

In general, you can think of the object model classes as being organized into categories that directly speak to these IDE concepts:

- ▶ Solutions and projects
- ▶ Windows and command bars (toolbars and menu bars)
- ▶ Documents
- ▶ Commands

- ▶ Debugger

- ▶ Events

Each of the objects in these categories touches a different piece of the IDE, and access to each object is typically through the root-level DTE2 object.

The DTE/DTE2 Root Object

The DTE/DTE2 object represents the tip of the API tree. You can think of it as representing Visual Studio itself, with the objects under it mapping to the various constituent parts of the IDE.

As mentioned previously, DTE2 is the most current version of this object, with DTE providing compatibility with previous versions. In this chapter, unless we specifically need to differentiate between their capabilities, we generically refer to the DTE and DTE2 objects as simply DTE.

The DTE properties are used to gain a reference to a specific IDE object (or collection of objects). Methods on the object are used to execute commands in the IDE, launch wizards, or close the IDE.

Table 13.2 shows the major properties and methods defined on the DTE2 object; they have been organized within the six object categories itemized in the preceding section.

TABLE 13.2   DTE2 Properties and Methods for IDE Access

Category	Property	Description
Commands	Commands	Returns a collection of Command objects; in general, a command is an action that can be carried out within the IDE such as opening or saving a file.
Debugger	Debugger	Returns the debugger object.
Documents	ActiveDocument	Returns a Document object representing the currently active document.
Documents	Documents	Returns a collection of Document objects representing all open documents.
Event Notification	Events	Returns the Events object for handling event notifications.
Solutions and Projects	ActiveSolutionProjects	Returns a collection of the Project objects representing the projects that are currently selected within the Solution Explorer.
Solutions and Projects	Solution	Returns the Solution object for the currently loaded solution.
Windows and Command Bars	ActiveWindow	Returns a Window object representing the window within the IDE that currently has focus.

13

TABLE 13.2   Continued

Category	Property	Description
Windows and Command Bars	CommandBars	Returns a collection of CommandBar objects representing all the toolbars and menu bars.
Windows and Command Bars	MainWindow	Returns a Window object representing the IDE window itself.
Windows and Command Bars	StatusBar	Returns a StatusBar object representing Visual Studio's status bar.
Windows and Command Bars	ToolWindows	Returns a ToolWindows instance, which in turns provides access to a few of the most prominent tool windows: the command window, error list, output window, Solution Explorer, task list, and toolbox.
Windows and Command Bars	WindowConfigurations	Returns a collection of WindowConfiguration objects; these objects represent the various window layouts in use by Visual Studio.

Category	Method	Description
Commands	ExecuteCommand	Executes an environment command.
—	LaunchWizard	Starts the identified wizard with the given parameters.
—	Quit	Closes Visual Studio.

NOTE

The mechanics of referencing and instancing a DTE object change slightly depending on whether you are writing an add-in or a macro, so we'll cover the specifics in the macro and add-in sections in Chapters 14 and 15.

In summary, the DTE object is a tool for directly interacting with certain IDE components and providing access to the deeper layers of the API with its property collections. If you move one level down in the API, you find the major objects that form the keystone for automation.

Solution and Project Objects

The Solution object represents the currently loaded solution. The individual projects within the solution are available via Project objects returned within the Solution.Projects collection. Items within a project are accessed in a similar fashion through the Project.ProjectItems collection.

As you can see from Figure 13.1, this hierarchy exactly mirrors the solution/project hierarchy that we first discussed in Chapter 4, "Solutions and Projects."

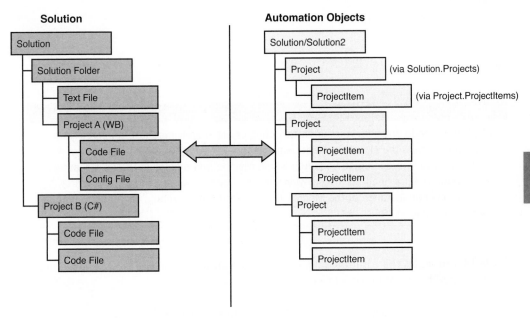

FIGURE 13.1   Mapping the solution/project hierarchy.

There are some mismatches here—solution folders, for instance, are treated as projects—but for the most part, the object model tree closely resembles the solution project tree that you are used to.

The Solution object and members enable you to interact with the current solution to perform common tasks such as these:

▶ Determining the number of projects in the solution (Count property)

▶ Adding a project to the solution based on a project file (AddFromFile method)

▶ Creating a new solution or closing the current one (Create and Close methods)

▶ Saving the solution (SaveAs method)

▶ Removing a project from the solution (Remove method)

You can also directly retrieve a reference to any of the projects within the currently loaded solution by iterating over the Solution.Projects collection. As an example of interacting with the Solution and Project objects, this Visual Basic macro code snippet removes the first project from the current solution:

```
Dim sol As Solution = DTE.Solution
Dim proj As Project = sol.Projects.Item(1)

If proj.Saved Then
```

```
            sol.Remove(proj)
Else
        ...
End If
```

> **NOTE**
>
> Most of the code snippets you see in this chapter are merely meant to reinforce how
> you would access the API component being discussed. We get into the specifics of
> exactly how to leverage these concepts within macros and add-ins in the next chapter.
> If you want to get a head start by playing with the code as we go along, you will first
> need to open an instance of the Macros IDE: Go to the Tools menu, select Macros, and
> then select Macros IDE.

Table 13.3 provides the combined list of the most commonly used properties and methods
implemented by the Solution objects.

TABLE 13.3   Primary **Solution/Solution2/Solution3** Type Members

Property	Description
AddIns	Returns a collection of AddIn objects associated with the current solution.
Count	A count of the project within the solution.
DTE	A reference to the parent DTE object.
FullName	The full path and name of the solution file.
Globals	Returns the Globals object, a cache of variables used across the solution.
IsOpen	Indicates whether a solution is open.
Projects	Returns a collection of Project objects representing all the projects within the solution.
Properties	Returns a collection of Property objects that expose all the solution's properties.
Saved	Indicates whether the solution has been saved since the last modification.
SolutionBuild	Returns a reference to a SolutionBuild object; this is the entry point to the build automation objects applicable for the current solution.
Method	**Description**
AddFromFile	Adds a project to the solution using an existing project file.
AddFromTemplate	Takes an existing project, clones it, and adds it to the solution.

TABLE 13.3 Continued

Property	Description
AddFromTemplateEx	Adds an existing project to a solution using the solution name.
AddSolutionFolder	Creates a new solution folder in the solution.
Close	Closes the solution.
Create	Creates an empty solution.
FindProjectItem	Initiates a search for a given item in one of the solution's projects.
GetProjectItemTemplate	Returns the path to the template used for the referenced project item.
GetProjectTemplate	Returns the path to the template used for the referenced project.
Item	Returns a Project instance.
Open	Opens a solution (using a specific view).
Remove	Removes a project from the solution.
SaveAs	Saves the solution.

Controlling Projects in a Solution

One of the things that the Solution object is good for is retrieving references to the various projects that belong to the solution. Each Project object has its own set of useful members for interacting with the projects and their items. By using these members, you can interact with the projects in various, expected ways, such as renaming a project, deleting a project, and saving a project.

See Table 13.4 for a summary of the most common Project members.

TABLE 13.4 Primary Project Object Members

Property	Description
CodeModel	Returns the CodeModel object associated with this project.
Collection	Returns a collection of Project objects for the current Solution.
DTE	Provides a reference back to the parent DTE object.
FullName	Provides the full path and name of the solution file.
Kind	Returns a string GUID indicating the type of project. Each project type is registered with Visual Studio using a GUID; consult the Visual Studio SDK documentation for a list that maps the project type GUIDs to their text description.
Name	Returns the name of the project.

TABLE 13.4   Continued

Property	Description
ParentProjectItem	Returns an instance of the parent Project. Some project types within Visual Studio are able to host or contain other project types; this property can be used to identify the host project for the current project (if there is one).
ProjectItems	Returns a ProjectItems collection containing each individual object within the current project.
Properties	Returns a collection of Property objects that expose all the project's properties.
Saved	Indicates whether the project has been saved since the last modification.

Method	Description
Delete	Removes the current project instance from the solution.
Save	Saves the project.
SaveAs	Saves the project. This method enables you to provide a new name for the project.

Accessing Code Within a Project

Beyond the basic project attributes and items, one of the cooler things that can be accessed via a Project instance is the actual code within the project's source files. Through the CodeModel property, you can access an entire line of proxy objects representing the code constructs within a project. For instance, the CodeClass interface enables you to examine and edit the code for a given class in a given project.

> **NOTE**
>
> Support for the different CodeModel entities varies from language to language. The MSDN documentation for each CodeModel type clearly indicates the source language support for that element.

After grabbing a CodeModel reference from a Project instance, you can access its CodeElements collection (which is, not surprisingly, a collection of CodeElement objects). A CodeElement is nothing more than a generic representation of a certain code structure within a project. The CodeElement object is generic, but it provides a property, Kind. This property is used to determine the exact native type of the code object contained within the CodeElement.

The CodeElement.Kind property is an enumeration (of type vsCMElement) that identifies the specific type of code construct lurking within the CodeElement object. Using the Kind property, you can first determine the true nature of the code element and then cast the CodeElement object to its strong type. Here is a snippet of C# code that does just that:

```
if (element.Kind == vsCMElement.vsCMElementClass)
 {
          CodeClass myClass = (CodeClass)element;
 }
```

For a better grasp of the code model hierarchy, consider the C# code presented in Listing 13.1; this is a "shell" solution that merely implements a namespace, a class within that namespace, and a function within the class.

LISTING 13.1   A Simple Namespace and Class Implementation

```
using System;
using System.Collections.Generic;
using System.Text;

namespace MyNamespace
{
    class MyClass
    {
        public string SumInt(int x, int y)
        {
            return (x + y).ToString();
        }
    }

}
```

If you map the code in Listing 13.1 to the code object model, you end up with the structure shown in Figure 13.2.

To get an idea of the complete depth of the code model tree that can be accessed through the CodeElements collection, consult Table 13.5; this table shows all the possible vsCMElement values, the type they are used to represent, and a brief description of the type.

TABLE 13.5   Mapping the vsCMElement Enumeration Values

Enumeration Value	Type	Description
vsCMElementAssignmentStmt		An assignment statement
vsCMElementAttribute		An attribute
vsCMElementClass	CodeClass	A class
vsCMElementDeclareDecl		A declaration

TABLE 13.5   Continued

Enumeration Value	Type	Description
vsCMElementDefineStmt		A define statement
vsCMElementDelegate	CodeDelegate	A delegate
vsCMElementEnum	CodeEnum	An enumeration
vsCMElementEvent	CodeEvent	An event
vsCMElementEventsDeclaration		An event declaration
vsCMElementFunction	CodeFunction	A function
vsCMElementFunctionInvokeStmt		A statement invoking a function
vsCMElementIDLCoClass		An IDL co-class
vsCMElementIDLImport		An IDL import statement
vsCMElementIDLImportLib		An IDL import library
vsCMElementIDLLibrary		An IDL library
vsCMElementImplementsStmt		An implements statement
vsCMElementImportStmt	CodeImport	An import statement
vsCMElementIncludeStmt		An include statement
vsCMElementInheritsStmt		An inherits statement
vsCMElementInterface	CodeInterface	An interface
vsCMElementLocalDeclStmt		A local declaration statement
vsCMElementMacro		A macro
vsCMElementMap		A map
vsCMElementMapEntry		A map entry
vsCMElementModule		A module
vsCMElementNamespace	CodeNamespace	A namespace
vsCMElementOptionStmt		An option statement
vsCMElementOther	CodeElement	A code element not otherwise identified in this enum
vsCMElementParameter	CodeParameter	A parameter
vsCMElementProperty	CodeProperty	A property
vsCMElementPropertySetStmt		A property set statement
vsCMElementStruct	CodeStruct	A structure

TABLE 13.5   Continued

Enumeration Value	Type	Description
vsCMElementTypeDef		A type definition
vsCMElementUDTDecl		A user-defined type
vsCMElementUnion		A union
vsCMElementUsingStmt	CodeImport	A using statement
vsCMElementVariable		A variable
vsCMElementVBAttributeGroup		A Visual Basic attribute group
vsCMElementVBAttributeStmt		A Visual Basic attribute statement
vsCMElementVCBase		A Visual C++ base

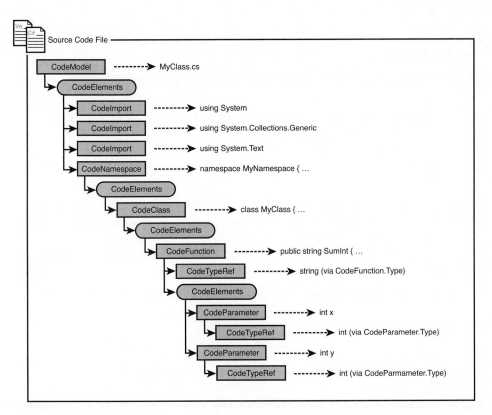

FIGURE 13.2   A simple code model object hierarchy.

Windows

The visible, content portion of Visual Studio is represented by Window objects, which are instances of open windows within the IDE such as the Solution Explorer, the Task List window, an open code editor window, and so on. Even the IDE itself is represented by a Window object.

Any given window is either a document window or a tool window. Document windows host documents that are editable by the Text Editor. Tool windows contain controls that display information relevant to the current context of the IDE; the Solution Explorer and Task List windows are examples of tool windows, and a VB source code file open in an editor is an example of a document window.

Referencing Windows

If you need to retrieve an instance of a specific window, you have a few different options, each optimal for a given situation. For starters, the main IDE window is always available directly from the DTE object:

```
Dim IDE As Window
IDE = DTE.MainWindow
```

Obviously, if you need to perform a specific action against the IDE window, this is your quickest route.

The DTE.ActiveWindow property also provides direct and quick access to a Window object, in this case the currently active window:

```
Dim CurrentWindow As Window
CurrentWindow = DTE.ActiveWindow
```

The tool windows within the IDE—that is, the command window, the error list window, the output window, the Solution Explorer, the Task List window, and the toolbox—also have a direct way to retrieve their object model instances: You use the DTE.ToolWindows property. This property returns a ToolWindows object that exposes a separate property for each of the tool windows.

This Visual Basic code grabs a reference to the Task List window and closes it:

```
Dim taskwin As Window
```

```
taskwin = DTE.ToolWindows.TaskList
taskwin.Close()
```

And finally, the fourth way to access an IDE window is through the DTE.Windows collection; this collection holds an entry for each IDE window. You can access a window from the collection either by using an integer representing the window's position within the collection, or by providing an object or a string that represents the window you are trying to retrieve.

The following code grabs a handle to the Solution Explorer window:

```
Dim windows As Windows2 = DTE.Windows
Dim window As Window = windows.Item(Constants.vsWindowKindSolutionExplorer)
```

Interacting with Windows

Table 13.6 itemizes the properties and methods available on each Window object.

TABLE 13.6   Window Object Members

Property	Description
AutoHides	A Boolean flag indicating whether the window can be hidden (applies only to tool windows).
Caption	The title/caption of the window.
Collection	The Windows collection that the current Window object belongs to.
CommandBars	A CommandBars collection of the command bars implemented by the window.
ContextAttributes	A collection of ContextAttribute objects; they are used to associate the current context of the window with the Dynamic Help window.
Document	If the Window object is hosting a document, this returns a reference to the document.
DTE	A reference to the root DTE object.
Height	The height of the window in pixels.
IsFloating	A Boolean flag indicating whether the window is floating or docked.
Left	The distance, in pixels, between the window's left edge and its container's left edge.
Linkable	A Boolean flag indicating whether the window can be docked with other windows.
LinkedWindowFrame	Returns a reference to the Window object that is acting as the frame for a docked window.
LinkedWindows	A collection of Window objects representing the windows that are linked together within the same frame.
Object	Returns an object proxy that represents the window and can be referenced by name.
ObjectKind	A GUID indicating the type of the object returned from Window.Object.
Project	A Project instance representing the project containing the Window object.
ProjectItem	A ProjectItem instance representing the project item containing the Window object.

TABLE 13.6   Continued

Property	Description
Selection	Returns an object representing the currently selected item in the window (for document windows, this might be text; for tool windows, this might be an item in a list; and so on).
Top	The distance, in pixels, between the window's top edge and its parent's top edge.
Visible	A Boolean flag indicating whether the window is visible or hidden.
Width	The width of the window in pixels.
WindowState	Gets or sets the current state of the window (via a vsWindowState enum value: vsWindowStateMaximize, vsWindowStateMinimize, vsWindowStateNormal).

Method	Description
Activate	Gives the window focus.
Close	Closes the window; you can indicate, with a vsSaveChanges enum value, whether the window's hosted document should be saved or not saved, or whether the IDE should prompt the user to make that decision.
SetSelectionContainer	Passes an array of objects to the Properties window when the Window object has focus. This property is mainly used for custom tool windows where you need to control what is displayed in the Properties window.
SetTabPicture	Specifies an object to use as a tab image; this image is displayed whenever the window is part of a tab group within the IDE.

Beyond the basics (such as using the Height and Width properties to query or affect a window's dimensions, or setting focus to the window with the SetFocus method), a few properties deserve special mention:

▶ The Document property gives you a way to programmatically interact with the document that the window is hosting (if any).

▶ The Project and ProjectItem properties serve to bridge the Window portion of the API with the Project/Solution portion; in a similar vein as the Document property, you can use these properties to interact with the project that is related to the window, or the project item (such as the VB code file, text file, or resource file).

▶ If you are dealing with a tool window, the SetTabPicture method provides a way to set the tab icon that is displayed when the tool window is part of a group of tabbed windows (for instance, the Toolbox window displays a wrench and hammer picture on its tab when part of a tabbed group).

▶ Again, specifically for tool windows only, the SetSelectionContainer can be used to supply one or more objects for display within the Properties window. This capability is useful if you have a custom window where you need to control what is displayed in the Properties window when the window has focus (all the standard VS windows already do this for you).

Listing 13.2 contains a simple macro illustrating the use of the Window object; in this example, each window is queried to determine its type, and then a summary of each window is output in a simple message box.

LISTING 13.2   VB Macro for Querying the Windows Collection

```vb
Imports EnvDTE
Imports EnvDTE80
Imports System.Diagnostics
Imports System.Windows.Forms


Public Module MacroExamples

    Public Sub InventoryWindows()
        ' Get collection of all open windows
        Dim windows As Windows2 = DTE.Windows

        ' Count the nbr of open windows
        Dim windowCount As Integer = windows.Count

        ' Local vars for looping and holding window and string
        ' results
        Dim idx As Integer
        Dim results As String
        Dim window As Window2

        results = windowCount.ToString + " windows open..." + vbCrLf

        ' Iterate the collection of windows
        For idx = 1 To windowCount

            window = windows.Item(idx)
            Dim title As String = window.Caption

            ' If the window is hosting a document, a valid Document
            ' object will be returned through Window.Document
            If Not (window.Document Is Nothing) Then
                ' Write this out as a document window
                Dim docName As String = window.Document.Name
                results = results + "Window '" + title + "' is a document window"
                    + vbCrLf
            Else
```

```
              ' If no document was present, this is a tool window
              ' (tool windows don't host documents)
              results = results + "Window '" + title + "' is a tool window"
                  + vbCrLf
          End If

      Next


      ' Show the results
      MessageBox.Show(results, "Window Documents", MessageBoxButtons.OK, _
          MessageBoxIcon.Information)

  End Sub


End Module
```

> **NOTE**
>
> If you want to embed your own custom control inside a tool window, you have to write
> an add-in and use the Windows.CreateToolWindow method. We cover this scenario in
> Chapter 14.

Text Windows and Window Panes

Text windows have their own specific object abstraction in addition to the generic
Window object: The TextWindow object is used to represent text editor windows. To
obtain a reference to a window's TextWindow object, you retrieve the Window object's
value and assign it into a TextWindow type:

```
Dim textWindow As TextWindow
textWindow = DTE.ActiveWindow.Object
```

The TextWindow object doesn't provide much functionality over and above the functionality found in the Window type; its real value is the access it provides to window panes.

Text editor windows in Visual Studio can be split into two panes; with a text editor open,
simply select Split from the Window menu to create a new pane within the window. The
TextWindow.ActivePane property returns a TextPane object representing the currently
active pane in the window, and the TextWindow.Panes property provides access to all the
panes within a text window:

```
' Get pane instance from collection
```

```
Dim newPane As TextPane2
newPane = textWindow.Panes.Item(1)


' Get currently active pane
Dim currPane As TextPane2
currPane = textWindow.ActivePane
```

One of the more useful things you can do with the TextPane object is to scroll the client area of the pane (for example, the visible portion of the document within the pane) so that a specific range of text is visible. This is done via the TextPane.TryToShow method.

Here is the definition for the method:

```
Function TryToShow( Point As TextPoint, Optional How As vsPaneShowHow, _
    PointOrCount As Object)
```

The TextPoint parameter represents the specific location within the text document that you want visible in the text pane (we discuss TextPoint objects in depth later in this chapter, in the section "Editing Text Documents"). The vsPaneShowHow value specifies how the pane should behave when scrolling to the indicated location:

▶ vsPaneShowHow.vsPaneShowCentered causes the pane to center the text/text selection in the middle of the pane (horizontally and vertically).

▶ vsPaneShowHow.vsPaneShowTop places the text point at the top of the viewable region in the pane.

▶ vsPaneShowHow.vsPaneShowAsIs shows the text point as is with no changes in horizontal or vertical orientation within the viewable region in the pane.

The last parameter, the PointOrCount object, is used to specify the end of the text area that you want displayed. If you provide an integer here, this represents a count of characters past the original text point; if you provide another text point, the selection is considered to be that text that resides between the two text points.

The TextPane object is also used to access the Incremental Search feature for a specific window pane. Listing 13.3 shows an example of this feature in action.

LISTING 13.3   Controlling Incremental Search

```
Imports EnvDTE
Imports EnvDTE80
Imports Microsoft.VisualStudio.CommandBars
Imports System.Diagnostics
Imports System.Windows.Forms
```

```
Public Module MacroExamples

    Public Sub IncrementalSearch()
        ' Grab references to the active window;
        ' we assume, for this example, that the window
        ' is a text window.
        Dim window As Window2 = DTE.ActiveWindow

        ' Grab a TextWindow instance that maps to our
        ' active window
        Dim txtWindow As TextWindow = window.Object

        ' Get the active pane from the text window
        Dim pane As TextPane2 = txtWindow.ActivePane

        ' Using the active pane, get an IncrementalSearch object
        ' for the pane
        Dim search As IncrementalSearch = pane.IncrementalSearch

        ' Try to find our IMessageMapper interface by looking
        ' for the string "IM"
        ' Configure the search:
        '    search forward in the document
        '    append the chars that we are searching for
        '    quit the search
        search.StartForward()
        search.AppendCharAndSearch(AscW("I"))
        search.AppendCharAndSearch(AscW("M"))

        ' To remove us from incremental search mode,
        ' we can call IncrementalSearch.Exit()...
        'search.Exit()

    End Sub
End Module
```

The Tool Window Types

In addition to having a Window object abstraction, each default tool window in the IDE—the command window, output window, Toolbox window, and Task List window—is also represented by a discrete type that exposes methods and properties unique to that tool window. Table 13.7 lists the default tool windows and their underlying types in the automation object model.

TABLE 13.7   Tool Windows and Their Types

Tool Window	Type
Command window	CommandWindow
Output window	OutputWindow
Task List window	TaskList
Toolbox window	ToolBox

To reference one of these objects, you first start with its Window representation and then cast its Window.Object value to the matching type. For instance, this VB snippet starts with a Window reference to the Task List window and then uses that Window object to obtain a reference to the TaskList object:

```
Dim windows As Windows = DTE.Windows
Dim twindow As Window = _
    DTE.Windows.Item(EnvDTE.Constants.vsWindowKindTaskList)
```

Tasks and the Task List Window

The TaskList object enables you to access the items currently displayed in the Task List window; each item in the window is represented by its own TaskItem object. The TaskItem object exposes methods and properties that enable you to manipulate the task items. For instance, you can mark an item as complete, get or set the line number associated with the task, and change the priority of the task.

You remove tasks from the list by using the TaskItem.Delete method and add them by using the TaskItems.Add method. The Add method allows you to specify the task category, subcategory, description, priority, icon, and so on:

```
Dim tlist As TaskList = CType(twindow.Object, TaskList)


tlist.TaskItems.Add("Best Practices", "Coding Style", _
    "Use of brace indenting is inconsistent", _
    vsTaskPriority.vsTaskPriorityMedium, _
    vsTaskIcon.vsTaskIconUser, True, _
    "S:\ContosoCommonFramework\Contoso.Fx.Common\Class1.cs", _
    7, True, True)
```

Table 13.8 provides an inventory of the TaskItem members.

TABLE 13.8   TaskItem Members

Property	Description
Category	The category of the task.
Checked	A Boolean flag indicating whether the task is marked as completed (a check mark appears in the check box next to the task).
Collection	The TaskList collection that the current TaskItem object belongs to.
Description	The description of the task.
Displayed	A Boolean flag indicating whether the task is currently visible in the Task List window.
DTE	A reference to the root DTE object.
FileName	The name of the file associated with the task (if any).
IsSettable	By passing in a vsTaskListColumn enum value to this property, you can determine whether that column is editable.
Line	The line number associated with the task.
Priority	A vsTaskPriority value indicating the task's priority level. Possible values include vsTaskPriorityHigh, vsTaskPriorityMedium, and vsTaskPriorityLow.
SubCategory	The subcategory of the task.
Method	**Description**
Delete	Removes the task from the Task List window.
Navigate	Causes the IDE to navigate to the location (for example, file and line) associated with the task.
Select	Selects or moves the focus to the task within the Task List window.

Listing 13.4 contains a short VB macro demonstrating the use of the TaskList, TaskItems, and TaskItem objects to iterate the list of user tasks and toggle their completed status.

LISTING 13.4   Toggling Task Item Completion

```
Imports EnvDTE
Imports EnvDTE80
Imports EnvDTE90
Imports Microsoft.VisualStudio.CommandBars
Imports System.Diagnostics
```

```
Imports System.Windows.Forms


Public Module MacroExamples

    Public Sub ToggleAllTasks()

        ' Reference the windows collection
        Dim windows As Windows = DTE.Windows

        ' Pluck the task list window from the collection
        Dim twindow As Window = _
            DTE.Windows.Item(EnvDTE.Constants.vsWindowKindTaskList)

        ' Convert the window object to a TaskList instance by
        ' casting its Object property
        Dim tlist As TaskList = CType(twindow.Object, TaskList)

        ' Iterate all of the task items in the task list
        For Each task As TaskItem In tlist.TaskItems
            ' Toggle the "completed" check mark on each user task
            If task.Category = "User" Then
                task.Checked = Not task.Checked
            End If

        Next


    End Sub
End Module
```

The Toolbox

Four objects are used to programmatically interface with the toolbox:

- ▶ **ToolBox**—An object representing the toolbox itself.

- ▶ **ToolBoxTabs**—A collection representing the tab panes on the toolbox.

- ▶ **ToolBoxItems**—A collection representing the items within a tab on the toolbox.

- ▶ **ToolBoxItem**—A discrete item displayed within a toolbox tab.

Figure 13.3 illustrates the Toolbox object hierarchy.

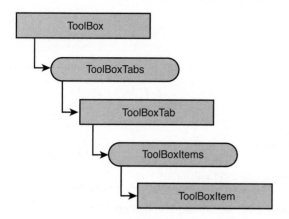

FIGURE 13.3   The Toolbox object hierarchy.

These objects are used primarily to add, remove, or alter the items hosted by the toolbox. For instance, you can easily add a custom tab to the toolbox by using the ToolBoxTabs collection:

```
Dim tBox As ToolBox
Dim myTab As ToolBoxTab
tBox = DTE.Windows.Item(Constants.vsWindowKindToolbox).Object
myTab = tBox.ToolBoxTabs.Add("My TBox Tab")
```

You can also add items to any tab with the ToolBoxItems.Add method, which accepts a name for the item to add, a "data" object representing the item, and a vsToolBoxItemFormat enum, which specifies the format of the item. The Add method uses the vsToolBoxItemFormat to determine how to interpret the "data" object value. For instance, if you want to add a .NET control to the tab created in the preceding code snippet, you can accomplish that with just one line of code:

```
myTab.ToolBoxItems.Add("ContosoControl", _
        "C:\Contoso\Controls\CalendarControl.dll", _
        vsToolBoxItemFormat.vsToolBoxItemFormatDotNETComponent)
```

Notice that the item, in this case, is represented by a path to the assembly that implements the control and that it has an item format of vsToolBoxItemFormatDotNETComponent.

Listing 13.5 contains a VB function that adds a tab to the toolbox, adds a control and a text fragment to the tab, and then removes the tab.

LISTING 13.5   Adding and Removing Items in the Toolbox Window

```
Imports EnvDTE
Imports EnvDTE80
Imports EnvDTE90
```

```vbnet
Imports Microsoft.VisualStudio.CommandBars
Imports System.Diagnostics
Imports System.Windows.Forms


    Public Sub AddAToolBoxTab()
        Dim toolBox As ToolBox
        Dim tabs As ToolBoxTabs
        Dim tab As ToolBoxTab
        Dim tabItems As ToolBoxItems
        Dim win As Window

        Try
            ' Get a reference to the toolbox
            win = DTE.Windows.Item(Constants.vsWindowKindToolbox)
            toolBox = win.Object

            ' Get a reference to the toolbox tabs collection
            tabs = toolBox.ToolBoxTabs

            ' Add a new tab to the ToolBox
            tab = tabs.Add("New ToolBox Tab")

            ' Make the added tab the active tab
            tab.Activate()

            tabItems = tab.ToolBoxItems

            With tabItems
                ' Add a piece of text to the toolbox.
                ' Clicking on the text will add it to
                ' the active document...
                .Add("Code Comment", _
                    "This is some text to add to the toolbox", _
                    vsToolBoxItemFormat.vsToolBoxItemFormatText)

                'Now add a control to the toolbox.
                'When adding a control, you need to specify
                'the path to the assembly; you can add all
                'classes from the assembly (shown below)
                'or just one of the classes (see MSDN
                'docs for that syntax)
                .Add("My Login Control", _
                    "C:\MyComponents\Contoso\LoginControl.dll", _
                    vsToolBoxItemFormat.vsToolBoxItemFormatDotNETComponent)

                'For demonstration purposes, let's remove
```

```
                'the items that we had just added, and then
                'remove the newly created tab...

                'Put up a messagebox to confirm the deletes
                MessageBox.Show("Click OK to delete the tab and added items.", _
                    "Delete Toolbox Tab Items", MessageBoxButtons.OK, _
                    MessageBoxIcon.Information)

                'Delete the tab
                tab.Delete()

            End With

        Catch ex As Exception
            MsgBox("Error: " & ex.ToString())
        End Try

    End Sub
```

Executing Commands in the Command Window

The command window is a tool window used to execute IDE commands or aliases. IDE commands are essentially ways to tell the IDE to perform some action. Some commands map directly to menu items (such as File Open), whereas others don't have menu equivalents.

The CommandWindow object permits you to programmatically pipe commands into the command window and execute them. You can also output a text string (for informational purposes) to the window and clear its current content:

```
' Get a reference to the command window
Dim cmdWindow As CommandWindow = _
    DTE.Windows.Item(Constants.vsWindowKindCommandWindow).Object

' Display some text in the command window
cmdWindow.OutputString("Hello, World!")

' Clear the command window
cmdWindow.Clear()
```

Listing 13.6 shows how to programmatically execute commands in the CommandWindow object.

LISTING 13.6   Executing Commands in the Command Window

```
Imports EnvDTE
Imports EnvDTE80
```

```
Imports EnvDTE90
Imports Microsoft.VisualStudio.CommandBars
Imports System.Diagnostics
Imports System.Windows.Forms

Public Module MacroExamples

    Public Sub ExecCommandWindow()
        Dim cmdWindow As CommandWindow = _
            DTE.Windows.Item(Constants.vsWindowKindCommandWindow).Object

        ' Display some text in the command window
        cmdWindow.OutputString("Executing command from the automation OM...")

        ' Send some command strings to the command window and execute
        ' them...

        ' This command will start logging all input/output in the
        ' command window to the specified file
        cmdWindow.SendInput("Tools.LogCommandWindowOutput cmdwindow.log", True)

        ' Open a file in a code editor:
        '    1. We use an alias, 'of', for the File.OpenFile command
        '    2. This command takes quote-delimited parameters (in this case,
        '       the name of the editor to load the file in)
        Dim cmd As String = "of "
        cmd = cmd &
    """C:\Contoso\ContosoCommonFramework\Integration\Integration.cs"""
        cmd = cmd & "/e:""CSharp Editor"""

        cmdWindow.SendInput(cmd, True)

        cmdWindow.SendInput("Edit.Find MessageTrxId", True)

        ' Turn off logging
        cmdWindow.SendInput("Tools.LogCommandWindowOutput /off", True)

    End Sub
End Module
```

Output Window

The output window displays messages generated from various sources in the IDE. A prime example is the messages generated by the compiler when a project is being built. For a deeper look at the functionality provided by the output window, see Chapter 11, "Debugging Code."

The output window is controlled through three objects:

▶ OutputWindow is the root object representing the output window.

▶ OutputWindowPanes is a collection of OutputWindowPane objects.

▶ OutputWindowPane represents one of the current panes within the output window.

Using these objects, you can add or remove panes from the output window, output text to any one of the panes, and respond to events transpiring in the window.

The following VB code fragment retrieves a reference to the output window and writes a test string in the Build pane:

```
Dim outWindow As OutputWindow = _
DTE.Windows.Item(Constants.vsWindowKindOutput).Object

Dim pane As OutputWindowPane = _
    outWindow.OutputWindowPanes.Item("Build")

pane.OutputString("test")
```

Using the OutputWindowPane object, you can also add items simultaneously to a specific output pane and the Task List window. The OutputWindowPane.OutputTaskItemString method writes text into the output window and simultaneously adds that text as a task to the Task List window:

```
Dim output As String = "Exception handler not found"
Dim task As String = "Add exception handler"
pane.OutputTaskItemString(output, _
   vsTaskPriority.vsTaskPriorityMedium,  "", vsTaskIcon.vsTaskIconNone, _
   "", 0, task, True)
```

Because most of the output window actions are conducted against a specific pane, most of the useful methods are concentrated in the OutputWindowPane object. For your reference, the OutputWindowPane members are itemized in Table 13.9.

TABLE 13.9   OutputWindowPane Members

Property	Description
Collection	The OutputWindowPanes collection that the current OutputWindowPane object belongs to.
DTE	A reference to the root DTE object.
Guid	The GUID for the output window pane.
Name	The name of the output window pane.

TABLE 13.9   Continued

Property	Description
TextDocument	A TextDocument object representing the window pane's content.
Method	**Description**
Activate	Moves the focus to the output window.
Clear	Clears the contents of the window pane.
ForceItemsToTaskList	Writes all task items not yet written to the Task List window.
OutputString	Writes a string to the output window pane.
OutputTaskItemString	Writes a string to the output window pane and simultaneously adds a task to the Task List window.

Listing 13.7 demonstrates controlling the output window by adding a new pane to the window, writing text into that pane, and then clearing its content.

LISTING 13.7   Writing to the Output Window

```
Imports EnvDTE
Imports EnvDTE80
Imports EnvDTE90
Imports Microsoft.VisualStudio.CommandBars
Imports System.Diagnostics
Imports System.Windows.Forms


Public Module MacroExamples

    Public Sub WriteToOutputWindow()

        ' Grab a reference to the output window
        Dim outWindow As OutputWindow = _
            DTE.Windows.Item(Constants.vsWindowKindOutput).Object

        ' Create a new pane in the output window
        Dim pane As OutputWindowPane = _
            outWindow.OutputWindowPanes.Add("New Pane")

        pane.OutputString("Text in the 'New Pane'")

        pane.Clear()

    End Sub

End Module
```

13

Linked Windows

Tool windows can be positioned in various ways within the IDE: You can float tool windows around within the overall IDE container; you can dock a tool window to one of the sides of the IDE; you can join windows together and pin and unpin them; and so on (see the section "Managing the Many Windows of the IDE" in Chapter 2, "The Visual Studio IDE," for an introduction to window layout).

A linked window refers to two or more tool windows that have been aggregated together. Figure 13.4 shows one common example of this; the toolbox and Solution Explorer window have been joined together in a common frame. Each window that is part of the frame can be viewed by clicking on its tab.

FIGURE 13.4   Linked windows.

By joining together two or more tool windows, you actually create an additional window object—called a linked window or window frame—that functions as the container for its hosted tool windows and is available as a part of the DTE.Windows collection.

By using the Window.LinkedWindows and Window.WindowFrame properties and the Windows2.CreateLinkedWindowFrame method, you can programmatically link and unlink any available tool windows. The Visual Basic code in Listing 13.8 demonstrates this process by doing the following:

1. You grab the window objects for the Toolbox window and the Solution Explorer window.

2. You programmatically join these two windows, effectively creating the linked window shown in Figure 13.4.

3. After joining the windows, you get a reference to the newly created linked window and use its LinkedWindows property to unlink the windows that were previously linked together.

LISTING 13.8   Linking and Unlinking Tool Windows

```
Imports EnvDTE
Imports EnvDTE80
Imports EnvDTE90
Imports System.Diagnostics
Imports System.Windows.Forms

Public Module MacroExamples


    Public Sub LinkUnLink()
        Dim windows As Windows2 = DTE.Windows

        ' Grab references to the solution explorer and the toolbox
        Dim solExplorer As Window2 = _
            windows.Item(Constants.vsWindowKindSolutionExplorer)
        Dim toolbox As Window2 = windows.Item(Constants.vsWindowKindToolbox)

        ' Use the Windows2 collection to create a linked window/window
        ' frame to hold the toolbox and solution explorer windows
        Dim windowFrame As Window2
        windowFrame = windows.CreateLinkedWindowFrame(solExplorer, _
            toolbox, vsLinkedWindowType.vsLinkedWindowTypeTabbed)

        ' At this point, we have created a linked window with two tabbed
        ' "interior" windows: the solution explorer, and the toolbox...

        MessageBox.Show("Press OK to Unlink the windows", "LinkUnLink", _
            MessageBoxButtons.OK, MessageBoxIcon.None)

        ' To unlink the windows:
        '    — Use the window frame's LinkedWindows collection
        '    — Remove the window objects from this collection

        windowFrame.LinkedWindows.Remove(toolbox)
        windowFrame.LinkedWindows.Remove(solExplorer)

    End Sub


End Module
```

Command Bars

A command bar is a menu bar or toolbar; from an object model perspective, these are represented by CommandBar objects. Because menu bars and toolbars are hosted within a window, you reference specific CommandBar objects via the Window object, through the Window.CommandBars property. In turn, every CommandBar plays host to controls such as buttons and drop-downs. Figure 13.5 shows the Solution Explorer tool window with its command bar highlighted.

Note that there are six buttons hosted on the command bar.

FIGURE 13.5   The Solution Explorer's command bar.

> **NOTE**
>
> Unlike the Windows collection, which holds only an instance of each open window, the CommandBars collection holds instances for every single registered command bar, regardless of whether the command bar is currently being shown in the window.

The VB code in Listing 13.9 queries the CommandBar object for the Solution Explorer window and prints out the CommandBar objects that it finds.

LISTING 13.9   Querying the CommandBar Object

```
Imports EnvDTE
Imports EnvDTE80
Imports EnvDTE90
Imports Microsoft.VisualStudio.CommandBars
Imports System.Diagnostics
Imports System.Windows.Forms

Public Module MacroExamples
```

```
Public Sub QueryCommandBar()
    Dim windows As Windows2 = DTE.Windows

    ' Grab reference to the solution explorer
    Dim solExplorer As Window2 = _
        windows.Item(Constants.vsWindowKindSolutionExplorer)

    ' Retrieve the solution explorer's command bar object
    Dim cmdBar As CommandBar = CType(solExplorer.CommandBars(1), CommandBar)

    ' Start building our output string
    Dim output As String = "Command bar contains: " + vbCrLf

    ' Get a reference to the controls hosted in the
    ' command bar
    Dim controls As CommandBarControls = cmdBar.Controls

    ' Count integer
    Dim i As Integer = 1

    ' Iterate the controls in the command bar
    For Each control As CommandBarControl In controls

        If control.Enabled Then

            output = output + i.ToString() + " " + _
                control.Type.ToString() + _
                ": " + control.Caption + vbCrLf

            i = i + 1

        End If

    Next

    MessageBox.Show(output, "Solution Explorer Command Bar", _
        MessageBoxButtons.OK)

    End Sub
End Module
```

FIGURE 13.6   Enumerating the buttons in a CommandBar.

Notice in Listing 13.9 that you have to explicitly cast the object returned from the Window.CommandBars property. This is, interestingly, not a strongly typed property, and it returns an Object instead of an actual CommandBar instance.

TIP

Use the CommandBar.Type property to determine whether a command bar is a toolbar or a menu bar. A value of MsoBarType.msoBarTypeNormal indicates that the command bar is a toolbar, whereas a value of MsoBarType.msoBarTypeMenuBar indicates that the command bar is a menu bar.

The CommandBar object properties and methods are documented in Table 13.10.

TABLE 13.10   CommandBar Members

Property	Description
AdaptiveMenu	For menu bars, this Boolean flag indicates whether the command bar has *adaptive menus* enabled. (Adaptive menus, sometimes referred to as *personalized menus*, are menus that alter their drop-down content based on projected or actual usage by the user; the intent is to display only those commands that are useful on the menu and hide the other nonessential commands.)
Application	An object representing the parent application to the command bar.
BuiltIn	A Boolean flag used to distinguish between built-in and custom command bars.
Context	A string indicating where the CommandBar is saved (the format and expected content of this string are dictated by the hosting application).
Controls	A CommandBarControls collection containing CommandBarControl objects; each of these objects represents a control displayed by the command bar.
Creator	An integer value that identifies the application hosting the CommandBar.
Enabled	A Boolean flag indicating whether the command bar is enabled.
Height	The height of the command bar in pixels.
Index	The index of the command bar in the command bar collection.
Left	The distance, in pixels, between the left side of the command bar and the left edge of its parent container.

TABLE 13.10   Continued

Property	Description
Name	The name of the command bar.
NameLocal	The localized name of the command bar.
Parent	An object that is the parent of the command bar.
Position	An MsoBarPosition enum value used to get or set the position of the command bar (for example, MsoBarPosition.msoBarTop).
Protection	An MsoBarProtection enum value that identifies the protection employed against used modification (for example, MsoBarProtection.msoBarNoMove).
RowIndex	An integer representing the docking row of the command bar.
Top	The distance, in pixels, between the top of the command bar and the top edge of its parent container.
Type	The type of the command bar (as an MsobarType enum value; for example, MsoBarType.msoBarTypeNormal).
Visible	A Boolean flag indicating whether the command bar is currently visible.
Width	The width of the command bar in pixels.
Method	**Description**
Delete	Removes the command bar from its parent collection.
FindControl	Enables you to retrieve a reference to a control hosted by the command bar that fits various parameters such as its type, ID, tag, and visibility.
Reset	Resets one of the built-in command bars to its default configuration.
ShowPopup	Displays a pop-up representing a command bar.

NOTE

Previous versions of Visual Studio actually relied on a Microsoft Office assembly for the CommandBar object definition (Microsoft.Office.Core). Visual Studio 2005 and later versions provide their own implementation of the CommandBar object that is defined in the Microsoft.VisualStudio.CommandBars namespace, although you will find some types that carry their nomenclature over from the MS Office assembly, such as the various MsoXXX enums.

Documents

Document objects are used to represent an open document in the IDE. To contrast this abstraction with that provided by the Window object, a Window object is used to represent the physical UI aspects of a document window, whereas a Document object is used to represent the physical document that is being displayed within that document window.

A document could be a designer, such as the Windows Forms designer, or it could be a text-based document such as a readme file or a C# code file open in an editor.

Just as you get a list of all open windows using the DTE.Windows collection, you can use the DTE.Documents collection to retrieve a list of all open documents:

```
Dim documents As Documents = DTE.Documents
```

The Documents collection is indexed by the document's Name property, which is, in effect, the document's filename without the path information. This makes it easy to quickly retrieve a Document instance:

```
Dim documents As Documents = DTE.Documents
Dim readme As Document = documents.Item("ReadMe.txt")
```

Using the Document object, you can do the following:

▶ Close the document (and optionally save changes)

▶ Retrieve the filename and path of the document

▶ Determine whether the document has been modified since the last time it was saved

▶ Determine what, if anything, is currently selected within the document

▶ Obtain a ProjectItem instance representing the project item that is associated with the document

▶ Read and edit the contents of text documents

Table 13.11 contains the member descriptions for the Document object.

TABLE 13.11   Document Members

Property	Description
ActiveWindow	The currently active window associated with the document (null or Nothing value indicates that there is no active window).
Collection	The collection of Document objects to which this instance belongs.
DTE	The root-level DTE object.
Extender	Returns a Document extender object.
ExtenderCATID	The extender category ID for the object.
ExtenderNames	A list of extenders available for the current Document object.

TABLE 13.11 Continued

Property	Description
FullName	The full path and filename of the document.
Kind	A GUID representing the kind of document.
Name	The name (essentially, the filename without path information) for the document.
Path	The path of the document's file excluding the filename.
ProjectItem	The ProjectItem instance associated with the document.
Saved	Indicates whether the solution has been saved since the last modification.
Selection	An object representing the current selection in the document (if any).
Windows	The Windows collection containing the window displaying the document.

Method	Description
Activate	Moves the focus to the document.
Close	Closes the document. You can indicate, with a vsSaveChanges enum value, whether the window's hosted document should be saved or not saved, or whether the IDE should prompt the user to make that decision.
NewWindow	Opens the document in a new window and returns the new window's Window object.
Object	Returns an object proxy that represents the window and can be referenced by name.
Redo	Reexecutes the last user action in the document.
Save	Saves the document.
Undo	Reverses the last used action in the document.

Text Documents

As we mentioned, documents can have textual or nontextual content. For those documents with textual content, a separate object—TextDocument—exists. The TextDocument object provides access to control functions specifically related to text content.

If you have a valid Document object to start with, and if that Document object refers to a text document, then a TextDocument instance can be referenced from the Document.Object property like this:

```
Dim doc As TextDocument
Dim myDocument As Document

doc = myDocument.Object
```

Table 13.12 contains the TextDocument members.

TABLE 13.12   TextDocument Members

Property	Description
DTE	The root-level DTE object.
EndPoint	A TextPoint object positioned at the end of the document.
Parent	Gets the parent object of the text document.
Selection	Returns a TextSelection object representing the currently selected text in the document.
StartPoint	A TextPoint object positioned at the start of the document.
Method	**Description**
ClearBookmarks	Removes any unnamed bookmarks present in the document.
CreateEditPoint	Returns an edit point at the specific location (if no location is specified, the beginning of the document is assumed).
MarkText	Bookmarks lines in the document that match the specified string pattern.
ReplacePattern	Replaces any text in the document that matches the pattern.

TIP

A text document is represented by both a Document instance and a TextDocument instance. Nontext documents, such as a Windows form open in a Windows Forms designer window, have a Document representation but no corresponding TextDocument representation. Unfortunately, there isn't a great way to distinguish whether a document is text-based during runtime. One approach is to attempt a cast or assignment to a TextDocument object and catch any exceptions that might occur during the assignment.

Two TextDocument methods are useful for manipulating bookmarks within the document: ClearBookmarks removes any unnamed bookmarks from the document, and MarkText performs a string pattern search and places bookmarks against the resulting document lines. A simple macro to bookmark For loops in a VB document is presented in Listing 13.10.

LISTING 13.10   Bookmarking For Loops in a VB Document

```
Imports EnvDTE
Imports EnvDTE80
Imports EnvDTE90
```

```
Imports Microsoft.VisualStudio.CommandBars
Imports System.Diagnostics
Imports System.Windows.Forms


Public Module MacroExamples

    ' Bookmark all 'For' tokens in the current
    ' document
    Public Sub BookmarkFor()
        Dim doc As Document
        Dim txtDoc As TextDocument

        ' Reference the current document
        doc = DTE.ActiveDocument

        ' Retrieve a TextDocument instance from
        ' the document
        txtDoc = doc.Object

        ' Call the MarkText method with the 'For' string
        Dim found As Boolean = _
            txtDoc.MarkText("For", vsFindOptions.vsFindOptionsFromStart)

        ' MarkText returns a boolean flag indicating whether or not
        ' the search pattern was found in the textdocument
        If found Then
            MessageBox.Show("All instances of 'For' have been bookmarked.")
        Else
            MessageBox.Show("No instances of 'For' were found.")
        End If
    End Sub

End Module
```

The other key functionality exposed by the TextDocument object is the capability to read and edit the text within the document.

Editing Text Documents

From a Visual Studio perspective, text in a text document actually has two distinct "representations": a virtual one and a physical one. The physical representation is the straight, unadulterated code file that sits on disk. The virtual representation is what Visual Studio presents on the screen: It is an interpreted view of the text in the code file that takes into account various editor document features such as code outlining/regions, virtual spacing, and word wrapping.

Figure 13.7 shows this relationship. When displaying a text document, Visual Studio reads the source file into a text buffer, and then the text editor presents one view of that text file to you (based on options you have configured for the editor).

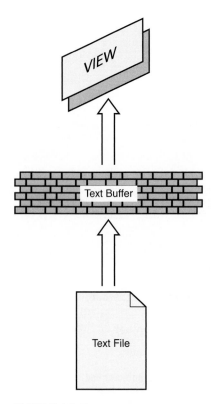

FIGURE 13.7   Presentation of text documents within the IDE.

Text in a document is manipulated or read either on the buffered text or on the "view" text that you see in the editor. There are four different automation objects that enable you to affect text; two work on the text buffer and two work on the editor view.

For the text buffer:

▶ TextPoint objects are used to locate specific points within a text document. By querying the TextPoint properties, you can determine the line number of the text point, the number of characters it is offset from the start of a line, the number of characters it is offset from the start of the document, and its display column within the text editor window. You can also retrieve a reference to a CodeModel object representing the code at the text point's current location.

▶ The EditPoint object inherits from the TextPoint object; this is the primary object used for manipulating text in the text buffer. You can add, delete, or move text using edit points, and they can be moved around within the text buffer.

And, for the editor view:

▶ The VirtualPoint object is equivalent to the TextPoint object except that it can be used to query text locations that reside in the "virtual" space of the text view (virtual space is the whitespace that exists after the last character in a document line). VirtualPoint instances are returned through the TextSelection object.

▶ The TextSelection object operates on text within the text editor view as opposed to the text buffer and is equivalent to the EditPoint interface. When you use the TextSelection object, you are actively affecting the text that is being displayed within the text editor. The methods and properties of this object, therefore, end up being programmatic approximations of the various ways that you would manually affect text: You can page up or page down within the view; cut, copy, and paste text; select a range of text; or even outline and expand or collapse regions of text.

Because the VirtualPoint object is nearly identical to the TextPoint object, and the TextSelection object is nearly identical to the EditPoint object, we won't bother to cover each of these four objects in detail. Instead, we focus on text buffer operations using EditPoint and TextPoint. You should be able to easily apply the concepts here to the text view.

Because EditPoint objects expose the most functionality and play the central role with text editing, we have provided a list of their type members in Table 13.13.

TABLE 13.13   EditPoint2 Members

Property	Description
AbsoluteCharOffset	The number of characters from the start of the document to the current location of the edit point.
AtEndOfDocument	Boolean flag indicating whether the point is at the end of the document.
AtEndOfLine	Boolean flag indicating whether the point is at the end of a line in the document.
AtStartOfDocument	Boolean flag indicating whether the point is at the beginning of the document.
AtStartOfLine	Boolean flag indicating whether the point is at the start of a line in the document.
CodeElement	Returns the code element that maps to the edit point's current location.
DisplayColumn	The column number of the edit point.
DTE	Returns the root automation DTE object.
Line	The line number where the point is positioned.
LineCharOffset	The character offset, within a line, of the edit point.
LineLength	The length of the line where the edit point is positioned.

TABLE 13.13   Continued

Property	Description
Parent	Returns the parent object of the EditPoint2 object.

Method	Description
ChangeCase	Changes the case of a range of text.
CharLeft	Moves the edit point to the left the specified number of characters.
CharRight	Moves the edit point to the right the specified number of characters.
ClearBookmark	Clears any unnamed bookmarks that exist on the point's current line location.
Copy	Copies a range of text to the Clipboard.
CreateEditPoint	Creates a new EditPoint object at the same location as the current EditPoint object.
Cut	Cuts a range of text and places it on the Clipboard.
Delete	Deletes a range of text from the document.
DeleteWhitespace	Deletes any whitespace found around the edit point.
EndOfDocument	Moves the edit point to the end of the document.
EndOfLine	Moves the edit point to the end of the current line.
EqualTo	A Boolean value indicating whether the edit point's AbsoluteCharOffset value is equal to another edit point's offset.
FindPattern	Finds any matching string patterns in the document.
GetLines	A string representing the text between two lines in the document.
GetText	A string representing the text between the edit point and another location in the document.
GreaterThan	A Boolean value indicating whether the edit point's AbsoluteCharOffset value is greater than another edit point's offset.
Indent	Indents the selected lines by the given number of levels.
Insert	Inserts a string into the document, starting at the edit point's current location.
InsertFromFile	Inserts the entire contents of a text file into the document starting at the edit point's current location.
LessThan	Returns a Boolean value indicating whether the edit point's AbsoluteCharOffset value is less than another edit point's offset.
LineDown	Moves the point down one or more lines.

TABLE 13.13   Continued

Property	Description
LineUp	Moves the point up one or more lines.
MoveToAbsoluteOffset	Moves the edit point to the given character offset.
MoveToLineAndOffset	Moves the edit point to the given line and to the character offset within that line.
MoveToPoint	Moves the edit point to the location of another EditPoint or TextPoint object.
NextBookmark	Moves the edit point to the next available bookmark in the document.
OutlineSection	Creates an outline section between the point's current location and another location in the document.
PadToColumn	Pads spaces in the current line up to the indicated column number.
Paste	Pastes the contents of the Clipboard to the edit point's current location.
PreviousBookmark	Moves the edit point to the previous bookmark.
ReadOnly	Returns a Boolean flag indicating whether a text range in the document is read-only.
ReplacePattern	Replaces any text that matches the provided pattern.
ReplaceText	Replaces a range of text with the provided string.
SetBookmark	Creates an unnamed bookmark on the edit point's current line in the document.
StartOfDocument	Moves the edit point to the start of the document.
StartOfLine	Moves the edit point to the beginning of the line where it is positioned.
TryToShow	Attempts to display the point's current location within the text editor window.
Unindent	Removes the given number of indentation levels from a range of lines in the document.
WordLeft	Moves the edit point to the left the given number of words.
WordRight	Moves the edit point to the right the given number of words.

13

Now let's look at various text manipulation scenarios.

Adding Text   EditPoint objects are the key to adding text, and you create them either by using a TextDocument object or by using a TextPoint object.

A TextPoint instance can create an EditPoint instance in its same exact location by calling TextPoint.CreateInstance. With the TextDocument type, you can call the CreateEditPoint method and pass in a valid TextPoint.

Because TextPoint objects are used to locate specific points in a document, a TextPoint object is leveraged as an input parameter to CreateEditPoint. In essence, the object tells the method where to create the edit point. If you don't provide a TextPoint object, the edit point is created at the start of the document.

This code snippet shows an edit point being created at the end of a document:

```
Dim doc As Document = DTE.ActiveDocument
Dim txtDoc As TextDocument = doc.Object
Dim tp As TextPoint = txtDoc.EndPoint
Dim ep As EditPoint2 = txtDoc.CreateEditPoint(tp)
' This line of code would have the same effect
ep = tp.CreateEditPoint
```

After creating an edit point, you can use it to add text into the document (remember, you are editing the buffered text whenever you use an EditPoint object). To inject a string into the document, you use the Insert method:

```
' Insert a C# comment line
ep.Insert("// some comment")
```

You can even grab the contents of a file and throw that into the document with the EditPoint.InsertFromFile method:

```
' Insert comments from a comments file
ep.InsertFromFile("C:\Contoso\std comments.txt")
```

Editing Text   The EditPoint object supports deleting, replacing, cutting, copying, and pasting text in a document.

Some of these operations require more than a single point to operate. For instance, if you want to cut a word or an entire line of code from a document, you need to specify a start point and end point that define that range of text (see Figure 13.8).

FIGURE 13.8   Using points within a document to select text.

This snippet uses two end points, one at the start of a document and one at the end, to delete the entire contents of the document:

```
Dim doc As Document = DTE.ActiveDocument
Dim txtDoc As TextDocument = doc.Object

Dim tpStart As TextPoint = txtDoc.StartPoint
Dim tpEnd As TextPoint = txtDoc.EndPoint

Dim epStart As EditPoint2 = txtDoc.CreateEditPoint(tpStart)
Dim epEnd As EditPoint2 = txtDoc.CreateEditPoint(tpEnd)
epStart.Delete(epEnd)
```

Besides accepting a second EditPoint, the methods that operate on a range of text also accept an integer identifying a count of characters. This has the effect of defining a select. For example, this snippet cuts the first 10 characters from a document:

```
epStart.Cut(10)
```

Repositioning an EditPoint   After establishing an EditPoint, you can move it to any location in the document by using various methods. The CharLeft and CharRight methods move the point any number of characters to the left or right, whereas the WordLeft and WordRight methods perform the same operation with words:

```
' Move the edit point 4 words to the right
epStart.WordRight(4)
```

The LineUp and LineDown methods jog the point up or down the specified number of lines. You can also move EditPoints to any given line within a document by using MoveToLineAndOffset. This method also positions the point any number of characters into the line:

```
' Move the edit point to line 100, and then
' in 5 characters to the right
epStart.MoveToLineAndOffset(100, 5)
```

The macro code in Listing 13.11 pulls together some of the areas that we have covered with editing text documents. This macro and its supporting functions illustrate the use of EditPoints to write text into a document. In this case, the macro automatically inserts a comment "flowerbox" immediately preceding a routine. To accomplish this, the macro goes through the following process:

1. A reference is obtained for the current document in the IDE.
2. The active cursor location in that document is obtained via the TextDocument.Selection.ActivePoint property.
3. An EditPoint is created using the VirtualPoint returned from the.
4. A second EditPoint is then created; these two points are used to obtain the entire content of the routine definition line.
5. The routine definition is then parsed to try to ferret out items such as its name, return value, and parameter list.
6. A string is built using the routine information and is inserted into the text document using an EditPoint.

LISTING 13.11   Inserting Comments into a Text Window

```
Imports EnvDTE
Imports EnvDTE80
Imports EnvDTE90
Imports Microsoft.VisualStudio.CommandBars
Imports System
Imports System.Collections
Imports System.Diagnostics
Imports System.Text
Imports System.Windows.Forms


Public Module MacroExamples

    ' This routine demonstrates various text editing scenarios
    ' using the EditPoint and TextPoint types. If you place your
    ' cursor on a subroutine or function, it will build a default
    ' "flower box" comment area, insert it immediately above the
    ' sub/function, and outline it.
    '
    ' To use:
    '    1) put cursor anywhere on the Sub/Function line
    '    2) run macro
    '    The macro will fail silently (e.g., will not insert any
    '    comments) if it is unable to determine the start
    '    of the Sub/Function
```

'

```
Public Sub InsertTemplateFlowerbox()

    ' Get reference to the active document
    Dim doc As Document = DTE.ActiveDocument
    Dim txtDoc As TextDocument = doc.Object
    Dim isFunc As Boolean

    Try
        Dim ep As EditPoint2 = txtDoc.Selection.ActivePoint.CreateEditPoint()

        ep.StartOfLine()
        Dim ep2 As EditPoint2 = ep.CreateEditPoint()
        ep2.EndOfLine()

        Dim lineText As String = ep.GetText(ep2).Trim()

        If InStr(lineText, " Function ") > 0 Then
            isFunc = True
        ElseIf InStr(lineText, " Sub ") > 0 Then
            isFunc = False
        Else
            Exit Sub
        End If

        ' Parse out info that we can derive from the routine
        ' definition: the return value type (if this is a function),
        ' the names of the parameters, and the name of the routine.
        Dim returnType As String = ""
        If isFunc Then
            returnType = ParseRetValueType(lineText)
        End If

        Dim parameters As String() = ParseParameters(lineText)
        Dim name As String = ParseRoutineName(lineText)
        Dim commentBlock As String = BuildCommentBlock(isFunc, name, _
        _returnType, parameters)

        ' Move the edit point up one line (to position
        ' immediately preceding the routine)
        ep.LineUp(1)

        ' Give us some room by inserting a new blank line
        ep.InsertNewLine()
```

```vbnet
        ' Insert our comment block
        ep.Insert(commentBlock.ToString())

    Catch ex As Exception
    End Try

End Sub
Private Function BuildCommentBlock(ByVal isFunc As Boolean, _
    ByVal name As String, _
    ByVal returnType As String, ByVal parameters As String())

    Try
        Dim comment As StringBuilder = New StringBuilder()

        ' Build up a sample comment block using the passed in info
        comment.Append("''''''''''''''''''''''''''''''''''''''''''''''''''")
        comment.Append(vbCrLf)
        comment.Append("' Routine: " + name)
        comment.Append(vbCrLf)
        comment.Append("' Description: [insert routine desc here]")
        comment.Append(vbCrLf)
        comment.Append("'")
        comment.Append(vbCrLf)
        If isFunc Then
            comment.Append("' Returns: A " & returnType &
            ➥"[insert return value description here]")
        End If
        comment.Append(vbCrLf)
        comment.Append("'")
        comment.Append(vbCrLf)
        comment.Append("' Parameters:")
        comment.Append(vbCrLf)
        For i As Integer = 0 To parameters.GetUpperBound(0)
            comment.Append("'        ")
            comment.Append(parameters(i))
            comment.Append(": [insert parameter description here]")
            comment.Append(vbCrLf)
        Next
        comment.Append("''''''''''''''''''''''''''''''''''''''''''''''''''")

        Return comment.ToString()

    Catch ex As Exception
        Return ""
    End Try
```

```vb
End Function
Private Function ParseRetValueType(ByVal code As String) As String
    Try
        ' Parse out the return value of a function (VB)
        ' Search for 'As', starting from the end of the string
        Dim length As Integer = code.Length
        Dim index As Integer = code.LastIndexOf(" As ")

        Dim retVal As String = code.Substring(index + 3, length - (index + 3))

        Return retVal.Trim()

    Catch ex As Exception

        Return ""
    End Try
End Function
Private Function ParseParameters(ByVal code As String) As String()
    Try
        ' Parse out the parameters specified (if any) for
        ' a VB sub/func definition
        Dim length As Integer = code.Length
        Dim indexStart As Integer = code.IndexOf("(")
        Dim indexEnd As Integer = code.LastIndexOf(")")

        Dim params As String = code.Substring(indexStart + 1, indexEnd
        ➡(indexStart + 1))

        Return params.Split(",")

    Catch ex As Exception
        Return Nothing
    End Try
End Function
Private Function ParseRoutineName(ByVal code As String) As String
    Try
        Dim name As String
        Dim length As Integer = code.Length
        Dim indexStart As Integer = code.IndexOf(" Sub ")
        Dim indexEnd As Integer = code.IndexOf("(")
        If indexStart = -1 Then
            indexStart = code.IndexOf(" Function ")
            If indexStart <> -1 Then
                indexStart = indexStart + 9
            End If
        Else
```

13

```
                indexStart = indexStart + 5
        End If

        name = code.Substring(indexStart, indexEnd - indexStart)

        Return name.Trim()

    Catch ex As Exception
        Return ""
    End Try
End Function

End Module
```

Command Objects

Every action that is possible to execute through the menus and toolbars in Visual Studio is generically referred to as a command. For example, pasting text into a window is a command, as are building a project, toggling a breakpoint, and closing a window.

For each command supported in the IDE, there is a corresponding Command object; the DTE.Commands collection holds all the valid Command object instances. Each command is keyed by a name that categorizes, describes, and uniquely identifies the command. The "paste" command, for instance, is available via the string key "Edit.Paste". If you want to retrieve the Command object mapping to the paste command, you pull from the Commands collection using that string key:

```
Dim commands As Commands2 = DTE.Commands
Dim cmd As Command = commands.Item("Edit.Paste")
```

You can query a command's name via its Name property:

```
' name would = "Edit.Paste"
Dim name As String = cmd.Name
```

Table 13.14 contains the members declared on the Command interface.

The list of all available commands is extremely long (nearly 3,000 total), and it is therefore impossible to cover every one of them here, or even a large portion of them. To get an idea, however, of the specific commands available, you can use the dialog box used to customize the Visual Studio toolbars. If you select the Customize option from the View, Toolbars menu and then click on the Commands tab, you can investigate all the various commands by category (see Figure 13.9). Another alternative is to programmatically iterate the DTE.Commands collection and view them that way. In fact, in Chapter 14, we use this as one scenario for showcasing add-in development.

TABLE 13.14   Command Members

Property	Description
Bindings	The keystrokes that can be used to invoke the command.
Collection	The Commands collection that the Command object belongs to.
DTE	A reference to the root-level DTE object.
Guid	A GUID that identifies the command's group.
ID	An integer that identifies the command within its group.
IsAvailable	A Boolean flag that indicates whether the command is currently available.
LocalizedName	The localized name of the command.
Name	The name of the command.

Method	Description
AddControl	Creates a control for the command that can be hosted in a command bar.
Delete	Removes a named command that was previously added with the Commands.AddNamedCommand method.

FIGURE 13.9   Using the Customize dialog box to view commands.

So, although we can't cover all the commands, you can learn how to perform common tasks with the Command objects such as executing a command, checking on a command's current status, and even adding your own commands to the command library.

Executing a Command

Commands can be executed in two ways. The DTE object has an ExecuteCommand method you can use to trigger a command based on its name:

```
DTE.ExecuteCommand("Window.CloseDocumentWindow")
```

The Commands collection is also a vehicle for launching commands through its Raise method. Instead of using the command's name, the Raise method uses its GUID and ID to identify the command:

```
Dim commands As Commands2 = DTE.Commands
Dim cmd As Command = commands.Item("Window.CloseDocumentWindow")
Dim customIn, customOut As Object

commands.Raise(cmd.Guid, cmd.ID, customin, customout)
```

Some commands accept arguments. The Shell command is one example. It is used to launch an external application into the shell environment and thus takes the application filename as one of its parameters. You can launch this command by using the ExecuteCommand method like this:

```
Dim commands As Commands2 = DTE.Commands
Dim cmd As Command = commands.Item("Tools.Shell")
Dim arg1 = "MyApp.exe"

DTE.ExecuteCommand(cmd.Name, arg1)
```

The Raise method also works with arguments: The last two parameters provided to the Raise method are used to specify an array of arguments to be used by the command and an array of output values returned from the command.

Mapping Key Bindings

Most commands can be invoked by a keyboard shortcut in addition to a menu entry or button on a command bar. You can set these keyboard shortcuts on a per-command basis by using the Command.Bindings property. This property returns or accepts a SafeArray (essentially an array of objects) that contains each shortcut as an element of the array.

Key bindings are represented as strings with the following format: "[scopename]::[modifier+][key]".

Scopename is used to refer to the scope where the shortcut is valid, such as `Text Editor` or `Global`. The *modifier* token is used to specify the key modifier such as "Ctrl+," "Alt+," or "Shift+" (modifiers are not required). And the *key* is the keyboard key that is pressed (in conjunction with the modifier if present) to invoke the command.

To add a binding to an existing command, you first need to retrieve the current array of binding values, add your binding string to the array, and then assign the whole array back into the `Bindings` property like this:

```
Dim commands As Commands2 = DTE.Commands
Dim cmd As Command = _
    commands.Item("File.SaveSelectedItems")

Dim bindings() As Object

bindings = cmd.Bindings

' Increase the array size by 1 to hold the new binding
ReDim Preserve bindings(bindings.GetUpperBound(0) + 1)

' Assign the new binding into the array
bindings(bindings.GetUpperBound(0)) = "Global::Shift+F2"

' Assign the array back to the command object
cmd.Bindings = bindings
```

> **NOTE**
>
> You can create your own named commands that can be launched from a command bar in the IDE (or from the command window for that matter). The Command object itself is added to the Commands collection by calling Commands.AddNamedCommand. The code that runs when the command is executed has to be implemented by an add-in. We cover this scenario in Chapter 14.

Debugger Objects

The automation object model provides a Debugger object that enables you to control the Visual Studio debugger. A Debugger instance can be obtained through the DTE.Debugger property:

```
Dim debugger As EnvDTE.Debugger
debugger = DTE.Debugger
```

With a valid Debugger object, you can do the following:

▶ Set breakpoints

- ▸ Start and stop the debugger for a given process

- ▸ Control the various execution stepping actions supported by the debugger such as Step Into, Step Over, and Step Out

- ▸ Issue the Run to Cursor command to the debugger

- ▸ Query the debugger for its current mode (for example, break mode, design mode, or run mode)

The following code starts the debugger if it isn't already started:

```
Dim debugger As Debugger2
debugger = DTE.Debugger

If debugger.CurrentMode <> dbgDebugMode.dbgRunMode Then
    debugger.Go()

End If
```

Automation Events

If your macro or add-in needs to be notified when a certain event occurs, various event objects are supported in all the automation object categories previously discussed. There are events for windows, events for editors, events for projects, and so on. For every event supported by the IDE, a corresponding class in the automation model allows you to hook the event and take action if the event is raised. The event objects tree is rooted in the DTE.Events property, as depicted in Figure 13.10.

Because events are handled differently depending on whether you are working with code in an add-in or code in a macro, we cover the details of handling events in Chapter 14. The basic premise, however, is fairly simple: You obtain a reference to the event object that you are interested in and then write an event handler that responds to one of that object's published events.

This code, for instance, is how you might handle the "build complete" event from inside a Visual Basic add-in:

```
Dim WithEvents bldevents As BuildEvents
bldevents = DTE.Events.BuildEvents
```

After instantiating a BuildEvents object, you now have to write the actual event handler:

```
Private Sub bldevents_OnBuildDone(ByVal Scope As EnvDTE.vsBuildScope, _
    ByVal Action As EnvDTE.vsBuildAction) Handles bldevents.OnBuildDone
        ' Code to handle the event goes here
    End Sub
```

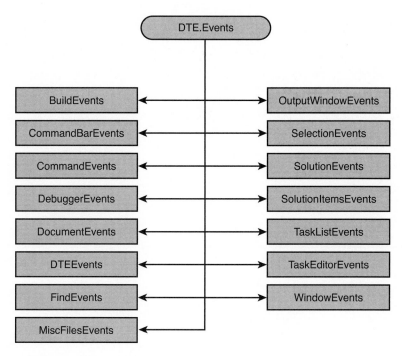

FIGURE 13.10   DTE Event types.

Summary

The Visual Studio automation object model is a deep and wide API that exposes many of the IDE components to managed code running as a macro or an add-in. In this chapter, we documented how this API is organized and described its capabilities in terms of controlling the Visual Studio debugger, editors, windows, tool windows, solutions, and projects.

We also discussed the eventing model exposed by the API and looked at the API's capabilities with regard to accessing the underlying code structure for a project, issuing commands inside the IDE, and editing text documents programmatically.

Using the methods and properties expressed on the automation objects, you can automate common tasks in the IDE and extend Visual Studio in ways that address your specific development tool needs.

In the next chapter, we directly build on the concepts discussed here and specifically walk you through the process of writing macros that talk to the automation objects.

CHAPTER 14

Writing Macros

Chapter 13, "Introducing the Object Automation Model," covers the API available for developers to customize, tweak, and control various portions of the Visual Studio IDE. This chapter takes that knowledge and shows you how to write macros that leverage the automation object model.

A macro's purpose is to provide you with an approach for writing your own task automation applets. In previous chapters, you saw many IDE features that automate repetitive tasks. The built-in refactoring support, IntelliSense word completion, code snippets, and other features certainly fall into that category. As you develop solutions with Visual Studio, you will find yourself performing additional repetitive tasks that beg for a solution, and macros are a solution. They are Visual Basic routines that interact with the automation object model to control various aspects of the IDE. Although macros can certainly be complex pieces of logic, their real value lies in the fact that it is relatively simple to write short, quick routines that take some of the manual pain away from the development process. Macros aren't used so much to add new functionality to the IDE as to batch together actions in the IDE and enable a single invocation point for those actions.

If you think about the common tasks that you perform while developing a Visual Studio solution, the macro's value lies in its capability to help you automate those tasks where it makes sense. Chapter 13 includes a macro sample that inserts a comment "flowerbox" at the start of a function or subroutine. The goal with that macro was to reduce the time required to fully comment routines. That particular macro wasn't complicated, nor did it solve a particularly egregious software engineering problem. Its intent, rather, was to take a small edge off a very manual component to the code-writing process: commenting your code. So the macro development process really starts with first identifying an opportunity for automation. The next step is to understand the

IDE objects you have to touch to effect a solution. The final step is tying those objects together with Visual Basic code in the form of a macro.

We have already covered two of the three pieces of knowledge that enable you to become proficient with macros: We discussed the automation object model in-depth in the preceding chapter, and we summarized the scenarios in which macros shine. The third and final piece is understanding the mechanics of writing a macro from start to finish and then executing the macro in the IDE.

Macros can be handcrafted or generated for you by recording certain actions within the IDE. In fact, Visual Studio even has a separate macro development environment—the Macros IDE—designed to help you quickly develop macro solutions.

Recording a Macro

The simplest way to create a macro is to record one: Just turn on Visual Studio's macro recorder and perform a series of actions in the IDE. The macro recorder turns your IDE interactions into macro code.

To start recording a macro, select Tools, Macros, Record TemporaryMacro (or press Shift+Ctrl+R). This immediately starts the recorder; a small toolbar, as shown in Figure 14.1, appears at this point to enable you to control the recording.

FIGURE 14.1   The Macro Recorder toolbar.

The three buttons on the toolbar enable you to pause and resume the recording, stop the recording, or cancel the recording. Pausing the recording does just that: The recorder stops recording your actions in the IDE, although it still remains active. Clicking the button a second time resumes recording. Stopping the recording causes the macro code to be generated and saved for later execution. Canceling the recording stops the recorder but does not save the macro.

With the recorder running, perform a series of actions in the IDE. Suppose that you want to have an easy way to expand all the project nodes (and their subnodes) in the Solution Explorer window. To record this action, you simply start the recorder, and then click on each of the project items in the Solution Explorer to expand them in their tree view. When you are finished going through every project and project item, click on the Stop Recording button. The macro is stored at this point as a "temporary" macro. It is not saved to disk at this stage, but you can immediately run it by selecting Run TemporaryMacro from the Tools, Macros menu.

> **NOTE**
>
> Only one temporary macro is stored at a time in Visual Studio. This means that if you record another temporary macro, the new macro simply replaces the current temporary macro. If you want to have the macro around for a while, you can store it on disk by selecting Tools, Macros, Save TemporaryMacro. If the Macro Explorer is not already displayed, this selection displays it.

Using the Macro Explorer

The Macro Explorer is the central tool within the IDE for managing macros. Macros are organized in projects and modules. For instance, the temporary macro that you just created shows up under the MyMacros project, under a module called RecordingModule, and it is called TemporaryMacro.

If you have selected to save the temporary macro, Visual Studio automatically places that TemporaryMacro node in edit mode with the name highlighted. This is your cue to type in a name for the macro. Pressing Enter commits the name change and causes the macro to be saved to disk. If you don't change the name, it is not saved.

Using the Macro Explorer, you can rename or delete macros and run macros.

To execute a macro, just double-click on its node in the Macro Explorer. This immediately runs the macro's code. While a macro is running or recording, you see an animated icon and a status message on Visual Studio's status bar (see Figure 14.2).

FIGURE 14.2   Macro indicators in the status bar.

TIP

Macros don't have any default or prebuilt notification mechanism that tells you when the macro has completed or if the macro has encountered an error. If you want to track a macro's progress, you need to edit the macro accordingly so that it outputs messages to the output window, through message boxes or other means.

To see the Visual Basic code responsible for implementing the macro, right-click on the macro in the Macro Explorer and select Edit to launch the Macro IDE. You can also launch the IDE by selecting Tools, Macros, Macros IDE (or pressing Ctrl+F11). The code generated by our prior recording attempt is shown in Listing 14.1. The commands for deleting or renaming a macro, macro module, or macro project are also located on the right-click menu in the Macro Explorer.

LISTING 14.1   Recorder-Generated Macro Code

```
Option Strict Off
Option Explicit Off
Imports System
Imports EnvDTE
Imports EnvDTE80
Imports EnvDTE90
Imports EnvDTE100
Imports System.Diagnostics


Public Module RecordingModule

    Sub TemporaryMacro()
DTE.ActiveWindow.Object.GetItem("ContosoCommonFramework\Architecture
➡Models").UIHierarchyItems.Expanded = True
DTE.ActiveWindow.Object.GetItem("ContosoCommonFramework\Class Libraries").
➡UIHierarchyItems.Expanded = True
DTE.ActiveWindow.Object.GetItem("ContosoCommonFramework\Class
➡Libraries\Contoso.Fx.Analysis\Properties").UIHierarchyItems.Expanded = True
DTE.ActiveWindow.Object.GetItem("ContosoCommonFramework\Class
➡Libraries\Contoso.Fx.Analysis\References").UIHierarchyItems.Expanded = True
DTE.ActiveWindow.Object.GetItem("ContosoCommonFramework\Class
➡Libraries\Contoso.Fx.Common\Properties").UIHierarchyItems.Expanded = True
DTE.ActiveWindow.Object.GetItem("ContosoCommonFramework\Class
➡Libraries\Contoso.Fx.Common\References").UIHierarchyItems.Expanded = True
DTE.ActiveWindow.Object.GetItem("ContosoCommonFramework\Class
➡Libraries\Contoso.Fx.Integration\Properties").UIHierarchyItems.Expanded = True
DTE.ActiveWindow.Object.GetItem("ContosoCommonFramework\Class
➡Libraries\Contoso.Fx.Integration\References").UIHierarchyItems.Expanded = True
DTE.ActiveWindow.Object.GetItem("ContosoCommonFramework\Consoles\AdminConsole").
```

```
➥UIHierarchyItems.Expanded = True
DTE.ActiveWindow.Object.GetItem("ContosoCommonFramework\Consoles\HelloWorld").
➥UIHierarchyItems.Expanded = True
DTE.ActiveWindow.Object.GetItem("ContosoCommonFramework\Consoles").
➥UIHierarchyItems.Expanded = True
DTE.ActiveWindow.Object.GetItem("ContosoCommonFramework\Consoles\AdminConsole\
➥Properties").UIHierarchyItems.Expanded = True
DTE.ActiveWindow.Object.GetItem("ContosoCommonFramework\Consoles\AdminConsole\
➥References").UIHierarchyItems.Expanded = True
DTE.ActiveWindow.Object.GetItem("ContosoCommonFramework\Consoles\HelloWorld\
➥Properties").UIHierarchyItems.Expanded = True
DTE.ActiveWindow.Object.GetItem("ContosoCommonFramework\Consoles\HelloWorld\
➥References").UIHierarchyItems.Expanded = True
DTE.ActiveWindow.Object.GetItem("ContosoCommonFramework\Consoles\HelloWorld\
➥XMLSchema1.xsd").UIHierarchyItems.Expanded = True
DTE.ActiveWindow.Object.GetItem("ContosoCommonFramework\Forms").UIHierarchyItems.
➥Expanded = True
DTE.ActiveWindow.Object.GetItem("ContosoCommonFramework\Forms\Contoso.UI.
➥WindowsForms.TestHost\Properties").UIHierarchyItems.Expanded = True
DTE.ActiveWindow.Object.GetItem("ContosoCommonFramework\Forms\Contoso.UI.
➥WindowsForms.TestHost\References").UIHierarchyItems.Expanded = True
DTE.ActiveWindow.Object.GetItem("ContosoCommonFramework\Forms\Contoso.UI.
➥WindowsForms.TestHost\Form1.jsl").UIHierarchyItems.Expanded = True
DTE.ActiveWindow.Object.GetItem("ContosoCommonFramework\C:\...\PortalSite\").
➥UIHierarchyItems.Expanded = True
    End Sub
End Module
```

14

Writing Macros with the Macro IDE

The Macros IDE, shown in Figure 14.3, is essentially a specialized version of Visual Studio, trimmed down and streamlined to support the macro development process.

Immediately, you can see that this is, in fact, the Visual Studio user interface that you are by now used to working with. Everything behaves the same: Tool windows can be docked, can float, can be pinned, and so on. The code editor window that you use to edit your macro code works the same with IntelliSense, outlining, and all the other productivity aids you have come to expect. Although the Macros IDE behaves identically to the full-blown Visual Studio IDE, there are some differences. For instance, it has only a subset of the tool windows and document windows supported in the full IDE. Language support in the code editor is limited strictly to Visual Basic (because that is the only macro language supported), and you can't design forms or any similar artifacts here.

FIGURE 14.3   The Visual Studio Macros IDE.

Working with Macro Projects

The Project Explorer tool window works on the same principles as the Solution Explorer; it presents a tree view of your work items. In the case of macros, the tree nodes are organized like this: project -> module. Individual macros are displayed in the code editor window (note that this is essentially the same as the Macro Explorer view, with the exception that the Macro Explorer's tree shows each individual macro by name).

In our case, we recorded a temporary macro, and it shows up under the MyMacros project, in the module named RecordingModule. If you look back at Figure 14.3, you see a portion of the code that was created when the macro was recorded; it is all contained in a Visual Basic sub called TemporaryMacro().

> **TIP**
>
> When you use the macro recorder, the code that it emits is automatically stored in the MyMacros project. To change this, just right-click any other macro project in the Macro Explorer and select Set as Recording Project.

Macro projects map one-to-one with a folder on disk; they are not the same as Visual Studio projects. By default, you have a MyMacros project (which maps to the folder MyMacros under Documents\Visual Studio 2010\Projects\VSMacros80) and a Samples project (which maps to a Samples folder under the same directory tree). Within each macro project directory, there is a .vsmacros file whose name is the same as the project directory's name. Thus, there is a Samples.vsmacros file in the Samples folder, and a MyMacros.vsmacros file in the MyMacros folder.

The .vsmacro file contains all the code for the individual macros (and modules) within the project that it maps to. This is a huge difference from the way that Visual Studio works with project files. A macro does not map to its own file like a project item does in, say, a Visual Basic class library project.

Sharing Macros

You might be surprised to learn that the default, native storage format for macros is binary. Technically, the .vsmacros file is a COM-structured storage file; within this file resides all the source code for every macro in the project. To share a specific macro module with others, you can export the module to a Visual Basic (.vb) file. To do so, perform the following steps:

1. Right-click the macro module in the Macros IDE Project Explorer.

2. Select Export ModuleName. The Export File dialog box launches (see Figure 14.4).

FIGURE 14.4   Exporting a macro module.

3. Select a location and filename, and the macro code is written into the file in plain text.

After you export a macro module, you can physically share it with other developers by passing the file around. Importing a previously exported macro file is easy: From the Macros IDE, select Project, Add Existing Item and select the macro .vb file to import; this places it into the macro project currently selected in the Project Explorer.

By sharing the entire .vsmacros file, you can also share entire macro projects at a time. It is often helpful in this scenario to change the default storage format from binary to text. You accomplish this from the primary Visual Studio IDE by first selecting a macro project in the Macro Explorer and then, in the property window, changing the Storage Format property from Binary to Text (see Figure 14.5).

FIGURE 14.5   Changing the macro project's storage format.

Immediately after changing this property value, Visual Studio converts the single binary macro project file to a series of plain-text files. Each module is represented by its own .vb file at this stage. See Figure 14.6 for a look at the files in the MyMacros folder, after the MyMacros project has been converted to text.

FIGURE 14.6   A macro project stored as text.

Adding a Project

Confusingly, the capability to add a macro project is not present in the Macros IDE. In other words, there is no File, Open command for opening a .vsmacro file. You can, however, do this in the Visual Studio IDE by selecting Tools, Macros, Load Macro Project. From there, you simply browse for the .vsmacros file that contains the project you want to load. If you want to create a new, empty macro project, select Tools, Macros, New Macro Project.

After a macro project has been added, it is immediately accessible in the Macros IDE.

Writing a Macro

If you revisit the code in Listing 14.1 that was generated for you when you recorded your Solution Explorer node expansions, you can see that it is straightforward, and represents a verbatim replay of what you manually accomplished in the Solution Explorer window. The macro references each individual item in the Explorer window by using the ActiveWindow.Object.GetItem method, passing in the object's name to get a UIHierarchyItem reference. From there, it is a simple property set to expand all the items below (by setting UIHierarchyItems.Expand = True).

The code is complete and works, but it's probably not exactly what you were looking for. For instance, it references the projects and project items that you expanded by their path and name. This means that the macro is certainly not generic (it would work only with this specific Contoso sample solution), and even then the code is fairly brittle. If you add or remove a project or project item, the macro won't know and it still tries to set the prior item's Expanded property. To really make the macro useful, you should rework the code. The advantage of using the recorder is that it produces a valid starting point for macro development. In fact, it has highlighted the use of an object, UIHierarchyItem, which we have not discussed. An eye for general program structure tells you that there should be a way to refactor these lines of code into a loop, recursively expanding nodes out in the tree until all have been expanded. Perhaps instead of just expanding or collapsing nodes, you can also try toggling the Expanded property on this object.

You edit macro code using the code editor just as you would edit any other document with Visual Studio. To rework this macro, you can start by establishing a recursive helper routine that takes in a UIHierarchyItem object, toggles its Expanded property to True, and calls itself for each sub item found in the UIHierarchyItems collection:

```
For Each subNode As UIHierarchyItem In node.UIHierarchyItems
    ExpandNodes(subNode)
Next
node.UIHierarchyItems.Expanded = True
```

NOTE

Unlike the editors in the main Visual Studio IDE, the text editor in the Macros IDE automatically saves the file you are editing when you close it. This is done without any prompting whatsoever. Unless you undo changes you have made while editing, they are committed after you close the editor, regardless of whether you have explicitly saved them.

Then, to kick things off, you need a parent, controlling routine that instantiates a window object (representing the Solution Explorer) and grabs the root-level UIHierarchy object from the window. From there, you loop the first level of nodes in the tree and call down into the recursive routine:

```
Dim tree As UIHierarchy
Dim explorer As Window2

explorer = DTE.Windows.Item(Constants.vsWindowKindSolutionExplorer)

tree = explorer.Object

For Each node As UIHierarchyItem In tree.UIHierarchyItems
    ExpandNodes(node)
Next
```

To go one step further, if you modify the recursive routine to take in a Boolean value, you now have a general-purpose routine that can either expand or collapse a series of nodes. Putting it all together, you end up with two macros: One expands all nodes in the Solution Explorer tree, and one collapses all nodes in the Solution Explorer tree. In Listing 14.2, you see these two macros as public subroutines called ExpandAll and CollapseAll. The private routine ExpandCollapseNodes is called by both of the macros. To run a macro in the Macros IDE, just press F5 or select Start under the Debug menu.

LISTING 14.2   Macro: Expand/Collapse All Solution Explorer Nodes

---

```
Imports EnvDTE
Imports EnvDTE80
Imports Microsoft.VisualStudio.CommandBars
Imports System
Imports System.Collections
Imports System.Diagnostics
Imports System.Text
Imports System.Windows.Forms


Public Module MacroExamples
```

```
' Expands all nodes in the Solution Explorer
Public Sub ExpandAll()
    Dim tree As UIHierarchy
    Dim explorer As Window2

    ' Reference to the solution explorer window
    explorer = DTE.Windows.Item(Constants.vsWindowKindSolutionExplorer)

    ' Reference to the UIHierarchy object obtained from the
    ' solution explorer window
    tree = explorer.Object

    ' Iterate the top level nodes, call recursive routine to
    ' expand each node
    For Each node As UIHierarchyItem In tree.UIHierarchyItems
        ExpandCollapseNodes(node, True)
    Next

End Sub

' Collapses all nodes in the Solution Explorer
Public Sub CollapseAll()
    Dim tree As UIHierarchy
    Dim explorer As Window2

    ' Reference to the solution explorer window
    explorer = DTE.Windows.Item(Constants.vsWindowKindSolutionExplorer)

    ' Reference to the UIHierarchy object obtained from the
    ' solution explorer window
    tree = explorer.Object

    ' Iterate the top level nodes, call recursive routine to
    ' expand each node
    For Each node As UIHierarchyItem In tree.UIHierarchyItems
        ExpandCollapseNodes(node, False)
    Next

End Sub

' Recursive routine for expanding or collapsing all of the sub nodes
' of a given UIHierarchyItem
Private Sub ExpandCollapseNodes(ByRef node As UIHierarchyItem, _
    ByVal expanded As Boolean)
    For Each subNode As UIHierarchyItem In node.UIHierarchyItems
        ' Re-call this routine with the new subnode as the parent node
```

14

```
            ExpandCollapseNodes(subNode, expanded)
        Next

        ' Perform the collapse/expansion
        node.UIHierarchyItems.Expanded = expanded

    End Sub
End Module
```

Compared with the code that the macro recorder emitted for you, there isn't a whole lot of similarity; but again, the recorded code was useful from an education perspective, alerting you to the approach and concept of using the UIHierarchy/UIHierarchyItem/ UIHierarchyItems objects to handle the node expansion.

Debugging

The debug experience with macros is similar to that of debugging other Visual Studio projects (which we covered in-depth in Chapter 11, "Debugging Code"). The runtime debugger in the Macros IDE supports all the familiar concepts of breakpoints and the Step Into and Step Over commands.

If you were unsure of your recursive code, you might choose to place a breakpoint in the recursive routine and monitor the progress of the macro. The Macros IDE also supports the Error List window, which flags any syntax errors for you. See Figure 14.7 for a glimpse of a breakpoint and the Error List window in the Macros IDE.

FIGURE 14.7   Debugging a macro in the Macros IDE.

NOTE

If debugging is taking place in the Macros IDE, the main IDE is inaccessible. You won't be able to perform tasks in the main IDE.

Handling Events

We cover the individual event classes in Chapter 13; every event exposed in the IDE is available via these automation classes. To handle an event in a macro, you need to have two things: an event definition and an event handler.

Every macro project has, by default, an EnvironmentEvents module. This module is automatically created for you every time you create a new macro project, and it implements event definitions for many of the automation events. If you need to handle any of the following event categories, the event definition is already taken care of for you:

▶ Core DTE events

▶ Document events

▶ Window events

▶ Task List events

▶ Search events

▶ Output window events

▶ Selection events

▶ Build events

▶ Solution events

▶ Solution item events

▶ File events

▶ Debugger events

▶ Project events

▶ Keypress events

▶ Code model events

Listing 14.3 shows the EnvironmentEvents source code (generated by Visual Studio) that is responsible for implementing these event definitions.

LISTING 14.3   EnvironmentEvents Module

```
Option Strict Off
Option Explicit Off
Imports EnvDTE
Imports EnvDTE80
```

```
Imports EnvDTE90
Imports System.Diagnostics

Public Module EnvironmentEvents

#Region "Automatically generated code, do not modify"
'Automatically generated code, do not modify
'Event Sources Begin
    <System.ContextStaticAttribute()> _
    Public WithEvents DTEEvents As EnvDTE.DTEEvents

    <System.ContextStaticAttribute()> _
    Public WithEvents DocumentEvents As EnvDTE.DocumentEvents

    <System.ContextStaticAttribute()> _
    Public WithEvents WindowEvents As EnvDTE.WindowEvents

    <System.ContextStaticAttribute()> _
    Public WithEvents TaskListEvents As EnvDTE.TaskListEvents

    <System.ContextStaticAttribute()> _
    Public WithEvents FindEvents As EnvDTE.FindEvents

    <System.ContextStaticAttribute()> _
    Public WithEvents OutputWindowEvents As EnvDTE.OutputWindowEvents

    <System.ContextStaticAttribute()> _
    Public WithEvents SelectionEvents As EnvDTE.SelectionEvents

    <System.ContextStaticAttribute()> _
    Public WithEvents BuildEvents As EnvDTE.BuildEvents

    <System.ContextStaticAttribute()> _
    Public WithEvents SolutionEvents As EnvDTE.SolutionEvents

    <System.ContextStaticAttribute()> _
    Public WithEvents SolutionItemsEvents As EnvDTE.ProjectItemsEvents

    <System.ContextStaticAttribute()> _
    Public WithEvents MiscFilesEvents As EnvDTE.ProjectItemsEvents

    <System.ContextStaticAttribute()> _
    Public WithEvents DebuggerEvents As EnvDTE.DebuggerEvents

    <System.ContextStaticAttribute()> _
    Public WithEvents ProjectsEvents As EnvDTE.ProjectsEvents
```

```
    <System.ContextStaticAttribute()> _
    Public WithEvents TextDocumentKeyPressEvents As
        EnvDTE80.TextDocumentKeyPressEvents

    <System.ContextStaticAttribute()> _
    Public WithEvents CodeModelEvents As EnvDTE80.CodeModelEvents

    <System.ContextStaticAttribute()> _
    Public WithEvents DebuggerProcessEvents As EnvDTE80.DebuggerProcessEvents

    <System.ContextStaticAttribute()> _
    Public WithEvents DebuggerExpressionEvaluationEvents As
        EnvDTE80.DebuggerExpressionEvaluationEvents
'Event Sources End
'End of automatically generated code
#End Region

End Module
```

Writing the Event Handler

In addition to defining the various event objects for you, the IDE can also be leveraged to insert the actual event handler skeleton code for you. First, open the EnvironmentEvents module in the code editor. Then use the type drop-down (the leftmost drop-down at the top of the code editor) to select the event class you want. Figure 14.8 shows the process of selecting the SolutionEvents type.

When you have the type selected, the declarations drop-down (the drop-down at the upper right of the code editor) holds a list of the events defined for that event object. If you are interested in receiving a notification, for example, every time a solution is opened, you select the Opened event. Immediately after you select this event, the event handler code is injected into the code editor. In this case, the following code results from the selection:

```
Private Sub SolutionEvents_Opened() Handles SolutionEvents.Opened


End Sub
```

You can leave this code as is in the EnvironmentEvents module (a reasonable practice), or you can cut and paste it into any other module in the project. With the event handler in place, you just need to worry about writing the code that deals with the event.

Every time a macro project that contains event handlers is loaded in Visual Studio, a security dialog box is displayed (shown in Figure 14.9).

This dialog box alerts you to the fact that the macro contains event interception code and enables you to disable the event objects in the macro, which is probably a good idea when you're opening a macro from an untrusted source. You also have the option to simply abort the project load process by clicking on the Don't Load Project button at the lower left of the Warning dialog box.

FIGURE 14.8   Selecting a macro event type.

FIGURE 14.9   Loading a macro project with event handlers.

Adding a New Event Declaration

If you need access to an event that isn't already declared for you in the EnvironmentEvents module, it is possible to add the event declaration manually. As a demonstration, let's add a new event handler for the WindowHiding event exposed by the WindowVisiblityEvents class. This event, which is not included by default, tells you whenever a tool window in the IDE is hidden.

Triggering Macros from Toolbars and Menus

If you want to provide quick access to the node expansion and node collapse macros, you can assign them as toolbar buttons or menu items in the main IDE. You do this through the Customize dialog box as shown here:

1. Display the dialog box by selecting Tools, Customize.

2. Select the Commands tab.

3. You can add your macro command button to a menu bar, toolbar, or context menu. Just pick the location you want on this dialog box, and then select the specific menu/toolbar you want to add the command to.

4. Click the Add Command button.

5. Select the Macros category in the categories list. Each individual macro in all the currently loaded macro projects will be displayed in the commands list box (following the format [Macro Project Name].[Macro Module Name].[Macro Subroutine Name]) See Figure 14.11 for an example where the ExpandAll macro has been selected.

FIGURE 14.11 Add a macro execution button to a Visual Studio toolbar.

6. Click OK to add the macro command button to the toolbar (in this example, we have added it to the Layout toolbar).

After you add the button or menu item. You can click on the Modify Selection button in the Customize dialog box to access a drop-down menu (displayed in Figure 14.12) that enables you to change the way the button or menu item appears within its host.

FIGURE 14.12   The Modify Selection drop-down.

Assigning Keyboard Shortcuts to Macros

To launch a macro via a keyboard shortcut, you need to assign the key sequence to the macro using the Options dialog box as described here:

1. Open the Options dialog box by selecting Tools, Options. You can also access this dialog box by clicking on the Keyboard button in the Customize dialog box (refer to the bottom of Figure 14.11).

2. Under the Environment node, select the Keyboard page.

3. In the Keyboard settings page, select the macro in the list of commands (you can filter this list by typing the name of the macro or by just typing macros in the text box labeled Show Commands Containing). Each macro is listed by its macro project, module name, and macro name.

4. Put the cursor in the Press Shortcut Keys text box and then press the key or keys you want to use to trigger the macro (see Figure 14.13).

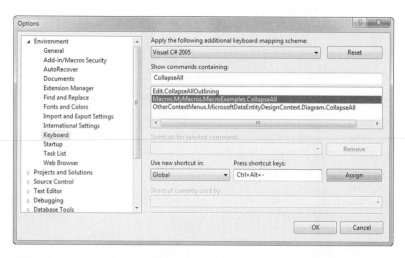

FIGURE 14.13   Assigning a keyboard shortcut to a macro button.

5. Click on the Assign button; you can now launch your macro by using the key combination that you entered.

NOTE

Visual Studio already has many different key combinations assigned to its various actions and commands. If you happen to press a key combination that is already in use, the command that currently uses that key combination is displayed in the drop-down at the bottom of the Options dialog box (see Figure 14.13). At this point, you can either choose a different set of keys to use, or you can overwrite the key assignments. Overwriting is probably not a good idea if you are replacing one of the more common commands: cut, open file, and so on.

Running Macros from the Command Window

As you have seen from the steps to trigger a macro via toolbar/menu and keyboard shortcut, each macro is exposed in the IDE via a command (see the section "Command Objects" in Chapter 13). The command window is purpose-built to execute commands, so macros can be run from the command window prompt as well.

With your cursor at the prompt in the command window, type the letter m to trigger the window's IntelliSense and thus display a list of all macros. Scroll down and select the macro you want to run; then press Enter. The macro executes.

Macros with Parameters   Although, in general, it makes sense for macros to execute without any required user interaction, it might sometimes be beneficial to write macros that accept parameters as part of their function/sub definition.

Consider the ResizeIDE macro in Listing 14.4. It takes in width and height values as parameters and then resizes the main IDE window according to those values.

LISTING 14.4   Resizing the IDE

```
Option Strict Off
Option Explicit Off
Imports EnvDTE
Imports EnvDTE80

Public Module MacroExamples

    Public Sub ResizeIDE(Optional ByVal width As Integer = 800, _
      Optional ByVal height As Integer = 600)
        Dim ide As Window2 = DTE.MainWindow

        ide.Width = width
        ide.Height = height

    End Sub
End Module
```

If you were to call this macro from the command window, you would have to pass these parameters in like this:

```
Macros.MyMacros.MacroExamples.ResizeIDE(800, 600)
```

> **NOTE**
>
> If you write a macro that accepts parameters, those parameters must be declared as optional, and you must provide default values for the parameters. Although you won't receive any errors, if you write a macro with non-optional parameters, the macro won't be registered. You won't see it in the Macro Explorer, and you won't be able to run the macro.

Summary

In this chapter, we described how to leverage the power of Visual Studio's automation APIs to create macros, add-ins, and wizards.

You saw that the macro recorder gives you a quick entry point into driving various components of the IDE, that the Macro Explorer provides a central place to manage your macro collections, and that Visual Studio provides a fully featured integrated development environment built specifically for macro development. Using these tools, you can record basic macros and use them as a starting point for more complicated macros, or you can craft macros from scratch using the Visual Basic programming language.

CHAPTER 15

Writing Add-ins and Wizards

If macros represent the quick and easy approach to automation then add-ins are their more complex, and more powerful, counterparts. Add-ins are compiled projects written in Visual Basic, Visual C#, even Visual C++. Add-ins are useful for covering more advanced extensibility scenarios up to and including surfacing your own custom forms, tool windows, and designers in the IDE.

Another related topic is that of creating and customizing Visual Studio wizards. Wizards are launched anytime you create a new project or add an item to a project. These wizards typically present one or more dialog boxes to capture preferences from the user and then use those preferences to create a project structure, generate default code, or perform even more complicated tasks. Wizards work in conjunction with template files to drive the initial structure for a code file or an entire project. The entire framework for wizards and templates is available to customize to fit your particular needs.

In the two preceding chapters, you have seen how the Visual Studio automation API is organized, and how you can write macros that interact with that API. Macros are an ideal way to control various items in the IDE. Within a macro, you have access to the entire automation object model, macros are easy to write, and they come complete with their own development environment. Even with all of these positives, however, there are limitations as to what a macro can do:

▶ A macro can't be used to create and display custom tool windows.

- A macro is incapable of exposing any sort of user interface beyond simple dialog boxes and message boxes.

- A macro can't implement a property page hosted in the Options dialog box.

- A macro can't dynamically enable or disable menu and toolbar items in the IDE.

- A macro can't be compiled and distributed as an executable binary.

Visual Studio add-ins can do all this and more. Put simply, add-ins present deeper IDE integration options to developers. So, what exactly is an add-in? An add-in is a compiled DLL containing a COM object that implements a specific interface, IDTExtensibility2, which provides the add-in with a direct connection to the IDE. As we have mentioned previously, you can write add-ins in your managed language of choice. Because we have spent so much time working with Visual Basic syntax in the macro world, in this chapter all the add-in examples are done in C#.

Creating Your First Add-in Project

The simplest way to get started with add-ins is to run the Add-in Wizard. As with the macro recorder, the wizard gives you a starting point for implementing your own add-ins. You can learn a great deal about the makeup of an add-in by examining the code the Add-in Wizard creates.

The Add-in Wizard launches whenever you try to create a new project of the type Visual Studio Add-in. From the File, New Project dialog box, select the Extensibility node in the project types tree (in Other Project Types, Extensibility). From here, you can see two project templates: Visual Studio Add-in and Shared Add-in (see Figure 15.1).

FIGURE 15.1   Selecting the Visual Studio Add-in Project Type.

We touch on the differences between these two project types in a bit; for now, we are interested in the Visual Studio Add-in template.

Click OK to start the Add-in Wizard.

Setting Add-in Parameters

The Add-in Wizard collects all the information necessary for defining the core parameters for the add-in project: the language you want to develop in, the application host, runtime information about the add-in (such as a description), and information for the About box. Let's briefly examine each of the wizard pages.

Selecting a Language

After an initial welcome page, the first piece of information you need to provide is the language you want to use for developing the add-in (see Figure 15.2).

FIGURE 15.2   Picking the add-in language.

The list of languages available depends on two things:

▶ The languages installed as part of your Visual Studio package

▶ The type of add-in (shared or Visual Studio)

Visual Studio add-ins support Visual C#, Visual Basic, and both managed and unmanaged Visual C++.

Picking an Application Host

After selecting a language, you are presented with a question about "application hosts." This screen is really just asking where you want the add-in to run.

Because you have indicated that this is a Visual Studio Add-in and not a shared add-in, your host options are the Visual Studio IDE or the Macros IDE (see Figure 15.3). Visual Studio 2010 has the capability to target multiple versions of the IDE. For instance, if you have Visual Studio 2008 installed side by side with Visual Studio 2010, you will have the option to host your add-in in both IDEs.

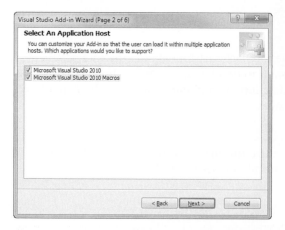

FIGURE 15.3   Selecting the application host.

NOTE

This is a good time to discuss the differences between a Visual Studio add-in and a shared add-in. A *shared add-in* is the moniker given for add-ins hosted inside a Microsoft Office application, such as Microsoft Word or Microsoft Excel. A Visual Studio add-in can be hosted only within the Visual Studio or Macros IDE. If you run through the Add-in Wizard for a shared add-in, the page that asks you to select an application host (or hosts) is populated with a list of the installed Microsoft Office applications; you won't be able to select Visual Studio as an application host for a shared add-in.

Describing the Add-in

The name and description you enter on page 3 of the wizard (see Figure 15.4) are visible in the Add-in Manager when the add-in is selected. This information is intended to give users an idea as to the add-in's functionality and purpose.

Setting Add-in Options

The next wizard page, shown in Figure 15.5, enables you to specify various add-in options. You can indicate whether you want the add-in to appear in the Tools menu, when you want the add-in to load, and whether the add-in could potentially display a modal dialog box during its operation.

Setting About Box Information

The second-to-last wizard page captures the text that Visual Studio displays in its About box (see Figure 15.6).

This is the place to include details such as where users can contact the author of the add-in, support and licensing information, copyright and version information, and so on.

FIGURE 15.4   Providing the add-in's name and description.

FIGURE 15.5   Setting add-in options.

FIGURE 15.6   Setting the add-in's About box text.

Finishing the Wizard

The last page of the wizard contains a summary of the options that you have selected. After you click the Finish button, the wizard starts creating the code for your add-in based on all the selections you have made in the wizard.

Because add-ins are DLLs, the Add-in Wizard creates the add-in source as part of a class library project in the IDE. The primary code file that is created implements a class called Connect. This class inherits from all the necessary COM interfaces to make the add-in work in the context of the IDE.

Listing 15.1 shows the Connect class as it was generated by the Add-in Wizard.

LISTING 15.1   Code Generated by the Add-in Wizard

```
using System;
using Extensibility;
using EnvDTE;
using EnvDTE80;
using Microsoft.VisualStudio.CommandBars;
using System.Resources;
using System.Reflection;
using System.Globalization;

namespace MyAddin1
{
    /// <summary>The object for implementing an Add-in.</summary>
    /// <seealso class='IDTExtensibility2' />
    public class Connect : IDTExtensibility2, IDTCommandTarget
    {
        /// <summary>Implements the constructor for the Add-in object.
        /// Place your initialization code within this method.</summary>
        public Connect()
        {

        }

        /// <summary>Implements the OnConnection method of the
        /// IDTExtensibility2 interface. Receives notification that
        /// the Add-in is being loaded.</summary>
        /// <param term='application'>Root object of the host
        /// application.</param>
        /// <param term='connectMode'>Describes how the Add-in
        /// is being loaded.</param>
        /// <param term='addInInst'>Object representing this
        /// Add-in.</param>
        /// <seealso class='IDTExtensibility2' />
        public void OnConnection(object application,
```

```
    ext_ConnectMode connectMode,
  object addInInst, ref Array custom)
{
  _applicationObject = (DTE2)application;
  _addInInstance = (AddIn)addInInst;
  if(connectMode == ext_ConnectMode.ext_cm_UISetup)
  {
    object []contextGUIDS = new object[] { };
    Commands2 commands =
      (Commands2)_applicationObject.Commands;

    string toolsMenuName;

    try
    {
      //If you would like to move the command to a different
      // menu, change the word "Tools" to the English version
      // of the menu. This code will take the culture, append
      // on the name of the menu, then add the command to
      // that menu. You can find a list of all the top-level
      // menus in the file CommandBar.resx.
      string resourceName;
      ResourceManager resourceManager =
        new ResourceManager("MyAddin1.CommandBar",
        Assembly.GetExecutingAssembly());

      CultureInfo cultureInfo =
        new CultureInfo(_applicationObject.LocaleID);

      if(cultureInfo.TwoLetterISOLanguageName == "zh")
      {
        System.Globalization.CultureInfo
          parentCultureInfo = cultureInfo.Parent;
        resourceName =
          String.Concat(parentCultureInfo.Name, "Tools");
      }
      else
      {
        resourceName =
          String.Concat(cultureInfo.TwoLetterISOLanguageName,
            "Tools");
      }
      toolsMenuName = resourceManager.GetString(resourceName);
    }
    catch
    {
```

```csharp
        //We tried to find a localized version of the word
        // Tools, but one was not found. Default to the en-US
        // word, which may work for the current culture.
        toolsMenuName = "Tools";
    }


    //Place the command on the Tools menu.
    //Find the MenuBar command bar, which is the top-level
    // command bar holding all the main menu items:
    Microsoft.VisualStudio.CommandBars.CommandBar
      menuBarCommandBar =
      ((Microsoft.VisualStudio.CommandBars.CommandBars)
      _applicationObject.CommandBars)["MenuBar"];


    //Find the Tools command bar on the MenuBar command bar:
    CommandBarControl toolsControl =
      menuBarCommandBar.Controls[toolsMenuName];


    CommandBarPopup toolsPopup =
       (CommandBarPopup)toolsControl;


    //This try/catch block can be duplicated if you wish to
    // add multiple commands to be handled by your Add-in,
    // just make sure you also update the QueryStatus/Exec
    // method to include the new command names.
    try
    {
       //Add a command to the Commands collection:
       Command command =
          commands.AddNamedCommand2(_addInInstance,
          "MyAddin1", "MyAddin1",
          "Executes the command for MyAddin1", true, 59,
          ref contextGUIDS,
          (int)vsCommandStatus.vsCommandStatusSupported+
          (int)vsCommandStatus.vsCommandStatusEnabled,
          (int)vsCommandStyle.vsCommandStylePictAndText,
          vsCommandControlType.vsCommandControlTypeButton);

       //Add a control for the command to the Tools menu:
       if((command != null) && (toolsPopup != null))
       {
          command.AddControl(toolsPopup.CommandBar, 1);
       }
    }
    catch(System.ArgumentException)
    {
```

```
        //If we are here, then the exception is probably because
        //a command with that name already exists. If so there
        //is no need to recreate the command and we can safely
        //ignore the exception.
        }
    }
}


/// <summary>Implements the OnDisconnection method of the
/// IDTExtensibility2 interface. Receives notification that the
/// Add-in is being unloaded.</summary>
/// <param term='disconnectMode'>Describes how the Add-in is being
/// unloaded.</param>
/// <param term='custom'>Array of parameters that are host application
/// specific.</param>
/// <seealso class='IDTExtensibility2' />
public void OnDisconnection(ext_DisconnectMode disconnectMode,
  ref Array custom)
{
}


/// <summary>Implements the OnAddInsUpdate method of the
/// IDTExtensibility2 interface. Receives notification when the
/// collection of Add-ins has changed.</summary>
/// <param term='custom'>Array of parameters that are host application
/// specific.</param>
/// <seealso class='IDTExtensibility2' />
public void OnAddInsUpdate(ref Array custom)
{
}
/// <summary>Implements the OnStartupComplete method of the
/// IDTExtensibility2 interface. Receives notification that the host
/// application has completed loading.</summary>
/// <param term='custom'>Array of parameters that are host application
/// specific.</param>
/// <seealso class='IDTExtensibility2' />
public void OnStartupComplete(ref Array custom)
{
}


/// <summary>Implements the OnBeginShutdown method of the
/// IDTExtensibility2 interface. Receives notification that the host
/// application is being unloaded.</summary>
/// <param term='custom'>Array of parameters that are host application
/// specific.</param>
/// <seealso class='IDTExtensibility2' />
```

15

```
public void OnBeginShutdown(ref Array custom)
{
}

/// <summary>Implements the QueryStatus method of the IDTCommandTarget
/// interface. This is called when the command's availability is
/// updated</summary>
/// <param term='commandName'>The name of the command to determine
/// state for.</param>
/// <param term='neededText'>Text that is needed for the
/// command.</param>
/// <param term='status'>The state of the command in the user
/// interface.</param>
/// <param term='commandText'>Text requested by the neededText
/// parameter.</param>
/// <seealso class='Exec' />
public void QueryStatus(string commandName,
  vsCommandStatusTextWanted neededText,
  ref vsCommandStatus status,
  ref object commandText)
  {
     if(neededText ==
        vsCommandStatusTextWanted.vsCommandStatusTextWantedNone)
     {
        if(commandName == "MyAddin1.Connect.MyAddin1")
        {
           status =
              (vsCommandStatus)vsCommandStatus.vsCommandStatusSupported
               ¦vsCommandStatus.vsCommandStatusEnabled;
           return;
        }
     }
  }

/// <summary>Implements the Exec method of the IDTCommandTarget
/// interface. This is called when the command is invoked.</summary>
/// <param term='commandName'>The name of the command to
/// execute.</param>
/// <param term='executeOption'>Describes how the command should
/// be run.</param>
/// <param term='varIn'>Parameters passed from the caller to the
/// command handler.</param>
/// <param term='varOut'>Parameters passed from the command handler
/// to the caller.</param>
/// <param term='handled'>Informs the caller if the command was
/// handled or not.</param>
```

```
/// <seealso class='Exec' />
public void Exec(string commandName,
  vsCommandExecOption executeOption,
  ref object varIn, ref object varOut,
  ref bool handled)
{
  handled = false;
  if(executeOption ==
     vsCommandExecOption.vsCommandExecOptionDoDefault)
  {
    if(commandName == "MyAddin1.Connect.MyAddin1")
    {
      handled = true;
      return;
    }
  }
}
private DTE2 _applicationObject;
private AddIn _addInInstance;
    }
}
```

At this stage, the add-in doesn't actually do anything. You still have to implement the custom logic for the add-in. What the wizard has done, however, is implement much (if not all) of the tedious plumbing required to do the following:

▶ Wire the add-in into the IDE

▶ Expose it on the Tools menu

▶ Intercept the appropriate extensibility events to make the add-in work

Now that you have a baseline of code to work with, you're ready to examine the source to understand the overall structure and layout of an add-in.

The Structure of an Add-in

The first thing to notice is that the Connect class inherits from two different interfaces: IDTCommandTarget and IDTExtensibility2.

```
public class Connect : IDTExtensibility2, IDTCommandTarget
```

The IDTCommandTarget interface provides the functionality necessary to expose the add-in via a command bar. The code to inherit from this interface was added by the wizard because the Yes, Create a Tools Menu Item box was checked on page 4 of the add-in wizard.

The IDTExtensibility2 interface provides the eventing glue for add-ins. It is responsible for all the events that constitute the life span of an add-in.

The Life Cycle of an Add-in

Add-ins progress through a sequence of events every time they are loaded or unloaded in their application host. Each of these events is represented by a method defined on the IDTExtensibility2 interface. These methods are documented in Table 15.1.

TABLE 15.1   IDTExtensibility2 Methods

Method	Description
OnAddInsUpdate	Called whenever an add-in is either loaded or unloaded
OnBeginShutdown	Called if Visual Studio is shut down while an add-in is loaded
OnConnection	Called when an add-in is loaded
OnDisconnection	Called when an add-in is unloaded
OnStartupComplete	Called when the add-in loads if this add-in is set to load when Visual Studio starts

The diagrams in Figure 15.7 and Figure 15.8 show how these methods (which really represent events) fall onto the normal load and unload path for an add-in.

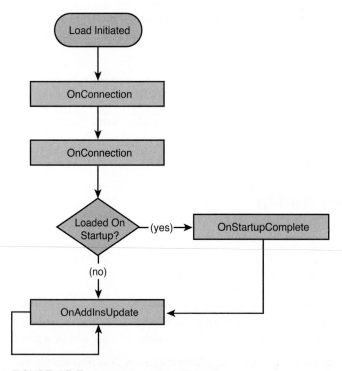

FIGURE 15.7   Load sequence of events.

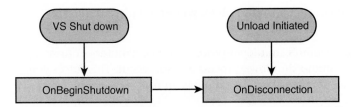

FIGURE 15.8   Unload sequence of events.

If you look back at the template code for the add-in, you can see that each one of these IDTExtensibility2 methods has been implemented. The OnDisconnection, OnAddInsUpdate, OnStartupComplete, and OnBeginShutdown methods are empty; the wizard has merely implemented the method signature. The OnConnection method, however, already has a fair bit of code to it before you even lift a hand to modify or add to the wizard-generated code.

Now you're ready to investigate what happens in each of the IDTExtensibility2 methods.

OnAddInsUpdate

The OnAddInsUpdate method is called when any add-in is loaded or unloaded from Visual Studio; because of this, the OnAddInsUpdate method is primarily useful for enforcing or dealing with dependencies between add-ins. If your add-in depends on or otherwise uses the functionality contained in another add-in, this is the ideal injection point for containing the logic that deals with that relationship.

Here is the OnAddInsUpdate method as implemented by the Add-in Wizard:

```
/// <summary>Implements the OnAddInsUpdate method of the IDTExtensibility2
/// interface. Receives notification when the collection of Add-ins has
/// changed.</summary>
/// <param term='custom'>Array of parameters that are host application
/// specific.</param>
/// <seealso class='IDTExtensibility2' />
public void OnAddInsUpdate(ref Array custom)
{
}
```

> **TIP**
>
> Because you don't know which add-in has triggered the OnAddInsUpdate method, you would need to iterate through the DTE.AddIns collection and query each add-in's Connected property to determine its current state.

OnBeginShutdown

OnBeginShutdown is called for every running add-in when Visual Studio begins its shutdown sequence. If an IDE requires any cleanup code (including perhaps resetting IDE settings that have been changed during the add-in's life), you would place that code within this method.

A user may elect to cancel Visual Studio's shutdown process. OnBeginShutdown fires regardless of whether the Visual Studio shutdown process was successful. This forces you, as an add-in author, to always assume that Visual Studio has, in fact, terminated.

Here is the OnBeginShutdown method:

```
/// <summary>Implements the OnBeginShutdown method of the
///IDTExtensibility2 interface. Receives notification that the host
///application is being unloaded.</summary>
/// <param term='custom'>Array of parameters that are host
application specific.</param>
/// <seealso class='IDTExtensibility2' />
public void OnBeginShutdown(ref Array custom)
{
}
```

OnConnection

OnConnection indicates that an add-in has been loaded:

```
public void OnConnection(object application, ext_ConnectMode connectMode,
    object addInInst, ref Array custom)
```

It accepts four parameters. The first parameter, application, is the most important; it provides a reference to the DTE object representing the IDE. You know from Chapter 13, "Introducing the Automation Object Model," that the DTE object is the key to accessing the entire automation object model. With macros, the DTE object is held as a global variable. For add-ins, the OnConnection method is the sole provider of this object, thus providing the crucial link between the add-in and its host IDE.

The second parameter, connectMode, is an ext_ConnectMode enumeration. It indicates exactly how the add-in was loaded (see Table 15.2 for a list of the possible ext_ConnectMode values).

TABLE 15.2   ext_ConnectMode Members

Member	Description
ext_cm_AfterStartup	The add-in was loaded after Visual Studio was started.
ext_cm_CommandLine	The add-in was loaded from the command line.
ext_cm_External	n/a (Visual Studio does not use this value.)
ext_cm_Solution	The add-in was loaded with a Visual Studio solution.
ext_cm_Startup	The add-in was loaded when Visual Studio started.

TABLE 15.2   Continued

Member	Description
ext_cm_UISetup	The add-in was loaded for UI setup (this represents the initial load of an add-in).

The addInInst parameter is actually a reference to the add-in itself. And last, the custom parameter is an empty Array object. This array is passed by reference and can be used to pass parameters into and out of the add-in.

The Add-in Wizard has taken the first two parameters, explicitly cast them to their underlying types, and assigned them into two class fields for later reference:

```
_applicationObject = (DTE2)application;
_addInInstance = (AddIn)addInInst;
```

The next block of code examines the ext_ConnectMode value. If this is the first time the add-in was loaded (for example, ext_ConnectMode is equal to ext_cm_UISetup), then the code does two things: It creates a Tools menu entry for the add-in, and it creates a custom, named command to launch the add-in (this named command is called when you select the add-in from the Tools menu).

```
if(connectMode == ext_ConnectMode.ext_cm_UISetup)
{
        object []contextGUIDS = new object[] { };
        Commands2 commands = (Commands2)_applicationObject.Commands;
    string toolsMenuName;

    try
    {
        //If you would like to move the command to a different menu, change the
        // word "Tools" to the English version of the menu.
        //  This code will take the culture, append on the name of the menu,
        //  then add the command to that menu. You can find a list of all
        // the top-level menus in the file
        //  CommandBar.resx.
        ResourceManager resourceManager = new _
                ResourceManager("MyFirstAddin.CommandBar", _
                Assembly.GetExecutingAssembly());
        CultureInfo cultureInfo = new _
                System.Globalization.CultureInfo(_applicationObject.LocaleID);
        string resourceName = String.Concat(cultureInfo.TwoLetterISOLanguageName,
                        "Tools");
        toolsMenuName = resourceManager.GetString(resourceName);
    }
    catch
```

15

```
{
    //We tried to find a localized version of the word Tools, but one
    //was not found.
    //  Default to the en-US word, which may work for the current culture.
    toolsMenuName = "Tools";
}
//Place the command on the Tools menu.
//Find the MenuBar command bar, which is the top-level command bar holding
//all the main menu items:
Microsoft.VisualStudio.CommandBars.CommandBar menuBarCommandBar = _
  ((Microsoft.VisualStudio.CommandBars.CommandBars)__
  applicationObject.CommandBars)["MenuBar"];

//Find the Tools command bar on the MenuBar command bar:
CommandBarControl toolsControl = menuBarCommandBar.Controls[toolsMenuName];
CommandBarPopup toolsPopup = (CommandBarPopup)toolsControl;

//This try/catch block can be duplicated if you wish to add multiple commands
//to be handled by your Add-in,
// just make sure you also update the QueryStatus/Exec method to include
// the new command names.
try
{
    //Add a command to the Commands collection:
    Command command = commands.AddNamedCommand2(_addInInstance, _
                "MyFirstAddin", "MyFirstAddin", _
                "Executes the command for MyFirstAddin", true, 59, _
                ref contextGUIDS,
                (int)vsCommandStatus.vsCommandStatusSupported
                 +(int)vsCommandStatus.vsCommandStatusEnabled,
                (int)vsCommandStyle.vsCommandStylePictAndText,
                 vsCommandControlType.vsCommandControlTypeButton);

    //Add a control for the command to the Tools menu:
    if((command != null) && (toolsPopup != null))
    {
        command.AddControl(toolsPopup.CommandBar, 1);
    }
}
catch(System.ArgumentException)
{
    //If we are here, then the exception is probably because a command with
    //that name already exists. If so there is no need to recreate the
    //command and we can
    //  safely ignore the exception.

}
```

> **TIP**
>
> You can see that the Add-in Wizard is quite liberal with its code comments; when you set out to write your own add-in, it is often useful to read the auto-generated comments and simply copy/paste relevant code snippets to duplicate functionality that the wizard has generated for you.

OnDisconnection

OnDisconnection fires when the add-in is unloaded from Visual Studio. This is the opposite action from that signaled by the OnConnection method. As with OnConnection, an enumeration—ext_DisconnectMode—is provided to this method that indicates how the unload action was initiated. For a list of the possible ext_DisconnectMode values, see Table 15.3.

TABLE 15.3   ext_DisconnectMode Members

Member	Description
ext_dm_HostShutdown	The add-in was unloaded because Visual Studio was shut down.
ext_dm_SolutionClosed	The add-in was unloaded because the solution was closed.
ext_dm_UISetupComplete	The add-in was unloaded after UI setup was complete.
ext_dm_UserClosed	The add-in was manually or programmatically unloaded. (This is used only if Visual Studio is still running; otherwise, ext_dm_HostShutdown will be used.)

Here is the OnDisconnection method:

```
/// <summary>Implements the OnDisconnection method of the IDTExtensibility2
///interface. Receives notification that the Add-in is being
///unloaded.</summary>
/// <param term='disconnectMode'>Describes how the Add-in is being
/// unloaded.</param>
/// <param term='custom'>Array of parameters that are host application
/// specific.</param>
/// <seealso class='IDTExtensibility2' />
public void OnDisconnection(ext_DisconnectMode disconnectMode, ref Array custom)
{
}
```

OnStartupComplete

If an add-in is set to load automatically during Visual Studio startup, the OnStartupComplete method fires after that add-in has been loaded.

Here is the OnStartupComplete method:

```
/// <summary>Implements the OnStartupComplete method of the IDTExtensibility2
/// interface. Receives notification that the host application has completed
/// loading.</summary>
/// <param term='custom'>Array of parameters that are host application
/// specific.</param>
/// <seealso class='IDTExtensibility2' />
public void OnStartupComplete(ref Array custom)
{
}
```

Reacting to Commands

Add-ins can react to commands issued within the IDE. If you recall from the discussion on commands in Chapter 13, and in Chapter 14, "Writing Macros," this is done through the concept of "named commands." A named command is really nothing more than an action that has a name attached to it. You already know that Visual Studio comes with its own extensive set of commands that cover a wide variety of actions in the IDE. Using the Commands/Commands2 collection, you can create your own named commands by using the AddNamedCommand2 method.

To repeat the dissection of the OnConnection method, the wizard has created a body of code responsible for creating a new named command, adding it to the Tools menu, and then reacting to the command. The IDTCommandTarget.Exec method is the hook used to react to an issued command. Here is its prototype:

```
void Exec (
    [InAttribute] string CmdName,
    [InAttribute] vsCommandExecOption ExecuteOption,
    [InAttribute] ref Object VariantIn,
    [InAttribute] out Object VariantOut,
    [InAttribute] out bool Handled
)
```

To handle a command issued to an add-in, you write code in the Exec method that reacts to the passed-in command.

CmdName is a string containing the name of the command; this is the token used to uniquely identify a command, and thus is the parameter you examine in the body of the Exec method to determine whether and how you should react to the command.

ExecuteOption is a vsCommandExecOption enumeration that provides information about the options associated with the command (see Table 15.4).

TABLE 15.4   vsCommandExecOption Members

Member	Description
vsCommandExecOptionDoDefault	Performs the default behavior
vsCommandExecOptionDoPromptUser	Obtains user input and then executes the command
vsCommandExecOptionPromptUser	Executes the command without user input
vsCommandExecOptionShowHelp	Shows help for the command (does not execute it)

The VariantIn parameter is used to pass any arguments needed for the incoming command, and VariantOut is used as a way to pass information back out of the add-in to the caller.

Finally, Handled is a Boolean that indicates to the host application whether the add-in handled the command. As a general rule, if your add-in processed the command, it sets Handled to true. Otherwise, it sets Handled to false, which is a signal to Visual Studio that it needs to continue to look for a command invocation target that will handle the command.

The code to handle the Tool menu command looks like this:

```
/// <summary>Implements the Exec method of the IDTCommandTarget
///interface. This is called when the command is invoked.</summary>
/// <param term='commandName'>The name of the command to execute.</param>
/// <param term='executeOption'>Describes how the command should
///be run.</param>
/// <param term='varIn'>Parameters passed from the caller to the command
/// handler.</param>
/// <param term='varOut'>Parameters passed from the command handler to
/// the caller.</param>
/// <param term='handled'>Informs the caller if the command was handled
/// or not.</param>
/// <seealso class='Exec' />
public void Exec(string commandName, vsCommandExecOption executeOption,
    ref object varIn, ref object varOut, ref bool handled)
{
    handled = false;
    if(executeOption == vsCommandExecOption.vsCommandExecOptionDoDefault)
    {
        if(commandName == "MyFirstAddin.Connect.MyFirstAddin")
        {
            handled = true;
            return;
        }
    }

}
```

15

Managing Add-ins

Visual Studio add-ins are controlled with the Visual Studio Add-in Manager, which enables you to do two things: load and unload any registered add-in and specify how an add-in can be loaded. To access the Add-in Manager (see Figure 15.9), select Tools, Add-in Manager.

FIGURE 15.9 Managing add-ins.

This dialog box always displays a list of any available add-ins on the local machine. Checking or unchecking the box next to an add-in's name causes the add-in to immediately load or unload. The Startup check box determines whether the add-in loads automatically when Visual Studio is started. The Command Line check box performs the same action if Visual Studio is started via the command line (such as when you are launching Visual Studio as part of an automated build scenario).

Add-in Automation Objects

To programmatically manage add-ins, you use the DTE.AddIns collection, which contains an AddIn instance for every currently registered add-in (whether or not it is loaded).

Assuming a valid reference to the DTE2 object, you can directly reference registered add-ins from the DTE.AddIns collection by using their names like this:

```
DTE2 _appObject;
AddIn addIn = _appObject.AddIns.Item("MyFirstAddin");
```

With a valid add-in object, you can use its properties to determine whether it is loaded, query its name, or retrieve the add-in's ProgID:

```
bool isLoaded = addIn.Connected;
string name = addIn.Name;

string id = addIn.ProgID;
```

> **NOTE**
>
> We use the term *registered* to denote an add-in that has been installed on the local machine and registered with Visual Studio. In versions before Visual Studio 2005, this meant that a Registry entry was created for the add-in. This concept was replaced in 2005 with XML files: Visual Studio looks for XML files with an .addin extension to determine the list of add-ins available to be loaded (an add-in is "loaded" when it has been connected to, and loaded within, an application's host process). These .addin files are created for you automatically by the Add-in Wizard, but they can be easily created or edited by hand as well. To get a feeling for the information and structure of these files, look in the Visual Studio 2010\Addins folder under your local Documents directory. Each registered add-in appears here; you can explore an add-in file by loading it into Visual Studio, Notepad, or any other text editor.

A Sample Add-in: Color Palette

To cap this discussion of add-ins, let's look at the process of developing a functioning add-in from start to finish. The add-in is a color picker. It enables users to click on an area of a color palette, and the add-in emits code to create an instance of a color structure that matches the selected color from the palette. Here is a summary list of requirements for the add-in:

▶ In a tool window, it displays a visual color palette representing all the possible colors.

▶ As the mouse pointer is moved over the palette, the control displays the Red, Green, and Blue values for the point directly under the mouse pointer.

▶ If a user clicks on the palette, it takes the current RGB values and emits C# or VB code into the currently active document window to create a new color structure that encapsulates the given color.

▶ The selection of language (for example, C# or VB) is a configurable property of the control.

Getting Started

To start the development process, you create a new solution and a Visual Studio Add-in Project called ColorSelectorAddIn. The Add-in Wizard creates a code base for you inside a Connect class just as you saw earlier in this chapter. The Connect class is the place where all the IDE and automation object model–specific code goes.

In addition to the core add-in plumbing, you also need to create a User Control class that encapsulates the user interface and the processing logic for the add-in.

Creating the User Control

First, you can work on getting in place a user control that has the functionality you are looking for. After you have a workable control, you can worry about wiring that control into Visual Studio using the Connect class created by the Add-in Wizard.

Add a user control (called PaletteControl) to the add-in project by selecting Project, Add User Control. After the control is added, you place nine controls on the user control design surface. First, add a picture box, which is used to display the palette of colors, stored as a simple bitmap in a resource file (in this case, we're using a color palette from a popular paint program as our source for the bitmap). With the palette in place, you now need six label controls to display RGB values (and label them as such) per the requirements. And finally, in the finest tradition of gold-plating, you also add a picture box that repeats the current color selection and a label that shows the code you would generate to implement that color in a color structure.

Figure 15.10 provides a glimpse of the user control after these controls have been situated on the designer.

Handling Movement over the Palette

With the UI in place, you can now concentrate on the code. First, you can add an event handler to deal with mouse movements over the top of the palette picture box. With the MouseMove event handler, you can update your label controls and the secondary picture box instantly as the pointer roves over the palette bitmap:

```
public PaletteControl()
{
    InitializeComponent();
    this.pictureBoxPalette.MouseMove +=
        new MouseEventHandler(pictureBoxPalette_MouseMove);
    this.pictureBoxPalette.Cursor = System.Windows.Forms.Cursors.Cross;
}

void pictureBoxPalette_MouseMove(object sender, MouseEventArgs e)
{
    // Get the color under the current pointer position
    Color color = GetPointColor(e.X, e.Y);
```

```
// Update the RGB labels and the 2nd pic box
// using the retrieved color
DisplayColor(color);

// Generate our VB or C# code for the Color
// structure
SetCode(color, _generateVB);
}
```

FIGURE 15.10   The PaletteControl user control.

Looking at the Code Generation Properties

The PaletteControl class exposes two properties. Code is a string property that holds the color structure code generated when the palette is clicked on, and GenerateVB is a Boolean that specifies whether the control should generate Visual Basic code (GenerateVB = true) or C# code (GenerateVB = false). Here are the field and property declarations for these two properties:

```
string _code = "";
public string Code
{
    get { return _code; }
}

bool _generateVB = false;
```

```
public bool GenerateVB
{
   get { return _generateVB; }

}
```

Implementing the Helper Routines

Whenever the mouse pointer moves over the picture box region, you need to capture the color components of the point directly below the cursor (GetPointColor), update the label controls and the secondary picture box control to reflect that color (DisplayColor), and then generate the code to implement a matching color structure (SetCode). Here are the implementations of these routines:

```
/// <summary>
/// Returns a Color structure representing the color of
/// the pixel at the indicated x and y coordinates.
/// </summary>
/// <param name="x"></param>
/// <param name="y"></param>
/// <returns>A Color structure</returns>
private Color GetPointColor(int x, int y)
{
    // Get the bitmap from the palette picture box
    Bitmap bmp = (Bitmap)pictureBoxPalette.Image;
    // Use GetPixel to retrieve a color
    // structure for the current pointer position
    Color color = bmp.GetPixel(x, y);

    // Return the color structure
    return color;
}


/// <summary>
/// Displays the RGB values for the given color. Also sets
/// the background color of the secondary picture box.
/// </summary>
/// <param name="color">The Color to display</param>
private void DisplayColor(Color color)
{
    // pull out the RGB values from the
    // color structure
    string R = color.R.ToString();
    string G = color.G.ToString();
    string B = color.B.ToString();
    // set our secondary picture box
```

```csharp
        // to display the current color
        this.pictureBoxColor.BackColor = color;
        // display RGB values in the label
        // controls
        this.labelRValue.Text = R;
        this.labelGValue.Text = G;
        this.labelBValue.Text = B;
    }


    /// <summary>
    /// Generates a string representing the C# or VB code necessary to
    /// create a Color structure instance that matches the passed in
    /// Color structure. This string is then assigned to this
    /// user control's _code field.
    /// </summary>
    /// <param name="color">The color to represent in code.</param>
    /// <param name="isVB">Boolean flag indicating the language
    /// to use: false indicates C#, true indicates VB</param>
    private void SetCode(Color color, bool isVB)
    {
        // Read in add-in settings from registry
        SetPropFromReg();

        string code = "";

        if (isVB)
        {
            code = "Dim color As Color = ";
        }
        else
        {
            code = "Color color = ";
        }

        code = code + @"Color.FromArgb(" + color.R.ToString() + ", " +
            color.G.ToString() + ", " +
            color.B.ToString() + ");";

        _code = code;
        this.labelCode.Text = _code;


    }
    /// <summary>
    /// Reads a registry entry and sets the language output fields
    /// appropriately.
    /// </summary>
```

```
private void SetPropFromReg()
{
    RegistryKey regKey =
      Registry.CurrentUser.OpenSubKey(@"Software\Contoso\Addins\ColorPalette");
    string codeVal = (string)regKey.GetValue("Language", "CSharp");

    if (codeVal == "CSharp")
    {
        _generateVB = false;
    }
    else
    {
        _generateVB = true;
    }

}
```

Signaling a Color Selection

Because you need some way for the control to indicate that a user has selected a color (for example, has clicked on the palette), you also define an event on the user control class that is raised whenever a click is registered in the palette picture box:

```
public event EventHandler ColorSelected;

protected virtual void OnColorSelected(EventArgs e)
{
    if (ColorSelected != null)
        ColorSelected(this, e);
}

private void pictureBoxPalette_Click(object sender, EventArgs e)
{
    OnColorSelected(new EventArgs());

}
```

> **TIP**
>
> To isolate and test the user control, you might want to add a Windows forms project to the solution and host the control on a Windows form for testing. Just drop the control onto the form and run the forms project.

With the user control in place, you are ready to proceed to the second stage of the add-in's development: wiring the user control into the IDE.

Finishing the Connect Class

The Connect class already has the basic add-in code; now it's time to revisit that code and add the custom code to drive the user control. The add-in should integrate seamlessly into the development environment, so you can use a tool window to display the user control that you previously created.

Harking back to the discussions of the automation object model, you know that the Windows2 collection has a CreateToolWindow2 method, which allows you to create your own custom tool windows.

> **NOTE**
>
> Prior versions of Visual Studio required you to create a shim control (using C++) that would host a control for display in a tool window. The tool window, in turn, would then host the shim. With Visual Studio 2005 and beyond (and the improved Windows2.CreateToolWindow2 method), this is no longer necessary. Now you can directly host a managed user control in a tool window.

Here is the method prototype:

```
Window CreateToolWindow2 (
    AddIn Addin,
    string Assembly,
    string Class,
    string Caption,
    string GuidPosition,
    [InAttribute] out Object ControlObject

)
```

Displaying the Tool Window and User Control

Because you want the tool window to be created and displayed after the add-in has loaded, this CreateToolWindow2 method call will be placed in the Connect.OnConnection method. First, you set up a local object to point to the DTE.ToolWindows collection:

```
// The DTE.ToolWindows collection
Windows2 toolWindows= (Windows2)_applicationObject.Windows;
```

Then you need an object to hold the reference to the tool window that you create:

```
// Object to refer to the newly created tool window
Window2 toolWindow;
```

And finally, you need to create the parameters to feed to the CreateToolWindow2 method:

```
// Placeholder object; will eventually refer to the user control
// hosted by the user control
object paletteObject = null;


// This section specifies the path and class name for the palette
// control to be hosted in the new tool window; we also need to
// specify its caption and a unique GUID.
Assembly asm = System.Reflection.Assembly.GetExecutingAssembly();
string assemblyPath = asm.Location;
string className = "ColorSelectorAddIn.PaletteControl";
string guid = "{62175059-FD7E-407a-9EF3-5D07F2B704E8}";string caption = "Palette
Color Picker";
```

Note that we have hard-coded a GUID to pass in to the CreateToolWindow2 method. Because our user control is a managed code control, and it is hosted in a native COM component (all tool windows in Visual Studio are COM-based), the add-in infrastructure needs some way to establish a viable calling interface for the control. This is done through the use of the GUID parameter.

You can use Visual Studio to generate your GUID by selecting Tools, Create GUID, and then selecting Registry Format. You can then directly copy and paste this into your code window.

With that in place, you are only a few lines of code away from creating and displaying the tool window:

```
// Create the new tool window with the hosted user control
toolWindow = (Window2)toolWindows.CreateToolWindow2(_addInInstance, assemblyPath,
    className, caption, guid, ref paletteObject);


// If tool window was created successfully, make it visible
if (toolWindow != null)
{
    toolWindow.Visible = true;
}
```

Capturing User Control Events

The add-in is missing one last piece: You need to react whenever the user clicks on the palette by grabbing the generated code (available from the PaletteControl.Code property) and inserting it into the currently active document. There are two tasks at hand. First, you need to write an event handler to deal with the click event raised by the PaletteControl object. But to do that, you need a reference to the user control. This is the purpose of the paletteObject object that you pass in as the last parameter to the CreateToolWindow2

method. Because this is passed in by reference, it holds a valid instance of the
PaletteControl after the method call completes and returns. You can then cast this object
to the specific PaletteControl type, assign it to a field within the Connect class, and attach
an event handler to the PaletteControl.ColorSelected event:

```
// retrieve a reference back to our user control object
_paletteControl = (PaletteControl)paletteObject;

// wire up event handler for the PaletteControl.ColorSelected event
_paletteControl.ColorSelected +=
    new System.EventHandler(paletteControl1_ColorSelected);
```

TIP

Getting a reference to the user control can be a bit tricky. If the user control is not a
part of the same project as your add-in class, `CreateToolWindow2` will return only a null
value instead of a valid reference to the user control. If you want to develop your user
control outside the add-in project, you have to make sure that the user control is fully
attributed to be visible to calling COM components. See the topic "Exposing .NET
Framework Components to COM" in MSDN for details on how this task is accomplished.

Inserting the Generated Code

You react to the ColorSelect event by grabbing the content of the PaletteControl.Code
property and writing it into the currently active document. Again, you use your automation object model knowledge gained from the preceding chapter to make this happen. The
DTE.ActiveDocument class holds a reference to the currently active document. By using
an edit point, you can easily write text directly into the text document:

```
TextDocument currDoc = (TextDocument)_applicationObject.ActiveDocument.Object("");
EditPoint2 ep = (EditPoint2) currDoc.Selection.ActivePoint.CreateEditPoint();
ep.Insert(_paletteControl.Code);
ep.InsertNewLine(1);
```

Exposing Add-in Settings

The final step is to make the add-in's language choice a configurable option. Users should
be able to indicate whether they want the add-in to emit C# or Visual Basic code. To do
this, you need to have a user interface in the form of an Options page (that displays in the
Options dialog box), and you need a place to persist the option selections.

Creating the Option Page UI

Add-ins can reference an Options page that appears in the Tools Options dialog box.
Again, as you did with the custom tool window, you build a user control to implement
the logic and the user interface for the Options page.

You start by adding a new user control to the existing add-in project. For this example, call this class PaletteControlOptionPage. Adding a label control and two radio button controls enables you to indicate the language preference for the palette add-in. Figure 15.11 shows the design surface of the Options page.

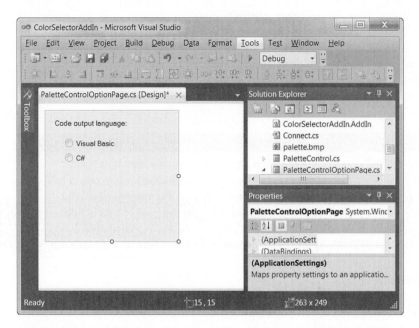

FIGURE 15.11   Designing the add-in options page UI.

The user control for the Options page needs to inherit from IDTToolsOptionPage:

```
public partial class PaletteControlOptionPage : UserControl, IDTToolsOptionsPage
{
    public PaletteControlOptionPage()
    {
        InitializeComponent();
    }
}
```

The IDTToolsOptionsPage interface defines five methods, outlined in Table 15.5.

TABLE 15.5   IDTToolsOptionsPage Members

Member	Description
GetProperties	Returns a properties object in response to calling DTE.Properties for this specific Options page
OnAfterCreated	Fires after the Tools Options page is created for the first time

TABLE 15.5   Continued

Member	Description
OnCancel	Fires if the user clicks on the Cancel button on the Tools Options dialog box
OnHelp	Fires if the user clicks on the Help button on the Tools Options dialog box
OnOK	Fires if the user clicks on the OK button on the Tools Options dialog box

These methods are called as the Options page progresses through its normal sequence of states, as you can see in Figure 15.12.

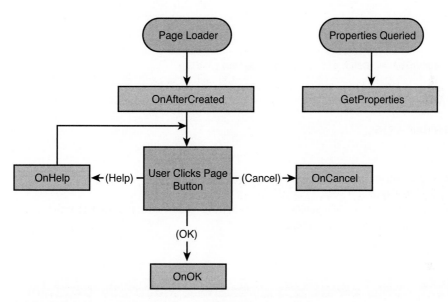

FIGURE 15.12   The Tools Options page action sequence.

By placing code within these methods, you can read in and store any configuration changes that a user makes through the Options page. In this case, you can keep things simple: Read in a value from a Registry entry as part of the OnAfterCreated method and update that same entry as part of the OnOK method:

```
public void OnAfterCreated(DTE DTEObject)
{
    // read our current value from registry
    // TODO: we should really include contingency code here for creating
    // the key if it doesn't already exist, dealing with unexpected values,
    // exceptions, etc.
    RegistryKey regKey =
        Registry.CurrentUser.OpenSubKey(@"Software\Contoso\Addins\ColorPalette");
```

```
    string codeVal = (string)regKey.GetValue("Language", "CSharp");

    if (codeVal == "CSharp")
    {
        this.radioButtonCSharp.Checked = true;
        this.radioButtonVB.Checked = false;
    }
    else
    {
        this.radioButtonCSharp.Checked = true;
        this.radioButtonVB.Checked = false;
    }
}
public void OnOK()
{
    string codeValue = "CSharp";    // our default value

    if (this.radioButtonVB.Checked)
    {
        codeValue = "VB";
    }

    // update the registry with the new setting
    RegistryKey regKey =
        Registry.CurrentUser.OpenSubKey(@"Software\Contoso\Addins\ColorPalette");
    regKey.SetValue("Language", codeValue);
}
```

> **NOTE**
>
> It is up to you to decide where and how you persist your add-in's settings. The Registry
> is one logical place; you could also elect to store your settings in an XML file that is
> deployed along with your binaries.

Registering the Options Page

The registration mechanism for an Options page is the same as that for an add-in: The
.addin file is used. By adding a few lines of XML, you can indicate to Visual Studio that an
Options page exists with the custom add-in. You can do this easily by editing the .addin
file right in Visual Studio (because it is automatically created as part of the project).

To include the necessary XML registration information, edit the .addin file and place the
following XML before the closing </extensibility> tag:

```
<ToolsOptionsPage>
  <Category Name="Color Palette">
    <SubCategory Name="Code Generation">
```

```
    <Assembly>C:\Users\lpowers\My Documents\Visual Studio 2008\Projects\
```

```
PaletteControlAddIn\PaletteControlAddIn\bin\PaletteControlAddIn.dll</Assembly>
      <FullClassName>PaletteControlAddIn.PaletteControlOptionPage </FullClassName>
    </SubCategory>
  </Category>
</ToolsOptionsPage>
```

You use the Category tag to specify the name of the option category displayed in the Tools Options dialog box. The SubCategory tag specifies the subnode under that category. The Assembly tag provides a path to the add-in's DLL file, and the FullClassName tag contains the full name for the add-in class.

With this final step complete, the add-in is fully functional. You can compile the project and then immediately load the add-in using the Add-in Manager. Figure 15.13 shows the add-in in action, and a complete code listing for the Connect, PaletteControl, and PaletteControlOptionPage classes (in that order) is provided in Listings 15.2, 15.3, and 15.4. The complete source code for this add-in can be downloaded from the Sams Publishing website.

FIGURE 15.13   The Color Selector Add-In.

LISTING 15.2 The Connect Class

```csharp
using System;
using Extensibility;
using EnvDTE;
using EnvDTE80;
using Microsoft.VisualStudio.CommandBars;
using System.Resources;
using System.Reflection;
using System.Globalization;
using System.Windows.Forms;

namespace ColorSelectorAddIn
{
    /// <summary>The object for implementing an Add-in.</summary>
    /// <seealso class='IDTExtensibility2' />
    public class Connect : IDTExtensibility2, IDTCommandTarget
    {
        #region Fields

        private DTE2 _applicationObject;
        private AddIn _addInInstance;
        private PaletteControl _paletteControl;

        #endregion

        /// <summary>Implements the constructor for the Add-in object.
        /// Place your initialization code within this method.</summary>
        public Connect()
        {
        }

        #region Events and Event Handlers

        private void paletteControl1_ColorSelected(object sender, EventArgs e)
        {
            try
            {
                TextDocument currDoc =
                  (TextDocument)_applicationObject.ActiveDocument.Object("");
                EditPoint2 ep = (EditPoint2)
                  currDoc.Selection.ActivePoint.CreateEditPoint();
                ep.Insert(_paletteControl.Code);
                ep.InsertNewLine(1);
            }
```

```
        catch (Exception ex)
        {
            MessageBox.Show("Exception caught: " + ex.ToString());
        }

    }

    #endregion

    /// <summary>Implements the OnConnection method of the
    /// IDTExtensibility2 interface. Receives notification that the Add-in
    /// is being loaded.</summary>
    /// <param term='application'>Root object of the host application.
    ///</param>
    /// <param term='connectMode'>Describes how the Add-in is being
    /// loaded.</param>
    /// <param term='addInInst'>Object representing this Add-in.</param>
    /// <seealso class='IDTExtensibility2' />
    public void OnConnection(object application,
        ext_ConnectMode connectMode,
        object addInInst, ref Array custom)
    {
        _applicationObject = (DTE2)application;
        _addInInstance = (AddIn)addInInst;

        if(connectMode == ext_ConnectMode.ext_cm_UISetup)
        {
            object []contextGUIDS = new object[] { };
            Commands2 commands = (Commands2)_applicationObject.Commands;
            string toolsMenuName;

            try
            {
                string resourceName;
                ResourceManager resourceManager =
                  new ResourceManager("ColorSelectorAddIn.CommandBar",
                    Assembly.GetExecutingAssembly());

                CultureInfo cultureInfo =
                    new CultureInfo(_applicationObject.LocaleID);

                if(cultureInfo.TwoLetterISOLanguageName == "zh")
                {
                    System.Globalization.CultureInfo parentCultureInfo =
                        cultureInfo.Parent;
                    resourceName = String.Concat(parentCultureInfo.Name,
                                                "Tools");
                }
                else
```

```
        {
            resourceName =
              String.Concat(cultureInfo.TwoLetterISOLanguageName,
              "Tools");
        }
        toolsMenuName = resourceManager.GetString(resourceName);
    }
    catch
    {
        //We tried to find a localized version of the word Tools,
        //but one was not found.
        //  Default to the en-US word, which may work for the
        //  current culture.
        toolsMenuName = "Tools";
    }


    //Place the command on the Tools menu.
    //Find the MenuBar command bar, which is the top-level command
    // bar holding all the main menu items:

    Microsoft.VisualStudio.CommandBars.CommandBar
       menuBarCommandBar =
       ((Microsoft.VisualStudio.CommandBars.CommandBars)
       _applicationObject.CommandBars)["MenuBar"];


    //Find the Tools command bar on the MenuBar command bar:
    CommandBarControl toolsControl =
      menuBarCommandBar.Controls[toolsMenuName];
    CommandBarPopup toolsPopup = (CommandBarPopup)toolsControl;


    //This try/catch block can be duplicated if you wish to add
    // multiple commands to be handled by your Add-in, just make
    // sure you also update the QueryStatus/Exec method to include
    // the new command names.
    try
    {
        //Add a command to the Commands collection:
        Command command = commands.AddNamedCommand2(_addInInstance,
          "ColorSelectorAddIn", "ColorSelectorAddIn",
          "Executes the command for ColorSelectorAddIn", true, 59,
          ref contextGUIDS,
          (int)vsCommandStatus.vsCommandStatusSupported+
            (int)vsCommandStatus.vsCommandStatusEnabled,
          (int)vsCommandStyle.vsCommandStylePictAndText,
          vsCommandControlType.vsCommandControlTypeButton);
```

```
            //Add a control for the command to the Tools menu:
            if((command != null) && (toolsPopup != null))
            {
                command.AddControl(toolsPopup.CommandBar, 1);
            }
        }
        catch(System.ArgumentException)
        {
            //If we are here, then the exception is probably because a
            //command with that name already exists. If so there is no
            //need to recreate the command and we can safely ignore the
            //exception.
        }
    }


    #region Create Tool Window

    // The DTE.ToolWindows collection
    Windows2 windows = (Windows2)_applicationObject.Windows;

    // Placeholder object; will eventually refer to the user control
    // hosted by the user control
    object paletteObject = null;

    // This section specifies the path and class name for the palette
    // control to be hosted in the new tool window; we also need to
    // specify its caption and a unique GUID.
    Window toolWindow;
    Assembly asm = System.Reflection.Assembly.GetExecutingAssembly();
    string assemblyPath = asm.Location;
    string className = "ColorSelectorAddIn.PaletteControl";
    string guid = "{62175059-FD7E-407a-9EF3-5D07F2B704E8}";
    string caption = "Color Selector";

    try
    {

      // Create the new tool window and insert the user control in
      // it.
        toolWindow = windows.CreateToolWindow2(_addInInstance,
            assemblyPath, className, caption, guid,
            ref paletteObject);

        // If tool window was created successfully, make it visible
        if (_toolWindow != null)
        {
```

```
                _toolWindow.Visible = true;
            }

            // retrieve a reference back to our user control object
            _paletteControl = (PaletteControl)paletteObject;

            // wire up event handler for the PaletteControl.ColorSelected
            //event
            _paletteControl.ColorSelected +=
                new System.EventHandler(paletteControl1_ColorSelected);

        }
        catch (Exception ex)
        {
            MessageBox.Show("Exception caught: " + ex.ToString());
        }

        #endregion

    }

    /// <summary>Implements the OnDisconnection method of the
    /// IDTExtensibility2 interface. Receives notification that
    /// the Add-in is being unloaded.</summary>
    /// <param term='disconnectMode'>Describes how the Add-in
    /// is being unloaded.</param>
    /// <param term='custom'>Array of parameters that are host
    /// application specific.</param>
    /// <seealso class='IDTExtensibility2' />
    public void OnDisconnection(ext_DisconnectMode disconnectMode,
        ref Array custom)
    {
    }

    /// <summary>Implements the OnAddInsUpdate method of the
    /// IDTExtensibility2 interface. Receives notification when
    /// the collection of Add-ins has changed.</summary>
    /// <param term='custom'>Array of parameters that are host
    /// application specific.</param>
    /// <seealso class='IDTExtensibility2' />
    public void OnAddInsUpdate(ref Array custom)
    {
    }

    /// <summary>Implements the OnStartupComplete method of the
    /// IDTExtensibility2 interface. Receives notification that
```

```
/// the host application has completed loading.</summary>
/// <param term='custom'>Array of parameters that are host
/// application specific.</param>
/// <seealso class='IDTExtensibility2' />
public void OnStartupComplete(ref Array custom)
{
}

/// <summary>Implements the OnBeginShutdown method of the
/// IDTExtensibility2 interface. Receives notification that
/// the host application is being unloaded.</summary>
/// <param term='custom'>Array of parameters that are host
/// application specific.</param>
/// <seealso class='IDTExtensibility2' />
public void OnBeginShutdown(ref Array custom)
{
}

/// <summary>Implements the QueryStatus method of the
/// IDTCommandTarget interface. This is called when the
/// command's availability is updated</summary>
/// <param term='commandName'>The name of the command to
/// determine state for.</param>
/// <param term='neededText'>Text that is needed for the
/// command.</param>
/// <param term='status'>The state of the command in the
/// user interface.</param>
/// <param term='commandText'>Text requested by the neededText
/// parameter.</param>
/// <seealso class='Exec' />
public void QueryStatus(string commandName,
    vsCommandStatusTextWanted neededText, ref vsCommandStatus status,
    ref object commandText)
{
    if(neededText ==
        vsCommandStatusTextWanted.vsCommandStatusTextWantedNone)
    {
        if(commandName ==
            "ColorSelectorAddIn.Connect.ColorSelectorAddIn")
        {
            status = (vsCommandStatus)
                    vsCommandStatus.vsCommandStatusSupported
                    |vsCommandStatus.vsCommandStatusEnabled;
            return;
        }
    }
```

15

```
        }

        /// <summary>Implements the Exec method of the IDTCommandTarget
        /// interface. This is called when the command is invoked.</summary>
        /// <param term='commandName'>The name of the command to
        /// execute.</param>
        /// <param term='executeOption'>Describes how the command should
        /// be run.</param>
        /// <param term='varIn'>Parameters passed from the caller to the
        /// command handler.</param>
        /// <param term='varOut'>Parameters passed from the command handler
        /// to the caller.</param>
        /// <param term='handled'>Informs the caller if the command was
        /// handled or not.</param>
        /// <seealso class='Exec' />
        public void Exec(string commandName, vsCommandExecOption executeOption,
            ref object varIn, ref object varOut, ref bool handled)
        {
            handled = false;
            if(executeOption ==
                vsCommandExecOption.vsCommandExecOptionDoDefault)
            {
                if(commandName ==
                    "ColorSelectorAddIn.Connect.ColorSelectorAddIn")
                {
                    handled = true;
                    return;
                }
            }
        }

    }

}
```

LISTING 15.3   The PaletteControl Class

```
using System;
using System.Collections.Generic;
using System.ComponentModel;
using System.Drawing;
using System.Data;
using System.Runtime.InteropServices;
using System.Text;
using System.Windows.Forms;
```

```csharp
using Microsoft.Win32;

namespace ColorSelectorAddIn
{
    [Guid("62175059-FD7E-407a-9EF3-5D07F2B704E8")]
    public partial class PaletteControl : UserControl
    {
        #region Fields

        string _code = "";
        bool _generateVB = false;

        #endregion

        #region Properties

        public string Code
        {
            get { return _code; }
        }

        public bool GenerateVB
        {
            get { return _generateVB; }
        }

        #endregion

        #region Ctor(s)

        public PaletteControl()
        {
            InitializeComponent();
            this.pictureBoxPalette.MouseMove += new
              MouseEventHandler(pictureBoxPalette_MouseMove);
            this.pictureBoxPalette.Cursor = System.Windows.Forms.Cursors.Cross;
        }

        #endregion

        #region Event Handlers and Delegates

        void pictureBoxPalette_MouseMove(object sender, MouseEventArgs e)
        {
            // Get the color under the current pointer position
            Color color = GetPointColor(e.X, e.Y);
```

```
        // Update the RGB labels and the 2nd pic box
        // using the retrieved color
        DisplayColor(color);

        // Generate our VB or C# code for the Color
        // structure
        SetCode(color, _generateVB);
    }

public event EventHandler ColorSelected;

protected virtual void OnColorSelected(EventArgs e)
{
    if (ColorSelected != null)
        ColorSelected(this, e);
}

private void pictureBoxPalette_Click(object sender, EventArgs e)
{
    OnColorSelected(new EventArgs());
}

#endregion

#region Private Routines

/// <summary>
/// Returns a Color structure representing the color of
/// the pixel at the indicated x and y coordinates.
/// </summary>
/// <param name="x"></param>
/// <param name="y"></param>
/// <returns>A Color structure</returns>
private Color GetPointColor(int x, int y)
{
    // Get the bitmap from the palette picture box
    Bitmap bmp = (Bitmap)pictureBoxPalette.Image;
    // Use GetPixel to retrieve a color
    // structure for the current pointer position
    Color color = bmp.GetPixel(x, y);

    // Return the color structure
    return color;
}
```

```csharp
/// <summary>
/// Displays the RGB values for the given color. Also sets
/// the background color of the secondary picture box.
/// </summary>
/// <param name="color">The Color to display</param>
private void DisplayColor(Color color)
{
    // pull out the RGB values from the
    // color structure
    string R = color.R.ToString();
    string G = color.G.ToString();
    string B = color.B.ToString();

    // set our secondary picture box
    // to display the current color
    this.pictureBoxColor.BackColor = color;

    // display RGB values in the label
    // controls
    this.labelRValue.Text = R;
    this.labelGValue.Text = G;
    this.labelBValue.Text = B;
}

/// <summary>
/// Generates a string representing the C# or VB code necessary to
/// create a Color structure instance that matches the passed in
/// Color structure. This string is then assigned to this
/// user control's _code field.
/// </summary>
/// <param name="color">The color to represent in code.</param>
/// <param name="isVB">Boolean flag indicating the language
/// to use: false indicates C#, true indicates VB</param>
private void SetCode(Color color, bool isVB)
{
    // Read in add-in settings from registry
    SetPropFromReg();

    string code = "";

    if (isVB)
    {
        code = "Dim color As Color = ";
    }
    else
    {
```

```
            code = "Color color = ";
        }

        code = code + "Color.FromArgb(" + color.R.ToString() + ", " +
            color.G.ToString() + ", " +
            color.B.ToString() + ");";

        _code = code;
        this.labelCode.Text = _code;
    }
    /// <summary>
    /// Reads a registry entry and sets the language output fields
    /// appropriately.
    /// </summary>
    private void SetPropFromReg()
    {
        try
        {
            RegistryKey regKey =
                Registry.CurrentUser.OpenSubKey(@"Software\Contoso\Addins\
                ➥ColorPalette");
            string codeVal = (string)regKey.GetValue("Language", "CSharp");

            if (codeVal == "CSharp")
            {
                _generateVB = false;
            }
            else
            {
                _generateVB = true;
            }
        }
        catch (Exception ex)
        {
            // error reading the registry; default to C#
            _generateVB = false;
        }
    }
    #endregion
}
}
```

LISTING 15.4   The PaletteControlOptionPage Class

```csharp
using System;
using System.Collections.Generic;
using System.ComponentModel;
using System.Drawing;
using System.Data;
using System.Text;
using System.Windows.Forms;
using EnvDTE;
using Microsoft.Win32;

namespace ColorSelectorAddIn
{
    public partial class PaletteControlOptionPage : UserControl,
      IDTToolsOptionsPage
    {
        public PaletteControlOptionPage()
        {
            InitializeComponent();
        }

        #region IDTToolsOptionsPage Members

        public void GetProperties(ref object PropertiesObject)
        {
            throw new NotImplementedException();
        }

        public void OnAfterCreated(DTE DTEObject)
        {
            // read our current value from registry
            // TODO: we should really include contingency code here for
            // creating the key if it doesn't already exist, dealing with
            // unexpected values, exceptions, etc.
            RegistryKey regKey =
              Registry.CurrentUser.OpenSubKey(@"Software\Contoso\Addins\
              ➥ColorPalette");
            string codeVal = (string)regKey.GetValue("Language", "CSharp");

            if (codeVal == "CSharp")
            {
                this.radioButtonCSharp.Checked = true;
                this.radioButtonVB.Checked = false;
```

```
        }
        else
        {
            this.radioButtonCSharp.Checked = true;
            this.radioButtonVB.Checked = false;
        }
    }


    public void OnCancel()
    {
        throw new NotImplementedException();
    }
    public void OnHelp()
    {
        throw new NotImplementedException();
    }

    public void OnOK()
    {
        string codeValue = "CSharp";    // our default value

        if (this.radioButtonVB.Checked)
        {
            codeValue = "VB";
        }

        // update the registry with the new setting
        RegistryKey regKey =
            Registry.CurrentUser.OpenSubKey(@"Software\Contoso\Addins\
            ➥ColorPalette");

        regKey.SetValue("Language", codeValue);

    }

    #endregion
    }
}
```

NOTE

If you have add-ins that were written for Visual Studio 2005, you need to make some minor updates to the source code to fully migrate features over to Visual Studio 2008/2010. Detailed migration steps are provided in the Visual Studio MSDN documentation. Search for the article "How to: Update Visual Studio 2005 Add-ins to Visual Studio 2008."

Creating a Visual Studio Wizard

Visual Studio makes heavy use of wizards to help guide developers through various tasks. The Add-in Wizard that we discussed in the previous sections is one such example of a New Project Wizard (it is launched when you try to create a new add-in project). There are also wizards for adding new items to projects. You can modify the existing Project/Add New Item wizards or create your own wizard complete with its own user interface. Finally, there are custom wizards that, like the other wizards, are responsible for generating code but are not called from a Visual Studio dialog box.

In the following sections, we focus on understanding the wizard landscape by creating a custom Add New Item Wizard.

Examining the Wizard Structure

Each wizard consists of two major components: a class that contains the code (and user interface) for the wizard and a .vsz file that provides information about the wizard to Visual Studio.

The IDTWizard Interface

To hook into Visual Studio's wizard engine, your Wizard class must implement the EnvDTE.IDTWizard interface. The IDTWizard defines a single method, Execute, that is called by Visual Studio whenever the wizard is launched. Here is the prototype for the IDTWizard.Execute method (in C#):

```
void Execute (
    Object Application,
    int hwndOwner,
    ref Object[] ContextParams,
    ref Object[] CustomParams,
    out wizardResult retval
)
```

The arguments passed to the Execute method are used to link the wizard to the Visual Studio environment and to pass relevant data to the wizard:

▶ **Application**—A DTE instance for the Visual Studio IDE.

- ▶ **hwndOwner**—A handle to the parent window; this window "parents" any user interface elements created by the wizard.

- ▶ **ContextParams**—For New Project/Add New Item wizards, an array of objects used to pass information about the type of wizard that was launched and various data necessary for the wizard to function, such as project name and install directory.

- ▶ **CustomParams**—An array of objects used to carry any custom parameters you define for your wizard.

- ▶ **wizardResult**—An enumeration value that indicates the results of the wizard.

The ContextParams parameter's content varies depending on the type of wizard. For instance, for a New Project Wizard, the third value in the ContextParams array represents the location where the project file is stored (called the LocalDirectory). But for an Add Item Wizard, the third value in the array is a pointer to a ProjectItems collection. Table 15.6 maps the various array elements to the three different wizard types.

TABLE 15.6   wizardResult Enumeration Values

Index	NewProject Wizard	AddSubProject Wizard	AddItem Wizard
0	WizardType enum	WizardType enum	WizardType enum
1	Project name	Project name	Project name
2	Local directory	ProjectItems object	ProjectItems object
3	VS install directory	Local directory	Local directory
4	FExclusive flag (create new solution or use current)	Name of added item	Name of added item
5	Solution name	VS install directory	VS install directory
6	Silent flag (run with or without UI)	Silent flag	Silent flag

To determine the results of the wizard, you look at the value placed in the wizardResult parameter. Table 15.7 lists the wizardResult enum values.

TABLE 15.7   wizardResult Enumeration Values

Member	Description
wizardResultBackOut	The user exited the wizard by clicking on the Back button.
wizardResultCancel	The wizard was canceled.
wizardResultFailure	The wizard startup failed.
wizardResultSuccess	The wizard startup succeeded.

The core content of the Execute method is entirely up to you. Within the body of the Execute method, you need to implement all the code necessary to do the work of the wizard and display its UI to the user.

> **NOTE**
>
> Although you probably think of wizards as a series of pages accessed by Next and Back navigation buttons, a wizard in Visual Studio's terms is nothing more than a COM object that implements IDTWizard. In fact, a wizard doesn't need to display a user interface at all. It could, for instance, merely use the parameters passed to it to do some work and then quit.

The .vsz and .vsdir Files

If you recall from our discussion of add-ins, every add-in uses an .addin file to register the add-in with Visual Studio. The .vsz files are the equivalent for wizards; they make Visual Studio aware of the wizard and its implementing class.

Here is a complete, sample .vsz file:

```
VSWizard 10.0
Wizard=ContosoWizard.AddNewClassWizard

Param=
```

The VSWizard line in this file identifies the version information for the wizard. The number 10.0 equates to Visual Studio 2010, and prior version numbers map to prior Visual Studio releases.

> **NOTE**
>
> The .vsz file format has not changed at all since Visual Studio 2003, so the version number is largely irrelevant; many of the wizards included with Visual Studio 2010 are labeled as version 6 files!

After the version number, a class ID is provided for the wizard. And finally, there are one or more (optional) Param lines. These lines define any custom parameters that you want sent to the wizard. Any parameters defined here come across in the CustomParams parameter in the Execute method.

Visual Studio has a specific folder hierarchy that it uses for storing wizard .vsz files; the folder where you place the .vsz file dictates exactly where the option to launch the wizard appears. As an example, if you want to create an Add Item Wizard for both Visual Basic and Visual C#, you need to place a copy of the .vsz file into both the Visual Basic and the C# folders. If Visual Studio 2010 is installed in its default location, you place the wizard files here:

```
C:\Program Files\Microsoft Visual Studio 10.0\VC#\CSharpProjectItems
C:\Program Files\Microsoft Visual Studio 10.0\VB\VBProjectItems
```

If you are creating a New Project Wizard, the files are placed in the VC#\CSharpProjects and the VB\VBProjects folders.

Wizard folders may also contain a .vsdir file. This file is used to provide Visual Studio with icon and other resource information about a particular wizard. The .vsdir file is also a plain-text file. Each line in the file represents a specific .vsz file/wizard and provides multiple fields (separated by the pipe character, |) with optional information about the wizard. Table 15.8 documents the valid fields for each .vsdir line, in order of their appearance. The optional fields are noted.

TABLE 15.8   .vsdir Options

Sort Priority	A number used to provide a relative grouping number for the wizard in the display dialog boxes. A wizard with a value of 1 is displayed next to other 1 wizards, and so on.
Description	The description of the wizard. This will appear whenever the wizard is selected in the Add Item dialog box.
DLL Path	A full path to the assembly containing the wizard's icon.
Icon Resource id	A resource identifier that points within the DLL to the icon to be displayed.
Flags	One or more bitwise values used to control certain wizard behaviors. See the MSDN documentation for a complete list. Optional.
Name	The name of the wizard to be displayed in the Name field of the dialog box (unlike the Localized Name, this field is required).

Here is a simple .vsdir file example with one wizard record:

```
CSharpContosoDataClass.vsz | | |1|Create a new Contoso storage
class|c:\ContosoFramework\Wizards\DataClassWizard.dll| | |Contoso Data Class
```

> **TIP**
>
> The .vsdir record provides a way to associate an icon resource to the wizard by enabling you to specify a DLL path and an icon resource ID. There is also a simpler way to accomplish this: Just create an .ico file, give it the same name as the wizard's .vsz file, and place it in the same directory.

Creating an Add New Item Wizard

Here are the basic steps for creating a wizard:

1. Create a new class library project; in this project, create a new class that implements the IDTWizard interface.

2. In the wizard class, write the code in the Execute method to perform the wizard's tasks and display its UI.

3. Create a .vsz file for the wizard.

4. Create or edit a .vsdir file to reference the new wizard and the .vsz file.

To solidify these concepts, let's look at them in action. We follow the development of a wizard from start to finish. In this case, the wizard is a C# Add Item Wizard. Its purpose is to collect some basic data from the user and then create a Tools Options page class (much like you manually did earlier in the chapter) that has been customized in accordance with the user's input into the wizard dialog box.

Implementing the Execute Method

The Execute method needs to do two things: display a Windows Forms dialog box to capture preferences such as class name; and process those preferences, generate a class that implements a Tools Options page, and add that class to the current project.

Creating the Dialog Box   First, the dialog box: It should look roughly like the dialog box in Figure 15.14 (there is nothing special about the implementation of this form, so we won't bother to detail all of its code here).

FIGURE 15.14   The wizard form.

When the user clicks on the OK button, you should set several properties on the form that mirror the selections made on the dialog box. For instance, if you implement this form as a class called WizardDialog, you need a WizardDialog.ClassName property, a WizardDialog.Category property, and so on. The last thing to do when the OK button is clicked is to set the form's DialogResult property. The Execute method on the wizard (which we examine in a moment) queries the DialogResult property to determine whether the user has committed the wizard or canceled it. Here is a look at the OK and Cancel button click event handlers:

```
private void buttonOK_Click(object sender, EventArgs e)
{
    // assign screen control values to our public
    // fields
    this.ClassName = this.textBoxClassName.Text;
    this.Category = this.textBoxCategory.Text;
    this.SubCategory = this.textBoxSubCategory.Text;
    this.UseRegistry = this.checkBoxUseRegistry.Checked;
    this.RegKey = this.textBoxRegKey.Text;

    // indicate dialog was accepted
    this.DialogResult = DialogResult.OK;
}

private void buttonCancel_Click(object sender, EventArgs e)
{
    // indicate dialog was cancelled
    this.DialogResult = DialogResult.Cancel;
}
```

Using a Template File   Remember, the purpose of this wizard is to generate some class code for us. There are two approaches we could take to generating the class code: You can generate every line of code using either the Code DOM API or brute-force string creation/concatenation, or you can use a template file. The template file approach is a bit simpler, and probably more efficient as well, so that is the approach we describe here.

The class template is a file that looks just like any other user control. Using the standard code created for a user control class, you substitute key areas with string placeholders. For instance, the class name is specified within the wizard, and thus something you should replace in the template class:

```
public class %TemplateClassName% : UserControl, IDTToolsOptionsPage
{
    ...
}
```

You also need the IDTToolsOptionsPage members—such as OnAfterCreated, OnOK, and so on—represented in the class. For most of these methods, you leave a simple System.NotImplementedException as a reminder to fill in code as necessary. For

OnAfterCreated and OnOK, however, you need the option of including a line of code to open the indicated Registry key:

```
public void OnAfterCreated(DTE DTEObject)
{
    // read our current value from registry
    // TODO: Include code to read from registry here
    %StartRegistryCode%
    RegistryKey regKey = Registry.CurrentUser.OpenSubKey(@"%TemplateRegKey%");
    %EndRegistryCode%
}
public void OnOK()
{
    //TODO: include code to save options
    // update the registry with the new setting
    %StartRegistryCode%
    RegistryKey regKey = Registry.CurrentUser.OpenSubKey(@"%TemplateRegKey%");
    %EndRegistryCode%
}
```

Again, you use placeholders here: The %StartRegistryCode% and %EndRegistryCode% delimits the OpenSubKey line of code. If the user unchecks the User Registry check box in the wizard, you eliminate everything between these two placeholders (including the place-holders themselves). The %TemplateRegKey% is used as a token for the Registry key value; this is something else that you collect from the user in the wizard's dialog box.

Executing the Wizard   The Execute method opens the wizard form and, if the user has not canceled the dialog box, uses the form's properties to call into a few internal routines responsible for generating the output class:

```
public void Execute(object Application, int hwndOwner, ref object[] ContextParams,
    ref object[] CustomParams, ref wizardResult retval)
{
    // instance the dialog for the wizard
    WizardDialog dlg = new WizardDialog();

    // show the dialog
    dlg.Show();

    // process the wizard results
    if (dlg.DialogResult == DialogResult.OK)
    {
        // Load template file, replace tokens, return content
        // as string
        string classContent = ReplaceTokens(dlg.ClassName, dlg.Category,
            dlg.SubCategory, dlg.UseRegistry, dlg.RegKey);
```

15

```
            // Put the returned string content into a file and
            // add the file to the current project
            // (3rd element of ContextParams is the current project's
            // items collection)
            ProjectItems projItems = (ProjectItems)ContextParams[2];
            AddFile(this.ClassName, classContent, projItems);

            retval = wizardResult.wizardResultSuccess;

        }
        // wizard was canceled; no action required
        else
        {
            retval = wizardResult.wizardResultCancel;
        }
    }
```

To react to the user clicking OK, you call three separate internal routines. The first, ReplaceTokens, opens the template class file and replaces the tokens (because this is a simple string substitution process, we won't reproduce the code here).

The second routine, AddFile, writes the new class content into a new file and adds it to the current project. Because this code might not be entirely obvious, here is one approach:

```
private void AddFile(string className, string classContent,
    ProjectItems projItems)
{
    // determine path to project files
    string fileName =
        Path.GetDirectoryName(projItems.ContainingProject.FileName);

    // use path and class name to build file name for class
    fileName = fileName + className + ".cs";

    // save class file into project folder
    using (TextWriter writer = new StreamWriter(fileName, false))
    {
        writer.Write(classContent);
        writer.Close();
    }

    // add the newly created file to the current project
    projItems.AddFromFile(fileName);

}
```

Last, you call UpdateXML; this routine opens the .addin file and adds the appropriate
<ToolsOptionsPage> node to the XML content:

```
private void UpdateXml(ProjectItems projItems, string category,
    string subCategory)
{
    // create string XML snippet
    string xml = "";
    xml += "<ToolsOptionsPage>\r\n";
    xml += "    <Category Name=\"" + category + "\">\r\n";
    xml += "        <SubCategory Name=\"" + subCategory + "\">\r\n";
    xml += "            <Assembly></Assembly>\r\n";
    xml += "            <FullClassName></FullClassName>\r\n";
    xml += "        </SubCategory>\r\n";
    xml += "    </Category>\r\n";
    xml += "</ToolsOptionsPage>\r\n";
    xml += "</Extensibility>";

    // iterate items in the project, looking for the
    // .addin file
    string projName = projItems.ContainingProject.FullName;
    foreach (ProjectItem itm in projItems)
    {
        if (itm.Name == projName + ".addin")
        {
            // open the .addin file's document object
            itm.Document.Activate();
            TextDocument txtDoc = (TextDocument)itm.Document.Object("");
            TextRanges nullObj = null;
            // add in the cat/sub-cat XML snippet
            txtDoc.ReplacePattern("</Extensibility>", xml,
                (int)vsFindOptions.vsFindOptionsFromStart,
                ref nullObj);

        }
    }
}
```

At this point, the wizard code is complete.

Creating the .vsz and .vsdir Files

All that is left to do is to "register" the wizard by creating the .vsz file and adding an entry
to the .vsdir file. The .vsz file is straightforward:

```
VSWizard 8.0
```

```
Wizard=ContosoWizards.ToolsOptionsPageWizard
Param=
```

The record you add to the .vsdir file looks like this:

```
ToolsOptionsPageWizard.vsz ¦ ¦ ¦1¦Create a new Tools Options Page
class¦c:\ContosoFramework\Wizards\ToolsOptionsPageWizard.dll¦ ¦ ¦Contoso Options
Page Class
```

With that, the wizard is fully functional and should be selectable from the Add Item
dialog box.

Summary

In this chapter, we described how to leverage the power of Visual Studio's automation APIs
to create add-ins and wizards.

You investigated the nearly unlimited potential for extending Visual Studio by using add-
ins that call into the automation API and expose their interfaces in a variety of ways,
including custom tool windows and dialog boxes.

And you also saw how to once again leverage the ubiquitous automation object model
and the built-in wizard engine to create your own custom wizards for adding new projects,
adding new project items, or executing nearly any other type of step-by-step process
within Visual Studio.

In the next chapter, we explore another, final way to extend Visual Studio using the
Managed Extensibility Framework.

We have seen in the preceding two chapters that there
are many different opportunities, and approaches, for
extending Visual Studio functionality. The add-in model, in
particular, is a powerful way to implement fairly robust
applications within the Visual Studio IDE. But Visual Studio
2010 introduces a brand new technology for extending
Visual Studio: the Managed Extensibility Framework (MEF).

MEF is actually a generic architecture pattern, API, and .NET
class library for enabling easy "plug in" extensions for any
.NET application. Visual Studio 2010 allows for MEF-based
extensions in the code editor, and will likely embrace MEF
more broadly across the entire IDE as time goes one.

This chapter introduces Microsoft's MEF and how the framework can be applied to extend the Visual Studio code editor.

The Extensibility Problem

Before getting into the architecture and code level details of
MEF, it is useful to understand the problem or question that
MEF is trying to answer. Put simply, that question is how
can developers allow their applications to be easily
extended by others, or conversely how can developers
extend existing applications in a simple way?

There are a variety of hurdles that have to be overcome in
this space. For instance, how can an application be open for
extensions, and yet closed so that its core functionality
can't be usurped against the intentions of its designers?
What developers are really after is a consistent solution that
enables dynamic applications to be created, and thus

enables other developers to extend those dynamic applications using well-known and understood mechanisms.

Creating Dynamic Applications

Prior to MEF, the work required to create a so-called open-ended, .NET application—that is, an application that allows others to contribute code and alter or add to its functionality—is not a trivial effort. The main issue here is one of discovery and instantiation. The "host" application (the application that supports extensions) needs to have a standard way of identifying and validating code meant to extend the host. And there needs to be a run-time activation approach as well: How is the plug-in code executed, and what portions of the host app can be affected by the plug-in?

This is where MEF enters the scene. It provides an architecture pattern and framework/API that host application developers and plug-in developers can use to enable these dynamic application scenarios.

In fact, MEF explicitly targets developers who are creating any of three different classes of applications:

▶ **Extensions**—Chunks of compiled code that enhance the functionality of an existing application. Extension developers need to be able to implement their components without having either access to the host applications' source, or even specialized knowledge of that source.

▶ **Extensible Frameworks/Host Applications**—Applications that need to support the dynamic addition of functionality via extensions.

▶ **Programming model**—The least common scenario; in this case, a developer is interested in creating a potentially new way of developing against an application platform. In this case, MEF can provide the building blocks that developers need to build their own extensible application platform.

Visual Studio is merely one example of a host application that clearly benefits from its ability to support rich add-ins that add value to the core feature areas delivered out of the box by Microsoft.

MEF Architecture

MEF achieves its goals through three different, but related, mechanisms:

▶ Dependency injection

▶ Structural matching

▶ Naming and activation

Let's walk through each of these concepts in an abstract sense and then see how they are physically implemented with MEF.

MEF Principles

Dependency injection is a software architecture term that refers to the concept of a framework or runtime "injecting" an external dependency into another piece of software. Handling this process is a core requirement for an extensibility framework.

Structural matching, also sometimes referred to as *duck typing*, is a style of feature discovery and typing in which a host determines the type of an object based on the properties and methods it exposes as opposed to its actual type in the object-oriented sense.

Finally, *naming and activation* is the "last mile" feature that puts all of the pieces together and enables an application to load and run the plug-in code in a predictable fashion.

When all three of these mechanisms are in place, you have a reasonable platform for building applications that can be dynamically composited at runtime. In other words, by exploiting an extensibility framework, you can deliver a flexible application that is capable of leveraging new features that are added dynamically over time; functionality that does not, in fact, require a wholesale replacement or upgrade of a core, monolithic executable.

Working with MEF

MEF applications are based around a small set of core concepts: the composition container, catalog, and parts. These are both abstract concepts and a physical API that you can interact with from managed code. All of the MEF classes live within the System.ComponentModel.Composition namespace and its children namespaces such as System.ComponentModel.Composition.Hosting.

Parts

An MEF *part* is the primary unit of functionality. Parts have a set of features that they provide (called exports); parts might also depend on features that other parts provide (termed imports).

Parts verbalize their exports and imports through contracts. At the code level, contracts are specified by using declarative attributes to declare their imports and exports (System.ComponentModel.Composition.ImportAttribute and System.ComponentModel.Composition.ExportAttribute, respectively).

Here is an example of a C# class declaring an export:

```
[Export(typeof(IMyExtensionProvider))]
internal class TestExtensionProvider
```

Composition Container

The *composition container* is the core of an MEF application and does all of the heavy lifting. It holds all of the available parts, handles the instantiation of those parts, and is the primary composition engine in MEF. In this context, composition can be thought of as the process of matching required services (imports) with published services (exports).

Host applications can instantiate a container via the
System.ComponentModel.Composition.Hosting.CompositionContainer class like this:

```
private CompositionContainer _container;
```

Catalog

The *catalog* is a sort of registry and discovery mechanism for parts, and is used by the
composition container. MEF provides a default set of catalogs, each one designed to
discover parts from a particular source or target: there is a type catalog for discovering
parts from a given .NET type (via the TypeCatalog class), an assembly catalog for discovering parts from an assembly (via the AssemblyCatalog catalog), and a directory catalog (via
the DirectoryCatalog class) for discovering parts that exist in a specified folder.

A fourth class, AggregateCatalog, enables you to combine multiple catalogs so that parts
from multiple catalog sources can be combined into one master catalog.

A catalog instance can be passed into the constructor for a CompositionContainer object.
We could write the following code to both create a new composition container, and
specify a catalog of parts that are to be discovered from within the specific assembly:

```
var catalog = new TypeCatalog(typeof(MyExtension));


CompositionContainer container =
    new CompositionContainer(catalog);
```

Figure 16.1 shows a diagram of the abstract MEF architecture.

FIGURE 16.1   A simplified view of MEF Architecture.

The Visual Studio Editor and MEF

Although the MEF is a general purpose extensibility framework applicable across a wide
range of application scenarios, it is particularly applicable to extending the Visual Studio
2010 code editor for one simple reason: The editor itself was built by Microsoft using MEF.

In other words, the code editor is comprised of a series of MEF parts. Adding additional parts to extend and change editor behavior is simply a matter of using the MEF design patterns and writing your own MEF parts to be discovered and used by the editor.

In Chapter 15, "Writing Add-Ins and Wizards," during our discussion of Visual Studio Add-in development, we talked about the need to understand two pieces of information in order to be successful with add-in development: You need to understand both the add-in process and you need to understand the API that Visual Studio exposes to add-ins.

With the editor (and with MEF), the same concepts apply. If you are to embark on an editor extension endeavor, you need to understand the extensibility mechanism (MEF), and the specific extensibility points (MEF exports) offered by the editor. Now that we understand the MEF process, we can examine how to create an MEF-based project within Visual Studio, and we can review the numerous extension points the editor exposes.

If you want to extend the editor, you need to know the exact editor extensibility points; in other words, you need to know which editor feature areas can be easily replaced or enhanced using your own MEF parts.

Editor Extension Points

The Visual Studio code editor has its own sort of API that it exposes via MEF. In other words, in MEF terms, there are a set of exports that the editor publishes that you can then use within your own MEF parts to extend the editor in virtually un-boundless ways.

With nearly 100% coverage of the editor's features, The following feature areas are valid extension points exposed by the Visual Studio editor:

▶ **Content types**—A content type in the context of a Visual Studio code editor is the type of text and syntax that can be parsed and understood by the editor. If you think about this from a languages perspective, Visual Studio content types map directly to the various syntax and text formats that Visual Studio understands such as C#, plain text, HTML, XML, XAML, and so on.

▶ **Classification types and classification formats**—Classification types are the types of text, appearing within a document, that the VS editor understands and looks for. In a typical C# file, for example, the editor recognizes numerical and string instances within the document because those are default classification types built into Visual Studio. For each classification type, a format can be defined as well. A classic example of this is the highlighting and text coloring that you see within the editor for things like string literals or comments.

▶ **Margins and scrollbars**—If you think of the physical layout of a code editor, its visual surface is dominated by the text area where the code actually lives, and this is surrounded by scroll bars and by a margin area (for instance, the area where we see breakpoint information). Those margins and scrollbars are both artifacts that can be customized with MEF parts.

▶ **Tags**—Tags are objects that enable you to associate data with different recognized types of text within an editor. For instance, the SquiggleTag is implemented by

16

Visual Studio to associate things like syntax errors with a chunk of text that is unrecognized. In this case, the data associated with the squiggle is the actual syntax error generated by the compiler; this data is manifested as a tooltip when you hover the mouse over the squiggle.

▶ **Adornments**—Adornments are visual objects that can appear within an editor. Physically, they are implemented as WPF objects, and they can exist at several different "layers" within the editor, so the adornment can actually occupy the same physical space as the text within the editor or float above text within the editor.

▶ **Mouse processors**—Mouse processors are extension points that enable you to capture and handle mouse input.

▶ **Drop handlers**—Drop handlers enable you to react to different types of objects as they are dropped on the editor surface. Visual Studio has a library of stock format types that it recognizes, including files, pen data, xaml, and tiff or bitmap images.

▶ **Options**—Using MEF, it is possible to define, store, and react to your own set of custom options within the editor.

▶ **IntelliSense**—We discuss IntelliSense extensively in Chapter 8, "Working with Visual Studio's Productivity Aids." You can write your own IntelliSense functionality using MEF.

Using the Visual Studio SDK

Besides understanding the editor extension points, there is another crucial step to take: installation of the Visual Studio SDK. The Visual Studio SDK, generally speaking, is a collection of tools and project templates that help developers customize the IDE. The SDK is particularly germane to the topic of editor extensions because it ships with a set of project templates and code samples that help kick-start your extension development efforts.

The SDK download links for Visual Studio 2010 are located at the Visual Studio Extensibility center on MSDN: http://msdn.microsoft.com/vsx.

After downloading and installing the SDK, you see a new set of project templates available when you launch the New Project dialog box (see Figure 16.2).

These templates all live under the Extensibility category. For the purposes of this chapter, the ones we are interested in are the four editor templates—specifically, the Editor Classifier, Editor Margin, Editor Text Adornment, and Editor Viewport Adornment templates.

Based on their names, and our prior list of extension points, you can get a good idea for the specific capabilities of each template. Seeing the extensions in action is as simple as running the template project; a new instance of Visual Studio launches with the extension running.

Every time you compile an extension project, the extension is copied over to Visual Studio's local folder where extensions are kept: %LocalAppData%\Microsoft\VisualStudio\10.0\Extensions\Company\Product\Version\. Keep in mind that extensions can be deployed by simply copying their binaries; they do not need to be deployed to the

GAC or otherwise registered. The default mechanism for deployment of extensions is the VSIX file (to refresh your memory on what VSIX is, consult Chapter 5, "Browsers and Explorers"). The VSIX file, when run, automatically creates the correct folder in the correct location and copies the extension binaries.

FIGURE 16.2   Project templates added by the Visual Studio SDK.

After an extension has been deployed in this fashion, you can manage via the Extensions Manager (located under the Tools menu), which we discuss later in this chapter.

Editor Classifier

The Editor Classifier template creates an MEF part that exports a classifier that handles syntax highlighting within the editor. This is implemented with a set of default classes that can be customized to implement your own classifier. By using this project as a starting point, you can direct the editor to recognize certain syntax and display the matching text in a certain way.

> **NOTE**
>
> As you examine the content generated by these extension projects, notice that the code generated for you maps directly back to the extension points previously discussed. For example, the Editor Classifier template relates directly back to the classification types/formats extension point.

The Editor Classifier project exports a new classifier type that is used by the editor when loaded in the IDE. The definition of the classifier—that is, the type of text that the classifier recognizes—is implemented in the EditorClassifier1 class. This class implements the

IClassifier interface, and has a GetClassificationSpans property that is responsible for recognizing a certain class of text. By default, this template simply recognizes any text; but you are free to tweak this code to parse out and match any sort of text pattern that you want.

> **NOTE**
>
> All of these MEF extension templates end up creating classes and types that are named after the project. By using the default EditorClassifier1 project name, we end up with classes such as EditorClassifier1, EditorClassifier1Form, and so on. If you have used a different name for your project, your type names should look different from those presented here.

Besides recognizing a class of text, a classifier is also responsible for how that text is displayed within the editor. For instance, keywords are shaded a different color, comments are colored, and so on. All of this work is performed within the EditorClassifier1Format class. The code generated for us sets the background color to a color (blue violet), and underlines the text, but we can change those details to whatever we want:

```
/// <summary>
/// Defines the visual format for the "EditorClassifier1" classification type
/// </summary>
public EditorClassifier1Format()
{
    this.DisplayName = "EditorClassifier1"; //human readable version of the name
    this.BackgroundColor = Colors.BlueViolet;
    this.TextDecorations = System.Windows.TextDecorations.Underline;
}
```

Editor Margin

The Editor Margin template creates a project that exports a margin that is displayed on one of the editor's borders. The main class here is the EditorMargin1 class, which derives from the WPF Canvas class and places a canvas with a child textbox (with the text "Hello, World!") at the bottom of the editor window (Figure 16.3).

Here is the code responsible for displaying the margin. Again, if you had a need to display meaningful data within a margin (code review comments? bug counts?), you can easily use the code here as a building blocking.

```
/// <summary>
/// Creates a <see cref="EditorMargin1"/> for a given <see cref="IWpfTextView"/>.
/// </summary>
/// <param name="textView">The <see cref="IWpfTextView"/> to attach the margin
 to.</param>
public EditorMargin1(IWpfTextView textView)
{
```

```
_textView = textView;

this.Height = 20;
this.ClipToBounds = true;
this.Background = new SolidColorBrush(Colors.LightGreen);

// Add a green colored label that says "Hello World!"
Label label = new Label();
label.Background = new SolidColorBrush(Colors.LightGreen);
label.Content = "Hello world!";
this.Children.Add(label);

}
```

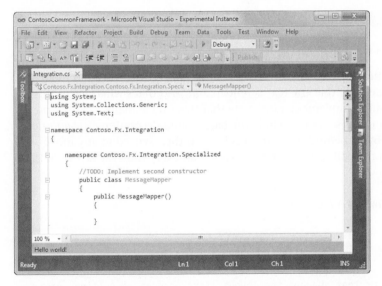

FIGURE 16.3   A "Hello World" margin added to the bottom of the code editor.

Editor Text Adornment

A text adornment is just what it sounds like: a graphical "markup" of text within the editor window. The Editor Text Adornment template creates a project that adorns every instance of the character A with a purple background and a red bordered box (Figure 16.4). As with the editor margin project, you use WPF objects.

FIGURE 16.4 Creating a text adornment in the editor.

Adornments reside on different "layers" within the editor. In this case, the adornment is implemented on the same layer that the text is rendered in, and that's what makes this specifically a text adornment implementation. Note that this isn't actually a case of the editor changing the font of those A's to include the background decoration. The adorner uses WPF to paint a red block behind the text. This block is then synced to any movements of the text within the editor (by re-creating its visuals every time the layout of the editor window changes):

```
public TextAdornment1(IWpfTextView view)
{
    _view = view;
    _layer = view.GetAdornmentLayer("TextAdornment1");

    //Listen to any event that changes the layout (text changes, scrolling, etc)
    _view.LayoutChanged += OnLayoutChanged;

    //Create the pen and brush to color the box behind the a's
    Brush brush = new SolidColorBrush(Color.FromArgb(0x20, 0x00, 0x00, 0xff));
    brush.Freeze();
    Brush penBrush = new SolidColorBrush(Colors.Red);
    penBrush.Freeze();
    Pen pen = new Pen(penBrush, 0.5);
    pen.Freeze();

    _brush = brush;
    _pen = pen;
}
```

Editor Viewport Adornment

The viewport adornment project is similar to the text adornment project, but it applies to a different layer of the editor—one where the text does not reside, which is a small but important distinction. Adorning the viewport in this fashion enables you to introduce visuals within the editor that aren't tied to any particular piece of text and can float in front or in back of the text layer.

The sample effect produced by this template places a simple purple box in the upper-right corner of the editor (see Figure 16.5).

FIGURE 16.5   An editor viewport adornment.

Structurally, the code is only slightly different than the code for the text adornment sample. The adornment class (ViewportAdornment1) uses the same WPF brush objects to paint its adornment. The key difference is the visual layer used by the factory class (ViewportAdornment1Factory). To compare and contrast the two, first examine the previous project's factory:

```
[Export(typeof(IWpfTextViewCreationListener))]
[ContentType("text")]
[TextViewRole(PredefinedTextViewRoles.Document)]
internal sealed class TextAdornment1Factory : IWpfTextViewCreationListener
{
    /// <summary>
    /// Defines the adornment layer for the adornment. This layer is ordered
    /// after the selection layer in the Z-order
    /// </summary>
```

```
[Export(typeof(AdornmentLayerDefinition))]
[Name("TextAdornment1")]
[Order(After = PredefinedAdornmentLayers.Selection,
    Before = PredefinedAdornmentLayers.Text)]
[TextViewRole(PredefinedTextViewRoles.Document)]
public AdornmentLayerDefinition editorAdornmentLayer = null;

/// <summary>
/// Instantiates a TextAdornment1 manager when a textView is created.
/// </summary>
/// <param name="textView">The <see cref="IWpfTextView"/> upon which the
/// adornment should be placed</param>
public void TextViewCreated(IWpfTextView textView)
{
    new TextAdornment1(textView);
}
}
```

And now, here is the viewport adornment factory:

```
[Export(typeof(IWpfTextViewCreationListener))]
[ContentType("text")]
[TextViewRole(PredefinedTextViewRoles.Document)]
internal sealed class PurpleBoxAdornmentFactory : IWpfTextViewCreationListener
{
    /// <summary>
    /// Defines the adornment layer for the scarlet adornment. This layer is ordered
    /// after the selection layer in the Z-order
    /// </summary>
    [Export(typeof(AdornmentLayerDefinition))]
    [Name("ViewportAdornment1")]
    [Order(After = PredefinedAdornmentLayers.Caret)]
    [TextViewRole(PredefinedTextViewRoles.Document)]
    public AdornmentLayerDefinition editorAdornmentLayer = null;

    /// <summary>
    /// Instantiates a ViewportAdornment1 manager when a textView is created.
    /// </summary>
    /// <param name="textView">The <see cref="IWpfTextView"/> upon which the
    ///     adornment should be placed</param>
    public void TextViewCreated(IWpfTextView textView)
    {
        new ViewportAdornment1(textView);
    }
}
```

Note the different layer order defined by each via the Order attribute ([Order(After = PredefinedAdornmentLayers.Caret)] versus [Order(After = PredefinedAdornmentLayers.Selection, Before = PredefinedAdornmentLayers.Text)]).

Using the Extension Manager

Before we detailed the editor extension points, we briefly mentioned the Extension Manager and its role. The manager is launched via the Tools menu, Extension Manager. The UI used by the extension manager is clean and simple (see Figure 16.6).

FIGURE 16.6   The Visual Studio Extension Manager.

The left pane manages the mode of the manager. You can manage installed extensions, browse extensions available online, or view updates available to any currently installed extensions. In Figure 16.6 you can clearly see all of the extensions that were installed as a result of running the four different extension template projects. You can uninstall or disable/enable any of the installed extensions using the middle pane. The right pane provides general information about the currently selected extension.

Selecting Online Gallery in the left pane allows you to browse and install extensions that are hosted online (Figure 16.7). You can post your own extensions online as well by visiting http://visualstudiogallery.msdn.microsoft.com/.

FIGURE 16.7   Browsing the extensions available online.

Creating Your Own MEF-Based Editor Extension

We have now covered all of the ingredients necessary to build your own extension. Let's walk through a simple example, end to end, and build an extension that displays some basic code metrics in a window in the corner of the editor. Functionally, we need to accomplish the following:

▶ Compute the required code stats by parsing the currently loaded code file

▶ Expose a set of properties on a WPF user control to hold those metrics; this user control also displays those metrics

▶ Display the WPF user control as an editor viewport adornment

Because this involves creating a new adornment pegged to the editor's viewport, we have the luxury of starting with the code produced for us by the Viewport Adornment template.

Create a new project using this template and name the project CodeMetricAdornment. Then, add a WPF user control title CodeMetricDisplayControl. Your baseline project structure should look like Figure 16.8.

FIGURE 16.8   Creating a new adornment project.

Now, open the CodeMetricAdornment class itself. Within the class, we \ add a field to hold a WPF user control object, and we get rid of the current Image field that is used by the template code:

```
private CodeMetricDisplayControl _displayControl =
            new CodeMetricDisplayControl();
```

We'll get to our code counting algorithm in a bit. Let's first focus on creating a simple WPF user control to display our code metric information. Add a new WPF UserControl to the project and call it CodeMetricDisplayControl. We need to display the three metrics, and their three labels, within the control; a grid works nicely for this.

Because the Grid is already included by default as the root arrangement element of our control, we just need to tweak its display a bit. Add three rows and two columns to the grid:

```
<Grid>
    <Grid.ColumnDefinitions>
        <ColumnDefinition Width="auto" />
        <ColumnDefinition Width="*" />
    </Grid.ColumnDefinitions>
    <Grid.RowDefinitions>
        <RowDefinition />
        <RowDefinition />
        <RowDefinition />
```

16

```
    </Grid.RowDefinitions>
</Grid>
```

Within the grid, add six TextBlock objects, three to hold our labels, and three to hold our actual counts:

```
<TextBlock Grid.Column="0" Grid.Row="0"
          VerticalAlignment="Center"
          x:Name="TextBlockLOC"
          Padding="5">Total Lines of Code:</TextBlock>
<TextBlock Grid.Column="0" Grid.Row="1"
          x:Name="TextBlockComments"
          VerticalAlignment="Center"
          Padding="5">Comment Lines:</TextBlock>
<TextBlock Grid.Column="0" Grid.Row="2"
          x:Name="TextBlockWhitespace"
          VerticalAlignment="Center"
          Padding="5">Whitespace Lines:</TextBlock>

<TextBlock Grid.Column="1" Grid.Row="0"
          VerticalAlignment="Center">0</TextBlock>
<TextBlock Grid.Column="1" Grid.Row="1"
          VerticalAlignment="Center">0</TextBlock>
<TextBlock Grid.Column="1" Grid.Row="2"
          VerticalAlignment="Center">0</TextBlock>
```

Within the CodeMetricDisplayControl class, add a property for each of these integers as well:

```
public partial class CodeMetricDisplayControl : UserControl
{
    private int _loc = 0;    // total lines of code
    private int _whitespace = 0; // whitespace (empty) lines
    private int _comments = 0; // total lines that are comments

    public int LinesOfCode
    {
        get { return _loc; }
        set { _loc = value; Refresh(); }
    }


    public int CommentLines
    {
        get { return _comments; }
        set { _comments = value; Refresh(); }
    }
```

```
public int WhitespaceLines
{
    get { return _whitespace; }
    set { _whitespace = value; Refresh(); }
}

public CodeMetricDisplayControl()
{
    InitializeComponent();
}

}
```

Note that in each setter, we are calling a Refresh routine. Let's write that routine, which updates the value of our TextBlocks to the current value held by our field for each of the code metrics:

```
private void Refresh()
{
    this.TextBlockComments.Text = _comments.ToString();
    this.TextBlockLOC.Text = _loc.ToString();
    this.TextBlockWhitespace.Text = _whitespace.ToString();
}
```

Disregarding any look and feel refinements, the WPF user control is now ready to go. Let's turn our attention back to the adorner class and write the code to actually count our lines of code, comments, and whitespace lines.

In CodeMetricAdornment, strip out all of the current WPF drawing code from the constructor. In its place add three lines that set the user control's properties based on the return values from a few private routines (which we implement next):

```
public CodeMetricAdornment(IWpfTextView view)
{
    _view = view;

    _displayControl.LinesOfCode = CountLOC(view);

    _adornmentLayer =
        view.GetAdornmentLayer
        ("CodeMetricAdornment");

    _view.ViewportHeightChanged += delegate { this.onSizeChange(); };
    _view.ViewportWidthChanged += delegate { this.onSizeChange(); };
}
```

The code to actually count our lines of code is straightforward. We take the IWpfTextView object provided by our adorner, and get the string representation for all of the current text in the editor window like this:

```
string code = view.TextSnapshot.GetText();
```

Now we can parse that string and return the various counts:

```
private int CountLOC(IWpfTextView view)
{
   string code = view.TextSnapshot.GetText();

   int count = 1;
   int start = 0;
   while ((start = code.IndexOf('\n', start)) != -1)
   {
       count++;
       start++;
   }

    return count;



}

private int CountWhitespaceLines(IWpfTextView view)
{
    string code = view.TextSnapshot.GetText();
    int count = 0;

    using (StringReader reader = new StringReader(code))
    {
       string line;

       while ((line = reader.ReadLine()) != null)
       {
           if (line.Trim() == "")
               count++;
       }

       return count;
    }
}

private int CountCommentLines(IWpfTextView view)
{
```

```
    string code = view.TextSnapshot.GetText();
    int count = 0;

    using (StringReader reader = new StringReader(code))
    {
        string line;

        while ((line = reader.ReadLine()) != null)
        {
            if (line.TrimStart().StartsWith("//"))
                count++;
        }

return count;
    }
}
```

We are almost done. The final piece that we need to change from the template code is to
re-write a piece of the OnSizeChange event handler. This was wired to position and display
the WPF Image control originally used by the template. Instead, we want this code to position and place our WPF user control. Change the code within OnSizeChange to this:

```
public void onSizeChange()
    {
        //clear the adornment layer of previous adornments
        _adornmentLayer.RemoveAllAdornments();

        //Place the image in the top right hand corner of the Viewport
        Canvas.SetLeft(_displayControl,
            _view.ViewportRight - _displayControl.ActualWidth);
        Canvas.SetTop(_displayControl,
            _view.ViewportTop + _displayControl.ActualHeight);

        //add the image to the adornment layer and make it relative to the
        //viewport
        _adornmentLayer.AddAdornment(
            AdornmentPositioningBehavior.ViewportRelative,
            null, null, _displayControl, null);
    }
```

Now the control is positioned and is in the adornment view layer. If you run the project
and then open a code file from within the IDE instance that is launched, you should
immediately see the fruits of your labor in the upper-right corner of the editor.

There is still one problem with our implementation. Although our code stats are displayed
correctly, they aren't updated when we change the text within the editor. To fix this, we

need to react to the adornment layer's IWpfTextView LayoutChanged event. We can hook this event inside of our CodeMetricAdornment constructor like this:

```
_view.LayoutChanged += this.OnLayoutChanged;
```

and then, create the event handler which updates our counts:

```
private void OnLayoutChanged(object sender, TextViewLayoutChangedEventArgs e)
{
    _displayControl.LinesOfCode = CountLOC(_view);
    _displayControl.CommentLines = CountCommentLines(_view);
    _displayControl.WhitespaceLines = CountWhitespaceLines(_view);
}
```

We could also make our WPF user control more compelling to look at by tweaking the XAML to add things like a background gradient, text coloring, and so on.

Figure 16.9 shows the final product, and Listing 16.1 contains the adornment class code. Full source listing for this project is available at this book's website.

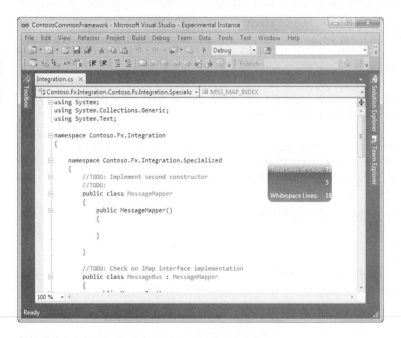

FIGURE 16.9   A simple code metric adornment .

LISTING 16.1   The CodeMetricAdornment class
_____

```
using System.IO;
using System.Windows.Controls;
using System.Windows.Media;
```

```csharp
using Microsoft.VisualStudio.Text.Editor;

namespace CodeMetricAdornment
{
    /// <summary>
    /// Adornment class that draws a square box in the top right hand corner of
    /// the viewport
    /// </summary>
    class CodeMetricAdornment
    {
        private IWpfTextView _view;
        private IAdornmentLayer _adornmentLayer;
        private CodeMetricDisplayControl _displayControl =
            new CodeMetricDisplayControl();


        public CodeMetricAdornment(IWpfTextView view)
        {
            _view = view;

            _displayControl.LinesOfCode = CountLOC(view);
            _displayControl.CommentLines = CountCommentLines(view);
            _displayControl.WhitespaceLines = CountWhitespaceLines(view);

            _adornmentLayer = view.GetAdornmentLayer("CodeMetricAdornment");

            _view.LayoutChanged += this.OnLayoutChanged;
            _view.ViewportHeightChanged += delegate { this.onSizeChange(); };
            _view.ViewportWidthChanged += delegate { this.onSizeChange(); };
        }

        public void onSizeChange()
        {
            //clear the adornment layer of previous adornments
            _adornmentLayer.RemoveAllAdornments();

            int buffer = 50;

            //Place the image in the top right hand corner of the Viewport
            Canvas.SetLeft(_displayControl,
                _view.ViewportRight - (_displayControl.ActualWidth
                + buffer));
            Canvas.SetTop(_displayControl,
                _view.ViewportTop + (_displayControl.ActualHeight
                + buffer));
```

```csharp
    _adornmentLayer.AddAdornment(
        AdornmentPositioningBehavior.ViewportRelative,
        null, null, _displayControl, null);
}

private void OnLayoutChanged(object sender, TextViewLayoutChangedEventArgs e)
{
    _displayControl.LinesOfCode = CountLOC(_view);
    _displayControl.CommentLines = CountCommentLines(_view);
    _displayControl.WhitespaceLines = CountWhitespaceLines(_view);
}

private int CountLOC(IWpfTextView view)
{
    string code = view.TextSnapshot.GetText();

    int count = 1;
    int start = 0;
    while ((start = code.IndexOf('\n', start)) != -1)
    {
        count++;
        start++;
    }

    return count;

}

private int CountWhitespaceLines(IWpfTextView view)
{
    string code = view.TextSnapshot.GetText();
    int count = 0;

    using (StringReader reader = new StringReader(code))
    {
        string line;

        while ((line = reader.ReadLine()) != null)
        {
            if (line.Trim() == "")
                count++;
        }

        return count;

    }
```

```
        }

        private int CountCommentLines(IWpfTextView view)
        {
            string code = view.TextSnapshot.GetText();
            int count = 0;

            using (StringReader reader = new StringReader(code))
            {
                string line;

                while ((line = reader.ReadLine()) != null)
                {
                    if (line.TrimStart().StartsWith("//"))
                        count++;
                }

                return count;

            }
        }
    }
}
```

Summary

In this chapter, we explored a new .NET library, the Managed Execution Framework, and how it can be used to write extensions for the Visual Studio editor. We discussed the overall architecture of MEF itself, including its extension discovery mechanisms and the core concepts of parts and imports/exports.

We also covered all of the specific Visual Studio 2010 editor extension points, and outlined the value that the Visual Studio SDK provides with its pre-stocked set of extension templates that target those editor extension points.

Finally, we walked through the creation of an editor extension that exploits the editor's adornment layer to display a running total of three different code metrics, all through the use of a WPF-based user control.

Creating ASP.NET Applications

Web development continues to be a major focus in the latest release of Visual Studio. As with its predecessors, the 2010 release continues to evolve the .NET web development experience. The new tool is packed with additional enhancements around caching, session-state storage, web forms, data applications, AJAX development, and deployment scenarios. There is also a new charting control and support for creating MVC (model-view-controller) standards-driven sites.

This chapter is focused on helping web developers leverage ASP.NET to create browser-based applications whose code runs on a server. These types of applications offer the broadest possible reach for web developers by targeting applications to work cross-browser and cross-platform with HTML-based compatibility. Of course, web development continues to evolve beyond the browser. For more information on such things as XBAP, AJAX, and Silverlight, see Chapter 20, "Creating Rich Browser Applications." If you are looking to develop XAML-based applications using Microsoft's WPF, see Chapter 19, "Creating Richer, Smarter User Interfaces."

We start by covering the basics of defining Visual Studio web projects and creating simple web forms. From there we move on to more advanced topics and demonstrate how you might build a cohesive user interface for your ASP.NET application that includes master pages, themes, Web Parts, and data binding. We then spend some time covering the major set of controls built into ASP.NET. We finish the chapter discussing how you deploy an ASP.NET application.

ASP.NET is a huge topic. We are not able to dig in on its every aspect. Instead, we concentrate on areas where you can leverage Visual Studio to increase your productivity in building web-based user interfaces. This is a key topic for all web developers.

We expect that as you build your ASP.NET interface, you will discover places that require further exploration. To that end, we try to point out some of them as we move through the chapter. Some examples include membership, user profiles, caching, website administration, and cross-page posting.

The Basics of an ASP.NET Website

Websites in Visual Studio start with a website project. The website project represents a connection between Visual Studio, the development version of your website (see Chapter 4, "Solutions and Projects," for more information), and a web server, be it local or otherwise. What is meant by website, however, continues to evolve and expand.

Simple HTML sites with just text, hyperlinks, and a few images are rarely created anymore or even discussed seriously as websites. Instead, .NET has pushed the definition of website well beyond the original ASP (active server pages) model that combined HTML with some server-side script. Nowadays, a website means user-interactive web forms; compiled code that links those web forms to a middle tier; master pages, styles, and themes that control the look of a site; configuration for such things as security, membership, and caching; database connectivity and data binding; and so on. The Visual Studio 2010 tools bring these concepts together to allow you to create rich, modern websites that offer an ever-higher degree of user interaction. In the following sections, we examine the makeup of the modern website and discuss how you create and configure them.

Creating a New Website or Web Application

Visual Studio allows you to create web both websites and web application projects. Both are represented by project templates that define default directories, configuration, web forms, and other related files and settings. A website is a simplified project template that is used to create websites that are typically deployed as a set of files. A web application project uses the standard Visual Studio structure of solution and project. This includes a project file that defines the content and structure of your site (a website does not contain this file). A web application project is used if you need specialized control over compilation, output assemblies, and class-to-page references. Websites are the preferred option for the majority of web developers. We focus on website templates in this chapter.

You create a new website using the New Web Site dialog box (File, New, Web Site). The New Web Site dialog box is somewhat different than the standard new project dialog box. Figure 17.1 shows an example. Notice that on the left side of the dialog box you are first asked to select a default language for your site (Visual Basic or Visual C#). You also select a template, .NET Framework version, location, and give your site a name.

FIGURE 17.1   When you create a new website you select both a language and a website template.

Selecting a Visual Studio Website Template

Visual Studio installs at least nine ASP.NET website templates by default. You pick a template based on your needs. However, the majority of sites are built with the standard template, ASP.NET Web Site. The following provides an overview of many of the ASP.NET templates:

▶ **ASP.NET Web Site**—Represents the standard ASP.NET website and starts with an App_Data directory, a Default.aspx web form, a web.config file, a master page (Site.master), style sheet (Site.css), and a Global.asax file. It also includes an Account directory that contains pages for managing login and user accounts. The JQuery scripts are also provided by default in this template (inside the Scripts folder). Of course, additional folders and files can be added as you build out your site. This is the template most commonly used to start a new website from scratch.

▶ **ASP.NET Web Service**—Represents a site focused on creating an XML-based web service (see Chapter 22, "Service-Oriented Applications," for more details). The template includes a service called Service.asmx that includes code for a basic web service, an App_Code directory to house the service's class files, an App_Data folder for housing data to which ASP.NET has access, and a web.config file for managing site configuration.

▶ **Empty Web Site**—Represents a website project devoid of all folders and files (except a web.config file). You use this project container as a starting point. It does not presume folders and files. Instead, you explicitly add these items yourself as required.

▶ **WCF Service**—Used to create a website that contains WCF services (see Chapter 22 for more details). Like the Web Service project template, the WCF Service contains the standard App_Code, App_Data, and Web.config files. However, the service file is a Service.svc file. This service stubs out a class that implements a configurable, WCF-based (and not simply XML-based) service.

▶ **ASP.NET Reports Web Site**—Creates a site for building web-based reports using the Microsoft Report Viewer tools. Creating this site not only creates an initial report in your project and sets appropriate references to Microsoft's report libraries, but it also launches a wizard to walk you through configuring the first report. This includes connecting to the data source, selecting data, and setting display options. You can then run reports in a web browser. The report viewer includes options for exporting reports as Excel and PDF.

▶ **Dynamic Data Linq to SQL Web Site**—Creates a site for building web applications that work with data. This site contains templates for pages that enable users to view, add, delete, and edit data. These page templates make it easy for you to work in most scenarios accessing data over the web. Of course the data access provided in this template is accomplished through LINQ to SQL.

▶ **Dynamic Data Entities Web Site**—Similar to the Dynamic Data Linq to SQL Web Site template. This template, however, access data using the ADO.NET Entity Framework.

TIP

You can find website starter kits to use as a basis for your new website. These kits do not ship with Visual Studio. Rather, you can download them. Starter kits include blogs, portals, e-commerce, small business, clubs, wikis, and many more. You can find out about these sites at http://www.asp.net/community/projects or refer to Chapter 7, "The .NET Community: Interacting Online," for more on connecting with community content.

Choosing a Website Location

In older versions of Visual Studio (before 2005), you were essentially stuck (or boxed in) when creating a location for your development website. You had to be running Internet Information Services (IIS) locally, and you had to store your web application inside the wwwroot folder structure. This model caused a number of problems. The first was that typically your application was spread all over your machine. You would have your solution file and .dll projects inside one directory and your web application buried on your C: drive in a special directory. The second was that this model forced development managers to allow IIS servers on every developer desktop (or not get work done). This typically broke standard policy. There were many more issues around IIS versioning, deployment, and more.

Visual Studio 2005 solved these issues. Options for connecting to the development version of an application were vastly expanded. You can now work with your application using a local IIS server (or not). You might instead want to work against the file system and use a local development web server (instead of a local instance of IIS). Or you might need to work against a remote server and connect to it via FTP or HTTP. Let's look at configuring these many website location options using Visual Studio 2010.

You define the location for your website (and consequently how you want to access it) when you first create it or connect to it. Recall that in Figure 17.1, there is a drop-down list next to the Location option (bottom left). This list contains the values File System, HTTP, and FTP. Each of these locations requires you to enter the appropriate location of your website and provide the appropriate credentials in order to create (or open) your site. Clicking the Browse button (right of the application name text box in figure 17.1) lets you navigate to the site's intended location. This button launches the Choose Location window. In the following sections, we look at the many options of this dialog box.

File System   The first option you have at the top of the Choose Location window is File System, which enables you to choose any directory on your machine in which to store the contents of your website. You can use this dialog box to navigate the file system and select or create a new folder to contain your site. Figure 17.2 shows this dialog box. The Create New Folder button is in the upper-right corner (along with the Delete button).

FIGURE 17.2   You can use the Choose Location dialog box to select a location on your file system in which to store your website content.

If you choose File System for your local website development, you do not need to have IIS on your machine. Instead, Visual Studio recognizes the content in the file system directory as a website and runs a local instance of ASP.NET Development Server. This server mimics IIS and can be run and killed on an as-needed basis. You end up with an instance of the development server running for each website you are currently browsing, debugging, or even building with Visual Studio.

Each development server instance is listed in your system tray. You can right-click an instance of the development server and navigate to the site it serves via a web browser, stop the server, or view its details. An example of the development server details window is shown in Figure 17.3. Here you can see the virtual and physical paths of the server, the port number, and the root URL. You also have the option to stop the running server using the Stop button.

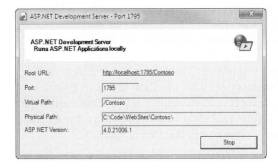

FIGURE 17.3   You can access the details of any running ASP.NET development server instance from the system tray.

TIP

By default, the development server runs on a dynamically generated port. However, you can force a specific port for your development server. To do so, you select the website in Solution Explorer and view its properties. You need to first set the property, Use Dynamic Ports, to false. This turns off the port assignments. You can then edit the Port number property. Figure 17.4 shows an example.

Local IIS   Visual Studio 2010 still enables you to configure a web application to use a local instance of IIS. This capability gives you the benefit of being able to run the server even when you're not developing. It also means you have more control over the configuration of your site using the IIS administration tool. However, in most scenarios, running a local version of IIS on a developer's machine is less than desirable. It takes up valuable system resources and often violates internal policies by exposing an extra server to the network.

To configure a local version of IIS, select the Local IIS option from the Choose Location dialog box. Figure 17.5 shows an example. Note that in the figure IIS (ASP.NET) is not installed locally on the machine. You can see that if you are running Visual Studio on Windows 7 (or Vista), you have some configuration to do. You must first get the IIS components installed. After it's installed, you need to launch Visual Studio with the elevated privileges of Administrator in order to select IIS.

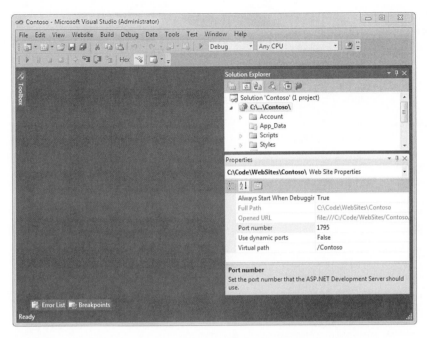

FIGURE 17.4   You can force a specific port number for your development server.

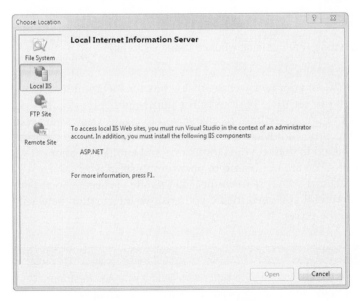

FIGURE 17.5   To use IIS, you must first configure your local machine and start IIS in the administrator context.

To install these options locally on Windows 7 or Vista, open the Control Panel window. From here you can select Get Programs (or Uninstall a Program) under the Programs area. On the left side of this window select the Turn Windows Features On or Off option. This launches the Windows Features dialog box as shown in Figure 17.6. Find Internet Information Services and drill down to make sure your ASP.NET and the ISAPI filters and extensions installed.

FIGURE 17.6   You use the Windows Features dialog box to install IIS locally.

You should now see more options in your new website dialog box for the Local IIS selection (see Figure 17.7). First, you can see three buttons in the upper-right corner of the dialog box. In order from left to right, these buttons enable you to create a new web application, create a new virtual directory, and delete a selected item. If you choose to create a new virtual directory, you are asked to define a directory name and a folder location where you want to store the site. You are not bound to wwwroot. Instead, you can create your site using any folder. You can also choose to connect to this site via Secure Sockets Layer (SSL). This capability is useful if you need to encrypt sensitive information between the development machine and the server.

TIP

If you're running Windows 7 (or Vista), you need to run Visual Studio with Administrator privileges in order to connect to IIS. To do so, right-click the shortcut to Visual Studio and choose Run as Administrator.

FTP Site   Another option is to work with your site across FTP (File Transfer Protocol). The New Website dialog box enables you to indicate where on a given FTP server your site should (or does) exist. To do so, you must enter the address of the server and the port and provide appropriate credentials. All FTP constraints apply to FTP sites; this means, for example, that passwords are not secure. Figure 17.8 shows the FTP website settings. Note that sites created using FTP are run in debug mode using the local ASP.NET Development Server. FTP is simply used to retrieve and store the files. Of course, you might have a web server that serves up the files from the FTP server. This server is independent and is not seen by Visual Studio.

FIGURE 17.7   After IIS is installed, you can select an IIS website as the basis of your project.

FIGURE 17.8   You can connect Visual Studio to a website on a remote server using FTP.

Remote HTTP Site   Finally, you can choose to communicate with a web server across HTTP for defining your website. This is typically a remote web server where you are doing shared development. The development server must have FrontPage Server Extensions applied to allow this type of connectivity from Visual Studio. Figure 17.9 shows an example of configuring a site's location to be a remote IIS server.

FIGURE 17.9   You can connect Visual Studio to a remote server over HTTP.

Choosing a Default Programming Language

Visual Studio 2010 enables you to mix the languages you use to develop the items in your site. When you create a web form or a class file, you can determine the language in which each individual item is written. However, when you create a new site, you set a default language for the site. This default language is set in the New Web Site dialog box (recall Figure 17.1, left-side pane). Setting this value tells Visual Studio how to generate your template files. In addition, it sets the initial value for the setting that controls the default language of any new items being added to your site.

Figure 17.10 shows a website with mixed code. There are two web files: one with a code-behind written in VB and one with a C# code-behind. This is acceptable. For class files, however, you must have like files in each directory that contains code. Notice the App_Code directory contains a C# class file. You cannot add VB class files to this directory. If you need to mix both VB and C# class files you have two options. First, you could consider putting your VB code into one class library project and your C# code into another. You would then add a reference from your website to these code libraries. Many web developers, however, prefer to keep their code in a single site structure. In this case, you can put VB code into one folder and C# in another. Refer again to Figure 17.10 for an example (the App_MoreCode folder). In this case, the compiler compiles code by folder; therefore, all code in a given folder must be of the same language.

FIGURE 17.10   You can mix both C# and VB code items in the same website.

Understanding the Makeup of Your Website

A typical website contains a number of different files including web forms, code files, style sheets, config files, images, controls, Javascript, and more. Keeping these many files organized and grouped together helps you find and support the items that make up your site. To this end, Visual Studio provides a number of "special" directories. The following sections provide a reference for the many directories and file types that are used to define a .NET website.

Directories   ASP.NET defines a number of folders that it uses to organize and recognize various files that make up your application. These folders have reserved names that mean something special to ASP.NET; therefore, you should use them appropriately.

You add an ASP.NET directory to your application via the context menu (right-click) for the site. Choose Add ASP.NET Folder from this menu. Figure 17.11 shows a web application with each of these special folders defined. Note that only those folders that contain an icon in addition to the folder icon are special folders in ASP.NET. Each of these special directories is listed in Table 17.1.

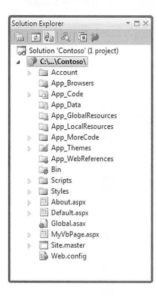

FIGURE 17.11   You can use the ASP.NET special folders to provide organization to the many files that make up your site.

TABLE 17.1   ASP.NET Directories

Directory	Description
Bin	This folder contains the compiled code (.dll files) that your application references. This might include external class libraries or controls you want to embed into your application (without embedding the source).
App_Code	This folder houses the class files that help define your application. For example, you could choose to put your business object or data access classes in this directory. All code in this directory is compiled into a single library. This includes code in any subdirectories. Therefore, all code in the directory must be of the same language.
App_Data	This directory contains data files used by your applications. This can be SQL Express files (.mdf), XML data, Excel files, and so on.
App_GlobalResources	This folder contains the resource files (.resx and .resources) that make up your application. You use resource files to abstract such things as string-based text and images from your actual application. In this way, your application reads from a resource file instead of being hard-coded with these values. This helps you support multiple language user interfaces, design-time changes, and related issues.
App_LocalResources	This folder also contains resource files. However, these files are specific to a page or control. They are not global to the entire application scope.

TABLE 17.1   Continued

Directory	Description
App_WebReferences	This folder is used to house and maintain references to web services. The files inside the folder include web service contracts (.wsdl) and schemas (.xsd) and other related items.
App_Browsers	This folder contains browser definition files (.browser). These files are typically used for mobile application support. Each .browser file defines the various capabilities for a given browser. This helps your user interface render appropriately for a specific device.
App_Themes	This folder contains subfolders that each define a specific theme (look and feel) for your application. Each theme folder contains one or more skin (.skin) files, a style (.css) sheet, and any theme-based images. See "Creating a Common Look and Feel," later in this chapter, for more on themes.

Files   Numerous files and file types define a typical ASP.NET website. Of course, there are files that you use often, such as web forms, user controls, classes, and configuration files; and then there are those that are rarer, such as skins, master pages, resources, and site maps. Table 17.2 lists some of the more common files that might exist in any given ASP.NET web application.

TABLE 17.2   ASP.NET Files

Item Template(s)	File Extension	Description
Web Form	.aspx	Defines an ASP.NET web form. This is the most common ASP.NET file. See "Creating Web Pages," later in this chapter.
Web Service	.asmx	Defines an ASP.NET XML-based web service. See Chapter 22 for more details.
Web User Control, Dynamic Data Field	.ascx	Represents an ASP.NET user control. User controls enable you to define your own version or combination of controls and reuse them throughout your site. The Dynamic Data Field control is another version of the user control used for creating custom displays of data.
No item template	.asax	Creates a global application class. This enables you to define code inside events that fire when IIS starts or stops an application, an error occurs, or a user initiates or terminates a session.

17

TABLE 17.2   Continued

Item Template(s)	File Extension	Description
Generic Handler	.ashx	A file used for creating a general, HTTP handler in your site. You can create a generic handler to receive an HTTP request, process it, and send information back in the response.
Class	.cs/.vb	Defines a class file. The extension .cs is a C# class file. The .vb extension is a class written in Visual Basic.
Master Page, AJAX Master Page	.master	Represents a master page. A master page is used to define common elements that might appear on multiple pages within a website. These might include menu items, navigation, headers, footers, and other related items. See "Master Pages," later in this chapter.
Web Configuration File	.config	Represents a configuration file for your web application. You use the configuration file to manage settings such as debugging and to store application-specific data (such as an encrypted connection string to a database).
Style Sheet	.css	Represents a cascading style sheet. It stores the styles of your application or theme. See "Style Sheets," later in this chapter.
LINQ to SQL Classes	.dbml	A LINQ to SQL class file. You create such a file to provide a class file that exposes LINQ queries against a given SQL database.
Report, Report Wizard	.rdlc	Enables you to create a web-based report that leverages the Microsoft reporting technology.
Site Map	.sitemap	Enables you to create a file that defines a map of your website. Sitemaps are used for various navigation controls within ASP.NET.
WCF Service, ADO.NET Data Service, AJAX-enabled WCF Service	.svc	Represents a WCF service. The ADO.NET Data Service item is another version of a service used specifically for working with data. See Chapter 22 for more information.
Skin File	.skin	Represents a skin for one or more controls in your application. A skin is defined for an application theme. See "Themes and Skins," later in this chapter.

TABLE 17.2   Continued

Item Template(s)	File Extension	Description
Jscript File, AJAX Client Library, AJAX Control Library, AJAX Client Behavior	.js	Used to create code files that contain java script. There are a number of item templates specifically for AJAX libraries (See Chapter 20).
HTML Page	.htm	A simple HTML page (no server-side processing of code).
Resource File	.resx	Used to create a resource file for storing things such as localized strings for different cultures and languages.

You add a new ASP.NET file to your application by right-clicking your site and selecting Add New Item. Figure 17.12 shows the Add New Item dialog box. Notice that you first select a language (left-side of the window). The many files that are available for selection are listed as item templates in the center. If you select a file type that belongs in a special directory, Visual Studio prompts you to put the file in that directory.

FIGURE 17.12   There are many file types you can add to a .NET website.

Controlling Project Properties and Options

ASP.NET applications have their own set of properties and configuration options. These properties control how an application works, gets built, works with the debugger, and so on. You access the properties for your website through the Property Pages dialog box. You can open this dialog box by right-clicking your website and selecting the Property Pages option. The following sections cover the many options of this dialog box.

References

The references in your application define the code that your application uses by reference. You add references to other projects in your solution, other .NET namespaces in the .NET Framework, third-party controls, and other .NET libraries. The code you reference is already compiled into a .dll file and exists on its own. In the case of project references, this code might get compiled each time your run the application. These .dll files might or might not be installed in the Global Assembly Cache (GAC). Figure 17.13 shows the References portion of the Property Pages dialog box.

FIGURE 17.13   You can manage the code your application references using the Property Pages dialog box.

> **NOTE**
>
> Web application projects use a different window for managing properties. In addition, the references are defined by a special folder called References inside the solution hierarchy. Again, we are focused on the website template.

Each current reference for the website is listed along with its associated reference type. Figure 17.3 shows two project references (BusinessDomain and DataServices). These references are to projects in the same solution as the website. They are automatically updated as the solution gets compiled. You could, of course, have specific .dll files you reference. These files are stored in the bin directory if they are simply local to your application. If they are global .dll files (used by more than just your application) they are stored in the GAC. You can see two such examples of GAC references (as indicated by the Type column) in Figure 17.3. You can also see the version being referenced (in this case, 4.0). From this dialog box, you can add a new reference, remove an existing reference, or refresh (update) the selected reference.

Adding a New Reference   You can add references to your ASP.NET applications (as shown by the Add button in Figure 17.13). Clicking this button brings up the three reference options shown in Figure 17.14. These options include a standard reference to a .NET class library (Add Reference), a reference to an XML web service (Add Web Reference), or a reference to a WCF service (Add Service Reference). We cover the two service-type references in Chapter 22.

FIGURE 17.14   You can select the type of reference you want to add to your application.

When you add a standard reference, you are making a connection to a .dll file that exists as part of another application or another project in your solution. Establishing this reference places a copy of the compiled .dll file into your website's bin directory. The namespaces, classes, and methods inside this .dll file are available for you to code against. The compiler also checks your application against any referenced .dlls to ensure that you are not breaking type constraints, method signatures, and the like.

When you select the standard Add Reference option, Visual Studio displays the Add Reference dialog box as shown in Figure 17.15. You can use the tabs across the top of the dialog box to find the specific item you want to reference. If, for example, you are looking to reference a namespace from the .NET Framework, you select the .NET tab. This tab locates items installed in your GAC, such as those in the System or Microsoft namespace. You can also set references to COM components, set references to other projects in your solution, browse for .dll files, and view recent references.

FIGURE 17.15   You use the Add Reference dialog box to reference code outside of your site.

Projects references represent those that exist in the current solution. These references work like any other with one exception. For your convenience, items marked as a project reference are automatically refreshed when those projects are recompiled. This ensures consistent type checking as your application is built.

Build

The Build page of the Property Pages dialog box enables you to control how your application is built using Visual Studio 2010. Figure 17.16 shows the options that are available. We cover each of these options next.

Start Action   The Start Action section of the Build page enables you to define how your application is compiled when you run it from the IDE. There are three options in this drop-down: No Build, Build Page, and Build Web Site (the default). Let's look at each of these options.

The No Build option tells the IDE to just launch the site in a browser without doing any compilation. In this instance, as pages and items are accessed in the browser, they are compiled. Instead of the errors showing in the IDE before you run the application, the errors are displayed in the browser as you find them.

The No Build capability can be great when you have a large application that contains pages that you are not working on or that have errors (and you intend to avoid). It also speeds the startup time because no pages are precompiled.

FIGURE 17.16   You can use the Build properties to control the version of the .NET Framework your site targets (among other things).

The Build Page option tells the IDE to compile only the current startup page or the page you're working on. This capability is useful if you work on only one page at a time. If the IDE finds errors, they are shown in the IDE before the page launches.

Finally, the Build Web Site option, which is the default setting, tells the IDE to build the entire website and all dependent projects before launching into the browser. This capability can be helpful if you are working on a small site by yourself. However, it can also cause longer build times on larger projects.

Target Framework   The Target Framework feature enables you to indicate (and change) the version of the .NET Framework your application targets. This means you can write ASP.NET applications using Visual Studio 2010 that target .NET 2.0, 3.0, 3.5, or 4.0. This is especially useful for those developers looking to upgrade their tools but who are restricted from upgrading their applications at present. Flipping this option compiles and checks your application against the target version of the .NET Framework. When your application runs, it calls code in the given target Framework.

Build Solution Action   There is a single option under Build Solution Action in the Build page for the professional edition of Visual Studio. Build Web Site as Part of Solution indicates whether Visual Studio should include the website as part of the solution's build. The default for this setting is true (or checked). In this case, when you choose Build Solution from the Build menu, the website is also built.

Accessibility Validation   The Accessibility Validation options in the Build page enable you to have Visual Studio check your web application for conformance with accessibility standards. These standards ensure that your application works for people with disabilities. The actual standards are covered in the next section. Here, you have two options for enabling validation: for the entire site or for just the current startup page. If these options are enabled, Visual Studio displays accessibility issues in the IDE when you run the application.

Accessibility

The Accessibility page of the Property Pages dialog box enables you to define what checks should be done relative to your site's conformance. Figure 17.17 shows the options for configuring the checks. There are three levels of checks based on two standards: the W3C's Web Content Accessibility Guidelines (WCAG) 1 and 2, and the U.S. government's standards for accessibility (Access board section 508).

FIGURE 17.17   You can use the Accessibility options to ensure your site is checked against accessibility rules (on by default).

A quick way to verify an entire ASP.NET as accessible-compliant is to run the page in a web browser, view the HTML source, copy the HTML from the page, and embed it as a separate HTML file in your solution. Visual Studio then checks to ensure that this new page is compliant on build.

For more information on building accessible applications, see "Walkthrough: Creating an Accessible Web Application" on MSDN.

Start Options

The Start Options page in the Property Pages dialog box enables you to define what happens when you start (or run) your application. Figure 17.18 shows the many options available. We look at each in the following sections.

FIGURE 17.18   You use the Start Options to configure what happens when you run your application from the IDE.

Start Action   The Start Action section of the Start Options page is useful for defining what happens when you start your application through the IDE. The first option, Use Current Page, tells Visual Studio to start the application using the current, active page in the development environment. This capability can be great for developers who work on one page at a time. The next option, Specific Page, enables you to set a startup page. This is akin to right-clicking a page and choosing Set as Start Page from the Solution Explorer. The third option, Start External Program, enables you to specify an .exe file to run (instead of the browser) when you start the application. The Start URL option enables you to send the browser to a different URL when running your application. This capability can be useful when debugging a web service. You might launch a client that uses your web service, for example. Finally, you can use the last option to tell Visual Studio to wait for a request (don't start anything). This, too, can be useful for a web service scenario.

Server   The Server section of the Start Options page enables you to specify a server to be launched for your application. Most applications leave this set to Use Default Web Server. This represents the file system websites. For scenarios that use IIS or FTP, you specify a URL to the actual server.

Debuggers   The Debuggers group of options on the Start Options page enables you to set the enabled debuggers used when running your application. By default, only ASP.NET is enabled. You can choose to turn off this setting. You can also add Native code, SQL Server, and Silverlight debuggers to the mix.

MSBuild Options

The MsBuild Options screen in the Property Pages dialog box enables you to control precompiling of your application. These options are specific to using the MSBuild compilation tool from the command line. Figure 17.19 shows an example. From here, you can set your precompilation output folder and manage related settings.

FIGURE 17.19   You can use the MSBuild Options dialog box to control precompiling options.

> **NOTE**
>
> You can get the same results from the Publish Web Site option in the IDE as you would with the MSBuild command-line application.

Silverlight Applications

The Silverlight Applications screen in the Property Pages dialog box enables you to manage settings for Silverlight applications to which your website connects. You can add a Silverlight application from here. You can then determine where the Silverlight application should copy its files (typically ClientBin). See Chapter 20 for more details on building Silverlight applications.

Creating Web Pages

ASP.NET web pages (also called web forms) make up the bulk of any given website. You create web pages to define your user interface. Web pages in ASP.NET have both a designer component and an event model. The designer enables you to define the controls and look of a given web page. The event model is used on the server to respond to user interaction (or events posted back to the server over HTTP). This section looks at the basics of both the web page's designer and its event model.

Adding a Web Page to Your Website

The first step to working with web pages is adding one or more to your website. To do so, you use the Add New Item dialog box and select Web Form from the item templates. Figure 17.19 shows an example of adding a CustomerEdit.aspx page to a website. Note that this figure is simply an alternate view of the same dialog box shown in Figure 17.12.

You have a few options when adding a new web page to your site. First, you can set the page's name. It is best to use a standard naming scheme and to make sure that the name also references the page's primary function. Web page names must be unique in a given directory. A good standard might be to indicate the data with which the page works followed by a user action for the page. In our example, this is CustomerEdit.aspx. The second option is the language on which the web form is based. Your website is typically either all C# or VB. However, it can be made up of a mixture of both languages. When you create a new page, the default language is chosen based on the default language for your website. However, you can use the left-side of the Add New Item dialog box to choose a different language for the page (see Figure 17.20).

FIGURE 17.20   You use the Add New Item dialog box to add Web Form pages to your site.

Next, you can indicate whether you want the code for the web page to be in a separate file. ASP.NET enables you to create a web form as a single file. This form includes both ASP markup and server-side code. In fact, you also get VB or C# IntelliSense inside the markup editor for these types of forms.

The dominant setting (and default) for most developers is code-behind (place code in separate file). Putting code in a new file enables you to manage that code independently of the UI markup. This can be a much cleaner development experience. However, some web developers prefer the simplicity of a single file model. In this case, your server-side code is placed inside a <script/> block.

In the case of the code-behind model, ASP.NET puts your code into what is called a partial class. This partial class contains only the code that you write. Code that is emitted by the tool or framework is not part of this file. Your code and the tool-emitted code are combined together during compilation. In this way, you are not burdened by code that is really not yours. Of course, the single-file model also excludes the tool-emitted code.

The final option on the Add New Item dialog box when adding a Web Form is Select master page. This setting tells the IDE that you want your new web form to use a master page for its default content and layout. We look at master pages later in this chapter.

Adding Controls to Your Web Page

You add controls to a web page by dragging them from the Visual Studio Toolbox to the web page. In the page designer, there are multiple views of your form: design, source, and split view. The design view enables you to build your form using drag-and-drop with a visual designer. This is similar to building a Windows, or WPF form. As you drag items onto the page, you see a visual representation of what they look like at runtime. This includes their layout with respect to one another. You can select an item on a page and use the property editor to change the look and behavior of the element.

Figure 17.21 shows a page in the design view. Notice the Toolbox on the left. This is the source of controls you can add to your page. In the center of the figure is the actual design surface. Notice that the Save button is selected. The properties for the Save button are shown on the right. You can use the property editor to make changes to how the control looks and acts. These changes are stored inside the markup for the page.

You can switch from Design to Source view using the buttons at the bottom of the page designer (refer to Figure 17.21). The source view enables you to see (and edit) the markup related to a web page. Here you can still drag controls from the Toolbox onto the editor, but instead of a visual representation, you get the markup code that represents the given item. You can then use the markup editor to change the values inside the markup. This includes setting property values for controls and changing layout information. Of course, Visual Studio provides IntelliSense for doing so. Figure 17.22 shows the same page as was shown in Figure 17.21 but now in source view. Notice that the Save button's properties are available for edit from IntelliSense. Editing markup in Source view might be a more familiar experience for coders.

The third view of your page is called split view. This gives you both markup and the visual design surface. The two try to stay in sync with one another. If you make a change in the

FIGURE 17.21 You can use the Toolbox to add controls to either the design view (shown) or the Source view of your page.

FIGURE 17.22 You can edit your page markup using Source view.

source view, for example, the design view tries to update itself or waits for you to click on it and then update. This can be useful if you do things both visually and through code (and have a big monitor). You end up doing a lot less switching back and forth between views. Figure 17.23 shows an example of the same page we've been looking at, now in split view. Notice how in both views it knows that the Save button is selected.

FIGURE 17.23   You use Split view to see both markup and design at the same time.

TIP

You can change how Visual Studio opens your web forms by default. You can choose between viewing in source view and viewing in design view. To do so, choose Options from the Tools menu. You then select the HTML Designer node from the tree. Figure 17.24 shows an example of this window. The Start Pages In group box enables you to modify this setting.

Responding to Events

When you write ASP.NET web pages, it is important to understand how the event model works. The event model represents how events are fired on the server when users make requests (or trigger actions). The ASP.NET event model is different from the standard Windows form event model because it combines events that process on a server with the nature of a web application delivered inside a web browser.

An ASP.NET page has less of an event model and more of a life cycle. The life cycle has a series of stages through which a page goes. In each stage, there is typically one or more events that get fired. The life cycle stages of an ASP.NET page are shown in Figure 17.25.

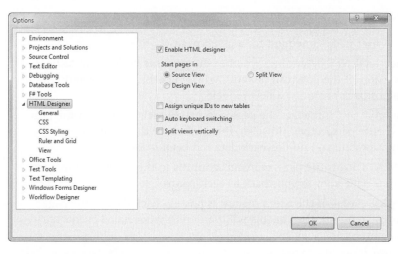

FIGURE 17.24   You can use the HTML Designer options to change how Visual Studio opens your web pages by default.

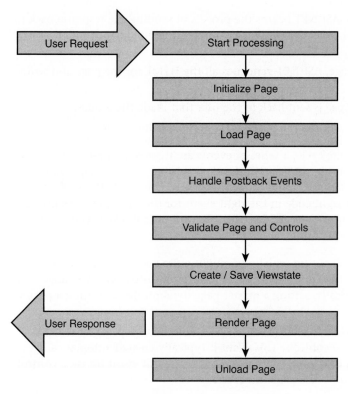

FIGURE 17.25   The ASP.NET page life-cycle stages.

Each stage in Figure 17.25 is described here:

1. **User Request**—A user makes a request for a given page.

2. **Start Processing**—ASP.NET determines whether the page life cycle needs to be executed or a version of the page can be returned from cache. It also determines if the request is a postback or simply a new request.

3. **Initialize Page**—ASP.NET initializes the page and makes each control on the page available from a code perspective. However, the controls at this point are not matched to any viewstate and no postback data has been loaded.

4. **Load Page**—ASP.NET loads the page, connects controls to their viewstate information, and connects data from the postback to each control.

5. **Handle Postback Events**—If the user's request is posting back data to the page (instead of a simple request), then at this point any postback-related events are called, such as a button's click event.

6. **Validate Page and Controls**—After the page has been loaded by the server, it gets validated. This means calling out to each control and ensuring that the Validation method is fired. Finally, the Page's IsValid property gets set at this stage based on the results.

7. **Create/Save Viewstate**—ASP.NET begins the process of sending the response back to the user. The first thing is to create the ViewState data and embed it inside the response.

8. **Render Page**—At this stage, ASP.NET generates all the HTML for the page and writes it to an output stream.

9. **User Response**—A response is sent back to the user that made the request.

10. **Unload Page**—ASP.NET unloads the page and discards it from memory.

As a page moves through this life cycle, a series of events are triggered. These events are where you place your code. It is important to understand this life cycle to help you understand the events, when they are fired, and what is available to you inside these events. You want to be sure to get the right code in the right event for the right job. Let's take a look at the basics of the web page event model. The following lists the key events in the page life cycle in the order in which they are fired:

1. **PreInit**—This is the first event for which you might write code. It gets raised before the initialize stage (refer to Figure 17.25). The PreInit event is useful if you are creating controls dynamically, setting a master page dynamically, or setting a page's theme dynamically.

2. **Init**—This event is called to create the controls used by the web page. It also initializes the properties of these controls. This event is typically created automatically by the IDE to set properties of controls on a given page. The init event for each control on the page is called prior to the page Init event.

3. **InitComplete**—This event is raised after the page Init event is called. It signals that view state tracking has been enabled. Any modifications to view state prior to InitComplete would be lost.

4. **PreLoad**—This event is called after the view state for the page and controls have been loaded but before the Load event.

5. **Load**—This event is called when the page is loaded and after the controls are initialized. This is a common event for web developers to use. You can use this event to determine whether a user is requesting a page or executing a postback (submitting data). You then call the appropriate code based on this information. Control Load events are also called during page load.

6. **Control Specific Event(s)**—Next, the page framework executes the event or events that are associated with the control the user used to submit the form (if any). For example, if a user clicked a button on your form, the button's click event is called after page load.

7. **LoadComplete**—Triggered after all initialization, loading, and control-specific events have processed. You can use this event to execute any code that requires the entire page to be loaded.

8. **PreRender**—This event is called just before the final rendering of the page is sent back to the browser. You can also use this event to make changes to the page after all events are called.

9. **PreRenderComplete**—Raised after the PreRender event has processed.

10. **SaveStateComplete**—Raised after the view state and control state information has been saved for the page. If you make changes to the page or controls at this point, those changes do not persist when the page is posted back to the server. However, the changes are reflected in the response.

11. **Render**—There is no Render event. However, the page calls the render method for each control on the page at this stage. This enables the control to output the markup to be sent to the browser.

12. **Unload**—This is the last event that is called for the page (after the page is rendered). The Unload event is first called for each control on your page. It then gets called for just the page. You use this event to do cleanup. For example, you might close page-level connections or do some form of logging. You cannot, however, make any changes that affect the response to the user. That was completed in the rendering stage (refer to Figure 17.25).

These steps represent the basic event model for a page. However, there are additional events for the page. In addition, user controls have their own events that are called during the control-specific event stage. Master pages can also add default processing for all pages. Understanding the events in any given page always help when you're debugging or trying to achieve a specific result.

> **NOTE**
>
> For more information on what happens inside the ASP processing framework, see "ASP.NET Application Life Cycle Overview" on the MSDN website. This article provides a detailed view of how ASP.NET works with user requests and renders a page. It also covers application- and session-specific events (inside global.asax).

Adding Page Event Handlers   There are a couple of ways to ensure that your event handlers are called by ASP.NET when a page executes. First, you can call them automatically. If you set the AutoEventWireup page-level attribute to True, then ASP.NET finds events that follow the Page_Event naming convention and automatically call them at their appropriate time. This approach can be convenient but requires you to recall each event's name so that you can define it appropriately.

You can also explicitly bind page events to methods in your code. In this way, you can use your own event names. You can also let Visual Studio generate the event names. You can add events to a page from the designer in a similar way you would bind events to controls: from the Properties window. However, to access a page's events, you must be in the Component Designer for the page. The Component Designer is another design view for a page. It is used to add components to the page such as event logging. You get to the component designer by right-clicking a page and choosing View Component Designer. After you have it open, you then open that page's Properties window. From there, you can select the lightning bolt icon to show all events for the page. Figure 17.26 shows an example.

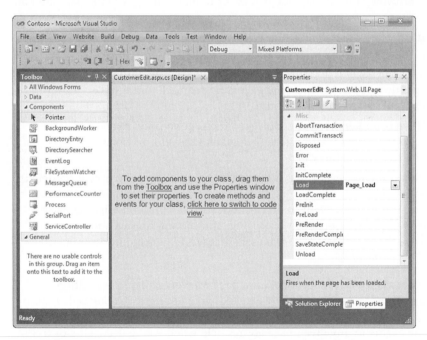

FIGURE 17.26   You can use the page's component designer to access the page events inside the Properties pane.

The right side of the figure shows the properties for the CustomerEdit.aspx page. Notice that the lightning bolt icon is selected from the Properties toolbar. This shows the events (and not the properties). You can double-click an event in this list to generate a method stub for the given event. You can also select an event from the list and then use a drop-down to choose a method already defined in your code and thus explicitly bind that method to the selected event.

Adding Control Event Handlers   You add events to controls in a similar manner. There is no component designer (thankfully) for a control. You simply select the control on a given page and view its properties in the Properties window. From the Properties window, you can select the lightning bolt icon to show all the events for the given control. You then double-click an event to add it to your code-behind. Of course, if you already have code written you can use the same window to select that code and thus bind it to the selected event.

Most events you add to a control are Action events. These are events that are based on user actions (such as button click). There are, however, other events. These events are typically used for special purposes and control developers only. Figure 17.27 shows an example of adding an event to the Click action of the Save button. Notice the additional events available for the Button control.

FIGURE 17.27   You can use the lightning bolt icon in the Properties pane to access control event handlers.

Designing Your User Interface

There is a lot that goes into building a good web user interface. So much so that some solid planning is typically in order before you start dragging controls onto forms. Your first step should be to consider your options, the needs of the users, and your maintenance requirements. You then put this information into some sort of design plan. Your design plan should include the following:

▶ Determine the type of information and user activity your site needs to support. You might make a list of the screen types in your system. For example, you might have pages that display report data, others that allow users to do data entry, still others that do searches, and so on. This helps you when deciding on the style elements required of your site.

▶ Decide whether you need to plan for multiple-language and culture information. This can have a big effect on how you build out the content items (such as labels, menu text, and the like) of your pages.

▶ Define the key areas of your site and how users navigate among them. This is often referred to as your site's taxonomy or sitemap.

▶ Determine what items go on all pages. This might include navigation, logos, design elements, footer information, and more. For example, you might make the key areas of your site into top-level menu items that go on all pages.

▶ Determine the style elements for your site. Or at least define the items that need to be stylized. As an example, you might determine that you need a consistent way to show page titles, navigation items, buttons, column headers, table data, and so on. Documenting these items enables you to plan upfront. You might also pass the list on to a designer and have the designer build out the styles for the application.

▶ Determine if your site will support a high degree of user interaction. If this is the case, you should consider creating an AJAX-enable site or perhaps using Silverlight (see Chapter 20).

▶ Decide whether you will support multiple themes to enable user-configurable options. You might, for example, need to rebrand your site depending on the user accessing it. In this case, you need to think about themes. You might also need to enable user customization of layout and content. In this case, you should consider using some of the portal controls.

These and many more decisions go into planning a good, web-based UI. Thinking through the items upfront pays big dividends down the road by saving you a lot of frustrating rework.

When you have your plan, Visual Studio 2010 is there to help. It enables you to create master pages for determining a common look and feel. There are controls for managing links and menus. You can support themes through skin files and style sheets. You can even allow users to participate in the customization of their layout using Web Parts. The following sections demonstrate the many features of ASP.NET that go into creating great web UIs.

Determining Page Layout and Control Positioning

An important consideration when building your web pages is deciding how controls are placed on a page. This is a big topic that continues to evolve. Many websites rely on tables of information for their layout. Each item on the page is in a table of columns and rows. Other sites place items on a page such that they do not move. If items overlap (such as when font sizes are increased), they show as overlap. There are others that build a page with no real layout at all at design time. They then rely on style sheets to apply a layout of the controls at runtime. And, of course, there are pages and sites that mix these options depending on the situation. The following list is meant to describe your options in more detail:

▶ **Flow Layout**—If you are comfortable with the dynamic nature of a web page in a browser, you might prefer to control your positioning through flow layout. This refers to your controls moving with the flow of the page. This capability is great if you intend to lay out your page with tables and place your controls within table cells. Using tables with flow layout is the most common method for laying out pages. Things are lined up with respect to how their neighbors are lined up. If an item moves down, for example, anything below that item also moves down in a relative fashion. This is the default setting in Visual Studio.

▶ **Absolute Positioning**—If you are used to building Windows forms, you might be more comfortable controlling the positioning of each individual item. In this case, you drag an item onto the form and move it around relative to other items. Where you drop it is where it is positioned (and where it stays). In addition, with absolute positioning, items are positioned based on their parent container. For example, if you put a button inside a div tag and set the position of the button to 5 pixels from the top and 5 pixels from the left, the 5 pixels in each case are counted from the bounds of the div tag (and not the page).

▶ **Relative Positioning**—This combines a flow layout with absolute positioning. With relative positioning, items are placed within the flow of a page. However, if you set an item's top and left properties, the distance defined by these properties is calculated based on the item's relative position on the page.

▶ **CSS Positioning**—CSS positioning is quickly becoming the standard for page layout as it offers the highest degree of flexibility and control. With CSS positioning, items are typically laid out on a page using flow layout. However, each item has a specific style defined either on the page or in a style sheet. Style sheets are the preferred choice so you do not have to redefine the styles on every page. The style has positioning information defined, including margins, heights, widths, and the like, which enables you to easily change the layout of a page (or entire site) by changing the style sheet (and not the pages themselves).

You might have situations in which you need to mix both flow and absolute layouts in a single page. For example, you could define a page that flows based on tables. Inside a given cell, you might set a panel control. This panel control might be set to allow only absolute positioning for items within the panel. Alternatively, you might add an image to a page that uses flow layout or CSS positioning. You might indicate that the image should be positioned as absolute or relative similar to how you would embed an image in a Word document.

Whichever path you choose, you should be consistent. You should define your layout strategy as part of your design plan. All the pages in the site should behave in a similar manner to make your maintenance easier. In addition, most pages are dependent on other page-like items (such as master pages and user controls). For this reason, you might want all of these items to be laid out on a page in the same way.

Setting How Controls Are Positioned

By default, Visual Studio is set to lay out items on your page using flow layout. That is, as you drag items from the Toolbox to the designer, the items are placed relative to one another. If you are using the two most common methods for controlling a page's layout (tables or CSS positioning) then flow layout is fine for your needs. Figure 17.27, presented earlier, shows a page in flow layout using a table to get relative positioning of controls.

You might run into a situation in which you need to absolute-position an item on a page that uses flow layout. For example, suppose in Figure 17.26 that we want to embed our company logo on the right side of the page. We could try to fit it in the table but would most likely be frustrated doing so because things can get out of line quickly.

Instead, we can use absolute positioning to control the position of the logo relative to the table. To do so, first select the image. Then, from the Format menu, choose the Position option. This brings up the Position dialog box, shown in Figure 17.28.

FIGURE 17.28   You can use the Position dialog box to change how a single element on a flow-layout page is positioned.

The Position dialog box enables you to indicate how a given, selected item should be positioned on the page. You can see that this is similar to positioning a graphic in a Word document. You choose the wrapping style and the positioning style—in our case, Absolute positioning. You can try to get the location and size information right. However, after you move to absolute position, you can change the position of the item just by dragging the item around.

TIP

The Format menu has the Set Position option. Use this for items you want to toggle between absolute and relative. After an item is set to absolute, you can drag the item to the right location.

Figure 17.29 shows the same image being dragged around the page. Notice that the IDE shows you the vertical and horizontal centers as lines up and down the designer. This helps you line up an item. If we were lining up a button or text box, the IDE would also show margin and space indicators to assist you. You can also use the arrow keys on the keyboard to tweak your positioning.

FIGURE 17.29   You can select an item set to absolute positioning and move it around the page using the mouse or arrow keys.

If you intend to use absolute positioning for your entire page, you do not want to have to manually select each item and choose Position from the Format menu, which would be tedious. Instead, you can set an option that tells Visual Studio how to add controls to a page by default. You set this choice within the Options dialog box (Tools, Options). Here you navigate to the HTML Designer/CSS Styling node. Figure 17.30 shows an example. Select the last check box (Change Positioning to Absolute) to indicate that from this point forward all controls should be added to a page using absolute positioning.

When you lay out a page using absolute positioning, all items must be put in their exact spot. For this reason, you must worry about margins and spacing issues. For example, Figure 17.31 shows the start of a page being built with absolute positioning.

17

FIGURE 17.30 You can use the HTML Designer options to change the default positioning for pages added to your site.

FIGURE 17.31 You can use absolute positioning to control the precise placement of controls within your page.

Here the Cancel button is being positioned to the right of Save and under the Name TextBox. You can see the margin indicators and alignment lines. However, if additional items need to be added between the TextBox and the buttons, each button has to be moved and repositioned. With flow layout, the items just move or you would insert a row in the table.

When an item is absolute-positioned on a page, the designer is simply changing the item's style behind the scenes. That is, it is setting the positioning details for each item using the style tag. For example, the following code shows the markup for the TextBox items in Figure 17.31:

```
<asp:TextBox ID="TextBox1" runat="server" CssClass="textBox"
  style="z-index: 1; left: 24px; top: 125px; position: absolute">
</asp:TextBox>
```

You can see here what is happening. The position attribute is set to absolute and the left and top positions are set. For this reason, items in the markup for absolute positioned pages do not typically follow in the order in which they exist on the screen. Rather, they are put into the markup in the order in which they are added to the page.

Also, notice that the code indicated something called z-index. This enables you to do layering in your output. Each item is on a layer (in this case, layer 1). Layers may overlap one another. You can change the layer in markup. Alternatively, you can use the Order option from the Format menu and choose either Bring to Front to bring the selected item(s) to the top layer or Send to Back to push all the items to the back-most layer.

Make Same Size   You can select a group of items and work to make them similar. To select a group, click each item while holding the Ctrl key. You can then choose to make the selected items the same size. You do so from the Format, Make Same Size menu option. Figure 17.32 shows an example with both buttons selected. Of course, you might be better served setting the size of buttons in a style sheet or theme (see next section).

Align Items   As discussed, you can use the guidelines to help line up your absolute-positioned items. Visual Studio also provides the Align options from both the Format menu and the Layout toolbar. You can see a glimpse of the Align menu options in Figure 17.32. Many of the sizing, ordering, and alignment options available from the Format menu are also accessible from the Layout toolbar. If you are doing a lot of absolute positioning work it is easier to have this toolbar loaded in the IDE. Figure 17.33 shows an example with the Layout toolbar highlighted. Notice that the two buttons are again selected. The option, Align Middles, is being clicked to ensure both buttons align horizontally at their center. There are, of course, many additional options on this toolbar including Align Lefts, Align Centers, Align Rights, Align Tops, Align Bottoms, the sizing options, the ordering options, and spacing options (increase vertical or horizontal spacing).

FIGURE 17.32 You can use the Make Same Size option on the Format menu to quickly set two or more controls to the same size (the first item selected is used as the size).

FIGURE 17.33 Use the Layout toolbar for quick access to alignment, sizing, ordering, and spacing commands.

> **TIP**
>
> If you use flow layout, you generally do not need to be concerned with the tab order of your controls (the order in which controls are accessed in the browser when a user presses the Tab key). That is because the browser tabs through the controls in the order they exist inside the page's markup. In flow layout, this order is the same order in which the controls are displayed. However, if you use absolute positioning, the controls in the markup could be in a different order than that of their display. In this case, you need to set the TabIndex property of each control to the order you want to have them accessed (1, 2, 3, etc.).

Creating a Common Look and Feel

When you create a website, you want the pages to look as if they all belong to one application. The navigation should be standard, the colors and fonts should match for like items, and sizing should be consistent. Users should not feel as though they are jumping sites simply by navigating from one page to the next. In addition, you don't want to have to manage this consistency across every single page in the site. This would be extremely tedious when you need to make a change to, for example, how all buttons in your site look.

Thankfully, you have the tools to support a consistent look across pages and make the management of it all much easier. Visual Studio 2010 provides support for building styles, managing them, and applying them to your pages. In addition, you can leverage style sheets at the site level, master pages, and themes. Let's take a look at all of these.

Styles and Style Sheets Basics

Styles and style sheets allow you to define a common look and behavior. You can then apply that common look to multiple items within your page and application. In this way, if you decide to change something, you can change it in one place and all the places that use the style will be updated.

Inline Styles A style simply defines the look of a given item. You can create inline styles that use the style attribute on a given form element to indicate how that element looks. In the following code, there is an inline style that sets the font, font size, and color for a label control:

```
<asp:Label ID="Label1" runat="server" Text="Edit Customer"
  style="font-family: Arial; font-size: large; color: Blue">
</asp:Label>
```

Inline styles do not offer much in the way of reuse. Instead, you have to define the style for every item on every page. This is okay for the occasional, unique circumstance.

However, it quickly becomes unmanageable if you are trying to keep like items on like pages looking alike. In these cases, it's best to abstract the style definition from the item by putting the style definition in a style class. In the above example, you might define the inline style as the title class in a style sheet (more on this in a moment).

Page-Level Styles   A style class can be defined in one of two places: in the page itself or in a style sheet linked to the page. If you define a style class in the page itself, it is applicable to only that page (and not the rest of the pages in the site). Styles defined at the page level are embedded in the <head> section of the XHTML. For example, the following markup abstracts the same style discussed previously into a page-level style:

```
<head runat="server">
  <style type="text/css">
    .titleText
    {
      font-family: Arial;
      font-size: large;
      color: Blue;
    }
  </style>
</head>
```

To apply this style to the form element, you set its Class property for HTML controls or the CssClass property for ASP.NET controls. The following shows an example for the Label control discussed previously:

```
<asp:Label ID="Label1" runat="server" Text="Edit Customer"
  CssClass="titleText"></asp:Label>
```

Element Styles (Style Rules)   You can create a style rule for an HTML element. This style rule applies for all HTML elements (and their related ASP.NET counterpart) of the given type automatically. That is, you do not have to assign the style to the element; it simply picks up the style.

As an example, suppose you want to manage how hyperlinks on your site look when a user hovers the mouse pointer over them. To do so, you can define a style inside a style sheet for the anchor tag's hover (A:hover) behavior. Inside the style, you might set the color, name, and size of the font. You might also turn off underlining when a user hovers over the link. After you've defined this style, you apply it to the page. All anchor tags on the page then use the given style definition. The following code shows an example:

```
a:hover
{
  font-family: Tahoma;
  font-size: 10pt;
  color: #0099FF;
  text-decoration: none;
}
```

Style Sheets   A style sheet represents a file that houses a set of styles to be applied to a page. In this way, you can abstract all your styles away from a page, centralize them, and manage them as a group. Visual Studio creates a default style sheet when you define a new website. This file is called Site.css and can be found inside the Styles directory. It contains definitions for many of the most common HTML elements that are stylized. This makes it a great starting point.

Inside a style sheet file you can add HTML element styles and your own style classes. The code for these styles looks just like the code we've shown thus far.

After a style sheet is defined, you link a page to a style sheet to use the styles defined inside the style sheet. A quick way to link a style sheet to a page is by dragging the style sheet from Solution Explorer to the form designer. This adds the link element to your code. You can also write this code manually. The link is added to the <head> section of the page as in the following example:

```
<head runat="server">
  <link href="StyleSheetMaster.css" rel="stylesheet" type="text/css" />
  <title>Edit Customer</title>
</head>
```

You assign style classes to form elements as discussed previously. Of course, HTML elements you define as styles simply pick up the style without you having to make explicit assignment. The Visual Studio designer shows style rendering during the design process. This way, you can see how your application will look as you build it.

TIP

The CSS definition enables you to define style hierarchies. This can be a great way to manage the look of a given area within your site without having to apply many styles to individual elements. For example, you might apply a specific style to a <div/> tag in your markup. Your style sheet might then define style hierarchies for elements within that <div/> tag. In this way, you apply a style to only one element on your page, but all the elements within might also pickup styles from the style sheet.

As an example, suppose you want to define a style for a user input form that has labels, text boxes, buttons, and related elements. You could define the style using a hierarchy and then enclose the form itself inside a <div/> tag. You then would only need to apply the style to the <div/> tag itself. The following shows an example of a hierarchical style definition:

```
.userForm
{
  font-family: Arial; /* default style */
  font-size: 10pt;
}


.userForm input /* input item style */
```

```
  {
    border-style: solid;
    border-width: 1pt;
    border-color: Gray;
    margin: 5px 0px 5px 0px;
  }


  .userForm span /* label style */
  {
    font-weight: bold;
    padding: 5px 5px 5px 5px;
  }
```

You can then apply this style to your form as in the following markup. Notice only the outer <div/> tag contains a style sheet definition.

```
<div class="userForm">
    <asp:Label ID="Label1" runat="server" Text="Name"></asp:Label>
    <asp:TextBox ID="TextBox1" runat="server"></asp:TextBox>
    <br />
    <asp:Button ID="Button1" runat="server" Text="Button" />
</div>
```

The results are shown in Figure 17.34. You can see how the items inside the <div/> tag picked up their styles. You can use this method for all sorts of HTML elements on your page. If you're using ASP.NET controls, however, you have to know how they render as HTML in order to define the appropriate style items. Alternatively, you can use themes for ASP.NET items (more on this later).

The Style Toolset
Thus far, we've looked at the basics of styles and style sheets. Of course, there is a lot more to creating styles, managing them, and applying them to your site. Thankfully, Visual Studio has a number of tools built-in to help us work with styles. Let's examine these tools.

Creating a Style Sheet   You can add one or more style sheets to an application through the Add New Item dialog box (refer to Figure 17.12). You can open a style sheet in the Visual Studio code editor. When you do, Visual Studio presents a Style Sheet toolbar, the Styles menu, and the actual contents of the style sheet. Figure 17.35 shows these items.

FIGURE 17.34   You can use hierarchical styles to simplify applying styles.

FIGURE 17.35   You can use the code editor to manage your style sheet markup.

The middle pane of Figure 17.35 shows the contents of the style sheet. You can manually edit the style sheet from here. Of course, being able to edit it requires you to have a decent working understanding of CSS. Visual Studio also provides IntelliSense to help guide you. As with anything, the more you work with it, the more familiar you become.

The CSS Outline pane (right-side of Figure 17.35) opens by default when you open a style sheet. You can use this pane to quickly find element styles and your custom classes. This is a simple view for style sheets that are not too complex. The Manage Styles window handles more complex scenarios (we cover this momentarily).

The Style Sheet toolbar has just a few options. The first one on the left launches the Add Style Rule dialog box. The second option (Build Style) opens the Modify Style dialog box. You can also right-click a style inside the editor to gain access to building the style using the Modify Style dialog box (more on this topic is coming up).The next button in the toolbar enables you to view the results in a browser window. Finally, the drop-down allows you to set a CSS standard (1.0, 2.0, 2.1) that you want to target.

Building a Style   You can code a style directly using the code editor or you can use the Modify Style dialog box to do so. The Modify Style dialog box provides access to key style attributes using an easy-to-use dialog box. After you build your style, the tool generates the correct markup and puts it in your style sheet file.

You can access the Modify Style dialog box by right-clicking inside an existing style, by selecting the Build Style option from the Style menu, or by clicking the Build Style option on the Style toolbar. Figure 17.36 shows an example. This figure represents the many options for controlling the font on a style. The Modify Style dialog box has many more options, such as backgrounds, tables, and borders. In addition, the Layout and Position items enable you to control how CSS positioning works.

FIGURE 17.36   You can quickly build your style definition using the Modify Style dialog box.

Clicking the OK button on the Modify Style dialog box saves your changes to the style sheet. Changes are saved as they appear at the bottom of the dialog box in the Description box.

Creating a Style Rule   A style rule is simply the definitions for a style element or a class (as in, h1 {}). You can create a new style rule by typing it directly into the editor (using the correct syntax, of course). You can also define a style rule by using the Add Style Rule dialog box. You access this dialog box by right-clicking in the style sheet editor pane, by clicking the leftmost button on the Style Sheet toolbar, or by selecting the Add Style Rule option on the Style menu. This dialog box is useful in that it lists the many HTML elements for which you can define style rules. It also enables you to define a style rule hierarchy. Figure 17.37 shows an example.

FIGURE 17.37   You can use the Add Style Rule dialog box to generate a style definition for an HTML element or custom class.

After you click OK, the style is saved to the style sheet. You can then edit the style's contents (see the previous section, "Building a Style").

Managing Styles   Visual Studio has a Manage Styles pane that enables you to easily work with and apply styles. This pane shows the styles available for a given page, enables you to create a new style, attach a style sheet to your page, apply a style to a control, and more. This makes working with styles a fluid and fast process.

You can access the Manage Styles pane from the View menu (View, Manage Styles). By default, the pane loads to the left side of the IDE. Figure 17.38 shows the Manage Styles pane loaded for the EditCustomer.aspx page.

There are a number of items to note here. The first is that the pane shows all styles available for use on the page. This includes those defined on the page (not shown but available under the grouping, Current Page) and those linked to the page through a style sheet (see the grouping, Site.css). You can use these groupings to copy items that are defined at the current page level into the style sheet (and vice versa). Visual Studio moves the markup code for you. Notice, too, that you can see a preview for the style selected. You also get the style's definition by hovering over it.

At the top of the Manage Styles pane are three options in the toolbar. From left to right they are New Style, Attach Style Sheet, and Options. Clicking the New Style button launches the New Style dialog box. This is a version of the Modify Style dialog box discussed previously. Figure 17.39 shows an example. Notice that the top of the dialog box is different. Here you can indicate the location of where you intend to define your new style (Current Page, New Style Sheet, or Existing Style Sheet).

17

FIGURE 17.38   You can use the Manage Styles pane to manage the styles in your site and apply them to your page elements.

FIGURE 17.39   You can use the New Style dialog box to define styles from Manage Styles.

The attach style sheet toolbar button (second from left) opens the Select Style Sheet dialog box. You use this dialog box to select an existing style sheet and attach (link) it to the page.

The Options button (top-right corner of the Manage Styles pane) enables you to filter how the styles are shown in the list. Options include categorizing styles by element, type, or order. You can also indicate that you want to see all styles, only those used on the current page, or only those used inside the items currently selected on the page.

Finally, you can right-click a style in the menu and execute one of many options. These include applying the style to the selected item in the designer and navigating to the code behind the style. You can also modify the style, delete it, or make a new style by copying the selected style. Figure 17.40 shows an example.

Applying a Style   There are many ways in which you can apply a style to a given element on a page. We've seen a couple already. In the previous section, you saw that you could select a style in the Style Manager pane and choose the Apply Style option from the context menu (refer to Figure 17.40). There is also a pane similar to Style Manager called Apply Styles (View, Apply Styles).

The Apply Styles pane behaves almost exactly like the Style Manager. One difference is that you can see a visual representation of the style on the style name itself instead of at the bottom of the pane as in the Style manager (see Figure 17.41). Click on the style name to apply it to your selection.

FIGURE 17.40   You can right-click a style and work with it from there including applying it to any selected items.

Another way to apply styles to your elements is in the markup itself. The good news is that both styles defined on the page and those linked as a style sheet are available inside IntelliSense. Figure 17.42 shows an example of applying the button style to an ASP.NET button control.

Finally, you can also set an item's style inside the Property window. Simply select an item and view its properties. The property, CssClass provides a drop-down of all styles available for the given element.

FIGURE 17.41   You can use the Apply Style.

FIGURE 17.42   You can apply styles from the markup editor using IntelliSense.

Editing Styles   There are various ways in which you can edit styles. You can right-click the code and choose Build Style to open the Modify Style dialog box. In addition, Visual Studio has the CSS Properties pane (View, CSS Properties) for editing styles. This pane enables you to see all the properties of a given style in a property editor form. Figure 17.43 illustrates this.

FIGURE 17.43   You can manage the CSS styles of a given element using the CSS Properties pane.

Notice that a Save button is selected. The CSS Properties pane then shows the rules and their style information for the selected item. You can edit the properties of the given style from this pane. An edit to a style here applies to wherever the style is defined. In this example, the edit is to the .button style defined on the Site.css style sheet file. The edit shows up immediately in the design window. It is also stored back in the .CSS file.

You can also use the CSS Properties pane to set and modify styles for individual items on the page. To do so, you first select an item on the page. You can then right-click inside the Applied Rules area of the CSS Properties pane and select, New Inline Style. This adds a style definition to the markup for the selected item. You can then use the CSS Properties section to set values for this specific item. The values are stored just with this item on the given page (and not in a style sheet).

Master Pages

Master pages were first introduced in Visual Studio 2005. They enable you to visually design a common look for your application in one file and then use that look in other files. This way you can centralize navigation, headers, and footers. In addition, when you derive a page from a master file, Visual Studio displays the contents of both pages at once inside the designer. This helps developers see how their page looks in the context of the overall site as they build it.

Creating a Master Page   You add a master page to your project through the Add New Item dialog box. You can have multiple master pages in your application. This capability can be especially useful if your application has more than one default layout (or look) for certain areas of the site. It is most common to have a master page that includes common navigation, common graphics, and a common footer. You can also nest master pages within one another (more on this to follow).

> **NOTE**
>
> The website template in Visual Studio 2010 includes a master page by default called Site.master. This can be a great starting point for customizing with your own details.

A master page defines the main HTML for the page. This includes the opening and closing HTML tags, head, body, and form. Inside the master page are one or more ContentPlaceHolder controls. These controls indicate areas on the page where content pages (pages that derive from the master) may place their content.

> **TIP**
>
> You can add a style sheet to a master page. In this way, all pages that use the master page are also linked to the style sheet.

Master pages also have their own code-behind file. This file should contain all code that relates to the workings of the master page itself. If there are working controls on the page, a menu for example, their code would go inside this code-behind file. In addition, the master page has its own set of page events (just like a standard .aspx page).

Figure 17.44 shows an example of a master page. Notice that this master page is laid out as a table using flow layout. The cell in the center row contains a ContentPlaceHolder control (named MainContent). This is the only place where content pages that use the master page can add their user-specific content.

FIGURE 17.44   Use a Master page to control the default look and navigation of your site.

Creating a Content Page   Users do not access master pages directly. Instead, they call the content pages that derive from the master. When they do, .NET combines the contents of both pages and returns a single response as if there is only one page.

You create a content page by selecting a master when adding a web page to your site. When you do, there is an option titled Select Master Page at the bottom of the dialog box (refer to Figure 17.20). When you select this option you are presented with available master pages in your application.

When your content page opens in design view, you see the content of the master page in the background. In the foreground you see Content controls for any ContentPlaceHolder controls that were added to the master page. This is where you add controls specific to your page. This provides a separation of functionality between what belongs to your page and what belongs to the master. You work with the page as you would any other ASP.NET web page. You add controls to the form and write event code in the code-behind file.

Figure 17.45 shows an example. This web page was created to edit a customer's profile; it is based on the application's master page. Notice that the content page has the same extension as any web form (.aspx).

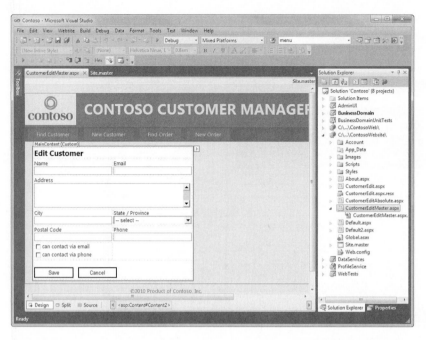

FIGURE 17.45   You add content to Content controls inside a page that uses a master page.

NOTE

Control layout and positioning can be important when you work with content areas. If, for example, you have turned on absolute positioning, the content placeholder acts more as a guide. Due to the nature of this layout option, the content placeholder cannot restrict you from placing your controls anywhere on the page. The flow layout option, however, has the opposite effect. Controls are allowed only inside the content areas unless otherwise marked as absolute-positioned.

TIP

You can use the Master object to reference the master page from the code within your content page's code-behind file. For example, suppose you have a label on the master page called LabelInstructions. You might need to set the value of this label from within each content page. You need to find the control used by the master page for the instruction text. You could then set the appropriate property on this control. The code to find the control on a master page looks like the following:

```
Label lb = (Label)this.Master.FindControl("LabelInstructions");
```

You could then use the variable, lb, to set the text on this label.

Adding Content to the <head/>   By default, master pages include a ContentPlaceHolder control inside the <head/> area of the HTML. This enables child pages to add information to the <head/> tag for the page such as a style definition or Javascript code. The following markup shows an example of this placeholder inside a master page:

```
<head runat="server">
  <link href="~/Styles/Site.css" rel="stylesheet" type="text/css" />
  <asp:ContentPlaceHolder ID="HeadContent" runat="server">
  </asp:ContentPlaceHolder>
</head>
```

The page that derives from a default master page includes a Content control for the <head/> area of the page. As an example, the following adds a <body/> style to the <head/> area of the child page.

```
<asp:Content ID="Content1" ContentPlaceHolderID="HeadContent" Runat="Server">
  <style type="text/css">
    body
    {
      font-family: Arial;
      font-size: 14pt;
    }
  </style>
</asp:Content>
```

> **TIP**
>
> You set the title for a page that uses a master page inside the @Page directive. The Title attribute is used for this purpose. This ensures a <title/> tag is appropriately added to your page. Adding a <title/> tag to a Content control does not work. Only the Title attribute of the @Page directive can be used for this purpose.

One drawback for public-facing sites that used prior versions of ASP.NET was that you could not easily set the meta tags for pages that derived from a master page. This made it difficult to add important keyword and description information used by search engines. Thankfully, version 4.0 of ASP.NET adds the MetaKeywords and MetaDescription properties to the Page class. This means you can now set these values as attributes of the @Page directive. You can also add the <meta/> tag to the <head/> section of a page or to the HeadContent Content control. The following shows an example:

```
<asp:Content ID="Content1" ContentPlaceHolderID="HeadContent" Runat="Server">
  <meta name="keywords" content="customer, shopper, edit" />
  <meta name="description" content="Used to edit a customer profile" />
</asp:Content>
```

Nesting Master Pages   Prior to Visual Studio 2008, you could have only one level of master page. You could not nest one inside the other and view the results in the designer. For example, a common scenario is to define a main master page to contain your site's frame, navigation, footer information, and the like. You might then create separate, sub-master pages for various content types. These sub-master pages would have their own, central design elements in addition to those defined by the main master page.

Visual Studio 2008 and beyond support this scenario. You can create a first master page. You can then create another master page and select a master page from which it derives. In this way, you build up a master page hierarchy. Figure 17.46 shows doing just that. Note the highlighted area, select master page.

FIGURE 17.46   You can use the Add New Item dialog box to create a master page that nests inside another master page.

With the new, nested master page, you can define master content inside the content placeholder defined by the main master page. You then add a new content placeholder inside your nested page. Pages based on this nested master page put their content inside this area. Of course, you can go multiple levels deep with nested master pages. The designer shows your various master pages during design.

Themes and Skins

Visual Studio 2005 first introduced the concept of themes for a website. This feature enables you to define one or more specific looks for the controls that make up your application. After you do, you can switch between them based on user preference, company affiliation, or similar factors.

At first glance, it seems that themes provide nearly the same experience as style sheets. However, themes go a few steps further. First, they leverage style sheets. Each theme can have an associated style sheet. Themes can also be applied in such a way as to work with an existing style sheet or to override it (see "Applying a Theme to a Site or Page," later in this chapter). The next difference is that themes enable you to embed graphic files as part of the themes. In this way, you can switch from one set of graphics to another based on a theme's name. Themes also enable you to define skin files for your ASP.NET controls. These skin files enable you to set property values of a control that fall outside mere styles (these property values must be non-behavioral, however). Lastly, a theme for a page can be set (and changed) at runtime. You can modify a property of the Page object to do so, which enables you to quickly switch your site's look.

> **NOTE**
>
> Unlike style sheets, only one theme can apply to a site at any given time.

Creating a Theme   Themes are created inside the App_Themes folder. Each theme gets its own theme folder. The name of the theme is the name of the folder (which must be unique). This ensures that there is no confusion when applying a theme. You apply a theme to a page or your site using the folder's name.

As an example, suppose you are building an application to manage customer details and orders. Assume that this application is accessed by different companies. Therefore, company A would manage its customers, and company B would manage its customers. In this scenario, the site owner might define a different theme for each company. Perhaps the theme is based on each company's colors, fonts, and graphics.

To create a theme, you typically follow a standard set of steps:

1. You must first create the App_Theme directory through the context menu. Right-click your website and choose Add ASP.NET Folder and then Theme. Alternatively, you might add a skin file to your application through the Add New Item dialog box and then Visual Studio creates the App_Theme directory automatically for you to house the `.skin` file. Remember to give your theme a name.

2. When you have the App_Theme directory, you can right-click on it to add a new theme folder, which you can find under the Add ASP.NET Folder menu. You should name the theme folder with the name of your theme.

3. Next, you add the files that make up your theme. These files typically include a style sheet, any images or resources, and a skin file.

Figure 17.47 shows the folder and file structure based on the example we discussed here. There are three themes: one called Contoso (company A), one called Fabrikam (company B), and a non-company theme (MainTheme).

17

FIGURE 17.47   You add themes to the App_Themes directory for your site.

Creating a Skin File   We have already discussed style sheets. What we need to look at now is defining a skin file. You can have one or more skin files in your theme. You might want to create a new skin file for each control you intend to skin. Alternatively, you might want to define a single skin file for your entire theme. The choice is yours.

Inside the skin file are control skin definitions called skins. You declare each skin just as you would write the markup for a given control on a web page. The syntax is similar. However, you omit the property assignments for the control that do not pertain to the skin.

There are two types of skin definitions: named skins and unnamed skins. A named skin is created by using the attribute SkinId. This enables you to define a unique name for the skin declaration. In this case, only controls in your site with this same SkinId are affected by the skin declaration. On the other hand, unnamed skins apply to all controls of a similar type. For example, if you want all your button controls to look a similar way, you create an unnamed skin for the button control. When you apply the skin to a page, all buttons pick up this look. Let's look at an example.

For this example, say you want to define a few skins to define your theme. You define named skins for the customer logo on the master page and the title labels on each screen. You then create unnamed skins for label, text box, button, and grid view controls.

Listing 17.1 shows the sample skin file. At the top are the named skins. Notice the use of the SkinId attribute. Again, this attribute is used when the skin is applied to specific instances of these types of controls (image and label in this case). Below this are the skins that apply to standard controls. There is one for all buttons, labels, text boxes, and grid views. Notice that the GridView definition includes definitions for the many parts of the control. You nest these definitions within the GridView definition as you would on any ASP.NET page.

You also need a similar file for company B (Fabrikam). To create it, you copy and paste this file to that company's directory. You then make minor edits to the image skin and the fonts and colors of the other skin definitions. We next look at applying these skins to the pages in the site.

LISTING 17.1   The Contoso Skin File

```
<%- named skins -%>
<asp:Image runat="server" SkinID="CustomerLogo"
 ImageUrl="~/App_Themes/Contoso/contoso.png"/>

<asp:Label runat="server" SkinID="TitleLabel"
 Font-Names="Arial Black"
 Font-Size="X-Large" />

<%- default, control skins -%>
<asp:Button runat="server" Width="80px" Height="24px"
 BackColor="#FFFFFF" ForeColor="MidnightBlue"
 Font-Name="Tahoma" Font-Size="10pt"
 BorderColor="#003399" BorderStyle="Solid" />

<asp:Label runat="server" ForeColor="MidnightBlue"
 Font-Names="Arial" Font-Size="Small" />

<asp:TextBox runat="server" Width="265px" BackColor="White"
 BorderColor="MidnightBlue" BorderStyle="Solid" BorderWidth="1px"
 Font-Names="Arial" Font-Size="Small" />

<asp:GridView runat="server" CellPadding="4" ForeColor="#333333" GridLines="None">
 <FooterStyle BackColor="#5D7B9D" Font-Bold="True" ForeColor="White" />
 <RowStyle BackColor="#F7F6F3" ForeColor="#333333" />
 <EditRowStyle BackColor="#999999" />
 <SelectedRowStyle BackColor="#E2DED6" Font-Bold="True" ForeColor="#333333" />
 <PagerStyle BackColor="#284775" ForeColor="White" HorizontalAlign="Center" />
 <HeaderStyle BackColor="#5D7B9D" Font-Bold="True" ForeColor="White" />
 <AlternatingRowStyle BackColor="White" ForeColor="#284775" />

</asp:GridView>
```

17

TIP

There is not much tool support for defining skin declarations. You are forced to manually enter this markup. However, a common shortcut can be to create a page that includes each control in the theme. You then use the designer to edit the controls on the page. Finally, you copy this markup from the page to the skin declaration and then delete any unwanted declaration code (including the ID tag).

Applying a Theme to a Site or Page   There are a few ways in which you can apply a theme. Each is meant to provide a different level of control. For example, you can set a global theme for an entire server. You can configure a theme for just one website. You can also choose to configure a theme at the individual page level. Finally, you can apply a single skin to a single control. You can see that these levels go from the very macro (server) to the granular (control). Most websites fall somewhere in the middle, like applying a theme at the page or site level.

You apply a theme at the page level by using the @ Page directive inside the page's markup. You have a couple of options here. You can decide that your theme should always trump all control settings. That is, if a developer explicitly sets a control value and that value is overridden by the theme, then the theme takes precedence. This type of declaration looks like the following:

```
<%@ Page Theme="Contoso" %>
```

Alternatively, you can set what is called a StyleSheetTheme at the page level. This indicates that the theme applies only where controls do not have explicit overriding values. In the previous declaration, the theme overrides local control settings. Using the StyleSheetTheme, you can set the theme to apply only to control settings that are not explicitly set. That is, if the control has a value for a given attribute, that value is used. If it does not, the theme's value is used. You set this type of theme for the page as shown here:

```
<%@ Page StylesheetTheme="Contoso" %>
```

You can define the theme for an entire website through the configuration file. This enables you to set a theme and then change it without recompiling your code. To do so, you add the Theme or StylesheetTheme (see the preceding example) attributes to the pages element inside the system.web node. The following is an example:

```
<system.web>
  <pages theme="Contoso" />
</system.web>
```

To define just the style sheet theme, use the following:

```
<system.web>
  <pages stylesheetTheme="Contoso" />
</system.web>
```

You can also set a theme inside your code. This capability can be useful if you are allowing users to choose their theme or you are dynamically setting a theme based on some user information. Recall the example with two companies: company A and company B. Remember, a theme file was defined for each. If you determine within your code that a member of company A (Contoso), for example, has logged in, then you set the theme this way:

```
Page.Theme = "Contoso"
```

You can make changes to a theme file or skin without recompiling your site. These changes are applied on the next browser refresh.

To set a theme for a single control, you use the SkinID attribute of the control. This ID can be set to reference a particular skin inside a skin file. The skin definition has the same skin ID as the one used inside the markup. You can set the skin ID from the markup or by using the Properties window for a given control open in the designer. The Properties window provides a drop-down list of skins that are available for the given control type. For example, to create an image control that picks up the skin definition you define this control as follows (in this case, the image control is inside the site.master page) :

```
<asp:Image ID="ImageLogo" SkinID="CustomerLogo" runat="server" />
```

You can also set the skin ID programmatically. The following is an example:

```
ImageLogo.SkinId = "CustomerLogo"
```

Figures 17.48 and 17.49 show examples of two different themes applied to the same web page, FindCustomer.aspx.

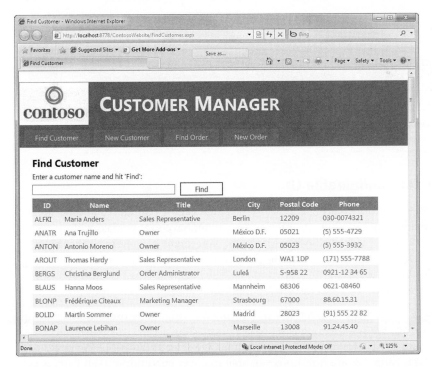

FIGURE 17.48   The Find Customer page with the Contoso theme applied.

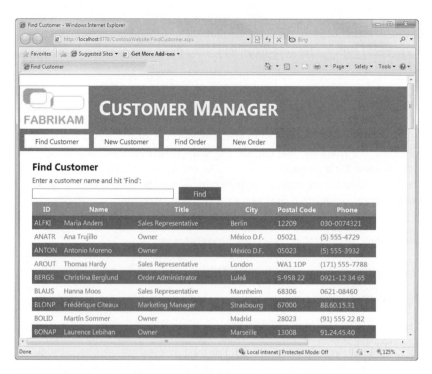

FIGURE 17.49 A second theme applied to the Find Customer page.

NOTE

One drawback of using themes is that you cannot see them applied to your page in the designer. Instead, you see only styles applied inline, at the page-level, or through a linked style sheet. To see your content with the theme applied you must run your page in a browser.

Creating a User-Configurable UI

ASP.NET provides support for creating a user interface that can be configured and personalized by each individual user of a site. As an example, if you have ever worked with Microsoft Office SharePoint Server or visited sites like MSN.com, you might have noticed that blocks of functionality define a given page. These blocks can be removed, added, moved around, and configured by users. To enable this functionality, the blocks all must work together as part of a portal framework. .NET has just such a framework built into the product.

The following sections provide an overview of creating a configurable user interface using the Web Part controls. We walk through the basics of building a Web Part page that enables users to monitor customers in a customer management application. We cover the many basics of Web Parts. We are not, however, able to cover everything. Web Parts is a big topic. This section should get you started in the right direction.

Working with the Web Part Controls

ASP.NET includes many Web Part controls and classes; the Visual Studio Toolbox alone defines 13 Web Part controls (see Figure 17.50). In addition, the System.Web.UI.WebControls.WebParts namespace contains nearly 100 classes. These controls and classes work together to manage the structure of a Web Part page, its personalization and configuration, and the presentation itself.

FIGURE 17.50   You use the many Web Part controls to provide web pages that allow for user customization.

When you create a basic Web Part page, you typically work with three types of controls: the WebPartManager, WebPartZone, and presentation controls themselves. The first control, WebPartManager, is actually required of all Web Part pages. It is the control responsible for managing the Web Parts on the page. You must define this control on each Web Part page and can define only one per page. The WebPartManager is responsible for tracking the controls and their zones throughout the page. It also manages the state that a page might be in, such as view or edit mode.

The second control, WebPartZone, enables you to manage the layout or "zones" of your page. A zone represents an area of the page where controls or features can be placed. To understand zones, you can think of your page in terms of horizontal and vertical content zones. For example, you might have a zone at the top of your page that presents the header for the application. Beneath this, you might have two vertical zones. The leftmost zone might be used for links and navigational controls. The middle zone might contain content Web Parts. Finally, you might have another zone at the bottom of the page to manage footer-type content.

Figure 17.51 shows an example of a Web Part page broken into zones. Of course, you can define any number of zones and lay them out as you like. This is simply one example.

> **NOTE**
>
> Zones also have associated styles. Each zone provides a common UI for controls within the zone. That is, they define a header, title, border, button style, and so on. This is known as the "chrome" for the controls in a given zone.

Last, you put controls into each zone of the Web Part page. These controls can be any .NET control that you want to be managed by the zone. You can also create your own user controls and Web Parts that can be placed in these zones. The advantage of the latter is that you can provide configuration capabilities for Web Parts. This enables users to edit a given Web Part's properties from within the web browser (similar to how Microsoft's SharePoint product works).

WebPartManager

```
Horizontal Zone 1



Horizontal Zone 2

   Vertical Zone 1      Vertical Zone 2




Horizontal Zone 3
```

FIGURE 17.51   You define multiple zones for a Web Part page.

Table 17.3 provides a brief reference to the primary controls that are used to manage a Web Part page. Each of these controls can be found on the Visual Studio Toolbox (refer to Figure 17.50). These controls are all zone controls (except the manager control). As such, they constrain what type of control should be added to the given zone.

TABLE 17.3   The Web Part Zone Controls

Control	Description
WebPartManager	This control tracks the zones on the page and the Web Part controls that are in those zones. Each Web Part page requires one (and only one) instance of this control.
CatalogZone	This control defines a zone that contains one or more CatalogPart controls. The CatalogPart control provides a list of Web Parts that are available for the page. When a user is editing the page, this zone is enabled. Users then use the CatalogPart control to select one or more Web Part objects and drag them into WebPartZones.
WebPartZone	You use this control for defining the primary zones of your user interface. You can add ASP.NET controls and Web Part controls into these zones. Most Web Part pages define two or more WebPartZones.
EditorZone	You use this zone for providing an area for users to edit and configure a given Web Part. The editor for a Web Part is defined as an EditorPart control. This zone contains these types of controls.

Creating a Web Part Page

You create a Web Part page using any standard web form (.aspx). For the following example, create a form titled MonitorCustomer.aspx. The next step is to drag a WebPartManager control onto this form. This control has no visual appearance on the form. Instead, it is simply necessary to create a Web Part page.

TIP

Inside Visual Studio's form designer, you can decide to show or hide controls that have no visual appearance. To do so, you use the View menu, Visual Aids submenu and check or uncheck the option ASP.NET Non-Visual Controls. Nonvisual controls show up as gray boxes inside the designer. The box typically contains a control's name and ID.

Defining Zones   Next, you add the zones to the page. Recall that the zones define where your Web Parts can exist and how they look and are sized. You can lay out your zones inside a table, use absolute positioning to place zones in specific areas, or use relative positioning. If you allow users to hide or close the controls in a zone, you might consider a table or relative positioning. If, on the other hand, your zones are static, you should use absolute positioning.

In our example, we use an HTML table. First, create three rows: the top for the page title, the middle to house Web Parts, and the bottom for a footer. Inside the middle row, define a new HTML table with three columns.

Each column contains a zone for the page. The left zone contains Web Parts related to customers, the middle zone contains information related to orders and statistics, and the rightmost zone allows users to modify the Web Parts displayed on the page. At this point, your form should look something like the one defined in Figure 17.52. Note that the page is shown without the theme definition applied.

Next you must lay out the zones inside the center row's HTML table. You can follow these steps to lay out the zones:

1. Place a WebPartZone control inside the first column of the table.

2. Set the HeaderText property of the first control to Customer Links. This enables people editing the page to see a zone name (and your intentions for the zone).

3. Set the first control's ID property to WebPartZoneCustomerLinks.

4. Repeat steps 1 to 3 for the middle column in the row. This time, call the Web Part zone Customer Statistics. This takes the most screen area and enables users of this screen to find orders and view stats.

FIGURE 17.52   You can use an HTML table to define the layout of a Web Part page.

5. Add a CatalogZone control to the rightmost column of the middle row. This Web Part enables users to customize what they see on the screen.

At this point, your Web Part page should look something like what's shown in Figure 17.53.

FIGURE 17.53   The Web Part zone controls added to the page.

The next step is to define the chrome for the Web Parts that are placed in the zones. Chrome refers to the styles such as header, links, and buttons. There are a lot of styles you can set for a given zone and its Web Parts. These include styles for when there is an error, styles for when things are inactive, and many more. These styles can be configured through numerous properties of the zone. You can also use the smart tag associated with the control to autoformat the zone. Figure 17.54 shows an example of the

FIGURE 17.54   You can use the AutoFormat dialog box to set many of the formatting properties of a zone control all at once.

AutoFormat dialog box. On the left are possible formats. On the right is a preview showing how the Web Parts in the zone look. This preview is based on actual content for the zone.

Use the AutoFormat option to set the chrome for each zone control. Set the customer links and customer statistics zones to Professional. Set the page Catalog Zone to Colorful.

Adding Web Parts to Zones   Now you're ready to add Web Parts to the zones you have defined. There are a few ways to go about this. You can create actual controls that implement the WebPart class. This method allows the most flexibility for creating Web Parts, but it also happens to be the most involved method. It also enables you to create user configuration for your Web Parts. This configuration is shown when a user edits a given Web Part. Of course, it is recommended for portal developers.

Alternatively, a quick way to create Web Parts is by defining a user control or simply by using a standard ASP.NET control. For instance, when you drag a control such as a Label onto the form, ASP.NET defines a Web Part around the given control. This makes for an easy way to create Web Parts.

For the example, you implement the latter method. You first create a Customer Links Web Part. This Web Part provides a series of links used to manage a customer. The following outlines the process for creating this web part:

1. Drag an ASP Label control inside the WebPartZone control for customer links.
2. This label is automatically turned into a WebPart control. You can see this in the markup. The <ZoneTemplate> element is added inside the <asp:WebPartZone> node. Inside this goes the Label control you added to the form.
3. Set a title for the Web Part by adding the title attribute to the Label control. This attribute is picked up by ASP and applied to the Web Part.
4. Add a few links within the confines of the <asp:Label> declaration. The final markup looks something like Listing 17.2. Here we omitted the style information that would normally go inside the Web Part zone; this omission is for the sake of clarity.

LISTING 17.2   The Customer Links Web Part

```
<asp:WebPartZone ID="WebPartZoneCustomerLinks" runat="server">
  <ZoneTemplate>
    <asp:Label title="Customer Links" ID="Label1" runat="server" Text="Label">
      <a href="FindCustomer.aspx">Find Customer</a><br />
      <a href="FindOrder.aspx">Find Order</a><br />
      <a href="CustomerDiscounts.aspx">Customer Discounts</a><br />
    </asp:Label>
  </ZoneTemplate>
</asp:WebPartZone>
```

Repeat this method for a few more Web Parts. For the example, you might create additional label-based Web Parts inside the <ZoneTemplate/> area of Customer Links. Some Web Parts might include Active Shoppers, Help, and a page Edit Mode indicator. In the Customer Statistics area you might add Web Parts for Find Orders and Top Products to round out the dashboard. You can try creating a couple of these as user controls (for more information on user controls, skip ahead to the "Working with the ASP.NET Controls" section later in this chapter). Also, try building out one or two of these Web Parts as tables nested inside a Label control. Figure 17.55 shows what your page might now look like inside the designer.

FIGURE 17.55   You can create any number of Web Parts inside a the WebPartZone control's ZoneTemplate markup section.

Enabling Users to Configure the Page   There are many options available for enabling users to customize the look and behavior of Web Parts. You can create editors for your controls that allow for full configuration on a per-control basis. You might have Web Parts that can connect (or talk to) other Web Parts. They typically require some sort of configuration. You might allow users to pick from a catalog of controls in order to determine which controls they would like to see on the page. It is also common to allow users to minimize, close, and move your controls from zone to zone. Here we look at a couple of these options.

First, let's configure our Web Part page to allow users to add Web Parts to the page as they see fit. This way users can determine which Web Parts they want to see on the page and where they want to see them. The following list defines the steps required to modify our Web Part page to allow for this level of user customization:

1. We start with a Web Part page that includes two label-based Web Parts: Customer Links and Help. The site also contains three user controls: Find Orders, Active Shoppers, and Top Products. It is these last three that we are going to turn into user-optional Web Parts. A user is able to add and remove these items from the page.

2. You use the CatalogZone Web Part to enable the management of a group (or catalog) of Web Parts. When the page was first laid out, we added this Web Part to the right-most zone. If you do not have it, add it.

3. Next, inside the CatalogZone Web Part add a DeclarativeCatalogPart. The control indicates that you declare all Web Parts that are managed in the zone. There are similar Web Parts such as PageCatalogPart, which manages all Web Parts on the page.

4. The next step is to declare the Web Parts that are managed inside the catalog by putting each user control's (or Web Part's) definition inside the DeclarativeCatalogPart section. Note you also need to add the tag, <WebPartsTemplate/>. Your markup should look like the following:

```
<asp:CatalogZone ID="CatalogZone1" runat="server"
  HeaderText="Manage Web Parts">
  <ZoneTemplate>
    <asp:DeclarativeCatalogPart ID="DeclarativeCatalogPart1"
      runat="server" Title="Select a Web Part">
      <WebPartsTemplate>
      <uc1:FindOrders ID="FindOrders1" runat="server" Title="Find Orders" />
      <uc2:ActiveShoppers ID="ActiveShoppers1" runat="server"
        Title="Active Shoppers" />
      <uc3:TopProducts ID="TopProducts1" runat="server" Title="Top Products" />
      </WebPartsTemplate>
    </asp:DeclarativeCatalogPart>
  </ZoneTemplate>

  </asp:CatalogZone>
```

5. The final step is to allow the user to enable editing to turn this catalog on. We will use a LinkButton control to do so. Add a LinkButton control to the bottom right of the page. Create an event handler for the LinkButton control's click event. Inside this event handler, you need to toggle the display state of the page between Browse (normal view) and Catalog (user Web Part selection view). The following code does just that:

```
protected void LinkButtonChangeContent_Click(object sender, EventArgs e) {
    if (LinkButtonChangeContent.Text == "Change Content") {
      WebPartManager1.DisplayMode =
        WebPartManager1.SupportedDisplayModes["Catalog"];
      LinkButtonChangeContent.Text = "Finished";
    } else {
      WebPartManager1.DisplayMode =
```

```
          WebPartManager1.SupportedDisplayModes["Browse"];
        LinkButtonChangeContent.Text = "Change Content";
    }
      }
```

The final step is to enable authentication for your site. Recall that personalization requires that the user be logged into the site. This way, the personalization information is persisted for the logged-in user. Authentication can be set up using the ASP.NET Configuration pages accessible from the Website menu in Visual Studio. From these pages you need to enable require authentication and then add yourself as a user. See "Configuring User Authentication" later in this chapter. Also, you need a page that allows you to log in to the site. Thankfully, these pages are part of the default website template and are found in the Account folder (Login.aspx). See "The Login Controls" later in this chapter for more details.

You should now be able to run the application, login, and select which of the three Web Parts you want to use. Figure 17.56 shows the page running in the browser. The user has clicked the Change Content LinkButton on the right to bring up the Manage Web Parts CatalogZone control. The user can select a Web Part from the list and indicate to which zone on the page it should be added. Notice, too, that the Active Shoppers and Find Orders Web Parts have already been added to the page by the user. Finally, the user can choose to add multiple versions of the same Web Part to the page if they like.

FIGURE 17.56   Users can use the CatalogZone editor to add Web Parts to predefined zones on the page.

Another common user customization is to allow for the moving of Web Parts between the zones and above and below one another. When the user is in the catalog mode, as in Figure 17.56, this feature is enabled by default. A user can select a Web Part and move it between zones and above and below other Web Parts. However, there are times when you want to allow users to move items between zones but require another level of trust before you let them use the catalog to add and remove Web Parts from the page. In this case, you need to provide layout editing independent of content editing.

To provide layout editing independent of content editing, you need to add another control that is explicitly for editing layout independent of content select by doing the following:

1. Add an EditorZone control to the page. Adding this control creates a zone where you can put EditorParts. It is typical for you to show this zone when your page is in edit mode. In the example, assume that you are using the zone but do not intend to display it to users.

2. Add the LayoutEditorPart control to the EditorZone you just created. This control should sit inside a <ZoneTemplate> tag. This web part allows for the page's layout to be edit-enabled.

3. Create a LinkButton control for allowing a user to turn on edit mode for the page. Label this control, Edit Layout. The design of your form should look something like that shown in Figure 17.57.

FIGURE 17.57   The LayoutEditorPart control enables users to edit the layout of the page.

4. Next you need to write some code for the LinkButton's click event. This code is similar to the code for the change content link button example. The following is an example:

```
protected void LinkButtonEditPage_Click(object sender, EventArgs e) {
  if (LinkButtonEditPage.Text == "Edit Layout") {
    WebPartManager1.DisplayMode =
      WebPartManager1.SupportedDisplayModes["Edit"];
    LinkButtonEditPage.Text = "Finish Edit";
  } else {
    WebPartManager1.DisplayMode =
      WebPartManager1.SupportedDisplayModes["Browse"];
      LinkButtonEditPage.Text = "Edit Layout";
  }
}
```

You can now run the page and view the results. When you click the Edit Layout LinkButton, the page goes into Edit mode (but not content selection). Here a user can move controls between zones, rearrange them, and toggle their close versus open state. Figure 17.58 shows this in action.

FIGURE 17.58 You can use the LayoutEditorPart control to enable users to work just with the layout of the page (and not the content displayed).

> **TIP**
>
> Web part personalization is persisted from session to session. If users (or developers) close controls, you need to give them a way to get them back. You can write some code to reset personalization for a page. You might give the user a reset link, for example. Inside the event for this link, you add code that resembles the following line:
>
> ```
> WebPartManagerMain.Personalization.ResetPersonalizationState()
> ```
>
> This removes any personalization settings and returns you to the defaults.

Working with the ASP.NET Controls

Visual Studio 2010 and the new version of ASP.NET introduce a few new controls and a number of control enhancements. We have already covered a few of the ASP.NET controls in this chapter, such as Web Parts, labels, and buttons. Our intent for the following sections is to provide broad coverage of the many other controls in ASP.NET. This includes the standard controls as well as controls for validation, login, navigation, and data. We also spend some time discussing user-defined controls.

> **NOTE**
>
> See Chapter 20, "Creating Rich Browser Applications" for coverage of the AJAX controls.

An Overview of the ASP.NET Controls

Controls render your user interface to the user's browser. ASP.NET controls are considered server controls. Server controls have a few basic tenants. They exist at design time (on the Toolbox) and you can manipulate their layouts and properties. They also have associated classes in the .NET Framework. The code in your site creates instances of these classes for manipulating a given control. In addition, all server control processing happens on the web server. That is, the code of the control executes (along with your code) and emits its HTML to be sent to the user's browser. When the user posts the page back to the server, ASP.NET rebuilds the controls and then reprocesses them to build a response back to the user.

> **NOTE**
>
> ASP.NET also supports the standard HTML controls. By default, these items are not available on the server. However, you can add the attribute runat="server" to any of these controls. This enables you to work with them in your code-behind class. In general, if you do not think you will ever need access to a control on the server, it's wise to simply use the HTML controls (without running them on the server).

The ASP.NET Control Features

The ASP.NET server controls are a set of abstract controls that render their UIs in many different forms back to a user's browser. They can emit HTML and JavaScript. They store state between requests, and some work with databases. The following list outlines some of the key features found inside the ASP.NET control model:

▶ **XHTML Compliance**—The ASP.NET controls are sent to the user's browser as standard HTML. All controls generate XHTML 1.1–compliant markup. This ensures that there are fewer surprises when your pages are being viewed in a web browser.

▶ **Browser Detection and Adaptive Rendering**—The ASP.NET controls can also adapt their markup output based on the requesting browser. Therefore, they can be both XHTML-compliant and browser-specific. This feature works by default for ASP.NET controls. This can save a lot of time because you don't have to try to code around the various browser types (see the note at the end of this section).

▶ **Event Model**—All the ASP.NET controls have the same server-side event model. You can write code to be called when a user triggers an event on the page, such as pulling down a drop-down or clicking a button.

▶ **Client Event Model**—The set of ASP.NET controls can participate in client-side events. That is, you can work to emit JavaScript as part of the control's rendering and call that JavaScript as part of the client's (browser's) event model.

▶ **State Maintenance**—ASP.NET controls (including the HTML controls) automatically maintain state between round trips to the server. For example, suppose that a user enters a value into a TextBox and posts the page to the server. If you send the response back to the user, the user's entry is still maintained inside the control. This saves you from having to code this feature into your pages when doing operations such as validation processing on the server.

▶ **Data Binding**—Many of the ASP.NET controls can be bound to data in your application. The data-binding model enables you to bind to many data sources such as a database, a business object, XML, and so on. In most scenarios, the binding requires little coding on your part.

▶ **Template-Based Layout**—Some of the ASP.NET controls provide templates to enable developers to define the control's layout. For example, you can use the ListView control to create a template that defines how the control renders when a user is editing data versus displaying it.

▶ **Skins and Style Support**—We have already described how themes and style sheets can be used to change the look of a site. Each ASP.NET control has support for both skins and CSS styles.

▶ **Data Entry**—ASP.NET controls support layout that makes data entry easier. You can, for example, define a tab order for the controls on a page; you can set the focus to a given control; you can even assign a hotkey (or access key) to a given control. All of this is done through properties on the control. The controls themselves generate JavaScript on the client to enable these features.

17

▶ **Validation**—There are validation controls built into ASP.NET. The server controls work with these validation controls and ASP.NET to provide a cohesive validation model for your pages. For example, you can group a set of validation controls and manage validation at the group level (think sections of your page).

This list represents some of the basic features of the ASP.NET control set. In addition, each control has its own set of features. You should experiment with each control to determine what works best for your situation. In the following sections, we discuss many of these controls.

> **NOTE**
>
> ASP.NET 4.0 provides additional browser rendering support. This is in direct response to the recent proliferation of browsers on mobile devices. In addition to IE, Firefox, Opera, and Safari, ASP.NET 4.0 includes browser definitions for Google Chrome, BlackBerry smartphones, and the Apple iPhone. These new capabilities also come with a new model for defining browser definitions. Therefore, expect to see even more support added to ASP.NET as more browsers with different capabilities come online.

The ASP.NET Standard Controls

There is a large set of what are called Standard controls in ASP.NET. These appear on the Toolbox in the Standard group (see Figure 17.59). Most pages you build draw heavily from this list. It includes label, text box, button, check box, radio button, calendar, and many more controls.

FIGURE 17.59   You use the Standard ASP.NET controls for most data-entry scenarios.

At design time, you drag one of these controls from the Toolbox onto the designer. You can then work with the control using the Properties dialog box. Each control has a host of properties for controlling appearance, behavior, accessibility, and more.

Refer to Figure 17.54 to see the Standard control list on the left. In the center, you can see controls for labels, text box, button, and check box. Notice that a text box has been selected. On the right is the property window for this text box. To access the events for a given control, you click the lightning-bolt icon on this property window.

There are many standard controls. Table 17.4 provides a list of a number of these, along with a brief description of its use.

TABLE 17.4   The Standard Controls

Control	Description
Button	Use the Button control when you expect a user to trigger an action on the page such as save, reset, or cancel. There are also the LinkButton and ImageButton controls. LinkButton behaves like a button but looks like a hyperlink. ImageButton is similar: It behaves like a button but you set an image to define its look.
Calendar	Use this control when you need to allow a user to see a set of dates and select one. Use the SelectionMode property to allow a user to select a day, a week, or a month.
CheckBox	Use this control when you want to allow a user to set a setting (yes or no, on or off). Again, there is an HTML equivalent if you do not need server-side processing.
DropDownList	Use this control to provide a list of options from which a user can select. You can bind the list to data. You can also respond to a user selecting an item from the list. If you have a lot of options from which a user might need to choose, consider the ListBox control. There is also the CheckBoxList control for a list of multi-select items and the RadioButtonList for a list of mutually exclusive items.
FileUpload	Use this control to enable users to push files from their local machines or networks up to your web server.
Image	Use this control when you need to populate an image on your page dynamically (using the ImageUrl property). Static images can use the HTML <img /> tag. There is also an ImageMap control that enables you to define sections of an image from which you can respond differently to user interaction.
Label	Use this control to provide text-based information to a user. You need a Label control only if you intend the text to be dynamic (set at runtime). If you have static text, you can typically just type it into the page using standard HTML formatting.
ListBox	Use this control when you want to allow a user to select one or more options from a set list. You can also data bind to this control.
Literal	You use the Literal control to write out HTML to the page. You typically use this control to build up markup dynamically in your code and add it to the page's rendering.

TABLE 17.4   Continued

Control	Description
MultiView	Use this control when you want to provide multiple views to a user based on the user's selection or the state of the system. For example, you might implement a read-only view and an edit view of the same data. Each view requires that you drag a View control onto the multiview. You then add the controls you want to display for the given view to this View control. You can get similar results with multiple Panel controls. However, the MultiView control provides additional management features for you.
Panel	Use this control as a container for other controls. It is especially useful when adding controls to a page programmatically. In this case, you can call the Panel.Controls.Add method to do so.
RadioButton	Use this control to provide a user with a group of items from which they may select only one. Use the GroupName property to group a set of radio buttons that need to work together.
Table	Use the Table control to build out tables dynamically in your code. If your tables are static, consider the HTML table control.
TextBox	Use this control to allow a user to enter text-based data on your page. The TextBox control has the property TextMode. Use this property to indicate that the user's entry is a single line (default), multiple lines, or a password.
Wizard	The Wizard control is similar to MultiView. However, it provides the additional capabilities needed for a wizard moving from step to step (or view to view) and back again.
XML	Use this control to display XML information. You can set the XML data using the DocumentSource property. You can also provide a transform file (XSLT) that defines formatting for the XML. You set the TransformSource property to your .xslt file.

Validation Controls

A set of validation controls is provided with ASP.NET. These controls enable you to indicate how user input should be validated for a page before the page is processed. In this way, you can ensure that a user has entered data in all the required fields and validate that this data meets your application's constraints.

Controls are always validated on the server and prevent an ASP page from processing if validation fails (see the page life cycle discussed previously). The controls can emit JavaScript to be run on the client, too (the EnableClientScript property is set to True by default). In this way, a user is notified of any page-level validation errors before having to submit the page to the server.

To use the validation controls, you drag them onto your form like any other control. You want to place them near the control they validate because they provide textual clues to the user as to what is wrong with the page. A standard process is to put the validation control to the right of the control it validates. You then set the ControlToValidate property of the validation control to another control on your form (the one you want to validate).

You then typically set the Text and ErrorMessage properties of the validation control. The Text property indicates the text that should be displayed by the validation control if the validation fails. The ErrorMessage property indicates the error message that should be displayed to the user inside a ValidationSummary control for the page. The ValidationSummary groups all error messages for a user in a single area.

As an example, take a look at Figure 17.60. Here you can see the validation control group in the Toolbox to the left. The page has a ValidationSummary control at the top (under Edit Customer). You can also see that both the name and the email text boxes have an associated validation control. The validation control for the email text box is selected. This is a RegularExpressionValidator control. With it you can use pattern matching to validate whether the user has entered a compliant email address. To the right, you can see this control's properties.

FIGURE 17.60   Use the ASP.NET Validation controls to ensure data is entered correctly for your forms.

Table 17.5 lists the validation controls provided in ASP.NET, along with brief descriptions of each.

TABLE 17.5   The Standard Controls

Control	Description
RequiredFieldValidator	Use this control for required fields on your page. You might combine a required field validation control with another control listed here.
RangeValidator	Use this control to validate whether a user's input is between a specified range. Use the Type property to indicate what type of range to validate, such as string, integer, double, date, or currency.
RegularExpressionValidator	Use this control to validate the pattern of the user's entry. You set the ValidationExpression property to a valid regular expression to do so. In addition, there are built-in regular expressions in Visual Studio. Clicking the ellipsis button in this property enables you to set standard regular expressions for such things as postal codes, email addresses, and phone numbers.
CompareValidator	Use this control to compare the user's input and validate based on this comparison. You can compare the input of the control being validated to a static value, another control, or a data type. Comparing to a data type allows you to ensure that the user has entered a valid value that can be converted to a given data type. Use the Type property to set this comparison.
CustomValidator	Use this control to write your own custom validation controls. You can write server-side validation and emit JavaScript to validate on the client.
ValidationSummary	Use this control to provide a summary of any validation errors raised by the page. The validation control's ErrorMessage property value ends up in the summary for each validation control that fails on the page.

The Login Controls

ASP.NET has a built-in set of login controls meant to provide a complete low-code (sometimes no-code) solution for managing and authenticating users. Figure 17.61 shows a list of all these controls in the Toolbox.

By default, the login controls use what is called ASP.NET Membership. This feature enables these controls to work with an authentication database and related features without your writing code. Membership allows for the creation of users and groups and the management of user data (including passwords). The membership services inside ASP.NET can work with a SQL Express database or Active Directory. You can also write your own custom provider that can be plugged into the model.

We look at configuring membership later in this chapter. First, let's examine the many login controls. Table 17.6 provides a brief overview of these controls.

FIGURE 17.61   You use the ASP.NET login controls to configure security for your site.

TABLE 17.6   The Login Controls

Control	Description
Login	This control provides the primary interface for challenging users for their credentials (usernames and passwords). You can format the look of the control as well as display other links and messages such as authentication errors.
	The control is set up to work with ASP.NET Membership by default. If you configure it, you do not need to write code. However, if you want to write your own code, you can use the Authenticate event to write your custom scheme.
LoginView	This control enables you to define two views of information: a view for users who are logged in to your application and a view for anonymous users. You add controls to each view to define what users see based on their current status.
PasswordRecovery	This control is used for users to recover their passwords. Typically, you configure this control to email users their passwords. However, there are additional options as well.
LoginStatus	This control shows the authentication status of the current user. Users are either logged in or not. If they are, the control enables them to log out. If they are not logged in, the control gives them the opportunity to do so.
LoginName	This control displays the username of the currently logged-in user.
CreateUserWizard	This control enables users to create their own accounts or helps in password recovery. Users can request an account (and fill in their details) with this control.
ChangePassword	This control enables users to enter their current passwords and new passwords. The control can then validate the passwords and make the change if successful.

17

Configuring User Authentication

You can create a login page (or control) by dropping the login control directly on a form. After you place it, you can begin to set the properties that define your application's security. Figure 17.62 shows an example. This page, Login.aspx, was created as part of the website template in the Account folder. Notice that the page takes advantage of a master page, too. The page does not offer much in the way of formatting within the designer; this is because it gets its formatting from a theme.

FIGURE 17.62   You can use the Login control to provide users a means to authenticate against your site.

Notice that the login control provides access to the Administer Website link. This link takes you to the Web Site Administration Tool (WSAT) for your site, where you can begin to define how authentication and authorization should work for your site.

> **NOTE**
>
> By default, user data is sent to the server from the client as plain text. Therefore, you should enable SSL and HTTPS for securing your site.

The WSAT is a web-based tool that enables you to configure your site, including security. Figure 17.63 shows the security tab for the tool. You can use the tool to define users' roles and access rules; you can also define application configuration (turn on tracing, for example) and select an administration provider. The default administration provider is configured for SQL Express (ASPNETDB.MDF). This is the place where the configuration data (such as users) for your site is stored.

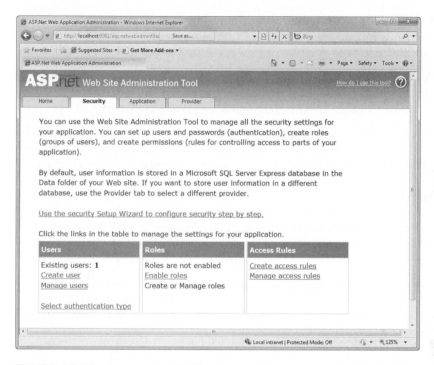

FIGURE 17.63   You use the WSAT tool to configure users and security for your site.

You can use the WSAT to change from Windows security to Internet security. The former is best when working on a LAN environment. The latter is required for most public-facing, secure sites. After you configure your security model to that of Internet, ASP.NET switches you over to using the membership database for user storage.

You can use the Security tab, shown in Figure 17.63 to configure the users, roles, and access for this database. Notice the three groups at the bottom of the screen: Users, Roles, and Access Rules. These groups provide links for managing the accounts in your system. Your login control automatically respects the information configured here. In addition, the WSAT updates your web.config file accordingly.

Site Navigation Controls

It can be easy to become lost on a lot of websites out there. If you don't provide good user navigation, chances are that users will complain (or stop visiting). ASP.NET provides a few controls to help deal with defining and controlling navigation. The controls include the following:

▶ **Menu**—You can use this control to create menus for your web page with Visual Studio. The menus support submenus and fly-out menus. You can even bind your menus to an XML data source.

▶ **SiteMapPath**—This control enables you to leave cookie crumbs as users navigate your site. That is, you can tell them where they came from and where they are. When you do, users can use this list to jump backward to a place they just were.

▶ **TreeView**—This control could always show hierarchical data. However, it can also be bound to an XML representation of your site called a site map. In this way, you can quickly define a navigation structure for your site that is updated in a single place.

Using the SiteMapPath Control

Recall that the SiteMapPath control is used to orient users in your site. You control this orientation definition through the use of a .sitemap file. You add this file to your site through the Add New Item dialog box. Inside it, you define the logical hierarchy of your site by nesting pages inside <siteMapNode> elements.

For example, if users start at a home page, the home page is your outermost node. As a user navigates into your site, you create nested nodes. Listing 17.3 shows a simple example that includes a three-tier definition: Home, Find Customer, Edit Customer. This makes a logical progression through the sample site.

LISTING 17.3   A .sitemap File

```
<siteMap xmlns="http://schemas.microsoft.com/AspNet/SiteMap-File-1.0" >
  <siteMapNode url="Default.aspx" title="Home"  description="">
    <siteMapNode url="FindCustomer.aspx" title="Find Customer"
      description="">
      <siteMapNode url="EditCustomer.aspx" title="Edit Customer"
        description="" />
    </siteMapNode>
  </siteMapNode>
</siteMap>
```

Figure 17.64 shows the results users see in their browsers. In this case, the `SiteMapPath` control was added to the master page so that it appears throughout the site. The control automatically picks up the content of the Web.sitemap file.

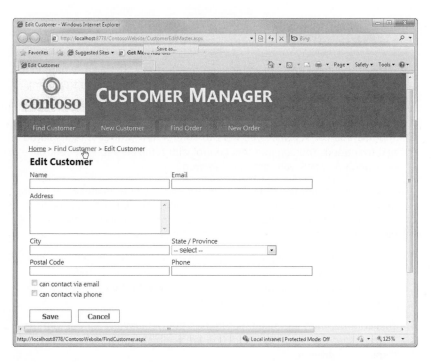

FIGURE 17.64   The SiteMapPath control uses a .sitemap file to provide navigation for users.

Data Controls

ASP.NET has a full set of controls that you can use for working with, displaying, and binding to data. These controls are meant to work with little to no additional code. Instead of writing code, you should be able to configure the controls to behave as you want. Figure 17.65 shows a list of all the data controls in the Toolbox.

Table 17.7 provides a brief overview of each of these controls.

TABLE 17.7   The Data Controls

Control	Description
AccessDataSource, EntityDataSource, LinqDataSource, ObjectDataSource, SiteMapDataSource, SqlDataSource, XmlDataSource	Several data source controls are available in ASP.NET. These sources can be configured to work with the source data and execute select, update, new, and delete methods. You use a data source control to bind to other controls (such as a GridView). The ASP.NET data source controls allow access to SQL Server data, Microsoft Access data, data contained in objects, XML data, data defined as a .sitemap file, and LINQ data.

TABLE 17.7   Continued

Control	Description
Chart	The Chart control enables you to create web pages that display data in a chart format. You can bind data to the control, display different types of charts, and allow for user interaction using AJAX. See "Chart Control" later in this section.
DataList	You use this control when you want to control how your data is displayed and formatted. You can use this control with templates to gain control over when and how your data is displayed.
DataPager	This control is new to 2010. This control allows you to manage the paging of data and the UI associated with that paging. You can use this control by itself or embed it as part of another control. This control was also discussed in Chapter 1, "A Quick Tour of Visual Studio 2010."
DetailsView	This control lets you display a single row of data (or row detail). You can display this row as an editable set of fields inside a table. The DetailsView control can be used in conjunction with the GridView control to obtain a master-detail editing structure.
FormView	This control offers the same features as the DetailsView control with the added benefit of being able to define the templates that make up the display of a given row.
GridView	This control is for binding to and working with tabular data. The control works with multiple data sources. It also allows sorting, paging, edit, add, and delete features.
ListView	This control is new in 2010. It simplifies the display of repeating data. The ListView control is driven based on user templates. In this way, you can configure how you want your UI to behave during operations such as view, edit, add, and delete. In addition, the ListView supports sorting, paging, and, of course, data binding.
QueryExtender	Allows you to define filters for data returned by from a data source.
Repeater	This control is a container for repeating data. You use the Repeater control with a template to indicate how the contents of the repeated data should be displayed. This ListView control can be a better alternative to Repeater.

NOTE

We cover ways to work with data and databases in Chapter 21, "Working with Databases." See "Data Binding with Web Controls" in that chapter.

Chart Control

New to Visual Studio 2010 and ASP.NET 4.0 is the chart control. This control enables you to define a chart from more than 25 different chart types. The chart can be bound to a data source (see Chapter 21 for details). When run, the chart control generates an image file (typically .png) and sends that image with your web page response. This provides a great addition to anyone looking to provide statistical or financial data in a graphical format over the web.

FIGURE 17.65   You use the Data controls in ASP.NET to allow users to work with data inside your website.

You can drag a Chart control from the Toolbox to your page. You can then configure the control in the designer or through markup. The designer provides a smart tag that lets you do much of the work to get the control set up (in addition to the Properties window), including defining a data source, selecting a chart type, and then configuring the data members of the chart.

Figure 17.66 shows a simple Column chart type. In this case, the chart is bound to a data source that aggregates product sales information by category. Notice that the X-axis is set to the category name while the y-axis is set to the sales figures. This information comes from columns defined in the data source.

User Controls

If you still can't find the perfect control, Visual Studio provides you with the framework to create your own controls. You can take the simple approach and define a user control. A user control works a lot like a web page. You can use the designer to lay it out. It also has a code-behind and the same event model as a web page. You can create a user control and then drop it on pages across your site.

Creating a User Control

You add a user control to your project from the Add New Items dialog box. You select the template, Web User Control (refer to Figure 17.20). User controls have the extension .ascx. You define the look of your control like you would a web page. You can use the designer to drag other form elements to the page from the Toolbox. In this way, user controls are composed of one or more existing ASP.NET controls.

FIGURE 17.66   You can use the Chart control to render data graphically.

As an example, recall the user controls discussed in the "Creating a User-Configurable UI" section. These controls could be added to a web page and used as Web Parts. Of course, you do not need to create a Web Part page to make use of a user control. You can put a user control on any ASP.NET page. Consider a control that enables a user to monitor product sales for a site similar to the one created in that section. You might define this control to allow a default set of common products as well as enable users to add their own products to the list. You can abstract this code into its own file and use it across pages.

Figure 17.67 shows an example. Here you see an .ascx user control with a SqlDataSource and GridView control. There are also controls to enable a user to type a product and add it to the monitored product list (the GridView).

Notice in the Solution Explorer the user control has a code-behind file. You can add a Page_Load event here to initialize the control. You can also add a button click event to handle what happens when the user clicks the Add button.

Adding a User Control to a Web Page

You can add a user control to a web page by dragging it from Solution Explorer onto the web form designer. Unfortunately, user controls do not have Toolbox support. However, they do have visual design support as shown in Figure 17.68. In this example, the user control, MonitorProductsUc.aspx has been added to a web form (ProductDashboard.aspx) which uses a master page (Site.master).

FIGURE 17.67   You can create a user control file to enable code re-use across the pages of your website.

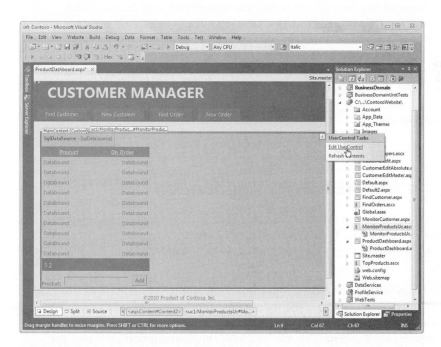

FIGURE 17.68   You can add a user control to a page by dragging it from the Solution Explorer to the web form designer.

You work with a user control added to your web page as a single control (and not with its constituent controls). The user control can expose properties like other controls. However, if you need to work with the inner workings of the user control, such as positioning individual elements, you have to open the user control file in the designer.

Of course you can add a control directly with markup, too. However, adding a control is just a little easier using the designer. When using markup, you need to first register the control with the page. This is done using the @Register tag. You want to place these tags under the @Page directive. The @Register tag should include the file for the user control (the src attribute), the name used for the user control type (tagname attribute), and the prefix used to help identify the tag (tagprefix). The following shows an example:

```
<%@ Register src="MonitorProductsUc.ascx" tagname="MonitorProductsUc"
  tagprefix="uc1" %>
```

After registering the control, you can reference the control using standard markup. The following code shows an example of the control registered above:

```
<uc1:MonitorProductsUc ID="MonitorProductsUc1" runat="server" />
```

MORE INFO

We have just scratched the surface of writing your own controls in ASP.NET. For instance, one drawback of a user control is that it is site-specific. That is, you cannot install it and use it across sites. You can, of course, copy and paste the file but then you run into versioning issues. Another limitation is that you cannot provide Toolbox and full design-time support (Properties window, smart tags, and so on) for user controls. If you want to provide both design-time support and installation, then you can create a *custom control*. Custom controls follow the same framework as the existing ASP.NET controls. You can even subclass and extend an existing control and turn it into your own custom version.

Creating an ASP.NET MVC Application

Visual Studio 2010 and .NET 4.0 introduce the ASP.NET MVC application template for building websites using a Model-View-Controller (MVC) architecture pattern. The MVC pattern itself is not something new. However, Microsoft's implementation of it for ASP.NET is new.

The pattern does away with the standard web-form model for developing pages. Instead, it creates loosely coupled objects that are highly testable. You trade the Page class, its lifecycle, the view state, and more for a loosely coupled architecture that promotes both code re-use and test-driven development. The ASP.NET MVC implementation preserves the ability to use master pages, style sheets, and standard markup for the layout of controls.

However, web developers will find writing functionality a much different experience using this application template.

Understanding ASP.NET MVC

The ASP.NET MVC application template works to de-couple your data and business logic (the model) from the display of that information (the view). It also places the code to handle interaction for the view and the model into a separate class (the controller). This separation changes the way you write web pages in ASP.NET.

With ASP.NET MVC, you can still create.aspx pages or .ascx controls to define the layout of your user interface. However, instead of writing code in the page's code-behind file, you use a controller class to manage the user processing. In addition, the code to define your domain objects and work with the database stays separate from the controller. Figure 17.69 shows an illustration of the ASP.NET MVC implementation.

FIGURE 17.69   An ASP.NET MVC application abstracts the model (data) from view (user interface markup), and the controller (code to connect the model and view).

The loosely coupled abstractions of an ASP.NET MVC implementation increase opportunities for re-use of your code and allow for test-driven development. Putting code into domain object and data abstraction layers has been a good practice for many years. In ASP.NET MVC, this is simply referred to as the model. In addition, having your user interface code in a separate class (the controller), decoupled from the intricacies of ASP.NET, makes it easier to write unit tests against that code.

The following provides additional details the three layers of ASP.NET MVC:

▶ **Model**—A model represents the code that is used for managing the data in your application. Model state is referred to as the actual data stored in a relational database (or similar). You can think of a model object in a similar way to domain objects in other architectures. As an example, you might create a Customer object that is used to represent a customer in your application. The attributes of a customer might exist inside a database. The Customer object in MVC would know how to work with a database to persist its state. It would also contain any business rules surrounding a customer. Of course, you might still implement a data access layer for your application and allow model objects to leverage that layer. You might also use the entity framework or LINQ to SQL to define your model (see Chapter 21 for more information on these items).

If you do not have (or need) domain objects you might not write a lot of code in the model. For example, if you rely on DataSet objects to work with the data in your database, you might access these DataSet objects directly from the controller and then pass them to the view. In this case, the DataSet objects themselves act like the model. In the same way, you may display a view of information that is wholly contained within the view (and does not rely on a model). In this case, you would process a request with a controller and display the results in a view without ever instantiating a model object.

▶ **View**—A view displays data to a user for their consumption and interaction. Views are the user interface components of your application (in ASP.NET, the markup). A view uses data provided by the model as its source information. This data is sent to it from the controller. For example, a controller might send the Customer data to a customer edit page in the view. That page might present the Customer data for edit using TextBox controls (among others).

▶ **Controller**—A controller is code you write to handle the user interaction and events inside an MVC application (often called input logic). Requests to your site are routed to a controller class. Your controller code knows how to handle user interaction, work with the model, and connect results to the right view. For example, when a page to edit customer details is requested, the controller works with the model to get the customer details, select the appropriate view, and provide the model data to that view. When the user hits the Save button, the Controller again takes over to move the data back into the model (and the model moves it to the database).

The Execution Model of an ASP.NET MVC Request

An application written using the ASP.NET MVC framework has a different processing model than the traditional, page-lifecycle of an ASP.NET application as discussed previously in this chapter. Just like the page-lifecycle, if you are writing ASP.NET MVC applications you need to understand how your code is processed by the framework classes inside System.Web.Mvc.

Like all web applications, the ASP.NET MVC processing starts with a user's HTTP request to a URL. The ASP.NET MVC framework maps URL requests to a controller class (instead of .aspx pages). You control this mapping through URL routing rules inside the Global.asax file. You use the Application_Start method to register your URL routing from a request to a specific controller. We walk through an example of this in an upcoming section ("Defining URL Routing to a Controller").

The controller class then processes the request, works with the model, and selects the appropriate view to display to the user. The view generates the HTML to be sent back to the user's browser for rendering. The following provides an overview of the ASP.NET MVC processing model:

1. A user requests a URL. This request is passed from ISS to the UrlRoutingModule class. This is an HTTP Module that serves as the front controller for routing requests.

2. The UrlRoutingModule parses the request and performs route selection ultimately using the MvcRouteHandler class to select one of the controller objects in your site to receive the request. You manage which of your controller objects receives the request using the Global.asax file's Application_Start method.

   Note: if no route is found, the request passes to ASP.NET. This enables you to mix both MVC and standard ASP.NET code in a single site.

3. After a controller class is identified, the MVC framework creates an instance of the controller and calls its Execute method.

4. An action method inside your controller is identified based on the request details. This action method is then called by the MVC framework. An action method is a method you write in your controller to handle the request and connect the model with the view.

5. An action method takes user input from the request (view), connects that information to the model, and then passes any response back as a specific MVC return type. The most common return type is ViewResult. It contains results to be passed to a view for display back to the user. Other return types include RedirectToRouteResult, RedirectResult, ContentResult, JsonResult, FileResult, and EmptyResult.

This processing model is much different than the standard ASP.NET model. Notice that it does not use postbacks but routes through a central controller class. If you have developed applications in ASP.NET this means you do not have the page life-cycle events or the view state. This means ASP.NET controls that rely on postbacks and view state do not work in MVC. This includes GridView, Repeater, and DataList. This tradeoff does come with a few benefits. We discuss these next.

When to Select MVC Versus Web Forms

There are many applications that should still be written as Web Form applications. ASP.NET MVC does not replace the Web Form technology. Instead, it is meant to provide an alternative for those development teams looking to have higher separation of responsibility, easier unit testing, and granular control of the HTML response.

ASP.NET MVC Advantages   There are many cases where an ASP.NET MVC application might be preferred. First, an ASP.NET MVC application works well for teams with a lot of separation of duties. If you have UI people writing view and others writing domain objects (models) then the separation of these items into their own files and layers is welcome.

Second, an ASP.NET MVC application supports test-driven development of not just your model but also your UI processing code. This comes from the UI processing code being separated from the actual display code (view). If you have ever tried to test the code associated with a traditional ASP.NET Web Form you know it is a difficult process. You need to load the page, its controls, and other related objects as part of your tests. ASP.NET MVC does not have this barrier to unit testing.

Finally, an ASP.NET MVC application has a higher degree of control over what gets sent as a response to the user. Typically you are controlling the actual HTML and Javascript that is output. However, this comes at the expense of being able to use the many ASP.NET controls and requires you to write more code than that of a traditional ASP.NET Web Form.

ASP.NET Web Form Advantages   The Web Form model is well-understood by many developers. It provides a great environment for rapidly building websites. An ASP.NET Web Form application can often seem more familiar to web developers that are used to event-driven programming. In addition, it takes advantage of the HTTP state model, server-side page and control events, and view state to preserve state between requests. Web Form pages often require less UI markup and fewer lines of code in your code-behind. Lastly, a Web Form application can be easier to follow than the loosely coupled MVC pattern.

> **NOTE**
>
> Traditional web forms and ASP.NET MVC can co-exist; neither excludes the other. If you build on ASP.NET MVC there still might be many times you create a standard ASP.NET page for certain scenarios such as simple data binding and display.

Creating an MVC Project

You create an ASP.NET MVC application using the Visual Studio template, ASP.NET MVC 2 Web Application. This is an application template and not a website template. Therefore, it has its own project file and is configured slightly differently.

You can access this template from the Add New Project dialog box (right-click your solution and Select Add, New Project or select the menu option File, New, Project). Figure 17.70 shows an example of creating a site based on this template. Notice this experience is not unlike creating other projects in Visual Studio.

FIGURE 17.70   You create an ASP.NET MVC project using the related project template.

Visual Studio gives you the option to create a related unit test project for your MVC site. Recall that one of the advantages of ASP.NET MVC is that you can more easily unit test your web code. Therefore, we suggest you select this option and allow Visual Studio to create a test project that references your web application. Figure 17.71 shows an example of the Create Unit Test Project that opens when you create a new ASP.NET MVC application. We are not going to re-cover unit testing in this chapter. For more information, refer to Chapter 9, "Testing Code."

FIGURE 17.71   Visual Studio gives you the option to create a unit test project that works with your ASP.NET MVC web application.

The ASP.NET MVC template organizes your code into a different structure than that of a standard ASP.NET website. This structure is based on a folder for models, views, and controllers. Figure 17.72 shows an example inside the Solution Explorer:

The folder structure of an ASP.NET MVC application tries to separate the various layers of your application into their own areas. For example, views are broken out into the Views folder. Within that folder, each area of functionality for your site has its own folder. The following provides more details of the folders inside an ASP.NET MVC site:

▶ **Models**—Use the Models folder for class files that define your business logic and work with your database. For example, you might write a Customer.cs class and store it here. You might also choose to keep your model in a separate .dll file and reference it from your website.

▶ **Views**—Use the Views folder for files related to your user interface. This includes web pages, user controls, and master pages. You add these files using the Add View dialog box (see "Creating a View" later in this chapter). Notice that there are multiple folders in the Views directory. Each controller should have a corresponding view folder. For example, if you create a CustomerController.cs class you would create a Views\Customer folder and place your views inside it. Notice, too, the Shared folder. This is for views shared across controllers such as Site.Master.

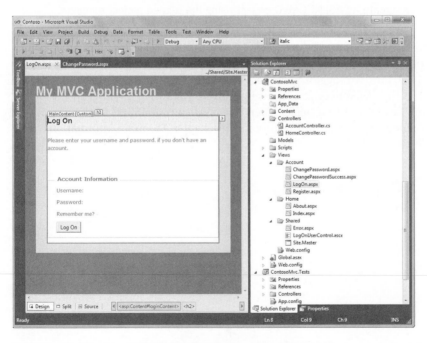

FIGURE 17.72   The ASP.NET MVC application template structures your site into different folders for the models, views, and controllers.

▶ **Controllers**—Use this folder for all controller classes in your application. Controller classes contain action code that connects user actions to the model and selects the appropriate response (typically a view). The ASP.NET MVC framework requires you append the word, Controller to the end of each controller class such as CustomerController.cs.

▶ **Scripts**—Use this folder to house your script files. By default, the ASP.NET MVC project includes AJAX foundation scripts and jQuery files in this folder.

▶ **Content**—Use this folder to house static site content for your site such as style sheets and images.

Creating Functionality Using ASP.NET MVC

It can seem like there are a lot of moving parts and a lot of code required to build applications with ASP.NET MVC. However, Visual Studio provides a lot of assistance for defining models, controllers, and views. This section walks through an example of using the ASP.NET MVC tools to create functionality that enables a user to view customers in a list, select a customer, and edit the customer's details.

Creating a Model

Recall that a model is the code used to interact with the data in your application. If you work with a database, this code typically returns lists of data and single records. It also lets users act on that data (add, update, and delete). If you already have a set of classes for working with your database and expressing your business logic you can use them for your model. If you don't have these classes you need to create them.

In the customer example, suppose you have a database that contains a Customers table (in this case we leverage the Northwind database for simplicity). You can write a custom class to express the properties and validation rules of a Customer object. You would also need to write functionality to get a list of customers, read a single customer, and update a customer in the database.

Alternatively, you can leverage the entity framework to create your model. This saves you from writing the model from scratch. The entity framework generates a class that can be mapped between a physical database and an object model. In this example, we use the entity framework (see Chapter 21 for more details).

To start, you right-click the Models folder inside of the Solution Explorer and choose Add New Item. From the Add New Item dialog box select the Data node on the left and the ADO.NET Entity Data Model item template. If your model contains many entities you might simply name it Northwind. In this case, we named it Customer.edmx. Figure 17.73 shows an example.

Adding the ADO.NET Entity Data Model item template launches the Entity Data Model Wizard. This wizard enables you to define a connection to a database and select which tables to include in your model. Figure 17.74 shows an example. Notice here the Customers table is selected. The namespace, Models, is used for the generated code.

17

FIGURE 17.73   You can define your Models using the entity framework.

FIGURE 17.74   You select the table(s) you want to include in your entity data model.

The actual model is shown in Figure 17.75 using the Entity Framework designer. The next step is to define a controller for working with your model.

FIGURE 17.75   Your data model class is stored in the Models folder.

Creating a Controller

Visual Studio provides an item template for creating a controller. You can access this template from the Add New Item dialog box. You can also right-click the Controllers folder in Solution Explorer and choose Add, Controller to bring up the Add Controller dialog box as shown in Figure 17.76.

FIGURE 17.76   You add a new controller to an ASP.NET MVC project using the Add Controller dialog box.

Here, you first specify a name for your controller using the naming standard, [Feature]Controller (in this example, CustomerController). Of course this serves as your class name. Notice that the dialog box provides the option to generate method stubs for the standard scenarios: Create, Update, and get Details. Selecting this option generates code that provides the right signatures to enable these scenarios. This can be a big help if you have these specific scenarios. You then need to add your code to work with the model inside the generated methods.

Remember, your controller classes can be unit tested. Again, this is one of the core benefits of ASP.NET MVC. If you are following test-driven development, you write your tests as you write your controller. We do not cover unit testing here, but you can refer to Chapter 9 for details.

The next step is to write some code to connect the CustomerController class and the Customer model. Here you add a variable declaration at the top of the controller that connects the model. This declaration creates an instance of the model. In our example, this is the northwndEntities1 model as shown in the following code:

```
//connect to model (northwind)
namespace ContosoMvc.Controllers
{
  public class CustomerController : Controller
  {
    private ContosoMvc.Models.northwndEntities1 _nwdEntities =
      new ContosoMvc.Models.northwndEntities1();
...
```

The next step is to write code that returns a list of customers to be displayed by a view. The ASP.NET MVC framework uses the controller's Index method to return a list of data from the model. The ASP.NET MVC framework uses the base class, ActionResult as the return type for most methods. An ActionResult tells the framework to perform an action. One such action is ViewResult. This is simply converting a model to a view. Therefore, the following code returns a ViewResult by calling Controller.View and passing in model data (a list of customers):

```
public ActionResult Index()
{
  //get all customers
  return View(_nwdEntities.Customers.ToList());
}
```

Next, we want users to be able to add a new customer to the database. This means that a user is presented with a blank view (more on this in a moment). They then should be able to enter customer details and send those details back to the controller. The controller then passes the customer to the model for an update to the database. Finally, the controller redisplays the customer list.

When addition records to the model, the ASP.NET MVC pattern expects the Create method. There are two versions of this method in the controller. The first takes not parameters and is used to enable a blank view of the data to be returned for saving. This method looks as follows:

```
public ActionResult Create()
{
  return View();
}
```

The second method handles the data posted by the user. In this case, the Create method expects a Customer object. It then calls the model to add the customer, save the changes, and return processing back to the list page (Index). The following code shows this method:

```
[AcceptVerbs(HttpVerbs.Post)]
public ActionResult Create(Customer customer)
{
  try
  {
    //insert customer
    _nwdEntities.AddToCustomers(customer);
    _nwdEntities.SaveChanges();

    //redirect back to the customer list page
    return RedirectToAction("Index");
  }
  catch
  {
    return View();
  }
}
```

Notice the attribute on the method listed above. This attribute, AcceptVerbs, indicates that this version of the Create method should be called as part of an HTTP POST.

The ability to edit a Customer is the final item from the example that you need to add to the Controller. The ASP.NET MVC framework expects the Edit method to be used for this purpose. Again, there are two versions of this method. The first enables a user to view a single customer's details in edit mode. It must get those details from the model and pass them to the appropriate view.

The following code shows an example:

```
public ActionResult Edit(string id)
{
  //select customer by id
  Customer cust = (from c in _nwdEntities.Customers
                     where c.CustomerID == id
```

17

```
                          select c).First();
    return View(cust);
}
```

Notice that the ASP.NET MVC framework uses the parameter name, id, by default to pass the id of the record to your method. This parameter was set up by the Index.aspx page (a view). If you want to change it, you can change it from the view. The following markup shows an example of how this is set up inside the Index.aspx page (we discuss views later):

```
<% foreach (var item in Model) { %>
  <tr>
    <td>
      <%= Html.ActionLink("Edit", "Edit", new { id=item.CustomerID }) %> |
      <%= Html.ActionLink("Details", "Details", new { id=item.CustomerID })%>
    </td>
...
```

Notice also that the code inside the Edit(string id) method uses LINQ to find the given customer inside the entities object. It then passes a Customer instance to a ViewResult and returns that from the method.

Next, you need a version of the Edit method that enables a user to post their changes for saving back to the database. These changes come back to the controller as a Customer instance. You then connect to your model for doing the update. The following code provides an Entity Framework example of doing so:

```
[AcceptVerbs(HttpVerbs.Post)]
public ActionResult Edit(string id, Customer customer)
{
  //get customer object that needs updating
  Customer custToChange = (from c in _nwdEntities.Customers
                           where c.CustomerID == id
                           select c).First();

  //update values
  custToChange.Address = customer.Address;
  custToChange.City = customer.City;
  custToChange.CompanyName = customer.CompanyName;
  custToChange.ContactName = customer.ContactName;
  custToChange.ContactTitle = customer.ContactTitle;
  custToChange.Country = customer.Country;
  custToChange.Fax = customer.Fax;
  custToChange.Phone = customer.Phone;
  custToChange.PostalCode = customer.PostalCode;
  custToChange.Region = customer.Region;

  //save changes
```

```
_nwdEntities.SaveChanges();

return RedirectToAction("Index");
}
```

At this point, you should have a model for working with customer data. In addition, you should have controller methods for showing customers in a list (Index), adding a new customer (Create), and updating an existing customer (Edit). The next step is to define views for each scenario.

Creating a View

You have two primary options for creating views. First, you can create a view without much assistance from Visual Studio. You do so by right-clicking the Views folder (or a sub-folder) and choosing Add, New Item. You can then select the view template and begin hand-editing your view.

The more common option for users of the ASP.NET MVC framework is to have Visual Studio generate a strongly typed view to one of your controller methods. This method saves you a lot of time in writing markup.

The first view in the example is to show customer data in a list. This view resides in the Views\Customer subfolder. You can right-click this folder and choose Add, View. You can also right-click the Index method inside the CustomerController.cs class and choose Add View (this is a shortcut as it fills out parameters of the Add View dialog box). In either case, the Add View dialog box is launched. Figure 17.77 shows an example.

FIGURE 17.77   You use the Add View dialog box to generate your view markup.

The Add View dialog box is used to set values parameters for generating view markup based on your model and controller. The View name is typically based on the user action.

Index.aspx should be the name for pages that show data in a list (and enable a user to select an item by its index). You can create a strongly typed view to ensure your view matches a model item. Selecting this option enables you to set a data class. In the example, this data class is Customer.

The next option, View content, enables you to indicate the type of view you want Visual Studio to generate. Your options include Create, Details, Edit, Empty, and List. In this case, we are displaying customers in a list. Therefore, select this option.

Finally, notice that the Add New dialog box enables you to select a master page. If you do, you can also indicate the content area to which you want to have your view added.

The markup that the Add View dialog box generates in this case is a HTML table that uses inline code (<% %>) to write out the details of the model to the browser.

You repeat this process to create views for Edit.aspx and Create.aspx. The following shows part of the Edit.aspx view. Note that many of the fields were omitted as their code structure is repetitive and to make the sample shorter:

```
<%@ Page Title="" Language="C#" MasterPageFile="~/Views/Shared/Site.Master"
  Inherits="System.Web.Mvc.ViewPage<ContosoMvc.Models.Customer>" %>

<asp:Content ID="Content1" ContentPlaceHolderID="TitleContent" runat="server">
  Edit
</asp:Content>

<asp:Content ID="Content2" ContentPlaceHolderID="MainContent" runat="server">
  <h2>Edit</h2>

  <%= Html.ValidationSummary(
    "Edit was unsuccessful. Please correct the errors and try again.") %>

    <% using (Html.BeginForm()) {%>

      <fieldset>
        <legend>Fields</legend>
        <p>
          <label for="CustomerID">CustomerID:</label>
          <%= Html.Hidden("CustomerID", Model.CustomerID) %>
          <label><%= Model.CustomerID %></label>
        </p>
        <p>
          <label for="CompanyName">CompanyName:</label>
          <%= Html.TextBox("CompanyName", Model.CompanyName) %>
          <%= Html.ValidationMessage("CompanyName", "*") %>
        </p>
        <p>
          <label for="ContactName">ContactName:</label>
```

```
                <%= Html.TextBox("ContactName", Model.ContactName) %>
                <%= Html.ValidationMessage("ContactName", "*") %>
            </p>
...ADDITIONAL FIELDS OMMITTED ...
            <p>
                <input type="submit" value="Save" />
            </p>
        </fieldset>

    <% } %>

    <div>
        <%=Html.ActionLink("Back to List", "Index") %>
    </div>

</asp:Content>
```

Defining URL Routing to a Controller

Before you can use your page, you must define a route to the page. You define these URL routing rules inside the Global.asax file. You use the Application_Start method to register your URL routing from a request to a specific controller. By default, the Application_Start method calls RegisterRoutes. This is where you add your specific routes from a requested URL to one of your controllers.

As an example, suppose you want the default page of your site to pass to the customer controller. The customer controller then processes the Index method (and thus display the Index.aspx page). To add this route you would call the MapRoute method of the RouteCollection object. You would pass it a route that includes the controller name (Customer) and the action method you want to be invoked (Index). The following shows an example of such a Global.asax file:

```
namespace ContosoMvc {
  public class MvcApplication : System.Web.HttpApplication {
    public static void RegisterRoutes(RouteCollection routes) {
      routes.IgnoreRoute("{resource}.axd/{*pathInfo}");

      routes.MapRoute(
        "Default",
        "{controller}/{action}/{id}",
        new { controller = "Customer", action = "Index", id = "" }
      );

    }

    protected void Application_Start() {
      RegisterRoutes(RouteTable.Routes);
```

17

```
        }
    }
}
```

Running Your MVC Application

The final step is to run your application. When a user requests a page, the request is processed by the routing engine. In this case, this passes control to your CustomerController class and the Index method is called. Figure 17.78 shows the results.

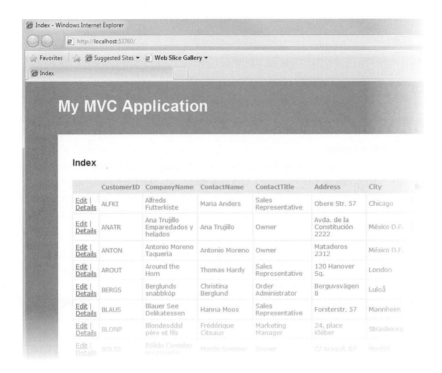

FIGURE 17.78   The ASP.NET MVC Application running in a browser.

Notice the Edit and Details links on the page. Clicking the edit link sends a request to your site in the following URL format:

```
http://localhost:53760/Customer/Edit/ALFKI
```

This URL is sent to the Customer controller. The Edit indicates that the Edit method should be called. The value after the edit is the customer id parameter sent to this method. Given that this request is an HTTP GET, the Edit method that does not have the AcceptVerbs(HttpVerbs.Post) attribute is called. This method returns an Edit.aspx view to the user. When the user clicks Save on that page, he sends a POST to the Controller and thus picks up the other Edit method that saves data to the model.

> **NOTE**
>
> You can walk through this sample by downloading the code from the website for the book.

Summary

In this chapter, we described how to create a web application and build web forms. In addition, we looked at how to leverage the features of ASP.NET to create a consistent (sometimes configurable) user interface. We also looked at the many controls in ASP.NET. Finally, we covered building web applications using the ASP.NET MVC template. Some key points in this chapter include the following:

▶ You can create a website using a local built-in server. You can also create your site on a remote server using HTTP (and IIS) or FTP.

▶ The website project property pages enable you to set what happens when you start your application from Visual Studio (among other things).

▶ You can create themes to switch the look and feel of your site without writing code or recompiling. The themes contain style sheets, images, and skin files.

▶ Web parts enable you to define a user-configurable user interface. You lay out this interface with zones and place Web Parts inside these zones.

▶ ASP.NET ships with login controls, Membership provider, and WSAT to help you manage the authentication of users on your site.

▶ Data controls inside ASP.NET make data binding, editing, and updating easier (often requiring no code). The new Chart control enables you to create graphical representations of data.

▶ You can create a user control to abstract re-usable code into its own file and leverage it across pages. A custom control, while more difficult to create, can provide installation and a better design-time experience for developers.

▶ You can use the ASP.NET MVC template to create a website that is easier to unit test, provides for separation of duties, and increases possibilities for code reuse.

17

Building Windows Forms Applications

One of the core goals for Visual Studio is enabling rapid Windows Forms construction. Using the Windows Forms Designer, the Controls Toolbox, and the various common controls provided by the .NET Framework, this chapter serves as your guide to the drag-and-drop creation of rich form-based applications. Specifically, we look at how best to leverage the built-in capabilities of the Forms Designer and the Visual Studio project system to quickly build a baseline form from scratch.

We don't worry about the code behind the form at this point; instead, the focus is on the user interface and Visual Studio's inherent Rapid Application Development (or RAD) capabilities with the Windows Forms Designer. In other words, we focus on the design-time capabilities of the IDE as opposed to the runtime capabilities of the form and control classes.

The Basics of Form Design

Designing the appropriate user interface for a Windows application is still part art and part science. In the Windows Forms world, a user interface is a collection of images, controls, and window elements that all work in synergy. Users absorb information through the UI and also use it as the primary vehicle for interacting with the application.

The task in front of any developer when creating a user interface is primarily one of balance: balancing simplicity of design with the features that the application is required to implement. Also thrown in the mix is the concept of standards, both formal and experiential.

Considering the End User

You can't start the design process unless you understand how the application will be used and who its intended audience is. Even applications that surface similar feature sets might need to provide significantly different user experiences. An application designed to store medical information might have the same data points and functions but would likely have a different persona if it was designed for the ordinary consumer as opposed to a physician or registered nurse.

Use cases and actual usability labs are both great tools for understanding user expectations, and they provide great data points for preserving that function versus simplicity of design balance.

Location and Culture

Location and culture figure into the equation as well. The typical form application used in the United States caters to this culture's expectations by anticipating left-to-right, top-to-bottom reading habits. In this environment, the most important elements of the UI are typically placed in the most prominent position: top and left in the form. Other cultures require this strategy to change based on right-to-left and even bottom-to-top reading traits.

Most controls in Visual Studio 2010 directly support right-to-left languages through a RightToLeft property. By setting this property to an appropriate RightToLeft enum value, you can indicate whether the control's text should appear left to right or right to left, or should be based on the setting carried on the parent control. Even the Form class supports this property.

Beyond the RightToLeft property, certain controls also expose a RightToLeftLayout property. Setting this Boolean property actually affects the overall layout within the control. As an example, setting RightToLeftLayout to True for a Form instance causes the form to mirror its content.

TIP

Search for "Best Practices for Developing World-Ready Applications" in MSDN for more detailed information on how to design an application for an international audience.

In addition, simple things such as the space allocated for a given control are affected by language targets. A string presented in U.S. English might require drastically more space when translated into Farsi. Again, many controls support properties designed to overcome this design issue; setting the AutoSize property on a control to True automatically extends the client area of the control based on its contained text.

Understanding the Role of UI Standards

Applications must also strive to adhere to any relevant standards associated with their look and feel. Some standards are documented for you by the platform "owner." Microsoft, for example, has a set of UI design guidelines documented within MSDN. The book Microsoft Windows User Experience, published by Microsoft Press, is included in its entirety within MSDN. By tackling topics such as "Data-Centered Design," "Input Basics," and "Design of Graphic Images," this book provides a structured baseline of UI design collateral for Windows application developers.

Design guidelines and UI standards are often specific to a given platform. The current look and feel expected from a Windows application trace primarily back to the "new" design that debuted with Windows 95. Windows XP further refined those expectations. Now, Windows Vista—the next-generation operating system from Microsoft—features an entirely new set of user experience guidelines.

Visual Studio 2010 surfaces some of these design guidelines and standards to make it easy to develop conforming interfaces. For instance, default button heights match the recommended standard, and Visual Studio assists developers with standard control positioning relative to neighboring controls by displaying snaplines as you move controls on the form surface. We cover this topic more fully later in this chapter.

De Facto Standards

Sometimes the influence of a particular application or suite of applications is felt heavily in the UI design realm. One example here is Microsoft Outlook. There are various applications now in the wild that mimic, for instance, the structure and layout of Microsoft Outlook even though they are not, per se, email applications. The Microsoft Outlook designers struck a vein of usability when they designed its primary form, and now other companies and developers have leveraged those themes in their own applications. A similar comment can be made about the visual appearance of the "Ribbon" toolbar made popular with Microsoft Office 2007.

Although there are limits, Visual Studio enables developers to achieve the same high-fidelity UIs used in Microsoft Office and other popular applications. In fact, if you look at the official Windows Forms website, you see demo applications written with Visual Studio showcasing how you can develop replicas of the Microsoft Outlook, Quicken, or even Microsoft Money facades (visit the "Downloads" page at http://www.windowsclient.net.

Planning the User Interface

Before you embark on the design process in Visual Studio, it is probably a decent idea to first draft a mock-up of the form's general landscape. This can be a simple pen and paper sketch; what we are looking for is a simple, rough blueprint for the application.

As a sample scenario, consider a Windows Forms application written for Contoso customer service representatives. The application needs to expose a hierarchical list of orders placed with Contoso, and it should enable the reps to search on orders and edit data.

Preliminary Design

A few basic components have been established as de facto standards for a Windows form: Menus, toolbars, and status bars are all standard fare and can certainly be leveraged within this fictional order application.

Beyond those staples, you know that you need to list orders on the screen and also provide for a region that shows order details. By borrowing liberally from an existing layout theme a la Microsoft Outlook, you might arrive at a tentative form layout plan like the one shown in Figure 18.1.

FIGURE 18.1   An initial layout plan.

It is important to pay some attention to the concept of resizing: How do the form's constituent controls respond relative to one another when a user resizes the form? What if a control element is resized because of a language change or a change in the underlying data? By fleshing out some of the resizing design intent now, you can save a mountain of work later. The prototype sketch in Figure 18.1 includes some simple text to remind you how to accommodate the different form regions during resizing.

Creating a Form

Although there are many different ways of approaching form design, the starting point for all of them within Visual Studio is the Windows Application project template. From the New Project dialog box, select this template, give the project an appropriate name, and click OK (see Figure 18.2).

FIGURE 18.2   Creating a new WindowsForms project.

The Windows Forms Application Project Type

Windows Forms Application projects consist of a default form class and, in the case of C#, a default static Program class. After creating the project, you are immediately presented with a blank, default form opened in the Windows Forms Designer. For a refresher on the basic capabilities and components of the Windows Forms Designer, reference Chapter 6, "Introducing the Editors and Designers."

Setting the Startup Form

Although the default project creates only a single form, you can, of course, add multiple forms at any time. This then raises the question of how to indicate at design time which form you initially want displayed at runtime (if any). There are two methods:

▶ For Visual Basic projects, the startup form is set using the Project Properties dialog box. The Startup Object drop-down in this dialog box contains a list of all valid form objects. You simply select the form you want launched on startup, and you're all set.

▶ For Visual C# projects, a slightly more complex approach is needed. The notion of a C# startup object is simply any class that implements a Main() method. Within the body of the Main method, you need to place a line of code that passes in a form instance to the Application.Run method, like this: Application.Run(new OrderForm()). Assuming that you have a class that implements Main and code that calls Application.Run in that Main method, you can then select the specific startup object via the Project Properties dialog box. The Program class, which is created for you during the project creation process, already implements the Main method, and by default runs the default form (Form1) on startup.

Inheriting Another Form's Appearance

If your form looks similar to another form that you have already developed, you have the option of visually inheriting that other form's appearance. Visual Studio provides an Inherited Form project item template to help you along this path.

To create a form that visually inherits another, select Project, Add New Item. In the Add New Item dialog box, select the Inherited Form item type (located under Visual C# Items, under the Windows Forms category). The Inheritance Picker dialog box then lists the available forms within the current project that you can inherit from. Note that you also have the option of manually browsing to an existing assembly if you want to inherit from a form that doesn't appear in the list. After you select the base form, Visual Studio creates the new form class; its code already reflects the base class derivation.

Form Properties and Events

A form is like any other control: You can use the Properties window in the IDE to control its various properties. Although we don't touch on all of them here, you should consider a few key properties as you begin your form design process.

Startup Location

You use the form's StartPosition property to place the form's window on the screen when it is first displayed. This property accepts a FormStartPosition enumeration value; the possible settings are documented in Table 18.1.

TABLE 18.1   FormStartPosition Enumeration Values

Value	Description
CenterParent	Centers the form within its parent form
CenterScreen	Centers the form within the current display screen.
Manual	The form positions itself according to the Form.Location property value.
WindowsDefaultBounds	Positions the form at the Windows default location; the forms bounds are determined by the Windows default as well.

TABLE 18.1   Continued

Value	Description
WindowsDefaultLocation	Positions the form at the Windows default location; the form's size is determined by the `Form.Size` property (this is the default setting).

Appearance

Given our discussion on the priority of UI design, it should come as no surprise that the appearance of the form is an important part of the overall application's user experience. For the most part, the default appearance property values are sufficient for the typical application. You should set the ForeColor and BackColor properties according to the color scheme identified for your application. Note that when you add controls to the form, most of them have their own individual ForeColor values set to mimic that of the form.

Some properties enable you to implement a more extravagant user interface. The Opacity property enables you to implement transparent or semitransparent forms. This capability might be useful for situations in which users want to see a portion of the screen that actually sits behind the form's window. In addition to the Opacity property, you use the Form.BackgroundImage property to set an image as the form's background. This property is best used to display subtle color gradients or graphics not possible with just the BackColor property.

Keeping in mind our goal of rapidly crafting the form, most of the activities within the designer described in this chapter consist of tweaking the form's properties and adding controls from the Toolbox to the form.

Form Events

Forms inherit the same event-driven architecture as other controls do. Certain public events defined on the Form class are useful as injection points across the continuum of a form's life.

Figure 18.3 shows the various stages (and corresponding events) from form inception to close. To react to a form event, you first need to create an event handler.

Creating an Event Handler   Visual Studio's Properties window provides a speedy mechanism for defining an event handler. First, select the form of interest. Then click on the Events button in the Properties window's toolbar. The window now shows a list of every event defined on the form. Double-clicking on the event creates a blank event handler routine and opens it in the code editor for you. The event handler has the correct arguments list and follows established standards for event handler naming (typically, object_eventname).

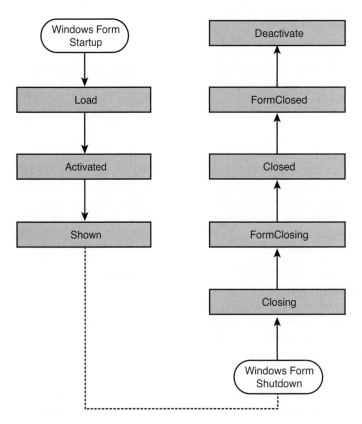

FIGURE 18.3   The events in the life of a Windows form.

The form needs to be opened in the IDE before the events can be accessed in the properties window. If the form is selected in the solution explorer, but not opened in the IDE, you can still edit the form properties but you won't be able to access the events in this fashion.

Figure 18.4 depicts the form events within the Properties window.

With the form in place, you can start placing controls onto its surface.

Adding Controls and Components

When you are building a form-based application, the user interface design really involves three separate tools within Visual Studio: the Forms Designer tool, which provides the canvas for the form; the Toolbox, which contains the controls to be placed onto the canvas; and the property browser, which is used to affect the form and its child controls, appearance, and behavior. This triad of IDE tools provides the key to rapid form construction with Visual Studio, especially as it relates to building a form's content.

FIGURE 18.4   Accessing Form events in the Properties window.

The term control technically refers to any .NET object that implements the Controlclass. In practice, we use the term to refer to the visual controls hosted by a form. This is in contrast to a component, which has many of the same characteristics of a control but doesn't expose a visual interface. A button is an example of a control; a timer is an example of a component.

Controls and components alike live in the Toolbox window (see additional coverage of the Toolbox in Chapter 6). Adding either a control or a component to a form is as easy as dragging its likeness from the Toolbox and dropping it onto the form's surface.

After you place a control on a form, the Windows Forms Designer paints the control onto the form to give you a WYSIWYG view of how the form will look at runtime. As we noted in Chapter 6, components are handled in a slightly different fashion. The Forms Designer has a special region called the component tray; any components placed onto the form are represented here. This enables you to interact in a point-and-click fashion with the component as you would with a control but doesn't place a representation onto the form itself because a component has no visual aspect to it.

Figure 18.5 highlights the component tray area of the Windows Forms Designer.

18

FIGURE 18.5   The component tray.

The Toolbox is customizable: You can add or remove controls from the Toolbox within any of the Toolbox tabs. Right-click anywhere in the interior of the Toolbox window and select Choose Items to launch the Choose Toolbox Items dialog box; from here, you can select or deselect the Toolbox control population. If a control doesn't show up in the .NET Framework Components tab or the COM Components tab of the dialog box, you can browse to the control's assembly and add it directly.

Control Layout and Positioning

When a few controls are on a form, the Windows Forms Designer is able to help automate some of the more common layout tasks, such as aligning a group of controls vertically to one another. We again refer you to Chapter 6 to see how you can leverage these productivity tools. But these layout functions, although nice from a design perspective, do nothing for you at runtime.

As previously noted, a control's runtime behavior within its parent form is an important area that needs attention if you are to implement your form according to your design intent. That is, you not only want controls to look a certain way, but also want them to act a certain way when the form is resized.

The simplest way to underscore the issue presented during a form resize is to look at a few figures. Figure 18.6 shows the simplest of forms: a label, a text box, and OK and Cancel buttons. The controls on the form have been carefully placed to maintain equal spacing;

the controls are nicely aligned in the vertical and horizontal planes; and, in short, this form looks just like the developer intended it to look.

FIGURE 18.6   Controls aligned on a form.

But then a user becomes involved. Figure 18.7 shows the results of resizing the form horizontally and vertically.

FIGURE 18.7   Form resize effects on design.

This appearance is clearly not what was intended; the nice clean design of the form has failed to keep up with the form's size. Perhaps the user resized the form in an attempt to get more room to type in the text box. Or perhaps the user tiled this application's window with other applications, causing its size to change. Whatever the reason, it is clear that further intervention by the developer is needed to keep the design "valid," regardless of the size of the form.

Just by viewing the before and after figures, you can decide on a strategy and answer the question "What should happen when a user resizes the form?" Figure 18.8 is a snapshot of the ideal; the text box has "kept pace" with the resize by horizontally extending or shrinking its width. The command buttons have kept their alignment with one another and with the text box, but they have not altered their overall dimensions. Plus, the label has stayed in its original location.

FIGURE 18.8   Reacting to a form resize.

Every form object has a resize event that fires whenever the form boundary size changes (most commonly as the result of a user dragging the form's border to increase or decrease the size of the form). Because every control has positioning properties such as Top, Left, Height, and Width, you could implement a brute-force approach to achieving the form shown in Figure 18.8. By writing several lines of code for each control, you can manually move or redimension the controls in response to the form size and the position of the other controls. But this approach is tedious at best and results in brittle code that has to be touched every time the layout and placement of controls are tweaked.

Thankfully, the Visual Studio Windows Forms Designer, in conjunction with some standard control properties, enables you to take all the common resize optimizations into account during the layout of the form. By anchoring and docking your controls, you can dictate their position relative to one another and to their position within the borders of the form.

Anchoring

Anchoring, as its name implies, is the concept of forcing a control's left, top, right, or bottom border to maintain a static, anchored position within the borders of the form. For instance, anchoring a label control to the top and left of a form (this is the default) causes the label to maintain its exact position regardless of how the form is resized. Each control's Anchor property can be set to any combination of Top, Left, Bottom, and Right. The control's property browser provides a convenient property editor widget, shown in Figure 18.9, which graphically indicates the sides of the control that are anchored.

Anchoring opposite sides of a control has an interesting effect. Because each side must maintain its position relative to the sides of the form, the control itself stretches either vertically or horizontally depending on whether the Top and Bottom or Right and Left anchors have been set. In fact, this is the exact behavior you want with the text box: You want its width and height to adjust whenever the form is resized. By anchoring all sides of the control, you get the behavior shown with the TextBox control in Figure 18.8; the control has automatically adjusted its dimensions (by stretching both horizontally and vertically) with no code required from the developer.

FIGURE 18.9   Setting the Anchor property.

By default, controls are typically anchored on their top and left sides. You might be wondering what happens if no anchors are specified at all. In that case, the control maintains its exact position regardless of form resize actions. This is, in effect, the same behavior as top and left anchors would have because forms have their top left-most points as their "origin."

Anchoring also solves the positioning problem with the OK and Cancel buttons. If you change their Anchor properties to Bottom, Right, they anchor themselves to the bottom right of the form, which is consistent with their recommended placement on a form. Because you aren't anchoring opposing sides of the control, you aren't forcing the buttons to resize; they are merely repositioned to keep station with the right and bottom edge of the form. Contrast this with the anchoring performed for the text box: Because you anchored all sides, you are not only keeping a uniform border between the edge of the text box and the form, but also causing the text box to stretch itself in both dimensions.

Docking

For the simple form in Figure 18.8, you can implement most of your layout logic using the Anchor property. But if you refer to the overall plan for the CSR screen (see Figure 18.1), you can see that you have some positioning needs that would be cumbersome to solve using anchors. For instance, the data entry region of the form should automatically

18

expand vertically and horizontally to fill any space left between the list of requests, the status bar, and the command bar. This is where the concept of docking comes to the rescue. Docking is used either to stick a control to a neighboring control's edge or the form's edge, or to force a control to fill all the available space not taken by other controls.

As with the Anchor property, the property browser provides a graphical tool to set a control's Dock property (shown in Figure 18.10).

FIGURE 18.10   Setting the Dock property.

Control Auto Scaling

The Windows Forms engine supports the capability to dynamically adjust a control's dimensions to preserve its original design proportions. This capability is useful if the form or control is displayed at runtime on a system with different display characteristics (resolution, DPI, and so on) than the system the form or control was designed on.

A simple example of this occurs when an application that uses a reasonable 9pt. font during design becomes almost unusable when displayed on a system whose default font size is larger. Because many UI elements auto-adjust based on the font of their displayed text (such as window title bars and menus), this can effect nearly every visual aspect of a form application.

Container controls (for example, those deriving from the ContainerControl class including the Form class and UserControl among others) starting with .NET 2.0 support two properties that enable them to counter these issues automatically without a lot of developer intervention: AutoScale and AutoScaleDimensions. AutoScaleMode specifies an enumeration value indicating what the scaling process should use as its base reference (DPI or resolution). Table 18.2 shows the possible AutoScaleMode values.

TABLE 18.2   AutoScaleMode Enumeration Values

Value	Description
Dpi	Scale relative to the resolution (96 DPI, 120 DPI, and so on.)
Font	Scale relative to the dimensions of the font being used
Inherit	Scale according to the base class AutoScaleMode value
None	No automatic scaling is performed

AutoScaleDimensions sets the dimensions (via a SizeF structure) that the control was originally designed to. This could refer to a font size or the DPI.

Using Containers

Containers are .NET controls designed to hold other controls. You can use containers in conjunction with the Anchor and Dock control properties to create intricate design scenarios. Although there are various container controls, the ones most applicable to control layout are the FlowLayoutPanel, TableLayoutPanel, and SplitContainer classes.

Both the TableLayoutPanel and the FlowLayoutPanel classes derive from the more generic Panel class. The Panel class provides high-level capabilities for grouping controls. This is beneficial from a placement perspective because you can aggregate a bunch of controls into one group by positioning them within a panel. This way, you can act on them as a group; for instance, disabling a panel control disables all of its child controls. The TableLayoutPanel and FlowLayoutPanel build on that functionality by also providing the capability to dynamically affect the positioning of their child controls.

The TableLayoutPanel

Consider a series of labels and text boxes for entering address information. They are typically arrayed in a column-and-row fashion. The TableLayoutPanel is ideal for implementing this behavior because it automatically forces the column and row assignment that you make for each of the controls. Figure 18.11 shows a series of label and text box controls embedded within a TableLayoutPanel. Notice that resizing the form (and thus the panel, which is docked to fill the form interior) causes the panel's controls to auto-adjust their alignment.

FIGURE 18.11   The TableLayoutPanel.

18

If an item within one of the cells extends beyond the cell's boundaries, it automatically overflows within the cell. This provides you with the same layout capabilities that HTML provides for web browser–based interfaces.

> **NOTE**
>
> When a control is added to a TableLayoutPanel, it is decorated with five additional properties: Cell, Column, Row, ColumnSpan, and RowSpan. These properties can be used to change the control's row/column position within the layout panel at runtime. The ColumnSpan and RowSpan properties are used the same way as their namesakes in the HTML world. In .NET, controls that imbue other controls with additional properties are called *extender providers*.

The FlowLayoutPanel

The FlowLayoutPanel has a simpler layout algorithm: Items are ordered either vertically or horizontally by wrapping control sets across rows or columns as needed. The two screens shown in Figure 18.12 illustrate the effect of resizing a flow layout panel containing a series of radio buttons.

FIGURE 18.12   The FlowLayoutPanel.

The SplitContainer

The SplitContainer control is a much enhanced alternative to the original Splitter control that was first included with .NET 1.0/1.1/Visual Studio 2003. This control represents the marriage of two panels and a splitter; the splitter separates the two panels either horizontally or vertically and enables a user to manually adjust the space (in the horizontal or vertical) that each panel consumes within the overall container.

Figure 18.13 shows the versatility of this control; two split containers, one embedded within a panel hosted by the other, are used to provide both vertical and horizontal resizing capabilities for the panels on a form (panel 2 isn't visible because it is the panel functioning as the container for the split container with panels 3 and 4). By dragging the split line to the right of panel 1, you can increase or decrease the horizontal real estate it occupies on the form. The same is true for the split line between panel 3 and panel 4; dragging this adjusts the ratio of space that both panels vertically occupy in relation to one another.

The ToolStripContainer

Many applications support the capability to drag and dock a toolbar, menu, and the like to any side of a form: top, bottom, left, or right. Visual Studio itself is an example of just such an application. By grabbing and dragging a Visual Studio toolbar, you can reposition it, for example, to the left side of the form. The ToolStripContainer control enables this functionality in your applications as well; it is a combination of four panels, each positioned on the four different edges of the containing form. These panels are used to host ToolStrip controls (more on these in a bit) and—at runtime—enable users to move tool strips within and between the four panels.

FIGURE 18.13   Resizing with the SplitContainer: a horizontal SplitContainer embedded in a vertical SplitContainer.

NOTE

Although the ToolStripContainer provides a convenient vehicle for snapping tool strips to the sides of a form, there is unfortunately no built-in support for "floating" tool strips.

The design experience is simple: You can shuffle controls around to the four different panels depending on where you want them positioned within the parent form. Figure 18.14 shows a ToolStripContainer in design mode. The smart tag offers up control over the visibility of the top, left, right, and bottom panels. Each panel is hidden by default. You can click on any of the arrows on the sides of the container to expand the corresponding panel and give you room to place tool strips within the panel.

Although it is convenient to be able to place items in a ToolStripContainer within the designer, the real benefit that you get from the control is the automatic support for dragging and dropping between panels at runtime. This means that, without writing a single line of layout or positioning code, you have enabled functionality that enables users to place their menus or toolbars wherever they want within the form. Figure 18.15 shows a toolbar, hosted in a ToolStripContainer, that has been redocked from the top panel to the left panel at runtime.

Multiple ToolStrip controls can also be stacked within any of the given panels in the ToolStripContainer. Figure 18.16 shows multiple command bars stacked within the rightmost panel. As noted later in the chapter, a control's z-order dictates its place within the stack.

18

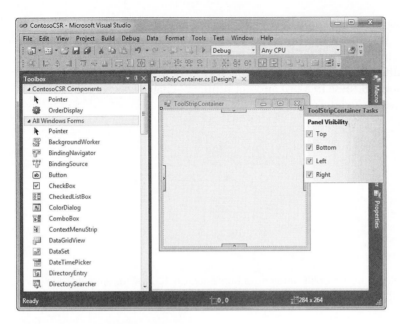

FIGURE 18.14   ToolStripContainer in design mode.

FIGURE 18.15   A toolbar positioned at runtime within a ToolStripContainer.

> **NOTE**
>
> The sharing of space—vertically or horizontally—within a tool strip container is some-times referred to as *rafting*. The tool strip controls are free to float anywhere within the panel.

There are a few other intricacies involved with form/control layout and positioning, but we have now covered the basics. With these concepts in hand and a general design for your form, you can start using the Windows Forms Designer.

FIGURE 18.16 Multiple toolbars stacked within the same panel.

Control Appearance and Behavior

A control's appearance is set via the same set of basic properties used to control form appearance: items such as ForeColor, BackColor, and Font all make an appearance on most controls.

Visual Styles

One item of interest is the capability for a control to automatically alter its appearance to conform to the currently selected "Desktop Theme" if it's running on Windows XP, Windows Vista, or Windows 7. This capability is enabled by a call to the Application.Enable VisualStyles method. This line of code is automatically included for you by default as the first line in the Main method. This location is ideal because it must be called before the controls in the application are actually created. If you remove the call, you can easily compare the appearance with and without the effects enabled. Figure 18.17 shows a form without visual styles enabled (left) alongside one with visual styles enabled (right).

FIGURE 18.17 The effects of Application.EnableVisualStyles.

Tab Order

By default, the order in which the controls on a form receive focus (tab order) is the same as the order in which they were placed on the form. To explicitly set the tab order for all the controls on a form, the IDE has a tab order selection mode.

To enter tab order selection mode, select View, Tab Order from the menu. The Windows Forms Designer annotates every control on the form with a number. This number represents that control's position within the overall tab order for the form. To set the tab order that you want, click sequentially on the controls; their tab order numbers automatically change as you click.

ToolTips

ToolTips are small "balloons" that display text as a user moves his or her cursor over a control. Typically, they are used to provide helpful hints or descriptions of a control's purpose, action, and so on. ToolTips are implemented with the ToolTip class and can be assigned to controls at design time.

The ToolTip class is an example of an extender provider (see the previous note on extender providers in our discussion on the TableLayoutPanel control). When you add a ToolTip component to a form, every control on the form now implements a ToolTip property that is used to assign a ToolTip to that specific control.

For illustration, if you wanted to add a ToolTip to a ToolStrip button, you would first drag the ToolTip component over to the form from the Toolbox. You would then select the ToolStrip button that you want to add the ToolTip to, and you would set its ToolTip property to reference the ToolTip instance on your form.

Working with ToolStrip Controls

Many of the standard, core visual elements of a form are realized with ToolStrip controls. A ToolStrip control functions as a container for other controls that derive from ToolStripItem. It can host various types of controls: buttons, combo boxes, labels, separators, text boxes, and even progress bars. The ToolStrip class itself is used to directly implement toolbars on a form and also functions as a base class for the StatusStrip control and the MenuStrip control.

ToolStrip controls come with an impressive list of built-in capabilities. They intrinsically support, for example, dragging an item from one tool strip to another, dynamically reordering and truncating items in the tool strip as users resize the strip or its parent form, and fully supporting different OS themes and rendering schemes.

All the different flavors of the ToolStrip control have some common traits:

▶ A design-time smart tag provides quick and easy access to common commands.

▶ In-place editing of child controls is supported (for example, a point-and-click interface is offered for adding, removing, and altering items within the ToolStrip, StatusStrip, or MenuStrip).

▶ An Items Collection Editor dialog box enables you to gain more fine control over child control properties and also enables add/reorder/remove actions against the child controls.

▶ Tool strips support a pluggable rendering model; you can change the visual renderer of a tool strip to a canned rendering object or to a custom object to obtain absolute control over the appearance of the tool strip.

From the initial form design, you know that you need menus, toolbars, and status bars, so the ToolStrip control and its descendants play a crucial role.

Creating a Menu

MenuStrip controls enable you to visually construct a form's main menu system. Dragging and dropping this control from the Toolbox onto the blank form automatically docks the menu strip to the top of the form (see Figure 18.18).

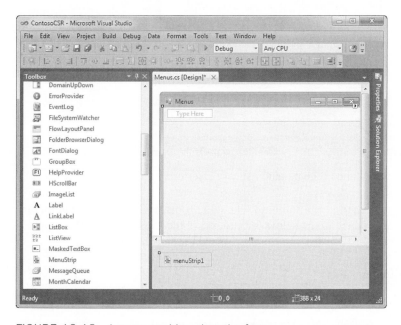

FIGURE 18.18   A menu positioned on the form.

18

After you place this control on the form, selecting the MenStrip control activates the smart tag glyph (smart tags are covered in Chapter 8, "Working with Visual Studio's Productivity Aids"). Clicking on the smart tag enables you to quickly do three things:

- ▶ Automatically insert standard items onto the menu
- ▶ Change the menu's RenderMode, Dock, and GripStyle properties
- ▶ Edit the menu items

Leveraging the capability to automatically equip a menu strip with a standard set of menus shaves a few minutes of design time off the manual approach. Figure 18.19 shows the result.

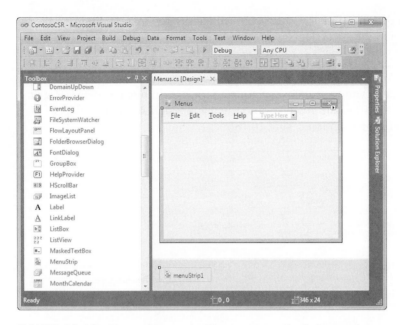

FIGURE 18.19 Menu with standard items automatically inserted.

Not only has the designer inserted the standard File, Edit, Tools, and Help top-level menu items, but it also has inserted subitems below each menu. Table 18.3 indicates the exact menu structure that results from using the menu's Insert Standard Items feature.

TABLE 18.3 Standard Menu Items

Main Menu	Menu Items
File	New
	Open
	Save
	Save As
	Print
	Print Preview
	Exit
Edit	Undo
	Redo
	Cut
	Copy
	Paste

TABLE 18.3   Continued

Main Menu	Menu Items
	Select All
Tools	Customize
	Options
Help	Contents
	Index
	Search
	About

If you want to manually add menu items into the menu strip, you can use the placeholder block within the menu strip labeled with the text "Type Here." Every time you type in the placeholder block, additional placeholders become visible, and a menu item is added to the menu strip (see Figure 18.20).

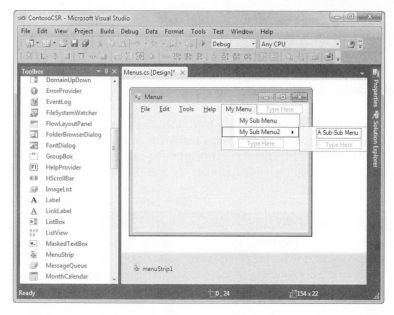

FIGURE 18.20   Manually adding menu items.

Creating a Toolbar

The next item up for inclusion on the form is a toolbar. Toolbars in .NET 2.0 and later are implemented directly with ToolStrip controls. As mentioned before, ToolStrip controls can host various child controls; each inherits from the ToolStripItem base class. Figure 18.21 shows the controls that can be implemented inside a tool strip.

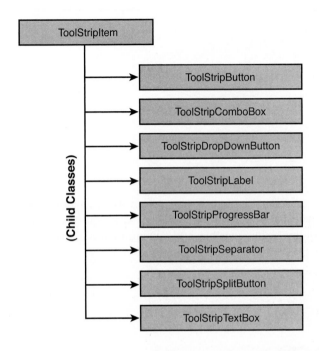

FIGURE 18.21 Classes inheriting from ToolStripItem.

In fact, the interactive layout features of the tool strip work the same way as the menu strip: Dragging the control onto the form will result in a blank ToolStrip control docked to the top of the form just under the existing menu control, and you can quickly add a roster of standard items to the tool strip by using its smart tag and selecting Insert Standard Items.

NOTE

Controls use the concept of *z-order* to determine their "depth" on the form. If two controls occupy the same space on a form, the control's individual z-order determines which of the two controls is on top and which is on the bottom. You control this layering in the IDE by right-clicking a control and using the Send to Back and Bring to Front menu commands.

Z-order plays an important role in the placement of docked controls. Docked controls are arrayed in increasing order of their z index on the form. For instance, if you select the ToolStrip and issue the Send to Back command, the order of the MenuStrip and ToolStrip containers is altered to place the ToolStrip first (at the top of the form) and the MenuStrip second (just below the ToolStrip instance).

Figure 18.22 shows the in-progress form with the added ToolStrip control.

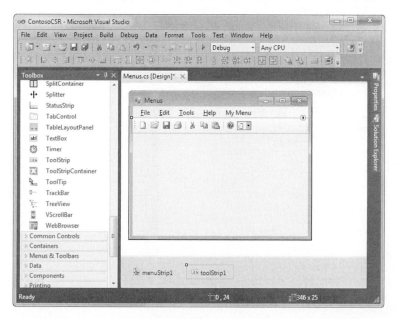

FIGURE 18.22   The main form with a complete menu and toolbar.

If you want to enable users to drag and drop the toolbar or menu onto one of the form's four sides, you use the ToolStripContainer. In fact, there is a shortcut option here: You can take any of the ToolStrip controls currently on the form and add them to a ToolStripContainer with just a couple clicks of the mouse. One of the items available via a tool strip's smart tag is the command Embed in a ToolStripContainer. If you issue this command against the toolbar that you just added to the sample form, Visual Studio does two things for you: It adds a ToolStripContainer to the form, and it places the selected ToolStrip into the container, specifically, in the top panel of the ToolStripContainer.

Creating a Status Bar

Status bars provide the user feedback on an application's current status, progress within an action, details in context with an object selected on a form, and so on. The StatusStrip control provides this functionality in starting with .NET 2.0/Visual Studio 2005, and it supplants the StatusBar control found in previous versions.

As with the other ToolStrip descendants, the StatusStrip control functions as a container; its capability to host labels in addition to progress bars, drop-downs, and split buttons makes it a much more powerful control than the StatusBar.

Figure 18.23 shows the fictional Contoso CSR form with a StatusStrip docked at the bottom of the form. In design mode, you see a drop-down button that holds a selection for each of the four supported child controls. For the purposes of this demonstration prototype, add a label control to report general application status and an additional label and progress bar to be used if you run into any long-running retrieval or edit operations.

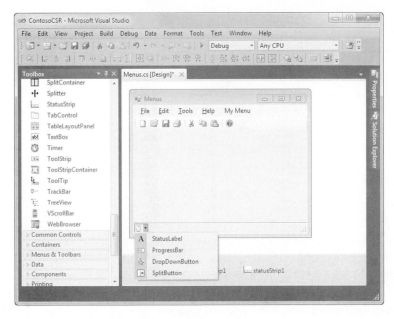

FIGURE 18.23   StatusStrip in design mode.

By default, child controls are added in a left-to-right flow layout pattern within the StatusStrip pattern. With just six clicks (two per item), you can add these controls to the strip. The in-place editing capabilities are great for quickly building out the look and feel of the strip; for greater control of the strip's child controls, you can use the Items Collection Editor dialog box.

Editing the StatusStrip Items   You use the StatusStrip's smart tag and select Edit Items to launch the Items Collection Editor dialog box. The editor provides direct access to all the hosted control's properties and also enables you to edit, delete, and reorder items within the status strip (see Figure 18.24).

By tweaking some properties here, you can improve the layout and appearance of your items. Figure 18.25 shows the default layout of the controls you added; ideally, you want the progress bar and its label control to sit at the far right of the status strip and the status label to sit at the far left to consume any remaining space.

FIGURE 18.24 The StatusStrip Items Collection Editor.

FIGURE 18.25 Default positioning of the StatusStrip items.

To make this happen, you need to set the Spring property to True for the leftmost label. This will cause the label to expand and contract to fill the available space on the status strip. Next, set its TextAlignment property to situate the text to the left of the label region and change the Text property to something more appropriate.

Figure 18.26 shows the fruits of our labor.

FIGURE 18.26 The final StatusStrip look and feel.

Displaying Data

So far, we have only touched on form elements that provide the basic framework user navigation, status, commands, and so on. However, the capability to access, display, and edit data from an underlying data store (relational or otherwise) is the real value of an application such as the fictional Contoso CSR application. We touch on the details of working with databases in the next chapter; here, we describe some of the basic controls used to display data in a form.

Hierarchical Data

The TreeView control is ideal for presenting data with hierarchical relationships and is thus a good candidate for housing the list of order records (which can be grouped by different criteria). First, add a SplitContainer control to partition the leftover interior space in the form into two discrete panels. Yet another panel houses the search function for orders; this is docked to the top of the left split panel. A TreeView dock-fills the remainder of this leftmost panel, and the right panel houses the data fields (text boxes, labels, radio buttons, and so on) for an individual CSR record.

TreeView controls present data as a list of nodes; each node can serve as a parent for additional nodes. Typically, with applications that front a database, you build the contents of the TreeView by binding to a resultset from the database, or by programmatically looping through the resultset and adding to the TreeView's node list through its API. But you also have control over the TreeView content in the designer by launching the TreeNode Editor.

The TreeNode Editor   The TreeNode Editor (see Figure 18.27) is a dialog box that acts much the same as the Items Collection Editor examined previously. It enables you to add, edit, and remove items from the TreeView control. You launch the editor dialog box by selecting Edit Nodes from the TreeView's smart tag.

FIGURE 18.27   Using the designer to edit nodes in the TreeView control.

Using the Add Root and Add Child buttons, you can insert new nodes into the tree's data structure at any given nesting level. Figure 18.27 shows manually inserted nodes with test data so that you can get an idea of what the order list would look like using the company as a parent node and order instances as child nodes under the corresponding company. Each item, or node, in the TreeView consists of two parts: an image and text. The image is optional; if you want to attach an icon to a node, you start by first assigning an ImageList control to the TreeView control.

Using an ImageList ImageList controls function as an image provider for other controls. They maintain a collection of Image objects that are referenced by their ordinal position or key within the collection. Any control that provides an ImageList property can reference an ImageList component and use its images. ListView, ToolStrip, and TreeView are some examples of controls that can leverage the ImageList component.

> **NOTE**
>
> Visual Studio 2010 ships with a large library of images that you can use with the TreeView or any other control that requires these types of standard graphics such as toolbars and menus. By default, the image files are placed in a zipped filed located at C:\Program Files\Microsoft Visual Studio 10.0\Common7\VS2010ImageLibrary.

An ImageList doesn't have a visual presence on a form; in other words, you can't see the ImageList itself. Its sole use is as a behind-the-scenes component that feeds images to other controls. Dropping an ImageList onto the designer puts an instance of the component in the component tray. You can then use the Images Collection Editor dialog box to add, edit, and remove the images hosted by the component. Changing the images associated with the image list automatically changes the images used by any controls referencing the ImageList.

Figure 18.28 shows a few images added within the Images Collection Editor. To enable the TreeView to use these images, you have to do two things:

1. Assign the TreeView.ImageList property to point to the instance of the ImageList component (in this case, ImageList1).

FIGURE 18.28 The Images Collection Editor.

2. Set the image associated with a node either programmatically or via the TreeNode Editor dialog box.

With the ImageList component in place and the TreeView dropped in the SplitContainer's left panel, the form is almost there from a design perspective. The remaining piece is the series of fields that display the data for a record selected in the TreeView control.

You could add this piece by just dragging a bunch of text boxes and labels over into a TableLayoutPanel and then docking the whole mess in the open SplitContainer panel. But because you really want to treat this as one cohesive unit to simplify positioning, eventual data binding, and so on, you instead create a user control for displaying a CSR record.

Tabular Data

The DataGridView control is the premium Visual Studio control for displaying data in a tabular format. It provides a row/column format for displaying data from a wide variety of data sources. Figure 18.29 shows a DataGridView with its smart tag menu opened; the smart tag menu provides fast access to the column properties of the grid control and also enables you to directly bind the DataGridView to a data source.

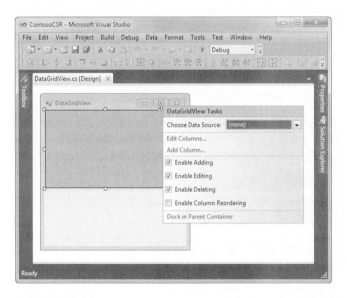

FIGURE 18.29   Configuring a DataGridView control with its SmartTag.

Data Sources   The DataGridView control supports various possible data sources. For instance, scenarios such as displaying name/value pairs from a collection are supported, in addition to mainstream support for datasets returned from a relational data store. If you select a data source for the grid, a column is added to the grid for every column that appears in the data source, and the row data is automatically provided inside the DataGridView control.

Data can be displayed in the grid control in an "unbound" mode as well; using the grid's row/column API, you can programmatically define the structure of the grid and add data to it at runtime.

Cell Types   Each individual cell in a DataGridView functions as if it is an embedded control. Each cell can express the underlying data that it contains in various ways; check boxes, drop-downs, links, buttons, and text boxes are all supported cell types. In addition to the data visualization possibilities, each cell also has its own set of events that can be hooked within your code. For example, you can hook the mouse enter and leave events for a specific cell.

We cover this control in depth in Chapter 21, "Working with Databases."

Creating Your Own Controls

If none of the stock .NET controls meets your specific needs, you can create your own controls for use on a Windows Form in three ways:

> ► You can subclass an existing control and modify or extend its behavior and appearance.

> ► You can create a user control by compositing together two or more existing controls.

> ► You can create a custom control from scratch, implementing your own visuals and behavior.

Subclassing an Existing Control

Subclassing an existing control is the best approach if your needs are only slightly different from one of the standard .NET Framework controls. By inheriting from an existing control class, you are riding on top of its behavior and appearance; it's up to you to then add the specialized code to your new control class.

For example, suppose that you want a text box that turns red anytime a numeric (that is, nonalphabetic) character is entered. This is easy to do with just a few lines of code sitting in the TextBox control's TextChanged event, but consolidating this behavior into its own class provides a reuse factor.

You start by adding a new user control to the project. User controls actually inherit from the UserControl class; because you want to inherit from the TextBox class, you need to

18

change the class definition by using the code editor. After you do that, you can place the new component on a form and use its functionality.

Working with an Inherited Control

Because TextBox already has a UI, you don't need to do anything with regard to the appearance of the control. In fact, it works just like any other text box control within the Windows Forms Designer (see Figure 18.30).

FIGURE 18.30   A control derived from TextBox.

The Properties window for the control behaves as expected, and double-clicking on the control immediately takes you to an open code editor window. In short, the design-time experience remains fully functional and requires no effort on the part of the developer.

Designing a User Control

A user control is technically the same as any other class that you author as a developer. Because a user control has a visual aspect to it, Visual Studio provides a designer, just as with Windows Forms, to help in the drag-and-drop creation of the control.

User controls are composite controls; that is, they are constructed from one or more existing .NET controls. As with a derived control, their user interfaces inherit from the native controls they are composed of, making them simple to build and use in the designer.

There are two approaches to the user control creation process: You can create a separate Windows Control Library project, or you can simply add a user control class to an existing Windows Forms project.

Creating a separate project enables the user control to live in its own assembly. If it is a separate assembly, you can treat the user control as the quintessential black box, giving you greater flexibility from a source control perspective and enabling you to share the control among multiple projects. For production scenarios, this is clearly the best route. However, for simple prototyping work, as you are doing here with the CSR form application, the ease and simplicity of just adding a new class to the existing project make this approach preferable to using the separate project approach. The class lives inside the same namespace as the form class.

If you were ever in a position to transition from prototyping to actual production development, nothing would preclude you from refactoring the control by simply copying the user control class file and embedding it in a separate control library project.

As soon as you add the user control class to the project, you are presented with the User Control Designer. The designer works in exactly the same way as the Windows Forms Designer; to build the user control, you drag components or controls from the Toolbox onto its surface.

Adding Controls

Obviously, the controls that you use to build your composite control entirely depend on how you envision the control's functionality. As an example, to create an order display control, you need to think about the underlying data structure of an order. An order record might contain the following:

▶ An order number

▶ A series of dates that capture the date the order was placed, date the order was shipped, and so on

▶ A list of items included on the order

▶ Billing information and shipping address

▶ Miscellaneous comments

Because this is a lot of information to try to cram onto one screen, you can turn to the TabControl. A tab control is another general-purpose container control that enables you to organize content across several pages that are accessed via tabs. Within each tab, you can leverage the TableLayoutPanel and implement most of the order fields with simple label and text box pairs.

As mentioned earlier, the whole process of getting these controls into the user control works identically to the Windows Forms Designer: You drag and drop the controls from the Toolbox onto the user control design surface. Figure 18.31 shows the OrderDisplay user control with its user interface completed.

FIGURE 18.31   Designing a user control.

Embedding the User Control

Now that you have a completed design for your user control, the only remaining step is to embed the control into your primary form. If you compile the project, Visual Studio automatically recognizes the user control class and include an entry for the control in the Toolbox. From there, you are just a drag-and-drop away from implementing the OrderDisplay control.

In Figure 18.32, you can see the OrderDisplay item in the Toolbox and the results of dragging it onto the form surface.

Creating a Custom Control

Custom controls represent the ultimate in extensibility because they are built from scratch. As a result, they are relatively hard to develop because they require you to worry not only about functionality but also about every single aspect of the control's visual appearance. Because the physical user interface of the custom control needs to be drawn 100% by custom code, a steep learning curve is associated with authoring a custom control.

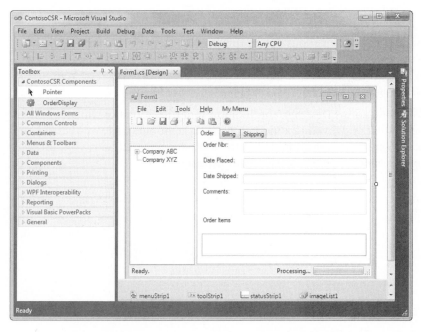

FIGURE 18.32   A user control displayed in the toolbox and on a form.

Because much of the work that goes into creating a custom control is at the code level, we won't try to tackle this subject with any useful degree of detail in this book. You should note, however, that the process starts the same way as with other control options: Visual Studio has a custom control project item template; adding this to your project gives you a baseline of code to start with. From there, it's up to you.

> **NOTE**
>
> The OnPaint event is where you place the code to draw your control's user interface. Although so-called "owner draw" controls can involve complex drawing code, the good news is that the Windows Forms Designer leverages whatever code you place in the OnPaint event in order to render the control at design time. This means that you can still rely on the Windows Forms Designer to provide you with a WYSIWYG experience even with custom controls.

Summary

In this chapter, we described the various design-time capabilities of the Windows Forms Designer tool. Windows Forms are a powerful presentation layer technology, and Visual Studio 2010 provides an array of tools for quickly building impressive, rich user interfaces based on this technology.

The role of the Windows Forms Designer, the Toolbox, and the Properties window were introduced in the context of delivering a modern, well-thought-out, standards-based user interface for a .NET Windows application. Using the tools documented here, you can wring the most out of your winforms development experience.

CHAPTER 19

Creating Richer, Smarter User Interfaces

With .NET 3.0, Microsoft delivered a brand-new set of technologies for powering the presentation layer in your applications: the Windows Presentation Foundation (WPF). WPF was designed from the ground up to leverage the strengths of both the Windows Forms development world and the Web Forms development world. At the same time, WPF attempts to overcome many of the obstacles that developers face when trying to build rich, compelling user interfaces that involve media and highly customized user interfaces, and that exploit all the horsepower available in modern CPUs and graphics processors.

WPF is intended to be a unifying platform with built-in, first-class support for data binding, audio, video, and both 2D and 3D graphics. Because WPF likely represents a significant learning curve for both new and experienced developers, we spend some time up front in this chapter discussing the basics before diving into the real target: how to use the Visual Studio WPF Designer tool (previously known by its code name "Cider") to build high-octane user interfaces for your Windows applications.

The Windows Presentation Foundation Platform

As a brand-new presentation layer framework, WPF brings a lot of new concepts and new coding territory with it—and can represent a fairly significant learning curve for developers. But let's take a brief look at the overall architecture of the WPF platform, and then dissect the programming model.

Physically, WPF is implemented with a series of three .DLLs:

- WindowsBase.dll

- PresentationFramework.dll

- PresentationCore.dll

Every presentation layer framework has to eventually paint pixels onto a screen, and WPF is no different. Implemented within its binaries is a composition and rendering engine, which talks to your hardware through DirectX. In addition to the rendering layers, there is also obviously a rich programming model that is implemented with deep support for things such as layout, containership (the capability for one element to contain another), and events/message dispatches. In short, it does all the heavy lifting to ensure that some very complicated user interface scenarios can be rendered on the screen with enough performance to appeal to a wide range of solution scenarios.

Figure 19.1 shows the logical architecture of the various WPF components. The actual rendering "engine" is contained within the Media Integration Layer component; PresentationCore handles interop with the Media Integration Layer, and PresentationFramework contains all the other magic necessary to make WPF successful as an end-to-end platform such as layout, data binding, and event notifications.

FIGURE 19.1   WPF logical architecture.

NOTE

Most of WPF itself is implemented in managed .NET code. The exception is the Media Integration Layer. When it comes to rendering the UI to the screen, WPF needs to optimize for performance over nearly all other concerns, and thus the Media Integration Layer is implemented as native code.

All of these WPF components work in concert to deliver an impressive laundry list of improvements to the state of the art with regard to presentation layer design, construction, and runtime support with .NET. Here is a small sample:

▶ **Media**—WPF supports 2D and 3D graphics, as well as WMV, MPEG, and AVI video.

▶ **Data binding**—WPF was built from the start to fully support the entire spectrum of data binding scenarios, up to and including LINQ and the Entity Framework.

▶ **Windows Forms Interoperability**—WPF applications can host WinForms components and vice versa. This is comforting because it means developers won't need to abandon the hard-won knowledge that comes with programming WinForms for many years.

▶ **Document Support**—WPF has several native constructs for building document-centric applications. For instance, there is a DocumentReader class for displaying fixed-format documents, and a FlowDocumentReader class for displaying documents with a dynamic layout. Think of a newspaper article, for instance, that automatically repaginates while remaining true to the column structure.

▶ **Animation**—Developers can create storyboard-based animations, and specify animation triggers and timers.

▶ **Control "look and feel"**—Controls in WPF have their appearance controlled by a template, which developers can replace or change to fully customize nearly every aspect of a control's "chrome."

▶ **Text**—There is rich typography support in WPF. Developers can manipulate a slew of font attributes (kerning; effects such as glow, drop-shadows, and motion blur; auto line spacing; and so on), and WPF developers can choose to have text rendered using ClearType technology or via two additional rendering modes introduced in WPF 4: aliased and grayscale.

During the initial beta cycles, Microsoft produced a series of prototype applications to showcase the new technologies in .NET 3.0, including WPF. Figure 19.2 shows a screenshot from the healthcare prototype. Although a static shot in black and white doesn't do the application much justice, you can get a good sense for the possibilities: The user interface for this application would have been extremely difficult to implement using Windows Forms technology.

For the most part, developers are free to not worry so much about the low-level architectural details of WPF; the programming model—and the tools which help us leverage that model—is where most developers will focus their energies.

Programming Model

The WPF class library consists of approximately 1,600 public types and more than 3,500 classes. As such, it has a considerably larger API surface than either ASP.NET or Windows Forms. As you would expect from a .NET class library, all of these classes can trace their ancestry back to System.Object. In addition, most WPF classes are based on so-called base elements: the UIElement, FrameworkElement, ContentElement, and

FrameworkContentElement classes. These classes are responsible for basic item presentation and layout capabilities and are contained within the System.Windows namespace.

FIGURE 19.2   An early, WPF-based, healthcare prototype.

In addition to these four base element classes, there are a few other important base classes that drive a lot of the functionality found in WPF:

▶ **Visual**—This class is the core rendering unit within WPF; UIElement inherits from Visual as do the higher level classes such as Button.

▶ **DispatcherObject**—This class implements the WPF threading model.

▶ **Control**—This is the base class for controls in WPF.

▶ **Application**—The Application class encapsulates all WPF applications; it provides application lifetime services, including the basic concepts of Run (to start an application) and Exit (to quit an application).

As you would expect, the WPF class library also provides all the major controls that you would typically find in a Windows application such as buttons, labels, list boxes, and text boxes.

The following snippet shows a WPF button control being instantiated, and the text Push Me is assigned to the button. Note that the control constructs are all familiar but that the actual object model is slightly different; the Button object in WPF does not have a .Text property as we would expect from an ASP.NET or WinForms button. Instead, it exposes a .Content property.

```
System.Windows.Controls.Button btn = new Button();
btn.Content = "Push Me";
```

Besides procedural code like that shown here, WPF also enables us to create and manipulate objects in a declarative fashion using a markup syntax called XAML.

Extensible Application Markup Language (XAML)

Extensible Application Markup Language, or XAML, is an XML dialect that can be used to describe the structure of a WPF application's presentation layer (for example, control instantiation, appearance, and layout).

XAML is a new "language," and is the principal way in which the various WPF tools create objects and set properties in a declarative fashion. As such, it is tempting to compare XAML to HTML: it certainly fills a similar role in that XAML and HTML are both declarative ways to describe objects. But XAML is actually tightly coupled to the .NET Framework. In fact, XAML is really a generic way to create and manipulate .NET objects. WPF tools, such as the WPF designer in Visual Studio, happen to leverage XAML, but strictly speaking, XAML is not a part of WPF. You can write an entire XAML application, for instance, using only the managed code language of your choice. But because XAML, as a programming model, brings several important advancements to the scene, it is heavily leveraged by all the Microsoft and non-Microsoft tools in the WPF world, and beyond. For instance, it is also used by Windows Workflow Foundation to describe workflows.

Just as we did previously, let's create a Button object and assign some text to the button—but this time, let's do all the work with XAML:

```
<Button Content="Push Me"></Button>
```

Alternatively, we could write this code like this:

```
<Button>Push Me</Button>
```

NOTE

XAML functionality is a subset of what is possible in .NET code. Or, to put it another way, anything you can do in XAML you can do in code, but not everything done in code can be done in XAML.

In a typical WPF application, XAML coexists with managed code through the same partial class paradigm introduced with ASP.NET. In other words, we may have a MainForm.xaml file with the look and feel of a window, and a MainForm.xaml.vb (or .cs) file that contains code that reacts to a user's input on that form. We see more of this in action a little later in this chapter when we take a close look at the WPF designer.

19

If XAML isn't necessary to create a WPF application, why is it desired? Given the fact that you can accomplish the necessary tasks to create UI objects in XAML or in managed code, why is XAML even in the picture? There are a few areas where the declarative syntax becomes tremendously important.

Syntax Simplicity   As is true with all XML-based languages, XAML is relatively easy for applications to parse and understand. Several developers have used this to their advantage and delivered lightweight tools for WPF development such as XAMLPad. This has also enabled tool vendors, including Microsoft, to rapidly release products into the market that understand XAML. Adobe Illustrator, for example, has a XAML plug-in that allows you to emit XAML, and of course Microsoft has not one but two design tools that read and write XAML: Expression Design and Expression Blend.

The boundary between XAML and code also turns out to be a nice dividing line between appearance and behavior. In this scenario, XAML is used to create the UI objects and the general look and feel of the application, while procedural code is used to implement the business logic, and to react to a user's input. This leads us directly to the other important advantage of XAML: collaboration.

Collaboration   If we separate appearance and behavior, we can also reap the benefits of improved collaboration among project team members—specifically, collaboration between designers and developers. Before WPF, designers would rely on "flat" bitmaps created with drawing programs, or would even rely on applications such as PowerPoint to mock up the user experience for an application. When that design is eventually handed off to the developer for implementation, there is an inherent disconnect: Programming tools don't understand 2D bitmaps or PowerPoint storyboards. They understand code and objects. And in the reverse direction, we have the same problem: Tools made for designers don't understand managed code. A developer can't implement a form in Visual Basic, for example, and hand it back to a designer for review and tweaking.

So developers are forced to re-create, as best they can, the vision delivered from the design team. This is a decidedly second-rate way to design and build applications. But with XAML, this situation changes dramatically. Because designers can now use tools that express their design in XAML (such as Microsoft Expression Blend), the developer can simply open that XAML file and provide the coding "goop" necessary to flesh out the desired features. In the process, we have 100% preserved the fidelity of the designers' original vision because the developer's tools are talking the same language. We also have full collaboration in the other direction: Changes that a developer makes to the designer's XAML can be instantly reviewed and tweaked within the designer's tools. This simple concept—the sharing of a codebase and language between design and development roles and tools—proves to be a powerful argument for leveraging XAML in your applications.

Now that we have covered the basics of WPF, let's see how we can start writing WPF applications using Visual Studio 2010.

Introducing the WPF Designer

We first introduced the WPF designer in Chapter 6, "Introducing the Editors and Designers." Let's recap the basics, and then move on to a more involved discussion of the WPF designer.

The WPF designer is the tool in Visual Studio that provides the WYSIWYG design surface for building WPF windows. In many ways, it behaves just like the designers we use for web forms and Windows forms. But it is in fact a brand-new tool, with some subtle differences over its IDE brethren. To see the designer in action, let's create a new project in Visual Studio. The project template we want to select is WPF Application, and it is located in the Windows category on the New Project dialog box (see Figure 19.3).

FIGURE 19.3   Creating a new WPF application.

This template takes care of adding the necessary WPF namespaces for us; the project also includes a file that implements the default window for the application: Window1.xaml. Double-clicking on the Window1.xaml file launches the designer, which is shown in Figure 19.4.

XAML and Design Panes

The WPF designer offers two different views: the visual representation of the window, and the XAML that implements the window. You can make changes to the window and its controls by either editing the XAML or changing elements on the design surface. Either way, the designer keeps both panes in sync.

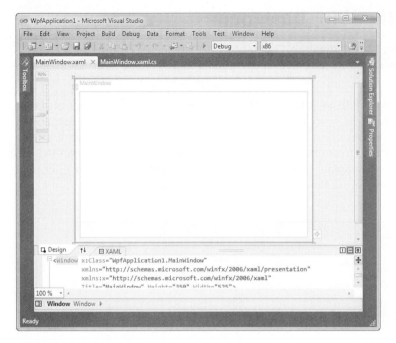

FIGURE 19.4   The WPF Designer.

You can configure the position and layout of the XAML and design panes in the following ways:

▶ The Swap button swaps the positions of the XAML and design panes with one another.

▶ The Vertical Split button tiles the panes vertically.

▶ The Horizontal Split button tiles the panes horizontally.

▶ The Collapse/Expand Pane button minimizes or restores the bottom or leftmost pane (depending on the view mode you are in).

Figure 19.5 shows the location of these pane management buttons on the designer.

TIP

If you are lucky enough to have a multi-monitor setup, the vertical split view is particularly helpful because you can display your XAML code on one screen and your visual design surface on another.

We interact with the designer in the same way we interact with other design surfaces or code editors: Controls can be placed on the design pane from the toolbox and then manipulated, and we can use the XAML pane to handcraft or alter XAML (with complete IntelliSense and formatting).

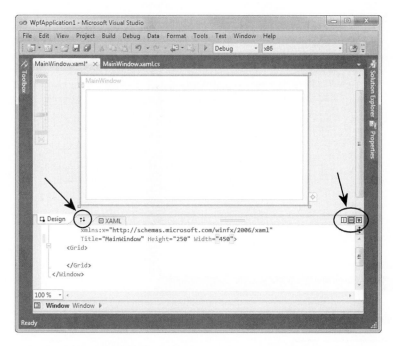

FIGURE 19.5   Controls for configuring the XAML and designer panes.

For the most part, control placement and positioning works the same as it does in the Windows Forms designer. There are a few minor exceptions: The WPF designer has some unique visualizations for displaying snap lines and control sizing (see Figure 19.6).

The Property Window

As expected, when you have a control selected in the designer, you can manipulate its attributes using the Properties window. The WPF Properties window has some surprises. For starters, it displays a small, thumbnail image of the currently selected control. Additionally, it supports two unique ways for locating control properties: besides the categorized and alphabetical display modes, you can group and sort properties by source. This is great for quickly looking at those properties, for instance, that have their value set explicitly in XAML, or have values that are currently being inherited down from a style. The WPF Properties window also enables you to search for properties of the control by typing in a search box. As you type, the window automatically filters the property list to just those that match your search criteria. Figure 19.7 shows an image of the Properties window.

The Zoom Control

One additional item is present with the WPF designer: a zoom slider control. Perched in the upper left of the design pane, this control can be used to zoom in or out on the current window from 10% to 2000% of the window's actual size. The shaded mark on the zoom control shows the 100% mark, and you can quickly toggle between 100% and 120% by clicking on the square button/region located at the bottom of the slider. Figure 19.8 shows the slider control, and Figure 19.9 shows our "Push Me" button (and container window) at 4x magnification.

19

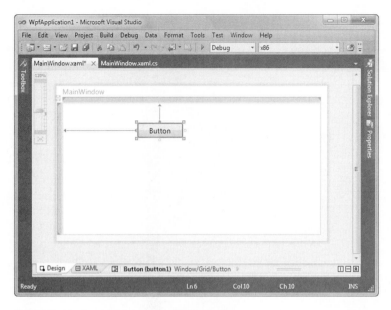

FIGURE 19.6   Sizing and positioning indicators.

FIGURE 19.7   The WPF Designer property window.

TIP

The zoom control is particularly useful when you have a complex form layout with a lot of snap lines and nested/layered controls amassed in a certain area. By zooming in on the area, you can get a crisp view of where things are positioned, and it becomes much easier to select or position the control you want instead of one of its neighbors. By zooming out, you can get a thumbnail look at your window to see how your overall look and feel is shaping up.

The XAML pane also has a zoom control. In the lower-left corner of the XAML editor pane there is a drop-down box that enables you to select a magnification percentage that can range from 20% to 400%.

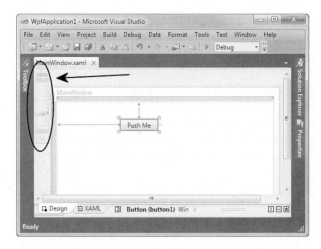

FIGURE 19.8   The zoom slider.

FIGURE 19.9   A button at 400% magnification.

Programming with WPF

With the basics out of the way, it's time for a more in-depth discussion of the various controls and technologies that you typically encounter when creating a WPF-powered application. After firmly grounding ourselves in these topics, we then move on to build a simple application, end to end, using the WPF designer.

Layout

Because software needs to present controls and data on a screen for visual consumption by users, the layout—or how things are arranged onscreen—becomes an important design feature. Good layout systems not only have to enable developers to structure controls in a coherent fashion, but also need to be robust in terms of how they handle things such as window resizing and flow.

In WPF, layout is exercised through a set of container controls called panels. Each panel is uniquely suited for a specific layout scenario, and the capability to combine them with one another means that the layout system in WPF can handle a large number of different control organization scenarios. The key point to understand with panels is that, as containers, they are responsible for the positioning (and in some cases, the sizing) of all the controls placed within. This means that the individual child controls themselves don't need to be aware of the specific layout system they are participating in—which greatly simplifies the code and architecture.

Table 19.1 lists the available layout panel controls.

Let's examine these controls, and their subtypes, one by one.

TABLE 19.1   The WPF Layout Panels

Class	Description
Canvas	A container control with no built-in layout logic
DockPanel	Panel that enables docking of its child elements
Grid	A container control that allows child objects to be positioned within columns and rows
StackPanel	A container control that implements horizontal and vertical stacking behavior for its child controls
WrapPanel	Panel that will automatically wrap elements to a new row as needed

The Canvas Control

The Canvas control is unique among all the layout controls because it is the only one that actually performs no layout at all. It is functionally similar to the GroupBox control that you might have used with a Windows Forms project: Child objects that are placed within a Canvas control are placed using coordinates relative to the canvas itself. There is no automatic resizing, flow layout, or positioning done on behalf of the child controls by the canvas. If any such logic is needed, you need to implement it yourself. This highlights the purpose of the Canvas control: providing the developer with the absolute control to position things as you want them positioned.

In Figure 19.10, we have a Canvas control with four buttons in a unique arrangement. They are all positioned relative to the sides of the Canvas container.

Here is the XAML:

```
<Window x:Class="ContosoAvalon.Canvas"
    xmlns="http://schemas.microsoft.com/winfx/2006/xaml/presentation"
    xmlns:x="http://schemas.microsoft.com/winfx/2006/xaml"
```

```
    Title="Canvas" Height="300" Width="300">
    <Canvas>
      <Button Canvas.Left="102" Canvas.Top="11" Height="23" Name="button1"
      Width="75">Button</Button>
      <Button Canvas.Left="47" Canvas.Top="38" Height="23" Name="button2"
      Width="75">Button</Button>
      <Button Canvas.Right="46" Canvas.Top="38" Height="23" Name="button3"
      Width="75">Button</Button>
      <Button Canvas.Left="102" Canvas.Top="99" Height="23" Name="button4"
      Width="75">Button</Button>
    </Canvas>
</Window>
```

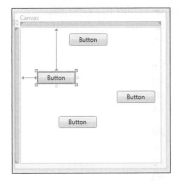

FIGURE 19.10   Buttons positioned within a Canvas control.

Note that we have provided coordinates that are relative to a specified side of the canvas. If we resize the window, the buttons move accordingly. Unless you absolutely need to manually specify control positions (as may be the case, for instance, if you are arranging controls in a nonstandard way or using controls to "draw" something in a window), it is recommended that you use one of the other panels that automatically perform the layout you need.

The DockPanel Control

Modern lines of business applications typically use some kind of docking arrangement for their controls: Toolbars may be docked at the top or sides of the window, a status bar may be docked at the bottom, and so forth. The DockPanel in WPF provides the capability to dock controls to one of the four sides of a window.

If we needed to create a window with a toolbar docked to the top and the left side of the window, with the remainder of the screen occupied by a canvas, we would do the following:

```
<Window x:Class="ContosoAvalon.DockPanel"
    xmlns="http://schemas.microsoft.com/winfx/2006/xaml/presentation"
    xmlns:x="http://schemas.microsoft.com/winfx/2006/xaml"
    Title="DockPanel" Height="300" Width="300">
```

19

```
        <DockPanel Name="dockPanel1">
            <ToolBar DockPanel.Dock="Top">
                <Button BorderBrush="Black">Button1</Button>
            </ToolBar>
            <ToolBar DockPanel.Dock="Left" MaxWidth="75">
                <Button BorderBrush="Black">Button2</Button>
            </ToolBar>
            <Canvas>
                <TextBlock>Canvas</TextBlock>
            </Canvas>
        </DockPanel>
</Window>
```

With the DockPanel, you can place more than one element in a certain dock position. Figure 19.11 shows six regions docked in a window: three of them are docked to the left, and three of them are docked to the top.

FIGURE 19.11   Docking controls within a DockPanel.

And here is the matching XAML:

```
<Window x:Class="ContosoAvalon.DockPanel"
    xmlns="http://schemas.microsoft.com/winfx/2006/xaml/presentation"
    xmlns:x="http://schemas.microsoft.com/winfx/2006/xaml"
    Title="DockPanel" Height="300" Width="300">
    <DockPanel Name="dockPanel1">
        <Button DockPanel.Dock="Left">Left #1</Button>
        <Button DockPanel.Dock="Left">Left #2</Button>
        <Button DockPanel.Dock="Left">Left #3</Button>
        <Button DockPanel.Dock="Top">Top #1</Button>
```

```
        <Button DockPanel.Dock="Top">Top #2</Button>
        <Button DockPanel.Dock="Top">Top #3</Button>
    </DockPanel>
</Window>
```

All the elements within a DockPanel are resized such that they stay docked in their designated position, and they entirely "fill" the window edge that they are docked to.

The Grid Control

The Grid panel is used for row and column arrangements, similar to an HTML table or to the TableLayoutPanel control in WinForms.

One common use for the Grid control is with dialog boxes or data entry forms where labels and values exist side by side and row by row; we can use the columns in the grid to align items horizontally, and the rows to align items vertically.

Columns are created in a grid through the use of the Grid.ColumnDefinitions element. For example, this XAML snippet would create a grid with three columns:

```
<Grid>
    <Grid.ColumnDefinitions>
        <ColumnDefinition></ColumnDefinition>
        <ColumnDefinition></ColumnDefinition>
        <ColumnDefinition></ColumnDefinition>
    </Grid.ColumnDefinitions>
</Grid>
```

In a similar fashion, the Grid.RowDefinitions element defines the rows within a grid:

```
<Grid>
    <Grid.RowDefinitions>
        <RowDefinition></RowDefinition>
        <RowDefinition></RowDefinition>
        <RowDefinition></RowDefinition>
    </Grid.RowDefinitions>
</Grid>
```

The WPF designer also has interactive features that allow for row and column addition, deletion, and sizing. Figure 19.12 shows a two-column, six-row grid placed in a window. Note that the designer shows the grid lines demarcating the rows and columns, and that there is a shaded border area to the top and to the left of the Grid control. Not only does this border area show us the current size (width or height) of a column or row, but we also can use this border area to create new rows or columns by just clicking where we want to place the new element. We can also drag the row or column lines to increase or decrease the size of the row or column.

FIGURE 19.12   Working with a Grid in the designer.

The dialog box shown in Figure 19.13 is easily achieved using a Grid panel (the XAML is shown in Listing 19.1). Arguably, the Grid control is the most flexible and relevant of the panel controls for almost all layout scenarios. For this reason, when you add a new window project item to a WPF project, the window by default already contains a Grid control.

FIGURE 19.13   Implementing a dialog box using the rows and columns of a Grid control.

LISTING 19.1   Implementing a dialog box with a Grid Panel

```
<Window x:Class="ContosoAvalon.Grid"
    xmlns="http://schemas.microsoft.com/winfx/2006/xaml/presentation"
    xmlns:x="http://schemas.microsoft.com/winfx/2006/xaml"
    Title="Grid" Height="300" Width="300">
  <Grid>
    <Grid.ColumnDefinitions>
      <ColumnDefinition Width="80"></ColumnDefinition>
      <ColumnDefinition Width="*"></ColumnDefinition>
      <ColumnDefinition Width="*"></ColumnDefinition>
    </Grid.ColumnDefinitions>
```

```xml
    <Grid.RowDefinitions>
        <RowDefinition></RowDefinition>
        <RowDefinition></RowDefinition>
        <RowDefinition></RowDefinition>
        <RowDefinition></RowDefinition>
        <RowDefinition></RowDefinition>
        <RowDefinition></RowDefinition>
        <RowDefinition></RowDefinition>
        <RowDefinition></RowDefinition>
    </Grid.RowDefinitions>

    <Label Grid.Column="0" Grid.Row="0">Name:</Label>
    <Label Grid.Column="0" Grid.Row="1">Street:</Label>
    <Label Grid.Column="0" Grid.Row="2">City:</Label>
    <Label Grid.Column="0" Grid.Row="3">State:</Label>
    <Label Grid.Column="0" Grid.Row="4">Postal code:</Label>
    <Label Grid.Column="0" Grid.Row="5">Date Hired:</Label>

    <TextBox Margin="5,5" BorderBrush="Gray" Grid.Column="1" Grid.Row="0"
    Grid.ColumnSpan="2"></TextBox>
    <TextBox Margin="5,5" BorderBrush="Gray" Grid.Column="1" Grid.Row="1"
    Grid.ColumnSpan="2"></TextBox>
    <TextBox Margin="5,5" BorderBrush="Gray" Grid.Column="1" Grid.Row="2"
    Grid.ColumnSpan="2"></TextBox>
    <ComboBox Margin="5,5" Grid.Column="1" Grid.Row="3"></ComboBox>
    <TextBox Margin="5,5" BorderBrush="Gray" Grid.Column="1" Grid.Row="4">
    </TextBox>
    <Label Grid.Column="1" Grid.Row="5">{Date}</Label>

    <Button Margin="5,5" Grid.Column="1" Grid.Row="6">OK</Button>
    <Button Margin="5,5" Grid.Column="2" Grid.Row="6">Cancel</Button>
  </Grid>
</Window>
```

There are three things to note in this XAML:

▶ We have used the concept of column spanning to get our controls to line up the way we want.

▶ We are using the Margin property on the child elements to give each label, text box, and so on, some room. Without a Margin specified, each control automatically fills the bounds of the cell it resides in, meaning that we have absolutely no border or gap between the controls (either horizontally or vertically).

▶ In the Grid's column definitions, we use an asterisk to denote a proportional size. In other words, the second and third columns equally share whatever space is left over after the first column has been rendered. We can adjust the proportion "ratio" by including a number as well (for example, `ColumnDefinition.Width="2*"`). We cover the details on grid sizing later in this chapter when we build a sample application.

The StackPanel Control

StackPanel controls implement a vertical or horizontal stack layout for their child elements. Compared with the Grid control, this is a simple panel that supports very little tweaking: you can select to stack children horizontally or vertically using the Orientation property, and after that the panel takes care of everything else. Each element within the StackPanel is resized/scaled to fit within the height (if stacked vertically) or width (if stacked horizontally) of the panel. Owing to the control's simplicity, the XAML is straightforward as well. Here, we are vertically stacking several check boxes, labels, a button, and a text box (see Figure 19.14 for the final product):

```
<StackPanel>
    <Label>Format Options:</Label>
    <CheckBox Margin="4" Height="16" Name="checkBox1">Perform Fast Format</CheckBox>
    <CheckBox Margin="4" Height="16" Name="checkBox2">Verify After Format</CheckBox>
    <CheckBox Margin="4" Height="16" Name="checkBox3">Enable Large Partition
     Support</CheckBox>
    <Label>Drive Label:</Label>
    <TextBox Margin="10,0" BorderBrush="Gray" Height="23" Name="comboBox2" />
    <Button Margin="80,20" Height="23" Name="button1" >Format</Button>
</StackPanel>
```

FIGURE 19.14   The StackPanel in action.

Another similar panel is the WrapPanel: this is essentially a StackPanel with additional behavior to wrap its children into additional rows or columns if there isn't enough room to display them within the bounds of the panel. See Figure 19.15 to see how the WrapPanel has auto-adjusted a series of buttons when its Window is sized smaller.

Styles and Templates

The capability to customize the look of a control in WPF, without losing any of its built-in functionality, is one of the huge advantages that WPF brings to the development scene. Consider the two slider controls in Figure 19.16: The top is the default style, and the bottom represents a restyled slider. Functionality is identical. We have simply changed the appearance of the control.

FIGURE 19.15   The WrapPanel.

FIGURE 19.16   The standard Slider (top) and a re-styled Slider (bottom).

Style is an actual class (in the System.Windows namespace) that is used in association with a control; it groups property values together to enable you, as a developer, to set them once and have them applied to controls en masse instead of having to set them individually on each control instance. Suppose, for instance, that your application uses a nice grayscale gradient for its button backgrounds. In addition, each button has a white border, and renders its text with the Segoe UI font. We can manipulate each of these aspects using Button properties; but it would quickly become laborious to do this on every single button. A Style enables us to set all of these properties once and then refer each button control to these properties by assigning the style to the button.

Here is the Style defined within a window in XAML:

```
<Window.Resources>
   <Style x:Key="GradientButton" TargetType="Button">
      <Setter Property="Margin" Value="2"/>
      <Setter Property="BorderBrush" Value="White" />
      <Setter Property="FontFamily" Value="Segoe UI"/>
      <Setter Property="FontSize" Value="12px"/>
      <Setter Property="FontWeight" Value="Bold"/>
      <Setter Property="Foreground" Value="White" />
      <Setter Property="Background" >
         <Setter.Value>
            <LinearGradientBrush StartPoint="0,0" EndPoint="0,1" >
               <GradientStop Color="Gray" Offset="0.2"/>
               <GradientStop Color="DarkGray" Offset="0.85"/>
               <GradientStop Color="Gray" Offset="1"/>
            </LinearGradientBrush>
         </Setter.Value>
```

19

```
        </Setter>
    </Style>
</Window.Resources>
```

To assign this style to any button within the window, it is as simple as this:

```
<Button Style="{StaticResource GradientButton}" Height="38" Name="button1"
Width="100">OK</Button>
```

This works very well for simplifying property sets. But what happens when we want to customize an attribute that isn't surfaced as a property? To continue with our button control, what if we wanted an oval shape instead of the standard rectangle? Because the Button class doesn't expose a property that we can use to change the background shape, we appear to be out of luck.

Enter the concept of templates. Templates enable you to completely replace the visual tree of any control giving you full control over every aspect of the control's user interface. A visual tree in WPF is the hierarchy of controls inheriting from the Visual class that provide a control's final rendered appearance. A good overview of WPF visual trees and logical trees can be found on www.msdn.microsoft.com. Search for the article "Trees in WPF."

> **NOTE**
>
> Earlier we mentioned that controls in WPF were "lookless"; templates are evidence of that fact. The functionality of a control exists separately from its visual tree. The default look for all the controls is provided through a series of templates, one per each Windows theme. This means that WPF controls can automatically participate in whatever OS theme you are running.

Templates are created via the ControlTemplate class. Within this class (or element, if we are implementing the template in XAML), we need to draw the visuals that represent the button. The Rectangle class in WPF can be used to draw our basic background shape. By tweaking the RadiusX and RadiusY properties, we can soften the normal 90-degree corners into the desired elliptical shape:

```
<Rectangle RadiusX="25" RadiusY="25" Width="100" Height="50"
Stroke="Black" StrokeThickness="1" />
```

We can also add some more compelling visual aspects such as a gradient fill to the button:

```
<Rectangle.Fill>
    <LinearGradientBrush>
        <LinearGradientBrush.GradientStops>
            <GradientStop Offset="0" Color="Gray" />
            <GradientStop Offset="1" Color="LightGray" />
        </LinearGradientBrush.GradientStops>
    </LinearGradientBrush>
</Rectangle.Fill>
```

> **TIP**
>
> To test the look and feel so far, type your "shape" XAML into the XAML editor, and tweak it as desired. After you are satisfied, you can copy and paste the XAML into the template. A better tool for designing user interfaces is Microsoft Expression Blend, but for simple design scenarios handcrafting the XAML or relying on Visual Studio's designer should be sufficient.

The text within the button is easily rendered using a TextBlock object:

```
<TextBlock Canvas.Top="5" Height="40" Width="100" FontSize="20"
TextAlignment="Center">OK</TextBlock>
```

After we are happy with the look and feel, we can "template-ize" this appearance by nesting everything within a ControlTemplate element. Because we need to refer to this template later, we provide a key/name:

```
<ControlTemplate x:Key="OvalButtonTemplate">
```

And finally, we embed the whole thing as a resource. A resource is simply a .NET object (written in XAML or code) that is meant to be shared across other objects. In this specific case, we want to be able to use this template with any button we want. Resources can be declared at any level within a WPF project: We can declare resources that belong to the overall window, or to any element within the window (such as a Grid panel), or we can store all of our resources in something known as a ResourceDictionary and allow them to be referenced from any class in our project. For this example, we stick to a simple resource defined in our parent window (for reference, this is the Window.Resources element that you see in the following code).

Listing 19.2 pulls this all together, and Figure 19.17 shows the resulting button.

FIGURE 19.17   A custom button template.

LISTING 19.2   Replacing a Button's Template

```
<Window x:Class="ContosoAvalon.CustomLook"
    xmlns="http://schemas.microsoft.com/winfx/2006/xaml/presentation"
    xmlns:x="http://schemas.microsoft.com/winfx/2006/xaml"
    Title="CustomLook" Height="300" Width="300"
    Background="#F8F8F8">
  <Window.Resources>
    <ControlTemplate x:Key="OvalButtonTemplate">
```

```
            <Canvas Width="100" Height="25" Margin="2">
                <Rectangle x:Name="BaseRectangle" Canvas.Top="0" RadiusX="25"
                 RadiusY="25" Width="100" Height="40" Stroke="DarkGray"
                 StrokeThickness="1">
                    <Rectangle.Fill>
                        <LinearGradientBrush>
                            <LinearGradientBrush.GradientStops>
                                <GradientStop Offset="0" Color="Gray" />
                                <GradientStop Offset="1" Color="LightGray" />
                            </LinearGradientBrush.GradientStops>
                        </LinearGradientBrush>
                    </Rectangle.Fill>
                </Rectangle>
                <TextBlock Canvas.Top="5" Height="40" Width="100" FontSize="20"
                 TextAlignment="Center">OK</TextBlock>
            </Canvas>
        </ControlTemplate>
    </Window.Resources>
    <Canvas>
    <Button Canvas.Left="49" Canvas.Top="44" Height="38" Name="button1"
     Width="93" Template="{StaticResource OvalButtonTemplate}" />
    </Canvas>
</Window>
```

Data Binding

Data binding, in its purest sense, is the capability of a control to be wired to a data source such that the control (a) displays certain items from that data source, and (b) is kept in sync with the data source. After the connection is made, the runtime handles all the work necessary to make this happen. It doesn't really matter where or how the data is stored: It could be a file system, a custom collection of objects, a database object, and so on.

So let's look briefly at how we can establish a data binding connection using WPF. The key class here is the System.Windows.Data.Binding class. This is the mediator in charge of linking a control with a data source. To successfully declare a binding, we need to know three things:

- ▶ What UI control property do we want to bind?

- ▶ What data source do we want to bind to?

- ▶ And, within the data source, what specific element or property or such holds the data we are interested in?

We can bind to either single objects (such as binding a string property on an object to a text box), or to collections of objects (such as binding a List<> collection to a list box). Either way, the mechanics remain the same:

```
Binding binding = new Binding();
```

```
binding.Source = _stringList;

listBox1.SetBinding(ListBox.ItemsSourceProperty, binding);
```

The preceding code snippet creates a Binding object, sets the source of the Binding object to our List<string> collection, and then calls SetBinding on our control (a ListBox), passing in the exact property on the control we want to bind to our data source, and the Binding object instance.

We can also assign data sources into a special object called the data context. Every FrameworkElement object, and those that derive from that class, implement their own DataContext instance. You can think of this as a global area where controls can go to get their data when participating in a data binding arrangement.

This ends up simplifying our data binding code quite a bit. We can set the context in our Window constructor like this:

```
this.DataContext = _stringList;
```

Now, we just point our ListBox to this data context using a tag within the ListBox's XAML element:

```
<ListBox Name="listBox1" ItemsSource="{Binding}" />
```

The binding object in this case automatically hunts for objects stashed within a data context somewhere within the object tree. When it finds one, it automatically binds the objects.

This works great for our simple List<string> example, but what if we are trying to bind a collection of custom objects to the list box? If we have a simple Employee class with a Name property and a PhoneNbr property, how could we bind to a collection of those objects and show the employee name? Our process would actually remain the same. If we create an Employee class, and then create a List<Employee> collection, all of this code still works. But there is a problem: Figure 19.18 highlights an issue we have to solve.

FIGURE 19.18   Binding a ListBox to a collection of custom objects.

We haven't yet told the binding engine how exactly we want our data to be represented within the list box. By default, the binding process simply calls ToString on every object.

One quick remedy would be to simply override the ToString method:

```
public override string ToString()
{
    return _name;
}
```

This corrects the problem in this instance. But a more robust approach involves the use of a DataTemplate. We cover that approach a little later, in the section "Building a Simple Image Viewer Application."

Routed Events

The standard way that .NET classes and controls raise and handle events is essentially the way that you perform these tasks in WPF. But the WPF libraries bring an important improvement to standard events. We call these routed events.

Consider a simple scenario: You have a Button control that consists of a background image and some text (see Figure 19.19). If you recall from our discussion of a controls template and visual tree, this means we actually have a few discrete elements that make up the button: a TextBlock, an Image, and the basic frame and background of the button.

FIGURE 19.19   A button with multiple elements.

These are separate objects/elements unto themselves. So the event situation becomes a little complex. It isn't enough to react to a click on the button background; we also have to react to a click on the button's text or the button's image. This is where routed events come into play. Routed events are capable of calling event handlers up or down the entire visual tree. This means we are free to implement an event handler at the Button level, and be confident that a click on the button's image or text will bubble up until it finds our event handler.

Routed events in WPF are broken down into three categories: bubbling events, tunneling events, and direct events:

▶ **Bubbling events**—These events travel up the visual tree starting at the initial receiving element.

▶ **Tunneling events**—These events start at the top of the control's visual tree and move down until they reach the receiving element.

▶ **Direct event**—These are the equivalent of "standard" .NET events: Only the event handler for the receiving element is called.

Events themselves, like nearly everything else in WPF, can be declared in XAML or in code. Here we have a button control with a MouseEnter event defined:

```
<Button MouseEnter="button1_MouseEnter" Height="23" Name="button1"
Width="75">OK</Button>
```

The event handler itself, in C#, looks like any other .NET event handler:

```
private void button1_MouseEnter(object sender, MouseEventArgs e)
{
    MessageBox.Show("MouseEnter on button1");
}
```

We have only scratched the surface on many of the basic programming concepts within WPF. But you should now be armed with enough knowledge to be productive writing a simple WPF application. Let's do just that, using the tools available to us in Visual Studio 2010.

Building a Simple Image Viewer Application

To illustrate the role that Visual Studio plays in WPF application development, let's build a sample application from scratch. In the tradition of "experience first," let's select something that can benefit from WPF's strong suits, namely visualizations and robust control layouts and templating.

Consider an image viewer application. We can use this application to view a list of image thumbnails and, after selecting a thumbnail, can view the image itself and even make changes to the image.

We target the rough design shown in Figure 19.20.

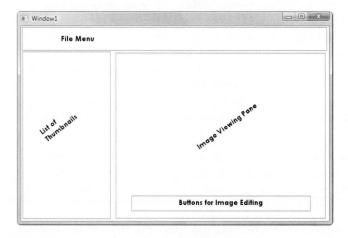

FIGURE 19.20   A sketch of an image viewer UI.

Here are our base requirements:

▸ When the application loads, it parses the images contained in the specified folder.

▸ Every image is listed in a list box; the list box shows image thumbnails and no text.

▸ When the user clicks on one of the items in the list box, the image viewing area is populated with the selected image.

▸ The user can then choose to manipulate the image: a black-and-white effect can be applied, the image can be rotated clockwise or counterclockwise, the image can be flipped, and it can be mirrored.

▸ In general, we try to use WPF's capabilities when possible to make the application more visually compelling; a standard battleship gray application is not what we are looking for here.

Starting the Layout

After creating a new WPF project, we double-click the Window1.xaml file and start designing our user interface. To start, a Grid panel and some nested StackPanel or WrapPanel containers provide the initial layout. Referring to the sketch design (Figure 19.20), one can envision a Grid with two rows and two columns to start. The top row holds the menu control (which should span both columns), and the bottom row hold the listbox of images in the left column, and another parent control in the right column which display the image and the editing buttons.

To get started on this layout, we can use the Grid control that has been automatically placed on our window during project creation. We could use the XAML pane for our window to quickly enter some XAML tags for the right elements, but let's see how quickly the WPF designer enables us to create a layout without typing anything. Select the grid within the designer; you can do this by either clicking within the designer, or clicking within the <Grid> element in the XAML pane. With the Grid control selected, notice two shaded border areas to the top and to the left side of the grid control. These are known as "grid rails." The grid rails enable you to quickly create columns and rows within the grid. If you move the mouse cursor over one of the grid rails, the cursor changes to cross-hairs. A grid splitter also appears; this visually indicates where the exact column or row divider is positioned within the grid. By clicking within the top grid rail, you can add a column; clicking in the left grid rail adds a row. Figure 19.21 shows an example of a grid selected in the designer, with the grid rails visible to the top and to the left of the grid.

For this project, move your cursor over the top grid rail and move the resulting column splitter so that it is approximately one-third of the way through the Grid's width. Now, click within the rail to create the two columns. Note that the designer shows us the exact width, in pixels, for each column (Figure 19.22).

Now, do the same within the left grid rail. Position the row splitter so that the top row has a height of about 30 pixels. Don't worry about getting this exact; we tweak the sizing a little later.

FIGURE 19.21   Grid with grid rails visible to the top and left.

FIGURE 19.22   Sizing columns within a Grid.

Add the List of Images

Drag a ListBox into the first column and first row. Initially, this ListBox has a height, width, and margin value set for it. Because we want this control to resize itself based on the size of the column and row that it sits within, we need to change these properties. Make sure the ListBox is selected within the designer, and then delete any values within the Height and Width properties. You should also set the VerticalAlignment and HorizontalAlignment properties to Stretch. And finally, set the Margin property to five (5).

You should now have a design surface that looks something like the window in Figure 19.23.

Add the Top Menu

The top menu control in our application will be used to open a folder selection dialog box. Drag a Menu control into the first column and first row. This control needs to span both of the columns in our grid, so resize it within the designer so it crosses the border between column one and column two. We can now make adjustments similar to those we made for our ListBox: Using the property window, remove any Height value, and set the Width to Auto. Set the HorizontalAlignment and VerticalAlignment properties to Stretch, and set the Margin to 5.

19

FIGURE 19.23   Our UI in progress.

We know we need to provide folder selection capabilities, so we title a main menu item as Folder, and include a subitem under that titled Open. To implement this design, use the property window and edit the Items property; a collection editor dialog box opens that enables us to add the Folder menu items. Via the Header property, we need to specify the text that is displayed for the menu (Figure 19.24) and also the name: FolderOpenMenuItem.

FIGURE 19.24   Creating a MenuItem.

After the Folder menu item has been created, select it and use the property window to edit its Items collection to add the final Open menu item. For this menu item, we also want to specify an event handler for its Click event. Make sure you have the Events tab selected in the property window, and then enter FolderOpenMenuItem_Click in the Click event (See Figure 19.25). Visual Studio automatically creates a stub for the event handler, and open it within the code editor for you. Because we aren't ready to implement this event yet, you can simply click back to the WPF designer within the IDE.

FIGURE 19.25   Wiring the Click event for our Open MenuItem.

Add the Image Viewer

The main screen area for this application is the image viewer, and its associated command buttons. This consists of a grid with two rows: the top row holds an Image control, and grows as we re-size. The bottom row is a static height and holds a StackPanel of buttons oriented horizontally.

Drag a Grid control from the toolbox into the second row and second column of our original parent grid. You configure the rows as indicated the same way you did for the root grid. For the image view box, we use an Image control. Drag one into the top row of the new grid and, as before, remove any Margin settings or Width/Height values.

And finally, drag a StackPanel into the bottom row of the new grid, remove any Margin settings, and set its Orientation property to Horizontal and the HorizontalAlignment property to Center. This panel is where we place our image manipulation buttons, which you can add now as well. Drag four buttons into the StackPanel, and adjust their margins and height/width until you get the workable look and feel you are after.

> **NOTE**
>
> While building this app, we have mostly relied on the WPF Designer's property window to tweak our control properties. But because the XAML code editor supports IntelliSense, and because XAML is fairly readable, you might find it faster and more productive to make the changes directly within the XAML. The bottom line here is that the IDE enables you to choose how you are most productive.

Grid Sizing Details

With all of our grids, columns, and rows now in place, we can think about how we want to handle sizing. In other words, how do we want our columns and rows to resize themselves if a user happens to resize the parent window? To configure the grid correctly, we need to understand the concepts of fixed, auto, and proportional sizing.

19

Proportional sizing, also sometimes referred to as "star sizing" is used to apportion row height or column width as a proportion of all available space. XAML-wise, proportional sizing is expressed with an asterisk inside the Row.Height or Column.Width properties. With star sizing, you indicate the proportional "weight" that you want the column to occupy. For instance, for a grid with two columns, if we specified a width on both columns of ".5*", we would end up with both columns taking up half of the available space (width wise) of the grid. Figure 19.22 shows some example column sizes using proportional sizing. If we just specify an asterisk with no weight (for example, Width="*"), we are instructing that column to take all of the remaining space.

Auto sizing causes the row height or width to grow or shrink as necessary to exactly fit whatever is currently placed within the row or column. So a row that is auto sized would be as tall as the tallest control it hosts. Note that in addition to the control height, other things can affect the space reserved for a control such as margins and padding.

And finally, *fixed* sizing works exactly like you think it would. You specify a width or height in pixels, and the column or row snaps to that dimension regardless of how the grid's parent control or window is sized.

With these details exposed, we can formulate a strategy for our layout. Figure 19.26 shows a revised sketch indicating our sizing scheme.

FIGURE 19.26   UI sketch with resizing notes.

The WPF Designer provides a way to directly indicate the sizing type for each row and column. Using the grid rails again, hover the mouse over the rail space for a column. A small toolbar pops up directly above the rail with three buttons. These three buttons correspond to the three sizing modes. Go ahead and cycle through all of the rows and columns in the designer, setting the height and width properties using the designer toolbar.

Here is a look at the current XAML with all of the basic elements in place:

```
<Grid>
    <Grid.RowDefinitions>
        <RowDefinition Height="Auto" />
        <RowDefinition Height="*" />
    </Grid.RowDefinitions>
    <Grid.ColumnDefinitions>
        <ColumnDefinition Width="Auto" />
        <ColumnDefinition Width="*" />
    </Grid.ColumnDefinitions>
    <ListBox Grid.Row="1" HorizontalAlignment="Stretch"
     Margin="5" Name="listBox1" VerticalAlignment="Stretch"
     Width="175" />
    <Menu Grid.ColumnSpan="2" HorizontalAlignment="Stretch"
     Margin="0" Name="menu1" VerticalAlignment="Stretch">
        <MenuItem Header="_Folder" VerticalAlignment="Center">
            <MenuItem x:Name="OpenMenuItem" Header="_Open"
             Click="FolderOpenMenuItem_Click"
             VerticalAlignment="Center">
            </MenuItem>
        </MenuItem>
    </Menu>
    <Grid Grid.Row="1" Grid.Column="1">
        <Grid.RowDefinitions>
            <RowDefinition Height="*" />
            <RowDefinition Height="Auto" />
        </Grid.RowDefinitions>
        <Image Grid.Row="0" Name="image1" Stretch="UniformToFill"
         Margin="5" VerticalAlignment="Center"
         HorizontalAlignment="Center" />
        <StackPanel Grid.Row="1" Orientation="Horizontal"
         HorizontalAlignment="Center" >
            <Button Width="50" Height="50" Margin="10">
             Button</Button>
            <Button Width="50" Height="50" Margin="10">
             Button</Button>
            <Button Width="50" Height="50" Margin="10">
             Button</Button>
            <Button Width="50" Height="50" Margin="10">
             Button</Button>
        </StackPanel>
    </Grid>
</Grid>
```

19

Storing the Images

With the UI elements in place, we can move on to the data binding issues (we come back later and give the UI more polish). The first task is to store the files in a collection of some sort. It turns out that there is a class in the System.Windows.Media.Imaging namespace that is suitable for our needs: BitmapSource. For a collection, a List<BitmapSource> object should work for the moment, but we need some way to populate the list. So let's create a wrapper class that both loads the list and exposes it as a property. Add a new class to the project with the following code:

```
public class DirectoryImageList
{
   private string _path;
   private List<BitmapSource> _images = new List<BitmapSource>();

   public DirectoryImageList(string path)
   {
      _path = path;
      LoadImages();

   }

   public List<BitmapSource> Images
   {
      get { return _images; }
      set { _images = value; }
   }

   public string Path
   {
      get { return _path; }
      set
      {
         _path = value;
         LoadImages();
      }
   }

   private void LoadImages()
   {
      _images.Clear();
      BitmapImage img;

      foreach (string file in Directory.GetFiles(_path))
      {
         try
```

```
        {
            img = new BitmapImage(new Uri(file));

            _images.Add(img);
        }
        catch
        {
            // empty catch; ignore any files that won't load as
            // an image...
        }
    }
  }
}
```

The LoadImages method in the preceding code is where most of the important logic is found; it enumerates the files within a given directory and attempts to load them into a BitmapImage object. If it succeeds, we know that this is an image file. If it doesn't, we just ignore the resulting exception and keep on going.

Back in our Window class, we need to create some private fields to hold an instance of this new class, and to hold the currently selected path. This is something we let the user change through a common dialog box launched from the Folder, Open menu item.

Here are the fields:

```
private DirectoryImageList _imgList;
private string _path =
  Environment.GetFolderPath
          (Environment.SpecialFolder.MyPictures);
```

Note that we have defaulted our path to the Pictures folder. To load up the list object, we write a ResetList method in our Window1 class:

```
private void ResetList()
{
    _imgList = new DirectoryImageList(_path);
}
```

Referring to our earlier discussion on data binding, we round things off by adding a few lines of code to the Window1 constructor: an initial call to ResetList, and a call to assign the data context to the Images property from the DirectoryImageList instance.

```
public Window1()
{
    InitializeComponent();
    ResetList();
    this.DataContext = _imgList.Images;
}
```

If we run the application now, we see a familiar sight (as in Figure 19.27): The data binding is working, but isn't quite the presentation format we want.

FIGURE 19.27 Initial data binding results.

Binding to the Images

Because our earlier trick of overriding ToString won't give us the right data presentation (an image, after all, is not a string), we need to turn to data templates. The DataTemplate class is used to tell a control specifically how you want its data to be displayed. By using a data template within the visual tree of the control, you have complete freedom to present the bound data in any fashion you want.

For this application, we are looking for images in the ListBox. This turns out to be quite easy. Create a Window1.Resources element in XAML, and create a DataTemplate that sets up the exact visualization we need:

```
<Window.Resources>
    <DataTemplate x:Key="ImageDataTemplate">
        <Image Source="{Binding UriSource.LocalPath}" Width="125"
          Height="125" />
    </DataTemplate>
</Window.Resources>
```

Then assign the DataTemplate to the ListBox:

```
<ListBox Grid.Row="1" Name="listBox1" ItemsSource="{Binding}"
 ItemTemplate="{StaticResource ImageDataTemplate}"/>
```

In our data template, the Image element is expecting a source URI for each image. So we use the UriSource.LocalPath that is provided on the BitmapSource object. If you now re-run the application, you should immediately see that our ListBox is now displaying thumbnail sized images (125 × 125) for every picture it finds in our local pictures directory.

We aren't done yet; clicking a thumbnail in the list box should cause the central Image control to display the indicated picture. By creating a SelectionChanged event handler and wiring it to the ListBox, we can update our Image.Source property accordingly.

The event is declared as expected within the ListBox XAML element:

```
<ListBox SelectionChanged="listBox1_SelectionChanged" Grid.Row="1"
 Name="listBox1" ItemsSource="{Binding}"
 ItemTemplate="{StaticResource ImageDataTemplate}"/>
```

And for the event handler, we cast the SelectedItem from the ListBox to its native BitmapSource representation, and assign it to our image control:

```
private void listBox1_SelectionChanged(object sender,
    SelectionChangedEventArgs e)
{
    image1.Source = (BitmapSource)((sender as ListBox).SelectedItem);
}
```

Button Event Handlers and Image Effects

With the images successfully loaded into the list box, and displayed in the central Image control, we can turn our attention to our four image editing/effects features:

- ▶ Black and white filter
- ▶ Image blur
- ▶ Rotate
- ▶ Flip

Because these four functions are controlled by the four buttons, we need to add some appropriate button images and events; we don't cover the button stylings here because they involve external graphics resources, but you can see how they turn out in the final screenshot (at the end of this chapter), or by downloading the source from this book's website.

The code for the events, however, is fair game. First, the XAML event declarations on each button:

```
<Button Click="buttonBandW_Click" Margin="20,0,0,0" Height="23"
 Name="buttonBandW" Width="30"/>

<Button Click="buttonBlur_Click" Margin="20,0,0,0" Height="23"
 Name="buttonBlur" Width="30"/>

<Button Click="buttonRotate_Click"  Margin="20,0,0,0" Height="23"
 Name="buttonRotate" Width="30"/>

<Button Click="buttonFlip_Click" Margin="20,0,20,0" Height="23"
Name="buttonFlip" Width="30"/>
```

19

Notice as you type these click events into the XAML pane that the XAML editor inter-venes with IntelliSense pop-ups that not only complete our Click declaration, but also create the corresponding event handler in our code-behind class!

To perform the image manipulations, we employ something known as a transform: the manipulation of a 2D surface to rotate, skew, or otherwise change the current appearance of the surface. We can handle our rotation feature directly with RotateTransform like this:

```
private void buttonRotate_Click(object sender, RoutedEventArgs e)
{
   CachedBitmap cache = new CachedBitmap((BitmapSource)image1.Source,
      BitmapCreateOptions.None, BitmapCacheOption.OnLoad);
   image1.Source = new TransformedBitmap(cache, new RotateTransform(90));
}
```

Our flip action ends up being just as easy, but uses a ScaleTransform instead:

```
private void buttonFlip_Click(object sender, RoutedEventArgs e)
{
   CachedBitmap cache = new CachedBitmap((BitmapSource)image1.Source,
      BitmapCreateOptions.None, BitmapCacheOption.OnLoad);
   ScaleTransform scale = new ScaleTransform(-1, -1, image1.Source.Width / 2,
      image1.Source.Height / 2);
   image1.Source = new TransformedBitmap(cache, scale);
}
```

The image blurring action is provided through a different mechanism known as an effect. By creating a new BlurBitmapEffect instance and assigning that to our image control, WPF apply the appropriate algorithm to the bitmap to blur the picture:

```
image1.BitmapEffect = new BlurEffect();
```

Path Selection with a Common Dialog Box

The last item on our to-do list is allowing the user to change the path of the picture files. WPF itself doesn't have any built-in dialog box classes to manage this, but the System.Windows.Forms namespace has just what we need: the FolderBrowserDialog class. This is launched from within the event handler for our FolderOpenMenuItem click event:

```
private void FolderOpenMenuItem_Click(object sender, RoutedEventArgs e)
{
   SetPath();
}

private void SetPath()
{
```

```
FolderBrowserDialog dlg = new FolderBrowserDialog();
dlg.ShowDialog();
_path = dlg.SelectedPath;
ResetList();
}
```

When a user selects a folder, we update our internal field appropriately, reload the DirectoryImageList class with the new path, and then reset our window's DataContext property to reflect the change. This is a perfect example of how seamless it is to use other .NET technologies and class libraries from within WPF. By adding the appropriate namespace and reference to our project, we just instantiate this class like any other class in our solution.

TIP

Because there are a fair number of controls that share the same name between WPF and WinForms (the ListBox control is one example), if you find yourself using classes from the System.Windows.Controls and the System.Windows.Forms libraries, you inevitably need to fully qualify some of your object names to avoid operating against the wrong class.

And with that, the application is functionally complete. For reference, we have provided the current state of the XAML and the code-behind listings in Listing 19.3 and Listing 19.4, respectively. If you really want to dissect this application, however, you should download the source code from this book's website. This enables you to see the improvements made with graphics resources and general look and feel, producing the final polished version shown in Figure 19.28.

FIGURE 19.28   After the finishing touches.

LISTING 19.3   The Image Viewer XAML Code

```xaml
<Window x:Class="WpfImageViewer.MainWindow"
        xmlns="http://schemas.microsoft.com/winfx/2006/xaml/presentation"
        xmlns:x="http://schemas.microsoft.com/winfx/2006/xaml"
        Title="Image Viewer Sample Application"
        Height="400" Width="550"
        Background="{DynamicResource BackgroundGradientBrush}">

    <Window.Resources>
        <DataTemplate x:Key="ImageDataTemplate">
            <Image Source="{Binding UriSource.LocalPath}"
                    Width="125" Height="125" />
        </DataTemplate>
    </Window.Resources>

    <Grid>
        <Grid.RowDefinitions>
            <RowDefinition Height="Auto" />
            <RowDefinition Height="*" />
        </Grid.RowDefinitions>
        <Grid.ColumnDefinitions>
            <ColumnDefinition Width="Auto" />
            <ColumnDefinition Width="*" />
        </Grid.ColumnDefinitions>
        <ListBox Grid.Row="1"
                HorizontalAlignment="Stretch"
                Margin="5" Name="listBox1"
                VerticalAlignment="Stretch"
                Width="175"
                ItemsSource="{Binding}"
                ItemTemplate="{StaticResource ImageDataTemplate}"
                SelectionChanged="listBox1_SelectionChanged" />
        <Menu Grid.ColumnSpan="2"
                Background="{DynamicResource MenuBackgroundGradientBrush}"
                HorizontalAlignment="Stretch"
                Margin="0"
                Name="menu1"
                VerticalAlignment="Stretch">
            <MenuItem Header="_Folder"
                    VerticalAlignment="Center">
                <MenuItem x:Name="OpenMenuItem"
                        Header="_Open"
                        Click="FolderOpenMenuItem_Click"
                        VerticalAlignment="Center">
                </MenuItem>
```

```xml
                </MenuItem>
            </Menu>
            <Grid Grid.Row="1" Grid.Column="1">
                <Grid.RowDefinitions>
                    <RowDefinition Height="*" />
                    <RowDefinition Height="Auto" />
                </Grid.RowDefinitions>
                <Image Grid.Row="0"
                        Name="image1"
                        Stretch="UniformToFill"
                        Margin="5"
                        VerticalAlignment="Center"
                        HorizontalAlignment="Center" />
                <StackPanel Grid.Row="1" Orientation="Horizontal"
                            HorizontalAlignment="Center" >
                    <Button Name="buttonBandW"
                            Style="{DynamicResource BWImageButtonStyle}"
                            Click="buttonBandW_Click"
                            Width="50"
                            Height="50"
                            Margin="10" />
                    <Button Name="buttonBlur"
                            Style="{DynamicResource BlurImageButtonStyle}"
                            Click="buttonBlur_Click"
                            Width="50"
                            Height="50"
                            Margin="10" />
                    <Button Name="buttonRotate"
                            Style="{DynamicResource RotateImageButtonStyle}"
                            Click="buttonRotate_Click"
                            Width="50"
                            Height="50"
                            Margin="10" />
                    <Button Name="buttonFlip"
                            Style="{DynamicResource FlipImageButtonStyle}"
                            Click="buttonFlip_Click"
                            Width="50"
                            Height="50"
                            Margin="10" />
                </StackPanel>
            </Grid>
        </Grid>
</Window>
```

19

LISTING 19.4   The Image Viewer Code Behind C#

```csharp
using System;
using System.Collections.Generic;
using System.Linq;
using System.Text;
using System.Windows;
using System.Windows.Controls;
using System.Windows.Data;
using System.Windows.Documents;
using System.Windows.Input;
using System.Windows.Media;
using System.Windows.Media.Effects;
using System.Windows.Media.Imaging;
using System.Windows.Navigation;
using System.Windows.Shapes;

namespace WpfImageViewer
{
    /// <summary>
    /// Interaction logic for MainWindow.xaml
    /// </summary>
    public partial class MainWindow : Window
    {
        #region Private fields

        private DirectoryImageList _imgList;
        private string _path =
            Environment.GetFolderPath(
            Environment.SpecialFolder.MyPictures);

        #endregion

        #region Ctor

        public MainWindow()
        {
            InitializeComponent();
            ResetList();
            this.DataContext = _imgList.Images;
        }

        #endregion

        #region Event handlers and delegates
```

```
private void FolderOpenMenuItem_Click
    (object sender, RoutedEventArgs e)
{
    SetPath();
}


private void listBox1_SelectionChanged
    (object sender, SelectionChangedEventArgs e)
{
    this.image1.Source = (BitmapSource)
                ((sender as ListBox).SelectedItem);
    this.image1.Effect = null;
}


private void buttonBandW_Click
    (object sender, RoutedEventArgs e)
{
    BitmapSource img = (BitmapSource)image1.Source;
    image1.Source =
        new FormatConvertedBitmap
            (img, PixelFormats.Gray16,
            BitmapPalettes.Gray256, 1.0);
}


private void buttonBlur_Click
    (object sender, RoutedEventArgs e)
{
    if (image1.Effect != null)
    {
        // if blur is current effect, remove
        image1.Effect = null;
    }
    else
    {
        // otherwise, add the blur effect to the image
        image1.Effect = new BlurEffect();
    }
}


private void buttonRotate_Click
    (object sender, RoutedEventArgs e)
{
    CachedBitmap cache =
        new CachedBitmap((BitmapSource)image1.Source,
            BitmapCreateOptions.None,
            BitmapCacheOption.OnLoad);
```

19

```
    image1.Source =
        new TransformedBitmap(cache,
            new RotateTransform(90));

}

private void buttonFlip_Click
    (object sender, RoutedEventArgs e)
{
    CachedBitmap cache =
        new CachedBitmap((BitmapSource)image1.Source,
            BitmapCreateOptions.None,
            BitmapCacheOption.OnLoad);
    ScaleTransform scale =
        new ScaleTransform(-1, -1, image1.Source.Width / 2,
            image1.Source.Height / 2);
    image1.Source =
        new TransformedBitmap(cache, scale);
}


#endregion

#region Implementation

private void SetPath()
{
    System.Windows.Forms.FolderBrowserDialog dlg =
        new System.Windows.Forms.FolderBrowserDialog();
    dlg.ShowDialog();
    _path = dlg.SelectedPath;
    ResetList();
}

private void ResetList()
{
    if (IsValidPath(_path))
    {
        _imgList = new DirectoryImageList(_path);
    }

    this.DataContext = _imgList.Images;

}

private bool IsValidPath(string path)
```

```
        {

            try
            {
                string folder =
                    System.IO.Path.GetFullPath(path);
                return true;
            }
            catch
            {
                return false;
            }
        }

        #endregion


    }

}
```

Summary

In this chapter, you had a brief introduction to Microsoft's new presentation layer framework, the Windows Presentation Foundation. We investigated the overall framework architecture and its programming model, including the new concept of using declarative markup to design and lay out a WPF client application's user interface. And we saw how the Visual Studio WPF Designer can be used to quickly craft compelling user interfaces using the same development processes we use when building Windows Forms or even ASP.NET applications.

We spent some time discussing the basics of control layout—a central theme in WPF—and covering the first-class data binding support that WPF enjoys.

As mentioned, developers trying to learn WPF will find that it is both a broad and deep subject. It is highly recommended that you spend some time with MSDN resources (such as the WPF developer center at www.msdn.microsoft.com/wpf) and then revisit this chapter to get a full sense of the skills and knowledge required to come up to speed on WPF development. Spending time with the design tools—free trials are available—is also highly recommended. See www.microsoft.com/expression for more information.

19

Creating Rich Browser Applications

Visual Studio 2010 enables developers to create great Web 2.0 applications. These applications give users a rich degree of interaction from within a browser. Sites with just text, images, and hyperlinks that refresh every time the user clicks the mouse are being reworked to give user a responsive UI similar to working in Windows. New sites are blurring the lines between what was thought possible with web applications and what was once strictly the domain of applications running natively on the operating system.

In this chapter, you learn about three browser-based technologies in Visual Studio 2010 you can use to create the next web. These include ASP.NET Ajax, WPF XAML Browser Applications (XBAP), and Microsoft Silverlight. With Ajax, you can create a rich experience that targets standard browsers on all platforms. WPF browser applications enable you to leverage nearly the full power of Windows Presentation Foundation (WPF) within a browser. Of course, this means your application must run inside a browser running on Windows. Finally, Silverlight applications can run inside a browser plug-in and provide a rich experience similar to that with WPF. In addition, Silverlight browser plug-ins are available for most browsers on most platforms.

Building Rich, Cross-Browser Interfaces with ASP.NET Ajax

With Visual Studio 2010, you can now more easily provide a high degree of user interaction within your ASP.NET applications. The tools include a set of controls, a code library, and access to a toolkit; all of these are available to help you embed client-side JavaScript in your user interface. This JavaScript can enable a richer user experience that includes modal dialog boxes, progress notification, partial-page updates, and much more. Collectively, this technology is known as Asynchronous JavaScript and XML (Ajax).

Ajax tries to break down the barrier between a thin, very dumb client and the server. In this way, it enables more real-time user interaction and at the same time offloads some of the server processing. Many activities can be done on the client without putting load on the server. In addition, in partial-page update scenarios, only the portion of the page being updated is sent to and from the server. This can increase the efficiency of the request and response.

The Ajax technology also enables you to continue to leverage the investments you've made in ASP.NET development. Ajax applications are built on the same ASP.NET control set you are used to. Ajax is simply an addition to these controls. In addition, because JavaScript is a standard (ECMAScript), it is part of all modern browsers (IE, Firefox, Safari) running on all platforms (Windows, Mac, and so on). Therefore, the web applications you build with it work cross-platform, cross-browser.

> **NOTE**
>
> Many ASP.NET controls have been using JavaScript on the client to provide better user interaction for a long time now. These include the validation controls for doing client-side validation, the Web Part controls for doing drag-and-drop of Web Parts across zones, the menu control, the TreeView control to open and view nodes, the calendar control, and more. The Ajax controls and Ajax Toolkit are simply a formalization of a direction web development had been heading for years.

The ASP.NET Ajax Controls

The ASP.NET Ajax controls are a set of four basic controls that serve one primary purpose: partial-page updates. Partial-page updates provide users a better experience when working with your application. Most web pages require a full refresh after the user has either requested or posted data to the server. This refresh of the page makes your entire page reload, which takes time and seems less than responsive to users—especially for large pages. A partial-page update submits only a portion of the page to the server for processing. In addition, the response returned from the server can be updated inside a portion of the page. This eliminates the refresh and makes your application more interactive to users. The ASP.NET Ajax Extensions controls work together to enable portions of a page to submit and then update independently.

The ASP.NET Ajax controls are used like any other ASP.NET control. You can drag a control from the Toolbox onto your form. You can then work with the control from the Properties window inside Visual Studio, inside your page's markup, and in your code file. Figure 20.1 shows you the list of Ajax controls available inside the Visual Studio Toolbox.

Notice the ScriptManager control in the Toolbox. This control is required on all pages that leverage the Ajax Extensions for partial-page update. You can only have one instance of this control on your page. It is responsible for adding the Microsoft Ajax Library to your page. This library is used in the asynchronous calling to and from the server during the partial-page update process.

FIGURE 20.1   You access the Ajax controls from the Visual Studio Toolbox.

Table 20.1 provides a list of all the Ajax Extensions controls shown in Figure 20.1. This list provides you a quick reference for understanding how each control is differentiated. We cover these controls in more depth in the coming sections.

TABLE 20.1   ASP.NET Ajax Controls

Control	Description
ScriptManager	All Ajax pages you write using the standard Ajax controls listed here require a single ScriptManager control on the page. It is used by ASP.NET to manage the other Ajax controls on the page, and handle partial-page rendering, globalization, localization, and more.
ScriptManagerProxy	A page may only contain a single ScriptManager control. You might have defined a master page that contains a ScriptManager control. In this case, a page that uses the master can take advantage of partial-page updates. However, if the child page needs to add additional script it can use the ScriptManagerProxy control to do so. The ScriptManagerProxy may also be used with user controls that might be placed on a page that already defines a ScriptManager control.
UpdatePanel	Use an `UpdatePanel` when you want to group items for partial-page update. Items inside an UpdatePanel that execute a postback to the server do so only for the panel (and not the rest of the page). In this way, you get an easy model for updating only portions of your page from the server without executing a full page refresh in the browser.

20

TABLE 20.1   Continued

Control	Description
UpdateProgress	The UpdateProgress control enables you to provide the user with status information as a partial-page update is processing on the server. The UpdateProgress is used in conjunction with the UpdatePanel control. When a partial-page postback is started, progress indication is made to the user. When the postback is complete, the user is again notified.
Timer	The Timer control provides a client-side timer that lets you postback the contents of an UpdatePanel at set intervals. In this way, you can trigger partial-page updates on a periodic basis.

Creating a Page that Supports Partial Update

You will find that the process of creating a page using the Ajax Extensions controls is very similar to creating standard pages. There are just a few things you need to worry about. In this section, you walk through an example of creating a ASP.NET page that supports partial-page update. You then build on this example to provide notification of server progress to the user's browser.

Partial-Page Update

A partial-page update posts only a portion of the page to the server; the server processes it, and then updates only that portion in the user's browser. This cuts down on overhead, increases speed, and decreases server processing; users also end up with a better experience. Only the section of the page with which they are working is updated. The page does not refresh and reload. This experience seems natural and faster to most users.

In this walk-through example, you create a web page that enables users to search for customer orders. We use the Northwind database as the source database. We then build the page such that when results are displayed, a user can page through them. When they do, the data pages are implemented as partial-page updates. This ensures that users do not feel as though they are performing a new search every time they select a new page of data.

To get started, create an ASP.NET website. By default, ASP.NET sites already support Ajax. Therefore, you do not need to do anything special beyond creating a basic ASP.NET website (see Chapter 17, "Creating ASP.NET Applications," for more information on creating websites). The following steps outline what is required to enable the example:

1. Create a new website application in Visual Studio (File, New, Web Site).

2. The default template uses a master page (Site.master). Open this page to view its markup.

3. Add a ScriptManager control to the master page. You can add it to any part of the page as it does not have a UI rendering. In this case, add it to the top of the page, after the opening form tag as the following markup shows:

```
<body>
    <form runat="server">
```

```
<asp:ScriptManager ID="ScriptManagerMain" runat="server">
</asp:ScriptManager>
```

...

Adding a ScriptManager control to the master page enables all pages that use the master to leverage the Ajax controls for partial-page updates.

4. Open the Default.aspx page. You turn this page into a form that enables users to search for customers in the database. Their search and subsequent data paging is done as partial-page updates.

5. The next step is to lay out a portion of the page. Add a page title, some instructions, a text box for users to enter a portion of a customer's name, a find button, and a label for the search results. Your page should look similar to Figure 20.2. Notice that the ScriptManager control displays on the master page in the designer.

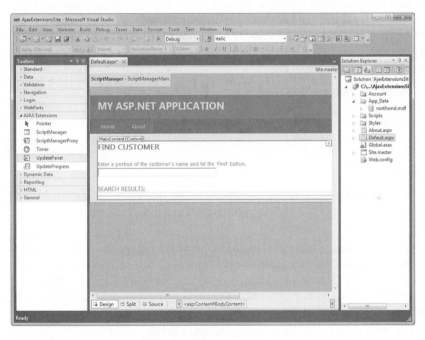

FIGURE 20.2   Add the basic layout items to your Find Customer page.

6. Next, add an UpdatePanel to the page; place it under the Search Results label. The UpdatePanel contains the portion of the page you want to partially update. The items placed inside the UpdatePanel are posted back to the server independently of the rest of the page and thus update independently. The user does not see a full page refresh when executing a find. The markup for your main content area should look similar to the following:

```
<asp:Content ID="BodyContent" runat="server"
  ContentPlaceHolderID="MainContent">
```

```
<h2>
    Find Customer
</h2>
<p>
  Enter a portion of the customer's name and hit the 'Find' button.
  <br />
  <asp:TextBox ID="TextBoxCustomer" runat="server"></asp:TextBox>
</p>
<h3>Search results:</h3>
<hr />
<asp:UpdatePanel ID="UpdatePanelResults" runat="server">
</asp:UpdatePanel>
</asp:Content>
```

7. The next step is to configure a GridView control to access some data. To do so, drag a GridView control from the Data controls group on the Toolbox. Put the GridView inside the UpdatePanel. You can use source or split view to verify that the control made it inside the UpdatePanel. The following shows an example of what the UpdatePanel markup should look like:

```
<asp:UpdatePanel ID="UpdatePanelResults" runat="server">
  <ContentTemplate>
    <asp:GridView ID="GridView1" runat="server">
    </asp:GridView>
  </ContentTemplate>
</asp:UpdatePanel>
```

8. Add the Northwnd.mdf file to your project. You can get this from the download code for this book or by searching for it on Microsoft.com. Add the file to the project's App_Data folder.

The next step is to connect the GridView control to a data source. In design view for your page, click the SmartTag (the arrow on the upper right) of the GridView control. Use the Choose Data Source option and select New Data Source. Follow along through the wizard. First, select a SQL Database in the Choose Data Source Type screen. You can use SqlDataSourceNwd for your data source ID.

On the Choose Your Data Connection screen, select northwnd.mdf from the drop-down. Hit the Next button and save your connection as ConnectionStringNwd.

When you get to the Configure the Select Statement step, select the radio button labeled Specify a Custom SQL Statement or Stored Procedure. Click the Next button to continue. You can use the Query Builder tool to build a SQL statement that joins the Customers and Orders tables. The following code provides an example. Notice that the WHERE clause uses the parameter @cust along with the LIKE keyword to define a user-specified value for the search.

```
SELECT Customers.ContactName, Customers.CompanyName, Customers.Phone,
       Orders.OrderDate, Orders.RequiredDate, Orders.ShippedDate,
       Orders.ShipAddress, Orders.ShipCity, Orders.ShipVia,
       Orders.Freight, Orders.OrderID
FROM Orders INNER JOIN Customers ON Orders.CustomerID =
                     Customers.CustomerID
WHERE (Customers.ContactName LIKE @cust + '%')
   ORDER BY Customers.ContactName, Orders.OrderDate
```

After defining the query, click the Next button on the wizard. You should now be on the Define Parameters page. Here you can define the source of the parameter you created in the prior SQL statement. For this example, you set the parameter value from your code-behind. This solves a known-issue when working with master pages. If you were not using master pages, you could set your parameter source to Form and indicate that the FormField is your text box used for data entry (TextBoxCustomer). However, because you are using a master page, configure your parameter as none. Figure 20.3 shows an example.

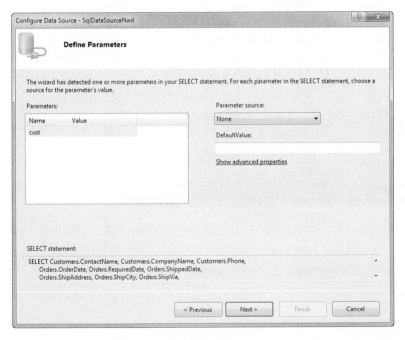

FIGURE 20.3   Use the Define Parameters screen to either link your SQL statement's parameters to your ASP.NET form or indicate no parameter source and thus use code to set the parameter value.

9. Next, double-click the Find button to generate an event handler in the code-behind file. Add code to set the data source parameter's DefaultValue property to the user's input from the text box. The following code shows an example:

```
protected void ButtonFind_Click(object sender, EventArgs e)
{
  SqlDataSourceNwd.SelectParameters["cust"].DefaultValue =
    TextBoxCustomer.Text;

}
```

10. The next step is to configure paging for the GridView control. You can do so from the SmartTag in design view; select the EnablePaging check box.

11. As an optional step, you can make the GridView display a bit better. From the quick actions smart tag, choose AutoFormat to apply a format to the grid. You can also use the Edit Columns link to bring up the column editor. Here you can change the column header text for each column, change the column order, and set formatting options for date values and currency.

You now have a customer search page that displays customer and order results to a user based on what she's entered. When the user clicks one of the paging buttons, the page partially updates. This is the result of the GridView being placed inside the UpdatePanel. Run the application and enter a couple of letters in the Find Customer text box field and click the Find button. In Figure 20.4, we've done just that. When you select a page link at the bottom of the page, the grid updates as a partial-page refresh.

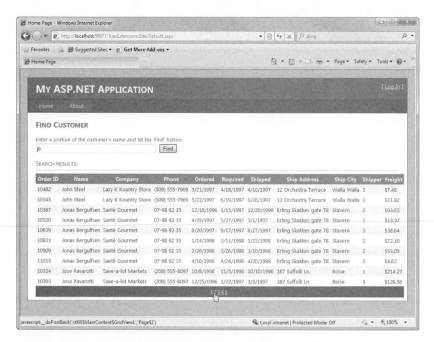

FIGURE 20.4   Your page does a partial-page refresh as users page through the data.

Notice that when you run the page, clicking the Find button does a full-page refresh, and paging does only a partial page-refresh. You can actually include the Find operation as a partial page refresh. To do so, follow these couple steps:

1. Move the TextBox and Button controls into the ContentTemplate area of the UpdatePanel control. Your markup for the content area should look similar to the following:

```
<asp:Content ID="BodyContent" runat="server"
  ContentPlaceHolderID="MainContent">
    <h2>Find Customer</h2>
    <asp:UpdatePanel ID="UpdatePanelResults" runat="server">
      <ContentTemplate>
        <p>
          Enter a portion of the customer's name and hit the 'Find' button.
          <br />
          <asp:TextBox ID="TextBoxCustomer"
          ➥runat="server"></asp:TextBox> 
          <asp:Button ID="ButtonFind" runat="server" Text="Find"
            onclick="ButtonFind_Click" />
        </p>
        <h3>Search results:</h3>
        <hr />

            <asp:GridView ID="GridView1" ...
```

2. From design view, select the UpdatePanel control inside the Properties window. Click the ellipsis button next to the Triggers property to launch the UpdatePanelTrigger Collection Editor. Add an item to this collection using the editor. Configure this item to trigger a postback when the find button's click event is raised. Figure 20.5 shows an example.

FIGURE 20.5   You can add a trigger to indicate a specific control will fire a partial-page update.

Run the page again. Notice that both the find process and the data paging result in partial-page updates.

Show Server Progress to the User

Users feel more comfortable when they receive immediate feedback after clicking somewhere on a web page and initiating an action. Of course, many server operations can take many seconds and longer. A better experience is to let the user know you are working on his request when either retrieving pages that have long operations (more than a second or so) or working across an occasionally slow network.

The ASP.NET Update progress control enables you to do just that. When a user clicks to execute a partial-page update, you can put up a wait notification or an animated .gif image. Then, when the page has finished, the wait notification disappears and a portion of the page updates. Let's look at building this into the find customer sample page.

In the preceding example, you implemented a partial-page update for finding a customer and paging through a GridView. In this example, you provide users with a progress indicator during the find process and the paging. To get started, you use the page created in the earlier walk-through. The following outlines the steps that should be applied to this page to implement progress notification.

1. The first step is to drag an UpdateProgress control to the page. Place the control under the GridView control but outside the UpdatePanel control. In this example, we show the progress indicator below the data pager. In this way, the user sees a progress indicator in the same area where his attention is focused.

   You can place an UpdateProgress control anywhere on the page but not inside the UpdatePanel itself. When the partial-page postback triggers, the client immediately kicks off the progress notification.

2. Next, you need to set a few properties on the UpdateProgress control for the page. You need to set the AssociatedUpdatePanelID property of the UpdateProgress control to the UpdatePanel control on the page. In this way, the two are linked. Because a given page might have multiple update controls, setting this property is required.

   You can also set the DisplayAfter property to the number of milliseconds the client should wait before display notification. In this example, set the value low (250 is a quarter of a second).

3. The last step is to define the message that is displayed to the user while he waits. You can put any HTML or markup inside the UpdateProgress control. You do so by dragging items onto the control in design view. In source view, you must create a ProgressTemplate node to house your markup.

   In the example, you can put the text "Please wait...." Also, if you have an animated .gif file that cycles back and forth or in a circle, you can add it here. The UpdateProgress markup should look something like the following:

```
<asp:UpdateProgress ID="UpdateProgressResults" runat="server"
  AssociatedUpdatePanelID="UpdatePanelResults" DisplayAfter="250"
  DynamicLayout="true">
  <ProgressTemplate>
```

```
        <div class="title" style="text-align: center; font-size: 10pt;" >
          <img src="images/rotation.gif" alt="waiting" />
          Please wait ...
        </div>
      </ProgressTemplate>

    </asp:UpdateProgress>
```

4. Optional: If you are running this example locally, you might not see much in the way of wait time. Therefore, you might introduce a wait time just to see it work. Of course, you would never do such a thing in a real application. To add a wait time, add code in the PageIndexChanged event of the GridView control to put the executing thread to sleep. The following code introduces a four-second delay:

```
protected void GridView1_PageIndexChanged(object sender, EventArgs e) {
  System.Threading.Thread.Sleep(4000);

}
```

You should now be able to run the application. If you added the find operation to the UpdatePanel, you should see the wait notification twice, after you click the Find button and again when the user pages through data. Figure 20.6 shows the page in action.

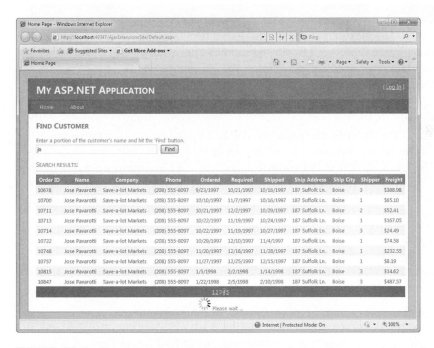

FIGURE 20.6   You can use the UpdateProgress control to show user information while waiting for a partial-page update to complete.

The ASP.NET Ajax Library/Control Toolkit

Microsoft worked with the development community to introduce an early version of Ajax inside of Visual Studio in the 2003/2005 versions. This support was referred to as ATLAS. From these early beginnings grew the Ajax Control Toolkit. Arguably, this toolkit represents one of the most successful open-source projects worked on jointly by a big company and the development community. This toolkit continues to evolve. The latest version has grown and is now called the ASP.NET Ajax Library. The library provides developer support for building Ajax controls, doing data-binding, and it works with JQuery. The library also includes new versions of the toolkit controls.

The Ajax Control Toolkit is a set of Ajax-based custom controls that provide many dynamic user activities inside the browser. There are controls for all sorts of features, including auto-complete as a user types, masked edit text boxes, password strength verification, modal pop-up dialog boxes, and many more. You can download the collection of controls either as full source or as a binary version. You can then leverage these controls inside your application.

The ASP.NET Ajax Library and Control Toolkit works with all modern browsers, including IE 6, 7, and 8. It also works with Firefox 3 and 3.5, Safari 4, Opera 10, and Chrome 3.

> **NOTE**
>
> We discuss the ASP.NET Ajax Library and Control Toolkit here because it has become a part of the Visual Studio developer's world. You can find tutorials and discussions on Microsoft's site: http://www.asp.net/ajaxlibrary/. You can get the source code from http://ajax.codeplex.com/.

Getting Started

Here we primarily cover the controls inside the ASP.NET Ajax Library. However, you should note that the library includes a lot of developer support for creating your own Ajax functionality. The latest version of the controls target the .NET Framework 3.5 SP1 or later; a Visual Studio 2010 / .NET 4.0 release is planned. You can download the source code or choose a no-source release version. Let's assume the latter because we are not covering the source code here.

The first step is to download the Ajax library zip file and extract it. There are several folders in the zip file. The Scripts folder contains the Ajax library script files. The AspNetAjaxBetaSamples folder shows how you can use the library. The WebForms folder contains the assemblies that make up the control toolkit and is our focus.

Two assemblies make up the control toolkit: System.Web.Ajax.dll and AjaxControlToolkit.dll. Let's look at how you can use the controls inside Visual Studio. The following steps show you how to get started with the ASP.NET Ajax Control Toolkit:

1. Create a new ASP.NET website with which to work. Alternatively, if you've created one for the previous walk-through, you can use it.

2. You want to add the controls to the Toolbox so that you can use them in your website. First, however, right-click the Toolbox and choose Add Tab to get a new area

on the Toolbox in which to house the Ajax Control Toolkit controls. Name this tab Ajax Control Toolkit or something similar.

3. Next, right-click in the area inside the new tab and select Choose Items. This enables you to select controls to add to this tab. Inside the Choose Toolbox Items, click the Browse button. Using the Open dialog box, browse to the location where you unzipped the toolkit. Navigate to the WebForms\Release folder. Select the AjaxControlToolkit.dll to import the controls into the Toolbox.

The controls in the toolkit should now be ready for your use. Figure 20.7 shows just a portion of the controls inside the Toolbox. Note that there are many controls listed here. Most of them provide a specific enough feature that you can understand them by name.

FIGURE 20.7   You can add the Ajax controls to the Toolbox for use on your web forms.

TIP

The ASP.NET Ajax controls are compatible with an ASP.NET MVC application (see Chapter 17). To use them in this scenario, you instantiate them in your JavaScript code using the Sys.create method. When you create a new instance of an extender control, you pass the name of the control as a parameter. The following code shows an example:

```
<script type="text/javascript">


Sys.require(Sys.components.calendar, function() {
```

```
    Sys.create.calendar("#input1");
  });
  </script>
```

Notice the use of the Sys.require method, which indicates that all scripts required by the calendar control should be loaded by the Script Loader.

The Controls in the Ajax Control Toolkit

The controls inside the Ajax Control Toolkit have full design-time support. They can be worked with from the Toolbox and dragged onto your forms for use. Of course, it's important to know how you can leverage each control for your specific purpose.

Table 20.2 provides a high-level overview of a sampling of the many controls in the toolkit. Remember, these controls execute the vast majority of their functionality on the client. This gives the user a more interactive experience. Use the list in Table 20.2 as a reference and starting point when building these features into your applications.

TABLE 20.2   ASP.NET Ajax Control Toolkit Controls

Control	Description
Accordion	Use the Accordion control to display several sections of information (or panes) that have a title and content. However, only one of the Accordion sections is open at a given time. As one opens, the currently open one closes, giving an accordion-like effect for a user.
AlwaysVisibleControlExtender	Use the AlwaysVisible control to float content on top of a web page that should always remain visible to the user. If the user scrolls the page, the AlwaysVisible content remains on top (and visible).
AutoCompleteExtender	The AutoComplete control is used to help users enter data in a list. As they type, data that starts with the letters they have typed is shown to the user in a pop-up under the text box. The user can select an item from this list.
CollapsiblePanelExtender	The CollapsiblePanelExtender enables you to easily define a panel on your form that the user can open and close. The panel has a title bar that includes the expand and collapse button.
AutoCompleteExtender	The AutoCompleteExtender control can respond to users' typing and provide them with options that they might be trying to type. It does so by attaching to a TextBox control and providing a pop-up panel with a list box. You populate the list box based on the user's typing as processed on the server. You might, for example, look up customer names as a user is entering an order.

TABLE 20.2   Continued

Control	Description
CalendarExtender	Use the CalendarExtender control to attach a calendar picker to any ASP.NET text box. The control enables a user to browse a calendar and select a date for populating a text box. The calendar control shows up when the user sets focus to the text box or clicks a button. When the user has selected the date, the calendar disappears.
CascadingDropDown	Use CascadingDropDown to populate a series of DropDownList controls based on a user's selection.
ConfirmButtonExtender	The ConfirmButtonExtender control is another pop-up type control. Use it when you want to define a button whose action requires a confirmation by the user (see an example later in this chapter).
FilteredTextBoxExtender	The FilteredTextBoxExtender control enables you to indicate the type of data a user can enter into a given text box. You might, for example, restrict entry to only numeric characters, only letters, only lowercase letters, and so on.
HoverMenuExtender	The HoverMenuExtender control provides users with a small menu of actions based on where they hover their cursors on the page. You might, for instance, provide a menu for edit, delete, and modify when a user selects a given item in a list. You attach a HoverMenuExtender to a given control on the page. In this way, you can get the context of where the user was when she selected an action.
ListSearchExtender	ListSearchExtender enables a user to type a letter in a ListBox or DropDownList and immediately select the first item in the list that starts with that letter.
MaskedEditExtender	The MaskedEditExtender control attaches to an ASP.NET text box and is used to both provide users with assistance when entering data and restrict the type of data they enter. For example, a user might need to enter a phone number in a certain format, such as (area code)-exchange-number. The MaskedEditExtender can enforce this format.
ModalPopupExtender	The ModalPopupExtender control enables you to create a window that pops up based on user action. This window is be modal on your page. That is, the page is disabled and the user has to respond to the dialog box to continue. This control is great for confirming a user's request and allowing for complex data-entry scenarios where another form is required.

20

TABLE 20.2   Continued

Control	Description
PasswordStrength	The PasswordStrength control attaches to a text box control and indicates visually to the user the strength of the password as the user enters it. You can use the control to set minimum password lengths, require non alphanumeric characters, and more.
PopupControlExtender	Use PopupControl to open (and close) a popup window that displays additional content to a user.
ReorderList	The ReorderList control creates a data-bound list of items that a user can reorder inside the browser. Users select an item and move it above and below other items (without accessing the server, of course). New items can also be added to the list by users.
SliderExtender	The SliderExtender control works with an ASP.NET text box to capture user input. A user slides a graphical element up and down or left and right across a range. The text box is updated as the user moves the slider.
SlideShowExtender	The SlideShow control is a set of buttons that enables a user to cycle through a set of images on your form. You can also set the control to automatically transition between slides on a timed interval.
TabContainer	The TabContainer control enables you to group areas of functionality for a page into logical tabs. A user can then click each tab and see the given functionality without refreshing from the server. Each TabContainer contains a TabPanel control. You place your ASP.NET controls onto the TabPanel control.
TextBoxWatermarkExtender	The TextBoxWatermark control extends the TextBox control to include a faded message when the TextBox is empty. When a user sets focus to the control the message disappears.

Using the Toolkit Controls on a Page

Notice that most of the controls in Table 20.2 include the "Extender" suffix . This indicates that the control extends an existing ASP.NET control. Or, put a better way, the control works with another control to provide its functionality. For example, a CalendarExtender works with a TextBox control. Those controls in the library without this suffix exist as standalone controls.

The Ajax Toolkit makes it easy to work with the controls—and even easier to work with the extender controls. To add an extender control to an ASP.NET control, you can use a smart tag action on the given control. The following steps outline adding a basic user confirmation pop-up window to a button control:

1. Create a new .aspx page for the sample.

2. Add a TookitScriptManager control from the Ajax control library to your page. This control works like the ScriptManager control. It provides the correct libraries for the Ajax controls to operate. In fact, open the Bin directory for your site after you add the control to the page. Notice that the Ajax library .dll files and their associated resource files are now added to your site.

3. Add a standard Button control to the page. Set the ID to ButtonSave and set the Text property to Save.

4. Double-click the button to add an event handler in the code-behind file. In the event handler, you might set the Text property of the button to something different just to confirm that user cancellation is working. The following is an example:

```
protected void ButtonSave_Click(object sender, EventArgs e) {
    ButtonSave.Text = "Saved";

    }
```

5. In design view for your form, select the button and its smart tag. Notice that there is an option for Add Extender. This option is added to Visual Studio by the Ajax Control Toolkit. Figure 20.8 shows an example. Select the option.

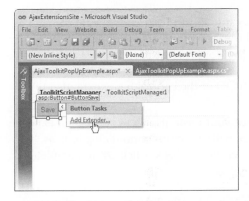

FIGURE 20.8   You use the Add Extender option to apply an Ajax extender control to an ASP.NET server control.

6. You should now be presented with the Choose an Extender dialog box (see Figure 20.9). Here you see all the extender controls. Select ConfirmButtonExtender. Notice that the ID is automatically set for the control based on the control you are extending. Click the OK button to continue.

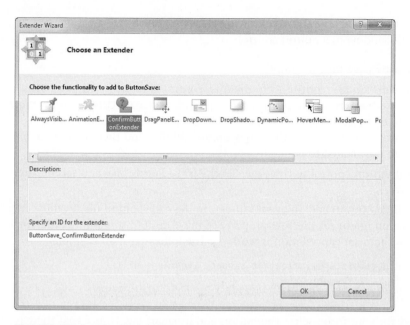

FIGURE 20.9 The Extender Wizard dialog box enables you to choose an extender control to apply to a standard ASP.NET control.

7. The control has no visual representation because it simply extends the button control. Therefore, you need to either find it in the properties window or switch to split or source view. From either place, set the ConfirmText property to a message that confirms the user's operation. Notice, too, that the extender control's TargetControlID was automatically set to the ID of the control being extended (in this case, ButtonSave).

8. Finally, run your application. You should see your form display as you would expect. Click the Save button and you are presented with a confirmation dialog box, as shown in Figure 20.10. Click Cancel to cancel the postback. Click OK to complete the postback on the server.

We've covered the Ajax basics that are built in to Visual Studio 2010 and those that are available in the ASP.NET Ajax Library and Control Toolkit. Our primary focus is on helping you use the Ajax controls to build better user experiences. Of course, there is more out there for those of you looking to build your own Ajax controls. This includes both the Microsoft Ajax Library and the ASP.NET Ajax Library. Both libraries make building Ajax extensions into your controls easier. The Microsoft Ajax library provides an object-oriented structure for those looking to build more JavaScript into their controls and pages. Visual Studio 2010 also has great support for debugging your client-scripts.

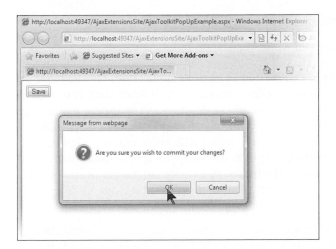

FIGURE 20.10   The ConfirmButtonExtender control in action.

Creating Unique, Rich Experiences on Windows via the Browser

In Chapter 19, "Creating Richer, Smarter User Interfaces," we walk through the process of creating Windows Presentation Foundation (WPF) applications using Visual Studio 2010. As you recall, these applications are based on XAML that is interpreted by the WPF portion of the .NET Framework and then rendered to the screen. WPF enables you to create user interfaces that leverage such things as vector-based graphics, scaling, and 3D effects in order to create unique user experiences for Windows. The applications we discussed in Chapter 19 are meant to be installed as standalone applications that run on the Windows operating system. However, similar WPF applications can be deployed to run in a user's web browser.

WPF applications built to target a web browser are called XBAP (for XAML browser application). An XBAP can be deployed through a simple ClickOnce URL and run as hosted inside the user's browser (the application does not leave the browser). Because of this, XBAP applications run inside a partial trust, security sandbox. For example, they do not have access to such things as the user's file system.

> **NOTE**
>
> WPF-based XBAP can run inside both Internet Explorer and Firefox. This ensures a larger reach for your application because the vast majority of users are standardized on one or the other. An XBAP does, however, require Windows and the .NET Framework on the client. If you need a fully cross-platform solution, you must build on ASP.NET or Silverlight.

Choosing Between WPF Standalone and WPF XBAP

There are specific scenarios in which an XBAP application has an advantage over ASP.NET, WinForms, or a standard WPF application. For one, you can use XBAP to easily create a user experience that typically does not exist inside a browser application. This includes Windows-like menus, context menus (right-click), interactive drill-down data, real-time spell-checking, masked edit controls, data list scrolling, hotkeys and shortcuts, managing the user's cursor, and many more features. This type of rich user experience is typically limited to a standalone Windows client. However, with XBAP, you can run a client with these features hosted directly inside the browser. In this way, you get the added benefits of easy deployment (and update), the use of the browser's security sandbox, and communication with your server (and web services) via HTTP. And, if you need it, your XBAP application can access isolated storage to save and recall data securely on a user's machine.

An XBAP application is a type of WPF application. The two are based on the same .NET Framework code. However, they have their similarities and their differences, which you need to understand when you make a choice for building your next user interface. Table 20.3 should help illuminate the options you have when comparing one to the other.

TABLE 20.3   ASP.NET Ajax Controls

Feature	WPF	XBAP
Installation	Typically installed on a user's machine using a .msi package or through ClickOnce. Can be uninstalled through Add/Remove Programs.	Installed inside the browser's cache (not a direct install on the machine). Installed via a ClickOnce URL.
User Access	A user can access via the Start menu, desktop shortcut, and so on. An .exe file is installed in the Program Files folder.	Accessed via the browser shortcuts (favorites) over HTTP. The .exe file is hosted in the browser.
Host/Process	Runs hosted in its own Windows process.	Hosted in the web browser's process.
Security	Typically runs with full trust on the user's machine. This means access to the registry, file system, and devices such as printers.	Runs in a partial trust sandbox. By default, no access to remoting, reflection, the file system, printers, WCF services, the registry, and more.
WCF Support	Can fully communicate with WCF services.	Cannot call WCF services from a browser application.

TABLE 20.3   Continued

Feature	WPF	XBAP
New Windows	Creates new, child windows similar to any Windows application.	New windows are "navigated" to in the browser and not popped open like a Windows application.
Updating	Requires some update strategy to get updates to the client or for the client to request updates.	Easily updated as the user hits the server to access. New versions can be deployed once to the server and all clients are updated.
Offline	A user typically has access to run the application when not connected to a server (offline).	Online only. Requires a connection to the server.

Creating a WPF Browser Application

Creating a WPF browser application is nearly the same as creating a standalone WPF application. Of course, there are a few things you need to consider to make sure your application is properly set up and configured to be deployed and run in a web browser. In this section, you walk through the basic steps of creating, configuring, and debugging an XBAP. From there, we discuss both security and deployment considerations.

To get started, you create a basic WPF browser application. We do not discuss the basics of UI design, layout, and coding because they were discussed previously, in Chapter 19. The first step is to create a WPF project. There is a special template in Visual Studio 2010 for XBAP applications. This template is called WPF Browser Application. Using this template gives you a head start on configuring your application to work in a browser. Figure 20.11 shows the New Project dialog box with the WPF Browser Application template highlighted.

When you create a WPF browser application, you get a project built on a similar template to a standard WPF application. This includes a default WPF form file and an app.xaml for configuration. In a WPF application your new files are typically named WindowX.xaml by Visual Studio (where X represents a number). In a XBAP, Visual Studio calls your WPF forms pages (PageX.xaml).

FIGURE 20.11   You use the Windows node of the New Project dialog box to access the WPF Browser Application template.

Each of these files is built on a different base class. A window file, for example, derives from System.Windows.Window, whereas a page file is built on the class System.Windows.Controls.Page. The app.xaml configuration file is a good place to set the page that should be viewed when the user first hits the application. Here there is an attribute of the Application node called StartupUri. You set this value to the name of your startup form in your application, as the following markup from an App.xaml file shows:

```
<Application x:Class="WpfBrowserWorkQueue.App"
  xmlns="http://schemas.microsoft.com/winfx/2006/xaml/presentation"
  xmlns:x="http://schemas.microsoft.com/winfx/2006/xaml"
  StartupUri="Main.xaml">
</Application>
```

Your next step is to build your WPF application as you would any other. You want to pay close attention, however, to the security restrictions of the sandbox in which your application is hosted (see later in this chapter). Other than that, you can use the many WPF controls to lay out your user interface. This includes menus, context menus, shortcut keys, and more.

You can run and debug your XBAP application like any other .NET application. Simply set any breakpoints you want and click the Start Debugging (or Run) button to will launch your application inside a browser.

Figure 20.12 shows the beginnings of a help-desk work tracking system running as a WPF browser application. Notice that the application is hosted in IE. Also notice the use of a menu bar, a status bar, a toolbar, context menus, and related features of Windows.

FIGURE 20.12   An XBAP application running in a browser provides WPF-like user interaction and functionality.

After you have your XBAP built to your satisfaction, you should deploy it to a web server for user access. We look at this process in a later section of this chapter. First, however, you need to be aware of the security surrounding any XBAP application you build.

TIP

XBAP applications can also be hosted within a frame in the browser. In this scenario, they can talk back to the owning parent web page via the BrowserInteropHelper.HostScript object.

Security Considerations

A WPF browser application is installed from a web server. By default, applications that originate from web servers are not (and should not be) trusted. Trust, in this case, refers to an agreement between an application and a user with respect to the user's machine and devices. You do not want applications that originate from the Internet, for example, to simply have access to your file system. Therefore, WPF browser applications run in what's called a sandbox.

This sandbox is controlled by your browser's security. By default, an XBAP application runs in what's called the Internet zone. This zone is low-trust, high-security. Figure 20.13 shows the Internet zone from the perspective of Internet Explorer. In this way, an XBAP has similar rights as would any application originating from the Internet (and therefore should be as secure).

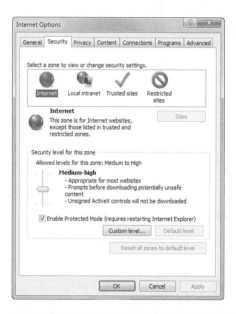

FIGURE 20.13   You can manage security from IE's Internet Options Security tab.

Clicking the Custom Level button shown in Figure 20.13 brings up the Security Settings dialog box for the given zone. XBAP applications have their own basic settings. These are highlighted in Figure 20.14. You can disable XBAP applications or ask the user before running them. By default, they are enabled in the Internet zone in IE.

FIGURE 20.14   You can set a custom level to control security settings for XBAP applications running in a browser.

When you run (or debug) your XBAP and it tries to go beyond the bounds of the sandbox, a security exception is thrown. Again, what your XBAP can do is controlled by the zone in which it resides. For the secure Internet zone, this means you need to avoid all the following when building your application:

▶ Remoting

▶ Private reflection

▶ Device driver access (like printers)

▶ Registry access

▶ Interop with other code (not .NET)

▶ WCF service calls (HTTP and web service calls are allowed)

▶ File system access (you can write a secure upload similar to a web page upload; in addition, isolated storage on the client is available)

If you need access to any of these items, it is best to consider a different deployment strategy. For example, you might switch to a WPF application that is deployed through a browser (and ClickOnce) but installed on a user's machine rather than simply hosted in the browser. In this way, the .exe is copied to the user's machine and installed as trusted (with access to the items previously listed).

It should be noted, however, that it is possible to run your XBAP application in a browser with full trust. This means giving your application rights inside the Local Intranet zone. A user gets a warning, but after the user confirms, the application has full access to the user's

20

machine from the browser. This should generally be avoided as a security best practice. If, however, it is used, it should be restricted to intranet applications at most.

You can use the Properties window for your WPF application to manage security by right-clicking the project file in Solution Explorer and choosing Properties. You then see the property editor inside of Visual Studio 2010. Figure 20.15 shows the Security tab of this window. Notice that you can toggle between full trust (WPF standalone) and partial trust (XBAP). You can also set the zone in which the application runs by default (Internet, Local Intranet, or custom). Selecting the Custom option enables the Edit Permissions XML button. Clicking that button enables you to change the permissions requested by your application in the app.manifest file.

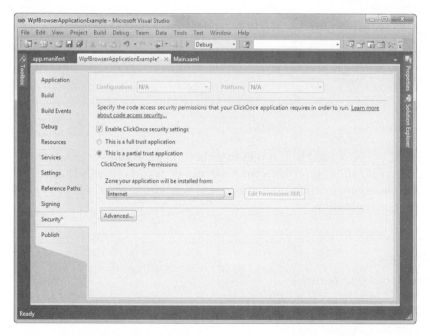

FIGURE 20.15   You can use the Security tab of the project properties window to change the security settings for your application.

Security and Site Navigation

You should be aware of how navigation works between content in your application and between any websites and your application. Each scenario comes with its own security restrictions.

First, application navigation security refers to the security applied when your application navigates between one page (.xaml file) and another. This type of navigation is allowed without concern for additional security. For example, you can create a new .xaml page and navigate to it in code as shown here:

```
Page2 p = new Page2();
this.NavigationService.Navigate(p);
```

You might write this type of code in response to a user action such as a menu item select or button click. Alternatively, you can use the Hyperlink element to give users a web-like behavior when navigating between pages in your site. The following markup is an example:

```
<Hyperlink NavigateUri="Main.xaml">
  Back to Main
</Hyperlink>
```

The other type of navigation security is called browser navigation security. This refers to navigation that happens between a website and your application. This type of navigation is allowed, provided that the user initiated the navigation from a hyperlink control in either the website or your WPF application. In this scenario, the content being linked to should also be in the same zone.

Deploying a WPF Browser Application

Users access WPF browser applications from their web browsers. Therefore, you must deploy the applications to an IIS web server. You can then link to the XBAP from a standard HTML or ASP.NET page via a hyperlink. The application are then installed in the browser via ClickOnce. Chapter 12, "Deploying Code," covers ClickOnce deployments. The following is a review of the steps specific to deploying an XBAP application with ClickOnce:

1. When you are ready to deploy, the first step is to build your application. You typically set your build state to Release to ensure that you are not unnecessarily shipping debug code. You can set your Build state from the Standard toolbar. Then select Build Solution from the Build menu.

2. After you've built your application, you should see a number of files in the bin\release directory for your application. These files represent those you need to deploy. However, you can't simply copy these files out to your web server. You need a deployment file. To get this file, you need to run the Visual Studio Publish Wizard, which you can access via the Build menu (Build, Publish [application name]).

3. The first step in the Publish Wizard is to set a directory to where you intend to publish the application. For now, leave this as publish\. This creates a directory in your application and puts all the necessary files there. You can then copy them up to your web server.

4. The next step in the Publish Wizard is to indicate how users install the application. Here it is important that you indicate From a Web Site. Figure 20.16 shows an

20

example. The remaining steps in the wizard are not applicable to XBAP applications; simply click Next and then Finish.

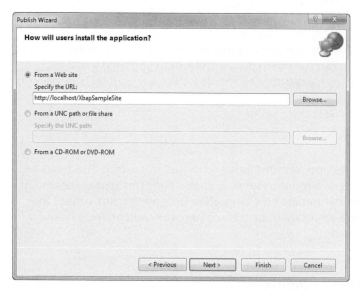

FIGURE 20.16   Use the Publish Wizard to indicate a URL to which you will publish your site for ClickOnce deployment.

5. Next, navigate to the folder created in the publish step ([your app]\publish) to observe its contents. In this folder, you see a couple of files and a folder containing other files. These items can be described this way:

   ▶ Publish.htm: This is an HTML file that contains a hyperlink to install your application. You can use this file to test the publication of your application. However, you typically do not deploy this file. An example of the file is shown in Figure 20.17.

   ▶ [ApplicationName].xbap: This file is called an XBAP manifest file where ApplicationName is the name of your Visual Studio project. The file is used to deploy your XBAP application. You create a web page (similar to publish.htm) to link to this file. IIS then passes this to ClickOnce to get the application installed.

   ▶ Application Files\[ApplicationName]_[version]\[ApplicationName].exe.deploy: This is the ClickOnce deployment file. This file contains your .exe.

   ▶ ApplicationFiles\[ApplicationName]_[version]\[ApplicationName].exe.manifest: This is a manifest file for your application and contains your application's metadata.

FIGURE 20.17   The Publish Wizard generates an HTML launch page for testing your XBAP deployment.

6. Your next step is to create an ASP.NET or HTML page for the user to initiate the installation. The important thing is that the page contains a hyperlink to the .xbap file. The following is an example:

```
<a href="WpfBrowserApplicationExample.xbap">Launch the Work Tracking
➥System</a>
```

7. The next step is to make sure that IIS is configured correctly. If you are already running IIS 7, there is no need to do anything. If, however, you are running an older version of IIS, you need to register the MIME types in IIS as listed in Table 20.4.

TABLE 20.4   XBAP Required MIME Types

Filename Extension	MIME Type
.application	application/x-ms-application
.deploy	application/octet-stream
.manifest	application/manifest
.xaml	application/xaml+xml
.xbap	application/x-ms-xbap
.xps	application/vnd.ms-xpsdocument

20

8. Your next task is to make sure that you create a website for your application. This can be done by creating a virtual directory in IIS.

9. The virtual directory you created in the preceding step is, of course, mapped to a physical folder (typically C:\inetpub\wwwroot\SiteName\). You need to navigate back to the publish directory, copy the files from there, and paste them into the physical folder of your website's virtual directory. You also need to paste your HTML file (default.htm) in the same folder.

All that is left is to run your application from a browser. When you do so, you should be presented with the default file for the site (typically default.htm for default.aspx). Figure 20.18 shows a launch page running at http://localhost/XbapSampleSite/.

FIGURE 20.18   You can create a launch page to kick-off your ClickOnce deployment.

Clicking the hyperlink in the center of the page installs the XBAP application in the user's browser (with a progress bar provided by ClickOnce). Figure 20.19 shows the application deployed and running from this URL.

Delivering Interactive Experiences Across Platforms

Microsoft continues its push to help developers and designers deliver a much richer user experience (similar to WPF) within a web browser. This technology is called Silverlight. With it you can create media-rich sites that include brochure-ware, interactive games, new shopping and buying experiences, interactive training, and sites that deliver video and audio. It was built to enable you to create truly rich, truly unique user experiences over the web.

FIGURE 20.19   The XBAP application deployed and running from a web server.

Because Microsoft Silverlight targets the web, it was built to work cross-platform and cross-browser. This means it works on Mac OS and Windows XP/7/Vista (there is even a Linux project called Moonlight underway by the community). In addition, Silverlight works on all modern browsers including IE 6 and 7, Firefox 2, and Safari. In all cases, it is a plug-in to the user's browser.

The Silverlight plug-in runs a smaller version of the .NET Framework. In this way, your development experience is similar to that of .NET. It does not, however, require the .NET Framework to be on the machine. Instead, everything that is required is inside the Silverlight plug-in.

You can write Silverlight applications similar to how you write WPF applications. The UI is marked up in XAML and the code-behind is C# or VB. You can also use Ajax, Python, or Ruby (and others) to work with Silverlight controls inside a website. In this section we walk through writing a simple Silverlight application. We then embed that application as part of a website. Let's get started.

Getting Started with Silverlight

Microsoft is evolving Silverlight at a fast pace. At the time of writing, the current, released version is Silverlight 3.0. However, there is also a beta of Silverlight 4.0. While we briefly discuss what is planned for the 4.0 release (see the end of this section), the content created by in the examples is all Silverlight 3.0 as that is the version shipping with Visual Studio 2010.

Creating a Silverlight Application

It's important to note that there are multiple ways you can leverage Silverlight. You can create a Silverlight application that runs self-contained in the browser. Alternatively, you can create a web page that embeds Silverlight as part of the page. This might be for video or to use a Silverlight control. You can also create an application that runs on the computer (without the need for a browser). This type of functionality opens up access outside of the Silverlight sandbox and is a major feature of the upcoming, 4.0 release. In this section, we highlight the browser scenarios for Silverlight applications.

Defining a New Silverlight Project

Your first step to building a Silverlight application is to create a Silverlight project. In Visual Studio 2010, you simply follow the standard File, New Project menu path. Figure 20.20 shows an example. Here you can select Silverlight Project to create an application or Silverlight Class Library (used to create a control).

FIGURE 20.20   You can use the Silverlight project templates to create a new Silverlight application in Visual Studio.

After selecting the Silverlight Application template in the New Project dialog box, Visual Studio presents you with the option to create a host project for your Silverlight application. Figure 20.21 shows this dialog box. You have the option to define your website name and select the website project type (web application, website, ASP.NET MVC website). In this example, we use the website option. You can also define your Silverlight version. This list is constrained by the versions installed on your machine. After you select to create a new website to host your application, Visual Studio generates a website template to go along with your Silverlight application. This template includes the files necessary to connect to your Silverlight application.

FIGURE 20.21   You can choose your Silverlight host application as part of the new Silverlight project process.

The Silverlight project template includes a default XAML page for defining your user interface (MainPage.xaml). The related website template includes both a .aspx and a .html test page that can be used to load the Silverlight application for testing. In also includes the Silverlight.js file which is used for working with Silverlight applications from a website. Figure 20.22 shows the two project templates as generated.

Building an Application

To build your application, you use the .xaml markup file to design your user interface and put any code you have in its code-behind. This should be a familiar process. In fact, the designer and code editor are just like WPF. You have a split design and XAML view. You also have a set of controls you can add to the design surface from the Toolbox. When doing so, you get the same alignment tools you would see in the WPF form designer. Let's build an example application.

In this example, you create a simple slide-show application. It enables a user to page forward and back through a set of images using Silverlight. As the user does pages through the images, the images render (without page refresh). Follow these steps to create this application:

1. First, create a new project as described in the previous section.

FIGURE 20.22   The as-generated Silverlight project template and the related website template.

2. Open the MainPage.xaml file. Set the controls DesignHeight to 600 and DesignWidth to 800. This file is actually considered a Silverlight UserControl. This control is embedded on a web page.

3. Add a Label control to the top of the page. Set its Content property to Image Slide Show. In the Text property group, set the font to bold and the text size to 18.

4. Add an Image control under the Label control. Set the image width to 640 and height to 480. Set the Stretch property to Fill.

5. Add an images folder to your application by right-clicking the project and choosing Add, New Folder. Navigate to the My Pictures\Sample Pictures directory on your machine. Copy these pictures into the newly created folder.

6. You can set the Source property of the Image control to one of the sample pictures. This might help you visualize your application in the designer.

7. Next, add two button controls to the bottom of the page. One on the left-side of the image. Set the Content property of this control to Previous. Place the other button control on the right side of the image. Set its Content property to Next.

   Figure 20.23 shows an example of what your markup and form should look like at this point.

8. Next you add event handlers that respond to the user clicking the Next and Previous buttons by double-clicking each button in the designer.

9. Now add some code in the code-behind to respond to these events. At the class level, we keep track of the images in a string array as well as the selected image index. We initialize the first image when the page loads, and in each of the button events we change images. Listing 20.1 shows the code you might write.

10. Run the application to see it working in your browser. Notice that you can set breakpoints in the code-behind file and debug as you would any other application. Figure 20.24 shows an example of the application running in IE.

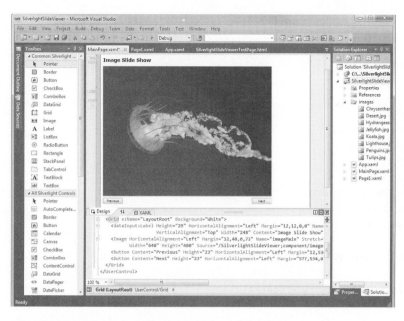

FIGURE 20.23   The Silverlight page in the designer.

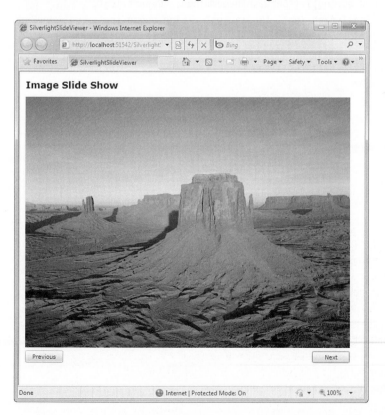

FIGURE 20.24   The Silverlight control shows images in the browser without refreshing.

LISTING 20.1   The MainPage.xaml Code-Behind

```
using System;
using System.Collections.Generic;
using System.Linq;
using System.Net;
using System.Windows;
using System.Windows.Controls;
using System.Windows.Documents;
using System.Windows.Input;
using System.Windows.Media;
using System.Windows.Media.Imaging;
using System.Windows.Media.Animation;
using System.Windows.Shapes;

namespace SilverlightSlideViewer
{
  public partial class MainPage : UserControl
  {
    //list of images
    string[] _images = new string[] {"Chrysanthemum.jpg", "Desert.jpg",
      "Hydrangeas.jpg", "Jellyfish.jpg", "Koala.jpg", "Lighthouse.jpg",
      "Penguins.jpg", "Tulips.jpg"};

    //used to track currently selected image
    int _selectedIndex = 0;

    public MainPage()
    {
      InitializeComponent();

      //set start image
      SetUri();
    }

    private void SetUri() {
      Uri u = new Uri("images/" + _images[_selectedIndex],
        UriKind.Relative);
      imageMain.Source = new BitmapImage(u);
    }

    private void buttonNext_Click(object sender, RoutedEventArgs e)
    {
      //check next value
      if (_selectedIndex + 1 < _images.GetLength(0))
      {
```

```
      _selectedIndex = _selectedIndex + 1;
    }
    //move to the next image in the list
    SetUri();
  }


  private void buttonPrevious_Click(object sender, RoutedEventArgs e)
  {
    //check previous value
    if (_selectedIndex - 1 >= 0)
    {
      _selectedIndex = _selectedIndex - 1;
    }
    //move to the previous image in the list
    SetUri();
  }
 }
}
```

Notice that the application is running in the website. In fact, the page that runs the application in the example is in the website template and is called SilverlightSlideViewerTestPage.aspx. If you open this page notice that it links to the deployment file for your Silverlight application. The following markup snippet shows this:

```
<body>
    <form id="form1" runat="server" style="height:100%">
    <div id="silverlightControlHost">
      <object data="data:application/x-silverlight-2,"
        type="application/x-silverlight-2" width="100%" height="100%">
      <param name="source" value="ClientBin/SilverlightSlideViewer.xap"/>
```

Notice, too, that the file referenced (SilverlightSlideViewer.xap) is actually copied to the ClientBin folder of the website. This gets updated as you build your Silverlight application.

In this case, the entire functionality is provided by the Silverlight control. However, because this control is actually embedded on a web page, you can add any additional markup or ASP.NET form controls to the page.

TIP

You can create Silverlight-only pages when you do not want your Silverlight to be embedded on a web page. In this case, add a Silverlight page item to your project instead of a Silverlight User Control.

Silverlight 4.0

Silverlight 4.0 promises to reset the bar for interactive, web-based applications. When released, developers should expect all of the following additions and improvements and more:

▸ A more complete, deeper set of controls to help build even richer, data-bound applications. This includes a RichTextbox control, masked edit controls, and enhanced DataGrid control.

▸ The ability to compile your Silverlight application and run it, without changes, as a standalone application on a desktop or deployed through a browser.

▸ Functionality for printing inside the Silverlight application.

▸ Additional support for Visual Studio including drag and drop data-binding.

▸ Support for the managed extensibility framework (MEF) when building composite applications (see Chapter 16).

▸ Built in support for webcams and microphones to enable person-to-person chat.

▸ Performance improvements including a 200% faster start up time.

▸ Multi-touch support for user gestures.

You can see from this list of just a few highlights that Silverlight 4 will be a big release.

Summary

In this chapter, we covered many options for enabling rich internet applications (RIA). These included creating standard web pages that leverage Ajax, building rich UIs inside a web browser running on a Windows Client using XBAP, and building cross-platform, media-rich solutions based on the Silverlight browser plug-in.

Which technology you use in your next application is really dependent on your content and your audience. The broadest possible user reach in order of most to fewest is ASP.NET and Ajax, then Silverlight, and finally XBAP. However, the highest degree of user interaction is the opposite order: XBAP, Silverlight (which is quickly catching up to XBAP and WPF), and then Ajax. You should carefully consider the technology you choose to use to build your next browser-based UI project. The good news is that with these technologies, you can provide new and exciting experiences for your users.

CHAPTER 21

Working with Databases

This chapter is all about how you can manage databases and build data-aware applications using Visual Studio 2010 and SQL Server.

Five different Visual Studio tools enable you to interact with a database and assist with building applications that leverage data from a database:

▶ Solution Explorer

▶ Server Explorer

▶ Database Diagram Designer

▶ Table Designer

▶ Query and View Designer

Collectively, they are referred to as the Visual Database tools. We introduced a few of these tools in Chapter 5, "Browsers and Explorers." Now we have the opportunity to explore how developers can use these tools to create database solutions.

In addition to the Visual Database tools, there are project templates available for enabling development of databases and creating application data tiers.

We start by examining how to build databases and database objects with the Visual Database tools. From there, we can cover the specifics of creating data-aware applications with data-bound controls.

Creating Tables and Relationships

The primary entities in any database are its tables. Tables are composed of a structure and data. Server Explorer is the Visual Studio instrument used to define or edit the structure or data of any table within a connected database. In fact, using Server Explorer, it is possible to create a new SQL Server database instance from scratch.

> **NOTE**
>
> As we noted in Chapter 5, the Express and Standard editions of Visual Studio refer to the Server Explorer as the Database Explorer. For simplicity, we always refer to this window as the *Server Explorer* in this chapter.

Creating a New SQL Server Database

Data connections are physical connections to a database. In Server Explorer, the Data Connections node has a list of every established database connection. To start the database creation process, right-click the Data Connections node and select the Create New SQL Server Database option. In the resulting dialog box (see Figure 21.1), you need to provide a server name, login credentials, and a name for the new database.

FIGURE 21.1   Creating a new SQL Server database.

This immediately creates the indicated database and add a connection to the new database under the Data Connections node. Figure 21.2 shows the newly created Contoso database added to the list of connections.

Adding an Existing Database

Of course, you can also establish a connection to an existing database. Again, you right-click the Data Connections node; this time, though, you select the Add Connection option. The Add Connection dialog box (see Figure 21.3) is similar to the new database dialog box. You specify a data source, server name, login credentials, and database name/database filename to connect to the database.

FIGURE 21.2   The new database added to the data connections.

FIGURE 21.3   Connecting to an existing database.

Under each connection are folders for the following classes of database objects:

▶ Database diagrams

▶ Tables

▶ Views

- ▶ Stored procedures
- ▶ Functions
- ▶ Synonyms
- ▶ Types
- ▶ Assemblies

These folders are the launching point for creating corresponding objects within the database.

Defining Tables

The Table Designer is the Visual Studio tool you use to define or edit the definition for a table. Using the Server Explorer window, right-click the Tables folder under an existing connection and select Add New Table. The Table Designer opens in the main document pane of the IDE.

The designer is implemented in a tabular format; you add a row in the designer for every column you want to define in the table. For each table column, you specify a name, data type, and nullability. In addition to the tabular designer interface, a Properties window is present that provides complete access to all the different properties for any given column in a table (see Figure 21.4).

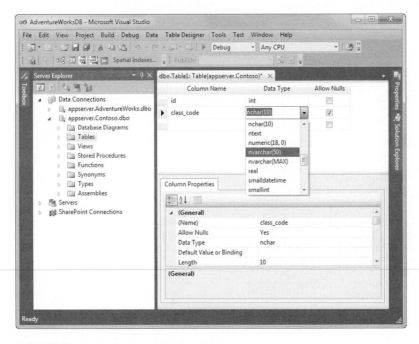

FIGURE 21.4   Defining a table's columns.

In addition to the basics, the Table Designer enables you to define a column, or group of columns, as part of the primary key for the table, or as part of an index.

Setting a Primary Key

With the Table Designer active in the IDE, a new Table Designer top-level menu item is available. You can use this menu, or the shortcut menu displayed whenever you right-click within the Table Designer, to access a list of useful actions. For instance, to create a primary key for the table, you select the column or columns that constitute the key and then select Set Primary Key from the designer's menu. A key icon indicates any primary keys defined in the table.

Creating Indexes, Foreign Keys, and Check Constraints

Indexes, foreign keys, and check constraints are all created using the same interface and process: Select the appropriate action from the Table Designer menu; use the settings dialog box to first add the index, key, or constraint; and then set its properties in the property grid. As an example, to create an index across one or more columns in the table, select the Indexes/Keys item from the Table Designer menu. In the Indexes/Keys dialog box (see Figure 21.5), you can add a new index and then set its properties in the property grid.

FIGURE 21.5   Creating an index.

Column population for the index is controlled with the index's Columns property; a separate Index Columns dialog box (see Figure 21.6) enables you to change the column membership and specify the sort order for each column.

Using the Database Diagram Designer

The aforementioned Table Designer and dialog boxes enable you to define tables and table-related constructs on a table-by-table basis. The Database Diagram Designer provides the same functionality in a more visual format. It enables you to build a diagram of the whole database showing tables, table columns, keys, and table relationships, and also enables you to create each of these items from within the Diagram Designer tool.

FIGURE 21.6   Column membership in an index.

Like the Table Designer, the Database Diagram Designer is implemented within the IDE's document pane. It has its own menu and toolbar associated with it; you can access many of the commands on the menu/toolbar through the designer's shortcut menu by right-clicking anywhere within the designer.

TIP

Within a diagram, you can change the view style on a per-table basis. Right-click the table and select one of the available Table views: Standard (shows column name, data type, and allow nulls), Column Names, Keys, Name Only, and Custom (you select the data you want to display). The Name Only view is particularly useful if you want to see an entire database diagram to get a sense of the relationships without necessarily caring about the table details themselves.

Creating a Database Diagram

To create a database diagram, right-click on the Database Diagrams node in the Server Explorer window and select Add New Diagram. A blank diagram opens, and the designer immediately displays a dialog box for adding tables to the diagram (see Figure 21.7).

FIGURE 21.7   Adding tables to a diagram.

After you've added a few tables, the diagram shows a graphical representation of the tables' columns and any relationships that the tables participate in. The diagram is fully interactive; you can directly edit column definitions, keys, relationships, and so on.

> Here is a quick shortcut for adding groups of related tables: Add a table to the diagram, select it, and click on the Add Related Tables button in the designer's toolbar. This automatically adds to the diagram any table in the database that has a current relationship with the selected table.

Modifying Table Definitions

Tables can be edited "in-line" within the diagram. To change column details, you click within the table and then enter column name information or change the data type and nullability rules. To add a column, just fill out a new row within the table representation in the diagram.

Building Table Relationships

Table relationships are easy to define within a diagram: Just drag and drop the primary key column from one table to the foreign key column on another table to automatically display the Foreign Key Relationship dialog box (Figure 21.8). This dialog box captures the general relationship information; note the text in the dialog box that clearly states that we are editing a new relationship. Because the relationship is new, we need to define the table columns that participate in the relationship.

FIGURE 21.8   Creating a foreign key.

Clicking on the Tables and Columns Specification property launches a second dialog box (Figure 21.9). Here, we establish a common one-to-many relationship between a category table and a product table. The product table has a category ID column that is foreign-keyed to the primary key on the category table. After committing the column assignments, you complete the relationship by changing any properties (if needed) on the relationship itself in the Foreign Key Relationship dialog box and then clicking OK.

FIGURE 21.9   Establishing foreign key column assignments.

Relationships are depicted within the diagram as a line between the two tables. The line indicates the direction of the relationship by showing a key on the primary key side and an infinity symbol on the foreign key side (or the "many" side) of the relationship. Figure 21.10 illustrates tables with one-to-many relationships as they appear within the Database Diagram Designer.

FIGURE 21.10   Table relationships in the Database Diagram Designer.

> **NOTE**
>
> By default, relationships enforce referential integrity. That is, they prevent any action (insert, update, delete) that would result in a mismatch of keys between the two related tables. This includes inserting a foreign key (FK) value when it doesn't exist as a primary key (PK) in the related table, changing a PK value that is referenced as a FK value, and so on.
>
> You can control whether a relationship enforces referential integrity through the Enforce Foreign Key Constraint setting in the Foreign Key Relationship dialog box. Relationships that do not enforce referential integrity are depicted as banded lines instead of solid lines within the Diagram Designer. You should also note that the Diagram Designer shows only relationships that have been explicitly defined through the process covered in the preceding paragraphs. Just having similarly named foreign keys and primary keys does not automatically create a relationship for you.

In addition to one-to-many relationships, you can model one-to-one, many-to-many, and reflexive relationships using the Database Diagram Designer.

One-to-One Relationships   You build a one-to-one relationship in the same way you create a one-to-many relationship. The difference is this: One-to-one relationships are between two primary keys instead of a primary and a foreign key. If you drag a primary key column from one table to a primary key column on another table, this automatically creates a one-to-one association. These relationships are depicted with a key icon on both ends of the relationship line.

Many-to-Many Relationships   You create a many-to-many relationship with the help of a junction table. If you had to model a many-to-many association between an order table and an item table (an order can have many items, and an item can belong to many orders), you would first add a third table to the database to hold the foreign keys of this relationship.

After adding the junction table, you then establish a one-to-many relationship between the order and orderitem tables, and between the item and orderitem tables. The last step is to define the multicolumn primary key on the junction table. Figure 21.11 shows the results in the diagram.

Reflexive Relationships   A reflexive relationship is a relationship between a table and itself. A typical example used to illustrate reflexive relationship is that of a part table that relates back to itself to represent the fact that a part could be made up of other parts. In this case, the part table might carry a parent_part_id field that is meant to be a foreign key related to the employee table's primary key.

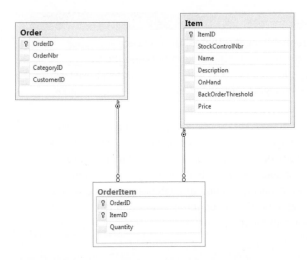

FIGURE 21.11   A many-to-many relationship.

To create a reflexive relationship, select the primary key column and drag it back onto the same table. The configuration of the key associations and the relationship values is the same as with any other relationship. Figure 21.12 shows a diagram of a reflexive relationship.

FIGURE 21.12   A reflexive relationship.

Working with SQL Statements

There is full support within the Visual Database Tools set for crafting and executing SQL statements against a connected database. This includes support for compiling SQL statements as stored procedures, creating views and triggers, and writing user-defined functions.

Writing a Query

The primary tool that facilitates the development of SQL statements is the Query/View Designer, which is a graphical tool that enables you to build queries with a point-and-click interface. After a query is constructed, this tool also enables you to view and interact with any results returned as a result of executing the query.

Now you're ready to put this tool through its paces.

Creating a new select query against a table is as simple as selecting the database in Server Explorer and then, under the Data menu, selecting New Query. An initial prompt gathers a list of the tables, views, functions, and/or synonyms to use as the target of the query (see Figure 21.13).

FIGURE 21.13   Adding tables to the query.

After you have selected the objects you want the query to target, the Query Designer opens. As Figure 21.14 illustrates, there are four separate panes to the designer:

▶ **Criteria pane**—This pane enables you to select, via a point-and-click diagram, the data columns to include in the select statement, sorting, and alias names.

FIGURE 21.14   The Query/View Designer.

▶ **Diagram pane**—This pane is similar to the diagram in the Database Diagram Designer; it graphically depicts the database object relationships. This makes creating joins a simple action of using existing relationships or creating new ones right within this tool.

▶ **Results pane**—After the query is executed, this pane holds any data returned as a result. Note that this pane is equipped with navigation controls to enable you to page through large resultsets.

▶ **SQL pane**—The SQL pane holds the actual SQL syntax used to implement the query. You can alter the statement manually by typing directly into this pane, or you can leverage the designer and let it write the SQL for you based on what you have entered in the diagram and criteria panes.

You can show or hide any of these panes at will. Right-click anywhere in the designer and select the Pane fly-out menu to select or deselect the visible panes.

Fine-Tuning the SQL Statement

To flesh out the select statement, you can indicate which columns from which tables you want returned by placing a check next to the column in the diagram pane. You use the criteria pane to specify a sort order, provide alias names for the return columns, and establish a filter for the resultset. As you select these different options, the designer turns them into SQL, visible in the SQL pane.

> **NOTE**
>
> We are using the AdventureWorks sample database in a SQL Server 2008 instance for most of this chapter. If you want to follow along, you can download a copy of this database and others by visiting http://www.codeplex.com/MSFTDBProdSamples. You can access the different database samples by their corresponding SQL Server version by clicking the All Releases link on the right of the CodePlex screen. AdventureWorks is also the sample database used by the SQL Server 2008 Books Online help collection.

Figure 21.15 shows the completed "Employee" query, with results visible in the bottom pane.

Specifying Joins and Join Types

When you add multiple, related tables to the Query Designer, the designer uses their key relationships to automatically build a JOIN clause for the query. You also have the option to create joins on table columns that don't have an existing relationship. You do this the same way that you specify relationships in the Database Diagram Designer: You select and drag the column from one table to another within the diagram pane. The columns to be joined must be of compatible data types; you can't join, for instance, a varchar column with an integer column.

Joins are created using a comparison operator. By default, this is the equal operator; in other words, return rows where the column values are equal across the join. But you have control over the actual comparison operation used in the join. As an example, perhaps you want the resultset to include rows based on a join where the values in Table A are greater than the values in Table B on the joined columns. You can right-click the join relationship line in the diagram pane and select Properties to see the properties for the join; clicking the ellipsis button in the Join Condition and Type property reveals the Join dialog box, shown in Figure 21.16.

FIGURE 21.15   Querying for order information in the AdventureWorks database.

FIGURE 21.16   Setting the join type and operator.

Other Query Types

By default, creating queries from the Server Explorer results in a select query. But the Query Designer is equally adept at building other query types. If you want, for instance, an insert query, you can change the type of the query loaded in the designer by selecting Query Design, Change Type.

Table 21.1 shows the different query types supported by the designer.

TABLE 21.1   Supported Query Types

Query Type	Comments
Select	Returns data from one or more tables or views; a SQL SELECT statement
Insert Results	Inserts new rows into a table by copying them from another table; a SQL INSERT INTO ... SELECT statement
Insert Values	Inserts a new row into a table using the values and column targets specified; a SQL INSERT INTO ... VALUES statement
Update	Updates the value of existing rows or columns in a table; a SQL UPDATE ... SET statement
Delete	Deletes one or more rows from a table; a SQL DELETE statement
Make Table	Creates a new table and inserts rows into the new table by using the results of a select query; a SQL SELECT ... INTO statement

> **TIP**
>
> If you just want to quickly see the data contents of any given table, you can right-click the table within the Server Explorer and then select Show Table Data. This initiates a new Query/View Designer with a SELECT * statement for the given table. By default, only the results pane is visible. This functionality is ideal for testing scenarios in which you need to quickly edit data in the database or observe the effects of SQL statements on a table.

Creating Views

Views are virtual tables. They look and act just like tables in the database but are, in reality, select statements that are stored in the database. When you look at the content of a view, you are actually looking at the resultset for a select statement.

Because views are implemented as select statements, you create them using the Query/View Designer tool. In Server Explorer, right-click the Views folder under the database where you want to create the view. From there, you build the select statement just as you would for any other SQL statement.

Saving the view refreshes the database's copy of the view's select statement.

Developing Stored Procedures

A stored procedure is a SQL statement (or series of statements) stored in a database and compiled. With SQL Server, stored procedures consist of Transact-SQL (T-SQL) code and have the capability to involve many coding constructs not typically found in ad hoc queries. For instance, you can implement error-handling routines within a stored procedure and even call into operating-system functions with so-called extended stored procedures.

For a given database, right-click the stored procedures folder in Server Explorer and select Add New Stored Procedure. A template for a stored procedure opens in the SQL Editor. The SQL Editor is a close sibling to Visual Studio's Code Editor; although it doesn't have IntelliSense, it does support syntax coloring, breakpoints, and the more general text-editing features (cut-copy-paste, word wrapping, and so on).

Figure 21.17 shows the beginnings of a stored procedure in the SQL Editor window.

FIGURE 21.17 The start of a new stored procedure.

With the template loaded into the SQL Editor, writing a stored procedure involves typing in the lines of code and SQL that perform the required actions. But stored procedure developers haven't been left out in the cold with regard to productivity in Visual Studio. You can leverage the power of the Query/View Designer to write portions of your stored procedure for you.

Using the SQL Editor with the Query/View Designer

As you build the body of the procedure, the editor window highlights and boxes in certain parts of the procedure. These boxed-in areas represent SQL statements that you can edit using the Query Designer. Consider the stored procedure featured in Figure 21.18.

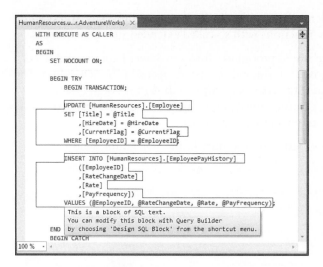

FIGURE 21.18   SQL statements in a stored procedure.

This procedure, from the AdventureWorks database, essentially consists of an update and an insert command. Both of these commands are contained within a blue-bordered box in the SQL Editor window. This is the editor's way of indicating that it has recognized a SQL statement within the procedure that can be designed using the Query/View Designer. If you right-click within the boxed-in area, the shortcut menu includes an option titled Design SQL Block. If you select this option, the Query/View Designer opens in a separate dialog box. Figure 21.19 shows the first of the two statements as they appear in the Query/View Designer.

FIGURE 21.19   Designing a query for a stored procedure.

Using the same process outlined before for writing queries, you can construct the SQL within the relative luxury of the Query Designer's drag-and-drop interface. Clicking OK on the designer dialog box will saves the query back into the stored procedure, updating the code in the editor window.

Notice that the Query Designer fully supports the use of parameters. When you fill in the parameter names in the New Value column (see the criteria pane in Figure 21.19), the designer is able to construct the appropriate SQL.

NOTE

The capability to create and edit stored procedures is supported only in Microsoft SQL Server. You cannot use the Visual Studio tools to create a procedure in, say, an Oracle database.

The Query Designer can also be pressed into play for inserting new blocks of SQL into a stored procedure (as opposed to editing existing SQL statements). First, in the SQL Editor window, right-click on the line within the procedure where you want to place the new query. From the pop-up menu, select Insert SQL. You can now use the Query/View Designer to craft the appropriate SQL. After you close out the dialog box by clicking OK, the new SQL is inserted into the procedure and can be saved into the database.

Debugging Stored Procedures

In addition to coding stored procedures, you can leverage the Server Explorer tool to help you debug them. With the stored procedure open in the SQL Editor window, set a breakpoint in the procedure by clicking in the Indicator Margin (for more details on the Indicator Margin and general editor properties, see Chapter 6, "Introducing the Editors and Designers"). With a breakpoint in place, right-click on the stored procedure's name in the Server Explorer tree and select Step into Stored Procedure (see Figure 21.20).

The SQL Debugger is also parameter-friendly. If the stored procedure uses any parameters, the debugger shows a dialog box to capture values for the parameters (see Figure 21.21).

You can quickly cycle through the list of parameters, supplying appropriate values. After you click OK, the stored procedure is executed. If you have set a breakpoint, execution pauses on the breakpoint (a yellow arrow is used to indicate the current line of execution within the editor, just the same as with the code editor window). With execution stopped, you can use the Locals and Watch windows to debug the procedure's code. See Chapter 11, "Debugging Code," for a more thorough treatment of the Locals and Watch windows as debugging tools in Visual Studio.

The Debug menu is used to control execution and flow. If you select Continue, the procedure continues running up to the next breakpoint (if present).

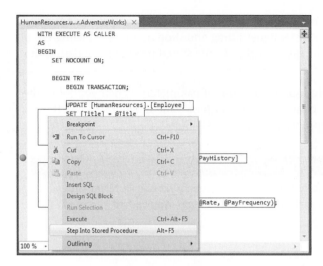

FIGURE 21.20   Stepping into a stored procedure.

FIGURE 21.21   Entering parameter values in the SQL Debugger.

Creating Triggers

Triggers are a type of stored procedure designed to run when the data in a table or view is modified. Triggers are attached to an individual table; when a query—an update, insert, or delete query—affects data in the table, the trigger executes.

Because a trigger is really a stored procedure with a controlled execution time (hence the name trigger), it can have quite complex SQL statements and flow execution logic.

To create a trigger, use Server Explorer and locate the table to which the trigger is to be attached. Right-click the table name, select Add New Trigger, and then use the SQL Editor to write the SQL for the trigger. When the trigger is saved to the database, it shows up under its related table in Server Explorer (alongside the columns in the table). Figure 21.22

shows a simple trigger designed to raise an error if an update statement changes the Availability column in the Location table.

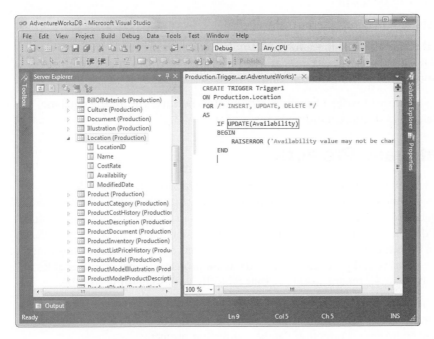

FIGURE 21.22   Creating a trigger.

Creating User-Defined Functions

User-defined functions are bodies of code/SQL designed to be reusable across a variety of possible consumers: stored procedures, applications, or even other functions. In that respect, they are no different from functions written in C# or Visual Basic. They are routines that can accept parameters and return a value. User-defined functions return scalar values (for example, a single value) or a resultset containing rows and columns of data.

One example of a user-defined function might be one that accepts a date and then determines whether the day is a weekday or weekend. Stored procedures or other functions in the database can then use the function as part of their processing.

Because user-defined functions are T-SQL statements with a format similar to stored procedures, the SQL Editor again is the primary tool for writing them. For each data connection visible in Server Explorer, a Functions folder contains any existing functions. To create a new function, you can right-click on this folder, select Add New, and then select the type of function to create. There are three options:

▶ **Inline Function**—Returns values as a resultset; the resultset is built from the results of a SELECT query.

- **Table-valued Function**—Returns values as a resultset; the resultset is built by programmatically creating a table within the function and then populating the table using INSERT INTO queries.

- **Scalar-valued Function**—Returns a single value.

After selecting the appropriate function type, template code for the function is delivered inside a new SQL Editor window. Feel free to use the Query/View Designer to construct any required lines of SQL within the function.

For the specifics on how to write a function and put it to best use within the database, consult your database's documentation.

Using Database Projects

Up to this point, we have discussed the use of the Visual Database Tools outside the context of a Visual Studio solution/project. Now let's investigate the role of the Database project type. Database projects in Visual Studio are used to manage the development and deployment of databases. essentially an offline version of a database. It mirrors a database through a set of .SQL files that contain the schema and object definitions for things such as tables, indexes, and stored procedures. With database projects, Visual Studio enables an end-to-end database development workflow that typically goes something like this:

- The DBA, who is typically the only person on a project team with access to the production database, uses VSTS Database Edition to create an initial database project and reverse engineer a production database into that project.

- The DBA is also typically responsible for generating test data sets for use in non–production databases.

- From there, the database developer gets involved. The database developer works within the confines of the database project to write the database code, changes schema items as needed to implement the required functionality, and writes unit tests that validate those changes.

- When done with a set of changes, the database developer checks the schema changes into the Team Foundation Server source control system.

- The DBA is then reinjected into the process. The DBA reviews the changes, compares the changes to the schema and data already in production, builds a deployment package containing those changes, and then oversees the deployment of those changes in a moderated way into production.

NOTE

Scripts are nothing more than SQL statements stored in a file. They are useful because they can be executed in batch to do such things as create tables in a brand-new database or add a canned set of stored procedures to a database. Because they are merely files, they can be transferred from computer to computer, enabling you to duplicate database structures across machines with ease.

The SQL scripts in the database project can create many of the database objects that we have already discussed: tables, views, triggers, stored procedures, and so on. Queries developed using the Query/View Designer can also be directly saved into a database project. In short, you use the Visual Database Tools in conjunction with a database project to create and save SQL scripts and queries.

Creating a Database Project

Database projects use the same project template system and "new project" process as all other Visual Studio project types. This means that we launch the creation process by selecting File, New, and then selecting one of the templates located in the Database/SQL Server/Advanced category on the New Project dialog box. Visual Studio ships with support for SQL Server 2005 and SQL Server 2008, and because these require different parsing and tooling support, they are both represented by different templates. In fact, we have three templates to pick from for both SQL Server 2005 and SQL Server 2008: One template uses a wizard to guide us through creating the project, the other creates an empty or blank database project for creating/manipulating objects within our database, and the third is a server project that enables us to create/manipulate global server objects or objects that reside in the master database (Figure 21.23).

FIGURE 21.23   Selecting the database project template.

Let's select the SQL Server 2008 Wizard template and walk through the wizard screens one by one.

> **NOTE**
>
> To be able to parse and validate the objects within a database project, Visual Studio needs to communicate with a local instance of SQL Server: This can be the Express Edition, Developer Edition, or Enterprise Edition of the particular database version you are targeting. If you do not have a local instance of SQL Server running, you see a dialog box at the start of the new project process prompting you to supply the path to a valid SQL Server local instance.

Project Properties

After we're past the initial welcome screen, we are prompted to specify how we want the project to be organized and which schema to use (see Figure 21.24). There are two options for organizing the project: by object type and by schema. With the Organize My Project by Object Type option selected, Visual Studio creates a schema objects folder with subfolders for your database objects such as tables and stored procedures. The Organize My Project by Schema option groups your project objects by the schema type that they belong to. For most database implementations, the default By Object Type setting is the most useful. The exception is those cases where the database itself has multiple schemas. Because this is true of the AdventureWorks database, we select the By Schema option.

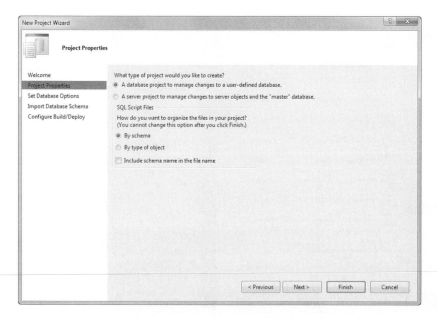

FIGURE 21.24   Setting properties of the database project.

To compare the different project organization approaches, examine Figure 21.25 and Figure 21.26. The first figure shows our database project organized by schema, and the second shows the same AdventureWorks database organized by object type.

FIGURE 21.25   A Database project organized by schema.

FIGURE 21.26   A Database project organized by object type.

Database Options

The next page of the wizard specifies the collation type to use and various collation and storage settings. Again, leaving settings these at the default is normal. In fact, in the next page of the wizard, you have the option to import these settings from the live database (in addition to its schema).

Import Database Schema

This page is where the database project really starts to enable the database development workflow: Although we can create an "empty" database project, most database developers will want to build their initial project from an existing database. This preserves the concept of a production database being the "one version of the truth." This is a recognition of the fact that we really want our test and development database environments to mirror the production environment in terms of structure. By reverse engineering a database into its component objects, Visual Studio enables us to create copies of a database, and that, in turn, enables developers to work in their own private sandboxes without worrying about affecting the product data store. Figure 21.27 shows the import schema page.

FIGURE 21.27   Selecting a database to use as the baseline for development.

The final step is to configure the build/deploy options, and these settings are provided on the final page in the wizard (Figure 21.28). Because the entire purpose of the database project is to enable developers to make changes to a database, it stands to reason that we also want a way to deploy those changes to a database. We need to indicate how we want to deploy our changes (we can opt to create a script, or create and execute that script), and where those changes should be deployed.

FIGURE 21.28 Setting deployment options.

This is the last page of the wizard; at this stage, Visual Studio has all the information needed to create the initial project. Clicking on the Finish button kicks off the project generation within Visual Studio. Refer to Figure 21.25 for a look at the end result; a fully populated database project within Visual Studio.

Note that each object in the database—be it a table, a stored procedure, an index, a key, or a constraint—is represented by a single .sql file. In addition to the schema files, we also have folders for holding data generation plans (more on these in a bit), and pre- and post-deployment scripts. Scripts placed into the pre- and post- folders are executed just before, or immediately after, deployment.

> **TIP**
>
> Pre- and postdeployment scripts are useful when you're deploying into a test environment. You can use predeployment scripts to initialize the environment, and postdeployment scripts to clean up after the deployment has finished.

The Schema View

In addition to the familiar Solution Explorer view, database projects also have a Schema View window (shown in Figure 21.29).

FIGURE 21.29   The Schema View window.

This explorer window looks similar to the Solution Explorer layout (especially if you have opted to organize your database project by object type and not schema), but it goes a step further to make SQL Server developers feel right at home in the IDE: It was designed to closely mimic the look and feel of the SQL Management Studio tool, right down to the icons used for the individual project items.

Because the Schema View window focuses exclusively on database objects, you won't find things like data generation plans here, or pre- and postdeployment scripts.

> **NOTE**
>
> Although the Schema View window is a powerful tool to use when managing database objects, it also has one annoying issue: It does not have a horizontal scrollbar like the Solution Explorer does, which means that if you have long object names, you actually need to widen the window in order to see the full name. Hopefully this is something that will be fixed in a future service pack.

Building and Deploying

The final item we haven't covered is the actual act of updating a schema in a database with the schema in a database project. You use the familiar build-and-deploy paradigm leveraged by other Visual Studio project types. In the context of a database project, the build process parses all the SQL files and identifies any files that have SQL syntax errors. If

21

the build is clean, the deployment actually updates the target database with the schema (or creates a new database if the target database doesn't exist).

We specified the default target database when we ran through the initial project creation wizard. You can also change this information at any time by right-clicking on the project in the Solution Explorer window and selecting Properties to open the properties window. The Deploy tab (see Figure 21.30) holds the settings that dictate how we deploy the changes we have made to the project.

FIGURE 21.30   Setting deployment options for a database project.

> **NOTE**
>
> You don't have to use Visual Studio to do the actual schema deployment. By building the database project, you are generating a SQL script file with all the necessary SQL commands. You can execute that script file from within any tool that understands T-SQL (including SQL Enterprise Manager itself). This is useful in situations in which the actual schema change is implemented by someone in the DBA role, who might or might not have Visual Studio installed, or who might have a specific tool that he or she is required to use for schema propagation.

A Note on Data Tier Applications

Another way to manage database development projects using Visual Studio is through a new concept introduced with SQL Server 2008 R2: Data Tier Applications, also referred to as DACs.

The concept of a DAC isn't that much different than the database project we have been discussing: it is meant to expose all of the database objects from a particular database in an "offline" fashion so that developers and DBAs can make and test changes against a database right from within the IDE. The key difference is in the approach: data tier application projects "compile" down to a .dacpac file. This file is a single unit of deployment, which contains all of the necessary database objects required by a given application: stored procedures, tables, server-side objects, management policies, and even user logins. A DAC does not contain any data.

The intent is to enable developers to work more in a declarative world (that is, we need to make these changes to a database for our application), instead of the current procedural world (that is, we need to execute these statements and scripts in this order against this database in order to run our application).

Visual Studio 2010 includes a new project type called Data-tier Application that can be found along side of the other SQL Server project types. These project types are only supported with SQL Server 2008 R2 (which, at the time of this writing, has not yet been released), and are not compatible with any other versions of SQL Server. Given the unreleased state of the technology, we leave this topic without investigating the specifics here. You should know that the Data-tier Application project looks and feels identical to the database project from within the IDE.

Creating Database Objects in Managed Code

Database objects are commonly implemented using some dialect of the SQL language. This is true with SQL Server as well. SQL Server 2005, however, introduced the capability of authoring SQL objects in managed code. So, instead of using Transact SQL, you can actually write your stored procedures, queries, views, and so on using your favorite .NET language.

The key enabler in Visual Studio that makes this happen is the SQL Server Project. Not to be confused with the formerly discussed Database Project, the SQL Server Project is a language-specific project type that provides class templates for implementing managed code versions of database routines.

Starting a SQL CLR Project

In the Add New Project dialog box, SQL Server CLR projects are located under the Database category. Creating a new SQL Server CLR project kicks off the same Add Database Reference dialog box that you have already seen with the Server Explorer and with the Database Project; the new project structure laid down by the project wizard is shown in Figure 21.31.

The SQL Server CLR project directly supports the creation of the following database objects:

- Stored procedures
- Triggers
- Aggregates

- ▶ User-defined functions

- ▶ User-defined types

FIGURE 21.31   A SQL Server CLR project.

The following sections look at how to go about creating a straightforward stored procedure.

Creating a Stored Procedure in C#

First, you add a stored procedure item to your project by using the Project menu and selecting Add Stored Procedure. A new class is added to the project. Listing 21.1 shows the base code that shows up within the new class file. You can add your custom code to the static void routine UpdateEmployeeLogin.

LISTING 21.1   The Start of a Managed Code Stored Procedure

```
using System;
using System.Data;
using System.Data.SqlClient;
using System.Data.SqlTypes;
using Microsoft.SqlServer.Server;


public partial class StoredProcedures
{
    [Microsoft.SqlServer.Server.SqlProcedure]
    public static void UpdateEmployeeLogin()
    {
        // Put your code here
    }
};
```

Managed code objects in SQL Server all leverage the .NET Framework data classes (that is, ADO.NET) to do their work. This means that stored procedures you write ends up instantiating and using classes such as SqlConnection and SqlCommand. The code you write is identical to data access code that you would write from within any other .NET project type: class libraries, web projects, and Windows forms projects. Because the common denominator is the use of ADO.NET classes, developers don't need to learn another language (such as T-SQL) to perform work in the database.

> **NOTE**
>
> It's outside the scope of this chapter to cover the relative merits or disadvantages of writing your database objects in managed code as opposed to T-SQL. Check out the whitepaper available on MSDN titled "Using CLR Integration in SQL Server 2005," by Microsoft. Although fairly old (it was written in November 2004), it is a great treatment of this subject and is highly recommended reading.

Listing 21.2 shows a fleshed-out C# routine that updates the AdventureWorks Employee table with login information. None of this code is complicated and it can be easily understood (and written) by anyone with C# data access experience.

LISTING 21.2   Managed Code for Updating Employee Login Values

```
using System;
using System.Data;
using System.Data.SqlClient;
using System.Data.SqlTypes;
using Microsoft.SqlServer.Server;


public partial class StoredProcedures
{
    [Microsoft.SqlServer.Server.SqlProcedure]
    public static void UpdateEmployeeLogin(SqlInt32 employeeId,
    SqlInt32 managerId, SqlString loginId, SqlString title,
    SqlDateTime hireDate, SqlBoolean currentFlag)
    {
        using (SqlConnection conn =
            new SqlConnection("context connection=true"))
        {
            SqlCommand UpdateEmployeeLoginCommand =
                new SqlCommand();

            UpdateEmployeeLoginCommand.CommandText =
                "update HumanResources.Employee SET ManagerId = " +
            managerId.ToString() +
                ", LoginId = '" + loginId.ToString() + "'" +
                ", Title = '" + title.ToString() + "'" +
                ", HireDate = '" + hireDate.ToString() + "'" +
                ", CurrentFlag = " + currentFlag.ToString() +
```

```
                    " WHERE EmployeeId = " + employeeId.ToString();

            UpdateEmployeeLoginCommand.Connection = conn;

            conn.Open();
            UpdateEmployeeLoginCommand.ExecuteNonQuery();
            conn.Close();


        }
    }
};
```

One line of code, however, deserves a more detailed explanation. The SqlConnection
object is created like this:

```
SqlConnection conn = new SqlConnection("context connection=true")
```

The connection string "context connection=true" tells the data provider engine that the
connection should be created in the same context as the calling application. Because this
routine is running inside a database, that means you are connecting to the host database
and run using the context (transactional and otherwise) of the calling application. Because
you are piggybacking on the context of the database that the routine is running in, you
don't need to hard-code a full SQL connection string here.

For comparison purposes, Listing 21.3 shows the same update query implemented in T-SQL.

LISTING 21.3   T-SQL for Updating Employee Login Values

```
ALTER PROCEDURE [HumanResources].[uspUpdateEmployeeLogin]
    @EmployeeID [int],
    @ManagerID [int],
    @LoginID [nvarchar](256),
    @Title [nvarchar](50),
    @HireDate [datetime],
    @CurrentFlag [dbo].[Flag]
WITH EXECUTE AS CALLER
AS
BEGIN
    SET NOCOUNT ON;

    BEGIN TRY
        UPDATE [HumanResources].[Employee]
        SET [ManagerID] = @ManagerID
            ,[LoginID] = @LoginID
            ,[Title] = @Title
            ,[HireDate] = @HireDate
```

```
        ,[CurrentFlag] = @CurrentFlag
    WHERE [EmployeeID] = @EmployeeID;
    END TRY
    BEGIN CATCH
        EXECUTE [dbo].[uspLogError];
    END CATCH;
END;
```

Building and Deploying the Stored Procedure

When you build your SQL Server project, the typical compilation process takes place. Assuming that your code will build, you can now deploy the resulting assembly to the database. Use the Build menu to access the Deploy command.

After the assembly has been deployed, you can test it by calling it from an application or from a query window. For detailed information on how to call managed assemblies and write them, consult the SQL Server Books Online.

Binding Controls to Data

You have now seen all the various ways you can use Visual Studio to create and manage databases. The following sections look at the tools available for consuming data within Windows forms, WPF, or web applications.

An Introduction to Data Binding

There is a common problem and solution pattern at hand with applications that front databases. Typically, data has to be fetched from the database into the application, and the application's user interface has to be updated to display the data in an appropriate manner. For large datasets, the concept of paging comes into play. Because it is inefficient to load in, say, a 100MB dataset, a paging mechanism needs to be pressed into action to enable the user to move forward and back through the data "stream." After the data has safely made it into the application's UI, the application-to-database flow needs to be handled. For any pieces of data that have been changed, those changes have to be reconciled and committed back into the database.

Data binding is the term given to the implementation of a design pattern that handles all facets of this round trip of data from a data structure, into an application's controls, and back again (see Figure 21.32). Although the data structure is most commonly a database, it could be any sort of container object that holds data, such as an array or a collection. .NET further stratifies the concepts of data binding into simple data binding and complex data binding. Both of these terms refer to a control's intrinsic capabilities in the larger context of the data-binding process.

Simple Data Binding

Simple data binding is the capability for a control to bind to and display a single data element within a larger dataset. A TextBox control is a great example of a control commonly used in simple data-binding scenarios. You might use a TextBox, for example, to display the last name of an employee as it is stored within the employee table of a database.

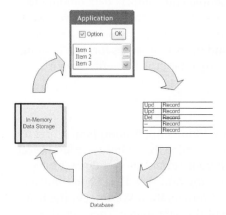

FIGURE 21.32   The data-binding process.

Support for simple data binding is widespread throughout both the Windows and web forms controls. When you use the built-in capabilities of the Windows and Web Forms Designer, it is trivial to add a group of controls to a form and simple-bind them to a dataset (more on this in a bit).

Complex Data Binding

The term complex data binding refers to the capability of a control to display multiple data elements at one time. You can think of this as a "multirow" capability. If a control can be leveraged to view multiple rows of data at one time, it supports complex data binding.

The DataGridView control (for Windows forms) and DataGrid control (for web forms) are premier examples of controls that were purpose-built to handle tabular (multirow and multicolumn) data.

Although the internals necessary to implement data binding are messy, complex, and hard to understand, for the most part the Visual Studio tools have abstracted the cost of implementing data binding out to a nice, easy, drag-and-drop model. Now let's look at how to rapidly build out support for round-trip data binding.

Auto-Generating Bound Windows Forms Controls

Although there are various ways to approach and implement data-bound controls with Visual Studio, they all involve the same basic two steps:

1. Establish a data source.

2. Map the data-source members to controls or control properties.

From there, the Visual Studio Form Designers are capable of generating the correct controls and placing them on the form. All the data-binding code is handled for you; all you need to worry about is the layout, positioning, and UI aspects of the controls.

As you might imagine, your form might have controls that use simple data binding or complex data binding or a mix of both. Now you're ready to look at the steps involved with creating a series of controls that leverage both simple and complex data binding to display information from the AdventureWorks Employee table. In this scenario, you work with the Windows Forms Designer. The ASP.NET Web Forms Designer works in a similar fashion, and you have a chance to investigate drag-and-drop approaches for data binding in the web environment in just a bit. As we have already established, the first step is selecting a data source.

Selecting a Data Source

In Visual Studio, make sure you are working inside a Windows Application project and use the Data Sources window to select a data source. If this window isn't already visible, select Show Data Sources from the Data menu in the IDE. If your current project doesn't have any defined data sources, you need to create one. Click the Add New Data Source button in the toolbar of the window to start the Data Source Configuration Wizard. On the first page of this wizard (see Figure 21.33), select the type of the data source. There are three options here:

- ▶ **Database**—The data source resides as a table within a relational database.

- ▶ **Service**—The data source is a web service that returns the data to be bound to the form controls.

- ▶ **Object**—The data source is an object that provides the data (this is useful in scenarios in which a business object from another layer of the application is responsible for delivering the data to the form).

- ▶ **SharePoint**—The data source is an object that is hosted within a SharePoint site.

FIGURE 21.33 Choosing the data-source type.

Because the concepts of data binding are most easily understood within the context of a database, we use the database data-source type as the underpinning for our walk-throughs in this chapter.

If you have selected the database data-source type, the second page of the wizard focuses on selecting the type of data model you use. Prior versions of Visual Studio simply enabled you to model your data using data sets. Visual Studio 2010 now also enables you to build an Entity Data Model, and use that as a data source for your binding. Entity Data Models are a feature of the Entity Framework, which we discuss later in this chapter. Regardless of the model you select, you need to indicate where the model gets its data (via connection string, and so on) and what data should be pulled into the model from the source database.

The final page of the wizard, shown in Figure 21.34, enables you to select which of the objects in the database should be used for the source data. You can select from any of the data elements present in any of the various tables, views, stored procedures, or user-defined functions in the database. For the purposes of this example, we have selected a DataSet model that pulls its data from the AdventureWorks database, and we have selected a few employee table data columns that are of interest: Employee ID, LoginID, HireDate, rowguid, BirthDate, SalariedFlag, VacationHours, SickLeaveHours, and CurrentFlag.

FIGURE 21.34   Selecting the data source objects.

At the conclusion of the wizard, your selected data source is visible in the Data Sources window (see Figure 21.35).

FIGURE 21.35   The Data Sources window.

If you have chosen to use a DataSet as your data model, behind the scenes, Visual Studio is really just using the data-source information collected in the Data Source Configuration Wizard to create a typed dataset. This dataset is then stored as a project item in the current project.

With the data source in place, you're ready to move on to the next step: mapping the data-source elements to controls on your form.

Mapping Data Sources to Controls
The really quick and easy way to create your data-bound controls is to let Visual Studio do it for you. From the Data Sources window, click on the drop-down button on the data-source name to reveal a menu (see Figure 21.36).

FIGURE 21.36   Changing the data table mapping.

This menu enables you to set the control generation parameters and really answers the question of which controls you want generated based on the table in the data source. By setting this to DataGridView, you can generate a DataGridView control for viewing and editing your data source. The Details setting enables you to generate a series of simple data-bound controls for viewing or editing data in the data source. For this example, select Details and then drag and drop the data source itself from the Data Sources window and onto a blank form.

Figure 21.37 shows the results. In just two short steps, Visual Studio has done all the following for you:

▶ Auto-generated a set of Label, TextBox, and DataTimePicker controls

▶ Auto-generated a tool strip with controls for navigating among records in the data source, saving changes made to a record, deleting a record, and inserting a new record

▶ Created all the necessary code behind the scenes to establish a connection to the data source, read from the data source, and commit changes to the data source

FIGURE 21.37   Auto-generated controls: viewing employee data.

You have essentially created an entire data-enabled application from scratch with absolutely no coding on your part.

The approach of using simple data binding might not fit into the user interface design, so you always have the option of working in the complex data-binding world and using the DataGridView as an alternative. Figure 21.38 shows the results of auto-generating a DataGridView instance using this same process.

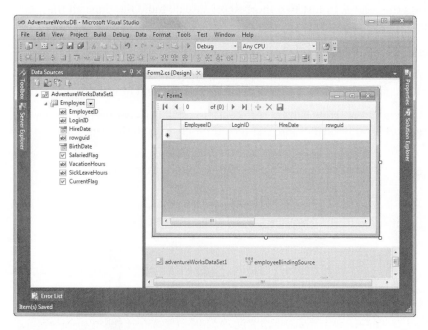

FIGURE 21.38   An auto-generated DataGridView.

Customizing Data-Source Mappings   Refer again to Figure 21.35 and look at the individual data elements that show up under the Employee data source. Each of these is displayed with a name and an icon. The name is, of course, the name of the data element as defined in the database. The icon represents the default mapping of that data type to a .NET control. For example, the Title field maps to a TextBox control, and the BirthDate field maps to a DataTimePicker control. Visual Studio actually attempts to provide the best control for any given data type. But feel free to manually indicate the specific control you want used. If you want to display the value of the Employee ID column in a label instead of a text box (in recognition of the fact that you cannot edit this value), it would be easy enough to change this before generating the controls by selecting the EmployeeID column in the Data Sources window and then clicking on the drop-down arrow to select Label instead of TextBox.

In addition to changing the control to data type mapping on an individual level, you can affect the general default mappings that are in place by selecting the Customize option from that same drop-down menu. The Visual Studio Options dialog box opens with the Windows Forms Designer page selected. Using the settings there (see Figure 21.39), you can specify the default control type that you want to apply for each recognized data type.

FIGURE 21.39   Customizing the UI representation for different data types.

Editing Typed DataSets

There is a designer provided solely for editing (and creating) typed datasets within Visual Studio: the DataSet Designer. This designer launches automatically when you open a DataSet project item such as the AdventureWorksEmployeeDataSet.xsd file that we just created when investigating data binding.

> **NOTE**
>
> Typed DataSet objects can be huge productivity enhancers over a normal dataset: Instead of using indexes into collections, you can reference tables and columns by their actual names. In addition, IntelliSense works with typed DataSet members, making coding against large data hierarchies much easier.

The DataSet Designer can be used to easily tweak datasets by changing any of the various constituent parts including the queries used to populate the dataset. Figure 21.40 shows the previously created AdventureWorksEmployeeDataSet open in the DataSet Designer.

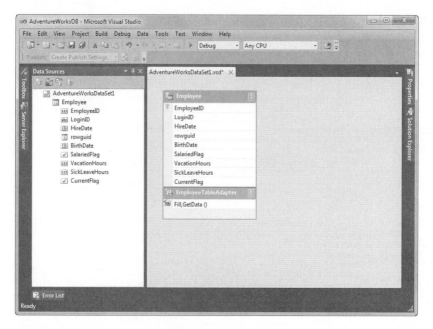

FIGURE 21.40   The Visual Studio DataSet Designer.

Note that each piece of the dataset is visually represented here, and we can interact with those pieces to effect changes. For instance, if we want to alter the query we originally constructed using the Data Set Configuration Wizard, we right-click on the Employee table on the design surface and select Configure to relaunch the query editor.

In the scenario we have been discussing, we are wiring the dataset directly to the results from a SQL query—but we can also use the DataSet Designer to create "unbound," new datasets. Adding a DataSet project item to our project enables us to start with a blank slate, adding tables, queries, and so on to the dataset to satisfy any storage requirements (or data retrieval requirements) that our application might have. This is especially useful for applications that read and write data but don't necessarily interact with a database. These dataset files can be used as simple file storage that you can easily bind later to a relational database.

Manually Binding Windows Forms Controls

In many situations, you don't want Visual Studio to create your data-bound controls for you, or you might need to bind existing controls to a data source. Data binding in these cases is just as simple and starts with the same step: creating or selecting a data source. Some controls, such as the DataGridView, have smart tag options for selecting a data source. Others don't have intrinsic data dialog boxes associated with them but can be bound to data just as easily by working, again, with the Data Sources window.

Binding the DataGridView

Grab a DataGridView from the Toolbox and drag it onto the form's surface. After you've created the control, select its smart tag glyph and use the drop-down at the top of the task list to select the data source to bind to (see Figure 21.41).

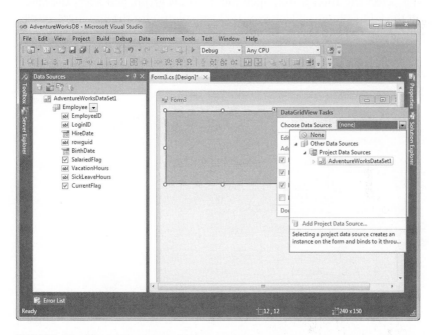

FIGURE 21.41   Selecting the control's data source.

With a data source selected, you have again managed to develop a fully functional application with two-way database access. All the code to handle the population of the grid and to handle committing changes back to the database has been written for you.

Customizing Cell Edits   The power of the DataGridView lies in its capability to both quickly bind to and display data in a tabular format and also to provide a highly customized editing experience. As one small example of what is possible in terms of cell editing, follow through with the Employee table example. When you auto-generated form controls to handle Employee table edits, you ended up with DateTimePicker controls to accommodate the date- and time-based data in the table. With the DataGridView, the cell editing experience is a simple text box experience: Each cell contains text, and you can edit the text and save it to the database. But you can provide a more tailored editing experience. You can use various stock controls (such as the DataGridViewButtonColumn, DataGridViewComboBoxColumn, and others that inherit from DataGridViewColumn; see

Chapter 18, "Building Windows Forms Applications") to display data within the columns of the grid.

For example, you can use the DataGridViewComboBoxColumn class to provide a drop-down edit for the Gender column in the grid. To do this, you first need to change the default column type. Select the grid control, open the smart tag glyph, and select the Edit Columns action. In the Edit Columns dialog box, find the column for the employee gender data and change its column type to DataGridViewComboBoxColumn (see Figure 21.42).

FIGURE 21.42   Changing the column type.

With the column type changed, you now need to specify how the grid should retrieve the list of possible values to display in the drop-down; the grid is smart enough to already know to use the underlying gender values from the table to select the one value to display in the grid. To handle the list of possible values, you could hard-code them in the column (see the Items property in Figure 21.42), or you could wire up a separate query—something along the lines of SELECT DISTINCT(Gender) FROM Employees—and have that query provide the list of possible values. Because constructing another query or data source is easy and doesn't lead to a brittle hard-coded solution, that's the approach we investigate here. To create a query to feed the combo-box column, you can visit the Data Sources window, select the Add New Data Source action, and follow the same steps you followed before to add the original Employee data source. This time, though, select only the Gender column.

After the data source is created, right-click on the data source and select Edit DataSet with Designer. We use the DataSet Designer to modify our query appropriately. In the designer (see Figure 21.43), you can see the Fill query and TableAdapter used to populate the dataset. If you click on the query (that is, click on the last row in the table graphic in the designer window), you can use the Properties window to directly edit the SQL for the query. By modifying this to reflect SELECT DISTINCT syntax, you can return the valid gender values for inclusion in the grid.

FIGURE 21.43   Changing the query for a data source.

Figure 21.44 shows the results. If you need to implement a cell edit control that doesn't currently exist, you need to create your own by inheriting from the DataGridViewColumn base control. This employee grid could benefit from a DateTimePicker control for the date- and time-based data such as birth date and hire date.

FIGURE 21.44   A drop-down within a DataGridView.

NOTE

If you look in the MSDN documentation, there is a specific example of creating a DataGridViewDateTimePickerColumn control and then wiring it up within the grid. Search for the phrase "How to: Host Controls in Windows Forms DataGridView Cells."

Binding Other Controls

For other controls that don't have convenient access to binding via their smart tag, you can leverage the Data Sources window. Drag a data source from the Data Sources window and drop it onto an existing control. The designer creates a new binding source, set it appropriately, and then make an entry in the control's DataBinding collection. If you try to drag a data element onto a control that doesn't match up (for instance, dragging a character field onto a check box), the drop operation isn't allowed.

Data Binding in WPF Applications

For the first time, Visual Studio 2010 has support for drag-and-drop data binding with WPF projects. The process is identical to the one we just covered for binding Windows Forms controls; we first need a data source added to our project. To change things up a bit, let's quickly build out a form that shows purchase orders and their detail line items.

First, create a new WPF project. Refer to Chapter 19 if you want to refresh your knowledge of the WPF project type and its designers/editors. Add the data sources in the same exact fashion as we did previously by using the Data Sources wizard. From the AdventureWorks database, we select both the PurchaseOrderHeader and PurchaseOrderDetail tables to be included in our data set (which we will call AdventureWorksPurchasingDataSet).

With the data source added, we build out a simple UI: on Window1, create a two column grid, and place a listbox in the left column of the grid. Name the listbox `listBoxPurchaseOrders`. At this point your workspace should look similar to the one depicted in Figure 21.45.

FIGURE 21.45   A UI and data sources added to a WPF project.

Now drag the PurchaseOrderID field from the PurchaseOrderHeader data source to the listbox. Although nothing appears to have changed visually, the listbox has actually been bound with a few lines of XAML:

▶ First, our data source has been referenced as a resource with the key AdventureWorksPurchasingDataSet (picking up from the name we gave the data set in the wizard).

▶ Additionally, a CollectionViewSource has been added with the appropriate binding path into the data set to pick up the Department table data.

▶ And finally, DisplayMemberPath, ItemsSource, and SelectedValuePath properties have been set on the listbox itself.

Besides the XAML modifications that were made by us, a series of statements have been added to the code file, within the Window_Loaded event. These statements are responsible for loading the data from the database via a table adapter object.

Listing 21.4 shows the current state of our XAML.

LISTING 21.4   XAML with Visual Studio Generated Data Binding

```xaml
<Window x:Class="AdventureWorksUI.MainWindow"
        xmlns="http://schemas.microsoft.com/winfx/2006/xaml/presentation"
        xmlns:x="http://schemas.microsoft.com/winfx/2006/xaml"
        Title="MainWindow" Height="350" Width="525"
        xmlns:my="clr-namespace:AdventureWorksUI"
        Loaded="Window_Loaded">
    <Window.Resources>
        <my:AdventureWorksPurchasingDataSet
            x:Key="AdventureWorksPurchasingDataSet" />
        <CollectionViewSource x:Key="purchaseOrderHeaderViewSource"
                            Source="{Binding Path=PurchaseOrderHeader,
            Source={StaticResource AdventureWorksPurchasingDataSet}}" />
    </Window.Resources>
    <Grid DataContext="{StaticResource purchaseOrderHeaderViewSource}">
        <Grid.ColumnDefinitions>
            <ColumnDefinition Width="150" />
            <ColumnDefinition Width="*" />
        </Grid.ColumnDefinitions>
        <ListBox Grid.Column="0" Margin="5"
                Name="listBoxPurchaseOrders"
                VerticalAlignment="Stretch"
                DisplayMemberPath="Name" ItemsSource="{Binding}"
                SelectedValuePath="DepartmentID"
                SelectedValue="{Binding Path=PurchaseOrderID, Mode=OneWay}" />
    </Grid>
</Window>
```

If we run the application at this stage, we see that we have a list of all of the purchase order IDs displayed in our listbox (Figure 21.46).

FIGURE 21.46   Data-bound purchase order headers.

Now, every time we select a purchase order ID in the listbox, we want to see its line items in the right column of our window. This is another, easy drag-and-drop operation requiring no hand-coding on our part. Grab the PurchaseOrderDetail data source that sits under the PurchaseOrderHeader data source, and drag it over into the right-most column of our WPF window (Figure 21.47 shows this drag-and-drop operation in progress). This has the net effect of creating a DataGrid control bound to the PurchaseOrderDetail rows that correspond to the currently selected PurchaseOrderHeader object in the listbox.

FIGURE 21.47   Adding a master-detail data source to the WPF form.

It's important that you grab the correct PurchaseOrderDetail object from the Data Sources window; by selecting the one that lies under the PurchaseOrderHeader, you are also grabbing the foreign key relationship between those two tables in the database, and that provides the context necessary for the WPF designer and editor to wire up the correct code to respond to selections in the listbox and display related records in the DataGrid.

Figure 21.48 shows the complete app that was accomplished with absolutely no coding required!

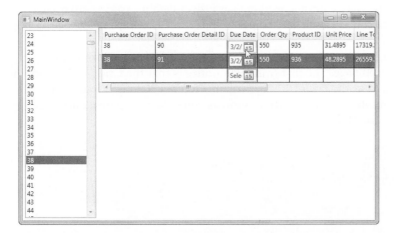

FIGURE 21.48   Master-detail data bound form in a WPF project.

Data Binding with Web Controls

Although the general concepts remain the same, data-binding web-based controls is a slightly different game than in the Windows forms or WPF world. The first obvious difference is that data sources for web forms are implemented by data-source controls in the System.Web.UI.WebControls namespace; there is no concept of the Data Sources window with web applications. Because of this, instead of starting with a data source, you instead need to start with a data control and then work to attach that control to a data source.

Selecting a Data Control

There are five primary controls you work with in a web application to deliver data-bound functionality:

- ▶ **GridView Control**—Provides a tabular presentation similar to the DataGridView control.

- ▶ **DetailsView Control**—Displays a single record from a data source; with a DetailsView control, every column in the data source shows up as a row in the control.

- ▶ **FormView Control**—Functions in the same way as the DetailsView control with the following exception: It doesn't have a built-in "default" for the way that the data is displayed. Instead, you need to provide a template to tell the control exactly how you want the data rendered onto the web page.

▶ **Repeater Control**—Simply renders a list of individual items fetched from the attached data source. The specifics of how this rendering looks are all controlled via templates.

▶ **DataList Control**—Displays rows of information from a data source. The display aspects are fully customizable and include header and footer elements.

For demonstration purposes, let's continue working with the AdventureWorks employee table and see how you can implement a data-bound web page for viewing employee records.

Using the GridView   First, with a web project open, drag a GridView control from the Toolbox onto an empty web page. The first thing you notice is that the GridView's smart tag menu is just as efficient as the DataGridView's menu. You are directly prompted to select (or create and then select) a data source as soon as you drop the control onto the web page surface (see Figure 21.49).

FIGURE 21.49   Selecting the GridView's data source.

Selecting the <New Data Source...> option uses a similar data-source wizard (refer to Figure 21.33) to collect information about your data source and add it to the project.

Once again, because of the data-binding support in the designer, you now have a fully functional application without writing a line of code. Figure 21.50 shows this admittedly ugly web page with live employee data.

Thankfully, you can just as easily put some window dressing on the table and make it look nice. By using the GridView's smart tag menu again, you can select the Auto Format option to apply several flavors of window dressing to the table (see Figure 21.51). And, of course, by applying a style sheet, you can really affect the look and feel of the page.

FIGURE 21.50   Live Employee records in the GridView.

FIGURE 21.51   Auto-formatting options for the GridView control.

Updating Data with the GridView   Creating the web grid was easy, and no data access coding was required on your part. The GridView you currently have is great for static reporting, but what if you want to edit data within the grid just as you did earlier in the Windows forms application? The key here is a set of properties on the GridView: AutoGenerateEditButton and AutoGenerateDeleteButton. When you set these properties to True, the GridView automatically includes an Edit link and a Delete link (shown on the previous figures). The Edit link comes fully baked with rendering code so that when it is clicked, that particular row in the grid becomes editable.

After changing the data in one or more of the columns, you can click on the Update link to send the data back to the database. For the update to work, however, you need to explicitly tell the data-source control (in this case, a SqlDataSource control) which query to use for processing updates. This is done with the SqlDataSource.UpdateQuery property. By specifying a parameterized UPDATE query in this property, you have fully informed the data source on how to deal with updates. You can take advantage once more of the Query Builder window to write this query for you: Select the data-source control on the web form, and in the Properties window select the UpdateQuery property. This launches the Query Builder window and enables you to construct the parameterized update command (see Figure 21.52).

FIGURE 21.52   Setting the UpdateQuery property using the Query Builder dialog box.

With that last piece of the puzzle in place, you now have a fully implemented and bound grid control that pages data in from the database and commits changes back to the database.

NOTE

To implement delete capabilities for a record, you perform the same steps using the DeleteQuery property and setting the AutoGenerateDeleteButton to True.

Data-Source Controls

As mentioned, data sources are surfaced through one or more data-source controls placed onto the web form. In the GridView example, the designer actually adds a SqlDataSource control to the form for you (based on your creation of a new DB-based data source). But there is nothing preventing you from adding one or more data-source controls to a web page directly. Just drag the control from the Toolbox onto the form surface. Table 21.2 itemizes the available data-source controls.

TABLE 21.2   Data-Source Controls

Control	Description
ObjectDataSource	Exposes other classes as data sources.
SqlDataSource	Exposes a relational database as a data source. Microsoft SQL Server and Oracle databases can be accessed natively; ODBC and OLE DB access is also supported.
AccessDataSource	Exposes a Microsoft Access database as a data source.
XmlDataSource	Exposes an XML file as a data source.
SiteMapDataSource	A special-case data source that exposes an ASP.NET site map as a data source.

After configuring the data source, you can then visit any data-aware control and bind it to the source.

Object Relational Mapping

We have spent most of this chapter covering the "standard" process for creating .NET applications that read and write data that resides in a database. Although Visual Studio and the ADO.NET libraries themselves do a lot to abstract away the difficult pieces of that process, problems still remain. In fact, there is one common problem that developers writing database-driven applications face: the mismatch between an application's normal object-oriented programming model, implemented in C# or Visual Basic, and the relational programming model surfaced in databases or datasets, implemented primarily with SQL.

In the object-oriented world, we manipulate objects via methods and properties, and each object itself can be (and often is) a parent or container for other objects. The relational database world is much more straightforward: Entities are implemented as row/column-based tables, and each "cell" in a table holds simple scalar values. The core issue is that you must change programming models when dealing with an application's internal framework or the relational database used as its data store—and translating from one to the other isn't a straightforward task.

As a simple example, rows from an invoice table are easily fetched into a dataset object using the various data-binding tools and classes discussed previously. But deriving a "native" Invoice object from the dataset involves two-way, manual translation and manipulation to get the core values to translate across this object/relational barrier. This highlights several issues: Do you abandon the dataset approach and read directly from the database into your applications' objects? Do you eschew the object approach and try to use the DataSet component throughout all layers of your application? Or is a hybrid approach best, maintaining strongly typed object collections in addition to the datasets?

Ideally, application developers would be free to work with and manipulate objects within the program's object model and have those objects and changes automatically stored in the database with little or no intervention. Not only does this keep the focus on core, well-understood object design patterns, but it also lets the individual developer work with his core language strength without having to learn or become expert in SQL. Pursuit of this goal obviously requires some sort of standard approach, and tooling support, for mapping objects to and from their equivalents within the relational database. And this is exactly what object/relational mapping tools do.

The term object/relational mapping (or O/R mapping) is used to refer to this general process of translating objects to and from databases. O/R mapping tools have been on the market for years now, and Microsoft has finally delivered O/R mapping support directly in the .NET Framework and in Visual Studio through two different but similar technologies: LINQ to SQL and Entity Framework. Let's briefly discuss both of these technologies, and their Visual Studio tooling, starting first with LINQ to SQL.

An Overview of LINQ

LINQ is an acronym for "Language Integrated Query." It is a component of the .NET Framework 3.5 and above that adds SQL-like querying capabilities to .NET objects. Specifically, it extends the core .NET languages—Visual Basic and C#—and the runtime to try to erase the object-to-database-entity barrier. Visual Basic and C# both support new query operators that operate over objects similar to the way SQL operates over tables in a database.

For example, you could query for all approved invoice objects like this:

```
var approved =
    from invoice in invoices
    where (invoice.Approved) == true
    select invoice;


foreach (Invoice invoice in approved)
{
    // do some work here
}
```

And runtime support is introduced for physically translating objects and methods to and from their database equivalents (primarily through the use of code attributes, as you see in a moment). This is a simple example of a class method mapped to a SQL Server stored procedure:

```
[Function(Name="HR.uspDeleteEmployee")]
public int uspDeleteEmployee([Parameter(Name="EmployeeID", DbType="Int")]
                            System.Nullable<int> employeeID)
{
    IExecuteResult result = this.ExecuteMethodCall(this,
            ((MethodInfo)(MethodInfo.GetCurrentMethod())), employeeID);
```

```
    return ((int)(result.ReturnValue));
}
```

LINQ comes in several different flavors, each targeted at a specific mapping problem:

- ▶ **LINQ to SQL**—This enables you to map objects to database entities.

- ▶ **LINQ to XML**—This enables you to query XML documents and map objects to XML document elements.

- ▶ **LINQ to Objects**—This specifically refers to the inclusion of .NET language syntax that enables queries to be written over collections of objects (as in our previous example with the approved invoices).

You need to be aware of one important fact regarding LINQ to SQL: although the technology is fully supported by Microsoft, it has been deprecated in favor of the Entity Framework. Some developers might still prefer to use LINQ to SQL because it is a lighter weight, and simpler ORM to implement.

> **NOTE**
>
> In 2007, Microsoft released a technology preview of a version of LINQ designed specifically for parallel execution. This technology, called PLINQ (for Parallel LINQ) has now been officially released as a part of .NET 4.0. In essence, PLINQ builds on the LINQ concepts by accepting any LINQ to XML or LINQ to Objects query, and executes those queries by optimizing for multiple CPU or multiple core scenarios.

If you are interested more in PLINQ or parallel programming in general, the Parallel Computing center on MSDN is a great start: http://msdn.microsoft.com/en-us/concurrency/default.aspx.

LINQ is a fairly broad and deep set of technology pieces, and covering even one in depth is outside of the scope of this book. We do, however, dig into the primary Visual Studio tool used when writing LINQ to SQL applications: the O/R Designer.

Mapping Using the O/R Designer

The first step in creating a LINQ to SQL application is typically the construction of an object model that is based on a given database definition. This is the exact function of the O/R Designer. It enables you to select a database and generate an object model that maps to the database's structure. Table 21.3 shows how the database components are mapped to object components.

TABLE 21.3   Default Database to Object Mappings

Database	Application Object
Table	Class
Table Column	Class Property
Foreign Key Relationship	Association
Stored Procedure/Function	Class Method

Adding Database Entities

The O/R Designer is the design surface for project items known as LINQ to SQL Classes, and so the first step in using the designer is to add a new LINQ to SQL Classes project item to a project. Figure 21.53 shows where this project item lives in the Add New Item dialog box.

FIGURE 21.53   Adding a LINQ to SQL Classes item to an existing project.

After you've selected the LINQ to SQL Classes item and added it to the project, the O/R Designer immediately launches (see Figure 21.54).

There isn't much to see yet because we haven't selected which database entities we want to represent within our object model. This involves the use of the second primary tool for performing the O/R mapping: Server Explorer.

By selecting a valid data source in Server Explorer, we can simply drag and drop a table over onto the left-hand side (the "data class" side) of the O/R Designer (see Figure 21.55).

Although nothing obvious happens after the table is dragged onto the data class pane (beyond having its visual representation in the designer), in reality potentially thousands of lines of code have been automatically generated to implement a class structure that mimics the table structure. In addition, all the attribute-based wiring has been implemented so that the LINQ engine can understand and process updates between the class object and the table's rows and columns.

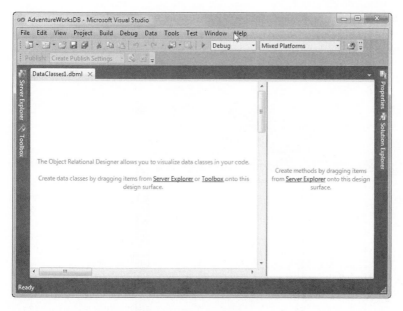

FIGURE 21.54   The LINQ to SQL O/R designer.

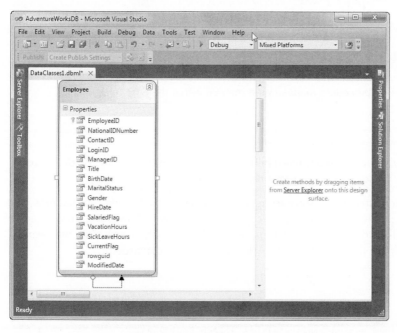

FIGURE 21.55   The AdventureWorks Employee table added to the O/R Designer.

This exact process is also used to create methods within our object model. We can, for instance, drag a stored procedure over onto the right-hand pane of the designer (the "methods" pane) to map a method within our object model to the stored procedure (see Figure 21.56).

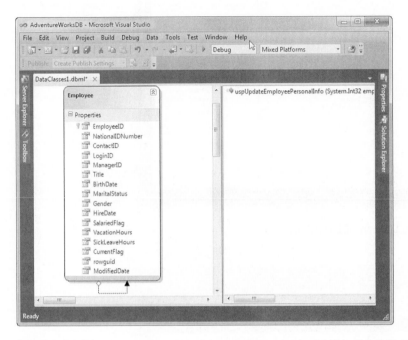

FIGURE 21.56   A stored procedure mapped as a method within the O/R Designer.

LINQ Code

Let's examine exactly what has taken place behind the scenes as a result of the drag-and-drop operation between Server Explorer and the O/R Designer.

For one, the connection string necessary to open a connection to the selected database is automatically stored in the app.config (or web.config) file for you. This is then leveraged by LINQ to make calls into the database when needed. In addition, a new class has been defined. Here is a snippet from the Employee class showing its constructor:

```
public Employee()
{
   this._Employees = new EntitySet<Employee>
                 (new Action<Employee>(this.attach_Employees),
                  new Action<Employee>(this.detach_Employees));
 this._Employee1 = default(EntityRef<Employee>);
```

```
OnCreated();
}
```

> **NOTE**
>
> The O/R Designer actually "de-pluralizes" entity names for you automatically. Many HR databases, for instance, might choose to implement an employee table and call it "employees" because it stores the data records for more than one worker. In an attempt to further push through the object model to data model impedance mismatch, the O/R Designer actually creates a class called "Employee" and *not* "Employees"; this correlates much better with the true intent of the class (which is to contain a single row/instance from the table and not the entire table).

You can see that LINQ marks up the object model with attributes to perform the magic linking between the objects and the database: Via the Table attribute, this class has been identified as a direct map to the HumanResources.Employee table.

Each column in the Employee table has also been implemented as a property on the Employee class. This snippet shows the EmployeeID property:

```
[Column(Storage="_EmployeeID", AutoSync=AutoSync.OnInsert,
DbType="Int NOT NULL IDENTITY", IsPrimaryKey=true, IsDbGenerated=true)]
public int EmployeeID
  {
    get
    {
      return this._EmployeeID;
    }
    set
    {
      if ((this._EmployeeID != value))
      {
        this.OnEmployeeIDChanging(value);
        this.SendPropertyChanging();
        this._EmployeeID = value;
        this.SendPropertyChanged("EmployeeID");
        this.OnEmployeeIDChanged();
      }
    }
  }
```

Beyond the Employee object, there has also been code generated for the data context. Here is a snippet of the class definition created automatically for us:

```
[System.Data.Linq.Mapping.DatabaseAttribute(Name="AdventureWorks")]
public partial class DataClasses1DataContext : System.Data.Linq.DataContext
 {

  private static System.Data.Linq.Mapping.MappingSource mappingSource =
        new AttributeMappingSource();

    #region Extensibility Method Definitions
    partial void OnCreated();
    partial void InsertEmployee(Employee instance);
    partial void UpdateEmployee(Employee instance);
    partial void DeleteEmployee(Employee instance);
    #endregion

  public DataClasses1DataContext(string connection) :
    base(connection, mappingSource)
  {
   OnCreated();
  }
  public System.Data.Linq.Table<Employee> Employees
  {
   get
   {
    return this.GetTable<Employee>();
   }
  }
 }
```

You can think of DataContext as the LINQ manager: It handles the connection back to the database, manages the in-memory entities, and marshals the calls necessary for data updates and any issues that might arise from concurrency and locking conflicts. In total, more than 500 lines of functioning code were emitted to make this all work. So, how do you actually use a LINQ object within your application? Read on.

Working with LINQ Objects

The goal with LINQ, again, is simplicity; LINQ classes look and behave just like any other class in our object model. We can create a new employee object, and set its properties like this:

```
Employee emp = new Employee();
```

```
emp.BirthDate = new DateTime(1965, 4, 4);
emp.Gender = 'F';
emp.LoginID = "templogin";
emp.MaritalStatus = 'M';
emp.Title = "Project Resource Manager";
...
```

To commit this new Employee object to the Employee table, we need to add the object to the Employees collection held by our data context, and then call the SubmitChanges method. Remember that the type is simply the default name given by the O/R Designer to our data context class; we can change this to anything we want.

```
DataClasses1DataContext db = new DataClasses1DataContext();
db.Employees.InsertOnSubmit(emp);
db.SubmitChanges();
```

In a similar fashion, employees can be removed from the collection (and then from the database):

```
db.Employees.DeleteOnSubmit(emp);
db.SubmitChanges();
```

We have really just scratched the surface here with regard to the intricacies and complexities of O/R application development using LINQ; but hopefully this overview of the O/R Designer can be used as a starting point for your O/R explorations in Visual Studio. Let's move on to the Entity Framework.

Working with the Entity Framework

Like LINQ to SQL, Entity Framework (or EF) is a technology that enables you to program against objects that are backed by tables within a relational database. And because they share that same overall goal, most of the concepts we covered with LINQ to SQL apply to EF-based applications as well. The notable difference with EF is the level of abstraction it provides. Whereas LINQ to SQL is a direct map of objects to database tables, EF maps database tables to an entity data model (EDM). From there, you can map objects to the EDM.

Within an Entity Framework's entity data model, there are actually two discrete models that are maintained by Visual Studio: the conceptual model (think application objects) and the storage model (the database that stores those application objects).

In Visual Studio, the Entity Framework models are used by adding an ADO.NET Entity Data Model item to your project. Just like our previous look at the LINQ to SQL Data Classes project item, the EF project item is located under the Data category in the Add New Item dialog box (Figure 21.57).

FIGURE 21.57   Adding the Entity Data Model project item.

When you add an entity model to your project, a wizard launches; this wizard gives you the option to start with an empty conceptual and storage model, or create a conceptual model from an existing database (Figure 21.58). In our case, we continue our walkthrough again using the AdventureWorks database.

FIGURE 21.58   Configuring the Entity Data Model with the wizard.

21

Editing the Entity Data Model

After the entity model is added to your project, you can make changes to that entity model using the Entity Data Model Designer. This is the visual design surface for your model. There are also two other windows displayed in conjunction with the model designer. The Model Browser provides a Solution Explorer-like view of both the conceptual model and the storage model for your entities, and the Mapping Details window shows exactly how objects in the conceptual model are mapped and linked to tables in the storage model. Figure 21.59 shows all three windows open within the IDE. Note that when we added the entity model to our project, we opted to build out the model using every existing table within the AdventureWorks database. Let's take a closer look at each of these windows.

FIGURE 21.59   Editing an Entity Data Model.

The Designer   The designer shows a familiar, visual view of conceptual model. Each object is depicted, along with its properties/fields, and relationships between objects are also clearly visible. In Figure 21.60, we see the now familiar Employee to EmployeeDepartment to Department relationships. These relationships were copied directly from the database foreign key relationships. On the design window itself, there is a small set of navigation buttons set just under the vertical scroll bar (highlighted for you in Figure 21.60). Because you might be dealing with hundreds or even thousands of objects within the designer, you need a way to zoom in and out on the design surface, From top to bottom, these buttons enable you to zoom in, zoom the diagram to 100%, zoom out, and zoom the diagram so that all objects are visible at once.

FIGURE 21.60   The entity model design surface.

Objects can be moved around on the design surface, but you can also use the designer to directly make changes to the model. For instance, you can select a property and change its name.

The Model Browser   The model browser window shows you all of the elements that are contained within both the conceptual model and within the storage model. This includes entities, tables, and relationships. You can use the model browser window to directly delete items from your models, or modify their properties. With large models, it is often easier to locate the entity you are looking for with the model browser than trying to visually find the object within the entity data model designer pane.

TIP

You can immediately show any model element within the designer by right-clicking the element within the Model Browser and selecting Show In Designer.

One of the coolest things about the model browser window is its search functionality. By typing a search term into the search box at the top of the window, you are able to see every instance of that term anywhere within the model. The vertical scroll bar actually graphically depicts everywhere within the model(s) that a search hit was found. If you examine Figure 21.61 closely, you see the results of a search for "Employee." 72 matches were found. Within the vertical scroll bar, you see "blocks" that represent where the match was found within the model hierarchy. Hovering over those blocks give you a tooltip that identifies the exact name that contains the match. This enables you to very quickly jump around your search matches within large models.

FIGURE 21.61   Searching within the Model Browser window.

The Mapping Details Window   We have discussed the idea of the conceptual model and of the storage model. But if these models lived in isolation, EF wouldn't be able to achieve its ultimate goal of linking code objects to database tables if there weren't some way of mapping between the two models. The Mapping Details window is the tool within the IDE that lets you view and edit all of the conceptual-to-storage model mappings.

Figure 21.62 shows the mapping details for Employee object. All of the mapping properties were preset for us because we chose to build out our conceptual model based on an existing database. When you select an entity with the designer, the mapping window will show an alphabetical list of all of the table columns. To the right of each column, is displayed the property that the column maps to on the object.

The mapping details window is also used to map an object to your own, custom functions for performing inserts, updates, or deletes. Click the two icons on the top left border of the mapping window to change between these two modes.

FIGURE 21.62   Mapping properties for the Employee object/table.

> **NOTE**
>
> You aren't limited to performing just a one-to-one map between objects and database tables. You could decide, for instance, that your conceptual model contains two Employee classes: HourlyEmployee and SalariedEmployee. You have the capability to create a function that filters the rows in the underlying Employee table and maps those rows to one or the other of these two objects. This is done quite easily in the Mapping Details window by adding a condition. Click the Add a Condition link within the window, and then specify a condition to apply against the SalariedFlag field on the table.

We have now covered the high-level overview of what the Entity Framework platform is and the tools and project items you use within Visual Studio to create EF-based projects. Now let's dig a bit deeper to see how we would use these tools to perform common EF tasks.

Querying Against the Entity Data Model

The real power of EF is the ability to perform SQL-like operations against a set of objects (for example, the objects you have defined in your entity data model) using a variety of different methods.

Because every object in EF is LINQ enabled, we could use LINQ to Entities to query for a list of salaried employees like this:

```
using (AdventureWorksEntities entities = new AdventureWorksEntities())
  {
     List<Employee> employees =
         (from e in entities.Employees
           where e.SalariedFlag == true select e).ToList();
  }
```

The AdventureWorksEntities object seen on the first line of code above represents our conceptual model; LINQ provides the syntax we need to iterate over those objects within the AdventureWorksEntities object.

EF also supports the ability to construct queries using the ObjectQuery class. This class lives within the System.Data.Objects namespace, and enables us to use standard SQL-like syntax for generating queries. Here is that same query, re-written using the ObjectQuery class:

```
using (AdventureWorksEntities entities = new AdventureWorksEntities())
    {
        ObjectQuery<Employee> query =
            entities.Employees.Where("it.SalariesFlag=@flag");

        query.Parameters.Add(new ObjectParameter("flag", "True"));

        List<Employee> employees = query.ToList();

    }
```

We could even query our objects using nothing more than standard stored procedures. This would be a two step process: First, we create a stored procedure in our underlying database (and thus our store model). Second, we map that stored procedure to a function within our model. With the function in place (here we have named it GetSalariedEmployees), we can call that function like this:

```
using (AdventureWorksEntities entities = new AdventureWorksEntities())
    {
        List<Employee> employees = entities.GetSalariedEmployees().ToList();
    }
```

Updating Data in the Entity Data Model

Because we are simply programming against standard .NET objects within the entity data model, updating data that resides in those objects is as simple as setting the object properties.

We can create a new Employee like this:

```
Employee newEmp = new Employee();
```

And set its properties like we would for any other object:

```
newEmp.SalariedFlag = true;
newEmp.HireDate = DateTime.Today;
newEmp.Title = "HR Manager";
```

We would then add the new employee to the entity data model like this:

```
entities.Employees.AddObject(newEmp);
```

And finally, we would need to tell the entity model to persist these changes to the database:

```
entities.SaveChanges();
```

In a similar fashion, we can delete objects by first referencing the object we want to remove, and then calling the DeleteObject method from our entities object. This code deletes the first employee in the employee table:

```
Employee firstEmp = entities.Employees.First();
entities.DeleteObject(firstEmp);
```

> **NOTE**
>
> We have discussed how to change data within entity data model, but what happens if either the database schema changes, or you want changes within your conceptual model to be made at the storage level as well? If you right-click on the entity data model designer, you see two options that essentially sync schema of the database with the object model or vice versa: Generate Database from Model and UpdateModelFromDatabase.

As you have probably guessed by now, Entity Framework is a vast and deep ORM platform. We have really only been able to scratch the surface here. If you intend on leveraging EF inside of your applications, we wholeheartedly recommend a book dedicated to the subject such as Julia Lerman's *Programming Entity Framework* from O'Reilly.

Summary

In this chapter, you read about the broad and deep support that Visual Studio 2010 has for building and managing databases, and also for creating applications that access data in a database. We discussed the suite of Visual Database tools, available right within the IDE, that function in synergy with one another and with the various Visual Studio designers to provide a seamless experience for writing queries, creating table structures, and crafting stored procedures. We also investigated the newfound support for writing SQL Server database procedures and functions using entirely managed code.

We spent some time discussing the basics of data binding—how it is a core problem space with many application development efforts and how the Visual Studio Web, Windows Form Designers, and WPF Designers and controls provide first-class support for simple to complex data-binding scenarios. In particular, we examined the role that these Visual Studio designers play in the data-binding world by enabling developers to rapidly build forms-based applications with sophisticated data needs without writing a single line of code.

And finally, we examined the built-in support that Visual Studio provides for mapping entire object models to a database using two different technologies: LINQ2SQL and Entity Framework.

Hopefully, by exposing you to all of these great built-in tools, we have started you on the road to becoming even more efficient in leveraging Visual Studio across a range of database interactions.

CHAPTER 22

Service-Oriented Applications

Services have transformed the way we think of the Web and how we leverage it to build software. Prior to services, the Web was mostly a means to deliver cross-platform user interfaces with low deployment costs. Of course, that was a huge deal (and remains so) for both Internet and intranet applications. Services have shown a similar potential to change the way we build our applications both for the Web and across networks.

At their core, services represent an interface (or set of methods) that provide black-box-like access to shared functionality using common formats and protocols. By this definition, a service should be loosely coupled with its clients and work across boundaries. These boundaries have, for a long time, prevented the true promise of reusable application components such as services. By working across boundaries such as process, machine, language, and operating system, services can truly be leveraged by the many potential clients that an organization might have today and tomorrow.

Visual Studio 2010 and the .NET Framework 4.0 enable developers to create service-oriented applications without having to dig into the inner workings of such things as SOAP, HTTP, Remoting, and WSDL. Instead, you can focus on creating services that solve your specific business problems. You can then let the Framework worry about your needs with respect to formats and protocols.

In this chapter, we first cover the fundamental concepts behind service-based applications. We then cover the two primary service technologies built into Visual Studio: ASP.NET Web Services and Windows Communication Foundation (WCF). The former enables you to build standard web services hosted by ASP.NET. The latter is Microsoft's framework that enables you to design and build service-oriented applications, capable of both consuming and hosting services over the web or over a network. For each section we discuss both creating services and writing service clients.

Service Fundamentals

A service defines a contract between a calling client and the service itself. In English, this contract states something like this: "If you send me data in this format, I will process it and return you the results in this other format." The format of this data and the communication parameters of these calls are all based on open standards such as XML and SOAP. Similar standards enable a client to often "discover" a web service and its contract and then work with it. These service standards apply across technology boundaries and therefore make services attractive for exchanging data between heterogeneous environments.

To help frame the benefits of services, it can be helpful to think of them within the context of the problems they were designed to solve. For example, many large companies have multiple applications that need to access and update similar information. They might, for instance, rely on customer data records inside a customer relationship management (CRM) system, an order-processing application, a shipping tool, a financial system, and a reporting package. In this case, the customer record is duplicated per system. This means the data may be contradictory (or out-of-date) in any one system. Companies might have band-aids in place such as batch processing that tries to keep the data in sync on a daily basis. Figure 22.1 illustrates this problem example.

What's worse, a company might have multiple systems that offer the same functionality (like two CRM systems). This can happen if the company has grown through acquisition and merger activities, or if each department has chosen its own technology. In fact, even if a company wrote all of these applications from scratch, you often see duplicate (or similar) code in each application for doing the same thing. This code, of course, has to be maintained and changes to it can often have unintended consequences on the other systems.

These problems are what service-oriented solutions are intended to solve. Consider that each of the applications in the prior example might work on different servers running different code on different operating systems. They often even have different database technologies. Therefore, a reusable component that could be plugged into each application could not be easily created. Even if it did, the need to centralize this information into a common view would still exist. For example, an update to a customer record in one system needs to somehow be recorded in the other systems.

What is required to solve this problem (and problems like it) is a common, shared interface into a centralized view of the data (in this case, customer data). This interface should be able to work across application boundaries such as protocols, data types, and processes. Architects recognized this problem but did not see a viable solution until the advent of

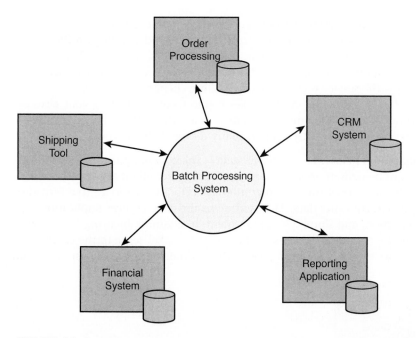

FIGURE 22.1 Heterogeneous applications often share data and have similar needs around that data. Nightly batch processing to update data across applications is not the best way to solve this dilemma.

the Web. With web technologies, the HTTP protocol was ubiquitous. Servers could talk to each other. Then along came the XML standard for describing messages. With these two technologies (HTTP and XML), applications running on different platforms had a way to communicate. They could send and receive structured messages over a common protocol, and thus web services were born.

Why ASP.NET Web Services and WCF

ASP.NET Web Services still maintain a dominant role in building service applications. They are great for communicating across the Internet. However, they are not always the most efficient means of communication. For example, if both the client and the service exist on the same technology (or even the same machine), they can often negotiate a more efficient means to communicate (such as Remoting). Service developers found themselves making the same choices they were trying to avoid. They now would have to choose between creating efficient, internal services and being able to have the broad access found over the Internet. And, if they had to support both, they might have to create multiple versions of their service or at least separate proxies for accessing their service. This is the problem Microsoft has solved with Windows Communication Foundation (WCF).

With WCF, you can create your service without concern for boundaries. You can then let WCF worry about running your service in the most efficient way, depending on the calling client. To manage this task, WCF introduces the concept of endpoints. Your service might have multiple endpoints (configured at design time or after deployment). Each endpoint indicates how the service might support a calling client over the web, via Remoting, through MSMQ, and more. WCF enables you to focus on creating your service functionality. It worries about how to most efficiently speak with calling clients. In this way, a single WCF service can efficiently support many different client types.

Consider our example from before. The customer data is shared among the applications. Each application might be written on a different platform, and it might also exist in a different location. You can extract the customer interface into a WCF service that provides common access to shared customer data. This centralizes the data, reduces duplication, eliminates synchronization, and simplifies management. In addition, by using WCF, you can configure the service endpoints to work in the way that makes sense to the calling client. Figure 22.2 shows the example from before with centralized access of customer data in a WCF service.

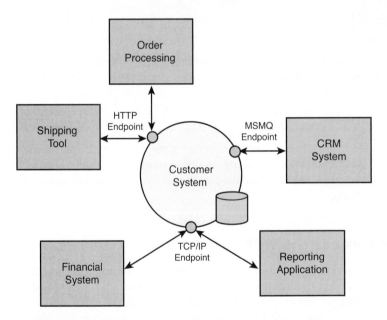

FIGURE 22.2   A centralized, service-oriented implementation of the customer data and service contract using WCF and multiple endpoints.

In the coming sections we cover creating both web services and those built on WCF. Visual Studio 2010 and the .NET Framework do a lot to abstract the intricacies or "plumbing" of building services away from everyday programming tasks. The result is a more productive development experience. You spend less time worrying about how to create a proper SOAP message or building communications channels and more time developing real business value.

ASP.NET Web Service Applications

22

Before getting started, it is important that developers understand the key concepts and standard terms around web services. This knowledge ensures that you know what is happening in your application. It also helps when you are reading the .NET documentation and articles related to building web service applications. Therefore, we have put together the following glossary of key terms related to web services:

▶ **Web Service**—A web service represents a cohesive set of application logic that performs actions and provides data. A web service groups this logic as methods that can be called over HTTP. Not all services are web services; only those that work over the Internet are considered web services.

▶ **Web Service Method (or Web Method)**—A web service method represents a method exposed by a web service. A web method can take parameters and return a response.

▶ **XML (Extensible Markup Language)**—XML is used to both represent and describe data in a platform-neutral manner. XML can be used to represent both simple and complex data elements and relationships. It is the XML standard that makes web services possible.

▶ **WSDL (Web Service Description Language)**—WSDL is used to describe the contents of a web service and its web methods. The WSDL provides the message data contracts that enable clients to work with a given service.

▶ **XSD (XML Schema Document)**—XSD contains a set of predefined types (string, decimal, and so on) and a standard language for describing your own complex types. An XML Schema Document (also referred to as an XSD) uses these types to describe (and restrict) the contents of an XML message.

▶ **SOAP (Simple Object Access Protocol)**—SOAP is an XML-based protocol for communicating between client and web service. It is helpful to think of SOAP as representing the format of the messages as they pass over the wire. SOAP wraps XML messages (in envelopes) for communication across the Web. Most SOAP messages are sent over HTTP. However, they can also be sent with transport protocols such as SMTP and FTP.

▶ **HTTP (Hypertext Transfer Protocol)**—HTTP represents the communication protocol used by web services to transfer SOAP-formatted (or encoded) messages. HTTP is also the way standard web page requests (GET and POST) communicate.

▶ **UDDI (Universal Description, Discovery, and Integration)**—UDDI is used to define a registry of web services. This capability is useful for the publication of services for developers to find and consume.

▶ **URI (Uniform Resource Identifier)**—URIs provide a means for locating items on the web. In most cases, URIs are URLs (uniform resource locators) that point to a given service.

▶ **DISCO (Discovery Document)**—A DISCO file provides information that links to other key elements of a web service. This includes links to XSDs, SOAP bindings, and namespaces. A program can use a DISCO file to determine how to work with a given web service.

▶ **WS-***—This term represents the overall standards for web services.

▶ **WSE (Web Service Enhancements)**—This is Microsoft's implementation of WS-* standards. WSE 3.0 was the latest version and was released with Visual Studio 2005. It enables web service transactions and enhanced security. WSE can still be downloaded as an add-in to Visual Studio 2005. For Visual Studio 2008 and 2010, these features were added to WCF.

Visual Studio makes building web services a similar experience as you would get when developing other classes and components. In this way, the complexities of SOAP, WSDL, XSD, and the like are abstracted (and auto-generated by the tool). You still have access and control over these low-level items if you need them. However, for the most part, you define a web service the same way you create a class. You then define web methods similar to the way you would define methods on a class. Visual Studio takes on the job of creating the appropriate schema contract for your method signatures and describing your web services in terms of WSDL. The .NET Framework then worries about properly packaging your data into a SOAP message and transmitting it across HTTP.

ASP.NET web services in .NET are built and delivered on the same framework that delivers ASP.NET websites. This means that web services share the same server technology (Internet Information Services, or IIS) as well as the same objects, such as `Application`, `Session`, and `Context`. In this way, developers who are familiar with delivering ASP.NET applications can leverage this experience for web services. You can take advantage of the built-in state management, authentication services, and performance of ASP.NET, for instance.

An ASP.NET web service is simply a web address to a web service file that contains the extension .asmx. The service has a standard http://... address. The .asmx file is used as the URI (uniform resource identifier) for the web service (similar to a web page). You write your code "behind" this file, and Visual Studio and .NET do the rest by attaching the appropriate WSDL and enabling the SOAP calls over HTTP. Let's take a closer look at how to leverage Visual Studio and ASP.NET to deliver web services.

The ASP.NET Web Service Project Template

A web service can be added to any ASP.NET website or web application project. Visual Studio used to provide a ASP.NET Web Service–specific template in prior versions. However, this template was removed in 2010 (you can still find it if you target 3.5 of the

Framework for your project). Removing this template is partly a reaction to the move to WCF (see the next section) and also a realization that you do not need a special website template to create a web service.

If you do plan to create service-layer or separate your services from any user interface elements you might consider creating an empty website to house your ASP.NET web services. You can do so using File, New, Web Site to launch the Add New Project dialog box as shown in Figure 22.3. Here, you can select the template ASP.NET Empty Web Site.

FIGURE 22.3   Consider using the ASP.NET Empty Web Site template for creating service-only ASP.NET sites.

As with defining a new website, you can indicate the location of the web service. You can choose a location by using the file system or by browsing to a web server using HTTP, or by leveraging FTP to indicate where to store the web service. In addition, you can define the default language in which the web service should be programmed (C# or VB).

Web Service Files

The only file in an empty website template is a basic web.config file that simply contains a line about compilation and the target version of the .NET Framework. Therefore, to create a service you must add it to the site. You do so by right-clicking the project in Solution Explorer and choosing Add New Item. This launches the Add New Item dialog box. Here, you select the .asmx template and provide a name for your service (this name will form part of the URI). Figure 22.4 shows an example.

FIGURE 22.4   Use the Web Service item template to add an ASP.NET web service to your website.

An .asmx file has both a markup and a code-behind file.

You can switch views by right-clicking the .asmx file. The markup file sits in the website and provides the file name for the URI. Typically, the markup contains only a single, @WebService directive. This directive indicates that the web service file is a pointer to the code for the service. The CodeBehind attribute indicates the location of the related service class file. The following shows an example:

```
<%@ WebService Language="C#" CodeBehind="~/App_Code/CustomerProfile.cs"
  Class="CustomerProfile" %>
```

Notice that this markup points to the code file called CustomerProfile.cs. Note that this file is inside the App_Code directory for the site. It has been moved in 2010. It used to be a file "under" the .asmx file similar to a web page's code-behind. The class file is where the logic for the service resides.

> **NOTE**
>
> You can define a web service as a single file (see the bottom of Figure 22.4), and both the directive and the code are stored together.

Finally, the @WebService directive uses the Class attribute to indicate a class contained inside the CustomerProfile.cs file. This class is the web service. The methods in this class are the web methods. Figure 22.5 shows the web service files in Solution Explorer and the default .asmx web service code from the template.

FIGURE 22.5   The ASP.NET Web Service code file has been moved to the App_Code directory for 2010.

Notice the code in Figure 22.5. This class is just a standard C# class (it could also be VB). It has using statements, the class definition, a method, and some attributes applied to both the class and the method. This programming model should be familiar to .NET developers.

Of course, you still have to let .NET know that this code is a web service. There are two ways the code does this. First, it uses attributes. The CustomerProfile class in Figure 22.5 is decorated with the WebService attribute. This defines the class as a web service. Notice also that the HelloWorld method has the WebMethod attribute applied. This attribute indicates that this method is a web method that can be called for the web service (you can have methods in the same class that are not defined as WebMethod).

Another way this class indicates itself as a web service is through inheritance. The class inherits System.Web.Services.WebService. This is actually optional. You could define a class as a web service without inheriting from WebService. However, through this inheritance, the class actually has full access to the ASP.NET features such as Session and Context objects. Having access to these objects provides many of the familiar ASP.NET features to web service developers.

Coding an ASP.NET Web Service

Now let's explore developing an actual web service with Visual Studio 2010. For this example, you develop the CustomerProfile example as an ASP.NET web service. This web service provides methods for retrieving customer information from a data store and saving changes to that information. Along the way, you look at the finer points of developing an ASP.NET web service. The following steps outline this process:

1. Create an empty ASP.NET website (name it Contoso.Web). Add a Web Service file (.aspx). Name this file CustomerProfile.asmx.

2. Next, remove the HelloWorld sample method and in its place create methods called GetCustomer, GetActiveCustomers, CreateCustomer, UpdateCustomer, and DeleteCustomer. Each method should be marked with the [WebMethod] attribute. Don't worry about the return types for now (just use void). Your file should look similar to the following code:

```
[WebService(Namespace = "http://contoso.com/")]
[WebServiceBinding(ConformsTo = WsiProfiles.BasicProfile1_1)]
public class CustomerProfile : System.Web.Services.WebService
{
  public CustomerProfile()
  {
  }
  [WebMethod]
  public void GetCustomer()
  {
  }
  [WebMethod]
  public void GetActiveCustomers()
  {
  }
  [WebMethod]
  public void CreateCustomer()
  {
  }
  [WebMethod]
  public void UpdateCustomer ()
  {
  }
  [WebMethod]
  public void DeleteCustomer()
  {
  }
}
```

3. Add a new class library project to your solution (File, Add, New Project). Call this project BusinessEntities. This project contains the actual definition for a simple

Customer class with a set of properties. Rename Class1.cs to Customer. Listing 22.1 shows a simple Customer class that aligns with the Customers table in the Northwind database.

LISTING 22.1   The BusinessEntities.Customer Class

```
using System;
using System.Collections.Generic;
using System.Linq;
using System.Text;

namespace BusinessEntities {
  public class Customer
  {
    public string Id { get; set; }
    public string CompanyName { get; set; }
    public string Name { get; set; }
    public string Title { get; set; }
    public string Address { get; set; }
    public string City { get; set; }
    public string Region { get; set; }
    public string PostalCode { get; set; }
    public string Country { get; set; }
    public string Phone { get; set; }
    public string Fax { get; set; }
  }
}
```

4. Next, create a second class library project called EntityServices and add a class called CustomerServices to this library. The EntityServices namespace provides the actual implementation of the code that executes on behalf of the CustomerProfile web methods. This code inside EntityServices does the actual work to get, save, and delete customer records.

    Of course this additional layer is optional. You could define all your execution logic right inside the web service. However, we are showing this example for two reasons. The first is that most applications leverage some existing code. It can be useful expose this existing code through web services. The second point is that this is just good design. Having the implementation code inside a separate object can lead to reuse, enable easier unit testing, and enable client scenarios that are more traditional (and do not rely on web services).

5. Add the northwnd.mdf database file to the EntityServices project (or create inside your developer edition of SQL Server). You can find the file in the downloadable content for this book.

6. You can now write the methods for retrieving, saving, and deleting a customer. First, add a reference from the EntityServices project to the BusinessEntities project. Next,

add a SaveCustomer, GetCustomer, GetActiveCustomers, and DeleteCustomer method to the CustomerServices.cs class in the EntityServices class library project you created. Listing 22.2 shows some basic sample code that works with the database table you created previously.

LISTING 22.2   The EntityServices.CustomerServices Class

```csharp
using System;
using System.Collections.Generic;
using System.Data.SqlClient;
using System.Data;
using System.Text;
using BusinessEntities;

namespace EntityServices
{
  public class CustomerProfile
  {

    string _dbConnect =
      @"Data Source=.\SQLEXPRESS;AttachDbFilename=C:\...\northwnd.mdf;Integrated
      ➥Security=True;User Instance=True";

    public DataSet GetActiveCustomers()
    {

      StringBuilder sql = new StringBuilder("SELECT CustomerID, CompanyName, ");
      sql.Append("ContactName, ContactTitle, Address, City, Region, ");
      sql.Append("PostalCode, Country, Phone, Fax ");
      sql.Append("FROM Customers");

      using (SqlConnection cnn = new SqlConnection(_dbConnect))
      {

        SqlCommand cmd = new SqlCommand(sql.ToString(), cnn);
        cmd.CommandType = CommandType.Text;

        cnn.Open();
        SqlDataAdapter adp = new SqlDataAdapter(cmd);
        DataSet ds = new DataSet();
        adp.Fill(ds);

        return ds;

      }
    }
```

```csharp
public Customer GetCustomer(string customerId)
{

  StringBuilder sql = new StringBuilder("SELECT CustomerID, CompanyName, ");
  sql.Append("ContactName, ContactTitle, Address, City, Region, ");
  sql.Append("PostalCode, Country, Phone, Fax ");
  sql.Append("FROM Customers WHERE CustomerID = @id");

  using (SqlConnection cnn = new SqlConnection(_dbConnect))
  {

    SqlCommand cmd = new SqlCommand(sql.ToString(), cnn);
    cmd.CommandType = CommandType.Text;
    cmd.Parameters.Add(new SqlParameter("id", customerId));

    cnn.Open();
    SqlDataReader dr = cmd.ExecuteReader();
    dr.Read();
    Customer c = new Customer();
    c.Address = dr["Address"].ToString();
    c.City = dr["City"].ToString();
    c.CompanyName = dr["CompanyName"].ToString();
    c.Country = dr["Country"].ToString();
    c.Fax = dr["Fax"].ToString();
    c.Id = dr["CustomerID"].ToString();
    c.Name = dr["ContactName"].ToString();
    c.Phone = dr["Phone"].ToString();
    c.PostalCode = dr["PostalCode"].ToString();
    c.Region = dr["Country"].ToString();
    c.Title = dr["ContactTitle"].ToString();

    return c;

  }
}

public void SaveCustomer(Customer customer, bool isNew)
{

  StringBuilder sql = new StringBuilder();
  SqlCommand cmd = new SqlCommand();

  //determine if update or save
  if (isNew)
  {
```

```
        //assume insert
        sql.Append("INSERT INTO customers (CustomerID, CompanyName, ContactName, ");
        sql.Append("ContactTitle, Address, City, Region, PostalCode, ");
        sql.Append("Country, Phone, Fax) ");
        sql.Append("VALUES(@customerId, @companyName, @contactName, ");
        sql.Append("@contactTitle, @address, @city, @region, @postalCode, ");
        sql.Append("@country, @phone, @fax)");

    }
    else
    {
        //assume update
        sql.Append("UPDATE customers set name=@name, email=@email, ");
        sql.Append("addressLine1=@addressLine1, ");
        sql.Append("addressLine2=@addressLine2, city=@city, ");
        sql.Append("state=@state, postalCode=@postalCode, ");
        sql.Append("phone=@phone, contactPhone=@contactPhone, ");
        sql.Append("contactEmail=@contactEmail ");
        sql.Append("WHERE CustomerID = @id ");
    }

    //add additional parameters
    cmd.Parameters.Add(new SqlParameter("@customerId", customer.Id));
    cmd.Parameters.Add(new SqlParameter("@companyName", customer.CompanyName));
    cmd.Parameters.Add(new SqlParameter("@contactName", customer.Name));
    cmd.Parameters.Add(new SqlParameter("@contactTitle", customer.Title));
    cmd.Parameters.Add(new SqlParameter("@address", customer.Address));
    cmd.Parameters.Add(new SqlParameter("@city", customer.City));
    cmd.Parameters.Add(new SqlParameter("@region", customer.Region));
    cmd.Parameters.Add(new SqlParameter("@postalCode", customer.PostalCode));
    cmd.Parameters.Add(new SqlParameter("@country", customer.Country));
    cmd.Parameters.Add(new SqlParameter("@phone", customer.Phone));
    cmd.Parameters.Add(new SqlParameter("@fax", customer.Fax));

    using (SqlConnection cnn = new SqlConnection(_dbConnect))
    {
        cmd.CommandType = CommandType.Text;
        cmd.CommandText = sql.ToString();
        cmd.Connection = cnn;
        cnn.Open();
        cmd.ExecuteNonQuery();
    }
}

public void DeleteCustomer(string customerId)
{
```

```
    string sql = "delete from customers where CustomerID = @id";

    using (SqlConnection cnn = new SqlConnection(_dbConnect))
    {
      SqlCommand cmd = new SqlCommand(sql, cnn);
      cmd.CommandType = CommandType.Text;
      cmd.Parameters.Add(new SqlParameter("@id", customerId));
      cnn.Open();
      cmd.ExecuteNonQuery();
    }

  }
 }
}
```

7. Next, add a reference from the web service project to both the BusinessEntities and EntityServices projects. You can do so by right-clicking the project in Solution Explorer and choosing Add Reference.

8. The last step is to write the code for the web methods defined inside CustomerProfile.cs. The GetCustomer method should take the parameter customerId and return a Customer instance. The CreateCustomer and UpdateCustomer methods should take an instance of the Customer class; they do not need to return a value. The GetActiveCustomers should return a DataSet object. Finally, the DeleteCustomer should take a customerId and not return a value. Listing 22.3 shows the sample code for the web service.

LISTING 22.3   Customer Profile Web Service

```
using System;
using System.Web;
using System.Web.Services;
using BusinessEntities;
using EntityServices;

[WebService(Namespace = "http://contoso.com/")]
[WebServiceBinding(ConformsTo = WsiProfiles.BasicProfile1_1)]
public class CustomerProfile : System.Web.Services.WebService
{

  EntityServices.CustomerProfile _custProfile =
    new EntityServices.CustomerProfile();

  public CustomerProfile()
  {
```

```
    }

    [WebMethod(Description="Returns a customer's profile")]
    public Customer GetCustomer(string customerId)
    {
        return _custProfile.GetCustomer(customerId);
    }

    [WebMethod(Description = "Returns all active customers.")]
    public System.Data.DataSet GetActiveCustomers()
    {
        return _custProfile.GetActiveCustomers();
    }

    [WebMethod(Description = "Create a new customer record.")]
    public void CreateCustomer(Customer customer)
    {
        _custProfile.SaveCustomer(customer, true);
    }

    [WebMethod(Description = "Update a customer record.")]
    public void UpdateCustomer(Customer customer)
    {
        _custProfile.SaveCustomer(customer, false);
    }

    [WebMethod(Description = "Deletes a customer record.")]
    public void DeleteCustomer(string customerId)
    {
        _custProfile.DeleteCustomer(customerId);
    }
}
```

TIP

When you're building a web service, it is best to group functionality into coarse-grained interfaces. You don't want web methods that do a number of fine-grained operations such as setting properties before calling a method. This chatty nature can be expensive when communicating across the Internet.

Of course, this approach is also contrary to most object-oriented application designs. Therefore, the use of a proxy object to bundle operations around a business object is ideal. The business object can be serialized and passed across the wire. On the other side, it can be deserialized and then worked with in an in-process manner (in which chatty calls are not expensive).

Now that you have built a simple web service, let's take a look at what defines this class as a web service. We return to this service example in a moment.

The WebService Attribute Class

The WebService attribute class (also called WebServiceAttribute) can be used to provide additional details about a given web service. You may apply this attribute when declaring a class as a web service. However, the attribute is not required. It merely gives context about a web service. For example, you used the WebService attribute on the CustomerProfile class declaration to provide details about the web service's namespace.

The following are the descriptive elements you can define with the WebService attribute class:

▶ **Description**—Used to define a description of the web service. This description is provided to consumers of your web service and in related documentation. You should always supply this web service description.

▶ **Namespace**—Used to declare the namespace for your web service (tempuri.org by default). This is similar to namespaces as you know them inside .NET. However, these namespaces are meant to be unique across the web on which they operate. Therefore, you should always define a namespace using a URL that you own and control. This can be a company Internet address, for example.

▶ **Name**—Used to define a different name for your web service. The name of your web service need not be restricted to the naming confines of .NET. Therefore, you can use this parameter to create a new name for your web service.

The WebService Class

The WebService class represents the base class for .NET web services. This is not to be confused with the WebService attribute class (see the preceding section). You derive from this class in order to use the common ASP.NET objects (Session, Application, Context, and so on). However, it is not mandatory that you do so. Visual Studio enforces this inheritance when you define a new web service, but you can remove this code if you have no intention of leveraging the ASP.NET objects within your web service. If you choose to derive from WebService, you access these ASP.NET objects the same way you would inside any web application.

The WebMethod Attribute Class

The WebMethod attribute class is used to indicate that a method in your service should be exposed via the web service. This declaration is mandatory for all methods that you intend to make available through the web service.

There are various parameters you can set when defining a web method. These parameters control how the web method operates. For the example, you set the Description parameter to document a description of the method. However, the following list provides a more comprehensive list of parameters on the WebMethod attribute:

▶ **Description**—Used to provide a description of the web method. This description appears to calling clients and on help documentation related to the web method.

▶ **EnableSession**—Used to indicate whether session states should be enabled for the given web method. Setting this value to True enables you to store and retrieve items in the session. If you set this parameter to True and inherit from WebService, you access the session from the Session object (WebService.Session). If you are not inheriting from WebService, you can still set this parameter to True. However, to get to the session object, you have to traverse the HttpContext.Current.Session path.

▶ **CacheDuration**—Used to indicate that the results of the web service should be cached for a specific duration. You set the duration (in seconds) for this parameter. Enabling this cache results in the caching of the response for every unique set of parameters passed to the web service (similar to ASP.NET output caching).

▶ **MessageName**—Used to define an alias or separate name for a given web method. This capability is useful if you intend to have overloaded methods that .NET supports but web services do not. In this way, you can keep your overloaded methods and then apply a unique name to each one using this parameter.

▶ **BufferResponse**—Used to indicate whether the entire response should be buffered in the server's memory before passing it back across the wire to the calling client. The default setting for this parameter is True. If you set it to False, the response is buffered in chunks of 16KB, with each chunk being sent to the client one at a time.

▶ **TransactionOption**—Used to indicate whether the web service should be the root of a transaction. By default, web services cannot be enlisted in other transactions. They can, however, invoke objects that participate in a transaction along with the single web service.

TIP

You can enable your ASP.NET web services to be called from client script using ASP.NET AJAX. This enables you to support partial-page updates when calling your web service from the browser. To do so, you decorate your service class file with the attribute, [System.Web.Script.Services.ScriptService]. See Chapter 20, "Creating Rich Browser Applications," for more details on AJAX.

Viewing the Formal Web Service Description

Visual Studio and the .NET Framework enable you to view a given web service inside the web browser. This capability can be useful for both testing a web service and discovering how one works (the messages they require and return). To access a web service, you first build (compile) it in Visual Studio and then access the .asmx file in a browser (you can also run your service using the Visual Studio debugger).

Figure 22.6 shows the CustomerProfile web service example in a browser window. Notice that all methods of the service are listed. Each method's description is also provided. This is the same description entered in the web method definition (WebMethodAttribute).

To see the actual formal description of the web service as it is defined in WSDL, you can select the link Service Description from the top of the page shown in Figure 22.6. When you click this link, the WSDL parameter is passed to the .asmx file on the QueryString.

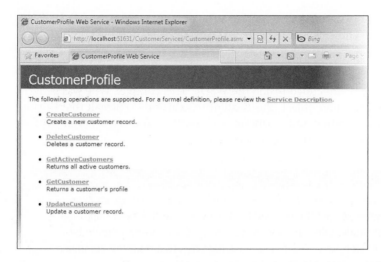

FIGURE 22.6   You can test your service by navigating to it in a web browser.

This tells ASP.NET to return the WSDL of the service. Try clicking the Service Description link in the example. Figure 22.7 shows a portion of what you see in your browser.

FIGURE 22.7   You can view the WSDL for your service inside the browser.

This WSDL conforms to the WSDL standards and can therefore be used by clients that want to access your service. These clients use this WSDL to understand how your web service operates.

As you scan the WSDL for the service notice how each service is defined. Also notice how the Customer complex type is embedded inside the WSDL. This complex type was generated based on the sample Customer object (BusinessEntities.Customer). Recall that this type is a return value to one method and a parameter to another. You can see that .NET is converting this to an XML type for use by web services.

NOTE

.NET ships with a tool named Disco.exe. You can find this tool at: C:\Program Files (x86)\Microsoft SDKs\Windows\v7.0A\Bin\NETFX 4.0 Tools (use the \x64 folder for 64-bit machines). Visual Studio uses this tool to generate files related to the understanding and discovery of web services. You can leverage this tool from the command line to generate these documents and store them for examination and use.

The documents created by Disco.exe serve as the input for client applications that consume the web service. These client applications are created using a related tool called WSDL.exe.

Viewing the Web Method

When you click on the web method name in the page as shown in Figure 22.6, ASP.NET generates a web form for you to use to test the given web service method. This form is accessed from the .asmx file (URI) with the QueryString parameter op (operation). You pass the name of the web method to this parameter. For the example, look at the web method named GetCustomer. Figure 22.8 shows this web form.

The top part of the form enables you to enter parameters for the web method and then invoke the actual web method using the HTTP POST protocol. This protocol is just one way to invoke the web method. Recall that you also use SOAP. This page shows actual examples of a SOAP request and response as well as the HTTP samples. These examples can be useful if you want to see how messages should be constructed for these protocols.

As an example, the following code shows a SOAP 1.2 message request for this web method. Notice that it indicates that the <customerId> element must be passed to the method. This is of the primitive type string.

```
POST /CustomerServices/CustomerProfile.asmx HTTP/1.1
Host: localhost
Content-Type: application/soap+xml; charset=utf-8
Content-Length: length

<?xml version="1.0" encoding="utf-8"?>
<soap12:Envelope xmlns:xsi="http://www.w3.org/2001/XMLSchema-instance"
xmlns:xsd="http://www.w3.org/2001/XMLSchema"
xmlns:soap12="http://www.w3.org/2003/05/soap-envelope">
```

```
  <soap12:Body>
    <GetCustomer xmlns="http://contoso.com/">
      <customerId>string</customerId>
    </GetCustomer>
  </soap12:Body>
</soap12:Envelope>
```

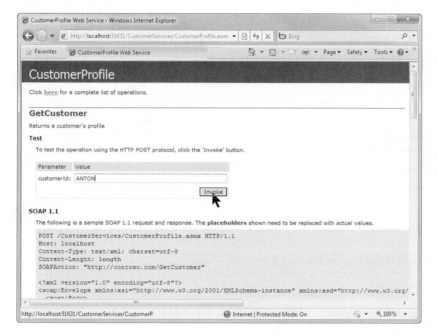

FIGURE 22.8   You can use the ASP.NET-generated form to exercise your web service.

The following shows the correlated SOAP response from the call. Notice here that the SOAP result is contained in the element <GetCustomerResponse>.

```
HTTP/1.1 200 OK
Content-Type: application/soap+xml; charset=utf-8
Content-Length: length

<?xml version="1.0" encoding="utf-8"?>
<soap12:Envelope xmlns:xsi="http://www.w3.org/2001/XMLSchema-instance"
 xmlns:xsd="http://www.w3.org/2001/XMLSchema"
xmlns:soap12="http://www.w3.org/2003/05/soap-envelope">
  <soap12:Body>
    <GetCustomerResponse xmlns="http://contoso.com/">
      <GetCustomerResult>
        <Id>string</Id>
        <CompanyName>string</CompanyName>
        <Name>string</Name>
```

```
          <Title>string</Title>
          <Address>string</Address>
          <City>string</City>
          <Region>string</Region>
          <PostalCode>string</PostalCode>
          <Country>string</Country>
          <Phone>string</Phone>
          <Fax>string</Fax>
        </GetCustomerResult>
      </GetCustomerResponse>
    </soap12:Body>
  </soap12:Envelope>
```

Invoking the Web Method

To invoke the web method, you enter a value for the parameters and click the Invoke button. Doing so executes the web service and returns the results. The results are sent back as XML. Figure 22.9 shows the results from the example.

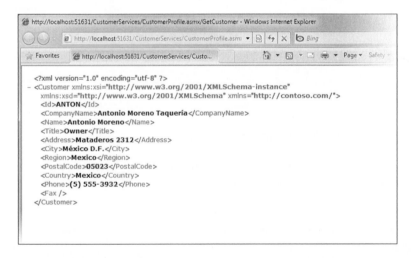

FIGURE 22.9   You can invoke your service using the browser and view the XML results.

NOTE

You can use this web page style only to invoke web methods that take simple (primitive) data types as parameters. If your web method takes a complex type (CreateCustomer, for example), then you can still see the request/response examples but cannot invoke the web method in this manner.

Consuming an ASP.NET Web Service

A web service can be consumed by any client capable of calling the service and managing its results. Visual Studio makes this task easy. It enables you to set a service reference to any service. This process is similar to setting a reference to another .NET library or COM component. After you define this service reference, Visual Studio generates a local proxy class for consuming the service. This enables you to program against the proxy class and not worry about writing service-specific code. Service references can be set inside most any .NET application, including Windows forms, WPF, console applications, and more. Let's take a look at this process.

Defining a Service Reference

You define a service reference for your project by selecting the Add Service Reference option from the context menu (right-click) for a given project. This will launch the Add Service Reference dialog box. You use this dialog box to browse to a service and add that service as a reference.

This dialog box was revamped in 2008 from prior versions of Visual Studio. It represents a unification of all service references including ASP.NET web services and those built on WCF. Figure 22.10 shows the initial screen of the Add Service Reference dialog box.

FIGURE 22.10   You can use the Add Service Reference dialog box to set a reference to an ASP.NET Web Service.

From the dialog box, you can type in the URI address of your service or click the Discover button to find services that already exist in your solution. After you've located services, you can see them on the list on the left. You can select the service interface and see its operations on the right. At the bottom of the form, you can set the namespace for your service reference. This defines the namespace that Visual Studio uses when generating service proxy code for you.

Clicking the Advanced button at the bottom of the Add Service Reference dialog box brings up the Service Reference Settings dialog box, shown in Figure 22.11. From here you can control how Visual Studio generates your proxy code. This includes the collections you want to map to and the scope of your proxy methods (public or private).

FIGURE 22.11   You can use the advanced settings to control how your service proxy code is generated.

Notice the Add Web Reference button at the bottom of Service Reference Settings. This option enables you to create a web reference in the style of Visual Studio 2005. Figure 22.12 shows an example. Prior to 2008 and WCF, this was the principal means of setting a service reference as there were only ASP.NET web services. This too generates a proxy class for you, the namespace of which is defined by the content of the Web Reference Name text box.

Getting back to the example, imagine you have a WPF application used for managing customer details. You need to bind this application to the CustomerProfile ASP.NET web service defined previously. For this example, assume that the WPF application exists independently of the service (in a separate process) and that the web service is deployed on a server and accessed by multiple, disparate clients.

FIGURE 22.12   You can create a basic, ASP.NET web reference.

NOTE

Note that if the client had direct access to the EntityService library, you would be better off bypassing the web service and setting a direct reference to EntityServices (and thus skip the overhead of the web service). For now, however, assume that they are separate processes and you need to create a reference to the web service. When we discuss WCF, we look at creating a single service to efficiently handle both local clients and those that call out of process.

In the example, both the WPF application and the service are in the same solution. Therefore, you can use the Add Service Reference dialog box and click the Discover button to find the service. Refer to Figure 22.10. Set the service namespace to CustomerProfileService and click OK to close the dialog box and generate the code used for the reference.

Viewing the Web Reference

You can now program against the service proxy that was generated. You can also see the generated code. Select Show All Files from Solution Explorer. Then, navigate to the Service References folder. Here you can see the CustomerProfileService reference. Figure 22.13 shows this along with the proxy service class open in the editor.

FIGURE 22.13   The generated service reference proxy.

The generated proxy class is a C# class that encapsulates and abstracts the intricacies of calling the web service. This enables developers to work with the service the same way they might work with any other .NET component or class. The contents of the proxy class include methods that mimic the web methods and objects that are used for the parameters (such as the Customer object).

If you update or modify your web service, you need to update the service reference. To do so, you right-click the service reference and choose Update Service Reference. This instructs Visual Studio to refresh the reference and regenerate code as necessary.

Calling the Web Service

You can call the web service the same way you would call any other .NET class. This capability is courtesy of the proxy class that was generated for you. However, it does require that you understand a little bit about WCF as the proxy generated is based on this technology.

We cover WCF in the coming section. However, for now, we focus on creating a SOAP client version of the CustomerProfileService. You reference the CustomerProfileService namespace (set when you added the service reference) and then create a new instance of the CustomerProfileSoapClient class. The following code is an example:

```
CustomerProfileService.CustomerProfileSoapClient _custProfileSrv =
  new CustomerProfileService.CustomerProfileSoapClient();
```

This SOAP client class gives you access to the web methods (GetCustomer, GetActiveCustomers, CreateCustomer, UpdateCustomer, and DeleteCustomer). To wire up these methods to the CustomerManager application, you can add a DataGrid control and a set of buttons to the MainWindow.xaml page. An example is shown in Figure 22.14.

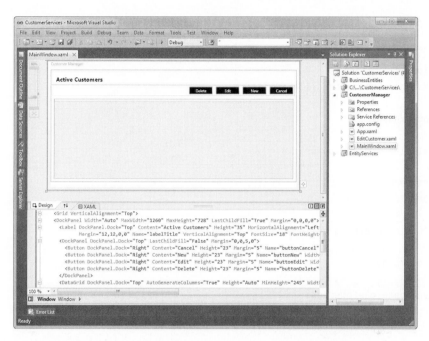

FIGURE 22.14   The main page for the Customer Manager application.

You can find the code for this sample in the downloadable content for this book. However, let's take a look at what happens when the user clicks the Edit button. Doing so will launch the EditCustomer.xaml window. This window expects the selected customer id as a parameter. The following code shows how we get this value from the DataGrid, pass it to the window's constructor, and then show the dialog box.

```
private void buttonEdit_Click(object sender, RoutedEventArgs e)
{
  System.Data.DataRowView rv = (System.Data.DataRowView)dataGrid1.SelectedItem;
  string custId = rv.Row["CustomerID"].ToString();
  EditCustomer edit = new EditCustomer(custId);
  edit.ShowDialog();
}
```

The code for the EditCustomer.xaml page takes the customer id value and passes it to the CustomerProfile service (through the proxy). The result is a Customer object. This object is then attached to each control on the form. Listing 22.4 shows the code for this process.

> **NOTE**
>
> You could have also written this example using data-binding and even auto-generated much of these forms.

LISTING 22.4   The EditCustomer.xaml.cs code for loading a customer for edit

```
using System;
using System.Windows;
using CustomerManager.CustomerProfileService;

namespace CustomerManager
{
  public partial class EditCustomer : Window
  {
    private CustomerProfileSoapClient _custProfile =
      new CustomerProfileSoapClient();

    public EditCustomer(string customerId)
    {
      InitializeComponent();

      //todo: validate customerId
      //get a customer obect and load the controls for edit
      LoadControls(GetCustomer(customerId));
    }
    private Customer GetCustomer(string customerId)
    {
      return _custProfile.GetCustomer(customerId);
    }

    private void LoadControls(Customer customer)
    {
      textBoxAddress.Text = customer.Address;
      textBoxCity.Text = customer.City;
      textBoxCompany.Text = customer.CompanyName;
      textBoxFax.Text = customer.Fax;
      textBoxId.Text = customer.Id;
      textBoxName.Text = customer.Name;
      textBoxPhone.Text = customer.Phone;
      textBoxPostalCode.Text = customer.PostalCode;
      textBoxRegion.Text = customer.Region;
      textBoxTitle.Text = customer.Title;
    }
```

```
    private void button1_Click(object sender, RoutedEventArgs e)
    {
      this.Close();
    }
  }
}
```

The calls to CreateCustomer, UpdateCustomer, and DeleteCustomer are similar; you can examine them by downloading the code for this book. Note that this is a simple example. To round this out, we would add data validation and a few other bells and whistles. However, it demonstrates how calls are made to the CustomerProfileSoapClient proxy to call the appropriate web methods.

Figure 22.15 shows the final results. Here the Customer dialog box is shown in response to the user clicking the Edit button. If the user clicks the Save button, the UpdateCustomer web method is called and the customer list refreshed.

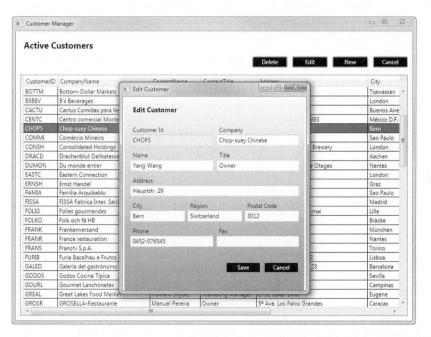

FIGURE 22.15   The CustomerProfile service being called from a WPF application.

> **NOTE**
>
> To debug your ASP.NET web service from a client application, you need to either have the service running in the same solution or attach to the ASP.NET worker process responsible for hosting the service. Refer to Chapter 11, "Debugging Code," for details on doing just that.

ASP.NET Web Service Exceptions

.NET can make it easy to forget that you are calling a web service. When you deal with proxy classes, you often get used to working with a web service as if it were no different from any other method. However, this can be dangerous. Web methods are different. One big difference is the way in which you throw exceptions from a web service. The following sections explore how to throw exceptions.

Creating a Web Service Exception

Fortunately, the SOAP specification describes how an exception is thrown over the Web through this protocol. These exceptions can be business logic exceptions or those generated by .NET when processing a call. The important point is that if you wrap these exceptions appropriately, the client should be able to understand how to manage them.

.NET provides the SoapException object for wrapping an exception for SOAP transmission. This class has a number of parameters that you might not be used to working with when throwing exceptions. The parameters and properties include the following:

▶ **Message**—Used to define a descriptive message of the exception. If you are passing a standard .NET exception through SOAP, you can set the Message property to the Message property of the standard exception.

▶ **Code**—Used to indicate whether the error was server- or client-related. You set the property to ServerFaultCode if the client passed the message correctly but the server failed to process the request (was down or broken). You set this value to ClientFaultCode if the client passed a bad message or bad parameter values.

▶ **Actor**—Used to set the value to the URI of the web service. The actor is the code that caused the exception.

▶ **Detail (Optional)**—Used to pass more information about a given error. The Detail property can include nothing or as much detail as you want to include about the exception.

Listing 22.5 shows a new version of the GetCustomer web method. This version checks to see whether the customer exists. If not, it throws a SoapException with the Code property set to ClientFaultCode. Note that the listing assumes a using (imports in VB) statement for System.Web.Services.Protocols.

LISTING 22.5   Creating a SOAP Exception

```
[WebMethod(Description="Returns a customer's profile")]
public Customer GetCustomer(string customerId)
{
  Customer cust = _custProfile.GetCustomer(customerId);
  if (cust == null)
  {
    SoapException soapEx = new SoapException("Could not find Customer",
      SoapException.ClientFaultCode, Context.Request.Url.AbsoluteUri.ToString());
    throw soapEx;
```

```
    }
    return cust;
}
```

WCF Service Applications

Like web services, Windows Communication Foundation (WCF) services have their own set of terms. It is important that you have a baseline understanding of these before discussing the key concepts around WCF service applications. The following list details these key terms related to WCF services.

> **NOTE**
>
> It is not imperative that you understand all of these terms to work with WCF. However, it can be helpful to have a cursory understanding when you are creating and configuring these services.

- ▶ **WCF Service**—A WCF service is a set of logic that you expose to multiple clients as a service. A service might have one or more service operations (think methods). A WCF service is exposed to clients through one or more endpoints that you define. Each endpoint has a binding and behaviors (see the "Endpoint" entry in this list). In this way, you can create a single service and configure it to work efficiently with multiple clients (such as HTTP, TCP, and Named Pipes).

- ▶ **WCF Client**—A WCF client is an application generated by Visual Studio to call a WCF service. You can create a WCF client by adding a service reference to a client application. The client application is the actual application that consumes the results of the WCF service. Think of the WCF client as the go-between or proxy that helps connect your client code to the WCF service.

- ▶ **Host**—A host is a process that runs (or hosts) the WCF service. This process controls the lifetime of the service. This is similar to how ASP.NET provides a host for web services. You can write your own service host or allow a service to be self-hosted.

- ▶ **Contract**—Contracts define your WCF services. This is essentially the public contract you guarantee between your service and any clients. There is a service contract that defines the content of the service (such as its operations). There is also an operation contract for each service operation. This contract indicates the parameters and return type of the service operation. There are also message, data, and fault contracts.

- ▶ **Endpoint**—Endpoints are configured for each service operation. An endpoint is where messages for your service are sent and received. Each endpoint defines both an address and binding for communicating with a service. For example, you might have one endpoint that works with SOAP over HTTP. You might have another endpoint for the same service that enables the service to work with MSMQ. In this way, you can add and configure endpoints to your service independently of actually coding the service. This ensures that your service can be configured to work efficiently with both existing and new clients.

▶ **Address**—An address is a unique URI for a given service. The address is used by calling clients to locate the service. The URI also defines the protocol that is required to reach the address such as HTTP or TCP. Each endpoint you define for your service can have its own address.

▶ **Behaviors**—A behavior defines how an entire service, a specific endpoint, or a specific service operation behaves. You can define behaviors for such things as security credentials and service throttling.

▶ **Binding, Binding Element, and Channel**—Endpoints have bindings that define how the endpoint communicates. A binding includes information about transport, encoding, and security. For example, you can configure an endpoint's binding to work with the HTTP transport encoded as text.

A binding is made up of binding elements. Each element represents a single portion of the binding. You might, for example, have a binding element for the encoding and another for the transport. Binding elements and their configuration are implemented as channels. The binding elements are stacked together to create this channel. In this way, the channel represents the actual implementation of the binding.

Visual Studio provides various tools that make building WCF services easier. If you know that you intend to host your WCF service inside a website under IIS then you can actually add a WCF service to a website using the item templates. However, if you want to host outside of IIS or to consider a different time, you can create a WCF project. In either case, you then define your service contract (as an interface). Next, you implement the service contract. Finally, you configure communication endpoints for the service. After your service is complete, you pick a hosting model and deploy it accordingly. Clients can then access the service. Let's take a look at each of these steps.

The WCF Project Template

You can use Visual Studio to create a WCF service project in much the same way as you define other projects (File, New, Project). From the Add New Project dialog box you can select the WCF node under either C# or Visual Basic. This enables you to choose a WCF service project template. Figure 22.16 shows this dialog box.

Notice that there are a few WCF service templates from which to choose. These templates enable you to create WCF services based on your specific needs. There is a template for working with Windows workflow called WCF Workflow Service Application. The Syndication Service Library enables you to create a syndication service like an RSS feed. The template, WCF Service Library, enables you to create a basic WCF service and then deploy it to a host at a later time (see "Hosting and Deploying a WCF Service" later in this chapter). The final template, WCF Service Application, creates an ASP.NET website and a WCF service. This template provides a default host for the service (IIS). We use this template in the example.

FIGURE 22.16   Use the WCF project templates to define your WCF service application.

WCF Service Application Files

The actual WCF Service Application project that is created through the Visual Studio template contains an interface for defining your service contract (IService1.cs), a file that represents the URI of your service (Service1.svc), and a related class file for implementing the service code (Service1.svc.cs). The project template also includes a Web.config file for configuring the service, and the appropriate .NET references. Figure 22.17 shows a new project based on the template. Here the generated code for the start of the CustomerProfileService interface is depicted in the code window.

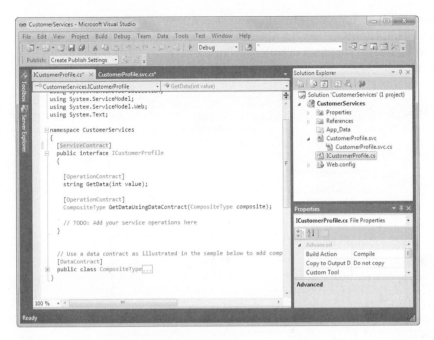

FIGURE 22.17   The WCF Service Application creates a service hosted in a website.

The service interface class (shown as ICustomerProfile.cs in the figure) is an interface you use to define your service contract. A contract includes the service operations and the data contract. Having the interface split into a separate file helps abstract all the WCF attributes and contract items away from your actual service logic.

The class is defined as a WCF service through the use of the ServiceContract attribute at the top of the class. In addition, the service operations (or service methods) are indicated as such through the OperationContract attribute applied to the method (GetData).

The actual service class (listed in the Solution Explorer as CustomerProfile.svc.cs) implements the service interface as follows:

```
namespace CustomerServices
{
  public class CustomerProfile : ICustomerProfile
  { ...
```

You place your service logic inside the class that implements the service interface. You might decide to actually put business code here or you might choose to call out to another library that contains the actual implementation code. Let's look at an example.

Creating a WCF Service

Now that you've seen the standard WCF service project template, it's time to walk through creating a WCF service with Visual Studio 2010. For this example, we develop a WCF version of the CustomerProfile service we created earlier in the ASP.NET web service section. Like that service, this service accesses the Customer object defined back in a BusinessEntities library (Listing 22.1) and the EntityServices implementation code (Listing 22.2). The latter provides methods to retrieve customer information from a data store and save changes to that information. The following steps outline the process of exposing this functionality as a WCF service:

1. Start by creating a new WCF Service Application project. Name the project, CustomerServices.

2. Use the Refactor, Rename option to rename the interface and service file to ICustomerProfile.cs and CustomerProfile.svc respectively.

3. Copy the BusinessEntities and EntityServices projects you created in the previous section to the folder for your project. Right-click the solution and choose Add, Existing Project to include both of these projects in your new solution.

4. Open the EntityServices.CustomerServices class and modify the database connection string as required.

5. Right-click the CustomerServices project and choose Add Reference. Add project references to both EntityServices and BusinessEntities.

6. Open the ICustomerProfile file. Remove the sample code in the file and in its place add method definitions for GetCustomer, GetActiveCustomers, CreateCustomer, UpdateCustomer, and DeleteCustomer. Each method definition should be marked with the [OperationContract] attribute. Your code should look similar to that in Listing 22.6.

LISTING 22.6   The ICustomerProfile Interface Definition

```
using System;
using System.Collections.Generic;
using System.Linq;
using System.Runtime.Serialization;
using System.ServiceModel;
using System.ServiceModel.Web;
using System.Text;
using BusinessEntities;
using System.Data;

namespace CustomerServices
{
  [ServiceContract]
```

```
public interface ICustomerProfile
{
  [OperationContract]
  Customer GetCustomer(string customerId);

  [OperationContract]
  DataSet GetActiveCustomers();

  [OperationContract]
  void DeleteCustomer(string customerId);

  [OperationContract]
  void CreateCustomer(Customer customer);

  [OperationContract]
  void UpdateCustomer(Customer customer);

}
}
```

7. Next, open the CustomerProfileService.cs class file. Here you implement the code for the interface defined in the preceding step. To start, remove the code inside the class definition. Next, put your cursor inside the ICustomerProfile interface implementation on the class declaration line. You should see a small smart tag under ICustomerProfile. Click it and choose Implement Interface ICustomerProfile. Figure 22.18 shows an example. Clicking this option stubs out your service methods.

FIGURE 22.18   Use the smart tag in the code editor to implement the service interface.

8. The next step is to write the code to connect your service methods to the EntityServices class library code. Remember, the CustomerServices project is simply a service-based proxy for the methods in the EntityServices library. Listing 22.7 shows what your code might look like.

LISTING 22.7   The CustomerProfile.svc.cs Implementation Code

```
using System;
using System.Collections.Generic;
using System.Linq;
```

```csharp
using System.Runtime.Serialization;
using System.ServiceModel;
using System.ServiceModel.Web;
using System.Text;
using BusinessEntities;

namespace CustomerServices
{
  public class CustomerProfile : ICustomerProfile
  {

    EntityServices.CustomerProfile _custProfile =
      new EntityServices.CustomerProfile();

    public Customer GetCustomer(string customerId)
    {
      return _custProfile.GetCustomer(customerId);
    }

    public System.Data.DataSet GetActiveCustomers()
    {
      return _custProfile.GetActiveCustomers();
    }

    public void DeleteCustomer(string customerId)
    {
      _custProfile.DeleteCustomer(customerId);
    }

    public void CreateCustomer(Customer customer)
    {
      _custProfile.SaveCustomer(customer, true);
    }

    public void UpdateCustomer(Customer customer)
    {
      _custProfile.SaveCustomer(customer, false);
    }
  }
}
```

9. The last step is to mark the Customer object you created in the first example as serializable. This class was inside the BusinessEntities library. Doing so tells WCF it can serialize the data inside the class for passing between client and service. Use the

DataContract attributes of the System.Runtime.Serialization namespace (you might need to add a reference to this namespace). You mark the class as a DataContract and each property as a DataMember. Listing 22.8 shows this revised code.

LISTING 22.8   Marking the Customer Class as a DataContract

```
using System;
using System.Collections.Generic;
using System.Linq;
using System.Text;
using System.Runtime.Serialization;

namespace BusinessEntities
{
  [DataContract]
  public class Customer
  {
    [DataMember]
    public string Id { get; set; }

    [DataMember]
    public string CompanyName { get; set; }

    [DataMember]
    public string Name { get; set; }

    [DataMember]
    public string Title { get; set; }

    [DataMember]
    public string Address { get; set; }

    [DataMember]
    public string City { get; set; }

    [DataMember]
    public string Region { get; set; }

    [DataMember]
    public string PostalCode { get; set; }

    [DataMember]
    public string Country { get; set; }

    [DataMember]
    public string Phone { get; set; }
```

```
    [DataMember]
    public string Fax { get; set; }
  }
}
```

That's it. You now have a simple WCF service hosted inside a web server. Next, we take a look at using Visual Studio to test the WCF service.

Running and Testing Your WCF Service

Whether you created a WCF Service Application (hosted in a website) or a WCF Service Library (hosted independently of the service definition), Visual Studio provides you a mechanism for running and debugging your services without having to deploy them first or write your own service client.

Visual Studio ships with a host application that you can use to host, run, and test your services. To use the Visual Studio WCF Service Host and the WCF Test Client you first set your service application as the startup project in Visual Studio (right-click on the project in Solution Explorer, Set as Startup Project). This is the same for the Service Library and the Service Application projects. You can then run the application in debug mode.

Running your application launches the Visual Studio WCF Service Host (minimized in the system tray) and the WCF Test Client used for testing your service. Figure 22.19 shows the WCF Service Host.

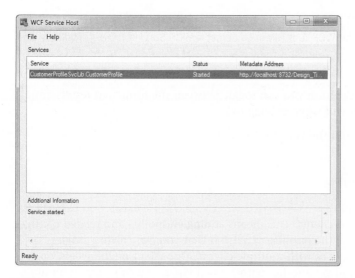

FIGURE 22.19   You can access the WCF Service Host application from the system tray.

The WCF Test Client presents your service and its operations. Figure 22.20 shows the CustomerProfile service written as a WCF Service Library running inside this test client.

Notice the ICustomerProfile interface. You can expand this to see your service operations. If you double-click a given service, you get the test client on the right. Here we have selected the service operation GetCustomer, entered a customerId value, and clicked the Invoke button to view the results.

FIGURE 22.20   You can use the WCF Test Client to select a WCF Service Library, invoke it, and view the results.

Notice that at the bottom of the form you can toggle between the formatted results and XML. The XML view can be useful when debugging.

To stop testing, select File, Exit in the WCF Test Client.

Configuring a WCF Service

You've seen the basics for creating a WCF service. After your service exists, you can edit its configuration to support various clients. This means adding endpoints and related configuration information. Remember, the promise of WCF is that you can create a single service and then optimize it to work with multiple clients. One client might access via HTTP, another through TCP, and yet another with Named Pipes. You can support all of these clients (and more) through configuration.

The WCF Service Library template contains an App.config file. The WCF Service Application contains the file, web.config. Both files define your service configuration. Typically you edit the web.config file using the XML editor in Visual Studio.

However, when dealing with service library projects and multiple endpoints it can be easier to edit this information using the Service Configuration Editor tool. To access this tool, right-click the config file and choose Edit WCF Configuration. Figure 22.21 shows the WCF Service Library of the CustomerProfile service open in the tool.

FIGURE 22.21   You can use the WCF Configuration Editor to manage the endpoints used to call your service.

22

TIP

This same editor can be used to edit WCF configuration files outside of Visual Studio. This can be helpful if your edits are post-development. Simply run the tool SvcConfigEditor.exe to launch the same dialog box.

You can use the tool to set individual settings on specific elements of your configuration. However, the tool is best used through its wizards. In fact, there is a wizard for defining a new endpoint. The following steps guide you through creating a new TCP endpoint for a WCF Service Library version of the CustomerProfile service.

1. To get started, select the Endpoints folder (nested under the CustomerProfileSvcLib.CustomerProfile service). Next, from the Tasks pane (bottom left), select Create a New Service Endpoint (top of the list). This launches the New Service Endpoint Element Wizard dialog box as shown in Figure 22.22.

FIGURE 22.22   The first step of the New Service Endpoint Element Wizard is to select a service.

2. The first step in the wizard is to select the service for which you are defining the new endpoint. Figure 22.22 shows this step. Select the service from the example, ICustomerProfile.

3. The next step is to select the communication mode of the service. You can choose from TCP, HTTP, Named Pipes, MSMQ, and Peer to Peer. For the purposes of the example, choose TCP. Figure 22.23 illustrates this step.

FIGURE 22.23   The second step is to select an endpoint communication mode.

4. Next, you need to specify an address (or URI) for locating the service. In the example, set this to net.tcp://localhost/CutomerProfile. You host the service at this address. Calling clients are then able to reach the service from here. Figure 22.24 shows entering this value.

FIGURE 22.24   You need to set the address for the given endpoint.

5. This should complete the New Service Endpoint Element Wizard. You should see a summary of the endpoint (as shown in Figure 22.25). Click the Finish button to complete the operation.

6. Next, you need to make sure that port sharing is enabled for the service. This enables multiple clients to access the same TCP port on the machine. To do so, select the Bindings folder from the configuration tree. In the Tasks pane select New Binding Configuration to launch a dialog box that asks you to select a binding type (see Figure 22.26). Select netTcpBinding and click OK.

7. In the Binding properties window find the property PortSharingEnabled and set its value to True as shown in Figure 22.27. Also, set the binding's name to Port Sharing Binding.

8. Next, in the configuration tree, select the endpoint you created through the wizard. Find its BindingConfiguration property and set it to the name of the binding configuration you previously created (should be PortSharingBinding). Figure 22.28 shows an example.

You can now close the Configuration Editor (File, Close). You should be able to open the App.config file and see the <netTcpBinding> element and your new <endpoint> element.

You can run the newly configured service using the Visual Studio host. Before doing so, however, you most likely need to enable port sharing for TCP on your computer by using

the command line. Launch a command window using Run as Administrator. Navigate to
c:\Windows\system32. Type the following command (exactly as it appears):

```
sc.exe config NetTcpPortSharing start= demand
```

FIGURE 22.25   The wizard provides a summary of your endpoint configuration. Review this
before clicking the Finish button.

FIGURE 22.26   Use the Create a New Binding dialog box to add a binding for TCP.

FIGURE 22.27   Ensure that PortSharingEnabled is set to True for your netTcpBinding.

FIGURE 22.28   Set the BindingConfiguration of your TCP endpoint to the PortSharingBinding you just created.

You should get a message indicating success. You can now run your service application. This time, you should see the host for both the HTTP and TCP endpoints as shown in Figure 22.29.

Consuming a WCF Service

You consume a WCF service in the same basic manner as described previously when consuming an ASP.NET web service. You start by adding a service reference to your project. Visual Studio then generates a proxy class for calling your service. You use this proxy class to call your service from your client application.

FIGURE 22.29   You can see the new TCP endpoint in the WCF Test Client.

The following walks you through configuring the CustomerManager application created previously in this chapter to work with the WCF Service Library version of the WCF service:

1. Copy the CustomerManager application from the previous example into your project directory. In Solution Explorer, right-click the solution file and choose Add, Existing Project. Select the CustomerManager.csproj file.

2. Make sure that the CustomerManager application in your solution contains no service references. If it does, right-click it and delete it. Also, be sure to remove the App.config file because it might contain service configurations. It is re-created.

3. Right-click the CustomerManager project and choose Add Service Reference to launch the Add Service Reference dialog box. You can use the Discover button to find the WCF services in the solution. In our example, there are two WCF services: one built and hosted inside a website and another built as a WCF Service Library. The latter can be identified by the naming Design_Time_Address. Select this one. Set the namespace for the reference to CustomerProfileService and click the OK button. Figure 22.30 shows an example of this step.

4. You should now have a new service reference and a new App.config file. You can use the WCF Configuration Editor for client configuration files as well. Right-click the App.config file in the CustomerManager application and choose Edit WCF Configuration to open the configuration (as shown in Figure 22.31). Select the Client folder. Note that there are two client endpoints: one for HTTP and one for TCP. Note their names (you need them shortly) and close the editor.

FIGURE 22.30   You can use the Add Service Reference dialog box to set a reference to a
WCF service.

FIGURE 22.31   You can use the WCF service configuration editor to view and edit WCF client
configurations.

5. The final step is to change the way you create an instance of the service. Look back at the code inside the MainWindow.xaml.cs and EditCustomer.xaml.cs. Here you created an instance of CustomerProfileSoapClient. You need to change this code to create an instance of CustomerProfileClient. This is an instance of the WCF client proxy generated by the service reference.

Recall that there are two endpoints for this service. You pass the endpoint you want to use into the constructor of the service. This is done by the name of the endpoint. In this case, we call the TcpEndpoint as both the client and the service are running on the same network (and same machine). The following code shows an example:

```
CustomerProfileService.CustomerProfileClient _custProfileSrv =
    new CustomerProfileService.CustomerProfileClient("TcpEndpoint");
```

That's it. You do not need to change the rest of your code in the CustomerManager application as the service proxy objects all have the same interfaces as before. You can now run the CustomerManager application and it connects to your WCF service.

Note that you could switch your constructor to call the HttpEndPoint and your code would work just fine (although it would have the added overhead of HTTP).

This still leaves a step undone. In this case, Visual Studio is hosting your WCF service. This is not a production solution. You need to pick a host, deploy the service to that host, and then perhaps change the configuration of the client accessing the service. Of course an easy option is to host in IIS. You can switch your reference to the WCF Service Application project (see downloadable content for this book) and you have a production-ready solution. Let's look at a few more options for hosting the WCF service.

Hosting and Deploying a WCF Service

For your services to accept requests, they have to be active and running, which means they need to be hosted in some runtime environment. Recall that when we covered web services, they were hosted for us by IIS. You can host your WCF services there too. However, there are additional options available to you.

You want to pick your host based on your needs. For example, if you have a peer-to-peer application, you might already know that each peer can host its own services. You also need to consider issues such as deployment, flexibility, monitoring, process lifetime management, security, and more. The following provides a brief overview of the WCF host options available to you:

▶ **Self-Hosted**—A self-hosted service contains the service within a running executable. The executable is managed code you write. You simply also embed one or more services within the executable. In this way the service is self-hosted. It does not require an additional process to execute. Instead, its lifetime is managed by the lifetime of the executable. When the executable is running, the service is listening for requests and responding accordingly. If not, the service is out of commission.

Self-hosted services are great when your clients need to communicate with one another. This is the case with peer-to-peer applications like Microsoft's Groove. Each client has services that can speak with the other clients.

To create a self-hosted service, you create an instance of the ServiceHost class inside your application. This class is passed an instance of your service. You then call the Open method of ServiceHost to begin hosting the service. When finished, you call the Close method.

▶ **Windows Service**—You can host your WCF service inside a Windows service application. A Windows service application is one that is installed as a service on a given machine. A Windows service can be configured to start, stop, and start up again on system reboot. In this way, they are very reliable and robust when you need services to simply stay up and running. They are also supported on all versions of Windows and Windows server.

To create a Windows service to host your WCF service, you create a class derived from ServiceBase. You then override the OnStart and OnStop methods in order to set up your service host. In the OnStart method you create a global ServiceHost instance and then call the Open method to begin listening for requests. You then simply call the Close method in the OnStop method.

Finally, you create an installer class for your service to install it in a machine's service directory. This class derives from the Installer class. You then compile the code and run installutil to get the service installed on a machine.

▶ **IIS**—IIS can host your WCF services. In this way you can take advantage of the many features built into this platform, including monitoring, high availability, high scalability, and more. You've seen how to create services hosted in a web site in the prior section.

▶ **WAS (Windows Process Activation Service)**—WAS was introduced with Windows Server 2008 (and available on Windows Vista/7). WAS gives you the benefits of IIS (health monitoring, process recycling, message-based activation, and so on) without the limitations of HTTP only. WAS works with HTTP, TCP, Named Pipes, and MSMQ. In addition, WAS does not require that you write hosting code (like the self-hosted and Windows Service options). Instead, you simply configure WAS to be a host of your service (like you would IIS).

As you can see, there are many options for hosting your service. Each has its own plusses and minuses with respect to setup, coding, configuration, and deployment. Depending on your needs, you should spend some time learning more about your host options. You can find a how-to on each option inside MSDN. Simply search for "WCF Hosting Options" and you should find how-to's on each host just discussed.

Summary

This chapter presented both ASP.NET web services and those built on WCF. You saw how .NET abstracts the programming of services and provides tools to make your life easier. In this way, you can concentrate on building business functionality (and not writing plumbing code). Some key points in this chapter include the following:

▶ Web services are based on open standards. .NET adheres to these standards to ensure that heterogeneous applications can all work together with web services.

▶ An ASP.NET web service consists of an .asmx file that points to the code behind the service. A web service works only across HTTP. This .asmx file represents the URI to the service.

▶ A WCF service can be created with multiple endpoints to efficiently support multiple clients across different communication protocols. WCF services work across HTTP, TCP, Named Pipes, and more.

▶ You consume a service by adding a service reference. This generates a local proxy client for your code to call.

CHAPTER 23

Embedding Workflow in Your Applications

There are many types of applications you might encounter as a developer. You might build user interface controls, websites, rich clients, frameworks, services, data-driven reports, and more. There is a specific class of applications, however, that are created to manage a business process. A business process might involve many other applications, systems, and people. You may have even written an application like this. For example, you might have a library for processing an order. There may be a method on this library that knows how to identify the order, read some state out of the database, and respond accordingly to the current request. It is likely that this code works with other code libraries, services, and systems. This type of code can be referred to as a workflow application.

A workflow is simply a set of related activities that must be logically processed in order to realize a specific business goal or task. There are workflows everywhere. For example, processing documents such as expense reports, timesheets, purchase orders, invoices, and financial appropriations requests all represent possible workflows. In addition, tasks such as renting a movie, processing a loan, and reserving a hotel room are also workflows. You might have already written code like these examples (whether or not you called that code a workflow).

Visual Studio 2010 and the .NET Framework 4.0 rewrote much of Windows Workflow Foundation (WF). If you are familiar with prior versions you should note that some of the concepts are the same but most of the coding is new. Here we focus first on the fundamentals of the new model. We then cover the many activities that you use to create your workflow, including managing messages, handling errors, storing data, and controlling the flow within your business process. Finally, we walk through the core steps of building a workflow including creating custom activities, defining sequences and flowcharts, hosting the workflow, running it, and working with persistence for long-running workflows. Let's get started.

> **NOTE**
>
> The WF tools and library is new for 2010. A lot of improvements have been made to creating and maintaining workflows. However, the SequentialWorkflowActivity and StateMachineActivity workflows from versions past are gone. In their place is a model based on activities that can host other activities. This new model is the focus of this chapter. Of course, you can still access the old model and its project templates by targeting the .NET Framework 3.5 for your given project.

Windows Workflow Fundamentals

You should think of a workflow as a series of activities that are interrelated to solve a specific business problem. These activities might call external code or services to accomplish their tasks. They typically also involve human intervention such as approval or some related form of processing. When an activity is complete, the next activity in the workflow gets executed until the specific workflow instance has completed. The workflow might have to pause during execution while waiting for a message or a user response. The workflow might be short-lived or long-running, spanning days or even months. In this way, a workflow mimics the needs of the actual business process.

Windows Workflow Foundation (WF) provides a set of activities for expressing workflows. You also write your own, custom activities that define steps in your business process. You then assemble both the base, WF activities and your custom activities using a graphical designer. Activities are assembled in some flow control mechanism such as another activity, a sequence, or a flowchart. Once complete, you then configure a host to handle the execution of your workflow and perhaps use the WF persistence service if your workflows are long-running in nature. Let's take a look at how this works.

The Components of a Workflow

Before you begin developing workflows, it's important that you understand the components that work together to help you build and run them. The basic parts involved with creating, hosting, and running a workflow include the workflow itself, a host process, the workflow runtime, the workflow runtime services, and a client application that communicates with the workflow. We describe these components at a high level in this section, and you can get to know more about each component in coming sections.

  ▶ **A Workflow**—A workflow is simply a collection of activity objects that work together to describe a process. The steps of a workflow are expressed as a hierarchy of activities. The top most, or outer, activity defines the workflow as a whole. It serves as an entry point and container for the workflow.

Most workflows are created from the base class activity and defined as XAML using a graphical designer. You can also create custom activities that derive from CodeActivity or NativeActivity. An activity (and thus a workflow) can accept arguments and return values.

▶ **Workflow Host Process**—A workflow requires a host process in order to run. The host process can be any Windows process including ASP.NET, a WPF application, a WCF host process, a Windows service, and more. The host process uses the workflow runtime to invoke a workflow and interact with it.

▶ **The Workflow Runtime Engine**—Workflows execute inside the workflow runtime engine. The host application tells the workflow runtime engine how it wants to invoke the workflow. The runtime engine is responsible for executing, maintaining, persisting if necessary, and leveraging other workflow services such as tracking and tracing.

▶ **Workflow Runtime Services**—The workflow runtime may take advantage of the base services provided by the workflow environment including persisting long-running services and providing tracking information.

▶ **Client Applications**—Workflows are typically executed by a host application in response to a client application request. For example, you might write a client application to submit a purchase request. This client application calls the host process and asks for a workflow instance to be created. It might then receive notifications or call back into the runtime (typically through the host) to query for information about a running workflow (such as status).

Figure 23.1 illustrates how these many components come together to form a solution.

Notice in the figure the workflow that is being executed by the workflow runtime. This workflow is typically created in Visual Studio as a separate project. You then use the graphical workflow designer to describe your process by connecting activities, defining arguments and variables, and creating dependencies among the activities. You can also define your workflow using code-only (C# or VB) or using markup (XAML).

Your workflow is compiled into an assembly and referenced by a host application that you create. Alternatively, you can invoke a workflow dynamically at runtime (using a XAML file (outside of a compiled assembly). The host application can be an ASP.NET site, a web service, a Windows Service, or any other .NET process. The host is responsible for managing client requests with respect to the workflow.

The host manages requests by working with the workflow runtime engine. It is the workflow runtime that creates instances of your workflow. It uses the workflow scheduler service to run the workflow based on how it was invoked. The runtime might also use the persistence service to save long-running workflows or to reactivate a saved workflow.

Clients communicate with a host through whatever mechanism you choose. In fact, you can combine the client and host as a single application. This can be useful for testing purposes and in applications in which workflows are relevant only when the client is running. A common scenario is to host a workflow inside a WCF service host or ASP.NET.

Workflow Host Process/Application
(ASP.NET, WinForms, WPF, WCF Host, Console, Windows Service, etc.)

`WorkflowInvoker.Invoke(new MyWorkflow());`

Workflow Runtime Engine

A Workflow
(an Activity That Groups
Other Activities)

Workflow Runtime Services

← Communicates →

Client Application

FIGURE 23.1   A Windows process is used to host a workflow. The host invokes the workflow.
Client applications communicate with the workflow runtime via the host.

Now that you have a good foundation, let's look at the tools Visual Studio exposes for
building workflows. We return to each of these concepts in the coming sections and
demonstrate how they operate.

The Workflow Project Templates

You create a new workflow project like any other (File, New Project). Selecting the
Workflow tab in the templates tree exposes four workflow project templates. You can
create workflow projects in either Visual Basic or C#. Figure 23.2 shows an example of this
dialog box for C#.

The Activity Library

The basic workflow template in this list is Activity Library. It is used to define a project
that contains only workflow definitions. That means no host or client is in the project
template; only the workflow itself is there. You are expected to create your own host and
client applications to make use of the Activity Library workflow. This is the most common
scenario after you learn to build workflow applications.

WCF Workflow Service Application

The Workflow project templates also include two templates that combine a workflow host
and the workflow library: WCF Workflow Service Application and Workflow Console
Application. The WCF Workflow Service Application template creates a web site to host a

FIGURE 23.2   You select the Workflow node on the Installed Template tree to access the work-flow project templates in Visual Studio.

WCF service that exposes your workflow. The workflow has a ReceiveRequest for starting the workflow and a SendResponse for completing the service and returning a message to the caller.

Workflow Console Application

The Console application template creates a console application that serves as both host and client for working with your application. This is a great way to learn and test your workflows as you do not need to concern yourself with creating these items and can instead focus on the workflow itself. When you are ready to release, however, you will typically remove the Console application and switch this to a library (.dll) project.

Activity Designer Library

The final template, Activity Designer Library is used to create a design-time experience for any custom activities you create. You use a version of the WPF XAML editor to define graphical representation of your custom activity. You can also create areas inside your activity where you expect other activities to be placed. Note that you can also create simplified workflow designers that you can expose to end users to enable them to config-ure portions of your workflow.

The Workflow Designer

When you create a new workflow project you typically interact with the designer to define your workflow (unless you are only creating CodeActivity types). This tool enables you to express your workflow in terms of a collection of connected activities. You also use the tools to work with each activity to configure its properties and set up relationships. Figure 23.3 shows an example of the workflow designer inside Visual Studio 2010.

FIGURE 23.3   The many parts of the workflow designer in Visual Studio.

Notice first the center of the screen. This is the design surface for a workflow. This is a basic workflow activity in the process of being created. There is an outer Sequence activity that houses the steps within the workflow (If and Assign activities). Tools for zoom, fit to screen, and overview are in the lower right of the designer. These tools are useful because a workflow can become quite large and therefore you need to be able to find and focus on different areas.

You drag activities to the design surface from the workflow Toolbox shown on the left of the screen. Notice the many activities that can be used to express a workflow. We cover these in a moment.

The bottom right of Figure 23.3 shows the Properties window for the selected workflow activity. In this case, an If activity is selected. You can use the Properties window to set a display name for an activity, access the expression editor for defining a condition, connect an activity to code, and set many other configuration values depending on the selected activity.

The bottom center of the screen is used to define variables, arguments, and imports statements. The Imports area is where you set the namespaces your workflow is using or imports. Variables are used to store data in a workflow much like you would use them in your code. Arguments are used to pass data into and out of a workflow. More on these items in a moment.

The Workflow Item Templates

You add items to a workflow as you would any other project (right-click the project file, choose Add, and select New Item). This launches the Add New Item dialog box as shown in Figure 23.4. From this dialog box, you can add one of four item templates to your project: Activity, Activity Designer, Code Activity, and WCF Workflow Service.

FIGURE 23.4   You can add new activities to your workflow projects using the Workflow item templates.

The following provides an overview of each of the item templates shown in Figure 23.4:

▶ **Activity**—Use the Activity template to create a workflow using the designer or XAML markup. The Activity template defines an outer container that houses other activities that describe your business process.

▶ **Activity Designer**—Use the Activity Designer template to create a design-time appearance for the custom activities you create. This is useful if you intend to package an Activity and share it with other developers. You can provide a visual representation of your activity on the design surface and support drag-and-drop, configuration, and property settings. If you are simply creating workflows to use in your application you do not need to use this template.

▶ **Code Activity**—Use the Code Activity if you want to express an activity (or entire workflow) as code inside the code editor (VB or C#). The Code Activity does not have a designer. Instead, you create your workflow as a collection of Activity objects using code.

▶ **WCF Workflow Service**—Use the WCF Workflow Service template to create a workflow that is exposed as a WCF service (see Chapter 22, "Service-Oriented Applications," for details on WCF). This template creates a .xamlx file. The template is based on the WorkflowService class (and not the Activity class). By default, the template creates a Sequence activity that contains a ReceiveRequest activity for getting a call from a service client. It also contains a SendResponse activity for sending results back to the service client.

The two most common item templates are Activity and CodeActivity. Let's explore using both templates to express a basic workflow.

The Basics of Creating a Workflow

To get started with WF it is often easier to create a simple workflow to help better understand the core concepts. In this section, you create a workflow project that takes a number and determines if the number is odd or even and then returns an appropriate message. Of course you could write this code in a couple lines and do not need a workflow to express something so simple. However, keeping this example simple helps illustrate how workflows are created, hosted, and executed. We cover a more real-world example later in this chapter.

Creating a Basic XAML-Based Workflow

In this example, you create a single project to serve as the workflow library, the host, and the client. Note that this sample is available from the downloadable content for the book.

1. Open Visual Studio and create a new project (File, New Project).

2. Select the Workflow Console Application project template. Name this project EvenOddWfHostAndClient. It serves as the workflow library. We also use the Console application to host the workflow and interact with it.

3. Rename the workflow by changing both the filename and the class name. Open Workflow1.xaml in the designer.

4. To change the workflow's class name, select the workflow and view its Properties. Change the Name property to EvenOddWfHostAndClient.EvenOddWf.

5. To change the filename, right-click the file in Solution Explorer and choose Rename. Set the file name to EvenOddWf.xaml.

   Figure 23.5 shows an example of your workflow in Visual Studio. The renamed portions of the workflow are highlighted.

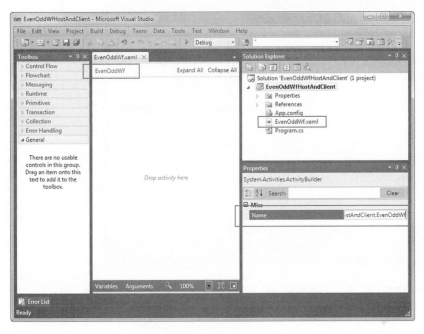

FIGURE 23.5   You use the Properties window of the workflow to rename the workflow class. Use Solution Explorer to rename the workflow file.

6. Define workflow arguments. The workflow should take a numeric value as an input. This argument serves as the number the workflow interrogates to determine if it is odd or even. It should also return a message to the user with the results of the workflow. To get started defining these arguments, double-click the EvenOddWf.xaml file in Solution Explorer to open the design surface.

7. Click the word Arguments at the bottom of the designer. This opens the Arguments editor. Click on the empty row in the Name column. Enter the name, NumberToCheck. Set the Direction to In to indicate this is an inbound parameter only. Set the Argument type to Int32 to define the data type.

8. Repeat the previous steps to define the output message parameter. Set Name to OutputMsg; set direction to Out to indicate this parameter can be read by the calling client as an output argument; set argument type to String.

Figure 23.6 shows an example of these arguments inside Visual Studio.

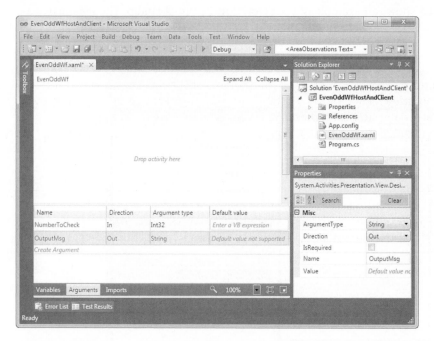

FIGURE 23.6   You can use the Arguments tab in the workflow designer to define inbound and outbound arguments for a given workflow.

9. The next step is to design the workflow itself. To get started, be sure the workflow is open in the designer and the Toolbox is visible.

10. From the Control Flow section of the Toolbox, add a Sequence activity to the workflow. This activity acts as a container for other activities; it tells the workflow engine to execute these activities in a linked sequence. Click on the Sequence name in the designer and rename it (DisplayName property) to Main Sequence.

11. Now is a good time to define the variable you will use to store the message before returning it to the client. Click the Variables tab at the bottom of the workflow designer; make sure you have the Sequence activity selected as variables in your workflow are scoped just like variables in code. Add a variable named result. Set its type to String and make sure the Scope is set to Main Sequence.

12. The next step is to define the if...then condition logic. From inside Control Flow section of the Toolbox, add an If activity to the Sequence activity. This activity defines the logic to determine if the input argument, NumberToCheck, is odd or even. Click on the If activity and set the display name to "If number is odd / even" to help make the workflow more readable.

13. Inside the If activity, position your cursor in the Condition text box. From the Properties window, click on the ellipsis button for the Condition property to bring

up the Expression Editor for the condition. Note that all conditions are written using VB syntax. A condition is also a boolean expression. In this case, you need to write an expression that determines if the number passed to the workflow is odd or even. The following shows an example of such an expression:

```
NumberToCheck Mod 2 = 0
```

14. The next step is to define what happens when the If condition results to true or false. From the Primitives section of the Toolbox, drag an Assign activity to the Then (condition=true) section of the If activity. In the Assign activity, set the left box to the result variable and the right box to Even.

15. Repeat these steps for the Else (condition=false) side of the If condition. Set the result variable to Odd.

16. The final step in designing the workflow is to set the output message for the return argument from the workflow. To do so, add another Assign activity to the bottom of the sequence. Set the left side of this activity to the out argument, OutputMsg. Click on the right side. From the Properties window click the ellipsis button on the Value property. Use the condition editor to define the following string concatenation:

```
"Your number " & NumberToCheck.ToString() & " is " & result
```

Your workflow should now look similar to that shown in Figure 23.7.

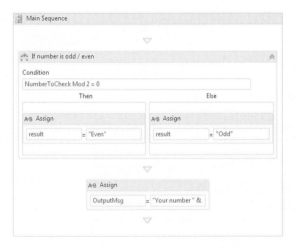

FIGURE 23.7   The final version of the EvenOddWf workflow in the designer.

17. Define a host program for the workflow and create a client to communicate with the workflow. In this example, both host and client are the Console application. Open the Program.cs file in the code editor.

18. The client code needs to enable a user to enter a numeric value to check. The code should validate this value before passing it to the workflow (we could do this in the workflow but we are trying to keep the workflow simple in this example). The client

code should call into the host and write out the results back to the user. The Main method in Listing 23.1 shows this client code.

19. The host code needs to invoke the workflow and pass in the NumberToCheck argument. This argument can be passed to the workflow when you instantiate it using property initializers. To get the return values from a workflow, you create an IDictionary generic collection and assign it to the results of the WorkflowInvoker.Invoke method. The EvenOddWfHost method shown in Listing 23.1 is an example.

Note that we separated this host code from the client just for clarity. We could have written this all in a single method.

LISTING 23.1   The EvenOdd Workflow Host and Client Code

```
using System;
using System.Linq;
using System.Activities;
using System.Activities.Statements;
using System.Collections.Generic;

namespace EvenOddWfHostAndClient
{
  class Program
  {
    static void Main(string[] args)
    {
      //client-code for user interaction
      Console.Write("Enter a number: ");
      string userInput = Console.ReadLine();

      //validate input and parse string to int (result)
      int result;
      while (!int.TryParse(userInput, out result))
      {
        Console.Write("Please enter a valid number: ");
        userInput = Console.ReadLine();
      }

      //call the workflow and write out results
      Console.WriteLine(EvenOddWfHost(result));

      //pause until user terminates
      Console.WriteLine("Press any key to close.");
      Console.ReadKey();
    }

    //separate host code from client code
```

```
  private static string EvenOddWfHost(int toCheck)
  {
    //create dictionary collection for out argument
    IDictionary<string, object> output;

    //invoke workflow, pass argument and get results (output)
    output = WorkflowInvoker.Invoke(
      new EvenOddWf() { NumberToCheck = toCheck });

    //return results
    return output["OutputMsg"].ToString();
  }
 }
}
```

23

20. Run the workflow and view the results. You can run the workflow like you would any other .NET program in Visual Studio. Figure 23.8 shows an example of the workflow running inside the console application.

FIGURE 23.8   The client running your workflow application.

Hosting and Invoking Workflows

In the previous example you used WorkflowInvoker to invoke the workflow. This class acts as your reference to the workflow through the runtime. In this way it is said to "host" the workflow. Of course you typically create your own host code to wrap this hosting. There are two other classes that you can use to invoke and manage a workflow. The following provides a description of all three workflow host classes:

▶ WorkflowInvoker—This class enables you to invoke a workflow similar to calling a method on another class. The workflow is invoked synchronously on the calling thread. Arguments are passed into the workflow and a result is returned.

▶ WorkflowApplication—This class enables you explicit control over executing workflows. This class is used for writing your own host that needs granular control over the execution lifecycle of workflows. You can use this class to tell the WF runtime when to load, run, persist, terminate, cancel, unload, resume, and more. In most cases, you would not need this level of control over your workflows but should instead rely on the WF runtime engine.

▶ WorkflowServiceHost—The third way to invoke workflows is through the WorkflowServiceHost class. You use this class when you want to host and expose your workflow using WCF. This class is typically used when your application is running multiple instances of a workflow on different threads.

Note that you do not need to explicitly use this class when you host your workflows inside of IIS or WAS (Windows Activation Services). Instead, these hosts actually work with WorkflowServiceHost behind the scenes; you do not need to write code for it to work. See the sample in the "Creating Activities and Workflow" section later in this chapter for details.

Express a Workflow as a Code Activity

In the earlier EvenOdd example you created a XAML-based workflow (you can actually right-click the file and choose View Code to view the XAML). You can also express workflows directly using code (VB or C#) by adding a Code Activity item template to your project (refer to Figure 23.4).

A Code Activity is a class file that derives from the CodeActivity class. You can use this class to write code that represents your entire workflow or you can create an activity that includes code to be used as part of another workflow. As an example, let's look at a couple ways we can replicate the EvenOdd workflow created previously using code.

To get started, let's assume you want to create the same functionality written previously but as a CodeActivity instance. Recall that the workflow returned an argument (OutputMsg). The good news is a Code Activity makes it easy to return a single value from a workflow. Instead of defining an out argument we can simply have the Workflow return a value.

To have the workflow return a value, you first indicate the workflow returns a type by passing the type name when you indicate inheritance. For example, the following line of code creates the new EvenOddWfSimpleCode class and indicates it inherits from CodeActivity and should return a string. Notice that you derive from CodeActivity<TResult>. This indicates that the workflow returns a value. If the workflow did not return a value, you simply derive from CodeActivity.

```
public sealed class EvenOddWfSimpleCode : CodeActivity<string>
{ ...
```

Remember that the EvenOdd workflow took an inbound parameter, too. You define this parameter at the class level as the type InArgument. The following code shows an example:

```
public sealed class EvenOddWfSimpleCode : CodeActivity<string>
{
  [RequiredArgument]
  public InArgument<int> NumberToCheck { get; set; }
...
```

To write the actual workflow code you need to override the Execute method of the CodeActivity class. If you derived from CodeActivity<TResult> the Execute method should return a value of the same type defined in TResult (in this case, string).

The Execute method takes a CodeActivityContext instance passed by the WF runtime engine. You use this context instance to access the actual properties (arguments) of the workflow instance. The following code shows the Execute method signature and the code to access the NumberToCheck argument:

```
protected override string Execute(CodeActivityContext context)
{
  //get the input argument value
  int numToCheck = context.GetValue(this.NumberToCheck);
...
```

You can now express your workflow using standard code. In this case, an If...Else statement and some string concatenation for the result. This is the best use of the CodeActivity class; when you need to write code instead of using the workflow activities. Of course, you can still use the workflow activities to express the steps in your workflow when working with code. We look at that example next. Listing 23.2 shows the full code listing for this simple Code Activity workflow. You can run it and get the same results as before. Note that the code to call the workflow is similar to that provided back in Listing 23.1. You can download this example from the book's website.

LISTING 23.2   The Code Activity Version of the EvenOdd Workflow

```
using System;
using System.Collections.Generic;
using System.Collections;
using System.Linq;
using System.Text;
using System.Activities;
using System.Activities.Statements;

namespace EvenOddWfUsingActivity
{
  public sealed class EvenOddWfSimpleCode : CodeActivity<string>
  {

    //define arguments
    [RequiredArgument]
    public InArgument<int> NumberToCheck { get; set; }

    protected override string Execute(CodeActivityContext context)
```

```
  {

    //get the input argument value
    int numToCheck = context.GetValue(this.NumberToCheck);

    string result = "";
    if (numToCheck % 2 == 0)
    {
      result = "Even";
    }
    else
    {
      result = "Odd";
    }

    return "Your number " + numToCheck.ToString() + " is " + result;
  }
 }
}
```

TIP

The CodeActivity class does have a drawback in that it does not support workflow Bookmarks. Bookmarks in WF enable a workflow to suspend (or wait) without holding on to a thread. You can then resume the workflow at a later time from the point of the bookmark. Again, those workflows derived from CodeActivity do not support this functionality.

Fortunately, there is the NativeActivity class. This too is a class used to create a workflow in code. You can change the inheritance structure of a CodeActivity to derive from NativeActivity and thus get the Bookmark capabilities. Of course, you might also have to make a few additional changes to support this new type.

Express a Workflow as an Activity Class

In the previous Code Activity example we didn't so much create a workflow (a set of activities executed by the WF runtime engine) as we did write some code that got called by the WF runtime. To create an actual workflow, you need to express the same thing defined by the designer inside your code. This means using the WF Activities from code (instead of the designer). This type of programming takes some getting used to as something as simple as an If...Then statement in C# or VB now needs to be expressed with Activity objects in your code. Let's look at an example.

One of the most straightforward ways to define an actual workflow in code is by deriving from the Activity class. Remember, a workflow is simply a collection of Activity objects.

You can still create arguments at the class-level scope (like you did with the Code Activity example).

However, instead of overriding the Execute method, you can create a default constructor for your workflow. Inside the default constructor you set up the actual activities in the workflow. This includes defining variables for the workflow. You then use the base class property, Implementation, to indicate which activities should be added to your workflow.

For example, the following code shows the start of the default constructor for the class, EvenOddWfActivity (another code-based workflow). Notice that a new Variable type called result is created. Next, this.Implementation is set to a new Sequence object and the result variable is scoped to the Sequence. This is just how you defined these items in the XAML-based version.

```
//create a constructor for the activity in order to define
//  the activity's implementation
public EvenOddWfActivity()
{
  //create an outbound variable in order to set the results of the activity
  Variable result = new Variable<string> { Name="OutputMsg", Default=null };

  //define the implementation as a new Sequence activity
  this.Implementation = () => new Sequence
  {
    //set the Sequence name and result variable
    DisplayName = "Main Sequence",
    Variables = { result },
```

Notice the use of property initializers for the Sequence object. This makes the code easier to read and understand. The next step is to add to the Activities property of the Sequence object to include the If and Assign activities. For the If activity, you need to define the Condition property, Then, and Else. In this case, you can set the Condition to a lambda expression to evaluate the NumberToCheck property. You use Assign activities to define both the Then and Else properties.

Finally, to define the result of the workflow to the result of the Activity execution you create a new Assign activity and set the To to an OutArgument and make it reference this.Result for the workflow context. You set the Value to an InArgument and concatenate the message.

Listing 23.3 shows an example (with lots of comments) on how you would express the EvenOdd workflow using code and the WF activity classes. Again, this can take some getting used to, but after you do it a few times it makes more sense (or you can always rely on the designer).

23

LISTING 23.3   The Activity Version of the EvenOdd Workflow

```
using System;
using System.Collections.Generic;
using System.Collections;
using System.Linq;
using System.Text;
using System.Activities;
using System.Activities.Statements;

namespace EvenOddWfUsingActivity
{
  //create a class that derives from Activity with a return type of string
  public class EvenOddWfActivity : Activity<string>
  {

    //define and inbound argument for the workflow
    [RequiredArgument]
    public InArgument<int> NumberToCheck { get; set; }

    //create a constructor for the activity in order to define
    //  the activitiy's implementation
    public EvenOddWfActivity()
    {
      //create an outbound variable in order to set the results of the activity
      Variable result = new Variable<string> { Name="OutputMsg", Default=null };

      //define the implementation as a new Sequence activity
      this.Implementation = () => new Sequence
      {
        //set the Sequence name and result variable
        DisplayName = "Main Sequence",
        Variables = { result },

        //add activities to the sequence (If, Assign)
        Activities =
        {
          //create the If Activity
          new If()
          {
            DisplayName = "If number is odd / even",

            //set the If Condition to a lambda expression that compares the
            //  inbound argument to Mod 2 = 0
            Condition = new InArgument<bool>((env) =>
              this.NumberToCheck.Get(env) % 2 == 0),
```

```
            //set the 'Then' parameter to a new Assign activity that sets the
            // variable, result, to "Even"
            Then = new Assign<string>
            {
              To = result ,
              Value = new InArgument<string>("Even")
            },

            //set the 'Else' parameter to a new Assign activity that sets the
            // variable, result, to "Odd"
            Else = new Assign<string>
            {
              To = result,
              Value = new InArgument<string>("Odd")
            }
          },

        //add a final Assign activity to the Sequence for setting the
        // outbound, return parameter of the Activity<TResult> object (Result)
        new Assign<string>
        {
          DisplayName = "Assign result to output argument",
          To = new OutArgument<string>(env => this.Result.Get(env)),
          Value = new InArgument<string>(env =>
            "Your number " + this.NumberToCheck.Get(env).ToString() +
            " is " + result.Get(env))
        }
      }
    };
  }
}
}
```

TIP

There are actually some good samples of writing workflows in code that can be down-loaded from MSDN. They may even already be installed on your machine. Look for the folder, WF_WCF_Samples. If you cannot find it, or just want to read the supporting documentation of these samples, search for "Windows Workflow Samples" on MSDN and you can navigate to a link that lets you download these samples. Of course you can get all the samples in this chapter from the downloadable content for the book.

Create a Dynamic Workflow

By default, your workflow definitions are compiled into the library in which they exist. This is fine if your workflows do not change often. However, there might be times where you need to tweak part of your workflow (set a threshold, change a condition) and do not want to recompile and redeploy your entire application. In this case, you can create a dynamic workflow.

A dynamic workflow is one that is not compiled into a class library or application. Instead, it may exist on its own or be part of the project but be defined in such a way as to not get compiled with the project. You then invoke the workflow using WorkflowInvoker.Invoke but pass the workflow file in dynamically by calling ActivityXamlServices.Load("fileName.xaml"). You can then modify the XAML for your workflow without recompiling your application. The next call to invoke an instance of your modified workflow loads the newly modified workflow file.

To configure a dynamic workflow that exists as part of a project, you first indicate that your workflow should not be compiled with the project. You do so through the Properties window for the given workflow file. You need to set three properties here:

- **Build Action**—From XamlAppDef to Content
- **Copy to Output Directory**—From Do not copy to Copy always
- **Custom tool**—from MSBuild:Compile to blank (remove this value)

Figure 23.9 shows an example of these property settings in the IDE.

FIGURE 23.9   You use the Properties window to indicate your workflow class should not be included in the assembly but copied to the output directory along with the assembly.

The next step is to change the way you invoke the workflow. You first set a using statement for the namespace, using System.Activities.XamlIntegration. You then change the WorkflowInvoker.Invoke call to pass the loaded workflow as the first parameter. Note that because this is not a strong type, you cannot use property initialization to set the inbound argument, NumberToCheck. In order to set this value, you define a type of IDictionary and add the named element there. You can then pass this Dictionary instance as another parameter to the `Invoke` method.

Listing 23.4 shows the EvenOddWfHost method revamped to load the workflow dynamically.

LISTING 23.4   The Activity Version of the EvenOdd Workflow

```
//separate host code from client code
private static string EvenOddWfHost(int toCheck)
{
  //create dictionary collection for out argument
  IDictionary<string, object> output;

  //create an input dictionary for input arguments to the workflow
  IDictionary<string, object> inputs = new Dictionary<string, object>();
  inputs.Add("NumberToCheck", toCheck);

  //invoke workflow, pass argument the loaded workflow, & inputs
  output = WorkflowInvoker.Invoke(
    ActivityXamlServices.Load("EvenOddWf.xaml"), inputs);

  //return results
  return output["OutputMsg"].ToString();
}
```

You can now build your project and change the workflow without recompiling by doing the following:

1. Open the project folder for your example. To do so, select the project in Solution Explorer and choose Project, Open Folder in Windows Explorer.

2. Navigate to the bin\Debug directory.

3. Open EvenOddWf.xaml in a text editor (such as Notepad).

4. Edit the final InArgument at the bottom of the file that does the concatenation of the results. Include the word "dynamic" in the concatenation.

5. Save and close the file.

6. Run the application (.exe) from the bin\Debug directory to see the modified workflow running without recompiling.

> **TIP**
>
> Workflows support full unit testing. You simply add a test project and set reference to the workflow namespaces. You can then call your workflow like you have seen in these examples. You then write assertions based on the results. For more information on writing unit tests see Chapter 9, "Testing Code."

Working with the Built-In Workflow Activities

It's helpful to keep thinking of a workflow as mapping the steps of your business process to a set of activities in your workflow. You might have activities that call internal code for validating a purchase order, reach out to web services to look up a price, or call a member of a referenced assembly to calculate taxes. Your activities might branch based on dollar thresholds. You might use the activities to execute approval tasks in parallel.

The activities in Windows Workflow are a rich set of tools designed to make all these business activities (and more) possible. This section provides a reference on how each of the Activity controls in the Toolbox is meant to operate.

Controlling Flow

The Control Flow activities enable you to manage how activities are executed within your workflow. If you think of a workflow as a tree of activities, the control flow activities provide instruction on how this tree gets navigated. Figure 23.10 shows an example of the Activities for controlling activity flow of execution.

FIGURE 23.10 Use the Control Flow Toolbox items to handle how the activities in a workflow are executed including sequencing, branching, and looping.

Notice that there are activities such as Sequence, While, DoWhile, and ForEach for managing order and branching. Control Flow also includes If, PickBranch, and Switch for handling branching logic. Table 23.1 lists each Activity and a description.

TABLE 23.1   The Control Flow Activities

Activity	Description
DoWhile	You can put other activities inside the DoWhile activity. The contained activities execute once and then continue to execute repeatedly until a condition is satisfied.
ForEach	The ForEach activity contains other activities in the Body. These activities are executed once for every item in a collection. The collection might be a variable, an argument, or some other data picked up by the workflow.
If	The If condition enables you to execute other activities if a condition is true or false. You can, of course, nest If activities like you would in code.
Parallel	You use a Parallel activity to contain a set of activities that can be executed in parallel (they do not require a specific sequence). See the note after this table.
ParallelForEach	You use a ParallelForEach to execute a contained activity for each item in a given collection. The activity contained in the body of the ParallelForEach are not executed in a sequence, one after another. Rather, they are scheduled asynchronously to be executed in parallel. See the note after this table.
Pick	The Pick activity provides an event-based model for controlling flow of your workflow. The Pick activity contains a group of Triggers and related actions. After a trigger complete, its corresponding action is executed and any other triggers executing or listening are cancelled.
Sequence	You use a Sequence activity to execute a set of activities in a specific order (top to bottom).
Switch	A Switch activity works just like a Switch (Select...Case) statement in code. You define a type for the Switch statement, set an expression to be evaluated, and then define cases. You can add activities inside each case to be executed when the expression evaluates to that case value.
While	The While activity executes activities contained within it when a set condition is true. It repeats until the condition is false.

23

> **NOTE**
>
> The parallel activities (Parallel and ParallelForEach) enable you to define activities to be executed in parallel. However, like past versions of WF, only a single thread is used to execute a workflow. Therefore, these tasks actually execute sequentially in a round-robin fashion. If, however, one of these activities blocks (waiting for input), it blocks other child activities of the parallel activity from executing until it finishes (unblocks).

Runtime and Primitives

The Runtime activities in the Toolbox enable you to communicate with the WF runtime engine to indicate persistence or termination of your workflow. The Primitives handle basics tasks such as variable assignment and writing text. Figure 23.11 shows these items in the Toolbox.

FIGURE 23.11   The Primitives activities enable you to do basic tasks in a workflow.

Notice the Persist activity. This is used to persist the workflow's state to physical storage so memory can be freed; it can be retrieved at a later time. You can configure your workflows to persist as-needed or you can explicitly indicate persistence using this activity. Workflows are persisted to an instance store using the WorkflowApplication or WorkflowServiceHost classes. The .NET Framework includes the SqlWorkflowInstanceStore class to persist workflows to SQL server. You of course need to enable persistence on your workflow and your workflow host (see "How to: Enable Persistence for Workflows and Workflow Services" in MSDN for details).

Table 23.2 lists each activity in the Runtime and Primitive areas of the Toolbox along with a description.

TABLE 23.2   The Runtime and Primitive Activities

Activity	Description
Persist	Indicates that the workflow runtime engine should persist your workflow state when this activity is reached. Persisting a workflow releases it from memory and provides a point of recovery when it is reloaded. The workflow is persisted to an instance store such as SQL Server.
TerminateWorkflow	Use the TerminateWorkflow activity to indicate to the workflow runtime that the given workflow should end when this activity is reached.
Assign	Use the Assign activity to assign a value to a workflow variable.
Delay	Use the Delay activity to indicate a TimeSpan object that sets a pause in the workflow. You might use the Delay shape to pause inside a loop; after an elapsed time you might check to see if what the workflow is waiting on has completed.
InvokeMethod	Use the InvokeMethod activity to execute a method on an referenced object. You set the TargetObject and MethodName properties to indicate both object and method.
WriteLine	Use the WriteLine activity to write a line of text to a specified TextWriter instance.

Error Handling

The error handling activities enable you to design the same Try...Catch error handling you would define for your code inside your workflow. Figure 23.12 shows these activities in the Toolbox. Table 23.3 describes the Error Handling activities shown in Figure 23.12.

TABLE 23.3   The Error Handling Activities

Activity	Description
Rethrow	Use the Rethrow activity to rethrow a caught exception after you are finished handling it (perhaps logging it).
Throw	Use the Throw activity to throw an exception from your workflow. You set the Exception property to "new up" an exception type to be thrown.
TryCatch	The TryCatch activity sets up three areas on your workflow: Try, Catches, and Finally. You can add activities to the Try section to be error-handled. You can define Catches to catch (and handle) specific error types.

FIGURE 23.12   The Error Handling activities enable you to implement Try...Catch error handling in your workflow.

Collection Activities

The Collection activities provide the basic activities required to add, remove, and clear items in a collection of objects. You can also test to see if a specific item exists within your collection. A collection in this case might be a variable defined as a List type. You might pass a collection of values to the workflow or pick this collection up by calling some code. You can then combine a looping control flow activity such as for ForEach to iterate over the collection, interrogate it, and make decisions to remove or add items. Figure 23.13 shows the Collection activities in the Toolbox.

FIGURE 23.13   The Collection activities enable you to work with collections of data (an ICollection object) inside your workflow.

The ExistsInCollection activity enables you to return a boolean indicating if a specific value exists in your collection. You define this activity by setting its Type property (it is a generic), a reference to the Collection you are checking, and the Item property to indicate the item in the collection for which you are looking. You can use the ExistsInCollection as the Condition to an If activity.

Table 23.4 provides a full list of the Collection activities and their usage.

TABLE 23.4   The Collection Activities

Activity	Description
AddToCollection<T>	Enables you to add an item to a collection by setting the Collection and Item properties.
ClearCollection<T>	Used to clear all items from a collection. You set the Collection property to indicate the collection to clear.
ExistsInCollection<T>	Use the ExistsInCollection activity to determine if a specific Item exists within the Collection you assign to the activity. The result is a Boolean that can be used as part of a condition.
RemoveFromCollection<T>	Enables you to remove a specific Item from a Collection you assign to the activity.

Supporting Transactions

The Transaction activities in the Toolbox enable you to group activities to be executed as a transaction. For sequential activities that execute without delay, you can use the TransactionScope activity. This is akin to using System.Transaction. For long-running transactions, you need to use the CompensableActivity (more on this in a moment). Figure 23.14 shows all the Transaction activities in the Toolbox.

The CompensableActivity enables you to handle long-running transactions. In this case, you might have committed portions of a transaction to a data store and then paused part of the workflow. If an error condition happens days or weeks later or a user cancels the request, you have to undo any previous work. CompensableActivity enables you to set this scenario up in your workflow. You add the long-running workflow activities to the Body of the CompensableActivity. You then add activities to a CompensationHandler to indicate what should happen when your workflow needs to compensate. Figure 23.15 shows an example of this activity.

Table 23.5 describes the full set of Transaction activities you can use to define and manage transactions in your workflows.

FIGURE 23.14   You use the Transaction activities to indicate transaction processing for your workflow.

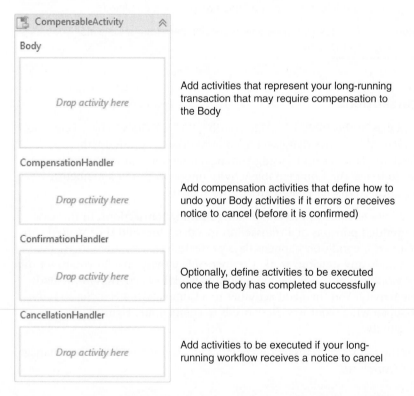

FIGURE 23.15   Use CompensableActivity to define transactions for long-running workflows.

TABLE 23.5   The Transaction Activities

Activity	Description
CancellationScope	Enables you to define a set of activities (a workflow) that can be cancelled. You use the Body to define the cancel-able scope. You then put activities inside the CancellationHandler to process what happens when the scope is cancelled.
CompensableActivity	You use the CompensableActivity to define a set of activities that should be executed if your long-running transaction fails. You might add a CompensableActivity to a Catch block in your workflow to undo work based on an error condition.
Compensate	Used to explicitly indicate that your workflow should compensate (call the CompensationHandler) based on some logic.
Confirm	Used to indicate that your workflow has completed and can be confirmed (calls the ConfirmationHandler).
TransactionScope	Enables you to define a set of activities that should executed together as a transaction. This is akin to participating in a System.Transaction transaction.

Managing Messages

Windows workflow provides a set of messaging activities that enable you to expose your workflow as a WCF service as well as call out to other services. There are a number of message-based activities, each designed to enable you to configure various message exchange patterns including Request-Response (or Send-Receive Reply). These activities also support correlation to make sure the right workflow instance gets the right message. Figure 23.16 shows the Messaging activities in the Toolbox.

FIGURE 23.16   You use the Messaging activities to define send and receive message constructs for your workflow.

The clearest way to learn the messaging activities is to create a message-based workflow, which you do in a moment. But first, take a minute to familiarize yourself with the Messaging activities defined inside Table 23.6.

TABLE 23.6   The Messaging Activities

Activity	Description
CorrelationScope	Enables you to group a set of activities that participate in message correlation. Correlation defines how messages are related one another and the right workflow instance.
	For example, you might add a Send activity and a Receive activity to a CorrelationScope. The CorrelationScope activity is then responsible for correlating the received message with the right workflow instance that initiated the send message. Alternatively, you can set the individual activities' CorrelationHandle property to get the same behavior without a CorrelationScope object.
InitializeCorrelation	Used to initialize message correlation without actually sending or receiving a message. This is useful if you need to define a correlation handle prior to sending or receiving a message.
Receive	Enables you to receive a message as part of your workflow. This represents a WCF service that receives the messages. You configure the Receive and Send activities like you would a WCF service and client.
ReceiveAndSendReply	Creates a Sequence activity that contains a Receive and a SendReply activity. This provides support for the common pattern of receiving a messaging and replying that the message was received. You set the Request property of the SendReply activity to the name of the Receive activity to which it is replying.
Send	Used to send a message from a workflow. You send the Endpoint property to indicate the binding (TCP, HTTP, etc.) and address to the destination. You can send a strongly typed message, an XmlSerializable type, or an untyped message.
SendAndReceiveReply	Creates a Sequence activity that contains a Send activity followed by a ReceiveReply activity. This provides support for sending messages and waiting for a correlated reply.
TransactedReceiveScope	Enables you to pass a transaction into a workflow as part of a message receive. You would typically add a Receive activity to the Request portion of the `TransactedReceiveScope` activity. You might then execute other activities in the Body and perhaps use a `Send` activity to send a response.

Creating a Message-Based Workflow

Recall the EvenOdd workflow from the earlier section. In this example, you create a version of the workflow that uses a message pattern to expose the workflow as a WCF service. The following outlines the steps to creating this workflow (this code is available as downloadable content for this book):

1. To get started, create a new workflow project as a WCF Workflow Service Application (File, New, Project). Name the project, EvenOddMessagingLib.

2. Rename the workflow service to EvenOddService in both the filename and the Properties dialog box for the workflow (the class name).

3. Delete the activity, Sequential Service, that was defined by default on the workflow.

4. Open the Toolbox and navigate to Messaging. Add a ReceiveAndSendReply activity to the designer.

5. Click the Variable tab at the bottom of the designer. Define a variable to contain the number being sent to the service to check for odd or even; call this variable numToCheck (Int32). Add a second variable to contain the response that will be sent back in the reply message; name this variable, result (string).

   Your workflow should now look similar to Figure 23.17.

FIGURE 23.17   Define the variables to contain the receive and send data for the messages of your workflow.

6. Next, configure the Receive activity. First, set the DisplayName to ReceiveNumToCheck.

   Second, set the OperationName to IsEvenOrOdd. The OperationName indicates the name of the service method.

   Third, use the Properties window to set CanCreateInstance to True (check the box).

Finally, click Define... (or View message...) in the Content section of the Receive shape. This launches the Content Definition window, which you can use to define the Message and indicate Parameters. In this case, create a new parameter called NumberToCheck (Int32, which is passed to the service method (IsEvenOdd) of the workflow. Use the Assign To column to assign this parameter to the variable, numToCheck. Figure 23.18 shows an example:

7. Now do a similar operation on the SendReply activity. Click the content area on the activity. Define a new parameter called OutputMsg (string), which serves as the output of the workflow. Map this parameter to the result variable. Figure 23.19 shows this example.

8. Next, add the If activity between the Receive and SendReply activities. Configure this activity as you did previously to define a condition to check to see if the number is divisible by two and then assign the results. Figure 23.20 shows the final workflow in the designer.

9. The next step is to write a WCF client to pass the appropriate message and receive the result (refer to Chapter 22 for details). Recall, however, that WCF can generate a default and even host your service by default in ASP.NET. Therefore, to test the service, right-click the EvenOddService.xamlx inside Solution Explorer and choose Set as Start Page.

10. Next, run the application. The WCF Test Client should launch as well as a local copy of the ASP.NET development server. Inside the WCF Test client, navigate to your service method, IsEvenOrOdd. Select this method and notice the test harness generates to the right of the dialog box.

FIGURE 23.18   Map the variable, numToCheck to the Receive message parameter, NumberToCheck.

FIGURE 23.19   Map the internal variable, result, to the OutputMsg parameter of the SendReply activity.

FIGURE 23.20   The message-based EvenOdd workflow inside the designer.

Use the Request section to indicate a NumberToCheck and hit the Invoke button. Notice the results in the Response section. Figure 23.21 shows an example.

FIGURE 23.21   The message-based EvenOdd workflow running inside the default, WCF Test Client application.

Note that you could also go back and connect the console application from the prior example to use this new message-based version.

Creating Flowchart Workflows

The Flowchart activities enable you to create a workflow using the well-understood flowchart paradigm. Processing starts at the top and works its way down. Along the way, different decisions are made and the workflow branches accordingly. The workflow might loop back on itself, but it eventually ends. Flowchart workflows are much like what you would draw on a whiteboard when describing your business process (a lot of boxes and arrows). Figure 23.22 shows an example of the flowchart shapes in the Toolbox.

If you have created a basic workflow then a flowchart workflow is easy to understand. You simply connect activities using arrows going from the top of the flowchart to the bottom. Diamonds (FlowDecision) indicate branching conditions in the flowchart. Table 23.7 describes the activities in the Flowchart Toolbox.

TABLE 23.7   The Flowchart Activities

Activity	Description
Flowchart	Enables you to connect activities using the flowchart paradigm.
FlowDecision	Enables you to indicate a condition that changes the direction of the activity flow.

TABLE 23.7   Continued

Activity	Description
FlowSwitch<T>	Enables you to create a switch (select...case) feature in your code. You draw lines from the FlowSwitch to other workflow activities that should be executed based on a value of the Switch expression.
	You can use this feature to execute state-machine like behavior for your workflows.

FIGURE 23.22   Use the Flowchart activities to create workflows based on the familiar model of a flowchart.

Creating a flowchart is really just a different way of expressing the workflow concepts discussed thus far. In fact, Figure 23.23 shows the EvenOdd workflow expressed as a flowchart. Notice how similar this workflow looks to the original. In addition, the host and client code did not change at all. You can review this sample using the downloadable content for this book.

Creating a Workflow Application

You have now covered all the built-in workflow activities. You have also seen a number of basic examples. It's time to put the basics to work in a bigger sample where you will learn more about things like hosting, messaging, persistence, and correlation with workflows. Let's get started.

> **TIP**
>
> This is a large sample application. We cover the highlights in the coming sections. If you are finding it difficult to follow along, you can open the solution from the downloadable content for this book. Please pay close attention to the ReadMe file for setting up the project to run correctly.

FIGURE 23.23   The EvenOdd example inside a flowchart-based workflow.

The Scenario: Travel Request

For this example, consider that you are working for the Contoso corporation and you need to automate and track the process of handling business travel requests. The following outlines the steps in this process.

1. A user initiates a travel request by filling out a travel request form. The actual form could be on a website, an InfoPath form, a rich client application, a mobile phone, or initiated via some other user interface application.

   Assume the form itself is connected to travel vendors for pricing and uses internal logic that calculates the total cost of the travel: airfare, rental car, per diem, parking, and mileage. The vendor provides a reservation id to keep track of the travel request before actually booking.

   Users are also asked to write a travel justification before submitting the request for approval.

2. The approval rules include a threshold. If the request is under $1,000 and the requestor is a manager or above, the request is automatically approved (and the workflow goes to step 5).

3. If, however, the request is more than $1,000 or the requestor is not a manager, the request requires an approval from the requestor's direct manager. In this case, the user's direct manager is notified of the request by checking his request queue on a website (we could send an email in addition to creating this log).

4. The manager can sign into the travel request application where he or she can review the request and approve or reject it. Note: For this example, we keep the security and user management stuff out for now (check the book's blog for updates to this example).

5. If approved, the travel reservations are booked using the reservation id provided by the travel vendor. The vendor provides a service for booking this travel. The request is then marked approved and complete.

Alternatively, if the request is rejected, the request is simply marked as complete.

The Application Project Templates

The first step with a scenario such as this should be to think it through, determine the general architecture of how this is created. This is where a simple diagram makes sense. Figure 23.24 shows the basic messaging structure, a bit of the workflow decisions, and the projects that are used to build this solution.

FIGURE 23.24   The Travel Request workflow has many connected parts, making a diagram essential.

Notice that Figure 23.24 alludes to a four specific projects inside the final solution. There are actually five in the final (a custom activity library). The following outlines each project, its type, and name.

Create the Projects

To get started, create a blank solution (File, New Project, Other Project Types, Visual Studio Solutions, Blank Solution). Name the solution Travel RequestSolution. Add the projects defined in Table 23.8 using the same names. Your Solution Explorer should look similar to Figure 23.25 (the figure shows an additional test project).

TABLE 23.8   The Flowchart Activities

Project	Template	Description
TravelDataLib	Windows\Class Library	Travel Data Library A class library used for communicating with the Travel Request database for storing requests and their state.
TravelManagerWeb	Web\Web site	Travel Manager Website The user interface for the application. It includes a home page (Default.aspx), a page for requesting travel (NewRequest.aspx), and a page for viewing pending requests and taking action (PendingRequests.aspx).
TravelRequestService	Workflow\WCF Workflow Service Application	Travel Request Workflow The workflow that defines the travel request business process. It is exposed as a WCF service.
UserLookupActivityLib	Workflow\Activity Library	<Not shown> A custom workflow activity to look up user information (such as the user's manager). This activity is used by the primary, travel request workflow.
VendorReservationService	WCF\WCF Service Application	Vendor Booking Service Simulates a vendor-based reservation system for handling a booking.

FIGURE 23.25   The project templates inside Solution Explorer.

Create the Database and Data Access Library

For this solution, you need to store the request details somewhere. You could implement an email based system that send details in emails and allowed someone to approve through their email client. In this case, however, you will create a simple table to store the travel request in a queue for approval and tracking (different from the workflow tracking service).

Creating the Database

To create the database we recommend you simply copy the TravelRequest.mdf file to your machine from the downloadable content for the book. However, if you want to create it from scratch you should follow the outline shown in Figure 23.26.

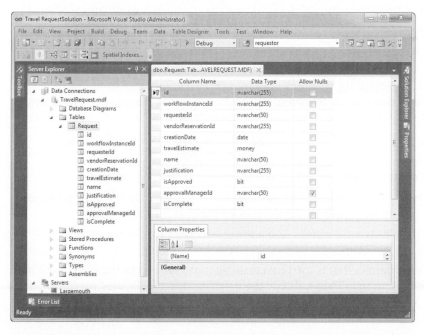

FIGURE 23.26   The TravelRequest.mdf acts as the queue of requests waiting approval from management.

The following provides the details for each column in the Request table:

- ▶ id—The primary key of the workflow request. It is stored as a GUID. The request id is used for message correlation in the workflow (connecting messages with the right workflow instance).

- ▶ workflowInstanceId—The GUID of the actual workflow. We store it here in case we need it. However, in this example it is not used.

- ▶ requesterId—The user name of the person requesting the travel.

- ▶ vendorReservationId—The GUID the vendor system (simulated) provides so the travel request can be booked after approval.

- ▶ creationDate—The date the request was made.

- ▶ travelEstimate—The estimated cost of the travel from the vendor system (simulated).

- ▶ name—The name or title of the request, such as Business travel to Seattle.

- ▶ justification—The reason the user is requesting the travel.

- ▶ isApproved—A flag indicating if the travel has been approved. Note that if isApproved is false and isComplete is true then the workflow has been rejected (and is no longer pending approval).

- ▶ approvalManagerId—The user name of the approving manager. You can use this to a greater extent in a later version after you wire up user logins to the site.

- ▶ isComplete—A flag indicating if the workflow has completed (is no longer waiting on anything such as an approval). After complete, it is closed for good.

Create the Data Access Library

The data access library is used in process by the travel request workflow to queue up approval requests and mark them approved or rejected. Because it is used in process it leverages the connection strings defined in the applications that reference it. The following walks you through creating the classes in the TravelDataLib project.

1. Delete Class1.cs and add a new file to the solution called TravelRequestMsg.cs.

2. Add a reference to the System.Runtime.Serialization namespace. This is used to define the DataContract.

   Add a reference to System.Configuration. This will be used to pull connection string information from the config file of the application that runs this code.

3. Open the TravelRequestMsg class. Add a using statement for the referenced namespace.

4. Define a DataContract that is used for passing a travel request to the workflow. This contract should, in many ways, mimic the database structure created previously. Listing 23.5 shows an example.

LISTING 23.5   The TravelRequestMsg DataContract to Be Passed to the Workflow

```
using System;
using System.Collections.Generic;
using System.Linq;
using System.Text;
using System.Runtime.Serialization;

namespace TravelDataLib
{
  //defines a travel request
  [DataContract]
  public class TravelRequestMsg
  {
    [DataMember]
    public string Id { get; set; }

    [DataMember]
    public string WorkflowInstanceId { get; set; }

    [DataMember]
    public string VendorReservationId { get; set; }

    [DataMember]
    public string RequesterId { get; set; }

    [DataMember]
    public DateTime CreationDate { get; set; }

    [DataMember]
    public double TravelEstimate { get; set; }

    [DataMember]
    public string Name { get; set; }

    [DataMember]
    public string Justification { get; set; }

    [DataMember]
    public bool IsApproved { get; set; }

    [DataMember]
    public string ApprovalManagerId { get; set; }

  }
}
```

23

5. Define two methods (in the TravelRequestDataAccess class) for working with the Request table. The first, Save, adds a record to the Request table. It is called in the workflow to store the request for approval and completion. The second, Complete, is used to mark the workflow complete (and either approved or not). Both methods take an instance of the TravelRequestMsg written in the prior step. Listing 23.6 shows an example of what this code should look like.

LISTING 23.6   The Save and Complete Methods Used for Working with the Request Data

```
using System;
using System;
using System.Collections.Generic;
using System.Linq;
using System.Text;
using System.Configuration;
using System.Data;
using System.Data.SqlClient;

namespace TravelDataLib
{
  public class TravelRequestDataAccess
  {
    //post a travel request to the queue (save to the db)
    public static void Save(TravelRequestMsg request)
    {
      string connectionString = ConfigurationManager.ConnectionStrings[
        "TravelRequest"].ConnectionString;

      StringBuilder sql = new StringBuilder("insert into request (id, ");
      sql.Append("workflowInstanceId, requesterId, ");
      sql.Append("vendorReservationId, creationDate, travelEstimate, name, ");
      sql.Append("justification, isApproved, approvalManagerId) ");
      sql.Append("values (@id, @workflowInstanceId, @requesterId, ");
      sql.Append("@vendorReservationId, @creationDate, @travelEstimate, ");
      sql.Append("@name, @justification, @isApproved, @approvalManagerId) ");

      using (SqlConnection connection = new SqlConnection(connectionString))
      {
        connection.Open();
        SqlCommand command = connection.CreateCommand();
        command.CommandType = CommandType.Text;
        command.CommandText = sql.ToString();

        command.Parameters.Add(new SqlParameter("@id", request.Id));
        command.Parameters.Add(new SqlParameter(
          "@workflowInstanceId", request.WorkflowInstanceId));
```

```
      command.Parameters.Add(new SqlParameter(
        "@requesterId", request.RequesterId));
      command.Parameters.Add(new SqlParameter(
        "@vendorReservationId", request.VendorReservationId));
      command.Parameters.Add(new SqlParameter(
        "@creationDate", request.CreationDate));
      command.Parameters.Add(new SqlParameter(
        "@travelEstimate", request.TravelEstimate));
      command.Parameters.Add(new SqlParameter(
        "@name", request.Name));
      command.Parameters.Add(new SqlParameter(
        "@justification", request.Justification));
      command.Parameters.Add(new SqlParameter("@isApproved", false));
      if (request.ApprovalManagerId == null)
      {
        request.ApprovalManagerId = "UNKNOWN";
      }
      command.Parameters.Add(new SqlParameter("@approvalManagerId",
        request.ApprovalManagerId));

      command.ExecuteNonQuery();
  }
}

public static void Complete(TravelRequestMsg request)
{
  string connectionString = ConfigurationManager.ConnectionStrings[
    "TravelRequest"].ConnectionString;

  StringBuilder sql = new StringBuilder("update request set ");
  sql.Append("isApproved=@isApproved, ");
  sql.Append("approvalManagerId=@approvalManagerId, isComplete=1 ");
  sql.Append("where id = @id ");

  using (SqlConnection connection = new SqlConnection(connectionString))
  {
    connection.Open();
    SqlCommand command = connection.CreateCommand();
    command.CommandType = CommandType.Text;
    command.CommandText = sql.ToString();

    command.Parameters.Add(new SqlParameter("@id", request.Id));
    command.Parameters.Add(new SqlParameter("@isApproved",
      request.IsApproved ? 1 : 0));
    command.Parameters.Add(new SqlParameter("@approvalManagerId",
      request.ApprovalManagerId));
```

```
        command.ExecuteNonQuery();
      }
    }
  }
}
```

Your data access library should now be complete. Notice the use of the TravelRequest connection string. You set this inside the configuration files that use this library.

TIP

As an alternate step, you might consider adding a test project to your solution and creating unit tests for these methods. This type of application can make it difficult to debug things such as a typo in your SQL. You need to create an app.config file to set the database connection string in the test class.

Create the Vendor Reservation Service

The vendor reservation service in this example is simply a simulated, third-party service that the workflow might call. It is here to round out the business case as well as demonstrate a useful feature of the workflow designer (more on this in the "Design the Workflow" section). Because it is simulated, we are not going to add too much to it. Follow these steps to define this simple, mock-object:

1. Start with the VendorReservationService WCF project. First, rename the service to TravelBooking.svc in Solution Explorer. You will need to open the class file and rename the class there, too. When you do so, you will want to use the smart tag to execute the rename refactor; otherwise, you will have to open the markup for the service (right-click TravelBooking.svc and choose View Markup) to rename the service in the markup.

2. Next, rename the service interface (IService1.cs) to ITravelBooking (both filename and interface name in the code). A rename in Solution Explorer should handle both. However, be sure to open the interface file and double check.

3. Inside ITravelBooking.cs, delete the CompositeType class. Then, remove the code inside the interface definition. Finally, add a method definition, BookTravel, that takes a string called reservationId. Your interface should look as follows:

```
[ServiceContract]
public interface ITravelBooking
{
[OperationContract]
void BookTravel(string reservationId);
    }
```

4. Then, open your service class (double-click TravelBooking.svc). Implement the new interface name at the class definition (`public class TravelBooking : ITravelBooking`).

5. Delete the code inside the TravelBooking.svs class (GetData and GetDataUsingDataContract).

6. Implement the ITravelBooking interface code inside the TravelBooking class. This code does not actually do anything; remember, this is for simulation and demo purposes. Listing 23.7 shows an example implementation.

LISTING 23.7   The BookTravel Service Method Is for Simulation Purposes

```
using System;
using System.Collections.Generic;
using System.Linq;
using System.Runtime.Serialization;
using System.ServiceModel;
using System.Text;

namespace VendorReservationService
{
  public class TravelBooking : ITravelBooking
  {
    public void BookTravel(string reservationId)
    {

      //TODO: write code to book the travel based on the reservation
      string rsvId = reservationId;

    }
  }
}
```

Create the Custom Activity Library

In this step you create two custom activities used for looking up a user to get her manager and to determine if the user is a manager. The actual logic of these services is not material. In a production system, these activities would most likely call out to Active directory or an HR system. They might also be exposed as services. However, in this example, they serve the purpose of demonstrating how you can create custom activities in a separate project and then use them in your workflows.

Create the IsManager Custom Composite Activity

The first activity checks to see whether the user is a manager. The following walks you through creating this activity:

1. Start with the UserLookupActivityLib project (an ActivityLibrary project). First, rename the Activity1.xaml file to IsManagerActivity.xaml. You also have open and then select the workflow in the designer and view its properties to change its class name to UserLookupActivityLib.IsManagerActivity.

2. As you can see, this custom activity is a XAML-based activity. Start by defining two arguments (click the Arguments tab at the bottom of the designer). You should expect the UserId (string) as an inbound argument. You pass the IsManager (Boolean) as an output argument.

3. Next, drag an If activity from the Control Flow area of the Toolbox to the design surface.

4. Edit the Condition of the If activity with some logic to determine if the user is a manager. In this case, the logic is secondary; you can use: UserId.EndsWith("mgr").

5. In the Then side of the If activity, use and Assign activity to set IsManager to True. Do the opposite for the Else condition.

Figure 23.27 shows what your IsManagerActivity should look like when complete.

FIGURE 23.27 You can use the workflow designer to quickly build custom, composite activities.

Create the GetUsersManagerActivity Custom Code Activity

The second activity looks up a user's manager based on her username. The following walks you through creating this activity.

1. Start with the UserLookupActivityLib project. First, add a Code Activity to your project. Name this activity GetUsersManagerActivity.

2. Change the inheritance of this activity to inherit from CodeActivity<TResult> where TResult is a string. This is used to indicate the activity's return (Result) type.

3. Next, define an input parameter to enable users of the activity to pass a username. Define this parameter as a InArgument<string> public property of the activity.

4. Override the Execute method to get the user's manager. This method can return a string value which is set to the result of the activity execution. Listing 23.8 shows an example of what your code might look like. Notice that the "lookup" simply appends "mgr" to the user name.

LISTING 23.8   Use CodeActivity<TResult> to Return a Single Value from Execute

```
using System;
using System.Collections.Generic;
using System.Linq;
using System.Text;
using System.Activities;

namespace UserLookupActivityLib
{

  public sealed class GetUsersManagerActivity : CodeActivity<string>
  {
    public InArgument<string> UserId { get; set; }

    protected override string Execute(CodeActivityContext context)
    {
      string userId = context.GetValue(this.UserId);

      //TODO: call code to lookup the user's manager

      return userId + "mgr";
    }
  }
}
```

You've now created both a XAML-based composite activity and a code-only activity. These activities are used in the workflow. In fact, you create a couple more code-only activities when you develop the workflow. We look at this work next.

> **TIP**
>
> You can actually define a designer for your custom activities. To do so, use the Activity Designer Library project template. You get a WPF-like designer for defining how your workflow activity should look and how users interact with it (such as setting sections that enable users to add other activities).

Design the Workflow (Travel Request)

It's finally time to design the actual workflow. The following sections take you through each step you need to get the workflow built and running.

Project Housekeeping

The following takes you through a number of configuration and housekeeping steps for the workflow project (TravelRequestService).

1. Add project reference to both TravelDataLib and UserLookupActivityLib. Right-click the project file; choose Add Reference; select the Projects tab; select both these projects.

2. Define a WCF service reference to VendorReservationService. Right-click the project file; choose Add Service Reference. Click the Discover button on the Add Service Reference dialog box. Select the TravelBooking.svc service. Name your service reference, VendorReservationSrv.

3. Define the database connection string. Open the Web.config file. Add a connection string to point to the TravelRequest.mdf file. Remember, this connection is used by the data access library so name the connection string TravelRequest. Your connection string should look similar to the following:

```
<connectionStrings>
  <add name="TravelRequest" connectionString=
    "Data Source=.\SQLEXPRESS;AttachDbFilename=C:\...\TravelRequest.mdf;
     Integrated Security=True;User Instance=True"
     providerName="System.Data.SqlClient" />
  </connectionStrings>
```

Data Access Custom Activities

You need to create two more custom code activities. These activities wrap the calls to add an item to the travel request queue and to mark the activity complete (and possibly approved). The following steps walk you through this process:

1. Start with the TravelRequestService project. Queue a travel request to the database by adding a new Code Activity to your workflow project. Name this activity TravelRequestQueueAddActivity.cs.

2. Add two input parameters to the activity. The first, TravelRequest, should take the full travel request message. Recall this type was defined as the DataContract in the data access project. The second, ManagerId, should be a string used for passing the user's manager to the request.

3. The Execute method should call Save on the data access library after setting the appropriate parameters.

Listing 23.9 shows an example of this code:

LISTING 23.9   The TravelRequestQueueAddActivity Custom Activity

```
using System;
using System.Collections.Generic;
using System.Linq;
using System.Text;
using System.Activities;
using TravelDataLib;

namespace TravelRequestService
{

  public sealed class TraveRequestQueueAddActivity : CodeActivity
  {
    //sends the travel request to the manager's queue (database)

    public InArgument<TravelRequestMsg> TravelRequest { get; set; }
    public InArgument<string> ManagerId { get; set; }

    protected override void Execute(CodeActivityContext context)
    {
      //get the travel request from the context
      TravelRequestMsg tRequest = context.GetValue(this.TravelRequest);

      //set workflow id for correlation
      tRequest.WorkflowInstanceId = context.WorkflowInstanceId.ToString();

      //set the approval manager to be notified
      tRequest.ApprovalManagerId = context.GetValue(this.ManagerId);

      //save the travel request
      TravelRequestDataAccess.Save(tRequest);


    }
  }
}
```

4. Indicate travel request is complete by adding a new Code Activity to your workflow project. Name this activity CompleteTravelRequest.cs.

5. Add three input parameters to the activity. The first, TravelRequest, should take the full travel request message. The second, ManagerId, should be a string used for passing the id of the manager doing the approval. The third, IsApproved, is used to indicate if the request has been approved.

6. The Execute method should call Complete on the data access library after setting the appropriate parameters.

Listing 23.10 shows an example of this code:

LISTING 23.10 The CompleteTravelRequest Custom Activity

```
using System;
using System.Collections.Generic;
using System.Linq;
using System.Text;
using System.Activities;
using TravelDataLib;

namespace TravelRequestService
{

  public sealed class CompleteTravelRequest : CodeActivity
  {

    //update the travel request with approval information

    public InArgument<TravelRequestMsg> TravelRequest { get; set; }
    public InArgument<string> ManagerId { get; set; }
    public InArgument<bool> IsApproved { get; set; }

    protected override void Execute(CodeActivityContext context)
    {
      //get the travel request from the context
      TravelRequestMsg tRequest = context.GetValue(this.TravelRequest);

      //set the approval manager doing the approval
      tRequest.ApprovalManagerId = context.GetValue(this.ManagerId);

      //set the approval status
      tRequest.IsApproved = context.GetValue(this.IsApproved);

      //save the travel request
      TravelRequestDataAccess.Complete(tRequest);
    }
  }
}
```

Design the Workflow

You are finally ready to create the actual workflow. The following walks you through this process.

1. Start by renaming your workflow inside the TravelRequestService project to RequestTravel.xamlx.

   Also, open the workflow and change the Name and Configuration name inside the Properties window to RequestTravel.

2. Delete the sequence that is shown by default.

3. Add a new sequence to the workflow. Set the Display name to Travel Request Approval Sequence.

4. Define variables by clicking the Variables tab at the bottom of the designer to define variables to be used by the workflow, including requiresApproval (Boolean), isUserManager (Boolean), isApproved (Boolean), managerUserId (string). Make sure your variables are all scoped at the sequence level.

   You also need to add a variable to hold the inbound message (travel request). To do so, add a variable called travelRequestMsg. In the Variable type drop-down, select, Browse for Types to launch the Browse and Select a .Net Type dialog box. In the Type Name box, enter Travel. This filters the list accordingly. Select the TravelRequestMsg type (from the referenced data access project).

   Finally, add a variable called processCorrelationHandle, which is used for message correlation to make sure the approval message is correlated to the right workflow instance. Follow the steps from before to set this variable type to System.ServiceModel.Activities.CorrelationHandle.

   Your variables should look similar to those shown in Figure 23.28.

Name	Variable type	Scope	Default
requiresApproval	Boolean	Travel Request Approval Sequence	True
isUserManager	Boolean	Travel Request Approval Sequence	False
isApproved	Boolean	Travel Request Approval Sequence	False
travelRequestMsg	TravelRequestMsg	Travel Request Approval Sequence	Enter a VB expression
processCorrelationHandle	CorrelationHandle	Travel Request Approval Sequence	Handle cannot be initialized
managerUserId	String	Travel Request Approval Sequence	Enter a VB expression
Create Variable			

Variables Imports   100%

FIGURE 23.28   The travel request workflow variables.

5. Define the message receive by adding a Receive activity to the top of the Sequence. This activity serves to define the WCF service that your workflow exposes to the client (travel request user interface).

6. Set the OperationName to ProcessTravelRequest. This defines the actual service method name.

7. Click the Content link on the Receive activity to bring up the Content Definition window. Here you define the message that this service expects from clients. Click on Message. In the Message data textbox type the variable name, travelRequestMsg to indicate that the inbound message should be mapped to this variable. Under Message type, select the TravelDataLib.TravelRequestMsg type. Figure 23.29 shows an example.

FIGURE 23.29   Configure the inbound message to the workflow.

8. *Important*: Select the Receive Request activity in the designer and view its properties. Set the CanCreateInstance to true (check the box). This indicates that this shape can create an instance of the workflow. If you miss this step, your workflow never processes.

9. The last step to configuring the Receive activity is to initialize message correlation. You must take this step or when your workflow waits for an approval and then an approval is sent the runtime engine does not know for which workflow the message is meant.

   From the Properties dialog box, select the ellipsis button on the CorrelationInitializers property.

   On the left-side of the Add Correlation Initializers dialog box click Add Initializer. Enter the variable name, processCorrelationHandle. On the XPath side of the dialog box select Query correlation initializer and set the key1 to Id:String using the drop-down that shows the message items from the travel request data contract. You use the Id as it is unique to each travel request, and, in this example, we are using content-based correlation (where Id is part of the message content).

   Figure 23.30 shows an example of setting this correlation handler.

10. Next, take a look at the Toolbox. You should see a few new sections that contain the custom activities you have created thus far. If you don't, build the solution and take a look again. In the new section, UserLookupActivityLib grab the GetUsersManagerActivity and drag it to the Sequence under the Receive activity. This is used to look up the user's manager information.

    Use the Properties window to set the user to lookup (UserId) to travelRequestMsg.RequesterId. Set the Result property (the manger's id) to the variable, managerUserId.

FIGURE 23.30   Initialize the content-based correlation to be used to correlate approval messages.

11. Again from the Toolbox, under the section TravelRequestService, select and drag the TravelRequestQueueAddActivity to the Sequence under the GetUsersManagerActivity. Recall this activity logs the request to the database.

Use the Properties window to set the ManagerId input parameter to the variable, managerUserId and TravelRequest to the travelRequestMsg variable.

12. From the Toolbox, drag an IsManagerActivity from the UserLookupActivityLib area to the workflow. Place it under the TravelRequestQueueAddActivity.

Use the Properties pane to set IsManager to the isUserManager variable and UserId to travelRequestMsg.RequesterId.

Your workflow should now look similar to Figure 23.31.

FIGURE 23.31   The first few steps in the travel request workflow.

13. The next step is to use the workflow activities to determine if the given request requires an approval. For this logic, you use a Flowchart activity. Drag it onto the Sequence under the IsManagerActivity. You can set the DisplayName to "Requires Approval?".

Notice that you can double-click this activity in its collapsed state to focus just on it. You use the navigation links at the top of the workflow to navigate back to the other layers of the workflow. Of course, you can expand all activities on the same window too.

The logic for the flowchart uses a Decision to check if the request is more than a $1000 dollars. If so, it uses an Assign to indicate requiresApproval=True. If not, you add another Decision to check isUserManager. If so, no approval is required (requiresApproval=False); otherwise an approval is required.

Figure 23.32 shows this flowchart in the designer.

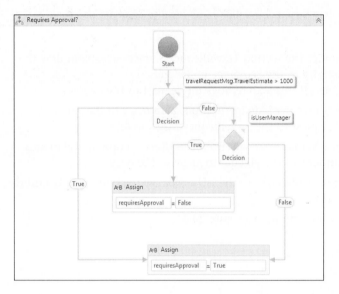

FIGURE 23.32   You can use a Flowchart activity to model the basic business logic of the workflow.

14. Add an If activity under the Flowchart in the Sequence. Set the DisplayName of this activity to, If Approval Is Required.

15. Set the If Condition property to the requiresApproval variable.

16. Add a Receive activity to the Then side of the If condition. Set the OperationName to ReceiveManagerApproval. This will become the name of the service method your workflow exposes for handling manager approvals.

    Use the Properties window to set the ServiceContractName property to IRequestTravelService.

17. Click the Define... (or View parameter...) link on the Receive activity (next to the Content option in the Receive designer). Inside the Content Definition window, set two parameters that you expect to receive from callers to this service: travelRequestId, String (for message correlation) and isApproved, Boolean. Be sure to

assign the isApproved parameter to the isApproved variable on the workflow. Figure 23.33 shows an example.

FIGURE 23.33   Set parameters for the If Approval Is Required, Receive operation.

18. The Receive activity is exposed as a separate service method of your activity. Therefore, it requires message correlation. Use the Properties window to set CorrelatesWith to processCorrelationHandle. Then select the ellipsis button on CorrelatesOn. Make sure you set key1 to the parameter, travelRequestId. Figure 23.34 shows an example of setting this correlation query parameter. Notice that you select travelRequestId and the tool takes care of the rest.

FIGURE 23.34   Set the travelRequestId parameter as the content-correlation query.

19. Inside the Else condition of If Approval Is Required, add an Assign activity. Set the variable isApproved to True. Recall that the else condition executes if the travel request does not require approval (under 1,000 and the user is a manager). Figure 23.35 shows the finished If activity.

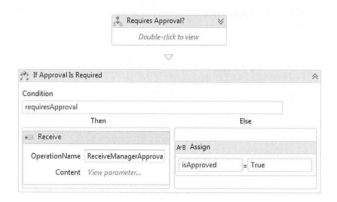

FIGURE 23.35 The completed If Approval Is Required If activity.

20. Add a final If activity to the bottom of the Sequence. This activity checks to see if the request was approved or if approval is not required (Condition: (isApproved) Or (requiresApproval = False)). If you are good to book the travel, then you need to send a message to the reservation system.

Recall that you set a reference earlier to the vendor reservation WCF service. When you did, Visual Studio was kind enough to generate a custom activity to call the BookTravel service method. It should be on the Toolbox (if not, rebuild your solution). Drag it to the Then area of the If condition. Use the Properties window to set the reservationId parameter to travelRequestMsg.VendorReservationId.

You can leave the Else section blank. Figure 23.36 shows an example of this If activity and the Properties window settings for BookTravel.

FIGURE 23.36 The If Activity for booking travel (or not).

21. Indicate that the workflow has completed. Drag the custom CompleteTravelRequest code activity (you created this earlier) from the Toolbox to the last step in the Sequence. Configure the input parameters IsApproved, ManagerId, and TravelRequest accordingly.

Figure 23.37 shows the final workflow (most shapes are collapsed).

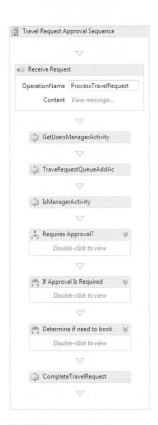

FIGURE 23.37   The final workflow Sequence activity (with all activities collapsed).

Adding the Workflow Persistence Service

Workflows disappear if the memory is cleared (a process ends, the machine reboots). If you want them to persist, especially for long-running workflows, you must define a persistence store.

Create the Store   WF ships with a default, SQL Server persistence store for you to use. It also defines how you can create and configure other persistence stores. In this example, we used the SQL Server persistence store.

To get started, you need a copy of SQL Server that you can use. We are using SQL Express in this example.

NOTE

To work with SQL Express, you might want to download the SQL Server Management Studio Express. It enables you to create SQL Express databases and run scripts. The fastest way we have found to install this locally (on Windows 7/Vista) is to use the Microsoft Web Platform installer and select it as an option. You can find this at http:/ /www.microsoft.com/web/.

The first step is to make sure you have this store installed and running. To do so, you need to create the database. You can call the database InstanceStore (or similar). You typically use a form of SQL Server Management Studio to create your database. You then run scripts in your database to set up the schema and logic. These scripts can be found in the directory (Windows 7/Vista):

```
C:\Windows\Microsoft.NET\Framework\v4.0.30319\SQL\en
```

There are two scripts you need to use to install the schema for your persistence store: SqlWorkflowInstanceStoreSchema.sql and SqlWorkflowInstanceStoreLogic.sql. These set up the instance store for SQL server.

Communicate with the Store   There are multiple ways you can communicate with the persistence store. You can create your own host application and use the workflow persistence services to communicate directly with a persistence store. This offers you a fine-grained approach to working with persistence.

For this example, however, the workflow is being hosted by WCF. This is great candidate to be hosted by WAS (Windows Process Activation Service) or IIS. In this case, you can simply configure the persistence store using the config file. When your workflow goes idle, it is automatically persisted for later use by the WF runtime engine. You can also use the Persist activity (and properties of other activities) to force a persist at key points in your workflow.

To configure persistence, open the Web.config file of the TravelRequestService. You then define a connection string as a service behavior called sqlWorkflowInstanceStore. The following shows an example. In this case the instance store is installed on SQL Express.

```
<behaviors>
  <serviceBehaviors>
    <behavior>
      <sqlWorkflowInstanceStore connectionString=
        "Data Source=.\SQLExpress;Initial Catalog=InstanceStore;Integrated Security
        ➥=True;Asynchronous Processing=True"
        instanceEncodingOption="GZip" instanceCompletionAction="DeleteAll"
        instanceLockedExceptionAction="BasicRetry" hostLockRenewalPeriod="00:00:30"
runnableInstancesDetectionPeriod="00:00:10"></sqlWorkflowInstanceStore>
```

Creating the Client Application (Request and Approval Forms)

In this final step you create a user interface for interacting with the workflow service.

Site Housekeeping

The following guides you through the basic housekeeping tasks required to get things started.

1. Open the TravelManagerWeb website in Solution Explorer.

   Add a Service Reference to the TravelRequestService (right-click the project, Add Service Reference). Navigate to RequestTravel.xamlx or select Discover from the Add Service Reference dialog box. Name this reference TravelRequestSvc. This serves as the WCF proxy to your workflow.

2. Add a regular, project reference to the TravelDataLib. You need this to define the message data contract to send to the travel request service.

3. Add new pages called NewRequest.aspx and PendingRequest.aspx. In the example code, we use the default master page from the website template. Therefore, make sure you select the Web Form using Master Page item template when creating these pages.

4. Open Site.Master. Change the menu items to include Home, New Request, and Pending Requests. The following shows this markup:

```
<div class="clear hideSkiplink">
    <asp:Menu ID="NavigationMenu" runat="server" CssClass="menu"
       EnableViewState="false" IncludeStyleBlock="false"
     ➡Orientation="Horizontal">
       <Items>
           <asp:MenuItem NavigateUrl="~/Default.aspx" Text="Home"/>
           <asp:MenuItem NavigateUrl="~/NewRequest.aspx" Text="New Request"/>
           <asp:MenuItem NavigateUrl="~/PendingRequests.aspx"
              Text="Pending Requests"/>
       </Items>
    </asp:Menu>
</div>
```

Create the New Travel Request Page

Follow these steps to create the new travel request page:

1. Open the NewRequest.aspx page.

2. Create the layout for the travel request. Figure 23.38 shows the layout for the new travel request web page. You can see this is pretty standard. There are two panels. The second panel (bottom) is hidden until after the request is sent. The top panel then is hidden and the bottom panel is shown.

3. The next step is to wire up the code-behind for the new travel request. In this case, you simulate working with the vendor service to get the reservation id. You do so by setting the reservation id inside the Page_Load event.

FIGURE 23.38   The new travel request web page.

4. Inside the click event for the request button you create the data contract to be passed to the workflow. You then call the WCF proxy that was generated when you added a service reference. Finally, you call the ProcessTravelRequest method (remember, this was the OperationName set to the Receive activity of the workflow).

   Listing 23.11 shows an example of this code.

LISTING 23.11   The NewRequest.aspx.cs Code-behind Class

```
using System;
using System.Collections.Generic;
using System.Linq;
using System.Web;
using System.Web.UI;
using System.Web.UI.WebControls;
using TravelDataLib;


namespace TravelManagerWeb
{
  public partial class NewRequest : System.Web.UI.Page
  {
    protected void Page_Load(object sender, EventArgs e)
    {
      if (!IsPostBack)
```

```
    {
      //init reservation
      TextBoxResId.Text = Guid.NewGuid().ToString();
    }
  }

  protected void ButtonRequest_Click(object sender, EventArgs e)
  {
    //TODO: add validation to form and object

    //create a travel request object to be passed to the workflow
    TravelRequestMsg tRequest = new TravelRequestMsg()
    {
      CreationDate = DateTime.Now,
      Id = Guid.NewGuid().ToString(),
      Justification = TextBoxJust.Text,
      Name = TextBoxName.Text,
      RequesterId = TextBoxrequester.Text,
      TravelEstimate = double.Parse(TextBoxCost.Text),
      VendorReservationId = TextBoxResId.Text,
      ApprovalManagerId = "Unknown",
      IsApproved = false,
      WorkflowInstanceId = "TBD"
    };

    //create the workflow service client object
    TravelRequestSvc.RequestTravelClient client =
      new TravelRequestSvc.RequestTravelClient();

    //start the workflow (pass the request)
    client.ProcessTravelRequest(tRequest);
    client.Close();

    //return to home
    PanelRequest.Visible = false;
    LabelResult.Text = "Travel request sent!";
    PanelResult.Visible = true;

  }
 }
}
```

Create the Pending Requests Page

The following guides you through creating the pending requests page.

1. Open the PendingRequests.aspx page.

2. Define two panels for the page. One shows the approvals pending queue. The other shows the result of a user action (and should thus be hidden to start).

3. Next, add a GridView control to the top panel.

4. Bind a GridView control to the Request table. You can do so walking through a wizard. You first select the Choose Data Source drop-down from the Grid View Tasks smart link. In the drop-down select New Data Source. This walks you through a wizard that lets you create a SqlDataSource control linked to the Request table. It also adds a connection string to the Web.config file and ultimately bind the Request table to the GridView control.

   Use the GridView smart tag to select, Enable Selection. In this case, users can select a single row in the GridView. When they hit the approve or reject buttons you determine their selection and process accordingly.

5. Add three buttons to the top of the form: Approve Selected Item, Reject Selected Item, and Refresh.

   Your form should look similar to that shown in Figure 23.39.

   Add event handlers to each button.

FIGURE 23.39   The new travel request web page.

6. Inside the code-behind, create a ProcessApproval method that takes an isApproved and message parameter. Add code to the Approve and Reject buttons to call this method.

7. Inside the ProcessApproval method, get the id (GUID) of the selected travel request to use for message correlation. Next, call the service client to reach back out to your workflow with an approval. Remember, this is the call to ReceiveManagerApproval.

Listing 23.12 shows what your code-behind should look like.

LISTING 23.12   The PendingRequests.aspx.cs Code-behind Class

```csharp
using System;
using System.Collections.Generic;
using System.Linq;
using System.Web;
using System.Web.UI;
using System.Web.UI.WebControls;

namespace TravelManagerWeb
{
  public partial class PendingRequests : System.Web.UI.Page
  {
    protected void Page_Load(object sender, EventArgs e)
    {
    }

    protected void ButtonApprove_Click(object sender, EventArgs e)
    {
      ProcessApproval(true, "Item approved!");
    }

    protected void ButtonReject_Click(object sender, EventArgs e)
    {
      ProcessApproval(true, "Item rejected!");
    }


    protected void ProcessApproval(bool isApproved, string message)
    {
      //get travel id fo the selected row
      string travelId = this.GridView1.SelectedRow.Cells[1].Text;

      //TODO: validate if already approved or completed
```

23

```
        //pass to the approval receive activity for correlation
        TravelRequestSvc.RequestTravelServiceClient client =
          new TravelRequestSvc.RequestTravelServiceClient();

        //start the workflow (pass the request)
        client.ReceiveManagerApproval(travelId, isApproved);
        client.Close();

        ShowResult(message);
    }

    private void ShowResult(string message)
    {
      PanelList.Visible = false;
      LabelResult.Text = message;
      PanelComplete.Visible = true;
    }

    protected void ButtonRefresh_Click(object sender, EventArgs e)
    {
      Response.Redirect("PendingRequests.aspx");
    }

  }
}
```

Running the Travel Request Workflow Application

You are nearly ready to run the application. First, however, you need to tell Visual Studio that you want to launch three projects when you click the Run button. This ensures the services are available to call.

To do so, right-click the solution and select Properties to launch the property pages for the solution as shown in Figure 23.40. Select the Multiple Startup Projects option. Indicate the Action, Start, for TravelRequestService, VendorReservationService, and TravelManagerWeb.

You are now ready to run the application! Click the Run button in Visual Studio. Give everything a minute to initialize.

Navigate to the NewRequest.aspx page from the Default.aspx page. Enter some basic travel request details as shown in Figure 23.41 and click Request.

FIGURE 23.40   Set the solution to launch three projects at startup.

FIGURE 23.41   A request for travel is posted to the workflow.

This sends your request to the workflow and shows you a confirmation in the web page. Navigate to the PendingRequests.aspx page. You should see your new request listed. Remember, this was written to the database through a custom activity added to the workflow. Figure 23.42 shows an example.

FIGURE 23.42   The request sits in the queue until being selected and approved.

Select your pending travel request (using the Select link on the left of the grid). Click the Approve Selected Item button. On the confirmation page, select to Refresh the grid. You should see your request as approved and completed. Note that you might have to click the Refresh button a couple of times; especially if you are pulling from persistence after letting the page site a minute or two. Figure 23.43 shows and example.

FIGURE 23.43   Request has been approved (and queue re-sorted).

Next Steps

This was a rather lengthy example. However, it should have answered the most pressing questions when building and hosting workflows. Of course, there are still a number of items left unfinished. We will do our best to tackle these issues and post blog entries and videos at visualstudiounleashed.com/workflow. These unfinished items include

▶ Add support for the workflow tracking service

▶ Add the ability to cancel the request

▶ Add user input validation throughout

▶ Add error handling

▶ Add the concept of actual, logged in users and managers

▶ Make the vendor reservation process more robust

Summary

This chapter presented the core, fundamental concepts for building applications that work with Windows Workflow Foundation. These included the components of all workflow applications: client, host, and workflow. A client is any application that calls into a host to work with a workflow instance. A workflow is a set of steps that solve a business problem. Your workflow is compiled and hosted inside a host application. The host application manages calls between the client and the workflow runtime.

We also covered the workflow designer and the many activities. This included all the built-in activities used for creating workflows as well as how to create your own, custom activities.

We hope this chapter serves as the foundation for you to explore additional concepts and services provided by the WF.

CHAPTER 24

Developing Office Business Applications

Microsoft Office is the well-known, best-selling suite of information worker productivity applications. We are all familiar with the word processing, spreadsheet, email, and form features provided by Microsoft Word, Microsoft Excel, Microsoft Outlook, and Microsoft InfoPath. But these applications are capable of more than just their stock features: They are a development platform unto themselves, a platform that can be extended and customized to build out line-of-business applications that leverage and build on the best-of-breed features offered by each application.

For instance, a purchase-order application could leverage the end user's familiarity with Microsoft Word to allow for data entry using a Word form, and reports and charts can be generated against purchase-order history using Excel.

In the past, the primary tool for extending Microsoft Office applications has been Visual Basic for Applications (VBA). With VBA, developers and even end users could create a broad range of solutions from simple macros to more complicated features that implement business logic and access data stored in a database. VBA offers a simple "on ramp" for accessing the object models exposed by every application in the extended suite of Microsoft Office: Project, Word, Outlook, InfoPath, PowerPoint, Publisher, and so on.

But starting with the first release of the Visual Studio Tools for Office (VSTO), developers now have a robust way to create Office solutions in managed code—Visual Basic and Visual C#—from directly within Visual Studio.

Visual Studio 2010 was released with the fourth generation of VSTO, which enables you to target the current (as of this writing) release of Office, Microsoft Office 2007, in addition to the forthcoming Microsoft Office 2010. The topic of using VSTO for Office development is a large topic that has entire books devoted to it; in this chapter we hope to simply introduce the concepts involved with VSTO and show how the Visual Studio Office project types can be used to quickly create powerful applications that leverage the existing power of Word, Excel, and Outlook. Some subjects we cover include these:

▶ Creating custom action panes

▶ Creating custom task panes

▶ Customizing the Office Ribbon

We specifically do not attempt to cover the object automation models for any of the Office applications, beyond the minimum necessary to understand the preceding concepts. For a more complete treatment of Office as a development platform, we recommend the VSTO team blog at http://blogs.msdn.com/vsto/, the book *Visual Studio Tools for Office 2007: VSTO for Excel, Word and Outlook,* by Eric Carter and Eric Lippert (Addison-Wesley Professional, 2009), and, of course, the various MSDN sections that cover VSTO (see the "Visual Studio Tools for Office" section later in this chapter).

Let's kick things off with a quick run-through of the various Office features that are available for customization.

> **NOTE**
>
> Although you can use Visual Studio 2010 to target both Office 2007 and Office 2010, we discuss only Office 2007 projects in this chapter. All the project types and methods for extending Office applications and Office documents are identical between Office 2007 and Office 2010.

An Overview of Office Extension Features

Because each Office application has a unique and specialized function, it should come as no surprise that the ways in which you can customize an Office application depend on which Office application we are specifically talking about. Although they all share a common, general layout for their user interface, there are intricacies involved with each of them that dictate different capabilities from within VSTO.

For instance, both Excel and Word deal with files as their central work piece, whereas Outlook deals with emails (which might be stored locally or on a server or both). So we can apply document-level extensions to Excel and Word, but this is not possible in Outlook. Conversely, the Outlook object model supports the concept of form regions, a concept absent in Excel and Word.

Office Features

Table 24.1 provides a matrix of the various features available for customization or extension within each Office application. We discuss each of these in the next section.

TABLE 24.1   Microsoft Office Extension Points

Application	Feature
Microsoft Excel 2007	Actions pane
	Task pane
	Data cache
	Ribbon
	Smart tags
Microsoft InfoPath 2007	Task pane
Microsoft Outlook 2007	Task pane
	Outlook form regions
Microsoft PowerPoint 2007	Task pane
Microsoft Word 2007	Actions pane
	Task pane
	Data cache
	Ribbon
	Smart tags

Some of these features are document-level features, and others are application-level features. The difference between the two is largely one of scope. Document-level customizations are attached to, and live with, a specific document, whether a Word .doc/.docx file or an Excel spreadsheet file. In contrast, application-level features are more global in reach and are implemented as add-ins to a specific Office application in exactly the same way that add-ins are created and implemented for Visual Studio itself (see Chapter 15, "Writing Add-ins and Wizards").

We look at the mechanics of how document-level and application-level solutions are differentiated in just a bit when we overview the VSTO project types. First, let's examine the features mentioned in Table 24.1. Understanding these features is key to determining how you might leverage Office using VSTO in your solutions.

Task Panes and Actions Panes

Task panes in Office are used to expose commands and features that are central to the task at hand without disrupting the user from focusing on the currently loaded document. See Figure 24.1 for a screenshot of a Microsoft Word 2007 task pane for merging form letters.

This task pane is able to guide the user through a series of steps while still allowing the loaded letter document to be visible. Task panes exist at the application level. Actions panes, on the other hand, are a type of task pane implemented at the document level.

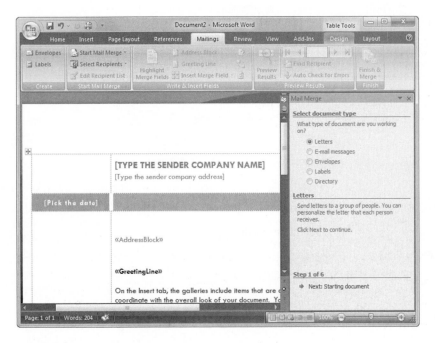

FIGURE 24.1   A Microsoft Word 2007 Action Pane.

Data Cache

A data cache refers to the capability of VSTO to store data locally within a document. This cache is also sometimes referred to as a data island. Because VSTO can read and write to the data cache, it is a useful tool for storing information needed by your Office add-in, or for shadowing data that resides in a database but is needed in certain disconnected scenarios.

Ribbon

The Ribbon is a user interface element that premiered with Microsoft Office 2007. It represents a new way to present features to users without using the traditional toolbars and menus. Commands in the Ribbon are grouped by task category, and within each task category commands are visually grouped with other similar commands. So with Word, for instance, we have a Review tab that consolidates all the commands related to document review. Because the Ribbon makes the most-used commands immediately visible and available, the Ribon attempts to avoid the problems caused by the menu bar paradigm in which items could be grouped and nested several layers deep (and thus, out of sight) within the menu system.

The tabs of the Ribbon and the command groupings within a tab are free to change from application to application depending on the context. Figure 24.2 compares the Ribbon home tab for Word and PowerPoint.

Microsoft PowerPoint 2007

Microsoft Word 2007

FIGURE 24.2   The Microsoft PowerPoint 2007 and Word 2007 Ribbons.

Smart Tags

Smart tags in Office function in a similar way to the smart tags present in the Visual Studio IDE (see Chapter 8, "Working with Visual Studio's Productivity Aids," to refresh your memory). Word is capable of recognizing various pieces of content as it is typed into a document, such as names, dates, financial symbols, and telephone numbers. When one of these items is recognized, it is flagged with a dotted purple underline. Hovering over that underline displays the smart tag icon, which can then be used to access a cascading menu with various options on ways to interact with that data. For instance, you might want to add someone's telephone number to your contact list. This action is easily executed from the smart tag menu for a telephone number (see Figure 24.3).

With VSTO, you can create your own smart tag recognizers and commands associated with them.

> **NOTE**
>
> If you are unable to see smart tags inside of your Word document, the feature is most likely disabled. To see which smart tags are enabled, click on the Office "pearl" at the upper left of the Ribbon, select Word Options, select Add-Ins, and then select Smart Tags in the drop-down labeled Manage at the bottom of the dialog box. Finally, click the Go button. The smart tags options screen lets you turn individual smart tags on or off.

Visual Studio Office Project Types

In general, there is a project type or family of project types available per Office application. In Figure 24.4, we see the various project types available by expanding first your chosen language node and then the Office node within the New Project dialog box.

FIGURE 24.3   A Smart Tag menu in Microsoft Word 2007.

FIGURE 24.4   The available Office project types in Visual Studio.

Note that we have the option of targeting either Microsoft Office 2007 or Microsoft Office 2010 applications. For the most part, the approach and capabilities remains the same between the two.

For Word and Excel, you see three project types each: an add-in template and two document-level templates. The document-level templates enable you to target either document files (for Word, this is referred to as the Word 2007 Document project template, and for Excel, this is referred to as the Excel 2007 Workbook project template) or Office template files (for example, you can customize a Word template).

As previously discussed, the difference between an application-level add-in and a document extension is one of scope: When you compile a VSTO project, just as with every other project type in Visual Studio, a managed code assembly is generated. That assembly can be attached or linked to an Office application (for example, Word or Excel), or to an Office document (for example, a .doc/.docx file or a .xls/.xlsx file). Document-level assemblies are loaded only when the document is loaded and are limited in scope to the document. Application-level add-ins are loaded during application startup (although this can be controlled by the user) and are more global in their reach.

> **NOTE**
>
> Although Visual Studio 2010 fully supports Microsoft Office projects right out of the box (at least with the Visual Studio Professional version), you also obviously need to have a copy of Microsoft Office and potentially various other components installed on your computer. See the MSDN article "How to: Install Visual Studio Tools for Office" for an in-depth look at VSTO requirements.

24

Creating an Office Add-in

To start creating your own Office add-in, create a new project in Visual Studio by selecting any of the Office add-in project types. Figure 24.5 shows the basic project structure created with a Word add-in project. We have a single code-file that establishes the startup entry point for the add-in, and provides us with the namespaces we need in order to access the Word automation object model.

FIGURE 24.5   A Microsoft Word 2007 add-in project.

There isn't anything terribly compelling about the developer experience so far. But VSTO provides a powerful set of visual designers you can use to craft your Office solution just as you would any other project in Visual Studio. To access these, we need to add a project item that has an associated designer. To start, let's see how to create a customized ribbon.

Customizing the Ribbon

Ribbon support within a VSTO project is enabled by adding a Ribbon project item to the project. Right-click on the project within Solution Explorer and select Add New Item. In the Add New Item dialog box (see Figure 24.6), you see two different Ribbon templates available for selection: Ribbon (Visual Designer) and Ribbon (XML). As their names suggest, the Visual Designer template provides you with a WYSIWYG design surface for creating your ribbon customizations. Because this design surface can't be used to build certain types of more advanced Ribbon features, the Ribbon (XML) item template is provided to enable you to handcraft ribbon features in XML. You need to use the Ribbon (XML) item if you want to do any of the following:

▶ Add a built-in (as opposed to custom) group to a custom tab

▶ Add a built-in control to a custom group

▶ Customize the event handlers for any of the built-in controls

▶ Add or remove items from the Quick Access Toolbar

FIGURE 24.6   Office project item templates.

For our purposes, let's select the Ribbon (Visual Designer) item and add it to our project. This adds the Ribbon1.cs file to our project. In a fashion similar to Windows Forms, this file has a designer and a code-behind file attached to it.

The design surface we are presented with is an exact replica of an empty ribbon (see Figure 24.7).

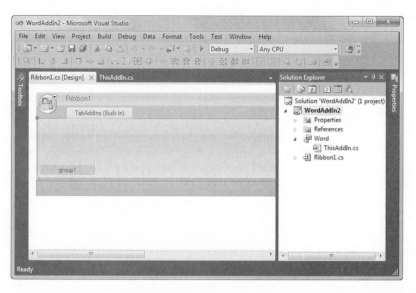

FIGURE 24.7   The Ribbon design surface.

There have been subtle look and feel changes to the Ribbon between Office 2007 and Office 2010. But the Ribbon itself is identical in terms of how you surface items on the Ribbon, and how you can modify the Ribbon from within an Office add-in.

Ribbons are composed of several elements: Tabs are used to provide the high-level task grouping of features, groups are used within each tab to provide more granular sectioning of the features, and controls reside within the groups to build out the custom user interface for the add-in.

With the Ribbon designer loaded, we now have access to Ribbon-specific controls over in the toolbox (see Figure 24.8). Adding controls to the Ribbon or adding new groups is as simple as dragging the desired control over to the Ribbon or group tab.

Adding Items to the Ribbon

To demonstrate, we can create our own custom group within the Add-Ins tab. Because we are presented with one group already by default, we can rename it to something more appropriate for our add-in. All the items in the Ribbon are modified via the properties window just as with all other Visual Studio project types. We simply click on the group, and then set its label property.

Groups act as containers on the design surface, enabling us to now drag and drop a button into the group. Figure 24.9 shows the beginnings of a custom ribbon for a purchasing system integration add-in. We have added two buttons, changed their ControlSize properties to RibbonControlSizeLarge, set their label properties to the text we want displayed in the button, and added some images to the buttons as well.

FIGURE 24.8   Office Ribbon controls in the IDE toolbox.

FIGURE 24.9   Creating a custom Office Ribbon.

TIP

The images used in this example were taken from the Visual Studio 2010 Image Library, but there is actually a cool way to reuse any of the icons that you see within Office. First, download the Icons Gallery Add-In from the Microsoft Download Center (search for "2007 Office System Add-In: Icons Gallery"). This download places an Excel file on your drive that, when opened, displays a gallery of the Office icons (see the Developers tab in the Excel Ribbon).

By hovering over an image of interest, you see its imageMso value. This is a string that can be plugged directly into a Ribbon button's OfficeImageId property. As long as an image isn't already set for the button, this causes the identified Office icon to be used. This is a real boon for UI design given the hundreds and hundreds of high-quality icons already available within Office. The image doesn't show in design-time, but does display correctly at runtime.

Adding more groups to our Ribbon involves more of the same drag-and-drop action from the toolbox. You can change the order of the groups in the Ribbon by selecting and then dragging a group to the left or right of any other existing groups.

> **NOTE**
>
> Notice that there is already a default tab implemented on the Ribbon called TabAddIns (Built-In). When you're creating a Ribbon for your add-in, its groups are automatically displayed under the Add-Ins tab within the target Office application. If you want to add items to one of the other default tabs in the Office application, or create your own tab, you have to use the Ribbon (XML) project item, and not the ribbon designer, to achieve that level of customization.

Handling Ribbon Control Events

Handling the events for our buttons is easy. Again, the idea behind VSTO is to provide Office customization capabilities using the same development paradigms already present in Visual Studio. This means we can double-click on a button to have the IDE automatically create and wire up an event-handler routine, ready to accept whatever code we need to write to implement the button's behavior.

To test this out, let's add the following to the Replace PO button:

```
private void buttonReplacePO_Click(object sender,
    RibbonControlEventArgs e)
{
    MessageBox.Show("buttonReplacePO_Click fired!");
}
```

If we run the project now by pressing F5, Word automatically launches; we can see our Ribbon customizations by clicking the Add-Ins tab. Clicking the Replace PO button yields the results shown in Figure 24.10.

Customizing the Task Pane

Task panes don't have a dedicated visual designer because they are implemented through the creation of a user control, which already has a design surface. To add a custom task pane to our Word add-in, right-click the project, select Add New Item, and then select the Windows Forms User Control item.

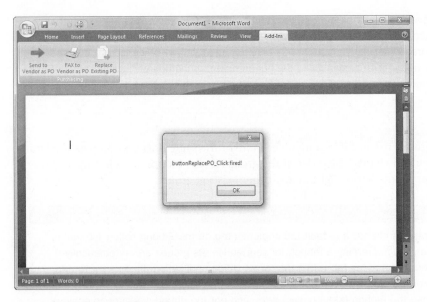

FIGURE 24.10   Testing a Ribbon button in Microsoft Word 2007.

NOTE

Because action panes are document-level concepts, we discuss those separately in the section "Creating an Office Document Extension" later in this chapter. The same general development process is followed.

After the user control is added and the designer is loaded, we can set about creating the UI and code-behind for the task pane. The only VSTO-specific action item here is wiring the task pane user control into Word's object model. All of that work is accomplished in code within the add-in class. First, to make our life a bit easier, we add a using statement to our add-in class (in this case, the ThisAddIn class):

```
using Microsoft.Office.Tools;
```

Then, we declare two local objects, one for the task pane and one for the user control:

```
private PurchaseOrderTaskControl poUserControl;
private CustomTaskPane poTaskPane;
```

And finally, we need the code to add the custom task pane to the application instance. We put this in the Startup event (for this example, ThisAddIn_Startup) so that the task pane is immediately available and visible when you run the add-in:

```
poUserControl = new PurchaseOrderTaskControl();
poTaskPane = this.CustomTaskPanes.Add(poUserControl, "Purchase Orders");
poTaskPane.Visible = true;
```

If you build and run the project now, you should see your task pane within the Word environment (see Figure 24.11).

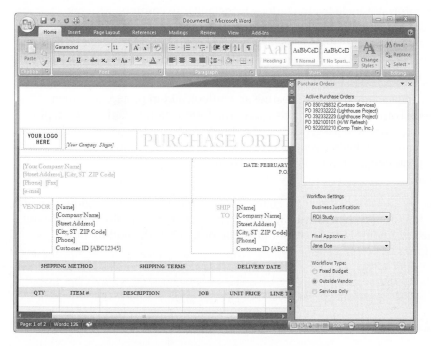

FIGURE 24.11   A custom task pane in Microsoft Word 2007.

TIP

Custom task panes action panes in VSTO do not directly support WPF user controls. There are ways, though, to surface WPF controls within a Windows Forms user control, thus giving you the ability to host a WPF-based task pane in Office. The key here is the use of the ElementHost control. This is a Windows Forms control that lives in the System.Windows.Forms.Integration namespace. In our example here, using WPF would be as simple as 1) adding an additional WPF user control to the project; 2) creating an instance of ElementHost; and 3) adding the WPF user control to the ElementHost with the ElementHost.Child property.

In essence, you need a Windows Forms user control hosting an ElementHost control which in turn hosts a WPF user control.

To dig more into the possibilities here, search msdn.microsoft.com for ElementHost.

Creating Outlook Form Regions

Let's turn our attention now to Outlook. As previously mentioned, Outlook has a unique extension point that is not available or relevant in Word or Excel; Outlook add-ins are capable of implementing form regions to any message class within Outlook. A message class is best thought of as the various entities that Outlook defines; these include notes, tasks, email, and so on. Put simply, a form region is the principal mechanism for developers to implement custom form fields within an existing form (for example, email, contact, or other custom forms not included in Outlook by default). To continue with our purchase order example from Word, perhaps a purchase order sent by email should have a set of editable fields and other UI associated with it. Those fields and UI could be implemented in Outlook 2007 as a form region. The best way to really understand form regions, is to jump right into the task of creating one.

Form regions are implemented by first creating an Outlook add-in project, and then adding an Outlook Form Region item. This trigger the form region wizard, which captures the information necessary to auto-generate a region class file. The first screen in the wizard is used to indicate whether you want to create a brand-new form region or use an existing one that was designed in Outlook itself. For our purposes here, select the Design a New Form option.

The second page in the wizard, shown in Figure 24.12, specifies where the region presents itself. There are four options here, with a graphic that illustrates the positioning behavior of the region. Select Adjoining to create our purchase order UI at the bottom of the Outlook email form.

FIGURE 24.12   Selecting the Outlook form region type.

The third page of the wizard (see Figure 24.13) queries for the name of the region, and which inspector display modes the region should support. Inspector is the Outlook term for the window used to view and edit a specific message class. For instance, when you compose a new email message in Outlook, you are actually seeing the email inspector in action.

FIGURE 24.13   Naming the form region and specifying the display mode.

The fourth and final page of the wizard (see Figure 24.14) associates the form region with any of the built-in Outlook message classes, or a custom message class implemented by a third party.

When finished, Visual Studio generates the code to match the form region properties provided in the wizard. You are now ready to construct the user interface for your region.

The visual designer for an Outlook Form Region looks identical to the Windows Forms UserControl designer: It is essentially a blank canvas that you drag controls onto. As with the other add-in types, your add-in class is where you link the user interface of your form region to Outlook's object model to perform the actual work of the add-in.

Figure 24.15 shows a completed Outlook form region attached to the mail message class (IPM.Notes).

Creating an Office Document Extension

There are various ways to customize Office documents themselves. You can host controls in a document, create action panes specific to a document, implement your own smart tags, and store data within a document.

FIGURE 24.14   Associating the form region with a message class.

FIGURE 24.15   An Outlook form region in action.

A document-level project is created using the same process we used for add-ins. This time, however, you select an Excel 2007 Workbook or Word 2007 Document project type. These project types use designers that represent the look and feel of an Excel workbook or a Word document.

Hosting Controls

Both Word and Excel have host items that function as containers for controls and code. A host item is essentially a proxy object that represents a physical document within either application. These are key to document-level customizations. For Word, we have the Microsoft.Office.Tools.Word.Document object, and for Excel, we have the Microsoft.Office.Tools.Excel.Worksheet object. Within Visual Studio, we build functionality using these host items through the use of designers. Each host item can host both Windows Forms controls and native Office controls.

> **NOTE**
>
> There is actually a third host item that represents an Excel workbook: Microsoft.Office.Tools.Excel.Workbook is a host item for enabling workbook-level customization, but is not an actual controls container. Instead, Workbook functions as a component tray and can accept components such as a DataSet.

Windows Forms Controls

Windows Forms controls can be added onto the document design surface just as if you were designing a Windows Forms application. In this example, we use an Excel workbook. The Excel 2007 Workbook project template automatically adds an .xslx file to our project, which includes three worksheets, each represented by its own class (these are the host items we discussed previously). These sheets have defined events for startup and shutdown, enabling us to perform work as the worksheet is first opened or closed.

The design surface for the worksheet looks identical to how the worksheet looks in Excel. From here, we can add Windows Forms controls to the worksheet by using the Visual Studio toolbox, and implement code in the code-behind file to customize the action of those controls. Figure 24.16 shows a workbook designer in the IDE with a few controls added.

> **NOTE**
>
> Creating an Office document project requires that your system allow access to the Microsoft Office Visual Basic for Applications project system. Normally, this type of access is disabled for security reasons. If access is disabled, Visual Studio prompts you to enable it before creating your Office project.

Host Controls

Host controls is the term applied to native Office controls. These controls actually extend objects found in the Word or Excel object models to provide additional capabilities such as event handling and data binding. Building out a document using host controls follows the same process as with Windows Forms controls. With a document-level project loaded, you see a tab in the Visual Studio toolbox that stores the host controls for the specific application that is targeted. For Excel, there is an Excel Controls tab, and for Word a Word Controls tab.

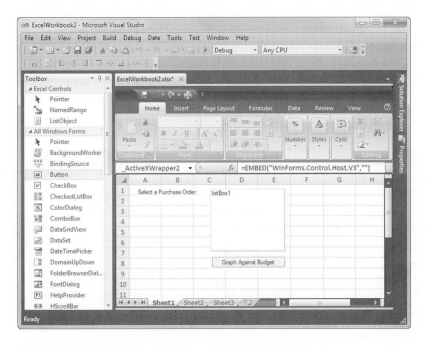

FIGURE 24.16   Adding controls to an Excel spreadsheet.

Table 24.2 itemizes the available host controls for both Excel and Word.

TABLE 24.2   Microsoft Office Extension Points

Project Type	Host Control	Function
Excel 2007 Workbook	ListObject	Displays data in rows and columns.
Excel 2007 Workbook	NamedRange	Represents an Excel range; can be bound to data and expose events.
Word 2007 Document	Bookmark	Represents a Word bookmark.
Word 2007 Document	BuildingBlockGalleryContentControl	Document building blocks are pieces of a document meant to be reused (a cover page, header, and so on); this control displays a list of building blocks that users can insert into a document.

TABLE 24.2 Continued

Project Type	Host Control	Function
Word 2007 Document	ComboBoxContentControl	A standard combo box.
Word 2007 Document	DatePickerContentControl	A standard date picker control.
Word 2007 Document	DropDownListContentControl	A drop-down list of items.
Word 2007 Document	PictureContentControl	Represents a document region that displays an image.
Word 2007 Document	PlainTextContentControl	Represents a block of text.
Word 2007 Document	RichTextContentControl	Represents a block of text; can contain rich content.

Creating an Actions Pane

In addition to customizing the interaction with users within a document, Windows Forms controls are used to craft custom actions panes. Actions panes should be used to provide contextual data and command options to users as they are editing/viewing a document (either a Word document or an Excel workbook file).

There are several reasons why you would elect to implement your document interface using an action pane. One reason is that the actions pane is "linked" to the document but is not an actual part of the document—the contents of the actions pane won't be printed when the document is printed. Another reason to implement an actions pane is to preserve the application's document-centric focus: You can read and page through an entire document while keeping the information and commands in the action pane in full view at all times.

Physically, actions panes are created with user controls and are represented by an Actions Pane Control item. Adding this item to your document project creates a user control class; you simply build out the user interface of the control as normal. In general, though, you likely want to dynamically add or remove controls from the actions pane depending on what the user is doing within the document that is open in Word or Excel. Providing this level of contextual relevance is the strong point and target of the actions pane in the first place.

Controlling Stacking Behavior

Because the actions pane functions as a toolbar container that can be docked and moved around by the user, there is a complete control layout engine for dictating how the controls within the actions pane should be displayed. The ActionsPane.StackOrder property works with a StackStyle enum to control layout behavior. The various StackStyle values are documented for you in Table 24.3.

TABLE 24.3   StackStyle Values

Value	Description
FromBottom	Controls are stacked starting from the bottom of the actions pane
FromLeft	Controls are stacked starting from the left of the actions pane
FromRight	Controls are stacked starting from the right of the actions pane
FromTop	Controls are stacked starting from the top of the actions pane
None	No stacking is performed (order and layout are manually controlled)

As we did with the custom task pane, after you have assembled a user control that you want to surface within the actions pane, you need to create a field variable to hold an instance of the control, and then add the control to the action pane.

So in the ThisWorkbook class, we add the following declaration:

```
private ActionsPaneControl1 approvalPane = new ActionsPaneControl1();
```

And the following line of code, inserted into the ThisWorkbook_Startup event, adds our user control to the workbook's action pane:

```
this.ActionsPane.Controls.Add(approvalPane);
```

Figure 24.17 shows a custom actions pane alongside its worksheet.

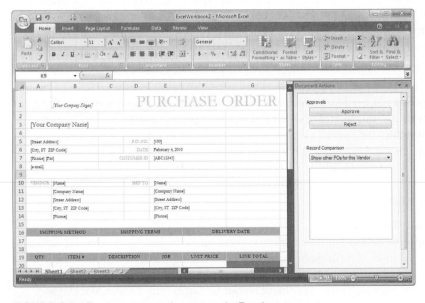

FIGURE 24.17   A custom actions pane in Excel.

Storing Data in the Data Cache

The data cache is a read/write location within an Office Word document or Excel workbook that can be leveraged by your Office application to store needed data. One common scenario is to bind host controls or Windows Forms controls in an actions pane or on a document surface to a data set stored in the document's data island.

Physically, this data island is implemented as an XML document that is embedded within the Office document. This XML container can host any data type that meets the following two requirements:

▶ It has to be implemented as a read/write public field on the host item (for example, the Word ThisDocument or Excel ThisWorkbook class).

▶ It must be serializable (the runtime uses the XmlSerializer to verbalize the object within the data island).

Most of the built-in .NET types meet these requirements. If you have written a custom type that also adheres to these requirements, it too can be stored within the data island.

Adding data to the data cache is easy. You mark the data type you want to store with the CachedAttribute attribute; assuming that the type meets the data cache requirements, and that you have created an instance of the type within your document-level VSTO project, it is automatically added to the data island.

DataSet objects turn out to be useful for conveyance within a data island. To declare a DataSet as cached, we write the following:

```
[Microsoft.VisualStudio.Tools.Applications.Runtime.Cached()]
public DataSet poDataSet;
```

This declaratively instructs the VSTO runtime to serialize the object and add it to the current document's data cache. The DataSet itself can be populated however you see fit.

There is also a way to imperatively cache an object in a document. Each host item exposes an IsCached method and a StartCaching method. By combining the two, you can check to see whether an object is already in the cache, and, if it isn't, add it to the cache. Using these two methods, we might end up with the following code to store our poDataSet object in a document:

```
if (!this.IsCached("poDataSet"))
{
    this.StartCaching("poDataSet ");
}
```

If you use the StartCaching() method, there is no need for the class to be decorated with the Cached attribute, but the object does still need to adhere to the other requirements for Office data island serialization. You can also use the StopCaching method on the host item to tell the VSTO runtime to remove the object from the document's data cache.

> **TIP**
>
> There is yet a third way to place an object into the data cache: the properties window. If you use the Data Sources window to add a data set to your project, you can create an instance of the data set and then select it in the designer. In the properties window for the data set instance, set the Cache in Document property to True. You also need to change the access type of the data set instance to Public.

Accessing the Data Cache

Many times, an Office business application relies on a server to function as a central repository for documents. This introduces a dilemma: the Office applications such as Word and Excel are not designed to be run in a server environment where many instances might need to be spooled up to serve multiple requests for document-level extensions. So far, we have been using objects within the Office object model to extend Office. And this implies that Office is installed on the machine running your assembly—something that is certainly not the case for typical server installations. Thankfully, one of the primary goals for document-level Office architecture is to enable the clean separation of data from the view of the data. Or, put another way, the VSTO architecture defines a way to access a document without actually using the Office client application. Instead, the VSTO runtime itself is used.

The key to accessing a document server side is the ServerDocument class. This class, which is part of the VSTO runtime and lives in the Microsoft.VisualStudio.Tools.Applications namespace, allows programmatic access to a document's data cache on machines that do not have Office installed. The process running on the server passes the path for the needed document into the ServerDocument's constructor, and then uses the CachedDataHostItem class and the CachedDataItem class to obtain either the schema or the XML or both from the document's data island.

As long as the target computer has the VSTO runtime installed, the following code could be used to access the purchase order data from a server-side purchase order spreadsheet:

```
string poFile = @"C:\ServerData\po39233202.xls";
ServerDocument poDoc = null;


poDoc = new ServerDocument(poFile);


CachedDataHostItem dataHostItem =
    sd1.CachedData.HostItems["ExcelWorkbook1.DataSheet1"];


CachedDataItem dataCache = dataHostItem.CachedData["CachedPO"];


//The dataCache.Xml property will contain the XML
//from the specified data island
```

Using the dataCache.Xml property, you can now deserialize back into the source data type, view the data, and so on.

Implementing Your Own Smart Tags

Office smart tags procedurally work like this: As a user types in an open document, the text is "tokenized" and then compared to all the terms/expressions that any of the smart tags in Office recognize. If the text is recognized by a smart tag, a list of actions is provided to the user (and displayed using the UI described previously when we first introduced the smart tag concept). So we have two parts to the process: recognition and action.

Using VSTO, you can create your own smart tags that define which text the tags recognize, and define the list of possible action items that are presented on recognition to the user.

Both Word and Excel implement classes that derive from the Microsoft.Office.Tools.SmartTagBase base class. For Word, this is the Microsoft.Office.Tools.Word.SmartTag class, and for Excel, this is the Microsoft.Office.Tools.Excel.SmartTag class. Both of these classes implement two important properties defined on the SmartTagBase class: Terms and Expressions. If your smart tag needs to match on simple text tokens, you can add them to the Terms collection. If more complicated matching is required, the Expressions property accepts a regular expression to perform its matching.

To determine how to configure your smart tag object, you need a little knowledge concerning how Office applications tokenize text. For instance, if a user types PO29302 into Word, the parser automatically creates two tokens out of that text: token 1 is PO and token 2 is 29302. Adding the string PO to the Terms collection would cause this text to be recognized by our smart tag because one of the tokens matches our term. We could also write a more complicated and robust regular expression that matches on "the letters PO preceded by one or more spaces, followed by any number of numerical digits, and then followed by one or more spaces" by using this: \sPO[0-9]*\s.

After you have determined what you want to match text-wise with your smart tag, you need to determine the list of actions available to users who click the smart tag. If you want to match on a purchase order number using the regex just shown, and then offer a user the ability to see the purchase orders details (perhaps within an actions pane or with an Outlook forms region), you define that action using the Action class (again, available in both Word and Excel). The Action class provides an event that you can hook to perform the custom work of performing the indicated action:

```
// Create the action object
DisplayPO = new Action("Display PO details");

// Add the action to the smart tag
POSmartTag.Actions = new Action[] { DisplayPO };
```

Listing 24.1 puts all of this together in a region that you can copy and paste into a Word document class (for example, ThisDocument) to create a custom smart tag, and Figure 24.18 shows the smart tag in action.

FIGURE 24.18   A custom smart tag implemented in Microsoft Word 2007.

LISTING 24.1   A Word Document Project with Custom Smart Tag

```
using System;
using System.Collections.Generic;
using System.Data;
using System.Linq;
using System.Text;
using System.Text.RegularExpressions;
using System.Windows.Forms;
using System.Xml.Linq;
using Microsoft.VisualStudio.Tools.Applications.Runtime;
using Tools = Microsoft.Office.Tools.Word;
using Office = Microsoft.Office.Core;
using Word = Microsoft.Office.Interop.Word;

namespace WordDocument1
{
    public partial class ThisDocument
    {

        private void AddPOSmartTag()
        {
            // Create the smart tag object
```

```csharp
        Tools.SmartTag poSmartTag =
            new Tools.SmartTag(
                "www.contoso.com#POSmartTag",
                "PO Smart Tag");

        // We want to match on a regex:
        poSmartTag.Expressions.Add(new Regex(@"\sPO[0-9]*\s"));

        // Define an action for the smart tag
        Tools.Action displayDetails =
            new Tools.Action("Display PO details...");

        // Add the action to the smart tag
        poSmartTag.Actions =
            new Tools.Action[] { displayDetails };

        // Add the smart tag to the document
        this.VstoSmartTags.Add(poSmartTag);

        // Wire up event handlers for the smart tag action
        displayDetails.Click += new
            Tools.ActionClickEventHandler(
            displayDetails_Click);
    }


void displayDetails_Click(object sender,
        Tools.ActionEventArgs e)
{
    // code would go here to reach out to the purchasing
    // system and surface the information in the current
    // document
}



private void ThisDocument_Startup(object sender,
        System.EventArgs e)
{
    AddPOSmartTag();
}



private void ThisDocument_Shutdown(object sender,
        System.EventArgs e)
{
```

```
        }

        #region VSTO Designer generated code

        /// <summary>
        /// Required method for Designer support - do not modify
        /// the contents of this method with the code editor.
        /// </summary>
        private void InternalStartup()
        {
            this.Startup +=
                new System.EventHandler(ThisDocument_Startup);
            this.Shutdown +=
                new System.EventHandler(ThisDocument_Shutdown);
        }

        #endregion
    }
}
```

Summary

In this chapter, we covered the capabilities present in Visual Studio 2010 for building on top of Microsoft Office applications and customizing their behavior at both the application level and the document level. In our discussion of Office add-ins, we covered the capability to add your own items, tabs, and groupings to the Ribbon, the construction of Outlook forms regions, and the development of custom task panes. In our discussion of Office document-level extensions, we illustrated the concepts behind hosting Windows Forms controls and native Office controls on a document's surface, building custom actions panes to provide context-aware actions and information to users, and using the data cache architecture to both read and write data to Office documents on the client and server side.

Finally, we presented how to craft your own smart tags.

Although we focused on only a few of the Office applications that can be customized using VSTO, we hope we have provided enough information around VSTO's projects and designers to get you started on your own investigation into Visual Studio and Office as a development platform.

CHAPTER 25

Developing Applications in the Cloud with Windows Azure

Cloud applications and cloud development is here. At the time of this book's release Microsoft makes good on its promise of production-ready cloud data centers located around the world close to abundant power sources. In fact, case studies that demonstrate the remarkable benefits of early movers to the cloud are already available from Microsoft and other cloud vendors.

As developers, we are eager to take advantage of all this computing power and simplified server management. This chapter covers the developer's perspective on using Visual Studio 2010 to build solutions for the cloud to be deployed on Windows Azure.

Azure Fundamentals

The first question most developers ask is, "What is Azure?" The answer is both simple and complex. At first glance, Azure is just a hosting model for your applications. This hosting model, however, is one built to provide an entirely new level of service to those applications it hosts. This is where Azure becomes interesting.

Yes, Azure is hosting. It is highly scalable (practically unlimited) data-center hosting to which you have immediate access to as little or as much as you want (depending on your needs and ability to pay). In fact, you can quickly (with a couple key strokes) scale up or down to meet demand. This is elastic scalability on demand. And, better yet, you have access to both emulate this data center and deploy to it directly from your development machine and Visual Studio.

Azure Platform Benefits

The Azure platform offers developers and infrastructure teams a new way of thinking about the deployment and management of their applications. The following provide an overview of the benefits of Azure from four of the primary perspectives:

▶ **Azure as an operating system**—Windows Azure is at its base an operating system designed to work across multiple servers (both physical and virtualized). In fact, you can think of Azure as an operating system exposed as a service. To make this possible, it includes what is called an application fabric (AppFabric). The AppFabric is responsible for handling the provisioning, scalability, fault-tolerance, load-balancing, failure detection, and monitoring of your applications. The AppFabric exposes the core services of Azure: compute (or hosting), data storage, service bus (discovering and connection of application services), and access control (based on claims and rules).

Developers can use the Azure services without ever really needing to think much about this operating system. It is simply the core that makes it all possible.

▶ **Azure as a hosting provider**—The Azure data centers are built using hundreds of connected computers that leverage virtualization and are managed by the Azure AppFabric. Of course, there are also many of these data centers resulting in thousands of computers and even more virtualized instances. Having this scalable, reliable, and available computing power available alleviates a lot of traditional headaches. Try to recall the last major, internet-scale application you built and hosted.

Azure alleviates the concerns of acquiring, installing, managing, troubleshooting, patching, and upgrading servers, load balancers, networks, data storage and the like. It's all just here in the cloud waiting for applications. This enables development teams to focus on the code and business problems; Azure handles the hosting, computing, replication, backup, fault-tolerance, network, and related demands.

▶ **Azure as a development platform**—The good news is that you get to leverage everything you know today about building .NET applications. It all works with Azure. This includes the tools (Visual Studio) and technologies (ASP.NET, Silverlight, WPF, WCF, WF, and so on) you use today.

Many applications port easily to the cloud with minor modifications. Of course, to take full advantage of the cloud services you might want to leverage the cloud data storage techniques in your applications; you might even consider SQL Azure for moving your SQL databases to the cloud.

The Azure SDK tools also indicate a local, DevFabric that emulates the cloud on your desktop. This includes emulation of running multiple instance, load balancing, and the Azure data storage mechanisms. This enables you to continue to debug and troubleshoot applications locally.

▶ **Azure as data and file storage**—The Azure platform gives you a number of options for storing data: tables, blobs, drives, and queues. We discuss each later in this chapter. However, what is important to know is that the platform takes care to secure your data (using claims-based access control) and to ensure your data is not compromised or lost. In fact, all data placed in the cloud is triple-replicated. Three copies are always maintained in case there is a failure (in which case the AppFabric automatically recovers for you).

If your needs are beyond these basic storage solutions you can get the full power of a scalable relational database using SQL Azure. We cover this in a later section.

You can see that cloud-computing with Azure offers many benefits. Let's get started building code for the cloud. This is the best way to familiarize yourself with the new concepts Azure introduces.

> **NOTE**
>
> Azure hosting is pay-as-you-go. There are set prices depending on your usage. You can get the latest details at microsoft.com/WindowsAzure. You can also find case studies for early adopters and much more.

Setting Up Your Development Environment

For the most part, you can create applications for the cloud as you would normally. This holds especially true for Web-related applications such as Silverlight, ASP.NET, WCF, and the like. Azure also allows for hosting more traditional applications using virtualized instances. However, our focus is developing and deploying to this new cloud and that means connected, hosted solutions.

The biggest change for your applications is that they are hosted via the AppFabric in a load-balanced scenario. You also have access to new data storage mechanisms, which can make it challenging to test your applications locally before moving to the cloud. Thankfully, the Azure SDK includes a local version of the AppFabric called the DevFabric. It can emulate running your application on multiple instances in a load-balanced cloud. It also includes emulation for storage of blobs, tables, and queues. The following sections walk you through getting your environment set up to build cloud applications locally than can be easily deployed to Azure.

Installing the SDK

The first step is to install the SDK. The Azure SDK does not ship with Visual Studio 2010 at present, so you need to download it and install it. Microsoft has released a few versions of this tool. The latest was released in June 2010 and is version 1.2 (which supports development against the .NET Framework 4.0). You can find the SDK easily by searching for "Windows Azure Tools for Microsoft Visual Studio." If you've installed a prior version of the SDK, you will want to download and install version 1.2.

If you have yet to install the SDK, you can do so through Visual Studio. First, use Visual Studio to create a new project (File, New, Project) and navigate to Cloud (for VB and C#). Here you see the Enable Windows Azure Tools option as a project template. Figure 25.1 shows an example of the dialog box you see prior to installing the SDK.

FIGURE 25.1   By default, you still need to install the Azure SDK in Visual Studio 2010.

NOTE

If you have installed the SDK, or downloaded and installed directly from the internet, skip ahead to "Azure Roles."

Clicking the enable Azure tools project template creates a simple Visual Studio project that loads an HTML page to give you a link to the download. Figure 25.2 shows an example of this project in the IDE. Next, click the Download Windows Azure Tools button, which takes you to a Microsoft download site where you can download the SDK (you will want to save it to your hard drive).

The SDK download is named VSCloudService.exe. You run this application to install the Visual Studio templates and the development fabric. The SDK includes all of the following items:

▶ Both C# and VB project templates for building cloud sites and services

▶ Tools to add, remove, and configure roles from the cloud (more on roles in a moment)

▶ The development fabric used to emulate the cloud locally (on your machine)

▶ The Azure development storage services

▶ Build and packaging services for deploying cloud services and applications

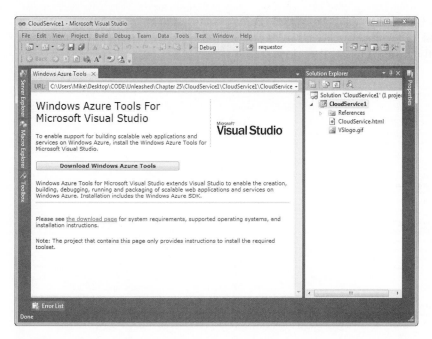

FIGURE 25.2   You need to download the Visual Studio tools for Azure (they work with Visual Studio 2008 SP1 as well).

Before you install the SDK you need to make sure your machine is running IIS7 and ASP.NET. If you try to install without these services, the SDK installer throws an error as shown in Figure 25.3.

FIGURE 25.3   You must be running IIS 7 with ASP.NET to use the Azure SDK.

You can install IIS7 and ASP.NET from the Windows Features dialog box (Start, Control Panel, Uninstall a Program, Turn Windows features on or off). Figure 25.4 shows the basic setup for installing these tools on Windows 7 or Vista.

FIGURE 25.4   You can install IIS7 and ASP.NET using the Windows Features dialog box.

The final step is to rerun the SDK installer (VSCloudService.exe) to check your version of Visual Studio and install the tools appropriately. Note that you can actually install the SDK on either Visual Studio 2008 SP1 or 2010. Figure 25.5 shows an example of the first screen in this setup.

That's it. You should now have your development environment prepped to begin building Azure applications locally. Note that you still have to create an Azure account for hosting. We cover that in a coming section. However, you can simulate an Azure application after the SDK has completed.

Azure Roles

Azure introduces the concept of roles in your application. Roles dictate your project type, how your application is hosted, and how you buy your Azure hosting. Today, there are basically two roles: Web and Worker.

You indicate your application's role inside its service model. The service model is the metadata that describes to the AppFabric how your application should be provisioned and hosted. You can set your role to either Worker or Web.

FIGURE 25.5   The Azure installation SDK detects your copy of Visual Studio and installs templates accordingly.

The Web role is used for creating applications that are to be exposed over the Web. This includes ASP.NET, ASP.NET MVC 2, and WCF-based applications. On the Azure side, Web role applications are executed under IIS7, ASP.NET 3.5 SP1/4.0 (this includes support for native code).

The Worker role is a bit different. It is meant to host background processing applications that are typically not web-addressable. Think of these as .DLLs hosted in a Windows Service. Of course these worker roles have access to the table, blob, and queue storage inside Azure. They can be great solutions for processing the user messages entered through a Web role (think Twitter). When you host, you have access to the .NET Framework and can run native code. It also includes a TCP port for communicating with your work role.

> **NOTE**
>
> Note that both roles (Web and Worker) are hosted on what amounts to Windows Server 2008 instances.

The Azure Project Templates

After your development environment is set up, you have a new project template option available when you click the Cloud link in the New Project dialog box. This template, called Windows Azure Cloud Service (see Figure 25.6), actually provides access to the cloud project types (web and worker roles).

FIGURE 25.6   The Azure Cloud service templates require an extra step when defining a project.

Selecting the Windows Azure Cloud Service template brings up another dialog box called New Cloud Service Project. This is where you actually define the projects that make up your cloud-deployment solution. This includes ASP.NET, WCF, and other project types. A separate dialog box enables you to add the projects that make up your solution so that the Azure tools can define the configuration scripts accordingly when generating your project templates. You can see an example in Figure 25.7.

FIGURE 25.7   The New Cloud Service Project enables you to set up one or more cloud applications in your solution.

You can always add a new Web or Worker role to your solution after it has been defined. Use the Project menu, Add New Web Role or Add New Worker Role.

Notice that the New Cloud Service Project dialog box enables you to move the various cloud project templates (left side) over to your solution (right side). To rename an item after you've moved it into your solution, click the pencil graphic in the upper-right corner. The red X removes it from the solution.

You can see there are many different templates from which to choose when building your cloud-based solution. Table 25.1 provides an overview of each of these templates and their uses.

TABLE 25.1   The Azure Project Templates

Project Template	Description
ASP.NET Web Role	Use this template to create a basic ASP.NET site that includes packaging and configuration information to be deployed to the cloud in the web role; it also includes references to the Azure services. See Chapter 17, "Creating ASP.NET Applications."
ASP.NET MVC 2 Web Role	This template creates an ASP.NET site based on the MVC 2 framework. See Chapter 17 for details on ASP.NET MVC 2.
WCF Service Web Role	Use this template to create WCF services you intend to deploy to the cloud. See Chapter 22, "Service-Oriented Applications."
Worker Role	A Worker Role application is one you deploy to the cloud to do some processing. It might work with your data to process it and perhaps call some of your other services. It might even serve as a host for your application or service. You can think of this project type as a Windows Service running on your behalf in your cloud space.
CGI Web Role	This project template simplifies the process of hosting FastCGI applications built with PHP on Azure. It provides a configuration template for your application.

25

Note that, by default, each of the project templates includes references to the Azure namespaces for use by your application. These include Microsoft.WindowsAzure.Diagnostics, .ServiceRuntime, and .StorageClient.

Azure Storage Options

Windows Azure provides a number of options for storing data for use by your application. You can store massive amounts of data in a cost-effective way using this platform. This data is kept close to your applications for fast access. It also is triple-replicated automatically to ensure failover. This section takes a look at the Azure specific data storage options. We review these when you create a sample application near the end of this chapter.

The Azure platform includes the following options for data storage: table, blob, queue, and SQL Azure (at an extra cost). Each of these items are outlined below.

> **NOTE**
>
> Azure storage services are built to scale using the same AppFabric discussed previously.

Table Storage

Despite what the name might suggest, the Table structure is not (and will never be, according to Microsoft) a relational database. For relational databases there is SQL Azure. However, many applications do not need the rigors (or constraints) of a full RDBMS. Instead, they need simplified, table-like storage. This is where the Table element comes into play.

The table storage is great for simple entity lists. The data is stored in name-value pairs where the name acts as the key and the value can be almost anything. You also partition (group) data into different tables by a key (there is no limit to the number of keys or partitions you can create). A partition simply indicates logical similarities among the items in a table. This is referred to as semi-structured data.

Azure table storage does not enforce schema. This means you can put different object types in the same table. You might, for example, have some objects with five properties and some with eight. It is up to your application to determine how to enforce schema. This can actually be somewhat liberating, especially in the smaller applications at which this type of storage is targeted.

It's worth repeating: Azure table storage is not a RDBMS. It does not support joins or stored procedures. It is for applications that do not demand and might never need the rigors of a full database (think blogs, image sharing, and other simple storage applications).

Blob Storage

Azure blob storage is like a file system. You can push any file into blob storage and use the file as you see fit. One benefit of blob storage in Azure is realized when you're working with large files. The files can be broken into blocks; each block can be uploaded in parallel. You can also access the entire file or only the block you need. You may even update the blocks of a file that have changes.

> **NOTE**
>
> In future releases of Azure, Microsoft intends to implement the concept of drives for mimicking computer drives in the cloud using blog storage.

Queue

Azure queue storage is a simple, lightweight message management system designed to exchange messages asynchronously. Messages can be sent to the queue. The queue persists these messages until they have been processed. This is a great solution for passing messages from system to system or between Azure roles (Web to Worker, for example).

A common pattern for using the queue storage is the Web role takes user input and then stores it in table storage. It might then post a task to the queue and report back to the user. A Worker role can then work in the background to pick up messages from the queue and process them (it might read back input from table storage based on a key inside the queue). If the worker role fails, the message goes back into the queue to be picked up later. After it's been processed, the message is removed from the queue and the table storage might get updated (and perhaps the user notified). In this way, queue storage helps to coordinate the work in your application.

> **NOTE**
>
> The data stores you create in Azure are accessible to your Azure Web or Worker applications through configuration. You define endpoints to access your data and configure these applications to connect to those endpoints. However, you also connect to these same endpoints outside of Azure; the data endpoints are independently accessible through a REST-based interface.

25

SQL Azure

If you need a relational database in the cloud, SQL Azure is there to help. It provides the full power of SQL Server but in a scalable, cloud-hosted solution (at an extra cost).

SQL Azure is much like SQL Server. However, there are some differences when it comes to boundaries, replication, and monitoring. SQL Azure provides partition-based boundaries; this is how SQL Azure scales, too, through partitioning your data across servers. It also automatically replicates your database in three places. It also gives you automatic failover, recovery, and monitoring support.

Coding against SQL Azure should be familiar to developers as it is SQL Server. This means the same code you write today works against SQL Azure.

SQL Azure also provides the Data Sync service, which enables features of the Sync Framework for synchronizing data from the database to a user's machine (for offline scenarios) or another server.

Like SQL Server, SQL Azure also allows you access to the other SQL services. This includes the Business Intelligence tools (BI) for creating cubes and doing data analysis, as well as the SQL Reporting Services (RS) for creating reports against your data.

Hello Cloud

To round out the fundamentals, let's look at building a simple Azure application and run it in the DevFabric. For this example, you create a simple, Hello Cloud application. The following outlines the steps in this process:

1. Start by opening Visual Studio in elevated privledge mode (right-click the shortcut and select Run as administrator).

   Create a new ASP.NET Web Role application in Visual Studio (File, New Project). Select Cloud from the list on the left of the New Project dialog box.

   Set the name of the solution to HelloCloud.

   Double-click Windows Azure Cloud Service to launch the New Cloud Service Project dialog box (refer to Figure 25.7).

   Select the ASP.NET Web Role and click the right-arrow to move this project into the solution. Use the pencil icon to rename the project HelloCloudWeb. Click the OK button to create the solution.

2. Navigate this solution in Solution Explorer. First, notice that Visual Studio has created an essentially blank ASP.NET site. However, open the References folder to see that there are references set to the Azure namespaces (among others).

   Open the WebRole.cs file in the website (see Figure 25.8). Notice that this code file includes information for the Azure runtime about starting and monitoring the web role application.

FIGURE 25.8   The default HelloCloud application in Visual Studio 2010.

Notice the other project in the solution. This is an Azure cloud service project used for configuring our role. More on this in a moment.

3. Open the Default.aspx page from the website. Add the text "Hello Cloud" to the top of the page. You can remove the other text inside the page.

4. Assume this application has to scale beyond a single instance in the cloud. Remember, you can emulate this scale on your development machine. To indicate the number of instances you have two options. Inside the HelloCloud Azure application you can edit the ServiceConfiguration.csfg XML file by hand. Alternatively, you can right-click the web role (Roles folder, HellCloudWeb) and choose Properties. This brings up an editor for the XML file and the web role. Figure 25.9 shows an example of this option.

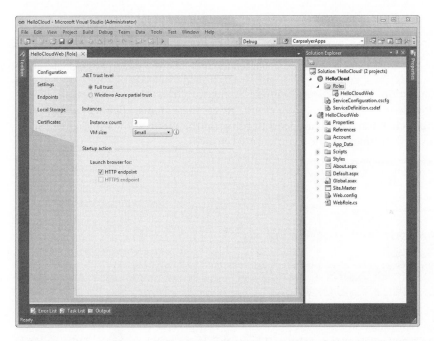

FIGURE 25.9   You can edit the settings of the web role using the Properties window. These settings are stored in ServiceConfiguration.csfg.

Using the Properties window, set the Instance count to 3 to indicate that you want to test the application as scaled for three instances. Figure 25.9 shows an example of this setting. Notice too that you can set VM size. Small is 1 core, 1.7GB of memory and 250GB of storage. For other size options, click the information (i) icon next to the VM size setting.

5. Run the application from the IDE. First, however, notice that the HelloCloud Azure application is actually set up as the startup project, which launches the application inside the DevFabric. Click the Run button in Visual Studio to get started.

6. If this is the first Azure application you have run, Azure initializes development storage. This creates your table, blob, and queue storage instances and can take several minutes. Figure 25.10 shows the dialog box that does this initialization.

FIGURE 25.10   The Azure data services are initialized the first time you run an Azure application.

7. After initialization, both the Development Storage and DevFabric services are running locally to emulate the Azure cloud. To see these items, click inside the task bar and right-click the blue Azure icon to bring up the menu shown in Figure 25.11. You can use this to manage the two Azure services.

FIGURE 25.11   You can access the Azure data storage and DevFabric from the taskbar.

8. Select the Show Development Fabric UI from the Azure task bar menu. This launches the Development Storage Service manager. You can see from Figure 25.12 that all three services are there: table, blob, and queue. You can start or stop services from this window. You can also navigate to the local storage for this service using the File menu, Open Azure Drive Folder in Windows Explorer.

FIGURE 25.12   You can manage the Azure data storage services.

9. Next, use the taskbar to open the Development Fabric. Notice that your HelloCloud application is running here. Expand the tree to see there are three instances running (per the configuration setting). Click one of these instances to see the startup script. Figure 25.13 shows an example.

FIGURE 25.13   You can see all three instances of the HelloCloud application.

10. You eventually see your application running in a browser. Figure 25.14 shows an example.

The next step is to deploy this application out to the actual cloud. We cover this process in a more robust example in the next section.

Building and Deploying an Azure Application

In this section you build a Web role project that takes advantage of Azure table storage. You then create an Azure account, package (publish) your project, and deploy it out to a staged instance in the cloud. Finally, you move your staged deployment into a production environment. Let's get started.

The Scenario

The scenario for this application is simple. We step you through creating an Azure deployed cloud application for providing feedback to the authors of this book. When complete, the site will be live for you to check out and leave your feedback. Of course, you are also able to download the full source.

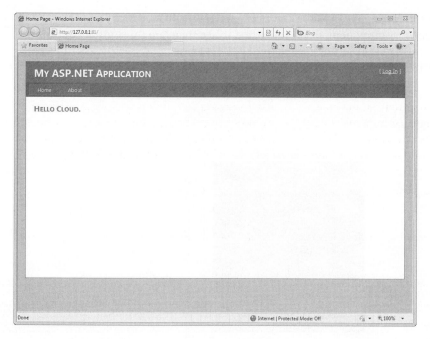

FIGURE 25.14   The Hello Cloud application running in an emulated Azure fabric.

Developing the Application

The components of the sample as defined within the pages of this book include a web role for enabling a user to leave their feedback and a data class for working with an Azure table. The Web role also contains a page for viewing feedback that has been posted by a user. This page is used to respond to user feedback.

> **NOTE**
>
> Note that a future version of this application will include a Worker role for pulling feedback from a queue and notifying the book's authors that there is feedback. When the feedback is sent, the item will be pulled from the queue.
>
> Check our blog www.visualstudiounleashed.com/azure for a video walkthrough of creating this worker role and adding it to the solution.

Create the Projects

The following outlines the steps required to create the projects used by this solution.

1. Launch Visual Studio as Administrator (right-click the shortcut and choose Run as Administrator).

2. Create a new cloud project (File, New, Project, Cloud, Windows Azure Cloud Service). Refer to Figures 25.6. Set the solution name to VS2010UnleashedFeedback.

3. Use the New Cloud Service Project dialog box to add a new ASP.NET Web Role (refer to Figure 25.7) to the solution. This is used for the user interface of adding feedback and viewing that feedback. Name this role UnleashedFeedbackWeb.

Create a Table Storage Data Model

In this section you write some code to work with the Azure table storage model. Recall that table storage is semi-structured (it does not enforce schema). You can define entities that you store in the table with a key and a set of properties. In this case, all your data has the same structure. However, we are free to add to the structure over time as long as we write the code to handle it.

The following walks you through creating a data class that serves as persistence to Azure table storage.

1. Add a new class library project to your solution (File, Add, New Project, Windows, Class Library). Name this project, FeedbackData.

2. Right-click the project template and select Add Reference. Navigate to the .NET tab and select System.Data.Services.Client. Repeat for Microsoft.WindowsAzure.StorageClient.

3. Rename Class1.cs to Feedback.cs (make sure to rename the actual class, too, if refactoring does not take care of it for you).

4. Open the class and add a using statement for Microsoft.WindowsAzure.StorageClient.

5. Indicate that your class inherits from the TableServiceEntity class, which serves as the base class for table entities. It defines both a PartitionKey and RowKey property.

   The PartitionKey is used to indicate how your data is grouped (and therefore accessed) in data partitions on Azure. Azure keeps like partitions together. However, it might separate different partitions on different nodes.

   The RowKey property is used as a primary key for the row. This makes it easy to access from Azure.

6. Add a default constructor to the object. Here you set the partition and row key. Set each as follows:

   PartitionKey—Set this to the current month and year to tell Azure to group table entries into month-year partitions. This gives us the opportunity to scale out our data across different partitions but requires us to access data using the partition key (one month at a time).

   RowKey—Write some code to set the row key to a unique value that indicates the latest date and time stamp. Data is returned sorted by RowKey to ensure the latest data is always returned at the top. We add a GUID to make sure it is unique.

7. Finally, add properties for the user to leave his feedback: Name, Email, FeedbackMessage, RequestReply, and ReplySent. Listing 25.1 shows the code for this class.

LISTING 25.1   The Feedback.cs Data Class

```
using System;
using System.Collections.Generic;
using System.Linq;
using System.Text;
using Microsoft.WindowsAzure.StorageClient;


namespace FeedbackData
{
  public class Feedback : TableServiceEntity
  {
    //define Feedback properties
    public string Name { get; set; }
    public string Email { get; set; }
    public string FeedbackMessage { get; set; }
    public bool RequestReply { get; set; }
    public bool ReplySent { get; set; }

    public Feedback()
    {
      //define a partition key to allow the data to be
      //  partitioned across nodes
      PartitionKey = "UnleashedFeedback" +
        DateTime.UtcNow.ToString("MMyyyy");

      //create a row key that sorts latest records to the top
      //  add a GUID to ensure the key is unique
      RowKey = string.Format("{0:10}_{1}",
        DateTime.MaxValue.Ticks - DateTime.Now.Ticks,
        Guid.NewGuid());
    }

  }

}
```

8. Create a class that is used by the Azure table service to set up the storage account access information and enables you to query against table data stored inside an

Azure table store. Add the newly created class to the project and name it
FeedbackServiceContext.

The Azure table service framework classes are built to work with the ADO.NET Data
Services. The TableServiceContext derives from DataServiceContext in ADO.NET
Data Services.

9. Make sure your new class, FeedbackServiceContext, inherits from
   TableServiceContext.

10. Add a constructor to the FeedbackServiceContext class that takes the storage creden-
    tials as a parameter and passes them into the base class.

11. Add a property to the FeedbackServiceContext of type IQueryable<Feedback> to
    expose the feedback table.

Listing 25.2 shows an example of this code.

LISTING 25.2   The FeedbackServiceContext.cs Class

```csharp
using System;
using System.Collections.Generic;
using System.Linq;
using System.Text;
using Microsoft.WindowsAzure;
using Microsoft.WindowsAzure.StorageClient;

namespace FeedbackData
{
  public class FeedbackServiceContext : TableServiceContext
  {
    public FeedbackServiceContext(string baseAddress,
      StorageCredentials credentials) : base(baseAddress, credentials)
    {
      //constructor sets the storage account access information
    }

    //expose the feedback table as a property
    public IQueryable<Feedback> Feedback
    {
      get
      {
        return this.CreateQuery<Feedback>("Feedback");
      }
    }
  }
}
```

12. Create the FeedbackDataSource.cs class, which is responsible for selecting, adding, and updating feedback data from the Azure table store. It includes the following methods:

Static Constructor—A static constructor that reads the table connection information from the configuration file. It also creates the table data based on the model (feedback class). This constructor is declared as static to indicate that initialization is called only once.

Default constructor—This constructor is used to initialize the data context class and set the retry policy (three times, three seconds between tries).

Select—This method returns an IEnumerable<Feedback> object that contains data selected from the table store using LINQ. In this case, the data is selected based on the partition (month year) passed to the method.

AddFeedback—This method takes a Feedback instance, adds it to the context (table), and then saves it.

GetFeedback—This method takes a partition key and row key. It uses LINQ to find the requested feedback item and returns it.

SetReplySent—This method enables you to mark an item in the table as having a reply sent back to the feedback. It looks up an item based on partition and row key. It then updates the ReplySent property and saves the data back to the data (table) context.

Listing 25.3 shows an example of these methods.

LISTING 25.3   The FeedbackDataSources.cs Class

```
using System;
using System;
using System.Collections.Generic;
using System.Linq;
using System.Text;
using Microsoft.WindowsAzure;
using Microsoft.WindowsAzure.StorageClient;

namespace FeedbackData
{
  public class FeedbackDataSource
  {
    private static CloudStorageAccount storageAccount;
    private FeedbackServiceContext context;

    static FeedbackDataSource()
    {
      //read connection information from config
      storageAccount = CloudStorageAccount.FromConfigurationSetting(
        "StorageCnnStr");
```

```
  //create the table based on the ServiceContext
  CloudTableClient.CreateTablesFromModel(
      typeof(FeedbackServiceContext),
      storageAccount.TableEndpoint.AbsoluteUri,
      storageAccount.Credentials);
}

public FeedbackDataSource()
{
  this.context = new FeedbackServiceContext(
    storageAccount.TableEndpoint.AbsoluteUri, storageAccount.Credentials);

  this.context.RetryPolicy = RetryPolicies.Retry(3, TimeSpan.FromSeconds(3));
}

public IEnumerable<Feedback> Select(string partitionMmYyyy)
{
  //select feedback for the given MonthYear
  var results = from f in this.context.Feedback
                where f.PartitionKey == "UnleashedFeedback" + partitionMmYyyy
                select f;
  return results;
}

public void AddFeedback(Feedback item)
{
  //add a row of feedback to the service (data) context
  this.context.AddObject("Feedback", item);

  //persist changes to the table
  this.context.SaveChanges();
}

public Feedback GetFeedback(string partitionKey, string rowKey)
{
  //get a single feedback item from the table
  var results = from f in this.context.Feedback
                where f.PartitionKey == "UnleashedFeedback" +
                  partitionKey && f.RowKey == rowKey
                select f;

  Feedback feedbackItem = results.FirstOrDefault<Feedback>();
  return feedbackItem;
}
```

```
public void SetReplySent(string partitionKey, string rowKey)
{
  //get the feedback item
  Feedback f = this.GetFeedback(partitionKey, rowKey);

  //mark reply as sent
  f.ReplySent = true;

  //update object and save to table
  this.context.UpdateObject(f);
  this.context.SaveChanges();
}


}


}
```

The feedback data source project is now complete. The next step is to wire this data access up to the website.

Create the Web Role Interface

The web role interface has two pages: Default.aspx enables users to submit feedback. ViewFeedback.aspx enables an administrator of the site to review and reply to that feedback. This section outlines the core steps and code for creating these interfaces.

1. Start by adding a project reference to the FeedbackData object, which is used for working with the table data.

2. Create the Default.aspx page and edit the Default.aspx page markup to include text boxes for entering feedback, validation controls, and a button for submitting feedback.

   In the sample version, we also put the main form inside a panel control. We added a second, hidden panel control to be shown to the user after he has submitting his feedback.

   Figure 25.15 shows an example of what this page might look like (we added a style sheet and master page).

3. The only code you need to add to this page besides the markup is a handler for the Submit Feedback button.

   Inside this handler, create a new instance of the Feedback class and initialize the properties to the values from the controls on the form.

   Next, create an instance of the FeedbackDataSource class. Call the AddFeedback method. You might also want to write out some trace information to help with troubleshooting.

   Listing 25.4 shows an example of this code.

FIGURE 25.15   Create a basic feedback form for users.

LISTING 25.4   The Default.aspx.cs Code-behind File

```
using System;
using System.Collections.Generic;
using System.Linq;
using System.Web;
using System.Web.UI;
using System.Web.UI.WebControls;
using FeedbackData;
using Microsoft.WindowsAzure;
using Microsoft.WindowsAzure.ServiceRuntime;
using Microsoft.WindowsAzure.StorageClient;
using System.Net;

namespace UnleashedFeedbackWeb
{
```

```csharp
public partial class Default : System.Web.UI.Page
{

  protected void Page_Load(object sender, EventArgs e)
  {
  }

  protected void ButtonSubmit_Click(object sender, EventArgs e)
  {
    //create a feedback item
    Feedback f = new Feedback()
    {
      Email = TextBoxEmail.Text,
      FeedbackMessage = TextBoxMessage.Text,
      Name = TextBoxName.Text,
      RequestReply = CheckBoxReply.Checked
    };

    //created the feedback data source
    FeedbackDataSource fDs = new FeedbackDataSource();

    //add the record to the table
    fDs.AddFeedback(f);

    //optional, log trace information
    System.Diagnostics.Trace.TraceInformation(
        "Added feedback item. Partition: {0}. Row: {1}. For: '{2}'.",
        f.PartitionKey, f.RowKey, f.Name);

    //reset the form
    PanelMain.Visible = false;
    PanelFinished.Visible = true;
  }
}

}
```

4. Add a new page to the site. Name it ViewFeedback.aspx. This page is used to select a partition of feedback (month year) and display it to an administrator. In this version, the admin can simply select an item and mark it as having been replied to.

5. Add a text box and button control to the page to enable a user to enter a partition to be returned from the database. You add code to the page to default this partition to the current month and year (we could have also implemented a calendar control).

6. Add a GridView control to the page. Select the smart tag to define a new data source to be bound to this control.

   In the Data Source Configuration Wizard, select Object as the data source type. Choose FeedbackDataSource as the object. If you can't find it, cancel the wizard and build the solution. Choose the Select method as the SELECT data method. Figure 25.16 shows an example.

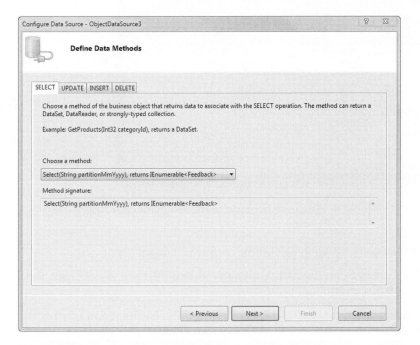

FIGURE 25.16   Create an object data of type FeedbackDataSource class.

   On the Parameters screen, set the parameters method to a Control and select the partition text entry field created earlier. Set the parameter's name to partitionMmYyyy. Finish the wizard.

   Finally, use the smart tag on the GridView to indicate that selection is allowed by checking the Enable Selection checkbox.

7. Next, add a label that can be updated to show the user which partition has been selected.

8. Finally, add a button that triggers an event to mark a selected item as replied in the table store.

   Figure 25.17 shows an example of what your page should look like.

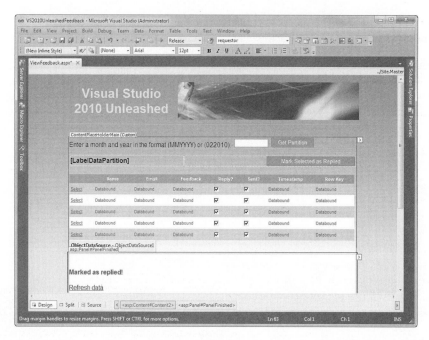

FIGURE 25.17   The ViewFeedback.aspx page is bound to the Feedback data class.

9. The final step is to write the code-behind for the ViewFeedback page.

   Add a Page_Load event to set the partition to a default month and year. Update the data source to use this month and year.

   Add code to the Mark Selected as Replied button to get the partition and row key and then call the FeedbackDataSource.SetReplySent method.

   Listing 25.5 shows this code.

LISTING 25.5   The ViewFeedback.aspx.cs Code-behind File

```
using System;
using System.Collections.Generic;
using System.Linq;
using System.Web;
using System.Web.UI;
using System.Web.UI.WebControls;
using FeedbackData;
using Microsoft.WindowsAzure;
using Microsoft.WindowsAzure.ServiceRuntime;
using Microsoft.WindowsAzure.StorageClient;
using System.Net;


namespace UnleashedFeedbackWeb.admin
```

```csharp
{
  public partial class ViewFeedback : System.Web.UI.Page
  {
    protected void Page_Load(object sender, EventArgs e)
    {
      if (!IsPostBack)
      {
        string partition = DateTime.UtcNow.ToString("MMyyyy");
        SetPartition(partition);
      }
    }

    protected void SetPartition(string partition)
    {
      //set the default partition to the current month and day
      TextBoxPartition.Text = partition;
      LabelDataPartition.Text = "Data shown for partition: " + partition;
      ObjectDataSource1.SelectParameters["partitionMmYyyy"].DefaultValue =
        partition;
      ObjectDataSource1.DataBind();
    }

    protected void ButtonMarkReplied_Click(object sender, EventArgs e)
    {
      //get selected item's row key and data key

      //created the feedback data source
      FeedbackDataSource fDs = new FeedbackDataSource();

      //todo: make more robus
      string partitionKey = TextBoxPartition.Text;
      string rowKey = GridView1.SelectedRow.Cells[7].Text;

      //mark as replied
      fDs.SetReplySent(partitionKey, rowKey);

      this.PanelMain.Visible = false;
      this.PanelFinished.Visible = true;


    }

  }

}
```

Configure the Web Role

The last thing you have to do before you can run your application in development mode is to configure the connection string for the table data. Recall this was referenced in the FeedbackDataSource class as StorageCnnStr. The following walks you through this process.

1. In Solution Explorer, navigate to the Azure project, VS2010UnleashedFeedback. Open the Roles folder. Right-click the UnleashedFeedbackWeb Web role and choose Properties.

2. You should see the Properties dialog box for Web role (refer to Figure 25.9 for an example). Select the Settings tab.

3. You need to add a setting for the connection string by clicking the Add Settings dialog box at the top of the screen.

   Name your new setting, StorageCnnStr.

   Set the Type as Connection String using the drop-down.

   Click the ellipsis button to bring up the Storage Connection String dialog box. Set this to Use Development Storage for now (you come back to this later). This is the setting you typically want to use when running locally (although your production data sources are addressable using endpoints and thus you could call them during development).

   Figure 25.18 shows the Storage Connection String dialog box. Click OK to close the dialog box. Your connection string settings should now look like those in Figure 25.19.

FIGURE 25.18   The Storage Connection String dialog box enables you to configure how you access the Azure data store.

4. The final step before you run the application is to set the environment for the configuration publisher by opening the WebRole.cs file inside the website. This class file sits in the root of your site and provides information that tells Azure how to start your

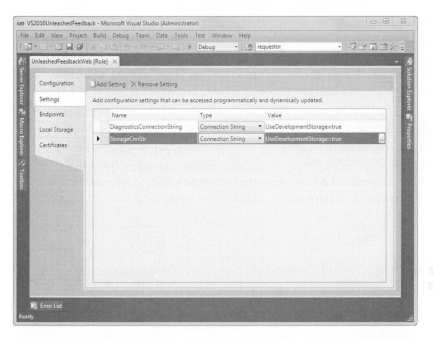

FIGURE 25.19   The StorageCnnStr configured to use development storage.

application. You need to add just a couple lines of code to the OnStart method. Add the following to this method after the line `RoleEnvironment.Changing += ..."`:

```
CloudStorageAccount.SetConfigurationSettingPublisher((configName,
    configSetter) =>
{
    configSetter(RoleEnvironment.GetConfigurationSettingValue(configName));
});
```

You can now successfully run your application locally on your machine and debug it using the local version of Azure table storage. Note, be sure that you are running Visual Studio in the elevated privileges mode (Run as Administrator) or you get a dialog box preventing you from running your application. Next up, we deploy to the cloud.

Subscribing to the Azure Services (Get an Account)

You are now ready to deploy your application to the cloud and we start by getting an account. If you already have an Azure account you can skip this step and go to the site and login. If, however, this is your first time setting up, the following steps walk you through the process of getting your account.

1. Start by visiting windowsazure.com.

2. Click the Sign Up Now button. If you don't see the button on the page, navigate to http://www.microsoft.com/windowsazure/account/ and click Get Your Account.

3. You should now see a page that shows you the options for purchase. You need to select a plan that meets your needs. Each plan has a different pricing structure. Thankfully, there is a nice comparison chart for you to use. Select a plan and click Buy.

TIP

Microsoft is offering MSDN Subscribers special rates for Azure that includes a free, eight-month, "kick-the-tires" configuration. In addition, MSDN subscribers are being offered special rates. For more information on the latter, visit http://msdn.microsoft. com/en-us/subscriptions/ee461076.aspx or refer to Chapter 1, "A Quick Tour of Visual Studio 2010."

4. The MicrosoftOnline Services Customer Portal opens for you to complete your transaction. This is a shopping experience site where you can add services and run through a checkout process. Figure 25.20 shows the Services tab on this site filtered for just Azure. Note that the same site is used for purchasing Office and Exchange online (among others).

FIGURE 25.20 You use the Microsoft Online Services Customer Portal to purchase your Azure services.

Click Buy Now to add any of these items to the service already in your cart. This is not necessary for the example. You only need the base account to complete this deployment and run it.

5. Click Checkout to walk through the purchase process. When you do, you have to agree to the terms and conditions. (See Figure 25.21.)

FIGURE 25.21   Walk through the checkout process to complete your Azure account setup.

6. Clicking checkout starts the registration process. You must enter address and company information for billing and tracking purposes. Finally, you provide billing information such as PO or credit card.

7. At the end of the checkout process, click the Proceed to Activation link to start the activation process. You have to enter a name for the subscription; this is just used to identify it on your billing.

You also must identify a site administrator. Note that you can have a separate account owner (owns the account and pays the bills) and a separate, technical administrator of the site.

8. Finally, you receive a confirmation email after your account is set up and ready to use. Click the links in this email to get started. If you lose the email, you can return to this website to view activation status (it can take a few minutes or up to 24 hours) and link out to your account.

You should now have an Azure services account for billing purposes. We now look at the technical configuration and deployment steps.

Creating a Storage Account

Now that you have an Azure account you need to configure it for both storage and hosting. The storage service is used to store data. In the example, it is the feedback data that gets stored in the Azure table storage. Configuring a storage account creates an addressable endpoint that your application uses to communicate with the data store. The endpoint requires an access key (shared secret), which is generated as part of this process. The following steps walk you through creating your Azure storage account.

1. Login to the Azure (you can link to it from the account confirmation email). Make sure you are on the Summary page and see My Projects. You should see the project you set up when you registered. Figure 25.22 highlights an example.

FIGURE 25.22   Click on your project in the My Projects list to configure.

2. Select the project by clicking on its name. You go to a site that shows the current state of the project. Because this is a new site, you should not see much here. However, there is New Service link in the top right of the page. Click this link to add a storage or hosting service to the project. Figure 25.23 highlights an example.

3. The New Service link takes you to the page shown in Figure 25.24. Click the Storage Account link to begin setting up your storage account.

4. Set a name and description that are used to identify the service in the management console. Figure 25.25 shows an example.

FIGURE 25.23   Click New Service to set up a storage or hosting service.

FIGURE 25.24   You can choose to create a storage or hosted service.

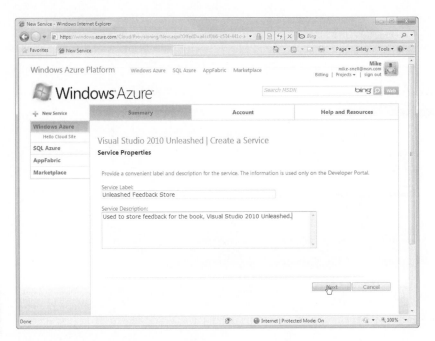

FIGURE 25.25   Set the label of the service so you can easily identify it inside the Azure management site.

5. Define the unique DNS name for addressing your storage service (see Figure 25.26). This name is used to generate an endpoint after you click the Create button at the bottom of the page. Enter a name in the provided text box and use the Check Availability button. Your name becomes part of the URI and therefore has to be unique across the AppFabric. This simply ensures your storage can be identified via an endpoint.

The other option on this page is Storage Affinity Group. Use this to set a label that the AppFabric can use to ensure the necessary parts of your application are co-located. If you do not need this, you can let the AppFabric decide how your items are deployed. In this case, however, we are indicating a label to make sure we keep the storage and host code close by. We are picking a data center region.

6. Click the Create button to generate the endpoints for your data store. This might take a couple minutes. It also generates a primary and secondary shared secret key to be used to authenticate callers to the service. Figure 25.27 shows an example. Note that you can use the Regenerate button to create new versions of the keys if they are compromised.

Your data storage account is now configured. You use this information in a moment when you deploy the application. First, however, you need to set up a hosting account.

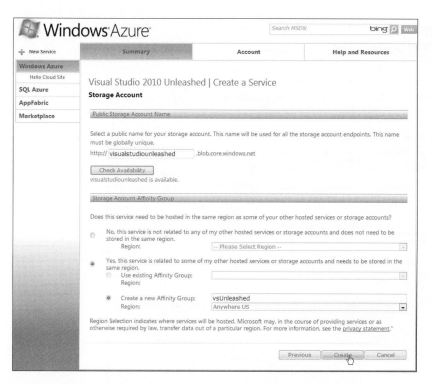

FIGURE 25.26   You must define a DNS name to access your storage. You should also create
an Affinity Group to make sure your data and hosted code get co-located.

Creating a Hosted Service Account

You now need to create a hosted service that is used to deploy the code. This service runs
under ASP.NET and responds to HTTP requests from users.

1. To get started, return to the Azure management web application summary page for
   your project (select Summary at the top of the page). You should now see the storage
   item (Unleashed Feedback Store) at the top of the page. Click the New Service link at
   the top right of the page (as you did previously in Figure 25.23).

2. This time, select the Hosted Services service (refer to Figure 25.24).

3. The first step is to define a service label and description as you did previously (refer
   to Figure 25.25). This time, name the service Unleashed Feedback Web.

4. The next step is to define a service URI. This time, the format is
   [servicename].cloudapp.net. This DNS name also has to be unique as it is a publicly
   addressable URI on the Internet. You should be able to use the same name you gave
   to the storage account.

   Again, on this same page, you need to select an Affinity Group. Because you set one
   up on the prior step, Azure assumes you want to use the same group (and you do,
   because this is part of the same application). Figure 25.28 shows an example.

FIGURE 25.27   The cloud storage account has been set up with endpoints and access keys (shared secret keys).

5. After you click Create on the page shown in Figure 25.28 you are taken to a page showing your hosted service. You should see two versions here: Production and Staging. Note that if you cannot see both versions, you can click the arrow bar on the screen to expand the list.

    This page enables you to deploy your solution to Staging, test it, and then deploy to production when you are ready. Figure 25.29 shows an example. Notice that you can also edit your affinity group, manage any certifications (for HTTPS), or delete the service all together.

Preparing Your Application for Publishing

Recall that the application you created has a connection string to an Azure table storage area. This connection string was set to work in your development environment. You need to modify this to work with production.

FIGURE 25.28   You set the DNS name for your hosted service along with an affinity group.

FIGURE 25.29   Your hosted service account includes a production and staging (test) version.

You have a couple options for doing so. First, you could deploy the application to Azure and then use the Azure website to edit the XML configuration that contains the XML string. Alternatively, you can set the connection string inside Visual Studio, and then deploy the version that is ready for production (and does not require additional configuration). The following walks you through taking the latter approach:

1. Return to your Visual Studio project and open the Roles folder in the VS2010UnleashedFeedback Azure project file. Right-click this file and view its properties. In this window, select the Settings tab from the far left. Figure 25.30 shows an example.

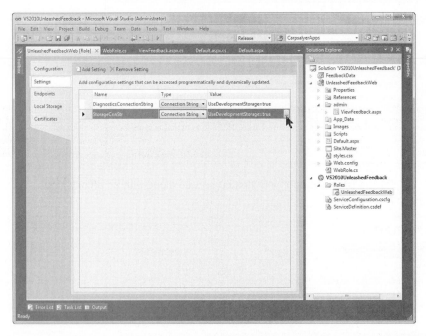

FIGURE 25.30   Return to Visual Studio to set the connection string to work with the Azure site storage account.

2. Select the StorageCnnStr line. Click the ellipsis button on the far right of the StorageCnnStr data row to open the Storage Connection String dialog box as shown in Figure 25.31.

3. Select the Enter Storage Credentials option. Inside the account name, enter the name you set for the storage account (visualstudiounleashed in the example, as shown in Figure 25.26). In the account key field enter your shared secret key that was generated for the storage services. You can get this information by returning to the Azure site and selecting the storage service (Unleashed Feedback Store). This key is the Primary Access Key, as shown in Figure 25.27.

   You can use the Use Default HTTP Endpoints option to indicate that your endpoints are set using your account name and the standard Azure naming structure.

FIGURE 25.31   Update the storage connection string to point to your Azure account.

4. Repeat these steps for the DiagnosticConnectionString (above the StorageCnnStr in the Settings tab). Here, you tell Azure where to write your diagnostic information.

   You should be able to select the same account name you entered for the StorageCnnStr. Visual Studio should then automatically fill in the account key. Also, be sure that HTTPS endpoints is selected. Figure 25.32 shows an example.

Use HTTPS for the DiagnosticConnectionString

FIGURE 25.32   Use HTTPS for the DiagnosticsConnectionString.

Your application is ready to deploy to the Azure site. The next section guides you through deployment. Don't forget to change your connection string back to Use Development Storage when you run the application in your local environment.

Publish and Deploy Your Application to the Cloud

There are two ways to deploy your application out to Azure. The first is a somewhat manual process using the windowsazure.com website. The other is through Visual Studio directly (this feature was added with the 1.2 version of the SDK). The following sections walk through each deployment option.

Publish and Deploy Your Cloud Service Manually

You have to create two files that are used to copy your site to the cloud. These two files are generated by Visual Studio (more on this in a moment).

The first file has the .cspkg extension. It is a compressed file that contains all the code in your site that requires deployment (.aspx pages, .dll files, images, and so on). The second file has the .csfg extension. It defines the configuration information for your site.

You can create the files required to publish your application from either the Build menu, Publish option or by right-clicking the project in Solution Explorer and choosing Publish. In either case, the Publish Cloud Service dialog appears. Figure 25.33 shows an example. Notice the Create Service Package Only option is selected. The other options allow direct deployment (we will look at that in a moment).

FIGURE 25.33   The published, ready-to-be-deployed Azure files.

Clicking OK in the Publish Cloud Service dialog instructs Visual Studio to generate the two files required for deployment. Visual Studio builds your application and packages the necessary files. It then opens your deployment files in a separate window for you to view them. Figure 25.34 shows an example.

Note that files are published to the folder [project name]\bin\[debug or release]\publish. Of course, if you are creating a final build you should switch your build option to release using the Visual Studio toolbar.

FIGURE 25.34   The published, ready-to-be-deployed Azure files.

Deploying to the Stage Environment   You are now ready to deploy your solution to the staged environment. This process involves moving the two files created during the Publish process to your Web role. Use the following process:

1. First, go to the Windows Azure developer portal site (windows.azure.com) and log in (if you have not already).

2. Click your project in the My Projects list. In this case, click the Visual Studio 2010 Unleashed project.

3. Select the Web role from the list of roles and services. In the example, this should be named Unleashed Feedback Web.

4. You should now be on the page used to manage your Web role (refer to Figure 25.29). Select the staging cube (click the arrow bar if the staging cube is not shown). Click the Deploy button to launch the Staging Deployment page. Figure 25.35 shows an example.

5. You can upload files from another area on your Azure system. In this case, however, you upload from your local hard drive. Click the Browse button under the Application Package to select the .cspkg file you generated previously.

    Do the same thing for the .cscfg file under the Configuration Settings area.

    Finally, define a name (label) for this deployment and click the Deploy button.

6. After deployment completes (which might take a minute), you should be returned to your Web role management page. You might see a progress bar as the deployment happens (servers are being requisitioned, services setup, and so on).

FIGURE 25.35   Set the files to be deployed and give your deployment a label.

You should also see that the Staging queue has the label defined in the previous step. It also has the Web Site URL set to a GUID, which enables Azure to create a staged, unique DNS entry for your site before you move it over to production. The staged cube is also longer empty. Figure 25.36 shows an example. Notice, too, that the site is stopped. There are options to Run, Delete, Upgrade, and Configure. You must first configure before you run the site.

7. You are now ready to click the Run button for the staging site (refer to Figure 25.36). This might take some time (five or more minutes). In addition, the DNS needs to propagate across Azure. If you return to the page during this time, Azure keeps you updated as to the progress. Finally, when the site is live, Azure marks it with a Ready checkmark.

8. You can now navigate to the site using the GUID-based URL under the staging cube. Test the site; if all looks good, you are ready to move to production (we talk about moving to production in a moment).

TIP

You can use the Upgrade button for a given hosted service to upgrade your application package and/or configuration. You can also upgrade a single role (web or worker) at a time.

FIGURE 25.36   The deployed site inside the Azure Staging cube.

Publish and Deploy using Visual Studio

You've seen how to publish manually using the Azure website. You can also publish automatically through Visual Studio. Recall the Publish Cloud Service dialog (refer to Figure 25.33), which has the option Deploy Your Cloud Service to Windows Azure.

To get started, you must provide credential to your Azure account, which is a one-time setup operation. You can do so with the Credentials drop-down, Add option. Figure 25.37 shows an example.

On the Cloud Service Management Authentication dialog you must provide both an x.509 v3 certificate and your Azure subscription ID. The former can be generated for you by Visual Studio if you do not have one. The latter comes from the bottom of the Account page in the Azure developer portal. Figure 25.38 shows an example.

Before closing the dialog, first grab the authentication certificate and post it to the Azure site. To do so, first click the link Copy the Full Path, shown in Figure 25.38.

Next, select the Account page on the developer portal. Select the link near the top that says Manage My API Certificates. This takes you to a page that enables you to upload your certificate. Click the browse button and paste in the path. Finally, click the Upload button to post your certificate to Azure. Again, this is a one-time procedure. The next time, you can just publish to the site.

FIGURE 25.37   You must set your Azure credentials to deploy directly from Visual Studio.

FIGURE 25.38   You can create an Azure authentication account.

Return to Visual Studio and click OK on the Cloud Service Management Authentication dialog. Visual Studio should now be communicating with your Azure site. You should be able to deploy to both staging and production. Figure 25.39 shows an example.

Visual Studio displays the Windows Azure Activity Log when you click OK to deploy to Azure. This shows you the status of your deployment and whether it succeeded. Figure 25.40 shows an example (the pane at the bottom of the image).

Promoting to Production

You have two options for moving to production. First, you can simply redeploy from Visual Studio but use the production option (refer to Figure 25.39). Alternatively, given that your site has been deployed and tested in staging, you can navigate to the Azure management page for your Web role and move stage to production.

FIGURE 25.39   Once authenticated, you can deploy directly from Visual Studio to Azure.

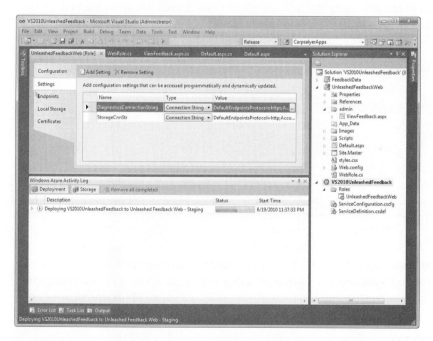

FIGURE 25.40   The Windows Azure Activity Log tracks the progress of your deployments.

Of course, you can also redeploy files (following the steps discussed earlier) to the Production cube. However, it is easier to click a button to swap staging and production (see Figure 25.41).

Once deployed (or swapped) you should be able to hit your site from the Internet using the DNS name you defined.

Click to Swap Staging and Production

FIGURE 25.41 You can swap staging and production for a quick stage deployment.

We would love for you to give this a test using the DNS we defined for our page. You can provide feedback to us on the book by entering the URL into a browser and visiting the deployed version of the site using the following URL: http://visualstudiounleashed.cloudapp.net/. Figure 25.42 shows an example.

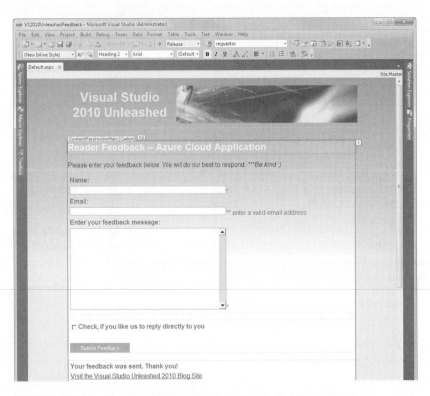

FIGURE 25.42 The site deployed and running in the Azure cloud.

We will try to keep the site up and running for some time after the book is published. We look forward to hearing from you.

Next Steps

This was another long example, but it hopefully answered the most pressing questions about using Visual Studio 2010 to build Azure solutions. There are still a number of items left to consider, however. We will do our best to tackle all of these issues and post blog entries and videos at visualstudiounleashed.com/azure. The items we plan to tackle include

- Add messages to an Azure queue after a user has left feedback. Create a Worker role to grab these messages and notify the administrators of the feedback.

- Move the site to a real domain name (and not cloudapp.net).

- Discuss tracing and monitoring cloud applications.

- Discuss moving the data storage over to SQL Azure.

- Demonstrate the access control security by locking down the ViewFeedback.aspx page.

> **TIP**
>
> Microsoft has also released a Windows Azure Platform Training Kit. You can find it on the Azure site. It includes additional labs, presentations, and videos on Azure.

Summary

This chapter presented the fundamentals of Windows Azure, which includes setting up your development environment to run a local version of the AppFabric and Azure storage services. You must download and install the SDK (version 1.2 at the time of printing) to get these items and the Visual Studio project templates.

The chapter also walked you through an example of building an Azure Web role application. You created an Azure account for both hosting and storage. Finally you configured and deployed your application to a production environment. You should be able to build on these fundamentals to create and deploy your own applications in the cloud.

Index

A

E

F

M

S

How can we make this index more useful? Email us at indexes@samspublishing.com

T

U

W

Z